THE RISE

OF CHILDREN'S

BOOK REVIEWING

IN AMERICA

1865-1881

THE RISE
OF CHILDREN'S
BOOK REVIEWING
IN AMERICA, 1865-1881

BY RICHARD L. DARLING

R. R. BOWKER COMPANY

NEW YORK & LONDON 1968

TO MY WIFE

PERSIS

On peut dédaigner la littérature enfantine...
à condition de tenir pour négligeable la manière
dont l'âme nationale se forme et se maintient.

PAUL HAZARD—LES LIVRES, LES ENFANTS ET LES HOMMES

TABLE OF CONTENTS

I

PROLOGUE

*Scream, O Eagle! "A bird in the air shall carry the voice, and
that which hath wings shall tell the matter." Great are thy
tidings! Thine enemy is become "a pelican of the wilderness,
an owl of the desert, a sparrow alone upon the house-top."
Therefore, O bird of good-omen! perch upon our columns,
and scream!
How shall our unsteady pen—shaken by a merry-dancing
pulse! attempt to write soberly today?* [1]

With exuberant outpouring the editor of the weekly *Independent*
greeted the fall of Petersburg and Richmond and the Southern retreat.
Within the week Lee himself would have surrendered. Before the month
had ended Lincoln would be dead, but the defeat of the rebel forces
would be accomplished. Not only did the *Independent* seem to be herald-
ing the end of a long and bitter war, but also may have recognized, however dimly, the beginning of a new era in the United States.

That the states, the Northern ones, had made progress during the war
years cannot be denied. The press of war had forced changes in the national life. But the burst of energy that was to come was without prece-
dent. Led by resurgence in the building of railroads, the national economy was moving into one of those post-war booms that have marked the
nation's history. Few could foresee the great depression that was so to

1

mar the seventies; the slowness of the recovery that would not bring a sound economy again until the eighties had almost begun.

The story of the times was told for the young in the pages of the weekly *Youth's Companion,* and in other periodicals and books for the young. The candidates for the nation's highest offices, the great reform movements, the pressures and the vices of the day were faithfully reported. Even the great depression of the period, following the crash of 1873, was reported to the youthful readers of children's magazines. The times were exciting and children, vicariously at least, took full part in them.

All things seemed on a grand scale. In 1872 the railroad titans added 7,379 miles to the railway network that could boast only 651 miles constructed in 1861, the year the Great Rebellion began.[2] And even in the depression year of 1875, nearly three times as many miles of rails were laid as had been built in the years before the war.

With the business boom came a great increase in population. The *Youth's Companion,* as soon as the 1880 census was complete, informed its readers that the nation consisted now of more than fifty million people, an increase of 11,600,000 since the 1870 census.[3] And though they did not announce it, the increase in the previous decade, despite the enormous casualties of the war, had been more than seven million. Even earlier, the young readers had been informed of the phenomenal growth of the cities.[4] New York had topped one million, and three other cities boasted a population of more than 500,000; fully twenty had more than 100,000.

Not every voice spoke so proudly of this growth. In 1868 *Farming for Boys* appeared, a book for the young with the avowed purpose of attempting to stem the tide of country boys departing for the wicked cities. The staid, Presbyterian *Hours at Home* welcomed the book.

The prevailing tendency of the age on the part of the young is to rush to the city, to prefer trade and commerce and professional life to agriculture; and nearly all that has been written for the young tends to foster and strengthen this tendency. But the aim of this book is to counteract this prevalent disposition to exchange the country for the city—to convince the country boy that the prospect of respectability, success in life, and happiness, is on the whole better for him there than in our great human hives—to convince our farmers' sons and the parents of city boys that argicultural employments are superior to others in their comparative freedom from temptation to vice, and in the sure rewards they bring in the long run to intelligently directed industry, and that it is a great mistake to suppose that the majority of those who exchange the farm for the city become great or rich. The fact is made manifest, in the personal history of a multitude of distinguished men, that the farm, and not the city, has been the birthplace of the leading minds of all the countries. . . .[5]

But this was not the spirit of the times. Horatio Alger, Jr., in *Ragged Dick,* and myriad tales that followed, told another story, of the fame and riches that an industrious boy might win if he turned to the metropolis.

Even the calamities of the age were on a grand scale. Chicago burned itself down grandly, with the most famous fire of the times. But Boston and other cities had great fires also. William T. Adams, in *Oliver Optic's Magazine: Our Boys and Girls,* described the effect of Boston's great fire on his publisher, Lee & Shepard.[6] Sixty acres of warehouses had burned, including Lee & Shepard's Milk Street warehouse. The firm's main office had been spared, but the plates for many of their publications had been melted down in the burned warehouse.

Entertainment frequently shared in the exuberance of the times. Perhaps the national sentiment is best typified in two great celebrations, Boston's Great Jubilee and Philadelphia's Centennial Exhibition. In an editorial, "The Great Jubilee," Adams described Boston's fete to his young readers. After a cutting remark at the rival city of New York, he declared that "the literary and musical metropolis of the United States of America set out to have the greatest musical feast the world has ever known; and . . . she has achieved a triumphant success." [7] Proudly, he described the chorus of 20,000 voices, the orchestra of 1,000 performers, and the four full military bands imported from Europe for the celebration.

Huge as it was, Boston's great celebration was dwarfed by the events in Philadelphia four years later. No doubt the lasting influence of the Centennial Exhibition was greater, also, for the entire nation, even the world, took part. The magazines printed photographs and drawings, which depicted the pavilions and the exhibits of various nations and of the businesses and trades at home. The book trade turned its attention to the Exhibition and published book after book, for young and old, which capitalized on the centennial interest in the nation's past. Perhaps the most interesting description of the exhibition appeared in the *Youth's Companion,* in an article, "The Event of 1876."

> *The opening of the Centennial Exhibition, on May 10th, was a grand and patriotic pageant, which will long make the year 1876 one of the most interesting in our history . . .*
>
> *The bright morning of the 10th of May, 1876, brought to Philadelphia a wonderful contrast to this old historic scene of 1776. The city was crowded with strangers from all parts of the world. Repre-*

3

sentatives from every civilized court were there. The broad avenues leading to Fairmount Park were thronged with people, and into the three hundred acres, set apart for the industrial palaces, where were gathered the arts and products of the nations, an inflow of people began. Under the terrace in front of the Art Gallery, tens of thousands became scores of thousands. The winged horses rose high in the air above them, and every heart beat with enthusiasm as the music of Wagner's Centennial March announced that the grand ceremony of opening the International Exhibition of 1876 had begun.

Then the President of the United States declared the Exhibition opened. The President and the Emperor of Brazil started the great Corliss Engine; the world's machinery was started into life; six hundred voices sang the "Hallelujah Chorus"; cannon thundered; the telegraph flashed the news to all parts of our own country and to countries over the sea; while all the bells of the city rung out for joy.[8]

The author described the events, beginning in March, 1871, with an act of Congress "providing for an exhibition of American and foreign arts, products and manufactures," up to the opening of the exhibition and the events, still to come, which would reach a magnificent peak on the Fourth of July, when descendants of revolutionary heroes would participate, and Bayard Taylor, Pennsylvania's own poet, would "celebrate in verse the nation's achievements for a hundred years." [9]

Religion did not fail to enter the spirit of the age. When Moody and Sankey ended a thirteen-week series of daily revival meetings in Boston, the *Youth's Companion* could report that more than three hundred meetings had been held with an average attendance of 5,000 souls. Though the writer admitted it would be difficult to judge the good accomplished, he quoted several testimonials to the effectiveness of the meetings.

The violence, the agitations, and the sins of the day were faithfully reported to the young. Martha F. Finley, never an author of high repute, but popular for generations, mixed a large portion of Ku Klux Klan activities into her *Elsie's Motherhood,* a portion which the reviewer for *Harper's New Monthly Magazine* thought of doubtful advantage to Miss Finley's girl readers.[10] Under the heading, "A Labor Revolt," the *Youth's Companion* lamented the great railroad strike that began on the 29th of July, 1877, and its results.[11] Not only was the editor opposed to such strikes, but he felt, they were surely doomed to failure. Even the sinister was reported, for the machinations of political bosses, particularly the notorious Boss Tweed, were dissected for the young.[12] The tragic flight of Chief Joseph across the Rocky Mountains until his surrender in northern Montana was also faithfully chronicled.[13] The *Youth's*

4

Companion revealed an admiration for the Nez Percé chieftain, praising his courage and skill, his kindness toward the wounded soldiers, that anticipated Helen Hunt Jackson's *A Century of Dishonor,* which exposed the treatment that the Indians had received on all sides at the hands of the white man.

Not all was violent, however. It was an age of great reform movements still, with the energies that had ended slavery turned to other worthy causes, causes with which the *Youth's Companion* was usually in full sympathy. Mr. Comstock's crusade against obscene literature was in full force in the seventies. The *Youth's Companion* reported that Mr. Comstock had been responsible for the destruction of more than twenty tons of the stuff, but that undoubtedly vast quantities were abroad and being read by the young.[14] A Brooklyn youngster, the child of a Sunday school superintendent, had been discovered in possession of the vilest kind of book. Parents had need take warning; not even Mr. Comstock could fully protect their children.

The march toward equal political rights for women was on. George M. Baker published a brief play, "Original Dialogues: Shall Our Mothers Vote," in the pages of *Oliver Optic's Magazine,* in which the Excelsior Debating Society argued in favor of women's suffrage.[15] One of the strongest reform movements was the temperance movement. The *Youth's Companion* was not alone in bringing to children's attention the dangers of strong drink.[16] Each year, intemperate books warning children of the evils of spirits poured forth from the American Temperance Union. Even the general book trade capitalized on the interest in this subject, almost outdoing the Temperance Union in their zeal to warn the young and, incidentally, to sell books.

Other events of great consequence were reported to the children in the pages of the *Youth's Companion,* such as the agitation for silver coinage[17] and the resistance to new labor-saving agricultural machinery in the West.[18] Nothing received more attention, however, than did the great depression that blighted nearly a decade. In 1876 the *Youth's Companion* reviewed the course of the slump in business.

It is a very wonderful circumstance that the whole world is at this moment passing through a season of great dullness in trade. There has not been before in modern times so universal a complaint of the kind as is now heard. In this country, as we all know too well, manufacturing and trade are almost at a standstill. The same is true of Great Britain, France, Germany, and the other commercial nations of the world.

The causes of this stagnation in business are various, but they are connected with each other. The evil seems to have begun in England,

5

and having been greatly aggravated by the consequences of our great panic of 1873, to have extended to all the countries with which Great Britain or the United States had large dealings.

There are some evidences that, so far as we are concerned, the long period of hard times is nearly over. We are now exporting more than ever before of the products of our industry, and millions of dollars' worth more than we are buying abroad. The result of this revival of an important branch of our trade will be very beneficial to us. . . .[19]

The benefits, however, were long in coming. The "Mercantile Failures," which disturbed the magazine earlier that year, were no more unhappy than the savings banks failures that were still continuing two years later.[20] When real promise of an upturn came, with the record harvest in 1878, the *Youth's Companion* was no longer so confident that the end was in sight.[21] It could only hope. Not until the beginning of 1880 did it declare that the depression had ended.

Meanwhile there are but few clouds in the world's horizon. Material prosperity is fast replacing the straitened time of the past few years; factories long shut are humming with labor; and the ships are once more heavy-laden with precious cargoes. Down to the very humblest occupation, restored confidence and reviving thrift are bringing greater comfort and more steady profits. It seems as if the whole world, after a long and uneasy rest, were starting forth on a new race of enterprise and peaceful rivalry.[22]

All these things had their effect on the period, but the one overwhelming event that cast its long shadow over the times was the Civil War. Everything was in some way touched by it. The great reform movements, by the need for energies to have a new outlet, the Indian problems by the westward movement of the war veterans, the boom and depression in business and trade by the pressures growing out of the war. Even at the beginning of the eighties a writer could not write about the war without being accused of bias and partisanship in some quarters, though others would praise his fairness.

Such was the world in which the child of the post-Civil War period lived. It was an exciting world and a troubled one. It was a world which some men defiled, but others did their utmost to improve. The public schools forged ahead, the great development of public libraries gained momentum, and, with the founding of the Chautauqua Assembly, adult education and home reading projects were fostered. Good or ill, it was a world from which children were not sheltered, a world brought into their homes each week in the pages of the most popular juvenile papers.

Children's books reflected the exuberance and freedom of the period. Real boys and girls, in ever greater numbers took their places in the literature of the children of America. Hans Brinker, Tom Bailey, the March sisters, and Tom Sawyer were new types of children in literature. In the hands of lesser artists the new freedom to depict natural children became overly exuberant and wild. A natural reaction against the sensationally wild adventures of some young fictional heroes had begun early in the period, but did not impede the gigantic strides in the creation of a children's literature that was really for children. Alice M. Jordan has aptly described the essence of this period in children's literature.

Could there be a wider gulf of separation between two types of book children than that between docile, earnest, literal, inquiring Rollo and mischievous, imaginative, harum-scarum, happy-go-lucky Tom? And yet this gulf was largely bridged in the fifteen years following the Civil War, that period of bad taste in architecture and house furnishings, of self-consciousness, of repressions and inhibitions. It is through consideration of the reading of New England children in the 1870's that we may trace some of the factors contributing to the greater freedom in the attitude toward children's reading. We shall discover a great fertility in the production of children's books, the first widespread awakening to the need of critical appraisal, the first wholehearted liberality toward children's tastes and interests, admitted without boundaries, without propaganda—in short, it was the beginning of a new era.[23]

Amy Cruse, writing about the reading available to English children, described this period as the richest years in reading that any generation has provided for its children, encompassing, as it does, *Alice's Adventures in Wonderland* and, by a slight extension, *Treasure Island*.[24] In between lie books by George MacDonald, Charlotte Yonge, Jean Ingelow, Juliana Horatia Ewing, Mrs. Molesworth, Dinah Craik Mulock, and others whose books were to please generations of children, as well as the art of Randolph Caldecott, Walter Crane, and Kate Greenaway. From America, she acknowledged, came some of the most popular of books. The Alcott books were welcomed by the reviewers and devoured by the children. Susan Coolidge's "Katy" books provided English children with their first really interesting school stories for girls, stories that could compare with the stories of England's own Tom Brown.[25]

Children's books made their way across the Atlantic in a continuing trade, so that the riches of each country were nearly doubled by those from the other. Lehmann-Haupt describes the situation in literature as unique, with England and the United States bound together by common language and by common traditions.[26] He feels that the nineteenth-century book world can hardly be understood without a realization of this relationship between the two countries. No less true was the effect of this relationship in children's literature. In general, it was the best books for children that weathered the trip across the Atlantic. In the introductory section of a column of reviews of children's books, a reviewer for the *Independent* described this trade.

> *Somebody has said that the Atlantic Ocean is a good literary strainer, only the best things getting through to the other side—a statement which is quite true in the case of juvenile literature. It is not easy for a British author to win reputation among American children, nor, when won, can he lose it any more readily.*[27]

The records in book-trade periodicals give us little clue to the actual number of books for children from abroad appearing in either country, but among the number of children's titles published each year were large numbers that had originated on the other side of the ocean.

The quantity of children's books was great. In no year did *Publishers' Weekly* list fewer than 250 children's books in its annual survey of "Juvenile Books of the Season," and often it listed more than 300. In England the number was even greater. The *Weekly Trade Circular* reported that 716 juvenile works appeared in England in 1871, including new works, new editions, and importations from the United States.[28] In America an average of 300 books, approximately, were listed in *Publishers' Weekly* each year, though this probably did not include all titles.

The period was a rich one for young readers. Books of a high quality and in large quantities were available to the young as they had never been before. Writer after writer commented on the great difference between the children's books of that day and those of earlier generations. A reviewer for the *Overland Monthly* applauded the change in children's books.

> *The old-fashioned stories, with a moral or pious reflection impending at the close of every sentence, or the clumsily adjusted mixture of didactic truth and saccharine rhetoric administered like sulphur and treacle for the moral health of the unhappy infant, are happily long since abandoned. The idea of pleasing children by writing down to their suppositious level and flavoring the work with a bland imbecility, has also exploded.*[29]

Even earlier, in 1868, the same periodical welcomed the change the new generation had brought to children's books.

> *Those of the present generation who drew their youthful inspiration from the pages of Mrs. Barbauld, Mrs. Edgeworth, and the ingenious story of Sandford and Merton, must look with considerable awe upon the glittering host who have succeeded them as entertainers of childhood. Dickens, Thackeray, Hans Christian Andersen, Laboulaye, Jean Macé and Mrs. Stowe—are the genii which the fairy godmother of the modern nursery summons to the amusement of "little Posterity." It was a great stride in the civilization of the world when it was discovered that it required first-class talent to entertain children, and that mere goodness, abstract morality and piety would not suffice. The next generation will be the wiser if not the better for such stories as "Ugly Duck" and "The Tin Soldier".*
>
> *Part of this improvement in children's stories is the choosing of subjects adapted to the localities, conditions and tastes of the little people. A boy's honest love of adventure is no longer studiously repressed.*[30]

Putnam's Magazine also heralded the change in literature for the young.

> *Verily there is a new era in this country in the literature for children. It is not very long since all the juvenile books seemed conducted on the principle of the definition of duty "doing what you don't want to," for the books that were interesting were not considered good, and the "good" ones were certainly not interesting. Most Sunday-school books were stories of unnaturally good and pious boys and girls, who, however, were not attractive enough to rouse a desire of imitation in the youthful breast.*
>
> *But now we have a different order of things, and books for children are about as varied in their scope as those for grown people.*[31]

Not every commentator was so enthusiastic about this change. *Old and New* lamented the great growth and change in children's books fearing that fictional children were all too likely to teach real children slang, the notion that they were accomplished enough to reform their own parents, and other undesirable things.[32] Books for children could no longer be considered, automatically, good for children. The answer to this problem was an increased need for criticism of children's literature. *Old and New* felt that the poor quality was largely due to a lack of proper reviewing. The writer urged education periodicals, Sunday school journals, and children's magazines to subject children's books to "a severe and unflinching criticism." [33]

Whether in response to the exhortation in *Old and New,* or for other

9

reasons, the period bloomed with reviewing of children's books. Between 1865 and 1881, thirty-six periodicals examined in detail for this study printed reviews and notices of more than 2,500 books, and editions of books, with more than 4,000 separate reviews. This was part of what Alice M. Jordan called "the first widespread awakening to the need of critical appraisal," and a large awakening it was indeed.[34] Most important periodicals of the day printed at least occasional reviews of children's books, a few printed a great many.

The periodicals themselves were constantly increasing in number, and, despite the great depression, by the mid-eighties the number published was many times larger than in 1865. Mott reports that 700 periodicals of all types were published in 1865.[35] By 1870 the number had increased to 1,200, and by 1885 had reached 3,300; though many of them were specialized, some were regional in their interest and had small circulations, and many were short-lived. Not least in this growth of periodical literature was the development of children's magazines of an unprecedented excellence. This general flowering of American periodical publishing brought with it a prodigious growth in book reviewing in which children's books received a large measure of attention.

In brief, both the publishing and reviewing of children's books reached a hitherto unequaled volume in the decade-and-a-half immediately following the Civil War. Yet no period in modern children's literature remains so misrepresented by later commentators, no period so misunderstood or so maligned. With almost willful blindness twentieth-century writers on children's books have dismissed the reviewing of children's books in this era as reviewing for which "children's books, if read at all when written about, were read for ulterior ends." [36] *A Critical History of Children's Literature,* published in 1953, stated that there had been no serious criticism of children's books until almost the third decade of the twentieth century.[37] Louise Seaman Bechtel went even further. In her anxiety to prove her thesis, she delayed the blossoming of the children's books themselves until after 1880, stating that "from 1880–1900 we had suddenly a wealth of good reading for young people." [38] Then she listed the major children's authors of the 1860's and 1870's as the writers of her period. Susan Coolidge's "Katy" books were even attributed by Bechtel to the twentieth century. A careful study of this period can only reveal how mistaken these writers were, how rich the period actually was in children's books of high quality, and in reviewing that compares well with the reviewing of children's books today. Perhaps, so far as informing the general public is concerned, it would not be extravagant to claim that the reviewing of children's books immediately after the Civil War was superior to that of our own time; for now the reviewing of children's books is left to a few papers and to those periodicals that cater to libraries and the educational world.

The period from 1865 to 1881, inclusive, has been chosen for this study for a number of reasons, in addition to the need to correct misconceptions. The year 1865 provides a good beginning year. Publishing ventures that had been postponed during the war years were begun again in 1865. The *Nation, Hours at Home, Our Young Folks,* and *The Catholic World,* all of which reviewed children's books, were founded in that year. Though none of the "classic" children's books were reviewed in American periodicals in 1865, it was in that year that William Worthen Appleton was sent abroad and returned with the 1,952 copies of the suppressed first edition of *Alice's Adventures in Wonderland,* which Carroll and Tenniel had rejected as unsuitable for the more refined English taste.[39] The book was reviewed in *The Nation* in 1866,[40] as was the first post-war American children's classic, Mary Mapes Dodge's *Hans Brinker; or The Silver Skates,* which had been intended for the 1865 Christmas trade, but was published just a little too late.[41]

In 1882, Caroline M. Hewins published her *Books for the Young,* and in the following year began her work for *The Library Journal* where she compiled each year a kind of anthology of reviews of children's books not unlike the *Book Review Digest* today. After 1881, then, the material on reviewing of children's books has been gathered into one place for those who would take the time to look at it. The previous seventeen years have been virtually untouched. It is with these years that this study deals. The study will examine criticism of children's literature and trends in children's publishing during the period.

Thirty-six periodicals have been examined for the study. This group of periodicals includes the most important literary magazines of the time, as well as a sampling of other types of periodicals: religious, educational, book-trade, and children's magazines, which were selected on the basis of the evaluation given them in Mott's *A History of American Magazines.* All major literary magazines of the period were included, and a sampling of other types of periodicals, based on Mott's evaluation, was also included. Every review of a children's book or a book recommended for children was studied.

The literature on book reviewing was used to define a satisfactory book review. This material is discussed in detail in Chapter 5 below, but in brief, the qualities looked for in reviews were these: (1) a summary of the book, including the action, characterization, and incident; (2) an awareness of the interests of children; (3) an evaluation of the book, relating it to children's literature in general; and (4) any comments of a special nature, such as analysis of illustrations, or of the print-

11

ing of the book. By such an examination, both the quantity and quality of reviewing of children's books will be demonstrated. It is hoped that a greater understanding of the children's books will result. An understanding of the children's books of an era is an important part of the understanding of the period as a whole.

2

THE PUBLISHING OF
CHILDREN'S BOOKS, 1865-1881

The publishing of children's books in the period from 1865 to 1881, cannot, of course, be divorced from publishing in general. Those things which affected the general publishing business affected the production of children's books. No publishers were devoted exclusively to the publication of books for the young. Separate departments and juvenile editors did not exist; yet this did not mean that the publication of children's books was by any means neglected. So greatly did it flourish, in fact, that some critics felt they must protest against the deluge of children's books that appeared each year. A writer in *Old and New* lamented, "Our fathers and mothers had not story books enough to read. Is it not a worse misfortune for our children that they have too many?" [1]

It is most difficult to provide exact figures to indicate the numbers of children's books published each year, though the incomplete records of the *Publishers' Weekly* indicate an average of around 300. But titles were omitted from that periodical's annual listings, and many new editions were probably omitted. Other titles lay on the borderline between children's books and adult books, so that they might be classified as either type. Beyond question, the number was large and formed a sizable percentage of the annual output, which, in 1874, reached more than 10,000 books for which copyrights were granted.[2]

Publishing of children's books in the United States was chiefly centered in the three cities of New York, Boston, and Philadelphia, in that order, as was the publishing industry in general. If the books reviewed represent a fair portion of the total, then New York had about twice as many publishers issuing children's books as Boston, and Boston about twice as many as Philadelphia. In actual titles published, however, this ratio does not hold, for Boston had several publishers who annually issued great numbers of books for children, including the king of publishers for children, Lee & Shepard, and Philadelphia was a major seat of prolific Sunday school publishing. Nevertheless, by sheer weight of numbers of publishers, New York was the leading publishing city for books for the young, as it was in the publication of periodicals that reviewed children's books.

New York's publishing for children was dominated by three types of publishers; the general trade firms, the American branches of British houses, and the firms which catered to, or were controlled by, religious denominations. Included in the first group were such major publishers as Harper & Brothers, D. Appleton & Company, G. P. Putnam's Sons, Charles Scribner & Sons, and Dodd, Mead & Company. Although Dodd, Mead came very close in the sixties to being a Sunday school publisher, the firm's output of children's books gradually became more diversified. Hurd & Houghton was a major New York publisher of children's books, but, after its merger with James R. Osgood, the firm centered its activities in Boston. The opposite situation prevailed in the case of E. P. Dutton & Company. Originally located in Boston, Dutton moved to New York in 1869.

Each of these firms published the works of at least a few well-known authors of children's books. Harper & Brothers had on its lists, among others, the English writer, Dinah Mulock Craik, Paul Du Chaillu, Thomas W. Knox, author of the "Boy Traveller" series, and Charles Carleton Coffin, whose historical books were popular for generations. Hurd & Houghton's best known author was probably Horace E. Scudder. Scribner published books by Mary Mapes Dodge and Frank R. Stockton, the editors of *St. Nicholas*. Dodd, Mead had the dubious honor of heading its list of children's authors with the name of Martha F. Finley, author of the interminable "Elsie Dinsmore" series. But it would be impossible to list here all the authors of the various publishers.

Robert Carter & Brothers and Anson D. F. Randolph headed the list of New York publishers who catered to the Sunday school trade. Though there were numerous other such publishers, more books were reviewed from these two publishers than from any others of their type. Books by Joanna and Julia Mathews, published by the Carters, were reviewed in almost every year of our period. Maria Charlesworth's pious stories issued from that house also, but their most famous author was probably Susan Warner, over whose *Wide, Wide World* Louisa May Alcott let Jo weep copious tears as she sat in the March family apple tree. A reviewer for *Hours at Home* neatly evaluated the contribution of Robert Carter & Brothers.

14

If the children of this generation go without pure, healthful, and elevating reading it will not be the fault of the Messrs. Carter. Possibly they may have published a stupid book, but they never published a bad one.[3]

The same description could apply equally to Anson D. F. Randolph.

Contributing large numbers of titles to the New York output of children's books, were the American branches of a number of important English publishing houses. Most important and most prolific of these were George Routledge & Son, publisher for both Kate Greenaway and Walter Crane, Cassell, Petter, Galpin & Company, Thomas Nelson & Sons, and Macmillan. Though they by no means issued all of the English children's books appearing in the United States, most of their children's books were imports or American editions of English works.

Though Boston had its share of Sunday school publishers, the general trade firms dominated the field of children's books. Lee & Shepard, Roberts Brothers, D. Lothrop & Company, A. K. Loring, Lockwood, Brooks & Company, and the various firms with which James R. Osgood was associated, dominated the field. Lee & Shepard, with a number of the most prominent and popular writers for children of the period, came the closest of any firm to being a publisher exclusively for children, though Roberts Brothers could probably claim to have had the most distinguished list of writers for children in America, including Louisa May Alcott, Susan Coolidge, and the English writer, Juliana Horatia Ewing.

Lee & Shepard must be considered the pre-eminent publisher of books for children in the United States during the period following the Civil War. There is ample evidence that the firm was considered the leader in production of juvenile literature at the time. *Putnam's Magazine,* in 1869, commented that "From the press of Lee & Shepard, Boston, we have a constant yield of juvenile literature, always of a popular, and often of an excellent quality." [4] In the *Independent,* in 1877, we find the comment that "there is hardly a poor juvenile on Lee & Shepard's list, for they seem bound to keep at the head of publishers of children's books." [5] *The Weekly Trade Circular* quoted a long description of the activity of Lee & Shepard from the *Boston Globe* which provides an interesting picture of the firm.

Among the publishing firms of the country, Lee & Shepard, of this city, are honorably distinguished by activity and enterprise. Indeed, their activity is insatiable. They are not content to be the great wholesale "jobbers" of books in the New England States, though their business must be immense in this department; they publish books of their own as well as sell all books published in any part of the country.

Their store on Washington Street resembles a bee-hive, the queen bee simply ensconced in a little room in the rear. This room is the objective point of authors who desire to get into print. Modestly penetrating through the throng of customers, they at last reach the sacred retirement of the publisher, who is to decide whether the births of their minds shall live or die. The space is very small, hardly sufficient to accommodate publisher and author, if either has a tendency to extend his legs. In this sanctorum, however, have been arranged the terms by which Oliver Optic, Elijah Kellogg, and Sophie May have made moderate fortunes. The publisher is shrewd, knowing, bright-eyed, exquisitely polite and frightfully sagacious, a man who has an instinct for selecting what will meet the needs of the popular mind, but who has at the same time a charming way of telling the horde of writers besieging him that they have just missed hitting the mark in white, and that he cannot venture his capital in the expensive operation of putting their manuscripts into octodecimo volumes. He is very benign in manner, but he is relentless in judgment. Meanwhile, the disappointed author hears the hum of bargaining in the front—thousands of volumes being sold by the indefatigable Lee, while he, the author, is discoursing in the rear with the benign but unconquerable Shepard.[6]

This varied activity did not prevent the firm from bankruptcy during the lean years of the depression.

One other Boston publisher should be mentioned. A. K. Loring did not have the long list of authors that Lee & Shepard could boast, nor yet the quality of Roberts Brothers' list. But it did have an author whose name would live on long after most of his books would be forgotten. Loring had the good fortune to be the publisher of Horatio Alger, Jr.

Philadelphia was the third most important publishing center, but in that city it was the Sunday school publishers that dominated the scene. Both Baptists and Presbyterians used Philadelphia as their center for production of books for the young. However, the names of three trade firms appear over and over in the reviews; J. B. Lippincott & Company, Porter & Coates, and Claxton, Remsen, & Haffelfinger. Lippincott led the field, but Porter & Coates could claim the exceedingly prolific Harry Castlemon as one of its authors. A reviewer for *Old and New* indicated the general attitude toward Philadelphia publishing in a review of two books from Claxton, Remsen, & Haffelfinger. "These are pleasing little stories of a Sunday-School description," he said, "with a certain quaint prettiness of binding which seems unsuitable for a Philadelphia book." [7]

Smaller numbers of children's books issued from other cities. Small, but regular, numbers of books came from Cincinnati, and, especially in the late seventies and the eighties, from Chicago. St. Louis produced a few children's books, some in the German language, and Baltimore a few, chiefly from the Catholic firm of Kelly, Piet, & Company. Several San Francisco books were reviewed, almost all from the house of A. Roman & Company, publisher of the periodicals, *Overland Monthly,* and *The Californian.* Cambridge, Massachusetts, Schenectady, and Troy, New York, each had a single publisher whose children's books were reviewed. Hartford, Connecticut, had two publishers, but one of them, the American Publishing Company, which published *The Adventures of Tom Sawyer,* was a subscription publisher rather than a trade publisher. The only books reviewed not from those cities were direct imports from England. Not a single children's book was reviewed which had been published in the states of the former Confederacy.

The period from 1865 to 1881 was a period of considerable instability in the publishing business, with both lean and full years. Boom, depression, great fires, and a basic weakness in the book trade contributed to the industry's troubles, as did cutthroat competition, particularly between rival editions of reprinted English works.

The boom that followed the termination of the war was as evident in book publishing, as in other sectors of the national economy. In the autumn of 1865, a writer testified in *Hours at Home,* that publishing was experiencing a new expansion.

> *The publishing trade of America is now, like other branches of commerce in the United States, assuming new and enlarged proportions on the deliverance of the nation from the incubus of civil war.*[8]

A letter dated October 10, 1866, to the editor of the *Independent,* described the flurry of activity in book publishing in Boston.

> *It is remarkable that, among all the threatening signs of the political sky, the manufacture of books is proceeding with almost unequalled energy. Printers and bookbinders never employed so many workmen, and it is not uncommon for them to work fifteen hours a day, sometimes extended to twenty. As they work usually by the piece, these long hours are their own choice, and are directly profitable.*[9]

In 1871, *Old and New* reported a busier summer than ever before in book publishing.[10]

By 1871, however, there were reports that belied the general prosperity. The March, 1871 issue of *The Literary World* devoted an editorial to "A Dull Season," describing a condition anything but prosperous.

> *Since the new year came in the publishers and sellers of books have had no reason to complain of a press of work. Trade has been univer-*

sally dull, and there are no trustworthy indications of an immediate improvement. At no time within our recollection have publishers been so reluctant to engage in new enterprises. Manuscripts are declined by hundreds, without examination, and an unknown author has but a poor chance of getting his book before the public. With the Spring a livelier state of things is hoped for; but there are no sound reasons for anticipating an active trade. So long as general business is dull, the book trade must suffer in common with other branches. While the people feel poor, as at present, they will rank books among the luxuries instead of among the necessaries of life.[11]

But the dullness of trade in 1871, was as nothing to the real depression which began in 1873.

At first, the advent of the depression was greeted with considerable optimism. *Publishers' Weekly* predicted in its September 27, 1873 issue that the financial panic of the previous Thursday would have no serious effect on the book trade.[12] Less than two months later it was predicting that the trade would improve with the holiday season.[13] But in each subsequent issue it acknowledged that trade was, after all, not good, blaming the difficulties on the psychological response of the buying public to the panic, rather than actual economic conditions.

The whole difficulty this season has been not that the country is poor, but that the people have become frightened, and the right way out of it is by courage, vim, and go-ahead-ativeness.[14]

Fewer books appeared that season than in the previous one, and the general lag lasted until the end of the decade. Each year many books for children were published, but the comments in literary periodicals indicated considerable uneasiness and concern. And a number of publishers were forced into bankruptcy. J. B. Ford & Company of New York, publisher of Mrs. Stowe, and Lee & Shepard of Boston, were only two of many publishers who suffered such reverses.

William T. Adams wrote an apologia for Lee & Shepard in an editorial entitled "Valedictory," for the final issue of *Oliver Optic's Magazine*. His brief explanation of the causes of the firm's misfortunes, with changes in detail, might have been the same for other firms as well.

It is not necessary to mention in detail the reasons which induce the publishers to suspend the publication of this Magazine. Their business misfortune has been recited all over the nation, in the newspapers and by word of mouth; and they have received the generous sympathy of the whole community, not the least from those who have suffered the most heavily by the calamity. Their heavy losses by the fire of 1872, and three other fires that followed close upon it, the financial panic of the succeeding year, and the unexampled business stagnation of the last two years, were the principal causes of their failure. Though unfortunate, their integrity has not been questioned, even by those who take the severest view of the case.[15]

Publishers' Weekly praised the efforts of Lee & Shepard to ward off failure, declaring, "They are honest men." [16]

That children's books in great number continued to appear was attested to by *Publishers' Weekly,* which declared that, despite its own predictions to the contrary, the number of books that appeared each holiday season was large. In 1875 the magazine had expected only a handful of books to appear at the holiday season, but there had been many, and in 1876, with still harder times, there were just as many.[17] *Scribner's Monthly,* in 1877, felt that the number of new books appearing might even be a sign of recovery.[18] Beginning in the same year, *Publishers' Weekly* began to see signs of improvement, but they were signs based on other indicators than the number of titles published. The crops of 1877 were good, an improvement which *Publishers' Weekly* hoped would bring a general upturn in business.[19] But when 1878 ended, the book trade had seen the worst year it had ever had, aggravated by bad spring weather in the West and by the epidemic of yellow fever in the South.[20] Not until after the harvests of 1879, a bumper crop year, did the long awaited improvement in business actually bring sizable relief to the publishers. *Publishers' Weekly* happily reported "The Turn of the Tide," as soon as the 1879 holiday season had ended.

> *The year just closed has brought at last the turn of the tide toward better times which has been so long hoped for and so long delayed. The fact that the value of the crops of this country this year exceeds last year's valuation by four hundred millions of dollars is at once suggestive of the source of the new prosperity and proof that it is real and not fictitious. This new total is largely increased by the value added by manufacturing processes, and the money which represents this new wealth has passed from one hand to another until at Christmas-tide the fair share of the surplus found its way out from the pockets of the people who have not bought books for years, into the bookstores.*[21]

But the end of the depression did not bring to an end all the troubles of the publishing business. Two problems peculiar to the business continued. One of these was the "unsystematic conducting of the book trade." [22] Various attempts were made to reform book selling, to limit discounts and bring order to the business. *Publishers' Weekly* devoted countless editorials to this problem. In 1874, an attempt was made to restrict discounts to 20 per cent, but *The Literary World* predicted it would not succeed.[23] In 1877, *Publishers' Weekly* reported that the problem still remained unsolved.

> *The passion for large discounts is by no means eradicated, and books are still often published at a much higher price than the normal rate, simply to permit a large discount. This holds especially true in juveniles.*[24]

The other unsolved problem was the need for international copyright. The failure of the Congress to approve an international copyright agreement no doubt proved an advantage to the unscrupulous, but was harmful to the publishing business in the United States as a whole, encouraging, as it did, a kind of competition which was undesirable. Though much has been made of American piracy of English works, many English writers were well paid for the American rights to their works. Often through, perhaps, faulty communication more than one publisher thought he had the rights to the same work so that rival American editions appeared. A bitter publishing war between Harper and Scribner arose, in part at least, from this situation, drawing comments from at least one reviewer.[25] Various editors championed the copyright cause, frequent articles appearing in *Scribner's Monthly,* as well as other magazines.[26] *Publishers' Weekly* made this issue a principal part of its policy.

This situation was disadvantageous for authors as well as publishers, though the condition improved for American authors after the British copyright made it possible for Americans to copyright their books by residing on British soil when their books were issued. *Publishers' Weekly* reported in 1871 that Louisa May Alcott had gone to England in order to protect her rights when *Little Men* was published.[27] But for British writers, there was no protection except the honor of the publishers. Most of them were, fortunately, honorable men, but there were notable exceptions. Walter Crane wrote a letter to the editor of *Scribner's Monthly* asking the magazine to draw the attention of its readers to the fact that the edition of *The Baby's Opera* with the imprint of McLoughlin Brothers of New York was an unauthorized edition, far inferior in reproduction of the pictures to the authorized edition of George Routledge & Son.[28] The editor responded with an enthusiastic appraisal of Crane's genius, and an earnest appeal to the public to boycott the pirated copy of Crane's work.

Mr. Crane is one of the most accomplished of the younger birth of English artists. He has already made a shining mark as a painter of "pictures," ordinarily so called, and a designer of picture-books for children. In this latter field he stands without a rival, and his work is as original as it is beautiful. There were of course some pretty children's books before these appeared. Cruikshank made several; Richard Doyle made one or two that were delightful; but Cruikshank's books had no color, and Doyle's color was not good;—the art of color printing which we have perfected, and which Walter Crane has known so well to employ, was not in use in those early days. Walter Crane has every charm. His design is rich, original, and full of discovery. His drawing is at once manly and sweet, and his color is as delightful as a garden of roses in June. And with these accomplishments he comes full-handed to the children—and to their parents and lovers too!—and makes us all rich with a pleasure none of us ever knew as children, and never could have looked to know. We are all his debtors for a substantial good,—for beautiful art brought to our every-day enjoyment for a valuable helper in the education of our children. And we join our earnest appeal to his quiet and modest one, that the American public will respect his work, will refuse to put into their children's hands, just because it is a little cheaper, a shabby travesty of a beautiful original.[29]

St. Nicholas discussed the same letter and warned its readers away from McLoughlin Brothers' pirated edition.[30]

Though the age was producing book illustrations of a quality hitherto unknown, at least in books for children, there remained considerable controversy over the quality of book manufacture, as well as the quality of writing for children. At the beginning of 1870 *Hours at Home* had nothing but praise for the new holiday books.

Another Holiday season is now fairly with us, and the booksellers' shelves glitter with the beautiful volumes which have for many months demanded in their production and ornamentation the imagination of artists and the best skill of engravers, printers, and binders. The year just ending, it is safe to assert, will be a notable one for the advance that it shows over all have gone before in the art of book manufacture; for the production of a volume which shall at once instruct the mind and delight the eye is indeed an art, and one of the finest of the fine arts too. Those of us who remember the gaudy Annuals which were once regarded as gems among Gift Books, in the light of these later days are almost ashamed to confess that we could once have been satisfied with the external glitter and internal vapidity of the volumes which we are now only too glad to tuck away behind more modest works on our library shelves, or to add to those attic libraries which we were willing to resign to rats and mice of a literary turn of mind.[31]

The *Literary World,* on the other hand, declared that the pictures "in American illustrated books are not always so good as they might be." [32] Most printing of pictures in the United States had been poor for several years, with the exception of a half dozen volumes, mostly from Boston. Field, Osgood, & Company, Hurd & Houghton, and the *Riverside Magazine* provided the only first rate examples of skill in the printing of pictures.[33]

The development of the heliotype process for printing illustrations played an important role after the early seventies. The process was described in a review of Jules Verne's *Five Weeks in a Balloon,* the illustrations for which had been reproduced by this method.

It may interest some of our readers to know briefly what the heliotype process is. A photograph of the object to be copied is taken upon a sensitized surface of chromated gelatin, the subjection of which to another chemical process leaves the negative so relieved that it can be printed from with ink, like type or wood-cuts, in an ordinary copper-plate or lithographic press. Thus are obtained the quality and truth of a photograph, combined with the durability and cheapness of an engraving. The process is similar to that known as the Albert-type. It has not yet been employed nearly to the extent it would be profitable and pleasant in this country, though quite extensively used in Europe.[34]

Five years later *Scribner's Monthly* claimed that "the books and pictures for young folks . . . show the marvelous advance which art and invention have made." [35] The writer felt that each year's output outdid that of the previous year. *The Dial* supported the judgment of *Scribner's Monthly,* stating the improvement in art was most apparent in the excellence of book production.

Year after year the execution displayed in this department of production shows an increase of refinement corresponding with the growth of aesthetic taste in the leading promulgators of the theory and practice of the fine arts. We have but to examine the fresh collections of children's books prepared for the holiday season to discern how far a genuine feeling for the beautiful and a correct appreciation of its laws and possible interpretations have been developed among us. Until recent years, the pictures in which color was invoked to lend its charms to form have been for the most part dismal in result. They were excrescences rather than embellishments, and perverted the sense they were intended to edify. Thanks to the broadening and strengthening of the foundations of art schools in our communities, the process of engraving and printing, as well as drawing and coloring, have been so advanced that paintings can be reproduced on the pages of our books with a high degree of skill and precision. Now that our artificers in lithography are attaining a mastery of color—the last and most sacred element of beauty,—we may look forward to an endless multiplication of enchantments by the inspired book-maker, who will add to the spells of literary genius the miracles wrought in the world of fine art.[36]

Publishers' Weekly, quoting from Charles F. Richardson in *The Independent,* reported a different appraisal of the merits of American book production. Great progress had been made during the Civil War, but the post-war period had been one of decline.[37] The post-war devotion to painting, architecture, and interior decoration gave little encouragement to the production of books.

People will not spend money for the intelligent adornment of what they have not time to read. Even among readers, art on the wall proves a dangerous rival to art on the book-shelf.[38]

One trend in house decoration, however, is of interest because of its peculiar connection to children's literature. Walter Crane's picture books provided the inspiration for a fad in wall decoration. A *Literary World* reviewer described some of the uses to which Crane's drawings were put.

We have seen them set as a substitute for tiles around a chimney-piece, inserted in book-cases and side-boards, employed by way of a frieze at the top of a tinted wall and as a dado at the bottom, used with excellent effect to fill the panels of a door, and, prettiest of all, to line the back of a shelved cupboard, in which ornamental china was kept. The effect of the superb and harmoniously blended reds and golds and blues behind the china was admirable. A nursery which we sometimes visit has a band of these pictures set round the room at the top of a chair rail. This band is an inexhaustible pleasure to the children who inhabit the room, and according to their nurse, "as good as a drawing lesson any day." [39]

But this was a passing fad and had only a remote connection with trends in children's books.

To evaluate the quality of the printing and decoration of children's books in the period following the Civil War is actually very difficult, for these books, like those of most later periods, show very great differences. Some of them were poor and unattractive indeed. Books from McLoughlin Brothers, for example, were often as inferior as Crane claimed their edition of *The Baby's Opera* was. Such books as Scudder's Bodley family series, from Houghton Mifflin, and Mary Mapes Dodge's *Rhymes and Jingles* from the firm of Scribner, Armstrong, & Company, were superior in printing and binding. Scudder's books attracted particular attention for their fanciful board covers.

Considerable disagreement existed also about the merits of the books themselves. *Lippincott's Magazine,* in 1870, felt that much of the writing for children was done by hack writers with the left-overs from their writing for adults.[40] The bookstores were filled with "pretty volumes full of vapid sentimentalism or diluted science." But the next year *Literary World,* though not denying that there were too many poor children's books, predicted that the number of such books would rapidly decrease, for children had little taste for much of the inane material published for their reading.[41] *Old and New* drew up a lengthy indictment of children's books, condemning both the writers and the publishers.

> *It is constant wonder how so many poor books get themselves published. The only explanation is in the low standard of the public—the publishers provide what will sell. Yet, while making for them this excuse, there is none for some of the tricks of trade which are practised. One is, the republication of books with changed titles, especially English reprints; which, issued by different houses, sometimes appear under three or four different names. Another, a late invention, and widely prevailing is selling books in series and in boxes. The former is not so objectionable, though often different volumes by the same author vary greatly, and it would be better if each could stand on its own merits; but what can be said of preparing a box with one good book in it, calling it a series with that name, and filling it up with four or five really worthless books for various ages and with no possible connection; and thus foisting upon the community what has proved else unsalable?* [42]

But at the beginning of the eighties, *The Dial* felt that adults, looking back at the books of their childhood, could only envy the contemporary child with books written by the best writers and illustrated by the best artists, while they had had only "the 'goodie' books in the Sunday schools; plain and clumsy to ugliness in their exterior, and mortally dry and unpalatable in their contents" and a few of the older classics.[43]

Even in the post-Civil War period, it was the Sunday school books that were judged to represent the poorest quality in books for the young. *Hours at Home* conducted what almost amounted to a crusade against the inferior books published for Sunday school libraries, with editorial comment and special articles appearing in various issues. If a searching examination of these books were made, the editor felt, the community would be shocked at the "mass of trashy, diluted, unnatural" books.[44] The preparation of such books was left entirely to "the whim of authors and the interest of publishers." [45] *Harper's* reviewer, not receiving as many as formerly to review, wondered if Sunday school library books might be improving or if the publishers were sending only the few better ones for reviewing.[46] Whatever it was, the criticism aimed at these books helped to focus attention on the qualities required for high quality in children's books, and had its influence on children's literature in general.

3

TYPES OF CHILDREN'S BOOKS

During the period from 1865 to 1881, children's books developed in ever greater numbers and in an ever widening range of form and content. Some of the forms were new, but for the most part they represented literary types that had been in vogue earlier, the great change was to be found rather in tone and attitude than in the types of books. But new or old, certain trends in children's books were characteristic of the period and provided the patterns in children's books for many years to come.

Perhaps the two most characteristic elements in children's literature at the time were the "quarto" or "children's quarto," and the ubiquitous series. *The Literary World* reported that the quarto was "by far the most attractive and popular form in which books for children are now made." [1] The quarto was a book, square in shape, half picture and half text, which was produced in particularly great numbers for the Christmas trade each year. *Literary World* reported that 300 children's quartos were announced in the United States and England for the 1879 trade.[2] Though many books of varied content were issued in this square shape, well-illustrated and printed on an excellent quality of paper, the more common type of quarto was one in which the pictures formed the original foundation, and the text was written to fit. The Bodley books of Horace E. Scudder were quartos, as were Knox's "Boy Travellers" books, Hezekiah Butterworth's "Zigzag Journeys," many of Frank R. Stockton's works, and countless others. This group was especially characterized by the reprinting of illustrations that had been used elsewhere previously, a fact frequently noted by the reviewers. A reviewer for *Hours at Home* commented that one set of illustrations was from *Harper's New Monthly*

Magazine and from various volumes of natural history and travel.[3] He did not, however, feel that they were any the less valuable for that reason. *Lippincotts' Magazine* described the pictures for Knox's *Adventures of Two Youths in Japan and China* as "veterans in service." [4] A glance through the back volumes of *Harper's* does, in fact, reveal the source of many of the illustrations for Knox's books. Scudder's and Butterworth's illustrations came from the stock of cuts held by their publishers also. Interestingly enough, an identical picture appeared in Horace Scudder's *Mr. Bodley Abroad* on page 157 with the caption "Climbing the Alps in Imagination," [5] and in Butterworth's *Zigzag Journeys in Classic Lands* as the frontispiece with the caption "Climbing Parnassus." [6] The picture shows mountain climbers attempting to pull and push three donkeys up a nearly perpendicular mountain, the donkeys' riders clinging valiantly to the necks of their steeds all the while. Probably Estes & Lauriat and Houghton, Mifflin & Company had bought copies of the same cut at one of the frequent auctions of the time. Both books appeared in 1880 so that it is impossible for one to have copied from the other.

This practice of writing books to fit available pictures placed a considerable burden on the authors, forcing them to put strange twists and turns into their stories in order to make them fit their illustrations, though surprisingly many of them read well despite this formidable obstacle to unity. Stockton was one of the most successful writers of this type of book, but he often wrote a brief story to fit each picture rather than a continuous narrative with many pictures. The *Literary World* effectively analyzed the difficulties of this type of book in a review of Susan Coolidge's *A Guernsey Lily.*

> *The book has no faults that we can discover; its defect, as a picture-story book, is that obviously the text was written to fit the pictures, and not the pictures made to fit the text. This, of course, may be a serious clog on a writer's independence, naturalness, and grace of movement, and such a book is to be judged more by its pictorial than its literary merit.*[7]

The surprising thing is that many passable books were written under just such circumstances.

The second striking characteristic of children's books was the series. Nearly every publisher had his share of series—"The Doll World" of Roberts Brothers, "Books for Girls" which Dinah Mulock Craik edited for Harper & Brothers, Charles A. Stephens' "Our Young Yachters" from J. R. Osgood & Company, and series by scores from the prolific authors of Lee & Shepard; the "Rosa Abbott Stories," "The Helping Hand Series," "The Proverb Stories," "Little Prudy's Flyaway Series,"

"The Charley Roberts Series," "The Elm Island Series"—until a reviewer for the *Independent* felt himself forced to comment on this "mania."

> *The fashion of publishing books in sets, which has been growing for sometime, seems now to be at its hight* [sic]. *Every other book is issued in some library or other; and since publishers follow, rather than create public taste, we infer that buyers prefer to purchase books of whose general nature they can tell something by the title of the series to which they belong.*[8]

Though these post-war series were undoubtedly the forerunners of the modern series of children's books, bane of the librarian, there were, in most of them, distinct differences from those of today. The average series of the sixties and seventies was not a series which, having begun with a single title that achieved popularity, was continued as long as the author and publisher could capitalize on children's interest in a popular character or set of characters. Rather, each series was planned as such from the outset and contained from four to six titles. Martha F. Finley's "Elsie Dinsmore" books were rather the exception than the rule, though, it is true, Rebecca Clarke, having finished a series with one group of characters, might write her next series about their cousins. Not that these series were any better than their modern counterparts, but only that they were slightly different is the point here. They were no worse than their modern equivalents and superior to some.

In general, a listing of the types and subjects of children's books from 1865 to 1881 would include practically every type that is read by twentieth-century children. A few types, fortunately, have disappeared. No more do we expect our children to read, with profit, such temperance tales as Mrs. J. P. Ballard's *Caught and Fettered* and Mary Dwinell Chellis' *All For Money,* M. Alice Sweet's *Coals of Fire* and Annette Lucille Noble's *The Queer House in Rugby* or the myriad other books for the young of the National Temperance Society and Publication House. The Congregational *Independent* reviewed them faithfully, though not often favorably. The few temperance tales reviewed elsewhere were, on the whole, even more unfavorably received. Surely only the authors and the misguided publication house felt that such stuff was truly the proper material for children's reading.

The Sunday school library book, typical of the book available to the post-Civil War child, has dwindled and all but disappeared. The committees and boards maintained by the various denominations were a major element of the publishing business rivaling the commercial trade itself. Each year they turned out books about pious children, miraculous conversions, and precocious young monsters who set themselves above their own parents in virtue. Even when the situations and characters were not impossible and unbelievable, these books tended to be dully didactic or overly sentimental. Mrs. Margaret Sangster's books for the American Tract Society were often sweetly sentimental, yet devoid of action and made plain to even the dullest reader where duty lay.

But piety and sentimentality were not left to the church publication committees alone. Dodd, Mead's Martha F. Finley was almost without rival in this field. Whether she wrote about the famous Elsie Dinsmore, in books which carried this heroine from childhood to old age, or about Mildred Keith, uprooted and carried away to pioneer in fever-ridden Indiana, Miss Finley knew that virtue resided always with the best people and was at no time more admirable than when that virtue was misunderstood or envied. The Keiths are insufferable in their feeling of superiority over all their Indiana neighbors. The reader looks to see them humbled and made human at last. But no, when fever sweeps the community, the true superiority of the Keiths, and especially of Mildred, is proven. Mildred, in her unflinching virtue, wins the recognition she has so deserved.[9] All the while, the youthful reader has wept while Mildred was misunderstood, while fever has struck her brothers and sisters, and even her saintly mother. What stony heart was unmoved!

Louisa May Alcott has described how another author's books could move readers to tears. Jo sat in the crotch of an apple tree, weeping constantly as she read Susan Warner's *The Wide, Wide World*. The postwar period found Miss Warner still busy with her pen. Others wrote in this same vein, even after Miss Alcott had pointed another way. Isabella Alden, writing under the pseudonym of Pansy, published sentimental books each year. Even as late as 1881, Margaret Sidney could launch her successful *Five Little Peppers* on a road to success based chiefly on a large measure of sentimentality. But Miss Sidney, like her characters, may have had better reason than some authors to believe that rather remarkable things may happen. She married her very successful publisher, Lothrop, so that the importance of succeeding by her own ability was of less moment.

Hurd & Houghton of New York issued in 1871 what may have been the last noteworthy example of a time-honored literary type. Mrs. Helen Aldrich De Kroyft's *The Story of Little Jakey* seems almost to belong to an earlier day, with its sad tale of the sorrows and early death of a noble, almost angelic child.[10] The story begins when the narrator first meets Little Jakey in the Institution for the Blind in New York, but deals mostly with the sad tale of the child's life as he tells it to this good lady: the earliest happy years with his mother and father, both painters, his father's degradation from drink, the sad leave-taking, the shipwreck in which the mother perished. The child was "A Wee Saint" who clearly belonged to God rather than to this world. Knowing this, the narrator devoted her energies to helping the child prepare for his eventual home. The sadness was all but unbearable when the end came.

We sprang to him, and leaning over his little form, and feeling that his pulse was really still, and his sweet breath hushed forever, Miss Wild exclaimed, "Why, the dear lamb is gone, surely gone" and it seemed that her heart would break, while she wept and sobbed over the little stranger who had so long shared her tender care. Then gently smoothing down his long white night robe, and pressing his little feet in her warm, loving hands,—

"The dear, tiny things," she said, "they are cold already. No light has blessed their journey through this world; but, God be praised, they are gone, treading now where there is light and love for all."

The beams of the morning were just glimmering through the shutters, when, with tears of pitying love dropping down over our cheeks, we kissed Little Jakey's dear mute lips farewell. Miss Wild closed down his dear eyes, and placed the wreath above his head again, and we bowed ourselves by his little lonely bed, while the angels bore his pure spirit away.[11]

A final chapter, with the title "Never More", describes the funeral of this blind, holy child who longed for wings so that he might fly to "Himmel vare Gott lives." But the days of weeping at the deathbeds of children were really over, and though even Miss Alcott extracted the full measure of tears at the bedside of Beth, a different tone pervades her work.

The March girls and two Toms, Tom Bailey and Tom Sawyer, typify the new in children's books after the war, and Little Jakey provides a somewhat exaggerated archetype of much that had gone before. Actually, Mary Mapes Dodge's *Hans Brinker; or, The Silver Skates* was the first important children's book in America to present truly real and believable children, though *Tom Brown's School Days,* from England, predates it. The Brinker children seem believable even today. Hans may seem almost too good, but he is not perfect, nor does he miraculously win the skates. His sister does, but we have seen from the beginning that no one can equal her speed in skating. If the story drags somewhat as the young aristocrats and their English visitor tour the major cities of the Netherlands, they do have adventures, and the reader suffers through the tourist's guide; his appetite for Hans's adventures even greater when he returns.

Hans Brinker dealt with real children, but real children in a far-off land, and a quaint land at that. Only two years away was the first part of that classic of American family stories, *Little Women,* which would make its author the queen of American writers for the young. What is there of adventure in this book? Very little. On the surface there is little to distinguish it from many another story about a family of girls. What is different is the freedom that pervades it, a freedom that is sometimes boisterous, sometimes headlong, sometimes unwisely used, but always tempered by family responsibility. The book was something new largely because, in showing this kind of freedom tempered only by kindly guidance, Miss Alcott was presenting a real American family, so life-like and believable that their names would become household words to generations of American children.

Thomas Bailey Aldrich, in his *The Story of a Bad Boy,* did, for the American boy, what Miss Alcott had done for girls. William Dean Howells quickly grasped the true novelty of this book.

> *Mr. Aldrich has done a new thing in—we use the phrase with some gasps of reluctance, it is so threadbare and so near meaning nothing—American literature. We might go much farther without overpraising his pleasant book, and call it an absolute novelty, on the whole. No one else seems to have thought of telling the story of a boy's life, with so great desire to show what a boy's life is, and so little purpose of teaching what it should be; certainly no one else has thought of doing this for the life of an American boy.*[12]

No matter what the adventure Tom was involved in, he was a recognizable boy, just the kind of bad boy most boys were or would have liked to be, "not so very, very naughty after all," as Miss Potter said of her two bad mice. Rather he was completely natural, doing foolish things, doing dangerous things, but never cruel or malicious ones. More than 90 years later, this book, which first appeared in the pages of *Our Young Folks,* is still available to young American readers, and has been offered as a premium to those children who would eat enough of a flavorless prepared cereal to earn a reward that had some zest and taste.

These three classics of American children's literature were only the beginning of a veritable flood of believable stories about real American children, some of them as great or greater than the pioneers, some of them poor, but a great many of them satisfactory books. Adeline Dutton Train Whitney wrote of recognizable girls and was, in her own day, compared with Miss Alcott as an outstanding writer for girls. It was Sarah Chauncey Woolsey, as Susan Coolidge, however, who produced in her "Katy" books, works which would rival Miss Alcott's in longevity, and would be nearly as popular in England as Miss Alcott's. Rebecca Clarke (Sophie May), too, was a writer in the realistic vein who, though surely not the genius Thomas Wentworth Higginson declared her to be, was by no means to be despised. If some of her stories seem to be more about children than for them, there is no denying that the children are real. Her greatest fault may well have been that she wrote too much, so that her books showed evidence of haste. Yet they were exceedingly popular.

Tom Bailey was to be excelled by a still greater Tom in the middle of the 1870's. It was natural that Tom Sawyer would call to the mind of the critic *The Story of a Bad Boy* and that the two would be compared. William Dean Howells has admirably described the appeal of Clemens' book to boy readers, in his description of Tom Sawyer's character.

> *In a word, he is a boy, and merely and exactly an ordinary boy on the moral side. What makes him delightful to the reader is that on the imaginative side he is very much more, and though every boy has wild and fantastic dreams, this boy cannot rest till he has somehow realized them . . .*
> *The local material and incidents with which his career is worked up are excellent, and throughout there is scrupulous regard for the boy's point of view . . .*[13]

Other writers contributed readable books to this wealth of realistic fiction for children. Frank R. Stockton contributed short stories, though his most notable ones might well be classed with fanciful writing. John T. Trowbridge wrote realistic, though sometimes somewhat improbable, stories in his "Jack Hazard" series, depicting a lower order of life along the barge canal. Noah Brooks spanned the continent in his *The Boy Emigrants,* a book for boys about the westward movement. Brooks himself had lived in California and worked with Bret Harte on the *Overland Monthly*. But his Western interests did not prevent him from contributing the first notable work in another new genre, the sports story. His *The Fairport Nine* was one of the earliest baseball stories.

The girls were not forgotten in fiction about the West. In 1878, Helen Hunt Jackson published *Nelly's Silver Mine* with a Colorado setting. Despite the implication of the title, the book was a relatively quiet one, realistic both in character and incident. A reviewer for *The Atlantic Monthly* declared it dealt with the less "barbaric side of Western frontier life" and was, therefore, a welcome relief.[14]

And there were books, certainly, from which the critic craved relief in a more quiet narrative. In the new rush of freedom in children's books many authors, at least in the eyes of their contemporaries, went much too far, so that one of the great outcries of the time was against "sensationalism" in children's books. Deservedly or not, much of the criticism of sensationalism was directed at one particular author, Lee & Shepard's

William T. Adams, better known to thousands of young readers as Oliver Optic. Adams was one of the most prolific of American writers, producing as many as four adventure books for boys each year, a few books for girls, and editing a magazine for young people. His is one of the great success stories of the day.

Both in popularity and in remuneration, Adams must have been one of the most successful authors of the time. *Old and New,* reporting in 1870 the most popular works of the previous three months at the Boston Public Library, declared that the novels of Oliver Optic and of Horatio Alger, Jr. were the most popular boys' books.[15] *Little Women* held the honors for novels read by girls. *Publishers' Weekly* reported convincing evidence of Adams' financial success. In an article devoted to the author, the magazine declared that he was writing two stories for the *Fireside Companion* for which he was to receive $2,500 each. It then quoted a comment from *The Watchman.*

We are acquainted with persons who would do the same thing for half the money, but can't find any one to offer them that half![16]

But the real testimony to Adams' success and to the success of the type of book he represents lies neither in his sales, nor in the sums of money he received for his stories. Rather, it lies in the profusion of attacks made on him and his writing. If countless children welcomed each new book from his pen, for his critics that was one more reason he should be suppressed. A reviewer for *The Nation* declared, "If we could have our way, the sale of them should stop immediately and entirely." [17] The *Penn Monthly* called his writing the "sensational, flashy 'Oliver Optic' books." [18] Though he may have had his defenders, they were far from vocal. But no one ever needed a defender less, for Mr. Adams could defend himself and had a forum from which to do so, his magazine.

In the third volume of *Oliver Optic's Magazine* he began the long series of editorials in which he defended himself and his writing. This first editorial seems not a defense of himself so much as a defense of the new freedom in children's literature.

Parents, guardians, and immaculate people do not insist that skating, base ball, coasting, and other boyish recreations, shall have a direct moral influence on the characters of the players. They are quite willing that they should enjoy themselves, so long as their sports do not have an evil or immoral tendency. The idea, if we comprehend the matter, is merely amusement, with a certain amount of physical development. Boys don't skate for the improvement of their systems, as a general rule; they skate for the fun of it.

Young gentlemen can obtain just as much physical exercise from sawing wood, hoeing potatoes, and other manual labor, as from skating, coasting, and base ball; but the unreasonable fellows refuse to consider hard work, especially if useful, as amusement. To a certain extent we feel willing to endorse their position, and to declare that there is not much fun in hoeing corn, as a steady employment.

The immaculate people, even, are willing that boys should play, purely for the fun of it; but they are not willing they should read for amusement. Condemning Jack Sheppard, Dick Turpin and "yellow-covered" literature in general, we think there is much to be read for "the fun of it"—many books that are exciting, interesting, or amusing, with no immoral or dangerous tendency in them. Boys may read for amusement, and will derive as much benefit, mentally, from the study of language as the bodily frame does from manly sport.[19]

By 1872 Adams was on the defensive. In another editorial, he declared that entertainment and a wholesome tone were all that should be demanded of a book for boys and girls. Even "sensation" was not to be feared, unless there were too much of it.

Therefore we say,—and it is a big "therefore,"—do not be afraid of interesting books, even if they do not contain information on all topics; do not be afraid of excitement, so long as it is healthy; do not keep young minds always on the high pressure system of instruction.[20]

If in this editorial he was on the defensive, in the next one he attacked. The editor of *The Christian Union* had accused Lee & Shepard of withdrawing its advertising because of unfavorable reviews of Adams' books, an allegation Adams declared emphatically to be false.[21] The truth, he declared, was that *The Christian Union* had dropped in circulation, and, in any case, Lee & Shepard had only advertised there because they were "dogged, hounded, teased, implored, persecuted" and offered half the periodical's normal advertising rate, 75¢ a line, instead of $1.50. Besides, Adams declared, a moral issue was involved. If his books were so bad, *The Christian Union* should not be willing to accept advertising of them.

If the defense against *The Christian Union* seemed petty, Adams' next venture in self-justification is touching. Delivering an address at the dedication of the Dorchester Branch of the Boston Public Library, Adams found himself introduced to his audience as Oliver Optic. Feeling that some criticism might be implied in that introduction, he described the beginning of his literary career, the inspiration he had received to write for boys from the Sunday school class he had taught there in Dorchester.

The address, which he printed in his magazine closes with an *apologia* for his writing.

> *When I began to write stories for the young I had a distinct purpose in my mind. How well I remember the books I read, unknown to my parents, when I was a boy! They were "The Three Spaniards," "Alonzo and Melissa," "The Mysteries of Udolpho," "Rinaldo Rinaldini," "Freemantle the Privateersman," and similar works, not found at the present time on the shelves of the booksellers, though, I am sorry to say, their places have been filled with books hardly less pernicious. The hero of these stories was a pirate, a highwayman, a smuggler, or a bandit. He was painted in glowing colors; and in admiring his boldness, my sympathies were with this outlaw and outcaste of society. These books were bad, very bad, because they brought the reader into sympathy with evil and wicked men. It seemed to me that stories just as interesting, just as exciting, if you please, could be written without any of the evil tendencies of these harmful books. I have tried to do this in the stories I have written for young people. I have never written a story which could excite the love, admiration, and sympathy of the reader for an evil person, a bad character. This has been my standard, and however others may regard it, I still deem it a safe one. I am willing to admit that I have sometimes been more "sensational" than I now wish I had been, but I have never made a hero whose moral character, or whose lack of high aims and purposes, could mislead the young reader.*[22]

Almost, those final lines amount to a recanting. Almost, they amount to an admission of guilt. But the most famous attack of all on Adams and other writers of his type was even then under way. And after that attack, his revenge would show no lack of self-confidence.

Louisa May Alcott was publishing in successive installments, throughout that year of 1875, her *Eight Cousins,* a mild little book about a girl, Rose, raised by a group of aunts. Nothing in the book had aroused controversy and the popularity of it seemed likely to equal Miss Alcott's earlier books. But the August installment contained a bombshell, for in this portion of the story Miss Alcott put herself forward as a leading critic of "sensational" books for boys. Mrs. Jessie and Dr. Alec had entered the room where Will and Geordie sat reading. Mrs. Jessie wasted no time in informing the boys that she disapproved of their books.

> *"I wish Rose would drive a bargain with Will and Geordie also, for I think these books are as bad for the small boys as cigars for the large one," said Mrs. Jessie, sitting down on the sofa between the readers, who politely curled up their legs to make room for her.*

"I thought they were all the fashion," answered Dr. Alec, settling in the big chair with Rose.

"So is smoking, but it is harmful. The writers of these popular stories intend to do good, I have no doubt, but it seems to me they fail because their motto is, 'Be smart, and you will be rich,' instead of 'Be honest, and you will be happy.' I do not judge hastily, Alec, for I have read a dozen, at least of these stories, and, with much that is attractive to boys, I find a great deal to condemn in them, and other parents say the same when I ask them."

"Now, Mum, that's too bad! I like 'em tip-top. This one is a regular screamer," cried Will.

"They're bully books, and I'd like to know where's the harm," added Geordie.

"You have just shown us one of the chief evils, and that is slang," answered their mother quickly.

"Must have it, ma'am. If these chaps talked all right, there'd be no fun in 'em," protested Will.

"A boot-black mustn't use good grammar, and a newsboy must swear a little, or he wouldn't be natural," explained Geordie, both boys ready to fight gallantly for their favorites.

"But my sons are neither boot-blacks nor newsboys, and I object to hearing them use such words as 'screamer,' 'bully,' and 'buster.' In fact, I fail to see the advantage of writing books about such people unless it is done in a very different way. I cannot think they will help to refine the ragamuffins, if they read them, and I'm sure they can do no good to the better class of boys, who through these books are introduced to police courts, counterfeiters' dens, gambling houses, drinking saloons, and all sorts of low life."

"Some of them are about first-rate boys, mother; and they go to sea and study, and sail round the world, having great larks all the way."

"I have read about them Geordie, and though they are better than the others, I am not satisfied with these optical[23] delusions, as I call them. Now, I put it to you, boys, is it natural for lads from fifteen to eighteen to command ships, defeat pirates, outwit smugglers, and so cover themselves with glory, that Admiral Farragut invites them to dinner, saying; 'Noble boy, you are an honor to your country!' Or, if the hero is in the army, he has hair-breadth escapes and adventures enough in one small volume to turn his hair white, and in the end he goes to Washington at the express desire of the President or Commander-in-Chief to be promoted to no end of stars and bars. Even if the hero is merely an honest boy trying to get his living, he is not permitted to do so in a natural way, by hard work and years of patient effort, but is suddenly adopted by a millionaire whose pocketbook he *has returned; or a rich uncle appears from the sea, just in the nick of time; or the remarkable boy earns a few dollars, speculates in pea-nuts or neck-ties, and grows rich so rapidly that Sinbad in the diamond valley is a pauper compared to him. Isn't it so boys?"* [24]

And so she continues, finally extracting from the boys a promise not to read another such book for a month. But Miss Alcott then proved herself a realist, for Geordie promised himself he would finish his book the moment the month ended.

Miss Alcott had unleashed a storm. Some of the critics scolded her, but they were gentle compared to the gentleman whose books she had called "optical delusions." His fury knew no bounds.

Appleton's Journal was amused by Miss Alcott's attack on her fellow author.

> *We wonder, by-the-way, if Miss Alcott realizes the risk she runs in deviating from her own proper field of story-telling and "dropping into" criticism? She devotes a couple of pages of "Eight Cousins" to denouncing the methods of her co-workers and disrespectfully characterizes certain well-known ornaments of current literature as "optical delusions." It is fortunate for her peace of mind, perhaps, that she has put the Atlantic between her and that din of warfare the first notes of which, as we understand, have already sounded.*[25]

Scribner's Monthly deplored her charge of undesirable language in the books of Oliver Optic, for this was her own greatest weakness.[26] She had attacked Optic "for teaching slang as eagerly as ever a 'hazed' Freshman retaliated upon Freshman when he became a Sophomore."

Mr. Adams, himself, did not spare her. In the September, 1875, issue of *Oliver Optic's Magazine* he reacted to her attack.

> *Miss Louisa M. Alcott is publishing a story in a magazine. It is called "Eight Cousins." The title was doubtless suggested by Miss Douglas's highly successful story, "Seven Daughters," published in our magazine. . .*
>
> *It is a critical story; or, at least, it contains a chapter of criticism. The topic is "Sensational Books for Boys," and she treats it as flippantly as though she knew what she was writing about. The mother of the two boys in the story says she "has read a dozen at least of these stories," from which we infer that Miss Alcott has read them; but, judging from some of the quotations she makes, she has read them with her elbows.*
>
> *She objects to "these popular stories," but she is very indefinite. She mixes things terribly. She quotes from one book and judges another by*

what she quotes. She quotes from the Optic books and then fastens upon them the sins of other books, as we shall presently show.[27]

Adams then defended himself, showing by quotations and statements that most of the evils cited by Miss Alcott were not to be found in his books, or were greatly exaggerated by that lady. The Farragut incident, he said, was more modest than she had indicated, though his quotation fails to dispel her charge. The army hero story was not nearly so extravagant as she had claimed. Much of what she said, he insisted, was "the critic's fiction and sensationalism" and did not appear in the books.

Then he turned Miss Alcott's method upon herself, showing that some passages could not be understood by boys, and that *Eight Cousins* had its own fair share of slang. By his final paragraph the reader wonders if he did not, finally, have the best of it.

Miss Alcott's criticisms are extremely sensational, as we have shown. She seems to have deliberately misrepresented the books she writes about. Her citations indicate that she had the book in hand from which she quoted, and we hardly think she could have made a tooth-pick out of the true cross without intending to do so. She could not have put that bar-room illustration into "Sunny Shores" without meaning to be untruthful. In a word, she has said enough to identify the Optic books, and then charged them with the faults of all the juvenile books published, her own included.

Ah, Louise, you are very smart, and you have become rich. Your success mocks that of the juvenile heroes you despise. Even the author of "Dick Dauntless" and "Sam Soaker," whoever he may be, would not dare to write up a heroine who rose so rapidly from poverty and obscurity to riches and fame as you did; but in view of the wholesale perversion of the truth we have pointed out, we must ask you to adopt the motto you recommend for others—"Be honest and you will be happy," instead of the one you seem to have chosen: "Be smart and you will be rich." [28]

Though the battle with Louisa May Alcott was the most famous one, it was by no means the only battle with another author of children's books in which William T. Adams was embroiled. The previous year his opponent had been Emily Huntington Miller, who had read a paper before the Chautauqua Assembly in which Oliver Optic was cited as an example of an author whose books were "trashy" and "sensational" and had a bad influence on their young readers.[29] Adams, in turn, accused Mrs. Miller of jealousy because her own books were not popular, and defended the heroes of his stories as honest boys whom Mrs. Miller might well imitate.

Adams took the brunt of the attacks on sensationalism in boys' books, but he was by no means the only offender. The name Horatio Alger, Jr., was often coupled with his, and, indeed, Alger got his start through the encouragement of Adams. Most of the criticisms aimed at Adams were equally applicable to Alger's books and to those of a goodly number of others. Harry Castlemon wrote books about the lower classes of the South, in which boys win successes no less remarkable than those of Adams' and Alger's boys. The Rev. Elijah Kellogg, another of Lee & Shepard's authors, wrote a less sensational type of story but Charles A. Stephens and James De Mille were frequent users of the Optic methods. The wild adventure books of Mayne Reid and William Henry Giles Kingston were imported from England, but did not compare in lasting popularity with a French import, Jules Verne. His books were as extravagant as any, but were built with such a semblance of truth that they were far more acceptable. In sheer numbers these books of adventure provided one of the largest groups of children's books of the era. If concern for their influence can be accepted as testimony to their popularity, they were also among the most in demand.

The period was not one of realism alone in children's books, for fantasy and fairy tales appeared each year. The best of these were not, however, by American authors. Those of lasting value were all from England. The first notable fantasy published in the United States after the close of the war was the Appleton edition of *Alice's Adventures in Wonderland,* which provided one of the chief fantasy types of the time. Mrs. Molesworth's *The Cuckoo Clock,* Jean Ingelow's *Mopsa, the Fairy,* Jane G. Austin's *Moonfolk,* and Eliza Tabor Stephenson's *Pansie's Flour-Bin* were all, more or less, indebted to Carroll's work.

Hans Christian Andersen provided the other main pattern in fantasy. E. H. Knatchbull-Hugessen, British Member of Parliament and writer of stories for children, found his inspiration in Andersen, though his writing was coarse where Andersen's was delicate. Horace E. Scudder was one of Andersen's greatest admirers, but an inadequate imitator of his master. New tales and new translations of Andersen's own works continued to appear.

Several American authors wrote in this vein. Scudder's earlier books for children were fantasy. Susan Coolidge, whose contribution in realistic stories was more durable, achieved her first notable success with *The New Year's Bargain,* in which two children strike a bargain with the months for a story and a gift from each of them. A reviewer in *Scribner's Monthly* declared the idea of the book to be "a conception by no means unworthy of Andersen himself, and so original and vivid as to entitle Susan Coolidge at once to a high place among writers for children." [30] Virginia W. Johnson won considerable praise for her *The Catskill*

Fairies. In this book a little boy named Job, left alone on Christmas Eve, found himself snowed in. As the hours passed, various creatures and animals told him stories. Only *The Nation* dissented from the general praise accorded the work, declaring it showed a "want of originality." [31]

Even these works, however, were not enough to establish American writers as equal competitors of English writers of fantasy for children. Successive years saw Lewis Carroll, George MacDonald, Mrs. Molesworth, Mrs. Ewing, Dinah Mulock Craik, and other English writers win the laurels on both sides of the Atlantic. All of them won the praise of American reviewers, and a lasting place in literature for children.

The Continent made its contribution as did England. The fairy tales of Edouard Laboulaye and of Jean Macé appeared in English translation. Wilhelm Friedrich Carové's *Story Without an End* was published in Sarah Austin's translation by Scribner, Welford & Company. Baroness E. Martineau des Chesnez's *Lady Green-Satin and Her Maid Rosettè*, still available in this country in the 1950's, was published by Porter & Coates in 1873. Countess de Segur's *Fairy Tales for Little Folk* had appeared in 1870, the same year that William Busch's *Max and Maurice; A Juvenile History in Seven Tricks,* still popular with German children, was first introduced to young American readers. It is doubtful that any subsequent generation of children had the same riches from abroad.

Various publishers issued annuals, richly illustrated and in brightly colored bindings, for the Christmas trade. To these regular annuals were added the bound volumes of children's magazines, providing anthologies of all the types of children's literature. Each year, collections of stories, old folk tales and literary tales for children appeared on the market. Perhaps the most notable anthology of the period was Horace E. Scudder's *The Children's Book* in 1881, in print for decades and still considered one of the best anthologies of children's literature.[32]

Poetry and verse were available in large quantities. Several editions of Mother Goose were printed, with a variety of different illustrations. Mary Mapes Dodge contributed to verse for the very young in her *Baby Days* and *Rhymes and Jingles.* Laura E. Richards began to publish her delightful nonsense verse in such volumes as *Five Mice in a Mouse Trap.* Edward Lear was reissued to add to the nonsense verse. Anthologies of poetry were numerous. Whittier collected his *Child Life,* which the *Appleton's Journal* reviewer declared was "more *about* children than *for* children." [33] This was the fault of many such anthologies. Francis Turner Palgrave's *Children's Treasury of English Song* was more consistently praised than any other for the high quality of the selection. Both *Appleton's Journal*[34] and the *Penn Monthly*[35] noted that Palgrave had included poems by Blake not included previously in children's anthologies.

40

Probably Elizabeth Barrett Browning and Christina Rossetti made the most famous contributions to poetry for children, though many other volumes of original poetry were published. Mrs. Browning's poetry in *Poems of Childhood* was mainly "mournful pieces," more suitable for mothers than for children.[36] The work of Miss Rossetti was generally praised and felt to be more suitable for the young.

A vigorous attempt was made to bring many of the classics of world literature to children through simplified versions, retellings, and editings. Chaucer, Spenser, and Ariosto appeared in children's versions. Shakespeare was redone repeatedly, both in prose and verse. There were various retellings of the ancient Greek stories, most outstanding being those of Alfred J. Church, who retold both Homer and Virgil for children. Church's Homer is still to be found in most children's libraries.

Sidney Lanier provided notable editions of famous works. *The Boy's Froissart* was welcomed everywhere as a valuable book, skillfully and tastefully edited. *The Boy's King Arthur* and *The Boy's Mabinogion,* following in successive years, were equally well received. These works were generally considered too difficult in the original, or, in the case of Malory, too poorly organized, for satisfactory children's reading. But when books, long a part of children's reading, were edited and condensed the reaction was very different.

The Californian had little patience with William T. Adams' *The Young Folks' Robinson Crusoe.*[37] The reviewer suggested that Adams gave a better performance in his own field than he did in condensing Defoe. The general reaction against the condensing of the classics was vociferous. *Harper's New Monthly Magazine* ran an editorial on the subject.[38]

The strangest examples of the rewriting of classics, however, were the books of Mary Godolphin and Mrs. Edward Askley Walker. These two authors attempted to rewrite such books as *Pilgrim's Progress, Robinson Crusoe, Swiss Family Robinson* and *Sandford and Merton* in words of one syllable. They were actually well received. *The Nation* declared that Mary Godolphin's *Robinson Crusoe in Words of One Syllable* "ought to put primers out of countenance, and make both teaching and learning to read a pastime." [39] For her *Swiss Family Robinson in Words of One Syllable, The Nation* had another judgment. This book was "monosyllabic in form at the expense of being trisyllabic in intelligibility." [40] Strange as these books were, they are in no worse taste than the countless rewritings and condensations that misguided educators have provided for the children of the twentieth century. Godolphin's books have an amusing quaintness, though their appeal to children is doubtful. Only a paragraph is needed to illustrate her method.

At length the time drew near for a ball, which Mrs. Merton meant to give. Dress and the dance were the sole things that the girls could now think of, but Maude was bent more on that which is good and true. Maude had been at work on a large roll of clothes, which she bade Hal to give to the poor folk he spoke of. When Hal took it from her his eyes were full of tears, for he saw in Maude's face the mark of a good and true heart. So much does real worth set off the looks! And Hal could but think, if all the rest of the girls were as good as Maude, they might spare all the pains they took to curl their hair and deck their forms.[41]

But fiction and belles-lettres, though the largest part, were far from the whole of children's literature. Great numbers of informational books for the young were published, some of them thinly disguised with story, and others straightforward information. History, travel, biography, and science made up the largest groups of informational books for children, though there were smaller numbers of other types of books.

Both the beginning and end of our period saw the publication of histories of the Civil War. The most highly praised history of the day was Thomas Wentworth Higginson's *Young Folks' History of the United States.* The *Literary World* hoped it would revolutionize the writing of school histories, but later books proved that it did not even revolutionize the preparation of histories by literary men, for Hezekiah Butterworth's *Young Folks' History of America* was a sorry work.[42]

Among other notable histories were Charlotte Yonge's series on England, Germany, Greece, Rome, and the Bible, and John D. Champlin, Jr.'s *Young Folks' History of the War for the Union. The Children's Crusade* by George Zabriskie Gray was treated as a children's book, though William Dean Howell's declared that it was not.[43] Many of the Civil War histories altered between 1865 and 1881. William M. Thayer's *A Youth's History of the Rebellion* was a partisan Northern picture of the war, while Champlin's *Young Folks' History of the War for the Union* was scholarly and judicious.

Three histories of Boston for young people appeared in 1881, Butterworth's *Young Folks' History of Boston,* Samuel Adams Drake's *Around the Hub,* and Scudder's *Boston Town.* Undoubtedly this threesome was indicative, in part, of Boston's consciousness of its own history, but it also indicated Boston's special interest in the reading and education of its young people. The three books invited comparison and comparisons of the three were made, though rarely a comparative judgment.

This interest in history was no doubt increased by the Centennial Exhibition in Philadelphia in 1876. Several of the histories of the United

States for children appeared about that time, as did many stories with a historical setting in revolutionary times. Charles Carleton Coffin's *Boys of '76* appeared in 1876, as did Will Carleton's *Young Folks' Centennial Rhymes,* Lucy E. and Clara F. Guernsey's *Washington and Seventy-Six,* William Henry Giles Kingston's *Virginia: A Centennial Story,* Charles H. Woodman's *The Boys and Girls of the Revolution,* and others.

Interest in history was accompanied by an interest in the lives of men who helped make history. Two series of biographies were especially popular and well-received, Edward Eggleston's "Famous American Indians" series, and George M. Towle's "Young Folks' Heroes of History" series. An interesting biography title was Horatio Alger, Jr.'s biography of President Garfield. With the title, *From Canal Boy to President,* Alger made the story sound like the life of one of his New York newsboys or bootblacks.

Travel and travelogue storybooks were in great popular demand. Virginia Haviland attributes the interest in travel to a number of factors; the development of trans-Atlantic steam navigation, the completion of the trans-continental railroads, polar expeditions, and Stanley's expedition to find Livingstone.[44] Undoubtedly, new contacts with Japan and the rest of Asia, following Perry's opening of Japan in 1854, also had its effect. Paul Du Chaillu's books for the young in the early post-war years were widely read, despite the annoyance of *The Nation* with the egotism and extravagance of Du Chaillu's supposedly factual tales.[45]

The travelogue storybook was the predominant form, however, in which this interest in travel was manifested in children's books. William T. Adams wrote his "Our Young Folks Abroad" series; Charles A. Stephens wrote a "Young Yachters Series," and a "Camping Out" series. Jacob Abbott's Rollo had travelled abroad, but these post-war travellers did not merely visit the countries; they had adventures in them.

The travelogue story book reached its peak with the series by Thomas W. Knox and Hezekiah Butterworth, and, to a lesser extent, Horace E. Scudder. In his "Young Travellers in the Far East" series, Knox sent two boys to travel through the countries of Asia with a schoolmasterish adult, fully capable of explaining local scenes and customs to the boys. Every place for which Harper & Brothers had an illustration was fair game for a visit by these tourists. The books seem pedestrian and decidedly stiff, but Knox had travelled and brought to them a wealth of information. Many reviewers felt that they were the best of their type.

Hezekiah Butterworth used another method. Many of the places to which the Zigzag Club made its journeys were places Butterworth had visited only in the library. But he mixed tales and history into his travelogues, thereby giving his books more the flavor that characterized Scudder's "Bodley" books, in which travel was only incidental to the telling of stories and the reciting of poetry. Their books, too, were dependent upon the pictures available in their publishers' warehouses, with the result that their narratives were frequently warped to fit the pictures.

History and its sister fields were not the only subjects in which children were provided with informational books. The post-Civil War period was greatly interested in science. Huxley was at the height of his reputation in England, and Professor Youmans had made himself Huxley's great spokesman in America. The *Popular Science Monthly* was founded in 1872, partly to bring Huxley's writings to American readers, and partly to propagate interest in scientific subjects. The children were not neglected. Jacob Abbott provided a "Science for the Young" series, which included such titles as *Heat, Light, Force,* and *Water and Land.* These, to coin a word, were "science-logue" story books, in which an instructor, not unlike Knox's, leads a group of boys through the world of science. Other writers provided the science without the sugar-coating of the story. John D. Champlin, Jr. wrote his *Young Folks' Astronomy* without fictional apparatus. Arabella B. Buckley, in her *The Fairy-Land of Science,* attempted to show that science itself was just as interesting as fiction, even fantasy. A highly praised book was *What Mr. Darwin Saw in His Voyage Round the World in the Ship "Beagle,"* an editing of Darwin's own book, keeping the graphic descriptions of the things he saw, but eliminating those sections of less interest to children.

Other types of books included works on musicians, on art, and even a book by M. L. Nesbitt called *Grammar Land,* which tried to turn grammar into fun by personifying the parts of speech. John D. Champlin, Jr., provided a *Young Folks' Cyclopaedia of Common Things,* and, to complete a reference set, a *Young Folks' Cyclopaedia of Persons and Places* Edward Everett Hale edited *Stories of War, Told by Soldiers, Stories of the Sea, Told by Sailors,* and similar anthologies, designed to arouse young people's interest in reading the originals from which Hale had taken his selections. Various kinds of how-to-do-it books were published, and much more of that type of material appeared in the children's magazines.

No brief discussion of trends in children's books in the decade and a half following the Civil War would be complete without some mention of children's magazines. This period might well be called the Golden Age of children's periodicals, for the greatest of them were published in those years. *Our Young Folks,* which was founded in 1865, set a standard that the best of them would follow. The *Riverside Magazine for Young People* excelled it in illustration, though not in the quality of literary contributions. It remained for *St. Nicholas,* under the editorship of Mary Mapes Dodge, to combine the qualities of the two earlier magazines into the greatest children's periodical of all. *Harper's Young Folks,* later *Harper's Round Table,* was another notable magazine of high quality.

In these, and in many other periodicals for children, appeared many of the stories that later were published in book form. Lucretia P. Hale's *Peterkin Papers* first appeared in *Our Young Folks,* as did Aldrich's *The Story of a Bad Boy,* Trowbridge's *Jack Hazard and His Fortunes,* and many others. Louisa May Alcott's *Eight Cousins* was first published in *St. Nicholas.* Noah Brooks' *The Boy Emigrants* first appeared there. Much of the material Scudder included in his Bodley books came directly from the pages of the *Riverside Magazine.* William T. Adams published many of his books first in *Oliver Optic's Magazine.* Others published in the *Youth's Companion* and other magazines of lesser fame. At no time during this period could children's books be separated from their magazines.

This was the world of children's books. Never before had children had books in such quantity nor dealing with such a variety of subjects. Never before had there been books of such quality either, but along with the truly excellent books there came great quantities of inferior books. With those books that provided delight and entertainment to children, while maintaining high moral standards, came others that, in order to entertain, were ever more wild and extravagant in incident, arousing complaints that they demoralized the children.

With this avalanche of books for the young, and with accompanying concern that many of the books were not good for children, it was natural that critics and commentators should come forth to attempt to set standards for literature for children and to create a body of critical writing in this field, aside from the book reviews. This criticism must be examined to gain proper perspective on the children's books and their reviews.

4

GENERAL CRITICISM OF
CHILDREN'S BOOKS

The criticism of children's literature which appeared between 1865 and 1881, though limited in quantity, provides considerable understanding of the movements in children's literature and of the attitudes of many of the reviewers. This body of criticism sets forth the standards that prevailed at the time and the purposes for which children's literature was felt to exist. Few periods have stated so clearly what a child's book should be and what it should not be.

Four critical papers best represent the contemporary attitude toward children's literature: an article, "Books for Our Children," in the *Atlantic Monthly,* by the Rev. Samuel Osgood, at that time a Unitarian clergyman; a series of articles with the general title "The Literature of Our Sunday Schools," in *Hours at Home,* by the Rev. George B. Bacon, a Presbyterian; the work of the Unitarian Ladies' Commission on Sunday-School Books; and the "Papers on Fiction and the Reading of School Children," presented at the 1879 conference of the American Library Association in Boston and reprinted in *The Library Journal.* Osgood's paper, appearing first, includes many of the ideas reflected in the work of the others. The papers presented to the American Library Association, near the end of the period, sum up the work of the earlier critics, question some of the standards, and pinpoint new problems aggravated by the increased use of public libraries by children.

When Samuel Osgood published his article, "Books for Our Children," in 1865, he was not providing a pioneer set of standards for children's books. The American Sunday School Union had set up standards for juvenile literature as early as 1830, according to Alice M. Jordan.[1]

Osgood's article, however, indicated a great change in attitude in thirty-five years. Jordan lists four major qualities which the American Sunday School Union felt a child's book must exhibit: (1) a moral and religious emphasis, (2) adaptation to the understanding of the child, (3) acceptable literary style, and (4) an American subject and attitude. The religious element was, however, held to be of far greater importance than the literary. Osgood reversed this emphasis and brought the needs of the child to the fore.

Osgood was one of the many New Englanders of the nineteenth century who combined a literary career with the career of clergyman. In 1835 he was editor of the *Western Messenger* published in Louisville, Kentucky, but by the early 1840's he had returned to New England. From 1849 to 1869, he was employed at the Unitarian Church of the Messiah in New York City, but in 1869 he resigned and, in the following year, took orders in the Protestant Episcopal Church. While at the Church of the Messiah, he had edited the *Christian Inquirer* and published articles on a variety of subjects.[2] His career exhibited that tolerance and liberality so characteristic of American Unitarianism. Certainly, it was a liberal spirit with which he wrote of children's literature.

Nowhere is Osgood's liberal attitude and the attitude of his generation more clearly indicated, than in his emphasis on the importance of heeding the needs and desires of childhood in producing juvenile literature. America, he felt, had produced no classics of juvenile literature largely because children's needs had been ignored.[3] In fact, the characteristic American children's book had been "a mistake," for it had been written in violation of children's first instincts.[4] Peter Parley made the mistake of trying "to make a precocious reasoning monster of the dear little child," but such mistakes should not be made again.

In order to forestall such repetition of error, Osgood set forth a description of the American child.

The American child is undoubtedly in some respects peculiar alike in temperament, disposition, and surroundings. He is somewhat delicate and sensitive in organization, and not as tough and thick-skinned, surely, as his English cousins. He grows up in the midst of excitement, with an average amount of privilege and prosperity unknown heretofore to the mass of children in any community. Our children are generally supplied with pocket-money to an extent unknown in the good old times; and the books that circulate among them at holiday seasons, and are sometimes found in school and Sunday libraries, often have a richness and beauty that were never seen fifty years ago on the parlor tables or shelves of parents. Reading begins very early among us; and the universal hurry of the American mind crowds children forward, and tempts them in pleasure, as in study and work, to rebel at the usual limitations of years, and push infancy prematurely into childhood, childhood into youth, and youth into maturity. The spirit of competition shows its head unseasonably, and there is a precocious fever of ambition among those who are taught almost in the cradle to feel that here the race for the highest prizes is open to all, and the emulation of the school is the forerunner of the rivalry of business, society, and politics. Our heads are apt to be much older than our shoulders, and English critics of our juvenile literature say that much of it seems written for the market and counting-room rather than for the nursery and playground. Yet we are not disposed to quarrel with the American child, or put him down at the feet of the pet children of Europe. He is a precious little creature, with rare susceptibilities and powers, whose very perils indicate high aptitudes, and whose great exposures should move us to temper not a little our pity for his failings with admiration for his excellence. Our boys and girls have done nobly, and the nation which they have now become may well prove its greatness by new wisdom and care for the boys and girls who are yet to grow up men and women and become the nation that is to be.[5]

This provided a picture of the American child as he differed from the English child, but not a picture of the child, as such, showing in what way he differed from the adult. Osgood next attempted to define this distinction, in order to determine differences in reading. Boys and girls are adults in *"nature,"* he said, but not in *"development."* [6] Everything that is contained in the adult is merely potential in the child. Children have intelligence and wills which should be taken into account in writing for them. Too many writers have treated children as though they were lacking in intelligence, were "little fools," giving them baby talk and twaddle, but those who did such writing were "great fools," failing to recognize that the child's mind was quicker and more intense than the adult mind.[7]

> *Children not only want the true thing said to them, but want to have it said in a true and fitting way; and no language pleases them so much as the pure, simple speech which the good old Bible uses, and which all our great masters of style follow.*[8]

Though there are real differences between children and adults, these differences lie in something other than in intelligence or in the quality acceptable in their literature. The best books are useful and pleasing to both. Rather, it is love, as passion, that distinguishes adult literature

48

from children's literature. Love is a part of human life, and of all literature, even children's literature, but not love in the form of passion. Love characterizes adult literature, but it is something else that takes that place in the literature of children, "a power quite as active and marvellous,—the mighty genius of play." [9]

Play, Osgood felt, was the key to children's literature. Children's books should be considered as a part of children's play, not their work. They must "win their way by their own charms." [10] This same element is also the distinctive one between literature for children and school books. One represents play and the other work. The best thing for the adult to do is to be honest and admit that study is work, rather than try to give children lessons disguised as playmates. "They are willing to have their pills sugared over, but do not like to have them called sugar-plums." [11] The adult has to realize that play requires no sacrifice of sense or purpose, but can carry "exalted characters or sacred truths" home to the children.

Even as play, children's literature requires all the "attention and emotion, the unities and the varieties of aesthetic art," and especially the varieties. Small children need "a variety of images in the easiest succession," as they find them in Mother Goose. The older the child, the greater the need for unity becomes, the organization of sensation. His literature should contain the symbolism of pictures in words, lines and colors; rich imagery and symbols opening to him "the gates of the whole world of truth and goodness and beauty." [12] It should teach him the difference between real beauty and shoddy imitations of beauty, between the truly excellent and the precious. Briefly stated, literature for children should teach them

> . . . to appreciate natural form, feature, and color, and composition, and so possess third senses and fancy with the materials and impressions of loveliness, that, when the constructive reason or the ideal imagination begins to work, it will work wisely and well.[13]

Osgood did not ignore the content of children's books, even though he so emphasized literary execution. He felt that the basic content of children's literature ought to be the great "universal and spiritual forces that bind us to our race and to God." [14] Beyond those universal things, American subjects should be included, especially the great ideas of the nation. The nation's strengths, however, not its weaknesses, should be illustrated.

He provided an admirable summary of what he wanted to see in children's books.

In claiming thus for our children's books this embodiment of wholesome truth in beautiful forms, we are not favoring any feeble dilettanteism, or sacrificing practical strength to pleasant fancy. Nay, quite the contrary; for it is certain that truth has power, especially with the young, only when it is so embodied as to show itself in the life, and to speak and act for itself. We believe in dynamic reading for children; and we now make a distinct and decided point of this, quite positive, as we are, that books are a curse if they merely excite the sensibilities and stimulate the brain, and bring on sedentary languor, and do not stir the muscles, and quicken the will, and set the hand and foot to work and play under the promptings of a cheerful heart.[15]

Osgood had thought carefully and well on children's books, stating a philosophy for them little different from that of the twentieth century. In fact, his emphasis on play is almost identical with the emphasis insisted upon by Paul Hazard, who has written with such wit on children's literature in our own time. His attitudes boded well for America's children.

When the Rev. George B. Bacon wrote his articles on children's literature, he was not attempting so ambitious a performance as had Osgood. Bacon's purpose was to reform the Sunday school library, rather than to set forth standards for children's books, but it was not possible to do the one without the other. While considering the requirements of a good book for the Sunday school, he found it necessary to consider the requirements of a good children's book.

The first problem Bacon found with religious juvenile books was that there were far too many of them.[16] He estimated that there had been five or six thousand volumes published for the Sunday school market, and, in view of the difficulty of getting reliable figures, even that estimate was probably a modest one.

Competing publishers and publishing societies keep the market full. "Favorite authors," known already by their dozen or half-dozen volumes, show a prolific celerity of production equal to that of the most popular contributors in the weekly story-papers. The increase of the number of houses in the book-trade which make a speciality of this literature, is another evidence in the same direction. That there must be "money in it," is evident enough from the rapid enlargement of the business, and from the rival circulars which come, like snow-flakes, from competing publishers, importuning country parsons and superintendents to "get the best," as in the battle of the dictionaries; evident enough, also, from the heavy discount which all the sellers can afford to make from the established prices of their volumes, and still live to sell and publish more.[17]

This profusion of publishing seemed an indication of the ephemeral nature of most of these books; yet books for Sunday schools should have some permanence. The Sunday schools should welcome good books, but should not be a haven for those that ought never to have been written.

One of the problems, he felt, was a lack of classification of the books in the libraries. Without some arrangement no one could know just what the books were.[18] Labelling a book a Sunday school book told nothing at all about it, but, by classifying it, the entire system would be strengthened. Books could honestly be themselves. If they were intended to be entertaining, they would not have to pretend to be religious. Real instruction could stand boldly forth without a wearisome tale.[19]

He described the history of literature for the Sunday school as having gone from "grave to gay," in his second article. Most of this paper was devoted to showing that these books had changed from morbid pictures of precocious children who died young, children whose sole purpose for living might be said to have been so that they could "be put in a memoir and published by the Tract Society," [20] to books of a very different nature. All the books, or nearly all, in the modern Sunday school were fiction, but fiction that was "stale and mouldy to begin with," and very poorly done.[21]

The modern Sunday school story had two major faults. First of all, it might teach "directly or indirectly, bad morality and bad religion." Secondly, it might have a bad effect simply because it was so inane. Though children's morals needed guarding, as great a need existed for guarding them from "virtuous twaddle." For a book to be religious did not make it good, for it could also be sentimental and false.[22] Too many authors tried to oversimplify truth, making things always turn out for the best in a way that life itself does not do. "It is softening of the brain which is to be apprehended, rather than hardening of the heart," Bacon declared.[23]

His third paper was devoted to a remedy for the situation. He felt that if Sunday school libraries could not be improved, then the Sunday schools themselves should be abolished; for the children could not be worse off if they had to find their own books, and possibly would be better off.[24] The books they found in the Sunday schools were prepared to appeal to them through their appetites, and their appetites had come to govern the very production of books. Bacon conceded that this was partly because the days of subjection of children were gone, but he felt the reaction had gone too far.[25]

A partial solution lay in defining the role of the Sunday school, in deciding whether it existed to entertain children or to instruct them. If they were to continue, some change needed to be made in the books kept in them. He suggested that factual books be included, travel, history, true adventure, and natural science. All of these would be preferable to the so-called religious fiction. Children would welcome them.

> *Indeed, a healthy child will, almost any time, choose fact instead of fiction, unless the fiction be of some most undisguised and wildly fantastic sort, such as a fairy story, or a nonsense story, or an allegory, or a fable. When he has fact he wants it genuine, and when he has fiction he wants it genuine. Give a child the chance to say what story you shall tell him, whether true or fictitious, and the chances are that he will choose the true one. Fictions made to look like truth, as are most of our religious "juveniles," are looked upon with wholesome aversion until the healthful taste of childhood becomes perverted and debased. There is a latent sense of the imposture, which provokes, in the prosaic, matter-of-fact mind of a hearty and robust boy, a just and natural resentment when he finds that what he has read is false. But fictions which upon their face are only fictions, making their appeal to the imagination, and moving in the unreal world of fancy,—these he will accept and heartily enjoy.*[26]

Bacon then praised the fanciful tales, their extravagance, their richness of invention, their "fascinating fidelity of detail," declaring them to be the very best kind of juvenile literature. He would not object, he said, if they were the only books in Sunday school libraries so long as they drove out the present ones. Sunday schools should have left two kinds of books, fact and fiction, each distinct from the other. There would be books of religious instruction, but good ones that made no pretense of being something else.

After listing the kinds of books that should be included in Sunday school libraries, Bacon made certain other suggestions. There would be better books, he felt, if there were no denominational publishing societies. The laws of supply and demand would have greater effect on the quality of books. Instead, the various denominations should devote their energies to the creation of a body that could do for their Sunday schools, what the Unitarian Ladies' Commission on Sunday-School Books had done for the Unitarians in selecting the best books for the young. Far more good was to be done in this way.[27]

This Ladies' Commission, and the lists of children's books which it published, had widespread influence on the children's literature of the time. Though its members were all Unitarians, and its work intended to serve the Sunday schools of that denomination, it won widespread approval from the periodical press and was imitated by other religious groups. Bacon was not the only non-Unitarian who praised its work.

Two articles concerning this organization appeared in *Old and New*.

One incorporated its annual report for 1871 which described the beginning of the Ladies' Commission and its method of work.

The Ladies' Commission on Sunday-school books originated in a meeting of ladies called at the Rooms of the American Unitarian Association, by Rev. Charles Lowe, Oct. 12, 1865. Mr. Lowe proposed, that, under the auspices of the Association, a library of Sunday-school books should be "selected with scrupulous care," so as to form "a collection that could be confidently recommended to the churches;" and he invited the ladies then present to organize for that purpose, and to ask the cooperation of others whom they thought competent to such a work.

Mr. Lowe's suggestion was promptly responded to, and a beginning made in a work which we trust has not been useless; but which has involved an amount of labor little expected by those who first put their hands to it.[28]

The list they had published consisted of three sections. The first was made up of books especially recommended for Unitarian Sunday schools. The second included books "highly recommended for their religious tone," but not adapted to Unitarian belief. The third part listed books that were good, but not of the type for Sunday schools. Out of a total of 3,554 books examined to the end of 1870, the ladies had rejected all but 977, nearly three-quarters of them. This highly selected list, they reported, had been very well received and extensively used.

The Ladies' Commission had about fifty members, divided into committees to read the books, each book being read by at least five members before it was voted upon. Because of the volume of work new members had been welcomed, mostly Boston ladies, but including corresponding members from Montreal, Chicago, Cincinnati, Milwaukee, New York, and elsewhere.[29] Each year, beginning in 1867, the Commission published either a catalog or a supplement to its existing catalog.

Publishers' Weekly published a report which included a tabulation showing the precentage of works the Ladies' Commission accepted each year from 1867 through 1873.[30]

The Catalogue of 1867 gives	*30 per cent*
The Supplement of 1868 gives	*24 per cent*
The Supplement of 1869 gives	*30 per cent*
The Supplement of 1870 gives	*18 per cent*
The revised catalogue of 1871 gives	*28 per cent*
The Supplement of 1872 gives	*22 per cent*
The Supplement of 1873 gives	*21 per cent*

Lee & Shepard made available to the ladies those books which they felt would be of interest to them, and the ladies subscribed to *Literary World* and to *Publishers' Weekly* in order to keep themselves posted on the current output of children's books. In addition, the ladies checked the book columns of the daily press so that no book might escape their attention.

In the same article the Commission gave a partial picture of what was included and excluded from their catalog.

> *While including in our catalogue a very wide range in subject and style, we have always been careful to exclude sensational books of every description, feeling very strongly that such reading, objectionable at all times, is peculiarly so to the class for whom we are working.*
>
> *We have met more than once both approval and objection on this score, but the arguments used against such exclusion, such as the popularity of such books, and their use in cultivating a taste for reading, have seemed to us applicable to circulating and public libraries, rather than to Sunday-school libraries, for which alone we attempt to provide in our regular work.*[31]

It was in the *Unitarian Review,* however, that the ladies actually enumerated the standards which they applied, listing those faults which were sufficient to exclude a book from their lists.[32] Poorness of execution was one of the most frequent faults. In this they included poor style, faulty structure, jumbled events, poor characterization and insufficient motivation, actions out of character, and stereotyped characters and incidents. They felt that adequate construction was rare, misuse of the English language all too common, with far too much use of slang. Another fault was what they called "mixed character," by which they meant that books started out with childhood, but moved rapidly into adulthood and the interests of adults. Many books, ostensibly for children, were really written about them in a way that was largely appealing to adults. The fourth major fault that could be laid to the writer was sensationalism, defined as exaggeration of incident, a lack of proper connection of cause and effect, and the "startling and often horrible character of events." In a few words the sensational was made up of "vulgar words" and "vulgar thoughts."

Sometimes they rejected books because of faults of the publishers, who issued series of uneven quality, using good books to float the poor. But the Commission's policy provided that in such cases the poor books cancelled out the good ones.

Only rarely did the Commission reject a book on doctrinal grounds alone. If the book was free from the other faults with which they were concerned, it was likely to have "positive merit." If it showed knowledge of human life and character, adequate style, and "correctness and purity" of language, it was likely to be accepted.

In general, the standards of the Ladies' Commission were negative, emphasizing those things that would cause a book to be excluded rather than accepted, but the effect was undoubtedly a good one. They emphasized literary qualities, not content. They forced the exclusion of the unrealistic religious novel which Bacon so strenuously objected to, and, though they were not so liberal in their standards as Osgood, they were exceedingly influential in improving the level of children's books.

If it is true that imitation is the sincerest form of flattery, or is even a testament to effectiveness, then the work of the Ladies' Commission was surely effective. In 1879, the *Literary World* announced that several Episcopal parishes of Cambridge, Massachusetts, had organized to provide the same scrutiny of books for their Sunday school libraries. The *Literary World* recommended the same thing for others.

> *The working of such commissions is easy and serviceable, and we see no reason why they should not be multiplied. Every large city might have its own. Existing libraries might be weeded, and future additions to them made under a censorship which should turn aside the poor and bad, and admit only the deserving and the valuable.*[33]

In the following year, *Literary World* announced the publication of the Episcopal commission's first list, and praised again the work of the Unitarian organization.[34] With such lists available, Sunday school books could be greatly improved. No Sunday school need have "twaddle," even though it might not have every good book available.

The fourth large contribution to the discussion of children's books took place at the Boston Conference of the American Library Association in 1879. The papers read at that conference were reprinted in the September-October issue of *The Library Journal* the same year under the general title, "Papers on Fiction and the Reading of School Children." Perhaps the papers might better be called a debate, than a discussion, for opposing views were presented, direct answers given, and the problems of children's literature clearly set forth by the members of the infant organization.

One of the first papers, by Kate Gannett Wells, emphasized the great need for parental supervision of children's reading in order to protect them from the books of such writers as Oliver Optic and Ouida, Louise de la Ramée, most famous for her adult *Under Two Flags,* but author also of such children's books as *A Dog of Flanders* and *The Nurnberg Stove.*[35] Ouida had been under frequent attack for the sensationalism of her novels. Miss Wells was, in a sense, the voice of reaction, for she would have sharply curtailed children's freedom, limiting their choice until they had reached seventeen or eighteen years.

Another paper, by Martha H. Brooks, a member of the Unitarian Ladies' Commission on Sunday-School Books, described the work of that commission, adding little that was new.[36] She did report that the publishers' habit of issuing books in boxed sets, which the Commission had so often complained about, was disappearing, but that their habit of reprinting older books, especially English books with new titles, continued and that many books were published in poor bindings. Her basic points were that children's books should be interesting, should look interesting, and should be free from both priggishness and sensationalism. Children should be given only the best.

Miss M. A. Bean presented an argument that has often bedevilled the public libraries.[37] Though stoutly maintaining she was not an enemy of "all juvenile literature," Miss Bean provided objections that applied to good and bad alike. Children read too many story books, with the result that they did poor work in school. She blamed "surreptitious reading during school hours," lack of attention, laziness, dislike of study, and poor memories on story books. She recommended that the books be of better quality and fewer in number, though it is difficult to see how this would have cured the problems she outlined.

The first revolutionary ideas were presented by S. S. Green, who not only defended fiction reading for the young, but also defended their reading such authors as William T. Adams and Horatio Alger, Jr. He insisted that sensational stories had their place in the collections of a public library and were far better reading for boys than the *Police Gazette* or dime novels. He commended the work of the Unitarian Ladies' Commission, but pointed out what he thought were weaknesses in their work so far as public libraries were concerned.

> *In using the catalogues of the Ladies' Commission it is important to remember that this organization seeks to provide books especially for children brought up under refining influences, and that were the ladies who compose it aiming to provide for the needs of public libraries they would use a little more latitude in the selection of books. Perhaps, also, the fact that gentlemen do not aid in making out the lists, limits somewhat their value.*[38]

The address of James Freeman Clarke did not enter into the controversy in the same way. He merely attested to the virtue of fiction, suggesting that care be taken not to stop children from reading fiction, but to raise their standards.[39] Thomas Wentworth Higginson, however, entered directly into the fray, defending the reading of the Optic-type books more strenuously than anyone else had done.

It is not a bad impulse but a good one which makes the child seek the reading you call sensational. The motive that sends him to Oliver Optic is just that love of adventure which has made the Anglo-American race spread itself across a continent, taking possession of it in spite of forests, rivers, deserts, wild Indians and grizzly bears. The impulse which leads him to Jules Verne is the same yearning of scientific imagination that has made the American the foremost inventor of the world. How much of the great daring of our American civil war was nurtured by tales of adventure, reaching lives that had until that war no outlet! You cannot repress those yearnings—you fortunately cannot. They are the efforts of the young mind to get outside its early limitations. You cannot check them by prohibition.[40]

For Mr. Higginson, the reading of adventurous fiction was almost a matter of patriotism, at least at first glance. But he makes other points which have a bearing on this attitude.

To begin with, the assumption of some of the previous speakers, as Mr. Higginson understood it, was that "boys are totally depraved and prefer bad fiction to good, and any fiction to fact." [41] To this he could not subscribe. If a boy refused to read a book because that book was dull, the refusal showed that the boy was intelligent. If we wish children to read good books, then the good books must be interesting. In closing, he agreed with Green that Oliver Optic should be supplied in the public libraries.

If, as Mr. Green has said, nothing takes hold of a neglected Irish boy, for instance, like Oliver Optic's stories, then I would give him Oliver Optic in copious draughts, and give it at the public expense; he will be all the less likely to supply himself with the Police Gazette *at his own cost.*[42]

William P. Atkinson took issue with Higginson. He believed that the reading of sensational books was a "mischievous influence," at least on the ordinary youngster.[43] Bright boys did not read Optic. His basic fear was that the youngster who began by reading Oliver Optic, would never rise to a higher level, but rather would come to read worse things.

Mellen Chamberlain attempted to summarize and evaluate what had gone before, though taking sides to some extent. He felt that prohibiting books was not the complete answer to the problem. Rather, librarians should, taking children where they were, attempt to lead them to better books. If one child was inspired to read better books, a kind of chain reaction should result, each child inspiring another, "and so on indefinitely." [44]

These papers cannot be considered literary criticism, in the strictest sense. They do, however, reflect important attitudes toward children's books current at the time, and do represent the ideas of leaders in the public library movement, just at the beginning of the development of children's rooms in libraries.

Very little was written about children's magazines, even though this was the period of their greatest flowering. The most important document was the prospectus for *St. Nicholas* which Mary Mapes Dodge published anonymously in *Scribner's Monthly* a few months before the beginning of her children's magazine was announced.[45] Mrs. Dodge was of the same spirit as Samuel Osgood, placing her major emphasis on children's reading as part of their play. "A child's Magazine is its pleasure ground," she declared.[46] She would exclude "old, lame jokes," the "wearisome spinning out of facts," and the "rattling of the dry bones of history." Instruction was to be permitted, but not preaching. Because they exist in life, harsh and cruel facts would be admitted, but only on condition that they "march forward boldly, say what they have to say, and go." [47]

An editorial in *Literary World* gave a formula similar to that of Mrs. Dodge for a children's magazine. After outlining the difficulties of producing a successful magazine for the young, the editor offered a prescription for good one.

> *Children like the real better than the ideal—stories whose personages and incidents they can liken to persons and events they have known. They do not care for juvenile prodigies of virtue, but prefer something "not too good for human nature's daily food." In poetry they like what is bright and jolly—not* Atlantic *poems razeed, we may say, like an elder brother's pantaloons, finical and mystical and incomprehensible. Finally, they do not want to find school-books in their magazines, under a thin disguise. Adults look to their monthly magazines not for instruction, but for entertainment; and that is what children ought to gain from the pages of periodicals professedly devoted to their interests. They have lessons enough at school; and it is hard for them to take up their magazine, in the long winter evening, anticipating an hour or two of quiet enjoyment, and run their heads against the very subjects—philosophy, natural history, or astronomy—that have puzzled their brains all day.*[48]

This criticism of children's books was not extensive. Some of it was, however, profound. Samuel Osgood searchingly examined what children's books should be, and provided not only standards for children's literature, but also philosophical justification for those standards. No other author wrote so comprehensive a study of children's literature, though other writers wrote in a similar vein, emphasizing the needs and interests of children, and literary quality. Even when there was disagreement, as there was in the papers presented at the American Library Association's Boston conference, there was little conflict as to what constituted high quality children's books. The disagreement was based on different points of view concerning the effects of certain types of books.

The philosophy enunciated by Osgood, and affirmed in part by others, provided an excellent standard for children's books. Indeed, our own age would subscribe to almost everything in Osgood's essay. Coming, as it did, almost at the beginning of our period, this critical statement provided the basic standard for the period, or, perhaps, codified attitudes which were common property. Many of his ideas were shared by the people who reviewed children's books. It would be difficult to prove that they had read his essay, for none of the reviewers mentioned him, though, since it appeared in the *Atlantic Monthly*, it is highly probable that most of them had. His ideas, however, are reflected in the reviews of children's books. He wrote an abstract essay setting forth general principles. The reviewers worked with specific books.

SOME NOTES ON
BOOK REVIEWING

Though book reviewing may be considered a development of the late eighteenth and nineteenth centuries, it was no longer an infant by the beginning of 1865. In fact, it was a well developed part of the literary world. Gard credits the *Edinburgh Review and Critical Journal* founded in 1802, as the periodical which originated the modern book review. He acknowledges that there had been reviews prior to that time, but says that "Whereas earlier reviewing had been mainly the work of publishers' hacks, this new journal gave vigorous and independent notice to the important books of each season." [1] The growth of book reviewing was rapid in the ensuing years.

> *In the century following the birth of these periodicals, what Wordsworth called the "inglorious employment" of reviewing underwent a prodigious growth. This was made possible by a vast increase in the number of books published each year, and by a corresponding increase in the number of periodicals in which books might be reviewed. Some of these journals were devoted almost exclusively to the discussion of literature and the reviewing of current books.* [2]

In this country the *North American Review* was founded in 1815. Its pages, and the pages of other journals which followed, were devoted, in large measure, to reviewing current books.

Though reviewing was at first the province of quarterly and monthly periodicals, the weekly and daily press began to review books also. [3] By the 1860's, a decade in which many new American periodicals were founded, a wide variety of periodicals included book reviews in each regular issue.

With the growth of reviewing as an important element in the reception of current literature, it was natural that reviewing itself should have been examined eventually, and various attempts made to define the function of the reviewer. The literature about book reviewing is large, but, not surprisingly, it shows a large measure of agreement among the writers who have turned their thoughts to the book review.

Perhaps the most helpful writing on this subject has been done by certain well-known reviewers and by a few important literary authors. Most writers agree that the review is a part of journalism, rather than a part of literature, or of literary criticism proper. Virginia Woolf describes the reviewer's function as "partly to sort current literature; partly to advertise the author; partly to inform the public," [4] while Leonard Woolf, in a note following the same essay, describes its function as "to give to readers a description of the book and an estimate of its quality in order that he may know whether or not it is the kind of book which he may want to read." [5]

Henry S. Canby adds a further dimension to the task of the reviewer.

To review a book is to discuss it in relation to literature, its literature especially, whether lyric poetry, mystery story, or character novel; to set it against this background and then to relate it to the interests and experience of the reader.[6]

To evaluate a given book, then, it would be most desirable to consider it in terms of its own kind. A children's book would be considered in terms of children's books.

Most writers, in considering this subject, agree that the reviewer's job is to keep the public informed about the current output of the publishers. W. Soskin says that the reviewer should keep the public "informed regarding the most important, most timely, most entertaining books published from day to day." [7] Rather than give an evaluation of the book as it will appear to posterity, the reviewer should "suggest the significance of the book in the contemporary literary pattern." [8] Herschel Brickell has the same point of view when he says "book reviewing . . . differs from literary criticism mainly in that it takes the short view." [9]

Gard goes into even more detail in distinguishing the difference between literary criticism and reviewing.

The book review is a specific and applied form of literary criticism, and is distinguished in several ways from criticism in general. In the first place, whereas criticism in general may be concerned with an author's entire work, or with that of a group of writers or of a period, the review is limited to a single book. While, of course, it may compare the book with others by the same author or by other writers, its interest is centered in the single work.

Another difference is this: while criticism in general often takes for granted that the reader is more or less familiar with the authors and books being discussed, the review takes less for granted.[10]

One of the jobs of the reviewer is to provide the reader with a description of the book so that the reader has some basis for understanding any judgment the writer makes about it.

The various writers, though differing in particulars, in general are seen to agree on what the function of the book reviewer is and on what the review itself must be. The reviewer is a kind of journalist whose job consists of bringing to the attention of potential readers the most interesting of the recent books. He provides some kind of description of the book's content and gives an evaluation of the book which will provide the reader with some notion of the book's possible standing within its own class. The reviewer is not, strictly speaking, a critic. Soskin, in fact, cautions that "if the reviewer is too much of an absolutist, too much of an eccentric who exercises his prejudices and peculiarly personal tastes in public, he is bound to fail." [11]

Very little, on the other hand, has been written about the reviewing of children's books. Anne Carroll Moore has written on this subject, but she points out no real difference between the reviewing of children's books and the reviewing of books in general. Perhaps the only special difference she indicates is the need to "keep in living touch with childhood by natural ways of communication." [12] She also emphasizes the great difficulty, as she sees it, of reviewing children's books, which she ranks in difficulty second only to writing for children.

Miss Moore's writing provides the basis for current opinion of the reviewing of children's books in the nineteenth century. In an essay which appeared in one of her collections she passed judgment on it.

For many more years than any of us like to recall, children's books, if read at all when written about, were read for ulterior ends. They were considered en masse *rather than individually, both in the educational field and in the publishing field. They were tagged for moralistic trends, for physical age limit, for collateral reading, for anything and everything save appraisal of them as books in relation to books in general.*

Standards of appraisal consistently applied to the consideration of children's books as holding a place in contemporary criticism were unknown in 1918 when I was invited to contribute a general article on the children's books of the year to the Bookman. *I had long felt the need for such recognition of children's books but I had looked for a seasoned critic to appear and carry forward such leads as Horace E. Scudder and Mary Mapes Dodge had given while editing the* Riverside Magazine *and* St. Nicholas.[13]

She reiterated this opinion in an address presented to the American Library Association at its Montreal meeting in 1934.[14] So common was the notion that no worthwhile reviewing of children's books had appeared earlier, that the authors of *A Critical History of Children's Literature* in 1953 dismissed as unworthy all criticism and reviewing of children's books before Miss Moore began reviewing without, apparently, feeling any need to cite an authority.

As the twentieth century approached the end of its second decade, library work with children had become an important and established phase of public library work. By this time, too, children's books formed a body of literature which had importance and significance. There was still lacking, however, informed and constructive literary criticism of children's books. On both sides of the Atlantic, there had been occasional reviews of books written for children. In many cases, such reviews were fallacious, dismissing the book as a mere children's book unworthy of sound appraisal, condemning it because it did not do what the reviewer thought should be done, ignoring the child's point of view or the fact that a new and important literary trend was evidenced.[15]

Mrs. Bechtel also attributed to Miss Moore "the first separate reviewing of children's books," and with no evidence to prove her statement.[16] That such statements were made indicates an appalling absence of scholarship.

Alice M. Jordan, in a book published in 1948, had hinted that there had been criticism of children's books as early as the end of the Civil War which was worthy of consideration. She said, speaking of a fifteen-year period beginning with 1865, that a new era of "liberality toward children's tastes and interests" had begun in both publishing and criticism of children's books.[17] Neither Miss Meigs and her collaborators, nor Mrs. Bechtel pursued Miss Jordan's remark. Had they done so they would have had to revise their statements.

That general criticism of children's literature existed and was of high quality in the post-Civil War period we have seen. In the chapters that follow it will be demonstrated that a large number of reviews of children's books appeared in American periodicals between 1865 and 1881, and that many, though not all, of those reviews represented sound reviewing, took into consideration the child's point of view, and were alert to new and important literary trends. There were reviews of the type which Miss Moore deplores, of course, reviews in which morals were considered more important than style, unity, or verisimilitude, reviews in which many things other than the book as a book were considered. But there were *many* excellent and lively reviews of children's books in which the reviewer honestly attempted to describe the book, to evaluate it in terms of other children's books, and to indicate to the reader whether it was a book he would want to read, or, more often, a book he would want to buy his children to read.

6

REVIEWING OF
CHILDREN'S BOOKS

As noted previously, more than 2,500 children's books were reviewed in more than 4,000 separate reviews in the 36 periodicals whose volumes were examined for this study. Though these periodicals represent only a small portion of the many hundreds of periodicals published in the United States during the seventeen years between 1865 and 1881, they include all the important book-reviewing journals, and representative periodicals from many special groups, such as religious periodicals, educational periodicals, and children's magazines. They represent a wide geographical distribution, including periodicals published in Boston, New York, Philadelphia, Chicago, St. Louis, and San Francisco. An exhaustive search of Southern periodicals failed to uncover a periodical which reviewed children's books during this period. A single review of Jean Ingelow's *Stories Told to a Child* in the *New Electic*, published in Baltimore, proved to have been quoted from another periodical.[1]

The periodicals can be classified fairly easily into convenient categories for discussion, though it might be possible to dispute the classification of some of them. For the purpose of discussing their reviews of children's books, they are divided into eight groups; literary monthlies, critical journals, scholarly reviews, religious periodicals, pedagogical journals, children's magazines, and a miscellaneous group which includes book trade periodicals and a scientific magazine. The eighth category, if it may be called a category, consists entirely of *The Nation,* which reviewed more children's books than any other magazine. By the very quantity of its reviewing it demands a chapter by itself.

The factors which may have influenced the tone and quality of the reviews have been discussed in previous chapters. A few other factors remain to be discussed. One important element affecting the amount of reviewing in a given periodical was undoubtedly the availability of reviewers. *The Nation,* with an imposing list of contributors available, was in an exceedingly advantagous position to provide unusual reviews. The *Atlantic Monthly* had, in its editor, William Dean Howells, a critic and reviewer of broad interests and excellent taste, who could make certain that the *Atlantic* reviews of children's books would be the best that any age could offer. *Harper's New Monthly Magazine,* though it underpaid him, had in Lyman Abbott, a reviewer of broad and liberal outlook who had, incidentally, a young family to which he could turn to gain a child's reaction to a given book. The *Literary World,* had, for a time at least, the services of Susan Coolidge who knew, as her own books so adequately prove, what was appealing to a child. Other periodicals, on the other hand, had reviewers with little understanding of the needs of children, though most of them were attuned to the prevailing spirit. A few, like *Catholic World,* were the prisoners of their own doctrine; but doctrinaire magazines exist in all times and places.

Another important factor was the availability of books for reviewing. An analysis of this problem remains to be made, but certain tentative conclusions can be drawn from the reviews themselves concerning the distribution of books to reviewers. Many books, for example, were distributed chiefly to those periodicals located in the same city as the book publisher. Boston books received more reviews in Boston, New York books received more in New York. Certain of the larger, and, presumably wealthier, publishers were able to distribute their books more widely and were able, therefore, to have them reviewed in more magazines. Some of the periodicals tried to review all or most of the books they received from the publishers. A comparison of the number of books received in a given volume of *The Nation* with the number of books reviewed in that volume shows that that periodical rarely failed to review a book which the publisher had supplied to it.

It is also possible, though exceedingly difficult to prove, that publishers refrained from providing review copies of books to periodicals which they feared would not review them favorably. Some evidence exists that the placement of advertising may have been influenced by reviews, and the same may have been true in the distribution of books for reviewing purposes.

The only direct testimony concerning review copies was in a report of the Unitarian Ladies' Commission on Sunday-School Books.

The hope of obtaining all such books from the publishers has proved vain. It is hardly worth their while to send large packages of books, of which but a very small proportion can be approved. But several of our largest publishing houses have never failed to respond promptly and cordially to any call from us.[2]

The situation of the Ladies' Commission was, however, somewhat different from that of the reviewing periodicals.

Considerable book reviewing, including reviewing of children's books, appeared in the daily press, though no attempt has been made to include it in this study. The scope and difficulty of assembling such material make it necessary that any study of reviewing of children's books in the daily press be made the subject of one or several separate studies. Whether such studies would repay the effort is, at least, open to question. An editorial in the *Literary World* charged that reviews in the newspapers were dictated by the counting room.[3] Proving or refuting that statement might provide an interesting study in itself.

Another area related to this study, but not a part of it, is the reviewing of children's books in English periodicals. Though it would not be desirable, or, indeed, possible, to examine English reviewing in detail in a study intended to survey the reviewing of children's books in American periodicals, it may be of some interest to take a brief glance at the reviews in one or two leading periodicals published on the other side of the Atlantic.

The *Athenaeum* reviewed a great many children's books each year, rarely less than fifty, and frequently almost a hundred, in reviews ranging in length from a few lines to 300 and more. The reader is immediately struck by the large number of prominent American children's books reviewed, such as *Little Women, An Old-Fashioned Girl,* other books by Louisa May Alcott, and various books by Susan Coolidge. The review of *An Old-Fashioned Girl* provides a good example of an *Athenaeum* review.

> *Let whoever wishes to read a bright, spirited, wholesome story get the 'Old-Fashioned Girl' at once! It is not our fault if the male readers who follow our advice should close the book with a pang of regret that Polly, the heroine—Polly the darling—is an entirely unattainable treasure. Neither will it be our fault if a standard is set up of a nice girl,—so high that most of the young ladies of their acquaintance shall seem to fall short of it; for Polly is a heroine in a book, and perhaps, after all, they would not have recognized how very good and pleasant she was, unless Miss Alcott had been there to tell them and to open their eyes. 'The Old-Fashioned Girl' is an American story, and there are little traits of life and manners which give a pleasant flavor of novelty to the tale; we have had several hearty laughs over the book,*

for it is full of fun. The picture of society amongst the young people in America is, we would hope, an exaggeration; and we heartily trust that the like fashions may never prevail in the school-rooms and nurseries of England; but if they should show themselves, we hope some "old-fashioned girl" like Polly Milton will come and drive them away.[4]

Miss Coolidge's books were equally well received in *Athenaeum* reviews. The reviewer declared that readers would read *The New Year's Bargain* with pleasure, "and then, we think, they will read it all over again, and like it the second time as much as they did the first."[5] He praised her *Mischief's Thanksgiving,* but expressed the wish that she would write more books about Katy, no matter how interesting other books from her pen might be.[6]

The *Athenaeum* failed to recognize the merit of *Alice's Adventures in Wonderland* when it appeared, declaring "that any real child might be more puzzled than enchanted by this stiff, over-wrought story,"[7] When *Through the Looking-Glass* was published, the magazine tried to make amends by including the earlier work in the praise lavished on its sequel in a long and carefully analytical review.[8] On the whole, however, the reviews differed very little from reviews in comparable American periodicals.

The Saturday Review of Politics, Literature, Science, and Art reviewed children's books also, though neither so many nor so fully as did the *Athenaeum.* Often there were only brief notices of a sentence or two for each book in a column devoted to holiday books. Other books received reviews of 150 or more words. Many American books were reviewed, often books by American authors whose books were not reviewed in the *Athenaeum,* such as Elijah Kellogg, Charles A. Stephens, and John T. Trowbridge. These reviews were most frequently printed with reviews of adult books under the heading, "American Literature."

The reviews in the *Saturday Review* were usually of high quality, taking into account the literary merit of a book and its appeal to children. Often a brief description of the action of a story was included. The review of Trowbridge's *Jack Hazard and His Fortunes* illustrates a common type of review.

Jack Hazard and His Fortunes, by J. T. Trowbridge, (Sampson, Low & Co.). This is a clever little story of American life, which will be found amusing by old readers as well as young. There is not only a good deal of quiet humour, but also for us on this side of the Atlantic there is a much greater freshness in the book, describing as it does a primitive kind of American life, than would be found in the same kind of book on English life. The hero's character, if not quite true to na-

ture, is nevertheless well drawn, though his amendment from his life of an outcast is certainly rapid. We doubt if he would quite so early as he is represented have felt all the horror of having "Sworn in his clean clothes." Mr. Trowbridge has evidently studied the philosophy of clothes, for he represents another character "as standing in all the dignity of a man insulted in his Sunday clothes." [9]

In general, an examination of the reviews of children's books in English periodicals reveals very little that is different from those in American periodicals. The English books appeared there earlier, the American books later than in American periodicals, but that was only to be expected. The same attitudes and the same methods can be found in both. The outstanding children's books, and many more that were not outstanding, were reviewed on both sides of the Atlantic, and on either side the reader was kept well informed of the qualities of the children's books that appeared each year. The chapters which follow will examine reviewing in various American periodicals.

7

THE NATION

On July 6, 1865, the first issue of one of the most outstanding American periodicals appeared. The weekly *Nation,* under the editorship of Edwin Lawrence Godkin, was, according to Mott, the best journal of its type to be published in this country.[1] Though its circulation was never great, its influence was far-reaching. Its purpose in its review section, "to criticize books and works of art soundly and impartially," was stated in a prospectus that appeared shortly before the first issue, and this purpose was maintained with a very high standard of reviewing.[2]

The Nation reviewed 42 children's books in its first half-year of publication, and from 19 to 64 in each subsequent year, hitting its high of 64 in 1881. During the seventeen years from 1865 to 1881, it reviewed more than 600 children's books in reviews ranging in length from a few lines to several hundred words. Every type of book published was reviewed, though the traditional Sunday school library book was only scantily represented. Though there were occasional reviews of children's books throughout the year, the bulk of the reviews appeared in three or four regular columns in November and December with the title "Holiday Books," "Gift Books for Youths," "Children's Books," or some other heading indicative of the seasonal nature of much of children's book publishing. Each column included several reviews and ran from a partial column of the two-column page to three or four pages.

None of the reviews in *The Nation* were signed though we do know who wrote a few of them. Haskell lists the names of eight reviewers of children's books in his index to *The Nation;* Titus Munson Coan, William Francis Allen, William Crary Brownell, Gaston Fay, Mrs. Clara

Barnes Martin, Frances Winthrop Palfrey, John T. Trowbridge, and George E. Woodberry.[3] Allen reviewed history and biography for the young. Trowbridge reviewed science books. The one identified section by Mrs. Martin was the entire column, "Children's Books" in the November 17, 1881 issue. Brownell reviewed a considerable number of works of fiction and other belles-lettres. So few reviews by the others are identified that it is impossible to see a pattern in the kinds of books they reviewed. Most interesting is the fact that a single column of reviews often included the work of several reviewers. Yet the tone and attitude of the reviews remained consistent. In fact, the general attitude toward literature for children remained consistent from the founding of the magazine to the end of our period, no matter who the reviewer. But the work of some of the individual reviewers will demand closer scrutiny later.

The Nation reviewers were particularly concerned that children's books should really be suitable for children. On numerous occasions they criticized a writer for having an eye cast at the parent while pretending to write for the child. In one review in 1868, the reviewer said that the best books for children were enjoyable for adults as well. "Imaginative literature of high quality has that faculty." [4] In a review the previous year, this principle was more clearly defined when the reviewer said that "in stories for boys there ought to be stories for men. But the two elements should be fused, not simply laid side by side." [5] Still another notion that *The Nation* objected to was that books about children were necessarily books for children.[6] This, they felt, was especially false when the book was an introspective one which was more likely to make adults feel like children again, but would miss the mark in arousing the interest of the children.[7]

Several books were singled out for praise for avoiding the danger of appealing to adults instead of children. Mrs. Molesworth's *Grandmother Dear* was a book with "wisdom, tact, humor, and good breeding . . . suggestive to parents without becoming a story *about* instead of *for* children." [8] The *Short Sermons to Newsboys* of Charles Loring Brace was another book written with the child's need and ability in mind, in language he could understand.[9] *Northern Lights: Stories from Swedish and Finnish,* translated by Selma Borg and Marie A. Brown, showed "thorough understanding of the child's character." [10]

Still other books were criticized for their failure to reach the child's level. Richard Henry Stoddard's *The Children in the Wood* was neither suitable for adults nor children.[11] For the former it was too simple; for the latter it was too obscure. Mrs. Barbauld's *Hymns in Prose for Children,* reissued in 1865, contained some good pieces for children, but many beyond their comprehension.[12] Elizabeth Barrett Browning's *Poems of Childhood* was guilty of still another fault of much literature intended for children.[13] These poems were too sad, suited more to the reading of mothers, than to that of their children. Perhaps the oddest book on which the judgment that the book was unsuited to the age for which it was intended was the anonymous *Alphabet in Rhyme* (American News Company, 1869). The reviewer's comment was that "it is an odd mistake that this writer has made in fancying himself a writer for children." [14] Even so noted an author as Susan Coolidge, did not escape the criticism that she sometimes was too concerned with the adult reading over the child's shoulder. Her *Eyebright* exhibited this fault.[15]

Much of *The Nation*'s criticism of children's books was devoted to literary qualities. Both the minutiae and the broader aspects of literary style and language received attention. Charlotte M. Yonge's *A Book of Golden Deeds of All Times and All Lands* was written in such pure and easy English that the reviewer considered it a book "well adapted for reading aloud in the family." [16] It was the simplicity and lack of literary pretension that commended Annie Douglas Robinson's *Picture Poems for Young Folks*.[17] These qualities gave many of the poems a ring of truth, the reviewer felt. The translation of Emile Achard's *The History of My Friends; or, Home Life with Animals* was "racy and mirthful." [18] George M. Towle's *Voyages and Adventures of Vasco da Gama,* the first volume in his "Young Folks' Heroes of History Series," received high praise.[19] It was well written, not with "fine writing," but not written down to the children either.

The reviewer's evaluation of *Maggie's Mistake; A School Girl's Story* deals with the point of view, rather than with style, and shows an awareness of one of the prejudices of children.[20] This story, he felt, was a good one which the children would like, despite the autobiographical form in which it was cast.

Frequently the reviews indicted a book for its poor style. Mrs. Henry Mackarness' *Children of the Olden Time* was a book with a good subject and a good plan, but written in a poor style.[21] It was even guilty of confusion in the use of pronouns. John Bonner's *A Child's History of the United States* used slang expressions that gave it a certain obscurity.[22] *Fairy Realm, a Collection of the Favorite Old Tales,* which had been retold in verse by Tom Hood was unsuitable for children both because its meters were too difficult, and because it used unsatisfactory jokes and overly complicated puns.[23] It was "long words and stilted expressions" which led the reviewer to condemn Sidney Daryl's *Told in the Twilight; or, Short Stories for Long Evenings*.[24] The reviewer quoted the phrase "advent into existence," used instead of "born" to illustrate this fault. *A Tale of a Nest* used language more difficult than the thoughts that it had to convey.[25] William Francis Allen, reviewing Charles H. Woodman's

The Boys and Girls of the Revolution, found the book too sentimental and too full of what he called "newspaper English." [26]

With three other books, it was the method of selection of material, quite as much as the writing, that earned the disapproval of the reviewer. In a column entitled "Bosh for Boys," two books by P. C. Headley were effectively disposed of.[27] The *Life and Military Career of Major-General Philip Henry Sheridan* and the *Life and Naval Career of Vice-Admiral David Glasgow Farragut* had the same faults. They were poorly written and contained irrelevant material. The author quoted from newspaper sources without ever acknowledging those sources. The book might have been better if the author had used his sources as sources rather than lifting from them wholesale, and he might have removed the profanity which marred the books.

It was the overall method of selection and composition that was criticized in Capt. C. W. Hall's *Drifting Round the World: A Boy's Adventures by Sea and Land.*[28] The book was so badly out of balance that more than half the world was crammed into less than the last hundred pages. And the style of writing was in itself defective for children's reading. The first sentence in the book had 71 words.

The comment that part of a book might better have been omitted was not confined to the more or less factual book. The reviewer said that Eliza Keary might well have left out half of the matter in *The Magic Valley; or, Patient Antoine.*[29] What remained would still have needed "harmony and fairy coherence" to make the book satisfactory. With Susan Coolidge's *Nine Little Goslings* it was the plots themselves with which the reviewer found fault.[30] The nine stories had good invention, admirable fancy, and sufficient variety, but the plots were often improbable.

Verisimilitude and probability received a great deal of attention from *The Nation*'s reviewers, particularly in characterization. Their objections to unnatural children amounted almost to a crusade, so vehement were they in condemning such characters. Anne G. Hale's *Fannie and Robbie* was declared worthless chiefly because of its characterization.[31] The reviewer felt that such unnatural goodness could only make young readers disgusted with goodness. In the same group of reviews *Frank Stirling's Choice* by Maria H. Bulfinch had one true-to-life character, Nanette, but the boys in the book were described as "the female Sunday-school teacher's ideals in boy's clothes." [32] *Miss Patience Hathaway; Her Friends and Her Enemies, and How She Returned Them Good for Evil,* by Warren I. Bradley, who wrote under the pseudonym Glance Gaylord, earned the reviewer's greatest contempt.[33] It was, he said, "a specimen of the worst of all sorts of writing for children." Not only the characters, but also the incidents were false and cheap. Mrs. Madeline Leslie's *Walter and Frank; or, The Apthorp Farm* received a treatment similar to Bradley's book.[34] It was "full of mistaken notions as to what it is possible or desirable for boys to do," the reviewer felt. The hero was a "cunning little prig." It would have been difficult to find a poorer book for a child. Martha F. Finley's nearly interminable "Elsie Dinsmore" series was criticized in *The Nation* for lack of sound and believable character creation. *Elsie's Children,* said the reviewer, "flows on unimpeded by any hindering deference to human nature." [35] George Cary Eggleston was called "an Oliver Optic of the better sort" because of the "impossible characters in improbable situations" in his *The Signal Boys; or, Captain Sam's Company.*[36]

On the other hand, books with fidelity to human nature were frequently praised highly for that reason alone. *Little Lou's Sayings and Doings* was declared sure to win the approval of the children.[37] It came, the reviewer said, close to "absolute truth of portraiture." Nellie Eyster's *Tom Harding and His Friends* was another book found to have good characterization.[38] The author understood boys, realizing that in books they should be presented as they are in life. Even when the author was not so successful in character creation, if he had achieved the appearance of truth, *The Nation* was apt to approve. William Henry Giles Kingston had not succeeded in making the characters in *Snow-Shoes and Canoes* really recognizable individuals, but since he managed to persuade the reader that they were real the book was recommended.[39]

Another trait *The Nation* considered of great importance in children's books was humor. Frank R. Stockton was singled out as the best American humorous writer for children, in the review of his *The Floating Prince, and Other Fairy Tales.*[40] "His drollery," the reviewer said, "is as spontaneous and unexpected and original as that in Alice's Adventures." [41] This characteristic was praised in almost every Stockton book reviewed in *The Nation. Ting-a-ling* was a "rollicking set of stories." [42] *What Might Have Been Expected* won unstinted praise.[43] It was one of the most amusing and thoroughly entertaining books the reviewer had read in a long time. After quoting amusing passages and describing certain particularly funny incidents he made the following remark.

> *It is a pleasant change to read an American story at once truly boylike, spirited, humorous, and distinctively* American, *that is neither slangy, nor underbred, nor full of impertinent young folks.*[44]

Mary Mapes Dodge's *Rhymes and Jingles* was another book with humor that delighted the reviewer.[45] These verses, many of them reprinted from the infant *St. Nicholas,* were described as "full of comical wise nonsense and the most felicitous absurdities of language."

The Nation did not, however, merely accept any humorous book for children as a desirable book because it was funny. The suitability of the humor for children was always the first consideration. Though E. H. Knatchbull-Hugessen's *Queer Folk* showed that the author had considerable inventive ingenuity, the reviewer found his humor crude and offensive to good taste.[46] The same charge of coarseness was made against the illustrations for William Busch's *Buzz-a-Buzz; or, The Bees.*[47] The humor in John Francis Maguire's *Young Prince Marigold, and Other Fairy Stories* had still another fault.[48] It was a dry humor that the children would not understand, though parents reading the book to their children might enjoy it.

A frequent device of the reviewers was to compare one book with others in its genre. Perhaps the most frequent comparisons were those in which they compared various fanciful tales to Lewis Carroll's *Alice's Adventures in Wonderland,* frequently unfavorably. *The Nation,* the only periodical to review the 1866 Appleton edition of *Alice's Adventures in Wonderland,* used that book as a kind of touchstone for its type. Jean Ingelow's *Mopsa, the Fairy* revealed "the imperfectly imaginative character of Miss Ingelow's mind," the reviewer said.[49] This book was a work of the fancy, a lower faculty, rather than of the imagination. *Alice* was a far superior book. Carroll's own *Through the Looking-Glass, and What Alice Found There* fairly cried out for such a comparison. And in certain ways the reviewer found it even better than the earlier work. Like *Alice's Adventures in Wonderland,* it was an exquisitely maintained dream but the idea of an inverted world seen through a looking glass seemed of a higher order of imagination than a rabbit hole world.[50] The reviewer found Alice's talk attractive in itself and well sustained, and many of the poems admirable, particularly "Jabberwocky" and "The Walrus and the Carpenter."

Another fanciful tale that a *Nation* reviewer felt could be considered the equal of *Alice* was George MacDonald's *The Princess and the Goblin.*[51] He considered this the best book for children or adults that MacDonald had produced, free from the preaching that so marred most of the author's works, and filled with admirable fancy, superior even to that in *Alice.*

> *The invention it shows is so innocent and poetical, the fancy is so ingenious without being artificial, that we would set it above even some of the most highly praised children's books of the day. In comparison with it, in regard to facility of fancy, even "Alice's Adven-*

tures" are cold and mechanical, though we dislike to say a word against a book which has that little girl in it.[52]

Most other books, like *Mopsa, the Fairy,* fared but poorly when compared with *Alice's Adventures in Wonderland.* Jane G. Austin's *Moonfolk; A True Account of the Home of the Fairy Tales,* in which the author expanded nursery rhymes into full-fledged stories, was obviously indebted to Carroll's books, but the reviewer felt that there was too much of it.[53] Charles G. Leland's *Johnnykin and the Goblins,* lacked the spontaneity and charm of Carroll.[54] The machinery of the book seemed awkward though the general plan was a good one. *Pansie's Flour-Bin* was an obvious imitation of *Alice.*[55] But the device of permitting the heroine to fall through a trap door, was "a poor substitute for the rabbit hole."

Two 1877 titles were more favorably compared with Carroll's books. The reviewer declared Mary De Morgan's *On a Pincushion,* which showed Carroll's influence, to be a very successful attempt to write an old-fashioned fairy tale.[56] He praised both its humor and the style of the narrative. Griselda, in Mrs. Molesworth's *The Cuckoo Clock* reminded the reviewer of Alice, but her story had real originality.[57] The tone, the style, the descriptions, and even the "gracious but effective moralizing" won his plaudits.

Another interesting comparison contrasted Edward Abbott's *Long Look House* with the instructional books of his father, Jacob Abbott.[58] *The Nation* reviewer felt that the father had done a better job than the son, for in *Long Look House,* the story itself was without interest and would be tiresome to children, though boys might be interested in some of the details of building a house.

Horace E. Scudder's *Stories from My Attic* was compared with the writing of Hans Christian Andersen. The book consisted of "graceful and gracefully written sketches and short stories," but was overly delicate, lacking in robustness and sometimes beyond the understanding of children.[59] Though Scudder's work brought Andersen's to mind, it was not of the same superior quality. One tale in Hackländer's *Enchanting and Enchanted,* translated from the German by Mrs. A. L. Wister, reminded the reviewer of Andersen.[60] The tales in this book seemed to him far superior to the average fairy tales.

Several other comparisons were used in *Nation* reviews. *Grimm's Goblins* was only "tolerable translation," inferior to others that had appeared.[61] But a first class American edition was still wanting. In still another type of comparison, the reviewer noted certain improvements in the 1868 edition of Edmund Routledge's *Every Boy's Book; a Complete Encyclopedia of Sports and Amusements.*[62] The previous year the book had been reviewed and, though several errors had been noted, it had been recommended.[63] The reviewer had particularly criticized the English editor for including baseball with "outdoor sports with toys," instead of with "athletic sports and manly exercises." In the 1868 edition this fault had been corrected.

The Nation reviewers were often concerned that whatever instruction a book for children attempted to convey should not overly burden the story. Robert Michael Ballantyne's *Deep Down; A Tale of the Cornish Mines* was judged a book "combining instruction and amusement in a more than ordinarily successful manner." [64] On the other hand, Edward Abbott never ceased to teach in his *Out-Doors at Long Look House*.[65] The reviewer declared the book to be "as realistic as the worst enemy of fiction could desire." Tongue in cheek, he concluded with the comment that this book confirmed his "doubt that Mr. Abbott is a born story-teller." Another book that failed to be entertaining, but was certainly instructive, was Helen C. Weeks' *An American Family in Paris*.[66] The information might just as well have come from a guide book, for the device of a family trip was "essentially unreal" and of little value to children.

Books written to win children for special causes, whether secular or religious, seldom won the approval of *The Nation*. In part, this disapproval is shown by the scarcity of books from the Sunday school presses among the books reviewed in the magazine and, in part, by the attitude revealed in the few reviews. In the introduction to a column, "Children's Books," in 1869, the reviewer lamented that there were too many children's books and listed sects and societies as parties partly responsible for this overabundance.[67]

Two books published by the American Unitarian Association were notable exceptions to *The Nation*'s general silence concerning the output of the sectarian press, and those two books may have been reviewed only because they were prize books, published as a result of the efforts of the Unitarians to improve the quality of Sunday school library books. One of them, Anna E. Appleton's *Stories for Eva,* was dismissed as a rather ordinary book of its type, too heavily loaded with piety.[68] The other, Mary C. Peckham's *Father Gabrielle's Fairy,* won the reviewer's approval.[69] He felt that the author had written as though she were more under the "influence of the idea that any work of fiction, however, is an artistic opportunity, than under the special inspiration of a Sunday school prize for a Sunday school book." Earlier, *The Child's Book of Religion* had been reviewed.[70] But it was a work specifically designed for religious instruction, rather than a pious story book.

But it was the publications of a secular society that brought the most thoroughgoing condemnation from *The Nation*. That society, the National Temperance Society, published many books for children in the post-Civil War period, intended to fill children's hearts and minds with the terrors of strong drink and tobacco. With characteristic wit, the reviewer said they were miscalled temperance books, but should rather be called "total abstinence books." [71] He described them as "foolishly and laughably bad." Mary D. Chellis' *Aunt Dinah's Pledge* was well-meant, but its effect was one of triviality.[72] The theme of all such books was too degrading to be suitable for the young. He concluded that all children's temperance books should be abolished. Archie Fell's *Gold and Gilt* was still another example of a temperance book with a good purpose, but which failed because it actually was based on a false view of life.[73]

The reviewers gave considerable attention to the moral and moralizing in children's books, condemning books that they considered immoral and praising truly moral books. But it was not a narrow, preaching kind of morality they sought, but rather that broader moral that twentieth-century reviewers, ashamed of the more old-fashioned word, have come to call the "theme." Conventional moralizing was not considered the essence of the moral by the reviewers of *The Nation*. *The Children of the Frontier* displayed an "unnatural tenderness of conscience," and contained a moral that the author lost no opportunity to emphasize.[74] In the same issue of the magazine, in a review of Andersen's *What the Moon Saw, and Other Tales,* the reviewer acknowledged the more basic morality in the work of a skilled artist.[75] Of Andersen's treatment of his moral, he said that "few pulpits know how to preach morality as well as he."

In the review of *A Sister's Bye-Hours,* by Jean Ingelow, it was the absence of the author's usual piety that won the reviewer's praise.[76] The book was filled with real religious feeling and sound examples of moral action, but avoided the conventional moral. Chauncey Giles' *The Magic Spectacles* was a type of moralistic fairy tale that the reviewer felt could only be written by a person with no imagination.[77] It used the fairy tale merely as a vehicle for instruction and preaching. The entire genre, the didactic fairy tale, could only be considered a "sorrowful failure." In a review of another book of fairy tales, the reviewer again indicated the magazine's attitude toward moralizing in the fairy tale.

> *Of course in every fairy tale there is a silken thread of reason that winds in and out through all the elusive transformations in the unreason of fairyland, but it is never obtrusive, it does not tell a child it is there to make him good . . . This must be considered a blemish in fairy tales, the office of which is to quicken the imagination rather than develop the conscience.*[78]

In the review of *Bessie Bradford's Secret* by Joanna H. Mathews, the reviewer indicated something of his attitude toward moralizing in realistic books for children when he asked why the author could not teach goodness by providing examples of it, instead of by showing the punishments that resulted from the absence of goodness.[79]

The Nation gave, perhaps, as much attention to morality in children's books as any periodical in the period, but with a difference from many of them. The reviewers of *The Nation* looked beneath the surface morality and the preaching that was provided in many books and discovered in the unreality of the story or the point of view of the author, a basic immorality which they found to be of far greater concern.

"Moral without moralization" [80] was the verdict of the reviewer of *Hans Brinker; or, The Silver Skates,* by Mary Mapes Dodge, but this kind of comment did not characterize the review, nor the reviews of other books still popular today, which were reviewed in *The Nation* when they first appeared. Three different editions of *Hans Brinker* were reviewed in the magazine between its first appearance in 1866 and 1881. The first reviewer recognized the merit of the book at the outset, declaring that Mrs. Dodge had written no better book for the young, praising its incident and action and the way in which facts were included in the story. In the second review, when a new edition appeared in 1873, the reviewer, while finding the edition less than worthy of the text, declared that *Hans Brinker* deserved to become a classic.[81] By 1879, when an inexpensive edition of the book was published, the reviewer felt that it had already achieved that status and was delighted to see another edition of so worthy a book.[82]

Alice's Adventures in Wonderland was another title whose merits were clearly discerned by *The Nation* reviewer, who called it "one of the best children's books we ever met with—a delightful addition to a delightful branch of literature." [83] He praised its humor, its dialogue and its creation of character. Not only the text, but also the illustrations, were superior. One of the few testimonies we have to the effectiveness of *The Nation* reviews concerned this book. Caroline M. Hewins wrote on April 9, 1869, from West Roxbury, Massachusetts, to describe to the editor how "the copy which was brought into our family by means of a notice in your paper, more than two years ago" was by that time nearly worn out from use by the family and by more than twenty other children to whom it had been loaned.[84]

Louisa May Alcott's books were reviewed, but not with the same glowing enthusiasm. The first part of *Little Women* was "an agreeable little story" well planned for the readers for whom it was intended and with good characterization.[85] The second part was entertaining and might "safely be put in the hands of young people." [86] In a way, the review of *An Old-Fashioned Girl* is more interesting, for in it the reviewer attempted to predict the future of Miss Alcott's books. The characterization in *An Old-Fashioned Girl* was not always natural but many portions of the book were "strictly true to nature." [87] On the whole, the reviewer felt she had done well, that she showed a natural sympathy with children. She was, he concluded, as good as any American writer of children's books, but not a writer whose books would live on, pleasing children in future generations. A brave prediction, perhaps, and not too surprising when one considers how much a part of her own time Miss Alcott was, but still a prediction that has not proved to be correct. That very sympathy "with the young and innocent and happy" of which the reviewer spoke, and an ability to create warm and lovable characters have kept vital Miss Alcott's books.

Still another book read today, which *The Nation* reviewed favorably, was Thomas Bailey Aldrich's *The Story of a Bad Boy*.[88] The bad boy, himself, the reviewer declared to be no worse than most boys, and amusing and interesting as well. The book deserved a high place in the output of children's books for the year.

Some of the very popular authors of the day fared less well. Although *The Nation* treated the first Horatio Alger, Jr. work it reviewed kindly, most of the books by that prolific author were condemned. *Paul Prescott's Charge,* despite some big words, was, the reviewer said, likely to be popular.[89] But *Rough and Ready* was a book that had no value whatsoever.[90] When *Risen from the Ranks; or, Harry Walton's Success* appeared, *The Nation* had no more patience. The book was reviewed only because of the extravagant claims of the advertisements. Only the young and ignorant, the reviewer said, "will absorb this sort of pabulum." [91] In a long review, which included many quotations from the book, not one thing was praised. Even the morality of it was a matter of "puling virtue," rather than basic morality.

William T. Adams' treatment ran a similar course. *The Yankee Middy* was clear and interesting, superior to most books for the same class of readers.[92] Less was said about *Work and Win,* except that the moral was in the preface, and, therefore, easily skipped.[93] But for *Seek and Find; or The Adventures of a Smart Boy,* a critical field piece was drawn into the line. The book was lively, but improbable, and the characters unreal. The reviewer could find nothing either improving or elevating. "If we could have our way," he said, "the sale of them should stop immediately and entirely." [94]

Though a majority of the books for children reviewed in *The Nation* were story books, a considerable number of factual books were also reviewed. Throughout the period studied, collections of folk tales received attention from the critics. The reviewer compared the tales collected by M. Frere in *Old Deccan Days; or, Hindoo Fairy Legends Current in Southern India* to the standard European folk tales and to the American

Br'er Rabbit stories but, despite similarities, found them fresh and different enough to be entertaining.[95] Children would like them and would not be harmed by them.

Just as highly recommended were the stories in *Slavonic Fairy Tales, Collected and Translated from the Russian, Polish, Servian and Bohemian,* by John T. Naaké, of the British Museum.[96] But the collection of Marie Pabke and Margery Dean, *Wonder-World Stories, from the Chinese, French, German, Hebrew, Hindoostanee, Hungarian, Irish, Italian, Japanese, Russian, Swedish and Turkish* received the highest praise.[97] The reviewer called it one of the best books of the year, a book that deserved a permanent sale. In the same column of "Children's Holiday Books", the third edition of Cornelius Mathews' compilation of American Indian legends *The Enchanted Mocassins* was reviewed.[98] William Elliott Griffis' *Japanese Fairy World; Stories from the Wonder-Lore of Japan,* though favorably reviewed, was felt to be wanting in literary finish.[99]

Several children's periodicals were reviewed, both in the children's books section and in the regular reviews of magazines. *The Little Corporal* was reviewed in an early issue.[100] The reviewer described it as a monthly children's newspaper, well-edited and well-printed, and wished it success. Later in the same year, 1865, it was again reviewed and declared to show "tact, taste, and care." [101] *Our Young Folks,* edited by Lucy Larcom, John T. Trowbridge, and, for a time, Mary Abigail Dodge, though deficient in its illustrations, was thought by *The Nation* to be the best children's magazine published in 1865.[102] When the *Riverside Magazine for Young People* was first reviewed in March 1866, the reviewer found in it a marked improvement in illustration.[103] In April, 1867, in the column, "The Magazines for April," *Our Young Folks* and *The Riverside Magazine* were judged the two best children's magazines.[104] In January, 1867, a special notice acknowledged the appearance of *Our Boys and Girls: Oliver Optic's Magazine,* finding that its chief difference from other children's magazines was that it was a weekly, while the others were monthlies.[105] By the time *St. Nicholas* appeared the regular reviews of magazines had been discontinued, but, even so, it is surprising that *The Nation* never reviewed this most important children's magazine of the century.

The reviews of children's books in history and biography, at least from 1876 on, are particularly interesting, for the majority of them are identified by Haskell as the work of William Francis Allen. It is possible that many of the other reviews were also by Allen though it is probably impossible to determine the authorship of any reviews not identified in Haskell's index, since he had available to him all the extant records of the magazine. Allen had been a schoolteacher, a principal, and an assistant superintendent of schools before he became a professor of classical languages and history at the University of Wisconsin in 1867, a post he held until his death in 1889.[106] In this chair, he had pioneered in the teaching of history by the topical system of study and had emphasized the use of original sources. To his reviewing of history books for children, he brought a broad background in that field which, however, he tempered with a knowledge of what appealed to children.

The earliest book which he is known to have reviewed was Charles H. Woodman's *The Boys and Girls of the Revolution,* a book published as part of the great upsurge of interest in the Revolutionary period during the 1876 centennial year.[107] The book was acceptable, but contained too much sentiment and had too much "newspaper English."

Two reviews in December, 1878, give a clearer picture of Allen's method of reviewing. His review of Charles Carleton Coffin's *The Story of Liberty* began with a description of the content of the book, followed be a severe criticism of the author's viewpoint and method.[108] The book was sensational in its method and extremely biased. So biased was it, that Allen feared that its effect might be to make fanatics of children. He suggested that any parents who bought Coffin's book might want to cut out pages 84–90, which dealt all too graphically with the horrors of the Inquisition.

The review of Elizabeth Stansbury Kirkland's *Short History of France for Young People* provides a more favorable judgment, but not one less searching.[109] Miss Kirkland's method, the telling of a consecutive story, made the book an excellent one for children. The faults of the book lay in the lack of bibliographic aids and maps, rather than in the text itself. The book needed a better table of contents, an index, and historical maps to make it more useful. He pointed out, as well, a few minor errors in the text.

In other reviews, Allen concerned himself with the illustrations, the interpretation of the historical events, and with the suitability of the author's method for the children for whom the books were intended. George M. Towle's *Raleigh, His Exploits and Voyages* contained two major defects.[110] Its illustrations were of the made-up variety, but history was better if the pictures were of real things. In addition, Towle's book contained apocryphal stories, yet did not indicate that there was doubt as to their authenticity. The interpretation accepted by Edward Eggleston in his *Montezuma and the Conquest of Mexico* was not that accepted by most historians.[111] Allen praised the book despite this fault, for its style was much more suited to children than Towle's.[112] He did not by any means, however, condemn all of Towle's work. His *Magellan; or, The First Voyage Round the World* was part of an excellent series and much better than "wretched books of sensational fiction." [113]

In the review of John D. Champlin's *Young Folks' History of the War for the Union,* Allen again mentioned bias, but this time to praise its absence.[114] Champlin's book was one he could recommend with enthusiasm. He felt that it was well-written, with a good narrative style and excellent use of incident, that it was fair in its treatment of controversial issues, and its illustrations and its index were both good.

Allen found Hezekiah Butterworth's style in his *Young Folks' History of America* far different from that of Champlin. Butterworth's style was "too heavy and formal" for children, better in the stories he had inserted from time to time, than in the main portion of the book.[115] Allen considered this book less successful than Butterworth's travel books, at least one of which, *Zigzag Journeys in Europe,* he had also reviewed.

Only for the review of Butterworth's *Zigzag Journeys in Europe,* among many reviews of travelogue story books in *The Nation,* is the reviewer identified. There is enough similarity, however, in the approach and in the comments made in other reviews of this type of book to indicate that others may well have been Allen's work. As in the reviews of factual books of history, the illustrations and the need for an index, as well as the presence of some errors, were frequently commented on.

Allen described the plan of *Zigzag Journeys in Europe* as a good one, entertainingly executed.[116] He commented particularly on the good maps and the interesting tales from history interspersed with the travels of the Zigzag Club. Though there were some errors in Thomas W. Knox's *Boy Travellers in the Far East, or Adventures of Two Youths on a Journey to Japan and China,* the reviewer described it as a "good and elegant" work.[117] Its style was reportorial, but the book was filled with information, good illustrations and contained nothing that was objectionably sensational. The book needed maps and an index to make it completely satisfactory. Besides the two titles already discussed, Butterworth's *Zigzag Journeys in the Orient,* Knox's *Boy Travellers in the Far East; Adventures of Two Youths in a Journey to Siam and Java,* and *Adventures of Two Youths in a Journey to Ceylon and India,* Edward Greéy's *Young Americans in Japan,* James D. McCabe's *Our Young Folks Abroad,* and Forbes E. Winslow's *Child's Fairy Geography, or a Merry Trip Round Europe* were reviewed between 1879 and 1881. To Colonel Knox went the honors from *The Nation* as the most successful writer of this type of book.[118] Knox had more humor than the others and, because he had actually travelled and seen some of the things he described, was able to assimilate his borrowed materials better, escaping the guidebook style that marred many of the others.

Another type of factual book frequently reviewed in *The Nation* was the book of science, or, sometimes, the science story book. Among the earliest reviewed were Jean Macé's physiology story books, *The History of a Mouthful of Bread, and Its Effects on the Organization of Men and Animals, The Servants of the Stomach,* and his *Grandpa's Arithmetic,* all translated from the French.[119] The first title was well-done and suited to the understanding of children, but the latter two were not so suitable. *Grandpa's Arithmetic,* in particular, used too cumbersome a method and was too difficult for children.

Two science textbooks for young people received long reviews in *The Nation.* Eliza A. Youman's *The First Book of Botany; Designed to Cultivate the Observing Powers of Children* introduced the scientific method into the school study of botany and encouraged examination of the actual plant instead of a mere memorization of theory; an innovation the reviewer welcomed.[120] Asa Gray's *Botany for Young People: How Plants Behave* was praised for its clarity and for the elegance of its illustrations.[121] In both reviews much of the space was devoted to a description of the author's method.

The reception accorded Edward Clodd's *The Childhood of the World,* was far less enthusiastic.[122] The book showed a confusion of science and religion and failed to make use of readily available information to be deduced from still existing primitive societies. *Half-Hours with the Animals: Narratives Exhibiting Thought, Sympathy, and Affection in the Brute-Creation* was a pseudo-scientific book, which *The Nation* found chiefly interesting for an anti-Darwinian reference.[123] The sympathy of the magazine with the scientific attitude of the day was further revealed by the recommendation given *What Mr. Darwin Saw in His Voyage Round the World in the Ship "Beagle",* which the reviewer considered just as readable and interesting for adults as for the children for whom it had been edited.[124]

The only review of a science book for children for which the reviewer was identified was *The Fairy-Land of Science* by Arabella B. Buckley reviewed by John T. Trowbridge, professor of physics at Harvard, where he encouraged students to do original research and was largely responsible for a change in the methods of science instruction.[125] He described Miss Buckley's book as a graceful attempt to show the forces of energy as fairies. The review was lengthy, much of its devoted to the author's method, which Trowbridge found fascinating.[126]

In most reviews of illustrated books, the reviewer commented on the illustrations, sometimes to praise them and at other times, to indicate the lack of skill either in the original design or in the engraving. But the most interesting comments on illustrations are those dealing with the four most prominent illustrators of the day, Walter Crane, Randolph Caldecott, Kate Greenaway, and Howard Pyle. Crane's artistry in his *Baby's Opera* was declared to be of the highest quality.[127] The full-page illustrations, the ornamental border, and even the cover were given high praise.

Again, in the review of Mary De Morgan's *Necklace of Princess Fiori-monde,* Crane's head and tail pieces and his initial letters were commended.[128] But it was in a review of Caldecott's *John Gilpin* and *House That Jack Built,* both described as "funny as well as clever," that both Caldecott and Crane received the comment, "Happy the generation that is brought up on such masters as Mr. Caldecott and Walter Crane!" [129] Once Caldecott's work was deplored by a reviewer, who felt that the humor in *The Babes in the Wood* showed a grievous lack of good taste.[130] But when *The Three Jovial Huntsmen* appeared, it was described as the work of a true master, both in conception and in execution.[131]

The genius of Kate Greenaway was also recognized by *The Nation* reviewers. In the review of her *Mother Goose,* it was proclaimed her best work.[132] "There is but one Kate Greenaway," the reviewer said. William Crary Brownell, reviewing Ellen Haile's *The Two Gray Girls and Their Opposite Neighbors* made the following statement concerning the illustrations.

It is illustrated by Kate Greenaway, M. E. Edwards, Lizzie Lawson, and others, though the drawings of the first are unhappily few in number, and those of the rest not particularly skilful.[133]

The Nation was one of the few periodicals that recognized the artistry of Howard Pyle's early children's book, *Yankee Doodle,* which appeared just before the end of 1881.[134] Only *The Critic* joined in its praise.[135] The reviewer felt that the illustrations were the first American works that approached Caldecott in skill. He considered the skill of Pyle's drawing to be superior to his use of color and particularly praised his feeling for perspective. Both *The Dial* [136] and *The Literary World* [137] condemned the book.

The Nation took note of most of the important special trends in the publishing of children's books, reviewing many of the books which characterized those trends. The children's quartos with stories created to fit the publisher's available illustrations were reviewed with comments on the way they were created. Mary Howitt's *Our Four-Footed Friends* was such a book.[138] Though pleasant enough in its way, the story was clearly invented to fit the pictures and did not amount to much as a story. Even less successful was Mrs. D. P. Sanford's *Houseful of Children,* in which the pictures were reasonably good, but the story obviously suffered from the need to fit a group of widely assorted and unrelated pictures.[139] The reviewer felt that the book, filled with an enormous number of characters and warped to fit the illustrations, would bewilder children.

Two books more favorably reviewed were Horace E. Scudder's *The*

Bodleys on Wheels, with illustrations from the *Riverside Magazine* and from Osgood's standard stock,[140] and Richard Markham's *Around the Yule Log,* illustrated with woodcuts from Dodd, Mead & Company's stock.[141] The reviewer described Scudder's book as an "ingenious pot-pourri." Markham's book, he felt, was superior to Scudder's in unity and verisimilitude, but was obviously an imitation of the former's Bodley family series.

The real genius in the creation of this type of book, in the opinion of *The Nation*'s reviewers, was Frank R. Stockton. Two of his books of this type were judged to be among the best books of their seasons. *Roundabout Rambles in Lands of Fact and Fancy* was the "very best book for children . . . in a long time." [142] For each of his illustrations, Stockton created a short story instead of the more usual continuous narrative. The reviewer felt that Stockton understood children's interests, had a real sense of artistic responsibility, good judgment and refined moral feeling. He praised the book for its humor and for the way in which violence was played down without "being in the least namby-pamby." To Stockton's *Tales Out of School* the reviewer gave the honor of first place among books of its type, calling it another *Roundabout Rambles,* filled with an "inexhaustible fund of amusement and instruction." [143]

As noted earlier, perhaps the oddest trend in children's books in the period was the rewriting of books in words of one syllable, with the intention of making them more readable and available to a wider audience. Several of these books were reviewed, at first with enthusiasm, but later with recognition of the obvious faults. Mary Godolphin's *Robinson Crusoe, in Words of One Syllable* was reviewed both in 1867 and 1868 when an American edition appeared. The reviewer considered the book successful, saying that it "ought to put primers out of countenance, and make both teaching and learning to read a pastime." [144] In 1868, the reviewer went even further, declaring that he could not name a book more worthy to be given to a young reader.[145] But in the review of the same author's *The Swiss Family Robinson, in Words of One Syllable,* though still maintaining that the method might have rendered the traditional primer obsolete, there was recognition of the defects in such a rewriting. The use of nothing but monosyllabic words had led the author into a ridiculous position. She had made her book, "monosyllabic in form at the expense of being trisyllabic in intelligibility." [146]

Related in purpose, but far different in result, was the trend to rewriting or editing of classics of literature to make them more available to children. The three Lanier books and several rewritings of Shakespeare were reviewed in *The Nation.* William F. Allen wrote the reviews of the Lanier books, emphasizing in his criticism the scholarliness and good taste of the editor's work. He declared that a boy could find no better reading than in *The Boy's Froissart,* which was handsome and well-printed, as well as edited with excellent judgment.[147] Both *The Boy's King Arthur*[148] and *The Boy's Mabinogion*[149] showed careful scholarship and the latter had "fine poetic feeling."

The Shakespeare rewritings invited comparison with the Lambs' work. Mary Seamer's *Shakespeare Stories Simply Told* were not as good as those of her well-known predecessors, but did include six more plays than they had.[150] Robert R. Raymond, in his *Shakespeare for the Young Folk,* professed to do "the skipping" for the children and attempted to make the plot and language more simple without departing so far from the original.[151] The reviewer felt that the book constituted an interesting experiment performed with good taste, but was not certain it would be a success with the children. The work of Mrs. Laura Valentine, *Shakespearian Tales in Verse,* received a far different treatment.[152] The verse was nothing but doggerel, and many of the plays selected were quite unsuitable for children. Not even the illustrations were satisfactory.

No periodical reviewed so many children's books as did *The Nation.* It may even be said that no magazine reviewed children's books so thoroughly or so well. Most of the reviews were long, running to 300 words or more, even when they were included in a column containing many reviews. The method followed was to make a general statement to open the review, often setting up a critical standard which would apply to the type of book in hand. This was followed by a description of the book, including quotations. Specific faults or virtues were pointed out and an overall judgment or recommendation made. The final few lines of the review concerned illustrations and the physical qualities of the volume.

In a few reviews the judgments of children were reported, or a reference made to the reviewer's own children. E. J. Kuntze's *Mystic Bell* was a book the reviewer said he would not buy for his own child.[153] The comments on Christina B. Rossetti's *Sing-Song; A Nursery Rhyme Book* were based in part on the reaction of a "limited little jury" to whom the book had been read.[154]

The reviewers were careful to point out errors, both in the knowledge of the author, and in the author's writing. Nellie Eyster called betting, "stealing," in her *Chincapin Charlie.*[155] In *Children with the Poets,* an anthology of verse, Harriet B. McKeever committed the more grievous error of making mistakes in the texts of several of the poems she included in her collection.[156] Mrs. E. Breckenbrough Phelps was taken to task for the bad grammar which disfigured her *Memoirs of Washington,* though faulty grammar was only one of many faults in that book.[157]

But the reviews were by no means confined to minute detail. They covered with broad scope and critical alertness the major portion of the children's books of the age. Posterity has not agreed with all the conclusions. Miss Alcott's books are still read, the opinion of one *Nation* reviewer notwithstanding. But most of their judgments have borne up well through the years, the books and authors with whom they were most severe having long since been forgotten.

The long-term validity of the reviewer's judgments is not, however, the crucial factor. Rather, it is that the reviews should bring to the attention of potential readers the books which are appearing in the market, and to help them in selecting those which they might wish to read or to own. This *The Nation* did eminently well. By reviewing a large number of books, by reviewing critically and in detail, and by treating children's books as a serious part of literature, the magazine provided its readers with an extensive analysis of the books they might want for their children.

8

LITERARY MONTHLIES IN
NEW YORK

Mott reports that after 1865 New York was clearly the leading center for magazine publishing.[1] Certainly that city had a larger number of literary monthlies that devoted space and critical comment to children's books than did any other in the country. Besides *Harper's New Monthly Magazine*, the most important holdover from the pre-war period, New York could boast that it had, during the period from 1865 to 1881, *The Galaxy, Putnam's Magazine, Appleton's Journal, Hours at Home,* and *Scribner's Monthly*, all of which reviewed some children's books. It is true that not all of these magazines lasted the entire seventeen years. *The Galaxy* ceased publication in 1878. *Hours at Home,* published by Scribner, gave way to the more lively *Scribner's Monthly*, which absorbed *Putnam's Magazine* somewhat later, as well as Boston's *Old and New* and the children's *Riverside Magazine. Appleton's Journal* was not actually a monthly until late in its career. It started as a weekly, for a time appeared three times a week, but became a true literary monthly in both style and format from 1876 until its demise. New York was the home of countless other magazines as well, but, among monthlies, those listed above gave it its greatest claim to distinction in literature, and were those which concerned themselves with literature for the young.

HARPER'S NEW MONTHLY MAGAZINE

The oldest of the New York monthlies was also the one which gave the greatest amount of attention to children's books. Mott does not list *Harper's* as one of those which made an outstanding contribution to

American literary criticism in the post-Civil War period, although it included a literary department.[2] This department was, at first, called "Literary Notices," but in December, 1868, its title was changed to "Editor's Book Table," and in December, 1869, to "Editor's Literary Record." That title was maintained through the period. According to J. Henry Harper, the book reviewing department was first conducted by George Ripley of Brook Farm fame, who was involved in the founding of the magazine.[3] He was succeeded in November, 1868, by Lyman Abbott, third son of the prolific writer of books for children, Jacob Abbott, later famous himself as editor of the *Christian Union* and *The Outlook*. Abbott began reviewing for Harper's in the sixties and, in the early seventies gained a considerable portion of his income from these reviews.[4] Abbott said his contract called for five or six pages of reviews each month.[5] Abby, his wife, actually read the fiction, and his reviews were based on her reports. Some of the reading of children's books was entrusted to their children, and some of it was made a part of the family reading, with the children and the adults of the family gathered together to listen as the stories were read aloud. In several reviews, to be discussed later, Abbott reported the reaction or evaluation of a particular book made by his own children. Abbott received $50 a month for his work for *Harper's*, a sum exactly equivalent to the monthly rent for his home in Cornwall, a few miles up the Hudson River from New York City.[6]

Though a few reviews of children's books had appeared in the magazine earlier, it was only after Abbott began conducting the review department that *Harper's* contained reviews of children's books in any considerable number. In fact, the entire book review department was expanded under his hand. Prior to 1869, the book review section appeared only intermittently and frequently was very short. In 1865, no reviews of children's books appeared and only two each year in 1866, 1867, and 1868. But in each subsequent year many more books for children were reviewed, except in 1876, the year Abbott joined the *Christian Union,* when there were only four. The year 1870 saw only nine reviews of children's books, but the following year there were eighty-two. This is, in part, accounted for by the fact that the late 1870 books, brought out for the Christmas trade, were reviewed in the post-Christmas issues. Both of these years were exceptional. It was more common for reviews of twenty to thirty-six children's books to appear each year. During the seventeen-year period from 1865 to 1881, more than 375 children's books were reviewed in *Harper's.*

Though fiction for children constituted a majority of the children's books reviewed, *Harper's* covered every type of book, including travel, history, science and natural history, poetry, music, biography, picture books, and a variety of others. Not only did the magazine review a great range in types of books, but also a great number of books by different authors. They range from the long-forgotten authors of the American Tract Society like Mrs. Sangster, the Mathews sisters, Julia and Joanna, authors of pious books published by Robert Carter & Brothers, the prolific authors of Lee & Shepard, Sophie May and Elijah Kellogg, to such still-popular authors as Mary Mapes Dodge, Susan Coolidge, and Louisa May Alcott. Nearly every literary type, religious stories, temperance stories, travelogue story books, fairy tales, adventure tales, sports stories, and stories of family life, was reviewed in *Harper's*.

At the beginning of a section of reviews Abbott commented that children's books ought to make up a considerable portion of the family library in most homes.[7] And to prove that this was no idle comment, he gave them an important place in the literary notices of *Harper's Magazine*. To his job of reviewing books for the young, he brought a kindly wisdom and an acute understanding of the children themselves, their tastes and their desires in books. If Abbott had a fault as a reviewer of juvenile literature it was, perhaps, that he was too generous, too ready to accept the judgment of children. But the parents of the seventies, seeking to select books for their children, must have felt that Dr. Abbott was one of the sounder guides. He had little patience with sensational stories. Both his father, Jacob Abbott, and his brother, Edward, writing books for the young, carefully avoided all traces of sensationalism. He felt, beyond question, that his own criticism and the criticism of others had some effect on the quality of children books. In January, 1871, he began a series of reviews with a comment on the improvement in children's books.

> *On the whole, taking the books before us as fair sample of what the year 1871 has in store for the little folks, we are inclined to congratulate ourselves and our readers on the fact, apparent, that abundant criticism is beginning to produce some results, and that, both in literary and art qualities, children's literature is undergoing a change greatly for the better. Albeit there is still abundant room for improvement in the future.*[8]

In December of the same year, he again commented on the seeming improvement in children's books, wondering if the books had really improved or if the editors were only sending their better books to the critics.[9]

In 1873, he again reiterated his feeling of the importance of children's books, prefacing a group of reviews with some general comments.

This literary recorder is not oblivious of the children, and intends to keep their parents advised from time to time respecting the character of books which are offered for their intellectual diet. The most important and influential books are not those which are the most ponderous, nor those which make the most stir in the world. The wise agriculturalist looks after the purity of his seeds as well as after the health of his fruit trees and the condition of his ripening grain; and the public, if it were wise, would not expend its criticism on maturer books, and leave those for the children to pass without examination. An unhealthy story-book in the Sabbath-school library will do more damage by far than the most heretical of treatises in the minister's study.[10]

This statement, ponderous as it is, might give the impression that Abbott's criticism was predominantly moralistic. He did give some attention to the moral values of children's books, reviewing many books intended for Sunday school libraries. He did comment on the information and instruction that the books would provide. He was, even at the time he was writing these reviews, a Congregational minister. But he was an enlightened and urbane churchman, with that broad point of view which typifies so much of the best thought of the nineteenth century, and it was this enlightened attitude that pervaded much of his criticism of children's books. Primarily, he considered children's books as their playground, and as a part of literature to be measured by literary standards. Even after 1876, when Abbott had become associate editor of the *Christian Union,* the same kinds of standards were used to evaluate children's books in *Harper's.*

In a great many reviews literary style was examined. Abbott described Horace E. Scudder's style in *Stories from My Attic* as "peculiarly genial in spirit and poetic." [11] In a review of E. H. Knatchbull-Hugessen's *Pussy-Cat Mew,* he made an even more detailed analysis of stylistic elements.

Humor is not ordinarily characteristic of fairy stories, or is at best of the most grotesque description. But these stories are told in a certain rollicking style, and with a curious admixture of the affairs and language of everyday life with that of the fairy world, which is very funny. The description, in the story of "The Four Pigs," of their housekeeping, is a capital example of a good grotesque.[12]

He described Paul Du Chaillu's style in *My Apingi Kingdom* as "an easy, pleasant, conversational style, without the slightest straining after effect." [13] Mrs. Ewing was praised for her unusual power of description in *Jan of the Windmill*.[14]

One peculiarity of style to be found in many children's books of the period was the use of baby-talk and of dialect to try to achieve realism. Joanna H. Mathews, a frequent user of childish language, was taken to task by Abbott for this use of baby-talk, despite the fact that he found much in her books worthy of praise.[15] While he found Helen Aldrich De Kroyft's *Little Jakey* a touching and pathetic story, he felt that the reader would grow weary of the German dialect which Miss De Kroyft employed in all of Little Jakey's conversation.[16]

Frequently an attempt was made to place a more or less absolute evaluation on a particular work or on a particular author. The reviewer of Laboulaye's *Fairy Tales* declared that work to be "the most charming collection of Fairy Stories which has appeared for a generation." [17] In the same year the reviewer declared that "of all writers of Fairy Tales we must, after due consideration and consultation with our own juveniles, give the first place to Monsieur Jean Macé." [18] By 1872, Abbott had found another author of fairy stories who had replaced Macé as the best, the English Member of Parliament and writer of children's books, E. H. Knatchbull-Hugessen.[19] In 1875 he gave almost as high an evaluation to Jane G. Austin's *Moonfolk,* declaring it the best fairy story of that year.[20]

Not all such evaluations were confined to fairy stories. The anonymous *John Whopper, the Newsboy* was the best work of its type since *Alice's Adventures in Wonderland*.[21] Dr. Abbott gave his greatest praise to his own father's work. "Mr. Abbott," he said, "at his best, is the very best living writer for youth." [22] Though later generations may not have confirmed such a judgment, the filial sentiment which, in part, gave birth to it is readily understood. And Jacob Abbott, though not deserving the title of best writer for children, was far from the poorest for children, and was one of the most influential in his time.

In a few reviews the work of one author was compared with that of another. James Greenwood's *The Adventures of Reuben Davidger* invited comparison with *Robinson Crusoe*. The review pointed out a resemblance between the two books, both in the "graphic minuteness of detail, and the sense of reality" of both characters and incidents.[23] But an even more interesting comparison was made between Edward Abbott's first children's book, *Long Look House,* and the writing of his famous father, Jacob. The younger Abbott had declared that his intention was to continue in the vein in which his father had worked, writing unsensational stories which, while they might amuse, would convey useful information to children. Virtually the whole of the *Harper's* review was devoted to a discussion of the similarities between the two.

The reader will insensibly compare it with the inimitable books of his father, Jacob Abbott. There is something in common in the works of father and son. Long-Look House is the reverse of sensational. It is full of useful information, and it is thoroughly healthy and pure in tone from beginning to end. But it is not as simple in language as it might be; incident is wanting; and we should expect that it would be found more useful for elders to read to the children than attractive for children to read to themselves.[24]

Occasionally Abbott indicated his evaluation of a book by equating it with others by the same author. In a brief notice of Rebecca Clarke's *Dotty Dimple at School,* he said that if a child had one of the books in the "Dotty Dimple" series, he would want the other four.[25] He called her *Little Folks Astray* a "worthy successor" to her other series.[26] In a notice of the last two volumes in Jacob Abbott's "Juno" series, he declared them to be equal to the first two and just as good as anything the author had ever written, "which is saying a great deal." [27]

When the opportunity presented itself, Abbott discussed similar books in a single review. Three books of verse, Mrs. Eliza Lee Follen's *Little Songs,* Mary Mapes Dodge's *Rhymes and Jingles,* and Lucy Larcom's *Childhood Songs,* for older children, provided him with one such opportunity. After describing and characterizing each collection, he contrasted them. Of the three, *Childhood Songs* contained more real poetry. It had "less of fancy but more of sentiment than *Rhymes and Jingles."*

The first two books will amuse, the third will develop, the first two will be the more attractive in the reading the third will be the sweeter in the memory.[28]

Little attention was given to action or to incident in the reviews in *Harper's,* except to outline briefly the plot or theme of a story. In the review of Edward Abbott's *Long Look House* lack of incident was mentioned.[29] Abbott described Caroline Dall's *Patty Gray's Journey to the Cotton Islands,* as a book with "incidents so commonplace that it is no wonder that she failed." [30] A particular incident was discussed in the review of *Salt-Water Dick,* by May Mannering, pseudonym of Harriet P. H. Nowell. Miss Nowell had ingeniously quieted a storm at sea by using literally the proverbial method of pouring oil upon the waters. Abbott could not approve. "A novel is no worse for children because it contains incidentally accurate information," he said. "Inaccuracy is nowhere so pernicious." [31]

Far more attention was given to character, particularly to the reality with which the author managed to invest his characters. But in these reviews we do not find a strict demand for complete reality. Abbott felt particularly called upon to defend the characters in his father's books. Discussing *August and Elvie,* he admitted that "critics say that such characters are unnatural," but he concluded with the statement that "they are certainly uncommon—more's the pity." [32] His father's purpose, he said, was to show how character should be, rather than how it is. But, by and large, Abbott looked for naturalness in character; at least, when his own father's writing was not involved. He criticized the characterization of Adalbert in *The House on Wheels,* a translation from the French, as exhibiting a kind of transformation "of the sort that rarely occurs except in children's books." [33] His evaluation of the portrayal of character in Horatio Alger, Jr.'s *Tattered Tom* was that Alger had "evidently studied his subject with care, and drawn his portrait from life." [34] Since Mayes reports that Alger usually used actual youngsters whose stories he knew as the basis for his books, or at least for the early chapters before Dame Fortune began to smile on his erstwhile paupers, Abbott's analysis of this book seems a good one, for he recognized a greater merit in the earlier chapters than in the later ones.[35]

The first part of his story, which contains the street Arab, is by far the best part of the book. No real interest is added to it by the plots and counterplots of the latter chapters, and "Tattered Tom" is more interesting by far in her original character than when converted into Miss Lindsay.[36]

Often Abbott felt that the author had gone too far in his attempts to create natural character, a complaint not infrequent in the reviews of other periodicals. John T. Trowbridge had gone too far in naturalness of character in *A Chance for Himself,* a sequel to *Jack Hazard and His Fortunes.* Abbott said that "in his anxiety not to draw model boys Mr. Trowbridge appears to have gone to the other and a worse extreme." [37] In *Stories of Vinegar Hill,* by Susan Warner, far too much slang and bad grammar had been employed in order to give the illusion of reality.[38] Even in C. Floyd's *Honest and Earnest,* a Sunday school book, which portrayed "naturally and graphically the misdoings of mischievous and careless but not malicious children, who are gradually developed into a higher religious life" he doubted the wisdom of showing such misbehavior in a child's book, and this despite the fact that the book was well done.[39]

Surprisingly, the review of John Habberton's *The Worst Boy in Town* expressed no objection to the mischief depicted. The reviewer saw elements in Habberton's book which were not, apparently, discerned by others.

If there is any sort of mischievous prank boys have not yet learned, or any ingenious trick or enterprise of which they are ignorant, Jack Whittingham, the "worst boy in town" of Mr. Habberton's sprightly tale, can fully enlighten their curiosity for further knowledge in that line. And if they read the record of Jack's career between the lines, they will also learn that they may be mischievous without being mean, malicious, or undutiful, and that when the time comes for them to give up "sowing their wild oats," their energies may be so directed as to make them industrious and honorable men.[40]

Harper's did not ignore the sensational books of the day, so often deplored by the more enlightened reading public, but rather criticized them severely and recommended interesting, non-sensational books as antidotes. In a group notice of a number of books published by Lee & Shepard, Abbott condemned all the books for this fault.

Sensationalism in grown folks' novels is bad enough, but it is in vain to cry out against Charles Reade, or even Sylvanus Cobb, while we feed our children on such highly seasoned diet as Pinks and Blues, Oliver Optic's Bear and Forbear, Charley and Eva Roberts' Home in the West, *or even Mrs. Samuel's* Springdale Stories. *Robbers, smugglers, counterfeiters, and murderers carry the heroes and heroines through a series of adventures that are only saved from being sensational by being stupid. That children read such stories with avidity is not surprising; but what possesses parents to purchase them and Sunday-schools to give them circulation? Of these books the "Springdale Series," in six volumes, is the least objectionable, and affords some compensation for its absurd story of the smuggler's cave, and its grotesque travesty on Eton, by really giving some useful information, and endeavoring, with some success, to point a moral.*

This sort of literature is the more inexcusable since there is no lack of what is at once really good and far more interesting.[41]

In another review, later in the same year, Abbott granted Oliver Optic's popularity with boy readers, but doubted that Optic, Mr. William T. Adams, was "always a safe guide, or . . . the best sort of inspiration." [42]

Oliver Optic and the publications of Lee & Shepard were not the only ones condemned for sensationalism. *Adventures by Sea and Land* published by Porter & Coates of Philadelphia, was guilty of the same fault. Abbott praised the appearance of the book, or rather, damned it with faint praise, saving his harshest strictures for its content, which he described in just sufficient detail to indicate its flavor.

96

It consists of a series of very sensational narratives so wildly improbable as to awaken the incredulity of even youthful and credulous readers. There are stories of pirate life, and sea-fights, and shipwrecks, and a hunting of wild beasts—stories of a kind that were more popular in our boyhood than they are now. The characteristic which commends a modern story is naturalness, and this, we are glad to believe, is true of juvenile stories as well as those for their elders.[43]

The Adventures of Robinson Playfellow was condemned as sensational. Abbott reported that this book, modeled on *Robinson Crusoe* as its title suggests, "purports to be a story of a young French marine, and forcibly suggests the boy's popular expression of incredulity, 'Tell it to the Marines.' "[44]

But frequently, he found books that could be useful in weaning boys away from such sensational stuff. Charles A. Stephens' *Camping Out* was such a book.[45] It would arouse the interest of boys in manly sports, in camping and in nature, and would be more entertaining to right-minded boys. In later years biographies were recommended as substitutes for sensational fiction. George M. Towle's *Voyages and Adventures of Vasco da Gama* was welcomed for this purpose.[46] Charles Lamb's *The Adventures of Ulysses*, republished in *Harper's New Monthly*'s "Half-Hour Series" in 1879, was also recommended as a good alternative to sensational fiction, since it would satisfy the demand for romantic adventure without the danger that the child's imagination would be developed in an unhealthy manner or his passions unduly stimulated.[47]

Despite the fact that certain of the sensational books were popular with the young, Abbott still placed a great deal of faith in the judgments of his own children, frequently reporting their reaction to a particular book in his reviews. Jean Ingelow's *Mopsa, the Fairy* was declared to be a splendid book by his son, and he was inclined to agree with his son's estimate after a mere glance through its pages.[48] In a notice of Jacob Abbott's *The Rolo and Lucy Books of Poetry*, which Dodd, Mead reissued in 1870, Lyman Abbott reported that "the popularity of the series has been attested to in our household, where little hands have almost utterly used up the first edition."[49] A latter day observer may be forgiven for wondering if the fact that the author was those children's grandfather might not have had something to do with the amount of wear the books received.

At times it was not the reading done by the children which was reported, but the reaction of the entire family on hearing a book read aloud. He found Mrs. Elizabeth Prentiss' *The Story Lizzie Told* to be "capital reading for Sunday afternoon; worth reading aloud, as we read it, to the whole family circle—children and grown folks."[50] An entire series was recommended for reading aloud, Jacob Abbott's "Science for the Young" which, Dr. Abbott reported, was being done in his family.[51]

A report of a different kind, and involving a different relationship of children to the story, appeared in the review of Rossiter W. Raymond's *The Man in the Moon.*[52] The following is Abbott's complete statement concerning the book.

> *Mr. Rossiter Raymond is in the habit of reading every Christmas, a story, prepared for the occasion, to the Sabbath-school of Plymouth Church. If we mistake not, this is the genesis of* The Man in the Moon. *In that case Plymouth Sabbath-school is to be congratulated on its good fortune. Mr. Raymond is a rare story-teller, and in his best mood when he is telling stories to children.*[53]

Abbott knew that he was not mistaken, actually, for he had, himself, been connected with Plymouth Church at various times. While a young lawyer in New York City he had attended regularly Henry Ward Beecher's services at Plymouth Church and had taught a Bible class in the Sunday school there.[54] Later still, after Beecher's death, he was acting pastor of Plymouth Church and, finally, its pastor. Perhaps he had heard Mr. Raymond read one or more of his stories to the Sunday school.

Age level was occasionally mentioned in *Harper's* reviews, particularly when the author seemed not to have gauged correctly the ability or interest of children. Abbott felt that *Little Women,* Part II, was "a rather mature book for the little women, but a capital one for their elders." [55] He objected to the fact that they were little girls in the first part, but were grown women with children of their own by the end of the second part. He had the same objection to *An Old-Fashioned Girl,* which, he declared,

> *is to our thinking quite as good a story, quite as fresh, unconventional, and true as "Little Women," though it will hardly be as popular with the little folks. In fact, it is written for an older audience, and in a literary point of view belongs in a class by itself, being neither quite young enough for a children's story, nor quite old enough for a novel.*[56]

It is interesting that Abbott recognized this book as something new, though it actually shared its quality with *Little Women,* a story for the in-between age and one of the earliest of "junior" novels. He saw Miss Alcott's work as a new class of writing.

In many other books, however, he discerned a failure on the part of the author to discriminate between what is appropriate for the young and what is appropriate for their elders. Julia A. Mathews' *Grandfather's Faith* was more suitable for the reminiscences of a grandfather than for the reading of his grandchildren.[57] Miss Mathews had simply failed to make a proper distinction. Abbott's successor, however, felt that Lizzie W. Champney's *All Around a Palette* was written with an adult audience in mind. It belonged "to that school of modern literature in which very abstract or poetic ideas, which only a mature mind can comprehend, are furnished with a pretense of being intended for children" but are actually aimed at their parents.[58]

On the other hand, a few books were praised for opposite qualities. Ellis Gray did not make the mistake of looking to the parents for appreciation of her *Long Ago*.[59] Abbott praised J. Lukin's *The Young Mechanic* for its simplicity and clearness. The author had "not fallen into the common mistake of explaining difficult operations to boys who do not understand the simple ones, but begins with the alphabet." [60]

Not all, by any means, of the attention went to the literary qualities of the children's books reviewed in *Harper's*. Abbott was a Congregational minister, and though he professed a liberal and enlightened evangelical Christianity, he was bound to consider the moral influence of books on children. Even had he not, by his own inclination, considered the moral effect of the books he reviewed, it is likely that the dominating influence of Fletcher Harper on the policies of the magazine would have assured such a consideration. Mott describes Fletcher Harper as the actual editor of the magazine for its first twenty-five years, though he was always an editor in the background.[61] In any case, there was no reason that he should ever have objected to Abbott's reviewing. Harper must have known well the kind of job Abbott would do when he employed him in 1868.

Harper's reviewed a large number of books frankly intended for Sunday school libraries, recommending a few, finding many of them unsatisfactory. *Tales from Alsace* had a "genuine religious spirit" and could be recommended for Sunday school libraries.[62] Abbott judged Katherine Williams' *Tiptoe* to be better than most Sunday school stories, since it was both more natural and more religious than most of them. Most Sunday school library books, he felt, gave children the idea that "piety and artificialness are synonymous terms." [63] *May's Own Boy* was described as a book suitable for Sunday reading, of which there were few enough at best.[64] He described Susan Warner's *Little Camp on Eagle Hill* as a vehicle for religious instruction, but felt that it was "free from heaviness or wearisomeness" despite this obvious purpose.[65]

In a review in 1871, Abbott took particular note of the quality of many of the Sunday school books from the house of Robert Carter & Brothers.

> With the numerous children's books which we receive from the house of Robert Carter and Brothers we have no other fault to find than that which Paul found with the Athenians—they are apt to be in all respects "too religious." This is emphatically true of Freddie Fighting His Way, and no less so of Little Primrose. The former talks like a half-blown theologian, and we quite agree with naughty Edgar and his impious Mamma, who "don't like such stuff for children." The moral of the latter's early death is, take care that you be not "too good for this world." [66]

On the other hand, he praised *Rose Marbury*, from the same publisher, as containing a better kind of religion. Particularly, it was praiseworthy because of the way it treated "the cold and selfish religionist in Aunt Fanny" one of the important characters in the story.[67]

Between 1878 and 1881, Abbott's successor reviewed a number of non-fiction books intended primarily for Sunday school libraries, two of them lives of Christ. The first one, MacDuff's *Brighter Than the Sun*, though its title was a poor one, was a book of "singular simplicity," and would, therefore, interest not only the ten to sixteen age group, for whom it was intended, but also even younger children, if read to them. The reviewer felt that the descriptions of the Holy Land, which were included, gave realism to the book.[68] But Richard Newton's *Life of Christ for the Young* was disappointing. Instead of a life of Christ, the book was actually a series of sermons. He found the illustrations especially bad, since they often had nothing whatsoever to do with the text, one of them actually a scene on the Rhine River.[69] He also reviewed Susan Warner's series written to illustrate Bible history, *Walks from Eden, The House of Israel, The Kingdom of Judah, The Broken Walls of Jerusalem,* and *The Star Out of Jacob* in a single review for the five titles, but his space permitted little more than a description of the books, which were written within a narrative framework.[70]

Harper's concerned itself more often with the moral influence of a book, than with any direct religious purpose. The attitude revealed was not a narrow one. As often as not, the books were found to have too much of moralizing in them. What was praised, was a general healthiness of moral tone, rather than any direct application of a moral maxim. At times the term "moral" was used to mean what would be called the theme today. At other times it was used to refer to the old-fashioned morals such as are attached to fables.

Often Abbott felt that an overdose of moralizing, either direct or implied, made the story poorer. He found Caroline Dall's *Patty Gray's Journey to the Cotton Islands* carried "such a cargo of moralizing," that would have sunk "even a story more buoyant." [71] In T.R.Y.'s *Belle Lovel*, the didactic purpose itself was worthy, but the author had not achieved that purpose in the story. The book, "like some unpleasantly good people . . . impairs its influence by a certain ostentation of moral excellence," he said.[72] His most emphatic criticism of moralizing, however, was reserved for Charlotte Tucker's *The Giant Killers,* one of many moralistic stories from the prolific pen of A.L.O.E.

> *It is an allegory, in which, however, the sugar-coating of story is so very thin that he must be a very stupid child indeed who does not recognize the medicinal moral underneath. A.L.O.E.'s stories in the field of modern fiction seem like an old-fashioned preacher, with his knee-buckles, and his stiff white choker, and his professional and stately air, in a modern assembly of ministers in their customary fatigue uniform.*[73]

Frequently, Abbott called the reader's attention to the good moral influence of a book, commending it for its general tone. When the Harpers republished Thomas Hughes' *Tom Brown's School Days* in 1870, he called it a "healthful book for boys." [74] He found Dinah Mulock Craik's *The Little Lame Prince* to be a book of good moral influence.

> *It is such a story as a loving mother with a fertile and pure imagination might tell her little ones, with no moral to be learned, but a moral life in it that will be the more readily communicated that it addresses the heart through the imagination.*[75]

He found John T. Trowbridge's *Doing His Best* to be considerably more healthy than *A Chance for Himself* had seemed the previous year. He said of *Doing His Best,*

> *We have not a very clear idea of what it is intended to teach, or whether it is intended to teach anything but a general lesson of self-dependence and manliness. It is however, very lively reading, with a good moral tone, but no distinctively religious influence either good or bad, with a fair sprinkling of wickedness, about such as boys, and men too, have to meet in ordinary life, but no profanity or vulgarity for the youthful reader to catch.*[76]

Abbott felt that society was achieving a more healthy attitude toward conventional morality in fiction. He felt that the popularity of Miss Al-

101

cott's *An Old-Fashioned Girl,* in which Polly's lover was reclaimed, was probably an indication of a decrease in the power of Grundyism in American life.[77] And he provided another proof in his own attitude toward James De Mille's *The Boys of Grand Prè School,* which, he said, "teaches no moral lesson, nor any other, but it will give the boys a hearty laugh, and . . . will do them no harm." [78]

Occasionally, an author went too far in reaction against narrow earlier attitudes. Mary N. Prescott, in *Matt's Follies,* had pictured too much mischief and mischief too serious to be completely healthy. "Miss Prescott writes," Abbott said, "as one who feels dissatisfied with the moralizing and commonplace fiction of past years, but has labored with a better intent than result to substitute something different." [79]

Abbott apparently had little patience with the general run of temperance stories, for he praised a few of them chiefly because they were unlike others. He felt that Julia McNair Wright's *The Best Fellow in the World,* a story warning of the dangers of moderate drinking, would not harm the youngster who read it, and might do him some good.[80] *The Seymours,* however, from the same publisher, the American Temperance Society, was of very doubtful moral effect.[81] In his review of Mrs. J. E. McConaughy's *The Fire Fighters,* Abbott expressed his general attitude toward temperance stories. Declaring this book to be an exception to the general run of such stories, he said, "We are not much enamored of the average temperance tale, which usually has little but good intentions to commend it." [82]

Several books were praised for their ability to instill manliness, or, at least, an admiration for that trait, in boy readers. Charles A. Stephens' *Camping Out* was praised for its treatment of the "manly sports" connected with camping.[83] *The Young Nimrods in North America; Hunting Adventures on Land and Sea* by Thomas W. Knox, had both this inspirational value and information as well.[84]

Harper's commented frequently on illustrations and illustrators in its reviews of children's books. The comments ranged from a mere remark, on the illustrations of *Appleton's Juvenile Annual for 1869,* that the pictures were merely average,[85] to fairly detailed analyses. Hammat Billings' illustrations for Dicken's *A Child's Dream of a Star* were described as having considerably less merit than the story. The reviewer said that "the star is overpowering in one or two cases, and the angels are unpleasantly ghostly; but the terrestrial pictures are exceedingly pretty." [86] Gustave Doré's designs for *Popular Fairy Tales* were warmly praised, for Abbott felt that Doré's genius was "peculiarly adapted to the quaint, queer, and often grotesque fancies of the old fairy tales." [87] Frölich's pictures for Charlotte Yonge's *Little Lucy's Wonderful Globe* had captured the essence of art for children, which lay in "simple and easily

102

comprehended forms." [88] Frölich was not, however, always correct in his drawing.

The only comments on the physical appearance of the books reviewed, other than on illustrations, were occasional statements that a book was a "quarto" in form. Mrs. D. P. Sanford's *The Captain's Children* was described as "a beautiful quarto," [89] and Thomas W. Knox's *Adventures of Two Youths in a Journey to Japan and China* as "an exceedingly beautiful quarto." [90]

All the most important types of children's books were reviewed in *Harper's* during the years between 1865 and 1881. A list of the fanciful tales for children reviewed would be a list of virtually every such tale published, but a few reviews indicate the reception of all the good ones. *Alice's Adventures in Wonderland* and a great many of the fanciful tales that followed in its wake were cordially welcomed. The attitude that permeates these reviews of fairy stories is, perhaps, best expressed in a review of Mrs. W. J. Hays' *The Princess Idleways*. The reviewer described the psychological fact that the imaginative and fanciful is essential to the child.

> *The transition from matters of fact, even when they are the most entertaining, to the marvels of fairy-land, is always delightful to a healthy-minded child, and often becomes an imperative necessity.*[91]

Though this review was written late in the period, the earlier reviewers, including Abbott, favorably reviewed most of the better fairy tales.

Several fanciful tales were reviewed in 1869, including Mary Wentworth's *Fairy Tales from Gold Land,* stories with a California setting from the house of A. Roman & Company of San Francisco. Their unusual setting was the only thing unusual the reviewer found in them.[92] *Alice's Adventures in Wonderland,* in the 1869 Lee & Shepard edition, received a favorable review in over a hundred words.[93] Jean Ingelow's *Mopsa, the Fairy* was reviewed the same year.[94] The reviewer reported the approval of one of his children. Other writers of fairy tales frequently reviewed in *Harper's* were E. H. Knatchbull-Hugessen and Mrs. Dinah Mulock Craik. Knatchbull-Hugessen was praised for the spiritedness of his style and for his ability to mix the everyday with the fanciful in an amusing manner.[95] Mrs. Craik's stories, the *Adventures of a Brownie,*[96] and *The Little Lame Prince,*[97] were imaginative, and, without being moralistic, contained a pureness of tone which Abbott found admirable.

Numerous books published chiefly for their informational value were reviewed, with each of the common types represented by a number of titles. These reviews also range in length from very brief notices to detailed analyses of the books.

103

Many books of science and natural history were reviewed. Both the number discussed and the attitude revealed showed an awareness of the increasingly important part science was playing in contemporary life; yet, at the same time, they show that the reviewer was aware that many people were deeply troubled by the implications of science and feared the effect of science upon their own beliefs and, especially, on those of their children. Abbott reassured the reader that his father's *Force* would present nothing that would lead children to consider religion and science as opposed to one another.

Parents, too, may rest assured that while Mr. Abbott will give, as he does, the results of the latest and best researches in the scientific world, he will write nothing that can awaken or confirm in the youthful mind the idea that science and religion are antagonistic; that on the contrary the incidental, but none the less powerful, effect of his writing will be to lead the reader to recognize in the works of God the wisdom, the skill, and the beneficience of their great creator.[98]

More often, the reviews dealt with the value of the subject or with the method the author used to present his subject. Jean Macé's *The History of a Mouthful of Bread* and his *The Servants of the Stomach* were described as "in a form so attractive that they will be read with pleasure." [99] These books presented science within a fictional framework, as did the books in Jacob Abbott's "Science for the Young" series. *The Fairly-Land of Science,* by Arabella B. Buckley, was a book of natural science presented in a manner "as engaging as a fairy tale." [100] In a long review of *What Mr. Darwin Saw in His Voyage Round the World in the Ship "Beagle,"* the history of the voyage was discussed, the method of abridging the book for children was analyzed, and the contents described.[101] The reviewer considered it one of the best books of science for children that had been published in many years. Jacob Abbott's *Water and Land* was praised for the excellent qualities of its style and method, which showed "clearness and precision of statement, amplitude of illustration, and fullness and freshness of scientific fact and theory." [102]

History for children also received a large measure of attention. In 1866, the third volume of John Bonner's *A Child's History of the United States* was reviewed.[103] This volume, which dealt with the Civil War, was characterized as "a graphic and spirited narrative" of the events it covered. The reviewer felt that the events were well selected and clearly described. He did not, as other critics did, suggest that Bonner was biased in his treatment of his subject.

A more detailed analysis was made of Isa (Knox) Craig's *Young*

Folks' History of England.[104] It was an admirable book, with a style both simple and attractive, with judicious handling of disputed questions, and with an excellent index so needed in a work of that type. The reviewer recommended it for anyone, child or adult, seeking a good brief introduction to English history.

Thomas Wentworth Higginson's *Young Folks' History of the United States* was analyzed in even greater detail.[105] The reviewer felt that Higginson's work was truly remarkable. The author had succeeded in making a really interesting book, though the odds would have seemed to be against success in a work which attempted to cover the entire span of the nation's history up to the Grant administration. Higginson's greatest achievement was in presenting the life of the people, not just the military and political events covered in the average history. Higginson was praised for his treatment of controversial subjects, such as the Civil War, with which he dealt "with great calmness and with judicial impartiality, though with no pretense at indifference and no lack of moral earnestness." [106] The index and the bibliography of books for further study were praiseworthy, but the illustrations were too profuse. The reviewer felt that much of the space given to pictures might better have been given to the author, especially since the imaginary pictures, a majority of those included, might better have been omitted.

Volumes in both Towle's and Edward Eggleston's series of biographies were reviewed. The longest review was given Towle's *Voyages and Adventures of Vasco da Gama.*[107] The reviewer discussed the author's qualifications for his task, which he felt were the best, but he did not devote many words to the actual book. In the review of *Pizarro* the next year, however, Towle's style was given more careful consideration.[108] His work was accurate, and the incidents selected were exciting and graphically portrayed, so that they ought to arouse a relish for history in young readers. Eggleston's *Pocahontas* and *Brant and Red Jacket* were described as accurate enough to be worth adult reading.[109]

Many "travelogue story-books" were reviewed in *Harper's,* the earliest being William T. Adams' "Young America Abroad" series. Earlier books by the same author had been noted with unfavorable comments, but this series, chiefly because of the information it contained about the countries the young Americans visited, was considered worth recommending.[110] Several of Charles A. Stephens' travel stories were reviewed, though in the review of *Off to the Geysers,* in which the young yachters visited Iceland, the reliability of the information presented was questioned by the reviewer.[111]

The more famous series by Horace E. Scudder, Hezekiah Butterworth, and Thomas W. Knox received longer reviews. Three of Scudder's Bodley family books were reviewed, but the first, *The Bodleys Tell-*

ing Stories, does not fit the travel story book classification.[112] *The Bodleys Afoot,* however, fitted the type on two counts. The Bodleys travelled around New England, and, in one of their many story-telling sessions, described an imaginary tour through South America, to which the review drew particular attention.[113] In the review of *Mr. Bodley Abroad,* the reviewer described the entire series as an excellent one.[114] He praised Butterworth's *Zigzag Journeys in Europe* for the entertaining manner in which the descriptions of people and places were presented.[115] Knox's *Adventures of Two Youths in Japan and China* had good content and a lively narrative.[116] The profuseness of illustration in each of these series was commented on favorably.

A number of classics rewritten or edited for children were reviewed. J. Moyr Smith's *The Prince of Argolis,* though well-illustrated, was dull.[117] Alfred J. Church's *Stories from Homer* was excellent, except for the archaic quality of the language.[118] A longer review of Barthold G. Niebuhr's *Greek Hero-Stories* discussed the value of the literary type for improving the mind of the child and for stimulating his imagination, praised the translation and illustrations, but gave most attention to the history of the work itself—how Niebuhr had told the tales for his own children.[119] Church's *Stories from Virgil,* unlike his earlier adaptation from the classics, was praised for its style, which was simple, yet elegant.[120] Sidney's Lanier's *The Boy's Froissart* was a book sure to appeal to children, and one in which the editor had adhered closely to the language of the original, or rather, to that of a good translation.[121]

Though it is not a real test of reviewers that they should judge the lasting appeal of a book it is, nevertheless, interesting to examine their judgments from that point of view. *Harper's* comes off rather well in such a test. *Hans Brinker, Little Women, Alice's Adventures in Wonderland, What Katy Did, Twenty Thousand Leagues Under the Sea,* and *Toby Tyler* were reviewed and recognized as books of unusual merit.

To characterize the reviews of children's books in *Harper's* is a difficult task. At least three different people wrote the reviews. Yet there is a similarity in tone running through the reviews that makes it impossible to identify an individual reviewer by internal evidence alone. Whether the reviews were by Abbott, by his predecessor, or by the man who took his post when he went to the staff of the *Christian Union,* the approach was still the same. It is even possible, though both J. Henry Harper and Abbott himself are silent on this point, that Abbott continued to write *Harper's* reviews after he joined *Christian Union.*

These reviews were concerned both with literary matters and with the wholesome influence each book might have. The reviews were not, perhaps, unusual; yet they represented common ideas toward children's books. They did not accept the overly pious books of an earlier generation. They expected children's books to please children, and, at the same time, looked for instruction in them. Though they welcomed books that made no pretense of teaching, there was not the same tolerance of books meant purely for pleasure that could be seen in the *Nation* and, as will be seen in the next chapter, in the *Atlantic Monthly*.

The reviews themselves differed greatly. Some were very brief, hardly more than notices, while others consisted of several hundred words. The method of treating the books also differed greatly. Some of the reviews were hardly more than descriptions of content, while others were as analytical as any review of an adult book in the same magazine. No one pattern can be said to have predominated.

Nevertheless, the reviews of children's books in *Harper's Magazine* were probably among the most influential of the period. The magazine had a large circulation, so that the reviews reached a large number of people. Equally important, few magazines reviewed so many children's books. Only the *Nation* and the *Literary World* reviewed more, and only the *Nation* covered the same span of years. Parents, who read *Harper's* reviews from 1865 to 1881, should have had no trouble in choosing their children's books wisely from a large selection.

THE GALAXY

In May, 1866, the first issue of *The Galaxy: An Illustrated Magazine of Entertaining Reading* appeared. Mott reports that it was founded with William Conant Church and Francis Pharcellus Church as editors and publishers in order to give New York a monthly that would be comparable in quality to Boston's *Atlantic Monthly*.[122] From the outset, *The Galaxy* was important for its literary criticism, which appeared in a department called "Current Literature."[123] But important as its general criticism may have been, the magazine made only a small contribution to the reviewing of children's books. In the nearly twelve years of its existence, reviews of only fifteen children's books appeared, all of them unsigned. The leading reviewers for *The Galaxy* were Richard Grant White, Edmund Clarence Stedman, Henry James, J. F. Meline, John Burroughs, and W. C. Brownell, but there is no clue whether any of them reviewed the few children's books.[124] Brownell reviewed a number of children's books for the *Nation* and may also have reviewed children's books for *The Galaxy*. This, however, is mere conjecture. One comment on the poor quality of illustrated books in 1870 was by J. F. Meline.[125] This criticism included illustrated books for children, but was not actually a review.

The fifteen children's books reviewed included ten fiction, two science and natural history, one each in poetry and history, and one, Rev. John

Hall's *Familiar Talks to Boys,* which should probably be classified as a book of sermons. The ten works of fiction included three translations and three books, *Hans Brinker, Little Women* and *An Old-Fashioned Girl* which are still popular. The others were well-known books in their own time, all of them reviewed in other periodicals as well.

The reviews of children's books were, in general, fairly long and tended to emphasize the literary qualities of the books reviewed. These reviews were not segregated from reviews of adult books, but were mixed with them in the "Current Literature" department. They usually included a description of the work, illustrative quotations and an evaluation. In two reviews the books were compared with other well-known works, but this was not the common practice. Usually the only reference outside the book was to the assumed interests of the children who would read it.

The review of Mayne Reid's *The Castaways* contained a comparison of that work to *Robinson Crusoe,* or, more exactly, it classified *The Castaways* as a book in the same genre as Defoe's classic.[126] Alexina B. White's *Little-Folk Songs* was declared to have the same kind of appeal as Mother Goose.[127] The poems made no attempt to teach, but were amusing and tender. The reviewer declared himself to be delighted that he found no sermons, no morals, and no "sentimental nonsense." [128] The book was forceful in its language and appealing in its rhythms. He declared it the best volume of verse for children to appear in fifty years.

In a few reviews, the harm or good a book might do to a child was discussed, but this discussion usually took a different turn from that which might have been expected. Bayard Taylor's *Boys of Other Countries,* for example, usually praised for the information it imparted, was praised by *The Galaxy* because it was "manly, simple and healthy." [129] The reviewer called it "a very good sort of book for those for whom it is intended, which, in these days of mawkish or feverish 'juvenile' literature, is saying much for it." On the other hand, Louise Chandler Moulton's *Bed-Time Stories* was condemned as a book not good for children.[130] It was filled with sadness and melancholy, so that the total impression was depressing. It was well-written in parts, but all of it was sad to greater or lesser degree, and with a sadness more suited to the adult reader than to the child. The reviewer found in it a kind of unreality, which, though pathetically true to a certain sort of life among children was better omitted. He quoted a passage to show the unnaturalness of some of the dialogue, and concluded with the statement that "on the whole we must protest against the book."

Martha F. Finley's *Elsie's Motherhood* was disposed of in even stronger terms. The characters were impossibly good, and the effect "revolting because it is monstrous." [131]

The three informational books reviewed were praised for their content, or for the method in which the material was presented. Eliza A. Youmans' *The First Book of Botany,* actually a textbook, was praised for its use of the new scientific method, which would lead the child away from the book itself to an examination of the actual plants.[132] The chief merit of Helen S. Conant's *The Butterfly Hunters* lay in its provision of information on catching and preserving insects, though the reviewer also found its mixture of adventure and lore a delight.[133] It was the style and method, however, which won the greatest praise for Higginson's *Young Folks' History of the United States.*[134] The reviewer praised the work for its unity, for its "succinct and logical manner," and for the "charm of novelty . . . maintained from the first." The Rev. John Hall's *Familiar Talks to Boys,* while not exactly an information book, might be included here. The reviewer, while not feeling that there was anything remarkable about the book, did feel that it contained "good sense, good feeling, sympathy, and good morals." [135]

The reviews in *The Galaxy* were of excellent quality. However, there were too few of them to constitute a major contribution to the reviewing of children's books. And just before the great increase in the reviewing of children's books that came in with the eighties, *The Galaxy,* never a financial success, sold its subscription list to the *Atlantic Monthly* and disappeared into history.[136]

APPLETON'S JOURNAL OF LITERATURE, SCIENCE AND ART

Appleton's Journal, which began publication on April 3, 1869, can be classified as a literary monthly only after it began its new series in 1876. It was a weekly most of the time before July, 1876, when it became a monthly and adopted the format commonly associated with the literary monthly of the period.[137] After a few volumes as a literary monthly, it became an eclectic magazine, borrowing from foreign periodicals nearly everything except its literary criticism.[138]

During the period the magazine was published as a weekly, the book reviews appeared in a department of "Literary Notes," which gave way in January, 1876, to "Books and Authors." When the monthly began, the reviews appeared in a "New Books" section, but from Volume III, New Series, to the end of 1881, the book department was called "Books of the Day." Through these changes in name, the character of the reviewing and book reporting changed very little. Book notices of adult's and children's books ranged from little more than listings to full scale reviews of several hundred words. Reviews of children's books appeared in the book department with adult books, without any attempt at segregation. From 1870, the second year of its publication, to the end of 1881,

Appleton's Journal printed reviews and notices of 85 children's books. More than half of the books reviewed were fiction, and nearly one-fifth of those were books by Jules Verne, the classification of which as children's books might be questioned, though not by children. Reviews or notices of *Hans Brinker* appeared on three different occasions. A considerable number of other kinds of books for children were reviewed, though only a few of each type, except poetry, nine of which were reviewed. Though many of the most noteworthy books were not reviewed, the list of those reviewed includes, besides the works of Jules Verne and Mary Mapes Dodge, Alcott's *Eight Cousins,* and Susan Coolidge's *What Katy Did.*

The predominant attitude revealed in the reviews was that books for children should be those children liked, not merely those adults felt the children ought to have in order to improve themselves. Repeatedly, *Appleton's Journal* praised a book because it was so much superior to the kind of book offered to children in an earlier day. Perhaps the review of *The Neptune Outward Bound,* a book of an old-fashioned type, revealed most clearly the magazine's standards for a good children's book.

> *Certainly the American boy, if we know him, cannot live upon such food as is set before him in "The Neptune Outward Bound," and even should he succeed in devouring it, that he should ask for a further supply, is incredible.*
>
> *We are always sorry when we are compelled to say anything in disparagement of a child's or boy's book. It is, of course, useless to apply severe standards—literary or logical—in our judgment of such a story; and it perhaps seems especially absurd to accuse a children's book of vapidity; but there is certainly a line to be drawn somewhere. A child's mind may not call for very solid meat, but it is a barbarism to stuff it with sawdust.*
>
> *When we say that "The Neptune Outward Bound" is a hopeless specimen of the dreariest class of children's literature, all experienced small boys, who have spent profitless hours in the selection of books from the average Sunday-school library, will know what we mean. It is a book that goes into the world with a prefatory note heralding its purpose: "Perchance this simple work may scatter a little seed, which shall produce an abundant harvest, and root out the poisonous plants that are springing up so profusely in our fair land.*[139]

The note struck here resounds throughout the *Appleton's Journal* reviews of children's books.

No book that had as its chief feature a moralistic or "preachy" tone could hope to win full approval. Sarah Kirby Trimmer's *The History of the Robins,* republished in 1875, was described as "highly 'moral' and commonplace," its virtue residing entirely in its illustrations.[140] John S. C. Abbott's *George Washington,* sometimes slovenly in style and with a "commonplace vein of moralizing which runs through it," was only saved from condemnation by the animation and picturesqueness of the narrative.[141] Even so, the reviewer felt that the book was "too sentimental to be entirely wholesome." *Bessie's Trials at Boarding School,* by Nora Perry, was another book with pointed morals, but the reviewer found it to be better than most of its type. The author better understood "the kind of influences that operate upon childish character," and created stories that were amusing.[142]

Often a book was praised as a good substitute for the earlier type of moralistic book. Frank R. Stockton's *What Might Have Been Expected* was good because he had avoided "the silly twaddle with which writers in former years supposed the minds of boys and girls should be fed." [143] The reviewer praised *Eight Cousins* despite its tendency to go, as he felt, almost too far in the other direction. Miss Alcott's stories, he said,

> . . . *tend to stimulate that pert "smartness" and self-assertion which are perhaps the most offensive characteristic of American children; but they are so much more wholesome, natural, and artistic, than the stuff for which they are offered as a substitute, that it would be less than ungrateful to insist upon their faults.*[144]

On several occasions a book was designated the "best," not necessarily in an absolute sense, but in a relative one. *Northern Lights* was described as one of the best children's books of 1873.[145] *Our Baby,* by Mrs. S. E. Warner, was the "best collection of graceful and happy babylyrics we have ever seen." [146]

Literary criteria predominated in the reviews of books for children in *Appleton's Journal.* Sometimes this only amounted to a statement that the book was readable, as the reviewer remarked of Coolidge's *What Katy Did,*[147] or that it was written well, as he said of Stephens' *Off to the Geysers.*[148] In other reviews more detailed literary analyses were given. *The Pearl Fountain,* by Bridget and Julia Kavanagh, was declared to possess "high literary merit," which the reviewer defined as "poetic fancy combined with a realistic method of treatment." [149] The common demand that realistic stories have a measure of reality led the reviewer to condemn John Habberton's *The Worst Boy in Town,* which was exaggerated, and untrue to nature, though some readers would consider it funny.[150] In the review of Joel Chandler Harris' *Uncle Remus, His Songs and Sayings,* one of the more complete explanations of literary merit was provided. After stating that no folklore surpassed the Uncle Remus stories in appeal to children, he numerated the qualities that explained their success, their "dramatic action, their realism, their shrewd insight into character, their gleams of poetic imagination and their genuine racy humor." [151] Another major achievement of the book was the skillful portrait of Uncle Remus himself.

In a number of reviews the style or the method of the author was discussed or characterized. Mrs. Joshua L. Hallowell was commended for avoiding the use of baby talk in her *Bec's Bedtime*.[152] The reviewer described the style of Frank R. Stockton's *What Might Have Been Expected* as "sprightly and engaging." [153] E. H. Knatchbull-Hugessen's style and method were much more completely analyzed. In the review of *Higgledy-Piggledy*, after quoting from the preface and describing the book the reviewer made the following critical comment,

> *Few modern writers of fairy-stories have Mr. Knatchbull-Hugessen's power of fusing the homely interest and incidents of "the humdrum present," and the supernatural creatures of a poetic and over-credulous past, into a homogeneous and artistic whole.*[154]

He continued by saying that these fairy tales had the "old-time directness, simplicity, and air of good faith; and, at least, they never attempt to put science and history into elfin or goblin costume."

Another approach used frequently in *Appleton's Journal* was to compare a book with those of other authors, or with earlier works by the same author. Both methods were used in the review of Henry M. Stanley's *My Kalulu*.[155] The reviewer found that he could praise this book, despite the fact that he had not been able to praise any of Stanley's earlier ones. He concluded the review with the comment, "the book carries us through enough exciting scenes to have furnished Capt. Mayne Reid with material for a small library." [156] In evaluating Jane G. Austin's *Moonfolk,* the reviewer placed the book in the same category as *Alice's Adventures in Wonderland,* declaring Miss Austin's book to be the "latest worthy addition" to the literary type.[157]

In reviews of two volumes, both poetry, the suitability of the work for children was considered. The reviewer felt that *Child-Life,* an anthology edited by John Greenleaf Whittier, was guilty of including poems that were "more *about* children than *for* children." [158] On the other hand, Edgar Fawcett's *Short Poems for Short People* were both about children and for them.[159] The children depicted were real children, with both the good and the bad combined in their natures. The poems were neither too sentimental nor too mirthful, but "treat of the familiar incidents of childhood in a light happy manner." He felt that these poems were something new in children's literature and deserved popularity.

Instruction in children's books received a fair share of attention, but the *Appleton's Journal* reviewer insisted that such instruction be well woven into the story. Stephens' *Off to the Geysers* agreeably combined adventure and instruction.[160] John T. Trowbridge's *The Young Surveyor,* on the other hand, failed to provide a real blending of the two.[161] Both the instruction and the story were, in themselves, good, but they were "mingled without being mixed." The reviewer felt that the boy reader would be all too likely to skip the section on surveying in order to continue with the story.

The reviewer felt that books intended primarily to be instructive should be pleasing as well. *The Childhood of Religions,* by Edward Clodd, which was described as a good popularization, praiseworthy both for its simplicity and for its sure foundation on the "rock of science," was also a worthy production because of its "pleasing guise." [162] *What Mr. Darwin Saw in His Voyage Round the World in the Ship "Beagle"* was charming because of the way fascinating personal observations were recorded and was an excellent introduction to natural history.[163] This book, adapting for the young, as it did, a work intended for adults, seemed to its reviewer so audacious a contribution to children's books that it was worthy of success for that reason alone. He praised the value of the illustrations, maps, and charts provided as well.

Most of the reviews of factual books in *Appleton's Journal* dealt with works in history and biography, ranging from a brief characterization of Coffin's *The Boys of '76* as "an excellent idea . . . admirably carried out," [164] to a 300-word review of George M. Towle's *Voyages and Adventures Vasco da Gama.* In the review of the latter, the idea of the series "Young Folks' Heroes of History," of which it was the first volume, was praised.[165] The style was "vigorous, animated, and rapid." Its only defects were the omission of the hero's early life and the absence of a map showing the hero's travels. Edward Eggleston's *Pocahontas* and *Brant and Red Jacket,* the reviewer said, combined the "attractiveness of romance with much of the instructiveness of regular history." [166]

It was the author's judicious treatment of a controversial subject that won the praise of *Appleton's Journal* in John D. Champlin's *Young Folks' History of the War for the Union.*[167] This book, the reviewer felt, should be read by all children in both North and South, for it avoided partisanship and emotion. It was a book that would provide a long stride toward the elimination of regional feeling. And to make it more attractive, it had an "agreeable and transparent style." [168] Its only defect was a single factual error which the reviewer called to the attention of the reader.

Several of the adaptations and rewritings of classic stories were reviewed. J. Moyr Smith's *The Prince of Argolis,* praised in other periodicals for the quality of its illustrations, was described here, too, as chiefly of value for its pictures.[169] The story was described as a burlesque on the story of Theseus and Medea, amusing, but little more. Alfred J. Church's *Stories from Homer* maintained the mood of the Homeric stories so effectively that it would appeal to both adults and children.[170] To Barthold G. Niebuhr, however, went the laurel for "the most successful attempt that has been made to render the old legendary tales of ancient Greece intelligible and interesting to children." [171] The reviewer compared them to Church's work, deciding that Niebuhr's *Greek Hero-Stories* was intended for younger children, and, as a result, gave less attention to detail. But it had much of the "spirit, animation, and charming simplicity" of the original. The review of Lanier's *The Boy's Froissart* stressed the value of the original work, and praised Lanier's handling of it.[172] Only the preface, which the reviewer felt was "written down" to children, did not seem worthy.

Considerable attention was given to illustrations, sometimes merely mentioned as attractive, at other times discussed in detail. The illustrations for Mrs. Dodge's *Rhymes and Jingles* were the best pictures for a child's book since Tenniel's for *Alice's Adventures in Wonderland*[173] In the review of Frank R. Stockton's *Tales Out of School,* the common method of illustrating children's quartos was discussed. After noting that the plan of *Tales Out of School* was similar to that of the same author's *Roundabout Rambles in Lands of Fact and Fancy,* the reviewer described the method.

The plan is the now familiar one of taking a lot of old woodcuts (of which publishers of illustrated books usually have a goodly store) and writing a story or abridging a narrative to suit. Usually the process of construction is apparent on the very face of the work, but Mr. Stockton is so fertile a raconteur, that he fairly deceives even those best acquainted with the sources from which he draws his material. It is amusing, for instance, to notice how closely he has stuck to the text, and yet how fresh-seeming he has rendered the thrice-familiar pictures and adventures of Sir Samuel Baker in the chapter purporting to narrate "Colonel Myles's Adventures in Africa and India." Besides the "conversion" of various books of travel and adventure, including one of Verne's fanciful narratives, the volume contains many curious bits of natural history.[174]

The pictures, themselves, formed a notable part of the volume.

The works of Jules Verne, one of which Stockton had rewritten in *Tales Out of School,* were faithfully reviewed in the pages of *Appleton's Journal* as they appeared in American editions. No less than ten titles were reviewed, including the *Tour of the World in Eighty Days, The Fur Country, From the Earth to the Moon, Journey to the Center of the Earth, Doctor Ox and Other Stories, The Wreck of the "Chancellor," The Mysterious Island,* volumes I and II, *Michael Strogoff, Hector Servadac,* and *The Exploration of the World.* Each book, except *The Fur Country,* was declared exciting and readable, especially for boys. The chief defect of *The Fur Country* was its lack of attention to details.[175] It was, on the other hand, Verne's close attention to detail that gave such an air of reality to his other books.[176] Even inaccuracy, such as the garbled geography of the western United States in the *Tour of the World in Eighty Days,*[177] and the "mistake of placing Grant's army between Lee and Richmond in the siege of that city" in *The Mysterious Island* [178] was not enough to destroy the effect of truth. Even when *Michael Strogoff* seemed to show the "weariness of over-production" it was still a "very readable and amusing book." [179] The reviewer felt that Verne's style could make the reader believe that the cow did, in actuality, jump over the moon.[180] To no other author of books for children and young people was so much space and attention given in *Appleton's Journal.*

Probably *Appleton's Journal* cannot be considered a major reviewer of children's books. Eighty-five reviews in twelve years makes only a small dent in the children's books of those years. Certainly the reviews and notices differed greatly from one another, from a brief sentence encompassing two very different volumes, Miss Alcott's *Aunt Jo's Scrap-Bag* and Christina Rossetti's *Sing-Song,*[181] to nearly 1,500 words devoted to Verne's *The Mysterious Island,*[182] with an average somewhere between 50 and 300 words. But the longer reviews were good ones, providing a picture of the content of the books, information on the method and style of the author, some detail on the illustrations, and a sound evaluation. If it was not a major reviewer of children's books, it was still a good one.

HOURS AT HOME

Mott lists *Hours at Home* among literary monthlies, though an examination of the volumes of the periodical reveal that it might almost be classified as a religious magazine of the Presbyterian denomination.[183] The magazine was founded in May, 1865, by Charles Scribner & Company. The first five volumes carried the subtitle, *A Popular Monthly Devoted to Religious and Useful Literature,* which certainly defined the tone of the contents, but this was changed to *A Popular Monthly of Instruction and Recreation* in the sixth semi-annual volume.

Hours at Home carried many articles on religion and religious subjects, as well as regular departments of unmistakably religious import,

115

including a monthly "Short Sermon for Sunday-School Teachers." The Rev. George B. Bacon's articles on "The Literature of Our Sunday-schools" appeared in successive issues in 1870. This religious emphasis was marked even in the reviews and notices of children's books. Many of the books were from publishing houses which concentrated on books for Sunday school libraries, such as W. M. Dodd and Robert Carter & Brothers. In a majority of the reviews the suitability of the book for Sunday school libraries was indicated.

The reviews and notices of children's books were very brief, rarely more than forty or fifty words, and frequently less. They appeared in the regular book review department along with reviews of adult books. In the eleven volumes published, during a period of five and one-half years, 98 reviews and notices of children's books appeared, chiefly of works of juvenile fiction with a religious purpose. In one issue, twelve books, not included in the 98, were listed with the comment that they were "books which no Christian parent need fear to put into the hands of his children." [184] This remark characterized the tone and attitude of most of the reviews of children's books in *Hours at Home*.

Only on a few rare occasions was any space given to the literary merits of a children's book, though there were a few notable exceptions. It was the pleasure that Jules Verne's *Five Weeks in a Balloon* would arouse that drew the attention of the reviewer, who said that "the ingenuity and invention of the author will excite the surprise and admiration of the reader." [185] Horace E. Scudder's *Stories from My Attic,* however, was given the most markedly literary review.[186] The reviewer called Scudder an American Andersen and described the volume as a "most dainty, tender, and exquisite volume." He found in it an amazing array of virtues.

> *An almost faultless style; a quiet but penetrating wit; a delicate and even quaint imagination; that subtile sympathy which throws a human interest about the animal, and eke the inanimate world— . . . and withal the beguiling art of story telling—these constitute the peculiar charm, and must make wide the popularity of the little book under notice.*[187]

More often consideration of the literary merit of a work was inextricably bound with the moral effect it would convey, or, at least, with the instruction it might provide. Mrs. Adeline Dutton Train Whitney's *A Summer in Leslie Goldthwaite's Life* was a book that might well "inspire a higher purpose of life." [188] It was the way in which Helen S. Conant mixed sound instruction in natural history with adventure that won the

116

critic's praise for her *The Butterfly Hunters*.[189] He had nothing but approval for Jean Ingelow's *A Sister's Bye-Hours,* for she had written,

> *a series of stories, some of them really charming, and all of them conveying healthful and useful moral and religious lessons. There is a grace and finish of style in this author which make her writings exceedingly attractive, and a moral atmosphere that is pure and bracing.*[190]

The reviewer could even overlook obvious defects when the book contained sound examples for children to follow. He readily acknowledged that the reader might doubt whether Elsie Dinsmore, in Martha F. Finley's *Holidays at Roselands,* was old enough to be a perfect judge of right and wrong, but despite the unreality of this element in her character, "her habit of referring every question to the Bible, and her carefulness to obey her father in everything which did not conflict with her conscience," provided a useful model, he felt.[191]

Even those books which might well have been praised for the pure delight they provided, *Hours at Home* found cause to praise for their morals. Despite the fact that Jean Ingelow's *Mopsa, the Fairy* contained, according to the reviewer, the most true pictures of fairy nature and was "exquisitely beautiful," the reviewer still found it necessary to point out how healthful it was.[192] The review of *An Old-Fashioned Girl* provides a striking illustration of this attitude.

> *There is such a jaunty, off-hand, bewitching air about Miss Alcott's last story of* An Old-Fashioned Girl *(Roberts Brothers), that somehow criticism seems to be an impertinence. All we can do, or at least want to do, is to say some pleasant word of recognition, and pass on. We wonder if the rising generation, and the risen too, know what a wholesome pill they are so eagerly devouring in the guise of a delightsome sugar-plum. For never was more sound principle, never more healthy sentiment nor timely doctrine and reproof presented in heartier, livelier, more "taking" style. If not a book for all time, it is precisely the book for a day, and that the one in which we live.*[193]

There were comments on illustrations in *Hours at Home*. Carové's *The Story Without an End* had the best colored illustrations the reviewer had ever seen.[194] But not even the "ingenious sugar-coating of his wholesome moral pills" could lead the reviewer to approve of the illustrations for Jacob Abbotts' *Juno and George* and *Mary Osborne*, which were "forlorn." [195]

Such was the reviewing in *Hours at Home,* at least of children's books. Though a surprising number of books were noted, none of the reviews were lengthy. Few of them gave any notion of the contents of the books, except to indicate the morals illustrated. Very little attention was paid to literary qualities. In almost every case, approval was bestowed on the basis of the healthful moral lessons the books contained.

The book review section was frequently signed by James Manning Sherwood, the editor of the magazine, but it is impossible to determine whether he wrote them all. Sherwood was a Presbyterian clergyman, who, if he wrote the reviews of children's books, must have had the Sunday school library in mind, and not even the kind of reformed Sunday school library which Rev. Bacon had pleaded for in the pages of Sherwood's own magazine. When the magazine was suspended in 1870 to make way for *Scribner's Monthly,* a new magazine under new editorship, children's literature gained. *Hours at Home* made but one notable contribution to the criticism of children's books, the series of articles by George Bacon on Sunday school library books.

PUTNAM'S MAGAZINE

In January, 1868, George Palmer Putnam, who had published an earlier magazine with the same name, began a new series, *Putnam's Magazine, Original Papers on Literature, Science, Art, and National Interests.*[196] This new series was to be short-lived, for it consisted of only five complete semi-annual volumes, and a sixth partial one before it was absorbed into the newly founded *Scribner's Monthly.* Mott says that Edmund C. Stedman was the magazine's book reviewer, as well as its associate editor, but some of the book review sections were signed by Richard Henry Stoddard.

During the brief life of *Putnam's Magazine* thirty-four reviews of children's books appeared in its pages, reviews of fiction chiefly, but with a sprinkling of other types of children's books, including several science books, most of which were cast in a fictional framework. The reviews averaged about 50 words in length, though a few were shorter and a few considerably longer, one running to nearly 250 words. The reviewer expressed his general attitude toward children's books in the final issue of the first year. Before beginning his actual reviews he commented on the children's books of the day.

Verily there is a new era in this country in the literature for children. It is not very long since all the juvenile books seemed conducted on the principle of the definition of duty "doing what you don't want to," for the books that were interesting were not considered good, and the "good" ones were certainly not interesting. Most Sunday-school books were stories of unnaturally good and pious boys and girls, who, however, were not attractive enough to rouse a desire of imitation in the youthful breast.[197]

The reviewer then proceeded to select books which he felt were likely to delight children.

Unlike *Hours at Home,* this periodical, in its reviews of children's books, never praised a book for its moral. In fact, almost the only mention of a moral appears in the review of Horatio Alger, Jr.'s *Ragged Dick.* The story was well told, and almost certain to be liked by boys, but there was "a certain monotony in the inculcation of the principle that honesty is the best policy." [198] But still, the reviewer said, it was a better book for the Sunday school libraries than most.

Instruction received a little more attention, but not as an exclusive feature without attendant pleasure. Jean Macé's *The History of a Mouthful of Bread,* the reviewer described as a charming enough book to make science attractive.[199] He praised Helen S. Conant's *The Butterfly Hunters* for the same reason.[200] But Mary Lorimer's *Among the Trees* had a little too much instruction in it. The reviewer confessed that "a little less Botany would have given us more pleasure, if less information, which we dare say ought to be dearer to us than it is." [201]

Most of the reviews, brief though many of them were, concentrated on the appeal of the book. William T. Adams' *Our Standard Bearer* was "brightly written, full of information, and attractive to his boy-readers." [202] The review of *Alice's Adventures in Wonderland* dealt chiefly with its appeal to children.[203]

On two occasions an evaluation of an author or work was made by using a comparison. The reviewer called Jean Ingelow's *Mopsa, the Fairy* her best book and "probably the best thing of its kind in English literature," a fairy tale true to its genre.[204] In the review of Horace E. Scudder's *Stories from My Attic,* he called Scudder "a man of delicate genius, who in these 'Stories' somehow reminds us of Hans Christian Andersen." [205]

The reviews in *Putnam's Magazine* were few. Some of them were so brief as to be almost mere notices, yet they had enough of the critical to qualify as reviews. Their point of view was certainly an enlightened one, reflecting the newer attitudes toward children and toward their books, accepting children's books as a part of literature, albeit a minor part, and considering them in terms of the children and what they would like.

The last issue of *Hours at Home* appeared in October, 1870, and the following month *Scribner's Monthly, an Illustrated Magazine for the People,* appeared in its stead. The older magazine had been wholly a publication of the Scribner house, but the new one was only partly a Scribner venture. *Scribner's Monthly* was published by a firm called Scribner & Company, in the ownership of which Charles Scribner, Josiah Gilbert Holland, and Roswell Smith each had a part.[206] With the December, 1870, issue, *Putnam's Magazine* and the *Riverside Magazine* were both absorbed by *Scribner's Monthly,* and in July, 1875, *Old and New* was purchased and merged in the new magazine. Having devoured one excellent children's magazine, the *Riverside, Scribner's Monthly* was father to an even greater one, *St. Nicholas.* In November, 1881, all relationship with the Scribner book house was severed, and the name of the magazine changed to *The Century Illustrated Monthly Magazine.*

Nearly 100 reviews of children's books appeared in the magazine between its founding in 1870 and the end of 1881, all of them in the regular department, "Culture and Progress," which dealt with literature and art. Frequently, a series of short reviews or notices would appear under a special sub-heading, "Children's Books," "Holiday Books," "A Sheaf of Juveniles," and other similar headings. Many longer reviews were not segregated from the reviews of adult books, but appeared under individual headings in that department. There were no reviews of children's books in the two 1870 issues, but thirty-seven books were reviewed in 1871, the largest number in a single year. Ten books were reviewed in 1872, but in subsequent years fewer, with a slight increase after 1878. It may well be that this falling off in the number of children's books reviewed resulted from the founding of *St. Nicholas* in which there were frequent notices and reviews of children's books.

The reviews themselves ranged in length from forty or fifty words, to well over a thousand, depending, in part at least, upon the editor's judgment of the importance of the books. Under the heading, "Two Books for Children," for example, *Eight Cousins* and Susan Coolidge's *Nine Little Goslings* had a review fully as long as those given most adult books.[207] The review of Higginson's *Young Folks' History of the United States* ran to more than 700 words. Most of them, however, were less than 100 words.

The reviews in *Scribner's Monthly* emphasized the literary qualities in children's books above all else, dealing with the characterization, the author's style and method and the quality of the book. Frequently one book was compared with another of the same type or with other books by the same author. Only in a limited way were the moral effects of a book considered, and then usually as a part of the total effect; glaring and obvious "morals" curtly dismissed.

In the review of *Eight Cousins* and *Nine Little Goslings, Scribner's* reviewer provided a good example of his reviewing method. Miss Alcott's characters, he said, talked with "the raciness of real life," although not all of them in this many-charactered novel were clearly delineated.[208] Only three or four actually came to life. Miss Coolidge's characters were better bred than Miss Alcott's, but they were not as real. Miss Coolidge's writing was graphic and showed considerable imagination. Miss Alcott's, on the other hand, too often seemed in danger of dissolving into the same raciness that she gave to the speech of her characters. Her use of slang was particularly undesirable. On the whole, however, he felt that Miss Alcott "keeps much higher laws than she breaks." In this lay her power. Miss Coolidge had greater artistic ability, but her writing was too much from an adult point of view to be as appealing to the young.

This method of comparing one author with another was more frequent and extensively developed in the *Scribner's* reviews than in others. Miss Coolidge's framework for *A New Year's Bargain* was "a conception by no means unworthy of Andersen himself, and so original and vivid as to entitle Susan Coolidge at once to a high place among writers for children." [209] The reviewer described *What Katy Did* as a book as good as those of Louisa May Alcott.[210] *Moonfolk,* by Jane G. Austin, brought *Alice's Adventures in Wonderland* to mind, but it lacked "the dash and unexpectedness of that more classic tale." [211] With Noah Brooks' *The Fairport Nine,* the comparison was with the same author's *The Boy Emigrants,* a better book, though *The Fairport Nine* was still a good one.[212]

Reality in characterization and verisimilitude in incident were frequently praised. The boys, in Bayard Taylor's *Boys of Other Countries,* behaved "precisely as boys might be expected to." [213] The reviewer praised Horace E. Scudder's ability to create individual characters in his *The Bodleys Telling Stories.*[214] Both of Noah Brooks' books reviewed in *Scribner's Monthly* were praised for their reality. *The Boy Emigrants* was a natural book, in which there was no "namby-pamby," but it nevertheless exhibited a wholesome atmosphere.[215] In *The Fairport Nine,* the boys were real rough and tumble boys.[216]

In several reviews books were praised for the style of the writing. The virtue of *Nine Years Old,* by Eliza Tabor Stephenson, lay in the manner of the writing, which manifested "quiet grace and clear tone." [217] Bayard Taylor's style was "clear and simple, without being puerile." [218] The writing of Juliana Horatia Ewing in *Jan of the Windmill* was "quiet and easy-flowing." [219] The reviewer felt that this was an unusually well-written book, with good character development, humor, and an appealing pathos.

Often the reviewer gave an over-all value judgment of a book. He dismissed Rebecca Clarke's *Little Folks Astray* as "a mere negation." [220] Rosa Abbott's *The Pinks and Blues* and Mrs. Bradley's *Proverb Stories* were called dime novels with morals added.[221] Of Marie Pabke's *Wonder-World Stories* he said that "not one is insignificant." [222]

A few books were condemned for their excessive didacticism, one for going too far in the other direction, and many were praised for a general moral atmosphere. The reviewer felt that Julia A. Mathews' *Lawrence Bronson's Victory* was a book that would have no interest for children because it was too didactic.[223] Its morals, he felt, would be skipped. On the other hand, John Habberton's *The Worst Boy in Town,* was one of the few books *Scribner's Monthly* declared to be immoral. This book was one "no judicious parent will knowingly put into the hands of his children." [224] The general attitude of the magazine toward morals in stories was best expressed in the reviews of Jacob Abbott's *Hubert* and *Juno on a Journey*.[225] In these stories the "moral" was an integral part of the action, and was more a matter of the general tone of the works than something explicit. This, he felt, was the only way that morals were of any value to children.

In theory, *Scribners' Monthly* was opposed to the combination of amusement and instruction in children's books in a "sugar-coated pill." Of one book that did so combine the edifying with the amusing, this time successfully, the reviewer said that "most sensible people revolt at the idea of administering knowledge to children in the disguise of amusement." [226] In the book he was reviewing, Frank R. Stockton's *Tales Out of School,* however, the author's literary talent had been great enough to enable him to avoid the usual failure. Charlotte Yonge had achieved the same kind of success in *Little Lucy's Wonderful Globe*. It was "a rare triumph to have combined in so much information with so much fun, to have made a geography into a fairy book." [227]

Humor was a characteristic praised wherever it appeared. The reviewer was almost in an ecstasy about Edward Lear's *Nonsense Songs, Stories, Botany and Alphabets*. "Blessed be nonsense!" he proclaimed.[228] He particularly praised the poem, "The Jumblies," which he believed to be a work of real genius. Humor was one of the qualities the reviewer found most winning in Frank R. Stockton's books, both in *What Might Have Been Expected*[229] and in *Tales Out of School*.[230] It was the humor which provided the very core of the review of Lucretia P. Hale's *Peterkin Papers*.[231] The reviewer enumerated the funniest scenes and described them as the kind children like.

Whenever the illustrations seemed particularly outstanding they received their full share of attention. Frölich's pictures for Charlotte Yonge's *Little Lucy's Wonderful Globe,* Tom Hood's *Puss and Robin,* and Henry Kingsley's *The Lost Child* received singular praise. After discussing the texts the reviewer said, "But it does not so much matter, after all, who does the rhymes or the narratives if Frölich does the drawing of the pictures, and children are to be pictured." [232] With the exception of a single picture, the illustrations in Kate Greenaway's *Under the Window* were excellent.[233] The reviewer felt that her drawing had the "very grace of an unconscious childhood" in it. One design only, that which accompanied the verse "Bugaboo," was a blemish on the book. He also found Rosina Emmet's pictures for *Pretty Peggy and Other Ballads* commendable, comparing her work with that of Caldecott, Crane, and Greenaway.[234]

Comparatively few informational books were reviewed in *Scribner's Monthly,* but those that were had long and detailed treatment, often in reviews of nearly 1,000 words. The method of reviewing these books was to describe the content of the book, to discuss the value of the subject, and to identify any deficiencies. John Lukin's *The Young Mechanic* was described as "the precursor of a new line of juvenile literature especially adapted to the necessities of Young America." [235] This statement preceded a lengthy description of the book, and a discourse on the needs of boys for materials of this type. In the review of Higginson's *Young Folks' History of the United States*, though granting that no better history for the young had been written, the reviewer felt there were weaknesses.[236] He found very specific omissions from John D. Champlin's *Young Folks' Cyclopaedia of Common Things* which should have been included.[237] Articles on the bicycle and on postage stamps were needed in an encyclopedia for children, and fuller lists of sources would have added to the value of the work. While praising Jules Verne's *The Exploration of the World* for its general accuracy, certain minor errors did not escape notice, particularly a reference to the "Gulf of Boston." [238] But the book was an entertaining as well as informative one, and of real value.

Scribner's Monthly included many important and long-lived children's books among those it reviewed. Four different titles by Louisa

May Alcott were reviewed, *Little Men, Eight Cousins, Aunt Jo's Scrap-Bag,* and *Jack and Jill,* four by Susan Coolidge, including *What Katy Did,* two by Mary Mapes Dodge, *Baby Days* and *Hans Brinker,* two editions of which were reviewed, two by George Mac-Donald, *A Double Story* and *The Princess and the Goblin,* and Edward Lear's *Nonsense Songs, Stories, Botany and Alphabets.* With but few exceptions, the list of books reviewed reads like a list of notable, if not great, books. The comments on and evaluations of some of these books are particularly interesting.

Though he did not question the justice of her popularity or the general worth of her books, the reviewer did not automatically endorse Miss Alcott's works, nor did he spare her some severe criticism. He read her *Little Men* aloud to some children before reviewing it in order to report their reaction as well as his own.[239] Finding it to have great fidelity to life and usefulness as a guide to raising boys, he declared it to be a better book, artistically and morally, than *Little Women.* The stories in *Aunt Jo's Scrap-Bag* were as though seen through rose-tinted glasses, but they were, nevertheless, attractive stories.[240] *Jack and Jill,* he felt, verged on sentimentality, but just managed to avoid it.[241] It was to *Eight Cousins* that he devoted his severest criticism, particularly to her language and her use of slang.[242]

The reviews of Mary Mapes Dodge's books were invariably laudatory. Both reviews of *Hans Brinker* took for granted that the work was an established classic, merely listing its virtues and defining its appeal.[243] The selection of pieces for her *Baby Days,* taken from the pages of *St. Nicholas,* showed excellent judgment the reviewer felt.[244]

The reviews of George MacDonald's books, and of those of Miss Coolidge, showed recognition of the high quality of their work. In fact, except for a few brief notices, largely of books considered unsatisfactory, *Scribner's Monthly* showed a keen sense of the importance of children's books, and of the need to review them carefully.

The method and style of these reviews often followed a recognizable pattern. The reviewer would describe the plot or action, usually briefly, and would point out incidents and situations that were particularly felicitous. He discussed the style and any special attributes of the books such as humor, strong character development, healthful tone, or naturalness. Almost always an evaluation was provided, and when there were notable illustrations they were mentioned. In some reviews, the books were related to other books of the same author, or to similar books by other authors. In brief, the reviews of children's books in *Scribner's Monthly* were thorough and of high quality.

In an eleven-year period nearly 100 books were reviewed, not a large number, but other children's books were reviewed in the same company's sister magazine, *St. Nicholas. Harper's Magazine* could claim to have reviewed more children's books than any other New York literary monthly, but *Scribner's Monthly* could claim the better reviews.

9

LITERARY MONTHLIES IN
BOSTON

If New York could claim more literary monthlies than Boston, "The Hub" had no reason to be ashamed of its contribution, for it had the most distinguished one, the *Atlantic Monthly. Old and New* was concerned that children's books should be criticized, but did not, itself, criticize them well. The *Atlantic,* on the other hand, provided excellent reviews of children's literature.

THE ATLANTIC MONTHLY

Only *Harper's New Monthly Magazine,* among literary monthlies, could claim in 1865 to have been on the scene longer than the *Atlantic Monthly.* But longevity, after all, is nothing but a stretch of years, and despite *Harper's* larger circulation figure, the *Atlantic* held undisputed pre-eminence among American literary magazines.[1] During the period from 1865 to 1881 three editors held the chair at the *Atlantic,* James T. Fields, William Dean Howells, and, for the greater part of 1881, Thomas Bailey Aldrich. Howells was the editor, however, with whom the magazine was largely associated in this period. He had become assistant editor in 1866, and then editor in 1871.[2]

Mott says that the book reviews of the *Atlantic* were always good, and were especially so during Howells' editorship.[3] They appeared monthly in a "Reviews and Literary Notices," department. During the seventeen years from 1865 to 1881 about 90 reviews of children's books appeared. Some of these were written by William Dean Howells, but the authorship of the majority is unidentified. Some of them may have been written by Horace E. Scudder, a frequent contributor, and one who always concerned himself with literature for children, but he is not identified as the author of any children's book review in the *Atlantic Monthly* indexes. He did, however, write an article for the magazine on Hans Christian Andersen that remains one of the best analyses of Andersen's art.[4]

Even before 1865, F. C. Hopkinson, in a review of Jacob Abbott's *Florence and John,* had attempted to describe in the *Atlantic* rules for writing children's books.[5] "How should a book for children be written?" he asked, and then he essayed an answer.

Three rules will suffice. It should be written clearly and simply; for young minds will spend little time in difficult investigation. It should have a good moral. It should be interesting; or it will generally be left unread, and thus any other excellence that it may possess will be useless. Some writers seem to have a fourth rule,—that it should be instructive; but, really, it is no great matter, if a child should have some books without wisdom. Moreover, this maxim is eminently perilous in its practical application, and, indeed, is seldom followed but at the expense of the other three.

To these three rules all writers of children's books profess to conform; yet a good book for children is a rarity; for, simple as the rules are, they are very little understood. While all admit that the style should be simple and familiar, some appear to think that anything simple to them will be equally simple to their child-readers, and write as nearly as possible in the style of "The Rambler." Such a book is "The Percy Family," whose author is guilty of an additional impropriety of putting his ponderous sentences into the mouth of a child not ten years old. Another and more numerous class, evidently piquing themselves not a little upon avoiding this error, fall into another by fancying it necessary to write down to their young readers. They explain everything with a tiresome minuteness of detail, although any observer of children ought to know that a child's mind does not want everything explained. They think that simplicity demands this lengthy discussion of every trivial matter. There is such a thing as a conceited simplicity, and there is a technical simplicity that in its barrenness and insipidity is worthy only of a simpleton.[6]

When Hopkinson required that a good children's book have a good moral, he apparently meant a good theme, for he said that "no book is good that is 'goody,' no book is moral that moralizes." Rather, he said that "our notion of a good moral is a strong, breezy, open-air moral, one that teaches courage, and therefore truth." [7]

These critical remarks, and those of Samuel Osgood in his 1865 article, indicate, to a large extent, the attitudes toward children's books reflected in *Atlantic Monthly* reviews. When the tyrannical role played by the *Atlantic* editors over the work of their contributors is considered, the relevance of these criteria for children's literature gains added significance.[8] No other American periodical so thoroughly outlined for itself, and for others also, standards for children's books.

This is the background from which the *Atlantic Monthly* reviews proceeded. For the first several years, beginning with 1865, only a few children's books were reviewed. In fact, until 1878, no more than four were ever reviewed in a single year, while in 1867, 1868, and 1874, none at all were reviewed, but in 1881, when forty-three books were given some sort of attention, the quality of the reviews greatly deteriorated. Prior to that time the reviews had been long, careful, and detailed, with fully as much critical attention as was given to adult books reviewed at the same time. For the most part, the reviews stood alone as part of the regular book review section, though in 1878 and 1879 a number of children's books were reviewed consecutively. In 1880, several were reviewed in a special column, "Holiday Books," and in January, 1881, ten books were grouped in a "Books for Young People" section. Beginning with the February, 1881 issue of the magazine a new department, "Books of the Month," was instituted, a department which frequently included a subsection, "Books for Young People." This department consisted of book notices, largely, rather than reviews. Most of the children's books listed were given only a sentence or two.

Though the *Atlantic Monthly* reviewed a few English books and a few books translated from French and German, most of its reviews were of original children's books by American authors. There is no particular evidence to indicate that this was a matter of policy; yet the result was nearly the same as though it had been. The books of Lewis Carroll, George MacDonald, and Mrs. Molesworth are conspicuously absent, and only *Mrs. Overtheway's Remembrances* by Julia Horatia Ewing was reviewed. In fact, the *Atlantic* showed a certain prejudice against English children's books. In January, 1878, the reviewer complained that American juveniles "for some years past have been almost driven from our book-seller's counters by the cheap and pretty illustrated wares of the London presses." [9] The next year the complaint was repeated even more forcefully.

We trust that the tide is turned, and that American children are again to form their ideas of life and society and nature from books that paint our own conditions, and not from English publications, which are as false to anything they are likely to know hereafter as they are inferior at their best to the best American writings for the young.[10]

On the other hand, and perhaps partly as a result of this attitude, many of the really outstanding American children's books were reviewed. *Hans Brinker; or the Silver Skates, An Old-Fashioned Girl,* and *The Story of a Bad Boy* were all given long careful reviews in its pages. *The Atlantic Monthly* printed the only review of Mark Twain's *The Adventures of Tom Sawyer,* though it must be said in defense of other periodicals, that the subscription method of publication which Twain used undoubtedly accounts for the paucity of reviews.

The vast majority of children's books reviewed in the *Atlantic* were fiction; well over half of those included. The next largest group consisted of eight travelogue story books, six history, biography, and travel, four natural history, four verse, and the rest, one or two in each group, included literature, music, folklore, and others.

The emphasis of the *Atlantic Monthly* reviews of children's books was on the literary qualities of the books primarily, as would be expected from the articles on children's literature printed in its pages. We find, in these reviews, much attention to characterization, style, and to an ability to please children. Very frequent comparisons were made with works that set standards.

Characterization was discussed at length in a considerable number of reviews. Howells, in reviewing *The Story of a Bad Boy,* praised Aldrich's character drawing and discussed in detail the various characters. *An Old-Fashioned Girl* was praised for "the truthfulness of many of the pictures of manners and persons." [11] Mrs. Abby Morton Diaz' *William Henry and His Friends* was described as having "singular fidelity to human nature." [12] The *Atlantic* reviewer, on the other hand, found Leora B. Robinson's *Patsy; A Story for Girls* and Campbell Wheaton's *Six Sinners; or School-Days in Buntam Valley* to be "as false to life and character as they are in taste." [13] Even Miss Alcott did not merit automatic commendation. In *Jack and Jill,* there was "nothing like real character drawing, and the air of life in the book is secured not by an endowment of the persons represented, but by the animation and cheeriness of the author." [14] The *Atlantic's* harshest words on this score were reserved for a Sunday school book published by the Congregational Publishing Society, Mary Dwinell Chellis' *Harold Dorsey's Fortune,* "one of those fictions which go a good way towards putting the reader out of patience with propriety." [15]

The plot or action of the story was discussed in several reviews. The reviewer of Mark Twain's *The Prince and the Pauper* said of it that it had no formal plot, but derived its effect from the way the story was told.[16] Similarly, Kate Tannatt Woods' *Six Little Rebels* was described as having no plot, but as gaining its effect from adventure and "a desultory succession of entertaining scenes." [17] *Nelly's Silver Mine,* by Helen Hunt Jackson, in a review that was largely laudatory contained, nevertheless, the statement that the book had some of the all-too prevalent conventionalism of juveniles.[18]

The *Atlantic Monthly* reviewed none of the books so often under attack for their sensationalism, the books of William T. Adams, or of Horatio Alger Jr., but rather noted the absence of sensational elements from the books it did review. *An Old-Fashioned Girl* was described as having "no sort of adventure or sensation." [19] *Two Cabin Boys,* a book of adventure by Louis Rousselet, was praised because it had "nowhere any sensationalism or extravagant adventure." [20] Frank R. Stockton's *A Jolly Fellowship* was described as having one rather sensational incident, but the reviewer felt that this was not fatal because the author had handled it with restraint.[21] Though the reviewer does not identify the situation in question, it was no doubt the storming of a fort which ended humorously rather than heroically. In a direct reference to the much attacked sensational books, the *Atlantic,* in reviewing two of the "Bodley" books, called Horace E. Scudder "the most serene and non-sensational story-teller for children, and therefore the best antidote for Oliver Optic & Co.'s 'Firewater' that we have." [22]

The *Atlantic* reviews frequently contained comments or evaluations on the style and method of the authors writing. Horace E. Scudder's style was admired on several occasions. His *Stories from My Attic* had "charming and suggestive writing," and "a style so charmingly simple and easy that we can no more give him up to the children than we can allow them Andersen altogether." [23] Reviewing *Doings of the Bodley Family in Town and Country* and *The Bodleys Telling Stories,* the *Atlantic* said Scudder "does everything with the complete finish that characterizes the work of those only who see their end from the beginning, and so are never in a hurry." [24] His method was then described and several quotations from the two books provided as illustrations of that method.

Sarah Orne Jewett's *Play Days* was described as a book of "gentleness and good-breeding," though this was only partly in praise of her writing, for the reviewer found in it a lack of inventive power and too much "mere graceful decoration." [25] Minute detail was praised in George Cary Eggleston's *The Signal Boys; or, Captain Sam's Company.*[26] A stylistic device used for rhetorical effect by Charles Carleton Coffin in the *The Story of Liberty,* the historical present tense, "leaves us a little jaded at last," the reviewer said.[27] The author's attempt to make his story dramatic gave the reader the impression that progress was "a series of frantic jumps." Coffin's *Old Times in the Colonies* depended too much on "declamation and a half-ranting style" to make history interesting, a method the reviewer considered unnecessary.[28]

The setting of the book was not ignored in *Atlantic* reviews. In several books accuracy and honesty in presenting a region of the country, or scholarly care in reproducing an historical period, constituted one of the real merits of the author's work. In *Nelly's Silver Mine,* Helen Hunt Jackson gave a presumably accurate picture of the calmer side of frontier life in Colorado, which the reviewer round a welcome change from the more extravagant pictures of the West.[29] Howells found Mark Twain's description of life in the Mississippi Valley to be one of the virtues of *The Adventures of Tom Sawyer.* Not merely was it the best picture of that region in a child's book, but it was "incomparably the best picture of life in that region as yet known to fiction." [30]

It was historical accuracy with which the reviewer was concerned in Elijah Kellogg's *Burying the Hatchet; or, The Young Brave of the Delawares,* a book in which the sensationalism of the title did not alter the basic honesty of the story. The book was called "an honest and every way admirable picture of life on the Pennsylvania frontier after Braddock's defeat." [31] The review included a comment on the religion in the story, but said that this was religion without cant and religion necessary to give a correct historical picture. In the review of Mark Twain's *The Prince and the Pauper,* the reviewer took great pains to show the method Twain used to provide a believable picture of the time of Edward VI.

> *However skillful in invention a writer may be, it is certain that his work loses nothing of effect from a studious harmonization with the period in which it is placed. In* The Prince and the Pauper *this requirement has been scrupulously observed. The details are not made obtrusive, and the "local color" is never laid on with excess; but the spirit of the age preceding that of Elizabeth is maintained with just the proper degree of art to avoid the appearance of artfulness. Critical examination shows that no inconsiderable labor has been given to the preservation of this air of authenticity; but the idea that the results of research are inflicted with malice aforethought is the last that would occur to any reader. On the other hand, if irrelevant phrases may be once or twice detected, their employment is obviously intentional,—the indulgence of some passing whim, the incongruity of which, it is taken for granted, will be excused for the sake of the fun. Such might easily be spared, no doubt, though they do no serious harm. It is in every way satisfactory to observe that the material accessories are*

*brought into view with an accuracy which coherently supports the
veracity of the narrative. Dresses, scenery, architecture, manners and
customs, suffer no deviation from historical propriety.*[32]

Like the *Nation,* the *Atlantic Monthly* was concerned that writers
of books for children should keep a proper point of view, writing for
children, not merely about them. George Zabriskie Gray, in his *The
Children's Crusade,* had just missed creating an excellent children's
book, though it was still a book that might be read to children.[33] Lack of
sufficient simplicity in writing, and lack of proper judgment in selection
made Abby Sage Richardson's *Stories from Old English Poetry* less than
a perfect child's book.[34] It was a more serious fault, however, that
marred *The Story of a Cat,* by Émile de la Bédollière. The reviewer felt
that children reading it would "have now and then a lurking suspicion
that they were made fun of." [35] The most common fault was that which
the *Atlantic* reviewer found in Rebecca Clarke's *Little Pitchers* and in
Mrs. Abby Morton Diaz's *The William Henry Letters.* Miss Clarke
wrote about children and their pranks and foibles in a way parents would
enjoy more than their children.[36] With Mrs. Diaz the reviewer was less
positive, merely suggesting the possibility that adults might enjoy more
than children "the reality of William Henry's boyishness." [37] But Horace
E. Scudder, the *Atlantic* felt, was a real master at pleasing the child. *The
Bodleys Afoot* showed the skill with which Scudder created children.[38]

Related, though certainly different in emphasis, were the discussions
of the treatment of boy characters in fiction. Most famous of the titles
discussed were *The Story of a Bad Boy, The Adventures of Tom Sawyer,*
and Charles Dudley Warner's *Being a Boy,* but there were a number of
lesser imitators who produced books more or less in the same genre which
were included. The first two were given long and careful reviews by William Dean Howells, while the Warner book had an even longer one.
These reviews had in common their concentration on the portrayal of
the "bad" boy.

Howells credited Aldrich with producing something completely new in
American literature, "of telling the story of a boy's life, with so great
desire to show what a boy's life is, and so little purpose of teaching what
it should be." [39] No one else had done this previously for an American
boy. Howells felt that at least part of the book's charm came from its
autobiographical basis. It contained all that a boy really is, and was told
so simply that it had been a real pleasure to boys and, incidentally, to
adults too. The picture of Tom Bailey which the author provided was
completely believable, whether fact or the product of his imagination.
Aldrich was, however, guilty on a few occasions of departing from his

point of view, so that it seemed to Howells almost as though someone else had done the writing.

Howells found *The Adventures of Tom Sawyer* an even more excellent presentation of a boy's life from a boy's point of view. He felt that "Tom Brown and Tom Bailey are, among boys in books, alone deserving to be named with Tom Sawyer." [40] But Tom Sawyer had not even the minor faults of *The Story of a Bad Boy*.

Warner's *Being a Boy* was not actually intended to be a boy's book, but the reviewer felt that it was one that might well be enjoyed by boys. He apparently referred to a boy's judgment of the book, for he said, "In fact, actual experiment had taught us that it will have a charm different in kind, but not in degree, for boys, and we would gladly see it in their hands, for they can get only good from it." [41] This book, too, the reviewer felt, was something new of its kind. It was a different kind of treatment of boyhood from that of Aldrich and Clemens. The boy Warner described, though identified as a New England country boy, was "the average boy John rather than any particular boy John." [42] Warner's method of presenting him differed markedly also. The reviewer found that, without being sentimentalized, these memories of boyhood "are touched with the greatest tenderness,—with the kind of compassion which one feels for one's own childhood, the sort of smiling regret one has for it." [43]

The lesser writers who attempted to gain a place because of the success of these books did not fare as well. When B. P. Shillaber's *Ike Partington* appeared, the *Atlantic* reviewer wondered if there was any longer a need "of entering a protest against the conventional boy of the story books." [44] Was not this trend perhaps going too far? "Besides, the lively boy has not been hidden under a bushel in juvenile literature of late," the reviewer said. When John Habberton's *The Worst Boy in Town* appeared, the *Atlantic* was certain the trend had gone too far. The reviewer called Habberton's book "a caricature and an offensive one." [45] *A Bad Boy's Diary* was named only as a warning to the writer and the reader.[46] The *Atlantic Monthly* had welcomed honest and realistic treatment of boy-nature in fiction, but it was not prepared to accept poor imitations of good literary work.

In his article on Andersen, Scudder had said that "to say there is humor is to say that there is real life." [47] The various reviewers for the magazine looked for and commented on humor in children's books. Abby Morton Diaz was described as a "humorist of the purest and kindliest quality." [48] The humor in Frank R. Stockton's *A Jolly Fellowship* provided "a capital accompaniment to the story." [49]

But the *Atlantic* did not like all kinds of humor. In one of its few pronouncements with which a modern critic might disagree, its reviewer described Laura E. Richards' *Five Mice in a Mousetrap* as "children's nonsense run mad." [50] He judged the pictures to be good, but the text "no more literature than a kaleidoscope is art."

The *Atlantic* reviews did discuss the moral of various stories, but a moral in the sense Hopkinson had suggested, rather than in the limited sense of a direct lesson to be taught the young reader. None of the books reviewed were conspicuous for moralizing tendencies, with the possible exception of Mrs. Whitney's *Real Folks,* which had too much of the didactic in it, yet was good whenever the author forgot to preach.[51] The kind of moral the reviewers looked for was of the sort described in *Hans Brinker.*

> *There is no formal moral, obtruding itself in set phrase. The lessons inculcated, elevated in tone, are in the action of the story and the feelings and aspirations of the actors.*[52]

Howells said Scudder's *Stories from My Attic* had "such unaffected religiousness of feeling that there seems to be no moral there." [53] In Helen Hunt Jackson's *Nelly's Silver Mine* the moral "pervades the book as a delicate perfume." [54] The children who read Mrs. Kate Tannatt Woods' *Six Little Rebels* would find no offensive moral, but rather that "gentle lessons of forbearance, charity, and unselfishness are impressed rather by the story than by any direct teaching of the writer." [55]

The *Atlantic* frequently compared one book with another, or one author with another. The comparison of *Tom Sawyer* with *Tom Brown's School Days* and *The Adventures of a Bad Boy* has been cited previously.[56] Not all such comparisons were so favorable. Howells compared Scudder with Hans Christian Andersen, finding similarities to Andersen in Scudder's writing, but a lack of Andersen's "richness of invention." [57] Emily Huntington Miller's *Captain Fritz, His Friends and Adventures,* a story of a French poodle told in the first person, was described as an imitation of Andersen's method.[58] Though the book was recommended, the reviewer declared that the author had not approached Andersen in skill.

Still another type of comparison was that used in the review of Mary De Morgan's *On a Pincushion, and Other Fairy Tales.* After lamenting that most modern fairy tales fail because of their authors' complete disbelief in fairies, the reviewer attributed to *On a Pincushion* the "blunt, homely character of the old fairy-tale morals," comparing the work to a standard literary form rather than to a single book or author.[59] Sarah Orne Jewett's *Play Days* was compared to books of "good breeding" in England and to "the noisy, ungrammatical, and boisterous type of young

America which gets recognition in books for young people," to both of which the reviewer felt Miss Jewett's book was vastly superior.[60]

Four adaptations or rewritings of well-known works were included among the books reviewed. One, Abby Sage Richardson's *Stories from Old English Poetry,* was

> *told with a good feeling for the originals; not always with simplicity, nor with perfect judgment as to what tales are best to tell young people, but prettily, and on the whole blamelessly.*[61]

Both *The Boy's Froissart* and *The Boy's King Arthur* were reviewed. *The Boy's Froissart,* the reviewer felt, had a little too much of Froissart, but was still a valuable addition to children's literature.[62] *The Boy's King Arthur* was given a longer and more detailed review, in which Lanier's editorial methods were described and commended.

> *In editing the book Mr. Lanier has shown excellent judgment; for in the first place he has ordered the confused succession of Sir Thomas Malory's book, and grouped the chapters according as they related to this or that knight; then he has carefully dropped out of sight all grossness, and he has quickened the narrative by the omission of episodical or dull chapters, the condensation into a paragraph of his own of what was drawn out unnecessarily, and the erasure here and there of superfluous sentences and words. Any one who has rambled through the apparently incoherent chapters of Malory will appreciate this service which a wise and sympathetic litterateur has rendered. He has not taken liberties with the text, but has corrected the looseness of the previous editor.*[63]

Still another edited book reviewed by the *Atlantic* was *What Mr. Darwin Saw in His Voyage Round the World in the Ship "Beagle,"* a book praised by all reviewers for making available to children a classic of natural history. The *Atlantic* had this to say of it.

> *We commend the book heartily for the wisdom of its conception, and its thorough acceptability. One could hardly choose a book for an intelligent boy which would more successfully appeal to his love of nature, or more pleasingly acquaint him with the great master of literature of science.*[64]

The attitude of the *Atlantic Monthly* toward the great English illustrators of children's books was like that toward English children's books in

135

general. So anxious was the magazine to find American books better than English, that the only references to such great illustrators as Walter Crane and Kate Greenaway were in comparison with Americans. The *Atlantic* found Scudder's "Bodley" books to have "as 'goodly outside' as the quaintest of the 'Walter Crane style' of imported literature." [65] While acknowledging that America had many imitators of Kate Greenaway, it was the absence of slavish imitation of her work that won the *Atlantic*'s praise for Miss A. G. Plympton's *The Glad Year Round,* which it called the "most throughly original and the best colored illustrated book of the season." [66] This book, the *Atlantic* felt, would establish Miss Plympton as one of the best American illustrators. But even this book owed something of a debt to Miss Greenaway.

The class of books to which this belongs was the immediate result of the introduction of the Kate Greenaway books; but while in all other cases the illustrators of these books on this side of the Atlantic have closely followed the teachings of Miss Greenaway, even adopting her costumes, Miss Plympton has made her book purely original and entirely American. The costumes worn by the children whom we see every day in the streets of the city or in the country are suddenly made very picturesque and beautiful under the skillful brush of this artist.[67]

The *Atlantic* reviewed a number of children's quartos, including several of Scudder's "Bodley" books. The reviewer described the author's method in constructing *Mr. Bodley Abroad.*

How or by what right the illustrations get where they are, and whether they suggest the text, or the text suggests them, is a secret of the author's clever workmanship into which we will not too nicely inquire; it is enough that they successfully complement each other, and seem always to be just what the children would naturally be interested in at the given moment.[68]

Margaret Vandegrift's *Clover Beach* struggled only "more or less successfully with an abundant supply of pictures," and the problem of working them in gave "a somewhat distracted air to the story." [69]

More attention was given to the content of the quartos than to their illustrations. The praise lavished on Scudder's volumes was in striking contrast to the criticism of Thomas W. Knox's *The Boy Travellers in the Far East; Adventures of Two Youths in a Journey to Siam and Java.* Though both authors were conveying information through the device of fiction, Scudder's work was consistently commended for the skill with which he made the information attractive. In Knox's book, however, the fictional apparatus was declared to be completely unnecessary, a device that slowed the narrative and made "a naturally stiff style more stiff." [70] Knox had neither "lightness or dramatic skill," qualities which might have improved the book, and made a mistake in supposing that fiction was necessary to make travel attractive to young people. His boys were indistinguishable from one another and from the adults in the book, while the characters in Scudder's stories were well portrayed and individual.[71] Though there may well have been greater skill in Scudder's writing, partisanship may well have tempered the reviewer's judgment.

By and large, the *Atlantic Monthly* judged informational books on the basis of their method rather than their content. George M. Towle's *Magellan* was only "moderately well done." [72] To the reviewer it seemed "a little stagey," and had a quality of indefiniteness. The reviewer felt that all books for children which dealt with history and science should be welcomed, since a separate children's literature was inevitable. This made him all the more sorry that in Towle's book "so good a chance has been so carelessly used." [73] Coffin's books of history were also guilty of being over dramatic. Coffin's *Old Times in the Colonies* was "a succession of shouts, and both scenes and pictures are liable to be hysterical." [74] In the review of *Life and Her Children,* a book dealing with lower forms of life, by Arabella B. Buckley, it was the content that was criticized.

We do not inquire into its scientific correctness; but we question the wisdom of giving children so much of the interior organization of animals, and of introducing them at once into the philosophy of natural selection.[75]

The *Atlantic* reviews rarely dealt with the correctness of an author's writing, but in a few cases they did. Louisa May Alcott, in *An Old-Fashioned Girl,* was guilty of "some poor writing and some bad grammar." [76] Rebecca Clarke's *Little Pitchers* was called "ungrammatical nonsense in print," which, despite the author's intention of reproducing the talk of children, the reviewer found unattractive.[77] One of the charms of Mary Esther Miller's *Brother Ben* and *The Bird Summer* were their lack of "cant and slang—the two black beasts of juvenile literature." [78]

With the exception of those appearing in 1881, the reviews of children's books in the *Atlantic Monthly* were of sufficient scope and critical quality to fully warrant the name review. A very few were less than one hundred words long, but most of them were from a few hundred words to several thousand. The longest, the review of *The Prince and the Pauper,* amounted to a full article in itself while many were only a little shorter. The reviews of *Hans Brinker, The Story of a Bad Boy,* and *The Adventures of Tom Sawyer,* among others, ran to well over a thousand words. Only after January, 1881, were the children's books given notices too brief to be really helpful to the reader. But even then, the children's books were accorded the same treatment as most adult books, and an occasional children's book was still given fuller attention. The review of *The Prince and the Pauper* appeared in the December, 1881, issue.

The method followed by the *Atlantic Monthly* reviewers was consistent with good book reviewing practices. After some brief introductory word, the review was concerned with providing some notion of what the book was about, indicating the qualities of the book which characterized it—in style, characters, setting, and so forth—and evaluating it. Sometimes the reviewer described what he found. At other times he made a statement about the book, and then quoted from it to illustrate his point. Wherever it was appropriate, comment was made on the illustrations, or on other special aspects of the book.

It is true that the *Atlantic* reviews occasionally used stock words of praise, such as "pretty," but the reviews always went beyond that word so that, by the end of the review, the reader understood why that adjective had been used. In fact, in all its true reviews, the *Atlantic* gave enough information for the reader to know what the book was about and how good it was. The reviews written by Howells were outstanding examples of good book reviewing, but the many unsigned reviews were of similar quality. The slightly more than 90 books reviewed or noticed represented, of course, only a small fraction of the children's books published, but included were many of the books and authors of greatest significance. There was certainly a high percentage of books with some pretension to literary merit. And it was as literature that the *Atlantic Monthly* gave its consideration to them. The standards of the magazine were, perhaps, as high or higher than those of any other literary magazine in America. It was those same standards that were applied to books for children.

OLD AND NEW

January, 1870, brought from Boston the first issue of a new monthly magazine, *Old and New,* which attempted to combine, in one periodical, the functions of both a literary monthly and a religious magazine. More than half the money needed to found it came from the American Unitarian Association.[79] Edward Everett Hale, already well known as an author and Unitarian clergyman, was the editor throughout its brief five and a half years existence, but not even his fame was able to make the magazine a popular one. Mott reports that its circulation was never more than 9,000.[80]

In the first issue of the magazine a book reviewing policy was set forth, and a goodly array of reviewers, to be known as the Examiner Club, were listed, including William Cullen Bryant, Orville Dewey, James Walker, Joseph Allen, and John Gorham Palfrey. Their duty, as the editor saw it, was to aid the American public in deciding among the books currently published, "which are best worth their buying and reading; what are best worth borrowing and returning; and, in instances where there is a great danger, what had best be neither bought or borrowed." [81] These reviews were to appear in a monthly department under the general title, "The Examiner."

Among a considerable number of reviews of religious and scholarly books, a few children's books were reviewed, and a larger number treated in brief notices. Only three children's titles had reviews of more than a hundred words, Edward A. Freeman's *Old English History for Children,* Charles and Mary Lamb's *Poetry for Children,* and Edward Clodd's *The Childhood of the World.* The more common practice was to discuss each book in one or two sentences. In some issues children's books were merely listed with no comment. Mott described the magazine as characterized by its "favorite premiums—chromos and croquet sets—." [82] Whatever the merit of such a judgment as far as the entire magazine is concerned, there would seem to be some justice in considering its reviews of children's books in the light of that description, for they are characterless and uninformative.

Most of the books were described and commended with a stock phrase such as "pleasing," "excellent," "delightful," or "lively." Often the reviewer commended a book merely on the basis that other books by the same author had been well received. Only in the few longer reviews was any idea of the content of a book indicated. The notice of Elijah Kellogg's *The Hard Scrabble of Elm Island* is typical of the method used in *Old and New.*

> The Elm Island series is an excellent set of books. Mr. Kellogg has a very manly way of writing; and his boys are capital fellows,—spirited and good workers. There are no better books for boys.[83]

Though the reader knew that *Old and New* approved of the book, little information was provided to indicate why. Similarly, of Rebecca Clarke's *Little Folks Astray,* the reviewer said only that "the author loses none of the vivacity and reality which have made all the Prudy books so popular." [84]

Not even when the magazine disapproved of a book did it provide a more extensive or informative treatment of the book in question. Paul Cobden's *Who Will Win?* and *Going on a Mission* did not meet with the reviewer's approval, yet the reader had no notion why not.

*These are two of the innumerable army of children's books, which
threaten to sweep away all the good old favorites by very force of
numbers. Our fathers and mothers had not story books enough to
read. Is it not a worse misfortune for our children that they have too
many?* [85]

The reader knew, certainly, that these books were not among those
he should provide for his children, but he could have had no idea from
this notice why his children should not read them. In a review of Mrs.
O'Reilly's *Giles' Minority; or, Scenes at the Red House,* the reviewer described it as "one of the huge class of children's books that are evidently
made to order, and are neither objectionable or to be commended." [86]

In a few reviews the *Old and New* reviewer appealed to the approval
of children themselves for his commendation of a particular book. The
review of Paul Du Chaillu's *My Apingi Kingdom* is entirely a report of a
young person's reaction to that book.

*The young reader to whom we confided this book for his opinion
was lost to civilization for several days, and only emerged to find out
the names of all Du Chaillu's other books, and put them down on the
list of things he wanted for Christmas presents.* [87]

James D. De Mille's *Lost in the Fog,* a boy reported, was sure to be good,
for any book with the initials "B.O.W.C." on its title page was always a
good one. [88]

Old and New occasionally recommended a book or a group of books
to Sunday school libraries. In one issue, seventeen books were listed and
declared to be books suitable for purchase by the librarians of Sunday
schools. [89] The list had been received from an authority in which the editor professed to have the highest confidence, probably the Ladies' Commission on Sunday-School Books of the American Unitarian Association, whose work had been described and praised in an earlier issue. [90]
The review of Edward Clodd's *The Childhood of the World* indicated
that his book had been approved for Sunday school libraries and was
included on the lists of the Ladies' Commission. [91]

In a special list in the December, 1871, issue of *Old and New,* the
subscriber was provided with a list of titles recommended for Christmas
gifts. [92] The list ranged in price from $1.75 to $120.00; from *Alice's Adventures in Wonderland* to the *Encyclopaedia Britannica.* The latter was
described as "a work no better in its kind . . . than the other." This
listing and a brief notice of Alcott's *Little Men,* were the only notices of
children's books still read by American children today. One book, no
longer a part of the reading of American children, but still beloved of all

140

German children, was reviewed in a notice most revealing of the attitudes that prevailed in the columns of *Old and New*. After describing William Busch's *Max and Maurice* as a book of the *Slovenly Peter* type, the reviewer concluded with a sentence condemning all books of this sort.

It speaks ill for the aesthetic development of our children, that we have noticed that none of the Christmas books with beautiful pictures, and pretty stories, seem to charm them so completely as the doings of these naughty little wretches.[93]

In an editorial comment, *Old and New* lamented that children's books were given so little critical attention.[94] Yet it was, perhaps, more guilty of this neglect than most of its rivals in the literary monthly field. Though it did provide brief notices of about thirty-three books, real reviews of three others, and a list of recommended books, it did not provide the type of information that would have enabled its readers to discriminate wisely among the juvenile publications of the time. Despite the literary reputation of the editor himself, and of some of the contributors to the magazine, most of the really critical statements concerning children's books did not deal with literary merit or lack of it, but with aspects of the books, such as the behavior of the children in *Max and Maurice,* which were offensive to gentility. The magazine praised the more vigorous work of the Ladies' Commission on Sunday-School Books, but its own work on children's books was superficial in method and limited in scope. At a time when American children's books had the vigor of a baseball game, *Old and New* could only bring to bear on them sufficient vigor for a weak game of croquet.

LITERARY MONTHLIES IN
PHILADELPHIA

LIPPINCOTT'S MAGAZINE

For many years Philadelphia had not had a first rate magazine, but this deficiency was corrected in January, 1868, when the first issue of *Lippincott's Magazine of Literature, Science and Education,* under the editorship of John Foster Kirk, appeared. From the outset, the quality of this new literary periodical was recognized,[1] and it attracted to its pages the work of an illustrious list of writers. Besides fiction and general articles, it included regular departments, one of which was "Literature of the Day." This reviewing department is characterized by Mott as "of unusually high grade, ranking with similar work in the *Atlantic* and the *Nation."* [2]

Whatever its virtues as a reviewer of general literature, *Lippincott's Magazine* paid scant attention to the children's books of the day, though its few reviews are of uniformly high quality. From its beginning in 1868 until the end of 1881, it reviewed only twenty-eight children's books, and only in 1881 when it reviewed nine, did it consider more than four a year. These reviews, except in 1881, were included with reviews of adult books. No children's books at all were reviewed in 1869, 1872–1876, or in 1879. In 1881 the nine reviews appeared in a special section of "Literature of the Day," under the sub-heading "Children's Books." None of these reviews were signed.

Though the number of reviews was small, the variety in types of books was extensive. Both realistic and fanciful fiction were included, as well as folk tales, literature, travel, history, natural history, a children's magazine, a holiday annual, and classics rewritten for children. Though many of the best known and most popular authors were never reviewed, several of the most significant authors were represented by at least one book. Both American and English authors were included, and one book adapted from the French, Marie E. Field's *The Wings of Courage,* which *Lippincott's* reviewer identified as originally the work of George Sand.[3]

The reviews, for the most part, emphasized the literary qualities of the books. In a review of Susan Warner's *Daisy,* the reviewer discussed the lack of plot, pointing out, however, that this lack might add to the verisimilitude of the story.[4] He questioned the wisdom of the use of the first person point of view in this story, since "Daisy's life presents an unbroken series of such very pious acts that the idea of vanity is rather too strongly suggested by the use of the first person in narrating them." [5]

The reviewer gave particular attention to characterization and to the scenes and incidents of stories. In the review of *Daisy,* he said that "the scenes and incidents throughout the book are well described, and the characters sketched with vigor." He found that Louisa May Alcott's writing in *An Old-Fashioned Girl* "is distinguished for delicate and faithful portraiture," [6] and that *Six Sinners* by Campbell Wheaton showed reality in its characters.[7]

A frequent method used to evaluate the books reviewed was to compare them with other books of a similar nature, or the author with another author of recognized ability. He called Frank Stockton's *Ting-a-ling* "a story ranking with Hans Christian Andersen's though totally different from it." [8] He compared Smith's *The Prince of Argolis* with Hawthorne's *Wonder Book,* praising the more recent work, yet placing it lower in quality than Hawthorne's classic.[9] In a review of John Habberton's *The Worst Boy in Town,* which he considered inferior on several counts, he compared the wood-chopping incident with the incident in which the boys whitewashed the fence in *The Adventures of Tom Sawyer,* but felt that Habberton's effort was not equal to Twain's.[10]

The reviewer commented more than once on humor in the stories. Of Leora B. Robinson's *Patsy: A Story for Girls,* he said "there is no lack of funny incidents in the book, but they are too crowded." [11] In the review of William Brighty Rands' *Lilliput Land,* he merely said that the book was amusing without any statement to indicate in what way the book was humorous.[12] The humor of *The Worst Boy in Town,* or rather its attempted humor, received severe criticism. The humor "fails to make itself apparent, and the incidents are likely to please only the most rudimentary tastes.[13]

Among the twenty-eight reviews were three reviews of adaptations for children. Here the criticism concerned itself to a large extent with scholarship rather than with literary merit as such. In the earliest of these reviews, that of Field's *Wings of Courage,* the reviewer was unusually severe.[14] He questioned the desirability of adapting the work at all, feeling that instead there should be an authentic translation of these fairy tales which would have great natural appeal to imaginative children. But even more serious was the failure to acknowledge George Sand's authorship of the original stories from which the adaptation was made.

His reviews of *The Prince of Argolis* and *The Boy's Froissart,* on the other hand, contained abundant praise. *The Prince of Argolis* was "written in a lively style, and combines exactness of detail with picturesqueness of description." [15] He praised the quality of the footnotes, which contained valuable instructive material, and the illustrations which followed the best authorities on the costume of the period. He found much to praise in Lanier's editing of Froissart, and, in fact, devoted a major portion of the review to a description of his method.[16] He concluded that the work was "performed in a quiet, scholarly way, with good taste and sincere feeling."

But not all the reviews confined themselves to criticism of a literary or scholarly nature. The many informational books reviewed demanded a different type of reviewing. We would expect that in addition to some consideration of the manner of the telling, the review would show some concern with the informative value of the content. The *Lippincott* reviewer, however, never lost sight of the fact that such books had to be interestingly written if they were to appeal to the young. In an early review of Parker Gilmore's adaptation for children of Lucien Biart's *Adventures of a Young Naturalist in Mexico* and of Paul Du Chaillu's *My Apingi Kingdom,* books of travel and adventure, he said that "books of adventure are no doubt among the healthiest reading which can be furnished to boys of average capacity." [17] He commented that Du Chaillu pretended to more information in his book than it actually contained, a comment with which the *Nation* concurred.[18]

The review of Donald G. Mitchell's *About Old Story-Tellers* dealt more with the content.[19] This book, which included biographical sketches of standard authors with extracts from their works, he described as "an excellent kind of criticism" for children, though he felt that some of the facts included might have been omitted, and other facts included to make it a better book for the young. Perhaps its greatest merit lay in its "expression of a hearty boyish enjoyment of the old stories."

Julia P. Ballard's *Insect Lives* was reviewed in a similar manner.[20] While praising the usefulness of the book, the reviewer suggested information that might have been included to make an even better book, such as the "length of days of each species." Despite the omission of useful material "the book, however, contains a good deal of information in a small compass, and given in a very simple and pleasant form."

In his review of Thomas W. Knox's *The Boy Travellers in the Far East; Adventures of Two Youths in a Journey to Japan and China,* the

144

reviewer digressed from the book in hand to discuss travel in general and the prevalence of things Japanese in American life.[21] His evaluation of this "travelogue story-book" form of children's book was the same as that of most other contemporary reviewers of children's books, that the use of fictional characters in a book of travel gave "a zest to the store of facts." [22] In an interesting comment on the illustrations, he called them "veterans in service," [23] a fact freely acknowledged in the prefaces to the books in this series.

Besides the strictly instructional value of certain books, the inspirational value was emphasized. Susan Warner's *Daisy* was described as having "a generous share of Christian as distinguished from moral instruction," [24] and Louisa May Alcott's *An Old-Fashioned Girl* contained "a decided acknowledgement of the superior claims of mental and moral worth." [25] In a review of a new edition of Margaret Scott Gatty's *Parables from Nature,* he dealt even more specifically with inspirational value. These parables, he said, "are so pervaded by fidelity to nature both in spirit and in fact, and so fitted to inspire that tender reverence in which children of the present day are sadly deficient, that they could not but do good." [26]

A few of these reviews reveal a concern with topical interests of the day that have little to do with the merit of the children's books as such. In the review of Knox's *The Boy Travellers in the Far East,* discussed above, the reviewer concerned himself with current popularity of foreign travel and with the influence of Japanese art and culture on American life. The review of Susan Warner's *Daisy,* contains an objection to Miss Warner's statement that the Negro race is superior to the white.[27] But in the review of Frank R. Stockton's *Ting-a-ling,* we find the most amusing reference to a topic of current controversy. Just two years before, Congress had appropriated the money to buy Alaska, but grave doubts remained as to whether the purchase had been a wise one. In praising Stockton's book of fairy stories, he called it "a more real addition to our possessions than any Alaska," a judgment that may have been influenced by Stockton's Philadelphia origin, in which the reviewer took particular pride.[28]

Lippincott's reviewer gave small consideration to the illustrations in the children's books reviewed, and even less to the illustrations as works of art in their own right. Much of his comment on illustration was concerned with the engravings in books of information. He praised the illustrations in *The Prince of Argolis* for their scholarly accuracy. In a review of Charles Carleton Coffin's *Old Times in the Colonies,* he credited the engravings with making it possible for the author "to realize his idea and make his historical sketches vivid and picturesque." [29] In a review of Cornelius Mathews' *The Enchanted Moccasins, and Other Legends of the American Indians* we find unfavorable comment on the illustration.[30] Of the pictures in this book he said "they . . . are neither numerous nor exquisite, but a book of this kind could very well dispense with all such aids to the imagination."

The reviews in *Lippincott's Magazine* varied in length from about 50 words on many books, particularly in the special section, "Children's Books" in January, 1881, to a very long review of over 1,500 words of *An Old-Fashioned Girl.* Though a majority of the books received 100 or fewer words, such books as *Daisy* and *Ting-a-ling* were reviewed at considerably greater length. As we have seen, *Lippincott's Magazine* tended to emphasize the literary qualities of the children's books reviewed, though not to the exclusion of other considerations. In most of the reviews, a brief synopsis of the action or the content was provided as well as an evaluation of the book, and particularly an evaluation in terms of the young readers for whom it was intended. The review of Juliana Horatia Ewing's *Jan of the Windmill* provides a good example of the method and style of the *Lippincott's Magazine* reviews.

> *Though this story does not profess to be written for children, it is evident that the writer had in view the youthful public which she had already succeeded in pleasing, and will perhaps please the more on this occasion, from not shaping her work expressly to suit it. The Scylla and Charybdis on which writers for children often make shipwreck are excessive simplicity and the introduction of thoughts and feelings foreign to the young reader. Both these faults are avoided in the book before us, in which clear expression of real thought shows that Miss Ewing understands as well the children for whom, as those of whom she writes. Little Jan's life at the mill and at the school is graphically described; and the pages relating the early studies from Nature of this second Giotto—the portraits of favorite pigs and the landscapes painted with the help of flowers and leaves, in which the sky was represented by violets—may delight as well old as young readers. A fit frame, too, for the figure of the dreamy little genius is the mill—such a one as poets in many tongues have celebrated, throwing a glamour around its homeliness and calling up images in keeping with the scenery. Something of this spell cannot fail to touch the fancies of all readers of this well-constructed and really charming tale.[31]*

Hackneyed words, such as "pretty," "pleasantly written," and "brightly written" are to be found in these reviews, but in every case enough additional information is included to give the reader sufficient data to decide whether or not he might want the book for his children.

Only one title was given a mere notice, an English children's magazine, *Good Words for the Young,* edited by George MacDonald. Here the reviewer merely reported that the editor's *Ranald Bannerman's Boyhood* and *At the Back of the North Wind* were appearing serially in it. Otherwise, the quality of these reviews is such that it can only be regretted that a mere twenty-eight books were reviewed through the end of 1881. Even on this point it must be acknowledged, to the magazine's credit, that the books reviewed were, for the most part, above the general average of children's books, and in the cases of *Jan of the Windmill* and *Ting-a-ling,* very good books indeed. And *An Old-Fashioned Girl* remains a popular girl's book even today.

PENN MONTHLY

Penn Monthly was founded in January, 1870 at Philadelphia, but it differed greatly from the slightly older *Lippincott's Magazine,* though Mott classifies both as literary monthlies.[32] Though it was apparently not particularly noted for its reviews it did contain a regular "New Books" department, in which, from 1873 to 1881, it reviewed seventeen children's books. The magazine concentrated its attention on sociology, politics, and art and was essentially serious and scholarly.

The reviews of children's books were included, with one exception, with the reviews of adult books. In 1873 two books were reviewed, in 1874 and 1875, one each, and in 1881 four. In 1876, however, nine were reviewed, six of them in a special section, "Some Books for Children." Two of the books included in this special section were, appropriately enough, Charles Carleton Coffin's *The Boys of '76* and Will Carleton's *Young Folks' Centennial Rhymes,* both written for the Centennial year being celebrated in Philadelphia and throughout the nation, and a third book, *Boys of Other Countries* by a Pennsylvania author, Bayard Taylor. One book included in the seventeen, Jules Verne's *Tour of the World in Eighty Days,* was not treated as a children's book, though reviewers in other periodicals considered it a book for boys.

The books reviewed show considerable variety in type, only six of the seventeen were fiction, while the rest included natural history, travel, biography, poetry, art, and one children's magazine. The only books it reviewed, however, which are widely remembered today are the Jules Verne title already mentioned, Mrs. Dinah Mulock Craik's *Adventures of a Brownie,* and Coffin's *Boys of '76,* which appeared in a new edition as late as 1924. This does not, of course, mean that other books reviewed were inferior, for many of them were popular and highly regarded at the time.

The *Penn Monthly* often tended to use the children's book or books in hand as the starting point for a discourse only partly related to the book. This was true of the review of Mrs. Craik's *Adventures of a Brownie.*

> *Children will always believe in ghosts and fairies. No process of civilizing can ever eradicate the supernatural elements from the minds of the small savages. For them the dark will aways teem with the old mysteries and the inexplicable sounds of night, or its yet more painful stillness, fashion mythologies too strong for all the philosophy of daylight. But whether this faith is to be fraught with misery or pleasure is a question that the exercise of a little tact can easily determine and care secure.*
>
> *How, in the old days of hideous goblin stories, which inspired a doubtful joy in the brightest sunshine and made night grisly, children were ever induced to go to bed alone, is beyond comprehension, and one is surprised that vigil-worn mammas had not long since devised the simple remedy of burning all this trash, and along with it a silly, prating maid or two to make way for better things.*
>
> *To teach the little people of the nursery that the little people of the moonshine are kindly in their pranks, that it is frolicsome and not malignant mischief that animates the powers of the air, is to drive away the lurking phantoms from beneath the crib and out of the dark corners, divesting bedtime of half its horrors.*
>
> *All this is apropos of the above charming little story by Miss Mulock about the tricks of Brownie—the "obliging goblin" who haunts every worthy fireside.*[33]

Though it might be said that the long introduction to this review deals with the needs of children, it certainly left little space for a discussion of the book itself.

In a few reviews style was considered. Bayard Taylor's *Boys of Other Countries,* though partly praised for the information it contained, was also praised for its "straightforward, simple style." [34] The style was a major consideration in the review of Jules Verne's *Tour of the World in Eighty Days.*[35] Here the reviewer noted that Verne gained verisimilitude by amassing details. The reviewer praised Coffin's *Boys of '76* for its "graphic quality" though he felt it showed signs of hasty writing,[36] and he referred to the verse in Carleton's *Young Folks' Centennial Rhymes* as "more or less felicitous." [37]

Sensationalism in fiction was severely criticized, though none of the books reviewed were accused of this fault. In the long introductory passage to the special section, "Some Books for Children" the reviewer lamented the unhappy state of boys' books since the Civil War, while recognizing an improvement in girls' books.

> *The ill effects of the war are to be seen in boys' books, the admirable works of Capt. Mayne Reid, and the prolific productions of Mr. Jacob Abbott being almost altogether supplanted by the sensational, flashy "Oliver Optic" books and the like. In books for girls there has been a somewhat different turn; and an undoubted improvement upon the old, sentimental, "goody" writers, is to be found in the realistic school of which Miss Alcott and Mrs. Whitney are shining lights. But this school gives already some indications of decline, and we may hope therefore for something soon still better.[38]*

This dislike of sensationalism appeared in the reviews when the books were praised for its absence. In a review of George Cary Eggleston's *The Big Brother,* the reviewer said that "it serves as a very good illustration of the fact which most writers for children seem to forget, that it is perfectly possible to give the little folks a really entertaining story without descending to sensationalism." [39] The reviewer shows some inconsistency, if it was the same reviewer, however, when he praises the same author's *Captain Sam* despite improbabilities which he recognized in its action.[40] He described Harry Castlemon's *Snowed Up* as a book of the Optic type, but found it "much superior in sentiment and moral tone." [41] The only book of fiction actually condemned was Helen Kendrick Johnson's *Roddy's Ideal* which he characterized as "sorry stuff," but this was because of the author's "facetiousness," rather than sensationalism.[42]

The *Penn Monthly* objected vigorously to obvious morals in children's books. The reviewer's only cause for concern with Eggleston's *The Big Brother* was that the moral was too obvious.

> *Our only fear is that the desire to instruct and to lead the children to think for themselves is too apparent; in other words, the moral is too thinly veiled; and we are all, not exclusively children, apt to turn from the moral of the story we read with a sort of impatient carelessness.[43]*

He described George M. Towle's *Marco Polo* as "worth a thousand of the unwholesome fictions, with platitudinarian morals, which are dished up for young readers every month," a somewhat exaggerated statement of the number of moralistic tales, but certainly a forceful one.[44]

The instructional value of a book was rarely mentioned in the *Penn Monthly* reviews, though the choice of books reviewed certainly revealed a concern with sound factual books for the young. Viollet-le-Duc's

Learning to Draw; or, The Story of a Young Designer, translated from the French by Virginia Champlin, was treated from the point of view of its instructional value, however.[45] The reviewer described the action of the story, in which, through a tale, drawing, geometry, botany, mensuration, comparative anatomy, and so forth, are taught to the reader, but he felt that the most important aspect of education—citizenship—had been omitted.

In Thomas Wentworth Higginson's *Young Folks' History of the United States* the reviewer found much to praise; its "clearness and grace of style," its bibliography, index, and appendices.[46] Its only fault seemed to be a failure to treat the civil history, in addition to the military history, of the Civil War. But what was particularly exciting was that the book represented a part of a new trend in straightforward and interesting writing of factual books for children, not only in history, but also in literature, science, and other fields as well.

The *Penn Monthly* was particularly conscious of the importance of scientific knowledge to society, and of the changes science was bringing. This is most obvious in a review of Edward Clodd's *The Childhood of the World.*[47]

> *The hope which the author very modestly expresses that his little book may interest an older class of reader than those for whom it was intended, is not doomed to disappointment. Very few will put it down without caring to make him the acknowledgment of having read it with pleasure and of being satisfied with its judicious method. In their eyes it will have the merit of showing what education means under the control of a more liberal ideal. True, it is no more than a hint of what the future is to bring about in the way of change. But this is certain, that studies that have been retained on account of their supposed disciplinary virtue will be rejected for others of immense practical importance. It is an honest owning of the claim that science makes upon the responsibility of those who have in training the minds that are to pass finally upon questions to which the present owes the simple duty of investigation. What we know is after all so much of what we are that the value of a single ascertained fact cannot be exaggerated. Knowledge is not only power, it is tolerance, virtue, charity. It apprehends the end of life. It comprehends the whole of character.*[48]

The magazine's severest words were reserved for a book which purported to be natural history, a translation of Émile Achard's *History of My Friends; or, Home Life with Animals,* but which actually dealt with the unhappy and violent deaths of various pets.[49] Besides this deficiency, the book was not one which would appeal to children, who would find it dull and ridiculous. The reviewer urged Mr. Achard not to "write another book for children until he knows something about the animal with two feet and no feathers."

The most amusing reference to current scientific developments appeared in the review of Edward Greéy's *Young Americans in Japan,* in which the reviewer amused himself with one section of the book by relating it to evolutionary theory.

> *Mr. Darwin's theory of the monkey as the progenitor of man receives incidentally a bit of proof in the descriptions of how monkeys are caught in Japan, viz., by cautiously exposing in a perfectly innocent way the intoxicating bowl, which Jocko, descending from safe vantage-ground, quaffs pleasantly and is thereby made a captive "as he goes rolling home."* [50]

In only one instance did the *Penn Monthly* reviewer compare one book with another; when he judged Will Carleton's *Young Folks' Centennial Rhymes,* a book about important revolutionary figures, which he considered less good than Coffin's *Boys of '76.*[51] He did, however, refer to the latter work as a good supplement to Higginson's *Young Folks' History of the United States.*[52]

Only in the review of *Boys of '76* was anything said about the illustrations, and then only that some of the pictures had appeared before in *Harper's New Monthly Magazine.*[53] The binding of *Young Folks' Centennial Rhymes,* colored red, white, and blue, was described as "more gaudy than tasteful."[54]

One other interesting aspect of the reviews in this periodical should be mentioned. The reviewer had confused George Cary Eggleston with his older brother, Edward, and praised *The Big Brother,* thinking he was praising a boy's book by the author of *The Hoosier School-Master,* which was written by Edward Eggleston.[55] Though such speculation is idle, it is impossible not to wonder if this incorrect identification of the author might have influenced the judgment of the book.

Although the reviews of children's books in the *Penn Monthly* are interesting from a number of points of view, there are not enough of them to be considered significant. Perhaps it should be considered surprising that a magazine of this type reviewed children's books at all, but one statement made by its reviewer, on the other hand, makes it surprising that there were not more. In the introduction to "Some Books for Children" he said,

> *Few people can be found who think it worth while to give much consideration to what sort of books their children shall read for their*

entertainment, or, perhaps better still, what they shall not *read. In a vague way it is felt that there should be some sort of control, but beyond the tabooing of actual "novels" and works positively vicious, it is not in general felt that duty requires us to go. Yet those of us who stop to think how much deeper, for the most part, are the impressions made on the mind by works of the imagination we read as children than by those we read as men and women, must be convinced that here is a subject it is dangerous to neglect. As there are men who can distinctly trace back a great part of their active love of honor and manliness to the reading of Scott's novels in youth, so there are those who can recognize a permanent influence exerted by imaginative literature at even a more tender age, and many more, doubtless in whom the influences have been entirely unconscious but still a power for good or evil. If when we do not avail ourselves of the aid of works of fiction in the moralizing of our children, is it not the least we can do to guard carefully against demoralizing them.*[56]

Certainly *Penn Monthly* itself did not give a great deal of consideration to children's books, despite the pretty lecture to its readers.

Few of the reviews considered matters of literary merit, though, indeed, a majority of the books reviewed were non-fiction, for which other criteria were more appropriate. The reviews ranged in length from about 50 words to about 700 words. Though often matters not connected with the actual merits of the book were dealt with at length, in every review some evaluation was provided which indicated a knowledge of the actual contents.

LITERARY MONTHLIES IN
THE MIDDLE WEST

THE LAKESIDE MONTHLY &
THE WESTERN MONTHLY

In January, 1869, in an attempt to provide Chicago with a first-rate literary magazine, *The Western Monthly* was founded.[1] At the beginning of 1871, the title was changed to *The Lakeside Monthly*. Mott characterized *The Lakeside Monthly* as a regional periodical, and most certainly its primary interests were in Chicago and the Middle West. Its reviews, however, revealed no special sectional emphasis. The five reviews of children's books which appeared included two books by English authors and three by American authors, none of whom were from the West.

The few children's books reviewed were accorded the same critical attention and the same amount of space given to adult books. Three of the books were discussed in considerable detail in reviews of over 1,000 words, while the other two were reviewed briefly in critical notices of about forty words each. Real concern for literary merit, and for suitability of the books for children is shown in the reviews, as well as a certain impatience with moralizing and with unnaturalness in character and action. None of the reviews were signed.

Most of the books reviewed were considered outstanding children's books of the time. One, *What Katy Did,* remains a popular book today, and was as popular in England as it was in America. Four of the books reviewed were fiction; the fifth was the widely acclaimed *The Childhood of the World* by Edward Clodd.

The reviewer gave special attention to the technique of writing fairy stories in his review of Jean Ingelow's *Mopsa, the Fairy.*

Miss Ingelow succeeds remarkably well in reconciling the boldest flights of fancy with a certain necessary degree of probability. Just here we think it is that so many writers in this field of literature fail. The fiction seems to be mere absurdity, and disgusts instead of pleases. There is an adroitness and tact displayed, too, in passing from one predicament to another, in "Mopsa," that is inimitable, and would alone stamp the author's genius; and the "That's all!" with which the story ends is so natural that we can hardly realize it does not fall from the lips of that dear old "auntie" of our childhood.[2]

In books that purported to be realistic he looked closely at their verisimilitude. *What Katy Did* he pronounced "genuine," and continued, "the author must know the little people by heart."[3] He said of Mary Abigail Dodge's *Little Folk Life* that it gave evidence that the author was at home in the nursery.[4] Louise Chandler Moulton's *Bed-Time Stories,* he found only a little better than the average. After stating that "the art of writing for children will never flourish until the practice is established of respecting childhood," he quoted a long passage from one story to illustrate unnaturalness in both the action and the dialogue.[5]

In the same review of *Bed-Time Stories,* preaching, obvious morals, and instruction in the guise of a story were inveighed against. They will, he said, "escape the detection of no child of sagacity sufficient to read."[6] On the other hand, the story should be basically a moral story, as was reaffirmed in the review of Miss Dodge's *Little Folk Life* when the reviewer said "Her little story is moral, without saying so, and of good flavor, without pretense of any sort."[7]

The Lakeside Monthly reviewer did not use comparisons with other books as a method of evaluating the book he was reviewing. He did, however, call attention to "certain unconscious resemblances" between incidents in *Mopsa, the Fairy* and the already widely-known and imitated *Alice's Adventures in Wonderland,* but he did not criticize Miss Ingelow for these parallels in the action of the two books.[8] In fact, he predicted that she had added "one more to the few truly successful child books."[9]

Like the reviewer for *Penn Monthly,* the *Lakeside* reviewer found Edward Clodd's *The Childhood of the World* the beginning of a new trend, but a new trend in the writing of scientific books for children, rather than a new trend in education. Not that he felt that the style of the book was perfect, but he judged it a good start in the right direction.[10] His greatest praise for the book, however, was reserved for its content, which he found particularly welcome because it would enable parents to present to children a truer picture of the development of the world, while formerly they had been teaching them what they did not themselves believe. He judged it "a triumph of juvenile literature."[11]

Perhaps the only picayune comment was that Miss Ingelow was guilty of two or three errors in English, which the reviewer carefully pointed out.[12] The most amusing comment, certainly, was that it was a relief that Miss Dodge, who used the name Gail Hamilton on her title pages, had returned to the nursery, a comment which must have brought a smile to the face of every *Lakeside* reader, for Miss Dodge was well known as a writer of polemic books on behalf of a number of causes and had recently published *The Battle of the Books,* an attack on her publishers, Ticknor & Fields, whom she accused of having dealt unfairly with her. The book, incidentally, had elicited more sympathy for the publishers than for the strident Miss Dodge.

The reviews in *The Lakeside Monthly,* despite their careful consideration of the books, were too few to make possible a high evaluation of the periodical as a reviewer of children's books. Of the many published, only a very small number were reviewed.

WESTERN

The only literary monthly published in St. Louis of any note was the *Western,* begun in 1866 as the *Western Educational Review.* In 1872 its name was changed to *Western; A Journal of Literature, Education and Art,* and in 1875 a new series was inaugurated which continued until the magazine ceased publication in 1881.[13] It is with the 1875–1881 series that we are here concerned. Mott says that the magazine continued, after it enlarged its scope, to have a schoolmasterish tone, indicating a continuing allegiance to its original purpose as an educational periodical. Certainly its reviews tend to verify his statement. Most of the books reviewed were textbooks and scholarly works, with only a few adult novels. Only five children's books were reviewed and all of them nonfiction. However, we have the unusual situation with this magazine of finding all the reviews signed. One review is signed with the initials B. V. B. D. and the other four, signed "EDITOR," were written by H. H. Morgan.

Of the five books reviewed, three were of historical nature, Higginson's *Young Folks' History of the United States* and his *Young Folks' Book of American Explorers,* and the anonymous *The Little Bugler,* "a record of personal experiences during the Civil War," which was published in St. Louis.[14] The other two were Alfred J. Church's *Stories from Virgil* and Annie Carey's *The History of a Book.* The reviews were short, ranging from 35 words to slightly more than 100.

The same reviewing technique was used by both B. V. B. D. and by H. H. Morgan. The review began with a general statement about the book or the author, continued with a description of the contents, and contained some evaluation of the work, and sometimes other comments.

B. V. B. D.'s review of *Young Folk's History of the United States* provides us with a typical example.

> *The book is written in a clear and entertaining style. The early history of the country, including what is known of the mound builders, the character of the Indians, the visits of the Northmen, the causes and results of the voyages of discovery, the colonial history, &c., is unusually full for a work of this description. Less space than usual is given to the events of war, it being the author's intention to especially emphasize the nation's progress in the arts of peace, and this he does with success. The treatment of war is strongly partisan in its character, but yet is far more just than naturally might have been expected from so partial a source.*[15]

Morgan's review of Church's *Stories from Virgil* followed the same pattern, listing those passages from Virgil which Church selected for retelling, and then commenting on the felicity of the choices.[16]

Only in the review of Higginson's *Young Folks' Book of American Explorers* did Morgan depart from this pattern.[17] He hardly considered the book at all, commenting that all Colonel Higginson's books were welcome, but devoted most of his review to a peroration on the values of American history. He completely neglected to characterize the book, so that the reader of the review was not aware that this book, merely edited by Higginson, was made up of extracts from the explorers' own accounts of their travels.

Only one reference was made to the children themselves in any *Western* review. Discussing Annie Carey's *The History of a Book,* Morgan said,

> *the information furnished will be valuable to many who lack opportunity for acquaintance with a treatise, while, for the younger reader, valuable instruction is conveyed without interfering with the pleasure which may be the sole motive for reading.*[18]

No consideration was given to illustration, though this may partly be explained by the fact that none of the books reviewed had remarkable illustrations. Morgan mentioned the physical book in his review of *The Little Bugler,* saying that it was "well printed." [19] In the same review, he noted that grammatical errors had crept in, though he blamed the editor or proofreader rather than the author. The only reference to current events was the one already quoted, in which B. V. B. D. felt that Higginson had been guilty of some partiality in his treatment of the Civil War.

The reviews of children's books in the *Western* are few indeed, and the books selected are, in a sense, all of a piece. All of them are books that would be useful for instruction, books that might well have formed a part of supplementary reading in a school, or, in the case of Higginson's *Young Folks' History of the United States,* been adopted as a textbook. The reviews themselves are adequate. It is only in the choice of books to be reviewed that we see the limitations of the periodical's particular emphasis, an emphasis which may, in part, explain its failure to consider more than a handful of children's books.

12

LITERARY MONTHLIES IN
SAN FRANCISCO

THE OVERLAND MONTHLY

San Francisco, in July, 1868, saw the publication of the first issue of a magazine, *The Overland Monthly,* which for a time, was a rival, in quality at least, of the literary monthlies of the Eastern seaboard.[1] The publisher was Anton Roman, who was later to found another San Francisco monthly, *The Californian,* which, after it took the name *Overland Monthly,* was to have an even longer life than the original periodical of that name. The chief interest, though not the exclusive interest, of the periodical was in California and the West. Bret Harte was its first editor, and in its pages he achieved his first important literary success, with his stories of California mining camps. An examination of only a few issues reveals the extent of its regional emphasis. Even in its reviews of children's books, its California loyalties were evident, though not to such an extent that its critical faculties were impaired.

Its book reviews, appearing in a monthly "Current Literature" department, were written in a lively and racy style that befitted a magazine published by the Golden Gate. Among those reviews, at times in a special subsection labelled "Children's Books," and at other times standing with the reviews of adult books, appeared forty-two reviews of children's books, six of them reviews of books by California authors and published in San Francisco. Other books included such outstanding titles as *Alice's Adventures in Wonderland, Little Men, Eight Cousins, The Story of a Bad Boy,* and *At the Back of the North Wind.* More than half the books reviewed in the *Overland Monthly* were fiction, both realistic and fanciful. No particular type of nonfiction was represented by more than one or two books. The emphasis of the magazine, both in its choice

158

of books to review, and in its method of reviewing them, was literary.

The reviewer concerned himself with truth to life in a very large number of reviews, both in action and in character. In the review of *Eight Cousins,* he was particularly concerned with the realism of the plot, pointing out that Miss Alcott's seeming perfection in plot construction arose from the fact that her plots did not come out too patly.[2] His greatest concern, however, was with reality in characterization. *Daisy,* by Susan Warner, he found to be a book with "exasperatingly perfect persons" and one in which the bad people, on the whole, were much better drawn than the good ones.[3] He praised the portrayal of the characters in *The Story of a Bad Boy,* but at the same time pointed out that even the hero was subordinate to the incidents.[4] His greatest praise of characterization was reserved for Miss Alcott. The characters in *Little Men,* he said, were "real living children" who revealed the author's "thorough insight . . . in the portrayal of children's characters." [5] After describing the aunts in *Eight Cousins,* the reviewer said that "in character analysis, Miss Alcott shows herself the true artist." [6] He had little patience for the "goody-goody" characters so typical of earlier children's books and of the contemporary Sunday school literature. He praised George MacDonald for taking "good care that his readers shall not mistake his hero for one of those consequential, priggish little monsters" in *At the Back of the North Wind.*[7] He felt, however, that Diamond's early death was a blemish on an otherwise admirable book, a "genial golden link between fairy-land and earth-land."

Though the *Overland Monthly* reviewed few of the books attacked for their sensationalism, it did not ignore this element in books. Of the sensational plot of Sir Samuel W. Baker's *Cast Up by the Sea,* it said that

the processes of digestion are seldom as painfully apparent in youth as in age, and highly spiced as Sir Samuel's book is, it will not perhaps hurt the boys seriously.[8]

Of sentimentality, and too great piety, he had more to say. *Cast Up by the Sea* had "a kind of sentimental beginning which most healthy boys will reject with infinite scorn, or skip with perfect indifference." [9] He found Susan Warner's *Daisy* "not harmful, except so far as a subject of milk-and-water diet may be harmful." [10] In the introduction to another review he provided a statement that could characterize the magazine's philosophy on this subject.

It was a great stride in the civilization of the world when it was discovered that it required first-class talent to entertain children, and that mere goodness, abstract morality and piety would not suffice.[11]

This attitude was also revealed by other statements found in the magazine.[12]

Though this method was not used often, the *Overland Monthly* reviewer did use comparisons with other books, not always in praise of the book he was reviewing. He found C. Clark's story, "The Man in the Moon," in *The Fairy Egg and What It Contained* by H. H. Weston, Clark and L. Gibbons, to be overly suggestive of the writing of Hans Christian Andersen.[13] On the other hand, he praised Jules Verne for creating an aura of reality by using the method of Robinson Crusoe; the piling up of details to the point where the reader could not but believe it all true, in his *Five Weeks in a Balloon*.[14]

Only in the review of *Alice's Adventures in Wonderland* was special attention paid to humor, and there it became the central theme of the review.[15] But another characteristic of *Alice* was commented on in several reviews. The reviewer praised the parodies on well-known poems in Carroll's work, and commented on this use of poems interspersed in other stories as well. Mrs. Washington Wright (Carrie Carlton) wrote poetic prose, he felt, but she wrote only prosaic poems in her *Inglenook; A Story for Children*.[16] Laura Preston's verse in *A Boy's Trip Across the Plains*, was not worth including, though he felt the legends she had inserted in the story were good enough to be retold elsewhere.[17]

On several occasions, the reviewer stressed the appeal to adults of a particular book, perhaps with the thought that, after all, some of these books would be read to the children by their parents. He called *Alice's Adventures in Wonderland* "the most originally entertaining and delightful child's story that ever grown reader enjoyed," indicating that the reviewer had found the same pleasure that succeeding generations of adults would find in it.[18] He called Andersen's *Fairy Tales and Sketches* "the loveliest stories ever written for the delight of little folks and children of larger growth." [19] He explained that it was the gentle satire underlying the fairy tales that helped to give them their appeal to adults. He also pointed out the fact that Louisa May Alcott's books were popular with adults as well as children.[20]

The reviewer was even more concerned, however, that the authors of children's books should have a real understanding of childhood and of what children desired in their books. Children's stories had improved greatly in recent years and this, he felt, was in part due to choosing subjects "adapted to the localities, conditions and tastes of the little people. A boy's honest love of adventure is no longer studiously repressed." [21] He praised more than one writer for an "honest, hearty appreciation of children." [22] In a characteristically lively way he described, in a review of Lukin's *The Young Mechanic,* the attitude of a child toward his book.

The verdict of boys, about the real merits of a book, is something which authors and publishers have learned to respect. The juvenile world, just now, is in a very critical mood. It refuses to read dull books; it mocks at all the goody and inane prattle once so current. This sharp discrimination is working a revolution in juvenile bookmaking. The writer must have something to say, and he must say it in the very best manner. The story must be well told, the scientific statements illustrated in the best style of modern art, or the youngsters toss the book into a corner, and it is never "dog-eared" or blurred by multitudinous readings. When a lad lies upon the carpet, his stomach downward, and his heels thrust up toward the ceiling, intent for hours upon sucking the juice out of a book, his judgment is well nigh infallible.[23]

The *Overland Monthly*'s reviews of nonfiction for children's emphasized, to a large extent, the writing and the method of the author, with lesser emphasis on instructional value, though that was not ignored. J. E. Taylor's *Geological Stories,* recommended for its value in interesting children in science, was examined to determine its readability for the young.[24] Of Abby Sage Richardson's *The History of Our Country,* the reviewer said that "all through the book there is plenty of the bright incident and brilliant description so necessary to make the study of history attractive to the young," and he discussed her ability to draw character.[25] It was the means by which the subject was made clear and understandable that was praised in Lukin's *The Young Mechanic.*[26]

Besides a special interest in California, there were only a few references in the reviews to important topical interests. The reviewer reported, in reviewing *The Young Mechanic,* that a whole industry had grown up to meet the demand of boys for lathes.[27] But far more important in terms of great problems that still troubled the minds and consciences of men, was a remark concerning the dedication of Henry M. Stanley's *My Kalulu* and a severe criticism of Mrs. Richardson's *The History of Our Country.* He pointed out that the dedication of *My Kalulu,* a very small part of the book to receive special mention, stated that the book was intended to pay tribute to "those who have aided in the suppression of slavery on the east coast of Africa." [28] But the review of *History of Our Country* shows a concern even closer to home, a concern with the need, with the Civil War ten years in the past, for writers of history to show an ability to appraise that struggle judiciously and calmly. This balanced judgment Mrs. Richardson's history lacked.

The book has one grave fault. Mrs. Richardson's writing lacks the repose of history. She too often allows her history to become a defense and justification of the American people, instead of a record of facts and a calm statement of the causes which produced them. This kind of writing, which disfigures many pages in the early part of the volume, almost destroys the historical value of her account of the great rebellion . . . Does not an account of a struggle like that deserve to be fairly written, without bitterness or assumed contempt? Any smart lad, after attentively reading these chapters, would conclude that there is another side, which has not been stated here. The time has now come when we have a right to expect that this kind of thing should disappear, and that those who undertake to write the history of our country should be able to bring to the study of the events of our own time some measure of the calmness and discriminating judgment which these events will inevitably receive from future historians.[29]

The greatest special interest of the *Overland Monthly* reviewers of children's books, arising from a strong sectional editorial emphasis, was their interest in California juvenile writers and in California publications. The magazine reviewed six such books, all of them published by A. Roman & Company of San Francisco, but most of them reviewed after Roman had sold the magazine to John H. Carmany & Company. The *Overland Monthly* confidently expected real California children's books to be written with a distinctive flavor and excellence that was clearly Californian. In an early issue, it said,

The "Rolo" series was perhaps the happiest adaptation to the seasonable wants of every New England country boy. And yet such a work would be partly incomprehensible to the California-bred youth, with his two seasons, his larger social privileges, and his more adventurous fields. The two volumes before us are, each in their own way, essays toward meeting these new conditions. In coloring, subject and style they are quite original. They will satisfy the wants of the juvenile Californian, and still not be without a certain charm for the children of the Atlantic seaboard.[30]

The same review ended with a call for California children's books.

The field of California juvenile fiction is open and inviting. The peculiar phases of domesticity, the color of romance and adventure in all society, and the rare glimpses of our out-of-door life and nature in her most fascinating outlines, all afford material that is characteristic of California, and may be captivating if not inspiring to the fancy of the rising generation.[31]

The *Overland Monthly* did not let its desire for local juveniles unduly influence its evaluation of the California books that did appear. The reviewer applied the same standards that he applied to other books. He found Mrs. Washington Wright's *Inglenook; A Story for Children* to be "a pretty truthful picture of a California mountain home with two or three natural young folks, the usual domestic details, and a slight dash of adventure." [32] He found Laura Preston's *A Boy's Trip Across the Plains* to be "a more vigorous story." [33] He must have felt, later, that he had been premature in feeling that these two books were the beginning of a California literature for children. Early in 1869, reviewing Clara G. Dolliver's *No Babies in the House and Other Stories for Children,* though he praised her style and her understanding of children, he was almost apologetic about the local color. [34]

At the end of the same year, the last review of California children's books appeared, a group review of three books. [35] Clara G. Dolliver's *The Candy Elephant,* he found to be "super-sentimental," relieved only by a little humor, while May Wentworth's *The Golden Dawn* had "Spanish nomenclature and a conventional New England sentiment." Both stories contained "fairies and poetical dolls, stuffed with sentimental sawdust." The only one of the three books which was praised was *Phebe Travers* by "Aunt Florida," which had realism in both character and detail, and showed understanding of children. Its local color was good, but it had the least about California in its pages. It was surely with just a touch of regret that the reviewer found himself forced to admit that California children's books were not fulfilling his earlier hopes.

> *We trust that we shall not be thought unpatriotic, nor as discouraging immigration, when we state that the merit of these California publications for children, by California writers, seems to be greatest when there is the least attempt to depict California life.* [36]

Whether because the high hopes of the magazine had been blasted, or because no other California juveniles appeared, the magazine reviewed no more children's books by Californians after 1869. A few of May Wentworth's "Golden Gate Series" received brief notices in Eastern periodicals, the quaintest one a statement, probably by Lucy Larcom, in *Our Young Folks,* "to think of California sending us children's books, as well as gold," but the reviewing of California juveniles was chiefly left to the *Overland Monthly.* [37]

Only in a few reviews were illustrations mentioned. In the review of *The Fairy Egg and What It Contained* the reviewer said "the book is happily illustrated, the illustrations plainly telling the stories, as the stories themselves naturally suggest the pictures." [38] He revealed his attitude toward illustrations in the review of Helen C. Weeks' *Four and What They Did.*

163

In the publication of this book, attention has been given to a cardinal point that is often omitted in books intended for children; namely, to make them attractive to the eye. The story may be interesting; but, if the first impressions are unfavorable, the verdict of the trundle-bed fraternity is against it.[39]

In the same review the attractive binding is praised. A special technical notice was paid to illustrations in the review of Verne's *Five Weeks in a Balloon,* where the process of heliotyping was explained to the reader.[40] The reviewer lamented that this system of reproducing photographs had not yet been widely used in America.

Most of the reviews in the *Overland Monthly* were long though, in a few cases, they were very short as on the two occasions when a group review labelled "Children's Books" appeared. These were actually brief notices lacking several of the attributes of real reviews. They did not indicate the content of the book and provided little information on which the reader could base a judgment. With these exceptions, however, the reviews ranged from about 100 words to over 1,500, with most books receiving a few hundred words. Fully as much space was given to Miss Alcott's books and to George MacDonald's *At the Back of the North Wind,* as to any adult novels.

The length and quality of the reviews were not the only indications of the importance the magazine granted to books for children. In the introduction to one of the "Children's Books" sections, the reviewer acknowledged the great possibilities for molding children through their books, declaring that inspiring themes could lead children to virtue. But he continued with this warning to would-be writers of such books.

Let Master Tommy discover a fascinating octavo, in blue and gold, dangling beside his distorted stocking-leg on Christmas morning, and his exultant, boyish heart will give a perceptible bound, as he ruthlessly turns to the title-page. But the doom of that book may be pronounced by the opening paragraph. For instance, let the first offensively suggestive injunction be "THOU SHALT NOT STEAL!" in leaded minion, and the pugnacious little tyrant, "by his minions led," will make off for the first accessible apple-orchard, or watermelon-patch (that is provided apple-orchards and watermelon-patches offer succulent inducements about Christmas time.) Young America brooks no such assault upon his integrity. Sanctimonious selections, which devout old dames consider amazingly proper and wholesome for the rising generation, are repudiated with a kind of ferocious disdain by the generation in question. They have an innate sense of the ridiculous impropriety of planting a heavy piece of artillery to batter down a bird's nest.

> To be a judicious and helpful writer for the young, is to deserve and exact perpetual veneration. An ancient Athenian orator compared the loss which the commonwealth suffered by the destruction of its youth, to that which the year would suffer by the destruction of the spring. The detriment which the public sustains from wrong predilections given to children by the mental pabulum prepared for their use, is an evil not less deplorable in its results; as it vitiates and enfeebles, and thus robs the world of beauty, excellence, and strength. Too much discretion could scarcely be exercised in the selections for juvenile libraries; and in the sweeping avalanche of this sort of literature, it is no sinecure to hunt out the gems from among the mass of verbal rubbish.[41]

With this exalted idea of the contribution of children's literature, the magazine, as we have seen, applied stringent standards in its evaluations of children's fiction; demanding realistic situations, believable characters, and possible actions, while demanding other suitable qualities in nonfiction.

The method and style of the reviews was such that the reader was informed about the book and his interest was aroused by the manner of the review. Usually enough of the content was described to provide a satisfying picture of the scope of the book; yet not so much that the reader would have felt that he was being given a dull outline. Characters were described in sufficient detail to reveal their basic qualities and to arouse interest in their fate.

The reviews in the *Overland Monthly* were unsigned and Mott gives no clue to their authorship in his history. There is enough similarity among the reviews of children's books, at least, to indicate that they either were written by the same person, or by people who had a similar attitude toward children's books. Since the editors changed more than once in the brief life of the periodical, it would seem unlikely that they had written them, but there is a distinct possibility that they might have been written by one of the assistant editors, Noah Brooks, who was the author of children's books. But this is only speculation. Their authorship is less important than their quality, which was as good as that of any magazine published at the time.

THE CALIFORNIAN

In January, 1880, a new attempt was made to provide San Francisco with a monthly literary magazine. This magazine was called *The Californian* for its first two years; then it became *The Californian and Overland Monthly*, and finally the second series of *The Overland Monthly*, called

165

by Ambrose Bierce the "Warmed-Overland." [42] Interestingly enough, the original publisher of this periodical was the same one who had founded the old *Overland Monthly,* though his connection with both periodicals was brief.

As far as reviews of children's books are concerned, the derisive comment of Bierce had some validity, for certainly they are but pale shadows of the reviews in the earlier magazine. They were few in number, only fifteen, they were shorter, only one running to 100 words, and they did not show the same deep concern with children's reading, the same attention to literary standards or the same careful attention to the books themselves.

Of the fifteen books reviewed five were fiction, four were travelogue story books, and the rest a miscellaneous lot, with no type represented by more than one book. Perhaps more significant, one-third of the books, including books of different types, dealt with the Orient, a fact that may be explained by California's, and especially San Francisco's commercial ties as the great port of the Eastern trade.

Though there were several reviews of fiction, no consistent pattern emerges from an examination of these reviews. The first novel to be reviewed, *The Loyal Ronins,* a translation from the Japanese of Tamenaga Shunsui by Shiuichiro Saito and Edward Greéy, was given only a few lines in a review with four other books, barely enough to tell the reader that the book was historical fiction and that "as a piece of literary *bric-a-brac* this book is unexcelled." [43] James Otis Kaler's long popular *Toby Tyler; or, Ten Weeks with a Circus* fared somewhat better. Its review opened with the statement that "it is a difficult thing to write a really good child's book with a moral that shall be at once interesting and impressive," continued with a two-sentence description of the action of the story, and ended with the remark that "the story is wholesome as well as interesting, and, on the whole, is much above the average of juvenile tales." [44] The review of *The Young Folks' Robinson Crusoe* said only that William T. Adams, the well-known "Oliver Optic," did better work in his own books than he did in adapting Defoe.[45]

In the review of John Habberton's *Who Was Paul Grayson?* we do get a reference to the needs of children.

The author of Helen's Babies *is not likely, by all appearances, to achieve another success. At all events his later works have tended further and further from that goal. Paul Grayson is one of the conventional "goody-goody" boys who is the model of the school, and the hero of a commonplace story. The peculiar atmosphere that surrounds boys Mr. Habberton had evidently not breathed for many years.*[46]

The longest review of a child's book was that of Thomas W. Knox's *The Young Nimrods in North America,* yet even here the reader learned surprisingly little about the book.[47] It contained adventure and fun, and a great deal of information, but no description of any part of the action, nor of the characters was provided.

The reviews of books about the Orient, while indicating, perhaps, the special interests of California, were disappointing. They included two books from Knox's "Boy Travellers" series, Tamenaga's *The Loyal Ronins,* discussed above. Greéy's *Young Americans in Japan,* and William Elliot Griffis' *Japanese Fairy World,* a collection of Japanese folk tales. None of them, however, received long reviews or reviews that indicated more than a cursory examination of the books. The Greéy book received one descriptive sentence.[48] Knox's *Adventures of Two Youths in a Journey to Japan and China* was reviewed in greatest detail, but the review gives little notion of the author's method, none at all of his pedestrian style.[49] Only the profuseness and beauty of the illustrations are treated adequately. *Adventures of Two Youths in a Journey to Siam and Java* was treated even more briefly.[50] The native Japanese illustrations were mentioned in the reviews of *The Loyal Ronins* and of *Japanese Fairy World.*[51]

A few other remarks made in the reviews are worth noting. In a review of Viollet-le-Duc's *Learning to Draw,* the reviewer noted that some of the author's statements were not within the comprehension of children.[52] He found a strange error in Hezekiah Butterworth's *Young Folks' History of America,* in which, on page 243, there was an illustration with the American flag "flying from the breast-works of Bunker Hill." [53]

There can be little question that *The Californian* was not a major reviewer of children's books, nor by any objective standards could its few reviews be said to be of good quality. It did, however, pay heed to one literary trend of the day, the travelogue story book, reviewing the two Knox titles, Greéy's book, and Horace E. Scudder's *Mr. Bodley Abroad.*[54] It reviewed two books that are still popular, Laura E. Richards' *Five Mice in a Mouse-Trap by the Man in the Moon*[55] and *Toby Tyler,* recognizing the merit of both of them. But when we consider that the publication of children's books had taken a great upswing in these two years, with the great depression at an end, the contribution of *The Californian* to the reviewing of children's books is very limited, indeed.

PERIODICALS OF LITERARY CRITICISM

Three important periodicals, devoted in large measure to the reviewing of books, flourished in the period from 1865 to 1881. The earliest was *The Literary World,* published in Boston beginning July 1, 1870. For a decade it held a unique place as a book review journal in America. In 1880, however, *The Dial* was founded in Chicago, and 1881 *The Critic* appeared in New York. All three included reviews of children's books though, in the period studied *The Literary World,* begun in 1870, reviewed far more than did the younger magazines.

THE LITERARY WORLD

Edited in its early years by S. R. Crocker, *The Literary World* provided a mild and tolerant kind of criticism of books, including children's books. Since none of the reviews were signed in the early years of the magazine, it is no longer possible to determine which reviews might have been written by Crocker himself, and which by others. The only signed reviews were two columns with the titles "Holiday Books for Children I" and "Holiday Books for Children II" which appeared over the signature of Susan Coolidge in December, 1877,[1] and January, 1878.[2] On one occasion, the editor reported that he was printing reviews of children's books dictated by a child "who has carefully read the books she describes, and in whose estimate we have reason to believe that a good degree of confidence may be felt." [3] Later a column of reviews appeared with the title, "A Child's Opinion of Some Children's Books." [4] It is possible that some of the reviews were written by Edward Abbott, who took over the editorship of the periodical from Crocker. His brother, Lyman Abbott, was reviewing children's books for *Harper's New Monthly Magazine,* and his father, Jacob Abbott, was the author of numerous books for children. Edward Abbott was himself author of *Long Look House* and other children's books.

Crocker set forth his critical theories in an early isue of his periodical.

> *Criticism means judgment, pure and simple; nothing more, nothing less. To criticise a thing is to make up an opinion of it after thorough examination. But in our day the word "criticism" has come to be synonym of censure, and a critic is of necessity a fault-finder. This misuse of the word criticism is not confined to the many, but obtains among the educated few—even among professed critics themselves. In the matter of book-notices it is especially frequent and glaring. Some of these* soi-disant *highest authorities in literature declare that a laudatory criticism is no criticism at all. The absurdity of this position appears at once on reference to the strict meaning of the word. The discovery of merit is as legitimate a result of criticism as the discovery of flaws. The true object of criticism is to set forth the real character of the object criticised or judged, and if the judgment deliberately made up is favorable, it is as properly critical as a well-founded adverse judgment of another object would be. Critical notices of books are such as give a fair estimate of their character,—be the estimate high or low.*[5]

In the second column, he reaffirmed this attitude, claiming that the critical basis of his paper had been vindicated by the number of subscriptions and letters he had received.[6]

The attitudes expressed here are apparent in the reviews of children's books. The reviews were tolerant, attempting to inform more than to condemn. The interest of *The Literary World* in books for children is amply demonstrated by the 660 reviews that appeared between 1870 and 1881. Few periodicals reviewed so many children's books, and even fewer reviewed them in such detail. Though there were reviews of 50 words or less, many ran to 2,000 or more words. In almost every volume long reviews are to be found. Crocker felt that the proper choice of children's books for the home was a serious matter to be given close attention. In an editorial addressed "To Parents and Guardians", he pointed out the need for parents to recognize the importance of books children read outside school and urged that more attention be given to their selection.[7] His own magazine did its utmost to help.

Crocker was virtually alone in attempting to define a children's book, or "juvenile." A correspondent, questioning the classfication of a particular book as a juvenile, received this reply.

A juvenile is, in our opinion, a book specially intended for the entertainment or instruction of the young; its personages may be adults or children, and its action may appeal equally to the young and mature. Its title to the name of "juvenile" lies in its adaptation to the young mind; there need not be a child or a young person in it,—e.g., "Robinson Crusoe." [8]

Not quite satisfactory though this definition may be, it is one more indication of the concern and the thought given to children's books by *The Literary World.*

Almost every conceivable type of child's book published during the period was reviewed in the magazine, from fantasy and other fiction, through biography, history, natural history, religion and science. The first was *Alice's Adventures in Wonderland* in a belated review intended more to pave the way for the forthcoming *Through the Looking-Glass* than to evaluate the first Alice book.[9] The last in the period studied was Howard Pyle's *Yankee Doodle.* In between, lay reviews of every important book for children published during more than a decade, as well as of many not so important.

The reviews, themselves, were concerned in a large measure with literary qualities and appropriateness for children. It was this latter quality that the reviewer noted particularly in Harry Castlemon's *The Sportsman's Club Afloat,* a book filled with the kind of adventure which children find especially appealing.[10] It was a similar virtue that won praise for John T. Trowbridge's *Young Joe.*[11] He understood both his subject and his audience. On the other hand Madeline Leslie's *True and False Pride,* was "rather above children's comprehension.[12] *Allie's Mistake,* by Rebecca Gibbons Beach, an attempt to write a "sentimental, holiday-flavored, 'kindly' fiction, for which Dickens, in his *Chimes and Carols,* gave the recipe" succeeded in being neither childlike nor appealing to children.[13]

Frequently the reviewer discussed the reality of the characters presented in children's books. Reviewing Elizabeth Stuart Phelps' *The Gypsy Series,* the reviewer praised her "genuine and life-like pictures of school life," as well as the naturalness of sentiment." [14] A goodly portion of the review of Mary G. Darling's *Battles at Home* was devoted to characterization. Before describing the characters and the incidents, the reviewer made this comment.

The reader will become conscious of an instant and instinctive concern with the fortunes of the five little people who are killing time in

Rev. Mr. Stanley's parlor, one dull afternoon. This concern is instantaneous, because the author brings up the boys and girls, one by one, and presents them in so charming a manner, and with such effective suggestions as to the character of each, that we at once accept them as personal friends.[15]

He also noted that the probability of this book would make it a far better medium of moral instruction than the all-too-common book which showed virtue and vice in such extremes that they were unbelievable.

One of the least temperate reviews printed in *The Literary World* concerned Cap. Mayne Reid's *The Castaways* "in which the most unreasonable incidents are thickly intermixed with a few facts of Natural History." [16] The reviewer said that the title should be taken as the proper instruction to children for treatment of the book itself. Elsie, in Martha F. Finley's *Elsie's Girlhood,* was called an "attractive character," though the reviewer granted that she was somewhat too perfect to be life-like.[17] Louisa May Alcott's *Eight Cousins* was treated anything but gently on the score of verisimilitude. The reviewer felt that Dr. Alec's method of educating Rose was fantastic, but not so fantastic as the notion that a houseful of aunts would have put up with it. Even more unbelievable to the reviewer was the transformation in Rose.

She seems to us an improbable girl, and the educational results claimed for Dr. Alec's system tax our credulity. The action of the story is not very likely, and none of the personages possess notable individuality or interest.[18]

Despite these flaws, he acknowledged that the book would probably be popular because of Miss Alcott's reputation.

The most frequent device used by *The Literary World* reviewers to show the style of an author was to quote liberally from the book at hand. Often they drew particular attention to the use of humor, and especially when humor was one of the most vital elements in an author's success. The reviewer called *Alice's Adventures in Wonderland* "infinitely laughable." [19] Humor was declared to be the very element in which Frank R. Stockton "seems to move and have his being," in the review of *A Jolly Fellowship.*[20] The reviewer quoted several passages to illustrate Stockton's happy gift.

In some reviews an attempt was made to analyze the source of the humor. Lucretia P. Hales' *The Peterkin Papers* provided one such opportunity.

What it is that makes the Peterkin Papers . . . so very funny, it would not be easy to say, but funny they indubitably are. We suspect a great part of the secret lies in the solemn and utterly matter-of-fact attitude of the author herself toward her own characters. She is never caught exchanging looks of sympathy with the audience, but is gravely considerate and sympathetic toward the absurdities of the remarkable moral, well-meaning, ridiculous Peterkins. Few things are droller in their way than the chapter which narrates the misadventures of "Elizabeth Eliza" in trying to summon a telegraph boy by the "District" system, pulling one wrong knob after another, and collecting first a fire brigade, then six hacks, and a squad of police, but retaining through all presence of mind enough to remember that a telegram must consist of ten words, and to frame her message accordingly.[21]

On a few occasions *The Literary World* drew on the comments of other critics to enforce its judgments. Discussing Rebecca Clarke's *Little Folks Astray,* the reviewer quoted from Thomas Wentworth Higginson's article in the *North America Review* in which Higginson had called Miss Clarke a genius.[22] The reviewer's conclusions concerning Mary G. Darling's *Battles at Home* were probably influenced by Louisa May Alcott, for he reported that he read the story with more than usual interest because she had praised it.[23]

To relate the book in hand to other books by the same author, to similar books by other authors, or to place the book in perspective with the genre of which it was an example, was a frequent practice in *The Literary World.* Elizabeth Stuart Phelps was compared to Miss Alcott in the review of her *The Gypsy Series.*[24] Miss Phelps was declared to have "a naturalness of sentiment hardly less remarkable" than Miss Alcott's. An interesting and fairly extended comparison was made of Mary Martha Sherwood's *Robert and Frederick* and Julia A. Mathews' *Jack Granger's Cousin.* The reviewer found the two books both alike and different.

> *It is droll to find two stories so nearly alike in subject and yet so different, as* Robert and Frederick *and* Jack Granger's Cousin. *Both are stories of school life, and of the influence of one boy over another, and in both cases the boys are relations; but one pair of cousins are English, the other American, and while* Robert and Frederick *has an old-fashioned quaintness which reminds one of the days prior to Miss Edgeworth,* Jack Granger *is eminently a book of our own period. A hearty sweet-natured book it is, and full of good lessons, and as the same can be said of its English pendant, either is recommendable as pleasant reading for boys.*[25]

The reviewers of *The Literary World* were not unconcerned with instruction and moral precept in children's books, though this concern cannot be called their basic one. On several occasions the reviewer questioned the suitability of a subject for children's books. But even when objecting to the morals of a book, the reviewer was careful to distinguish between his objections and the basic interest of the book to the child.

At other times, he was more concerned with the bad effect of that method so frequently referred to as "sensationalism", in which the author used a wild sequence of exciting but improbable incidents to cover an otherwise rather poor and shoddy story. On at least one occasion the reviewer praised the first book of an author, only to criticize severely the second, and not too different one, because of its sensational elements. When James D. De Mille's *Fire in the Woods* was published in 1871, the *Literary World* reviewer said that the author's books were "among the best that have recently been written for boys." [26] They were devoid of preaching any didacticism, and were throughly wholesome and interesting. A year later, admitting that his *Picked Up Adrift* would undoubtedly prove interesting to boys, the reviewer questioned the moral wholesomeness of Mr. De Mille's books.[27]

One of the authors most frequently praised in this regard was Elijah Kellogg. His books were highly interesting to boys, yet eminently improving.[28] Only as literary specimens did they leave something to be desired, but, the reviewer felt, even the errors in grammar, of which Mr. Kellogg was frequently guilty, could be forgiven an author who had so much to offer his boy readers. In a review of another Kellogg book, *Winning His Spurs,* the reviewer again praised the moral instruction the author conveyed.

We are glad to know that Mr. Kellogg's books are very popular; they deserve to be so; for they largely help to educate young readers morally and mentally, while affording them delightful entertainment.[29]

In more than one review, an author was critized for his choice of subject, even when his skill in presenting it was worthy of praise. The reviewer lamented that John T. Trowbridge, who was a "close observer of human nature" chose, in his boys' books, to portray a coarse side of life.[30] He then described the action of that author's *Bound in Honor* to illustrate his objection. In the review of Daniel Wise's *Roderick Ashcourt* basically the same criticism was made.[31] Wise had chosen a trust fund embezzlement as the subject of his book, a subject which the reviewer felt was totally unsuitable for a child's book, no matter how well-written the book might be. *Buried Treasure,* by Harry Castlemon, presented "some rather unwholesome company, not a little feverishly exciting incident, and a good deal of slang and coarse local dialect." [32] Its chief redeeming feature, and an historically interesting one, was that it presented a picture of "poor-white" life in the South.

Jacob Abbott's books were praised for their ability to instruct, though not especially for moral instruction. Rather, it was the author's ability to provide children with useful information, while at the same time entertaining them, that impressed the reviewer for *The Literary World*. He praised *Juno on a Journey* because it provided children with so much knowledge, yet in such a way that the children were barely aware that they were learning.[33] *Light,* which the reviewer said had the same excellent qualities as his earlier *Heat,* was a book that made "scientific lessons very palatable to the young." [34]

A few books published especially for Sunday school libraries were reviewed in the pages of *The Literary World,* but actually only a small representation of the many books issued by the Sunday school presses. N. I. Edson's *Silent Tom,* one of several $1,000 prize stories published by D. Lothrop & Company, was favorably reviewed.[35] The book was written "to enforce the necessity of active and earnest piety", but the reviewer found it acceptable since its characters were well-developed and believable. Other Sunday school library books did not fare so well. Mrs. Sherwood's *Stories on the Church Catechism,* an Episcopal book, was described as "rather flat." [36] *Young Folks' Bible History,* by Charlotte M. Yonge, was even less acceptable to the reviewer. It was "a childish book —milk for babes, and rather watery milk at that." [37] The severest condemnation given to one of these books was received by P. B. Chamberlain's *A Rare Piece of Work,* which was judged to be actually pernicious, despite its religious purpose.[38]

Only one of the many temperance books was reviewed in *The Literary World,* for the magazine considered them a poor class of books.[39] The one exception, Mrs. W. N. Cox's *Amy Garnett, the Alm's House Girl* was probably reviewed because the reviewer felt it showed promise that the author could produce better books by writing in a happier field. This book did have an interesting plot which lifted it above the common run of books of its type.

A special element severely criticized by *The Literary World,* as unsuitable for children's books, was the inclusion of love in the plot and incidents. Louisa May Alcott was roundly scolded on this score in the review of *Rose in Bloom.*

> *Miss Alcott improves in style, if not in originality and strength. Her last book, "Rose in Bloom," is one of her best, though the worm of torturing their little hearts with the agonies of love, is a mystery to us. ries by dressing up her boys and girls in the guise of grown folks and torturing their little hearts with the agonies of love, is a mystery to us. An excess of sentimental nonsense is the bane of all her stories.*[40]

Most of the popular and important authors of the day were reviewed in *The Literary World*. Nine of Miss Alcott's books were reviewed, all more or less favorably. Her *Little Men* received special attention when it was listed in an editorial as one of the outstanding books of the literary year.[41] Other authors given favorable reviews among those whose works are still read today were Mary Mapes Dodge, Lewis Carroll, Edward Lear, Susan Coolidge, Mrs. Ewing, Frank R. Stockton, Laura E. Richards, and Jules Verne.

Many of the most popular, though less enduring, authors fared well in the pages of *The Literary World,* especially in its early years. The works of Elijah Kellogg, for example, were praised consistently, except for a reference in the review of his *A Strong Arm and a Mother's Blessing*.[42] This book was "more to our taste than most of Mr. Elijah Kellogg's previous works," the reviewer said, though no earlier review in the magazine had anything but praise for his work. In a similar manner, after praising all her earlier books, the reviewer of Rebecca Clarke's *Twin Cousins* described it as the same kind of "strange polyglot made up of baby-talk, extraordinary grammar, and occasional slang" that marred her earlier works.[43] Prior to 1880 the works of Horatio Alger, Jr., and William T. Adams were consistently praised, but were not reviewed at all in 1880 or 1881. One can only conclude that the reviews were written by another hand at the beginning of the eighties.

Every literary type peculiar to the period was reviewed in *The Literary World*. Alfred J. Church's *Stories from Homer* was the first of the classics rewritten or edited for children to be reviewed.[44] The reviewer set a pattern in this review that was more or less consistently followed in reviews of other books of the same type. Though praising the effort and giving an over-all favorable judgment to the book, he objected to certain omissions and to certain incidents that Church had included. In the review of Storr and Turner's *Canterbury Chimes, or Chaucer Tales Retold for Children* less was found to criticize, except the inclusion of the tale of Gemlyn, the authorship of which was open to question.[45] But this was a matter of scholarship, rather than suitability for children. The review of Sidney Lanier's *The Boy's Froissart* suggests improvements that might have been made in the editing of the original work, while acknowledging that the book was a commendable one.[46]

Mary Seamer's *Shakespeare Stories Simply Told* was compared, not unfavorably, with the Lambs' tales.[47] Miss Seamer's works were likely to be less appealing to older readers, but were better suited to a child's understanding. The last two of Lanier's works of this type for children, *The Boy's King Arthur* and *The Boy's Mabinogion* were given more unreserved praise. *The Boy's King Arthur* was real literature and recom-

175

mended as a fitting substitute for sensational fiction.[48] The review of *The Boy's Mabinogion,* after describing Lanier's method, declared the book to be "one of the best of the holiday books of the season." [49]

Several of the children's quartos were reviewed in *The Literary World,* with attention frequently drawn to the intrinsic drawbacks of this particular type of children's book. Horace E. Scudder's *Doings of the Bodley Family in Town and Country* made no favorable impression.

> *Indeed, he has, we think, compromised his enviable literary reputation by engaging in so palpable a "job" of book making; and the want of humor and animation in the book may safely be attributed to his consciousness of the unworthiness of his work. The story is so simple that it often approaches the limits of silliness.*[50]

The reviewer granted that the illustrations were attractive, but found them to be unnaturally tied to the text.

The same author's *The Bodleys on Wheels* was treated more gently. The reviewer pointed out that the book gave the impression of having been written to fit its illustrations, but felt that the "author deserves the praise of having achieved a difficult task in a very perfect manner." [51] Olive Thorne Miller's *Little Folks in Feathers and Fur and Others in Neither* was another quarto which was praised for the author's ability to surmount the natural difficulty presented.[52] The reviewer felt that the book was superior in both purpose and performance to most of the children's quartos. Still another quarto which won praise was Miss Coolidge's *A Guernsey Lily,* which the reviewer declared would be good reading for children.

> *The book has no faults that we can discover; its defect, as a picture-story book, is that obviously the text was written to fit the pictures, and not the pictures made to fit the text. This, of course, may be a serious clog on a writer's independence, naturalness, and grace of movement, and such a book is to be judged more by its pictorial than its literary merit. Still, in this instance, he later is not by any means wanting, and the pictures are profuse, large, strong, and spirited.*[53]

That more specialized type of quarto, the travelogue story book, was generously reviewed in the pages of *The Literary World.* The earliest reviewed, Hezekiah Butterworth's *Zigzag Journeys in Europe* was described as "an extension of the 'Bodley-book' principle," clearly tieing it to the quarto tradition.[54] The reviewer informed the reader that the book was largely an Americanization of an earlier French book, and related it to Abbott's *Rollo's Tour in Europe.* Mr. Butterworth, he felt, had done a creditable job, creating a lively and instructive book, though he had made several errors, such as labelling Henry VIII's chapel as Westminster Abbey.

The real laurels, however, were reserved for Thomas W. Knox's *Adventures of Two Youths in a Journey to Japan and China,* which the reviewer declared "the boldest and most brilliant stroke for the favor of young readers which the present season has witnessed." [55] He compared Knox with Butterworth and Scudder, finding Knox superior. The book itself was beautiful in appearance and was written in a style appropriate to the author's subject and purpose. *Adventures of Two Youths in a Journey to Siam and Java* received the highest praise also, though qualified by the statement that the information was presented somewhat didactically. [56]

The reviewer had cooled toward Butterworth's method in the review of *Zigzag Journeys in the Orient.* [57] He found that the book had too much of the flavor of a guide book and encyclopedia to be completely appealing. James D. McCabe's *Our Young Folks Abroad* suffered from the same fault. It read like a guidebook and had a dry and didactic style. [58]

But he found Edward Greéy's *Young Americans in Japan* to be of superior quality. [59] Greéy had lived in Japan and, like Knox, wrote partly at least, from his own experiences. Though the book was a quarto, its style was lively, and the picture it provided of the country a really accurate one.

Many types of nonfiction for children were reviewed in the magazine, including science, biography, history, and several general reference books. Works in science and natural history were frequently recommended highly for younger readers. Reviewing two such books, Arabella B. Buckley's *Fairy-Land of Science* and William E. Damon's *Ocean Wonders,* the reviewer expressed his approval of that type of book for children.

> *While thoughtful people are anxiously questioning what to do with the mass of worthless or vicious reading now thrown into the hands of our youth, there is great reason for encouragement at the rapid increase in an interesting, and at the same time instructive and thoroughly healthy, juvenile literature. Few books of the class have a clearer ring than these two.* [60]

The Literary World was one of the many periodicals that heartily recommended *What Mr. Darwin Saw in His Voyage Round the World in the Ship "Beagle."* [61] Most of the lengthy review was devoted to a description of the method of the book and to its content.

A particularly interesting review of a work of natural history was that of Ernest Ingersoll's *Friends Worth Knowing.* [62] The book was praised for its careful and delicate style, and for the author's skill as an observer. But the most interesting element was the reviewer's discussion of the chapter on the buffalo and his fate, indicating the growing awareness of the need for conservation of wild life in America.

Works of biography and history received many reviews. The earliest was a review of George Zabriskie Gray's *The Children's Crusade,* which the reviewer insisted was not a juvenile book, though many other reviewers said that it was.[63] Isa (Knox) Craig's *Young Folks' History of England* was praised for its simplicity and intelligibility.[64] Higginson's *Young Folks' History of the United States* was given a longer review in which its avoidance of sectional bias, its index, illustrations, maps and bibliographies were praised. One paragraph is especially worth reproducing.

> *After reading this book, and comparing it with the school histories to whose perusal American youth have been heretofore condemned, we can no longer wonder that Americans have been reproached with ignorance of history. For the first time a man of genius has undertaken to tell the story of our country's growth,—not a pedagogue, cramped by routine, or a professional book-maker, thinking only of his copyright, but a man of culture, who knows not only history, but human nature, too, knows what is the pleasant side of learning, and how to hold it up to eager gazers. We trust that this admirable history—admirable not only as a literary composition, but as a pleasant and safe guide for the young to a knowledge of our national career—will open the eyes of educationists and the public to the fact that the preparation of text-books for the instruction of the young is too weighty and solemn a task to be entrusted to mere compilers, who put neither heart nor brains into their work.[65]*

Another review of a history of the United States contrasted sharply with this. Hezekiah Butterworth's *Young Folks' History of America* won no praise at all. Its reviewer reported that the work was not Mr. Butterworth's, but actually a reprint of Robert Mackenzie's *History of the United States,* which the original English publishers had expressly asked not be reprinted in the United States.[66] The reviewer cited errors and omissions which marred the text, and a totally inadequate index prepared for the American edition.

Sarah Brook's *A French History for English Children* was no more kindly treated.[67] The reviewer pointed out that though the book was well-made from a physical standpoint, it was without value. All dates were omitted, so that it was difficult to understand temporal relationships. The author was equally vague about names. But worst of all, her selection of incidents was not such as would be likely to interest children, and some

178

of them were irrelevant to the narrative. The book had no index, but that was not a drawback since it was not worth one.

An article which appeared with the title, "Boys' Books About Boston," is of special interest because the reviewer dealt with three books of history on the same subject, contrasting and comparing them.[68] Samuel Adams Drake's *Around the Hub,* Horace E. Scudder's *Boston Town,* and Hezekiah Butterworth's *Young Folks' History of Boston* appeared at almost the same time in the 1881 season, and invited comparison. The reviewer described the scope, content, and method of each book, and then made the following comments on them.

> *Mr. Drake's book is as if he were taking a party of boys about the city, pointing out the old land marks, and bringing to view their interesting associations with people and events of the past; Mr. Scudder's as if he had a lap full of grandsons and were telling them through a succession of winter evenings, in familiar conversations, the story of the city's growth and fortunes; Mr. Butterworth's as if he were writing Winthrop and Cotton Mather and Frothingham down to the capacity of readers in their early teens. The flavor of Mr. Drake's book suggests the out-of-doors, Mr. Scudder's the parlor, Mr. Butterworth's the library. Mr. Drake's appeals to the eye, Mr. Scudder's to the imagination, Mr. Butterworth's to a desire for knowledge for its own sake. All are illustrated, but it is probably a secret with the respective publishers where some of the pictures came from.[69]*

Volumes in both Edward Eggleston's and George M. Towle's series of biographies for the young were reviewed. Mr. Towle was praised in the review of the *Voyages and Adventures of Vasco da Gama* for his ability to tell a story and yet remain faithful to the truth.[70] His book was commended as a desirable replacement for the "trash which so abounds." His *Marco Polo* received equally high praise.[71] Though Eggleston received briefer reviews, his *Montezuma and the Conquest of Mexico* was judged to be a good book, with an excellent literary style.[72]

Two unusual works given long reviews in *The Literary World* were John D. Champlin Jr.'s *Young Folks' Cyclopaedia of Common Things* and his *Young Folks' Cyclopaedia of Persons and Places.* The earlier work was declared to be "a very successful embodiment of a very excellent plan." [73] The reviewer described its alphabetical arrangement, its index, and the accuracy of its information, recommending it to young and old alike, and commenting on the value of cultivating the habit in children of referring to such works. The *Young Folks' Cyclopaedia of Persons and Places* had more faults, but was still an excellent work which the reviewer could heartily endorse for any home.[74]

179

The most famous illustrators of the period were given special attention by *The Literary World* and were mostly praised. Caldecott had only one review. Mrs. Frederick Locker's *What the Blackbird Said,* which he had illustrated, the reviewer declared "as charming to read as to look at; which is saying a good deal where Caldecott is the artist." [75] Howard Pyle's only book for children published in the period was reviewed, decidedly unfavorably. The reviewer declared that *Yankee Doodle* was, to begin with, a silly ballad and that Mr. Pyle's illustrations did nothing for it, "showing neither pleasant sentiment, true humor, nor particularly skillful execution." [76]

For Walter Crane and Kate Greenaway, *The Literary World* pulled out all the stops. In June, 1877, an entire column was devoted to "Walter Crane's Picture Books." [77] The reviewer discussed in great detail Crane's drawing, his use of color, his concentration on detail, his humor, and his imagination, and reported the great influence Crane had even on home decoration. Crane, he declared, was foremost among artists who illustrated children's books. The reviewer discussed the two editions of *The Baby's Opera,* the authorized edition published by George Routledge & Sons, and the pirated edition of McLoughlin Brothers. Though he did not comment on the fact that the McLoughlin edition was pirated, he did find it somewhat inferior, especially in paper and coloring. He called the attention of the reader to several particularly felicitous drawings. *The Baby's Bouquet* was reviewed in equally glowing terms.[78] The reviewer felt that both reviewers and children were faced with an impossible dilemma if forced to choose between *The Baby's Opera* and *The Baby's Bouquet,* since both were nearly perfect. He was equally enthusiastic when Crane illustrated the work of another author, such as Mary De Morgan's *Necklace of Princess Fiorimonde.*[79]

Only Kate Greenaway earned the same praise from this magazine. As though to prepare for her advent, the reviewer, on several occasions referred to Miss Greenaway's influence and her followers before actually reviewing one of her books.[80] On the first day of January, 1881, a review of her *Birthday-Book for Children* appeared.

After all, there is but one Kate Greenaway. She has many imitators, but no rivals. Her pencil, her brush, and her colors are her own; and though we are sure she must be of a very generous and good-natured disposition, it is perfectly evident that she lends her tools to nobody. That is right. If she did, we are afraid we should not have had this bright and dainty Kate Greenaway's Birthday Book; which in its way is the gem of the season. It is a bijou of a book; a little bit of quarto, perhaps four inches square and two thirds of an inch thick, with capti-

vating corner vignettes on the covers, yellow edges, and a wealth of picture and verse within. The verses are by that worthy fellow workman of Miss Greenaway, Mrs. Sale Barker, and there are a picture and verse for every day in the year, three of each to every page, with a blank page opposite ruled in green to receive the birthday entries of the owner. Then for each of the months there is a full-page illustration in colors appropriate to the season, or otherwise. The daily pictures are of thumb-nail proportions, but are full of the artist's peculiar individuality. There are no children like Kate Greenaway's odd, whimsical little creatures; but so perfectly natural in every movement and expression, so picturesque in their costumes, so life-like in every attitude. There are nearly 400 of the pictures in all, and when we add that the book could almost be put in a watch-fob, we quite give a fair idea of its multum in parvo. *It is a quaint performance from cover to cover.*[81]

A long and detailed review was given to her *Mother Goose,* which the reviewer found equally superb.[82] Undeniably, reviews such as these gave the reader a full picture of what he could expect of the book itself. Probably no other American periodical of the period provided such excellent descriptive reviews of the work of important illustrators.

The reviews appearing in *The Literary World* ranged in length from 40 to 50 words up to more than 2,000, but all of them attempted to provide the reader with an accurate picture of what the book was about, the author's style and method, and some evaluation of the book's merits. That the judgments were very lenient there can be no doubt, but on the whole they were fair, emphasizing literary merit and the interests of children. The reviewers did point out small errors, but usually in factual works in which such errors were of importance. Attention was given to the moralistic in children's books, usually to point out a healthy atmosphere or attitude. Reviewing, as it did, more than 650 children's books in twelve years, *The Literary World* was a major source of reviews, rivaling the *Nation* in importance. Though its circulation was never large, it undoubtedly had a great influence in that type of American home where emphasis was placed on children's books.

THE DIAL

Founded, as it was, in May, 1880, *The Dial* made only a small contribution to the reviewing of children's books in the period from 1865 to 1881. The periodical was issued monthly from Chicago and was edited by Francis F. Browne, who had edited the earlier *Lakeside Monthly* in the same city. Mott reports that *The Dial* earned itself a reputation for criticism that was conservative, but honest.[83] Like other magazines of its type, its circulation was never great.

In the two years studied, 1880 and 1881, 54 children's books representing the varied output of those years were reviewed, seventeen in 1880 and thirty-seven in 1881. The reviews tended to be short, from 50 to 150 words. All were unsigned and consisted of a description of the book's content, a discussion of the illustrations and the physical book, and a brief evaluation.

Certain patterns can be perceived in the reviews, particularly an emphasis on literary quality. The reviewer described the style of Coffin's *Old Times in the Colonies* as "easy and familiar." [84] The *Tales of the Caravan, Inn, and Palace,* translated by Edward L. Stowell from the German of William Hauff, had "smooth, sumptuous diction." [85] The reviews, however, were so short that the reader had to depend entirely on the judgment of the reviewer, since few quotations were included. In the review of one book, Mary De Morgan's *Necklace of Princess Fiorimonde,* the reviewer called attention to a few stories that were too old for children.[86] In most reviews he merely said that the book would be successful or popular with children.

Very little attention was given to the instruction or the moral teachings of the books reviewed. Drake's *Around the Hub* was described as a book "as absorbing as it is instructive," but the emphasis of the review was on the high interest of the history.[87] The only important reference to the moral of a book was in a review of an 1881 edition of Thomas Day's *The History of Sandford and Merton,* in which the reviewer commented on the high moral character of the hero, who was "worthy of imitation by the boys of today." [88]

A new edition of *Little Women* was reviewed in 1880, but the comments were confined largely to the new illustrations.[89] Books by Stockton and Coolidge were reviewed, as well as James Otis Kaler's *Toby Tyler; or Ten Weeks with a Circus.* The review of *Toby Tyler* was a typical *Dial* review.[90] Two sentences outline the plot. A comment that the book was amusing and well written preceeded the conclusion that boys would be fascinated by the book, but unlikely to follow the example of its hero.

Among the more noted illustrators, both Kate Greenaway and Howard Pyle were reviewed. Kate Greenaway's *Birthday-Book for Children* and her *Mother Goose* were highly recommended. The *Birthday-Book* was described as a little gem,[91] and the *Mother Goose* as the "daintiest of juveniles." [92] The latter was praised for its form, action, finish, detail, for its "piquant costumes" and for the invention it revealed. Like the reviewer for *The Literary World, The Dial's* reviewer found Howard

182

Pyle's *Yankee Doodle* offensive.[93] He felt Pyle's illustrations were lacking in taste, and coarse rather than humorous.

Among the rewritten or edited classics, Lanier's *The Boy's King Arthur* and *The Boy's Mabinogion* were reviewed. In fact, they received two of the longest and most detailed reviews given children's books by *The Dial.* The reviewer considered *The Boy's King Arthur* one of the best books for children of that year, or of any year.[94] It was an excellent piece of editing, and in some respects even an improvement on the original. The review of *The Boy's Mabinogion* was partly devoted to the reviewer's regret that Lanier had died, but it too praised his editorial work highly.[95]

Four travelogue story books were reviewed, Knox's *Adventures of Two Youths in a Journey to Siam and Java* and his *Adventures of Two Youths in a Journey to Ceylon and India,* Butterworth's *Zigzag Journeys in the Orient,* and Edward Greéy's *Young Americans in Japan.* The reviewer called Knox's *Adventures of Two Youths in a Journey to Siam and Java* a genial and entertaining book, but the review was chiefly descriptive.[96] The second Knox book was given a longer review, chiefly devoted to a description of the author's method, but praising the pictures and pointing out one error of fact.[97] The same method was followed in the Butterworth review with the added comment that the popularity of the series was "well deserved." [98] The review of Greéy's book was more detailed, and included an account of the author's qualifications for his task.[99] The reviewer praised the narrative, the dialogue, and the author's picture of Japanese life.

Two volumes of history for children were reviewed, the work by Drake, *Around the Hub,* and John D. Champlin, Jr.'s *Young Folks' History of the War for the Union.* Drake was praised for his interesting style, and for the fullness of his account of Boston's history.[100] Champlin's work, a less literary one, was described as "serious reading for children" commendable particularly for its avoidance of a partisan point of view, and for its excellent maps, charts, and engravings.[101]

The Dial was particularly concerned with the physical qualities of children's books, commenting on the great improvement in the art of book production over that of an earlier generation. At the beginning of one series of reviews, the following comment appeared.

> *The effects of the late wide-spread impetus given to art-culture in this country are exhibited nowhere more sensibly than in the workmanship pertaining to the manufacture of books. Year after year the execution displayed in the department of production shows an increase of refinement corresponding with the growth of aesthetic taste*

in the leading promulgators of the theory and practice of the fine arts. We have but to examine the fresh collections of children's books prepared for the holiday season to discern how far a genuine feeling for the beautiful and correct appreciation of its laws and possible interpretations have been developed among us.[102]

In almost every review, the artistic appearance of the book and the quality of its illustrations and their reproduction was commented on.

Coming as it did, at the end of the period, *The Dial* cannot be considered a major contributor to the reviewing of children's books, though in the decade following it would be. But since the editor of this periodical was the same man who had earlier edited *The Lakeside Monthly,* a magazine which reviewed far fewer children's books, *The Dial* does serve to show the increasing concern with children's books in the decades following the Civil War.

THE CRITIC

Jeannette L. Gilder and Joseph B. Gilder founded *The Critic* in New York City in January, 1881. Published bi-weekly, it was chiefly devoted to the reviewing of books, though it included some reviews and discussion of fine arts, music, and drama, Mott's comment on their book reviewing is that it "was usually bright, incisive, and impartial, with a tendency to be conservative in judgments and not very profound." [103] Throughout most of its life, from 1881 to 1906, its circulation was around 5,000.[104]

Though *The Critic* was published only in the final year of the period covered by this study, it did review fcrty-three of the children's books of that year, and included a considerable variety in the types covered. Most of the reviews were short, around 50 to 100 words, though the review of Mark Twain's *The Prince and the Pauper* was longer. The reviews were unsigned, though it is possible they were written by one of the editors.

The point of view of the reviews of children's books was decidedly a literary one, for morals were mentioned only to indicate that they were unobtrusive, or that good manners and good behavior were presented in an undidactic manner.[105] A frequently used device was to compare a work with others of its type or with other works by the same author or illustrator. The reviewer quoted from Helen Hunt Jackson's *Mammy Tittleback and Her Family* to illustrate a resemblance to Wordsworth.[106] Frank R. Stockton's *The Floating Prince, and Other Fairy Tales* was compared with other nonsense books, Lear's, Carroll's, and Lucretia P. Hale's, and declared to be the best children's book to appear since.[107]

Kate Greenaway's *Mother Goose* was judged her best work, superior even to *Under the Window*.[108]

In a few reviews, the suitability of a work for children was questioned. The reviewer felt that Juliana Horatia Ewing's *Mrs. Overtheway's Remembrances* was too heavy for children, but too light for adults.[109] Flora L. Shaw's *Hector* was about children, but not really for them.[110] Of a different sort was the comment on Mrs. Laura Valentine's *Shakespearian Tales in Verse,* which the reviewer considered worthless. The children, he said, would be better off reading Edward Lear than King Lear at the age for which these jingles were suitable.[111]

Several books of lasting appeal were reviewed, with approval. James Otis Kaler's *Toby Tyler* was declared to have absorbing interest, and as the *Dial* reviewer had said, would be unlikely to encourage boys to run away from home.[112] The reviewer praised Mark Twain's *The Prince and the Pauper* as "a sweet and wholesome tale," but one less clearly for children than *Tom Sawyer*.[113] He also commented that "one shudders to think what it would have become in the hands of those who supply the literature of the Sunday-school libraries." After a long description of the action of the story, he commended the author's treatment of the historical period, and his use of local color and descriptive details. Laura E. Richard's *Sketches and Scraps* won unqualified approval.[114] The reviewer called it a brilliant book, with a fresh quality and almost too much variety.

Among illustrators, both Kate Greenaway and Howard Pyle were reviewed and praised. The reviewer declared that he had "seen no cleverer book for the young folks" than Pyle's *Yankee Doodle*.[115] The illustrator had caught the true spirit of the traditional poem. Not only was the work good, but the printing itself proved, the reviewer felt, that color printing in America had come into its own.

Often illustrators were praised for their ability to avoid imitation of either Kate Greenaway or Walter Crane. Lizzie Lawson's illustrations for C. L. Matéaux's *Old Proverbs with New Pictures* were judged to be original, or at least "not reflections of either Miss Greenaway or Mr. Crane." [116] Despite their resemblance to Miss Greenaway's illustrations, the pictures for Virginia Gerson's *Little Dignity* revealed some originality.[117]

Only one of the travelogue story books was reviewed in *The Critic,* James D. McCabe's *Our Young Folks Abroad,* which the reviewer described as a *Rollo in Europe* type of book.[118] He felt it contained "a really appalling amount of information," and was confusing because of the fiction mixed in it.

Three works of history were reviewed. Scudder's *Boston Town* was "easy and attractive reading," and had good illustrations.[119] Champlin's *Young Folks' History of the War for the Union,* while entertaining and lively, was declared to be biased.[120] Since this work was praised elsewhere for its objectivity, it would seem to be legitimate to question here the bias of the reviewer. But to Drake's *Around the Hub* went *The Critic*'s most enthusiastic praise for history for children. The reviewer called it "decidedly the best historical book of its kind for children that we have seen." [121] The absence of fiction made the book clearer and more interesting than other books of history for children which used a sugar-coating of fiction to provide a frame for history.

The quality of the reviewing in *The Critic* was high, and the number of books reviewed, forty-three, a considerable number for a single year. But like *The Dial, The Critic* appeared too late in the period to have had a great influence on the children's books of the period. Of periodicals whose chief function was the reviewing of current literature, only *The Literary World* could have had much impact by the end of 1881. All three, however, serve to indicate the importance attached to books for children in the years following the Civil War.

14

SCHOLARLY REVIEWS

Following the pattern of the great British quarterlies, America gave birth to several reviews in the nineteenth century, some secular, some religious, so that it is difficult in discussing them to be sure whether they always belong in a group by themselves or with religious periodicals. It must be admitted, however, that the same question could be raised concerning other types of American periodicals as well. In this study, *The New Englander,* which Mott calls a religious periodical,[1] is included with the *North American Review* and the *International Review,* while other more clearly religious quarterlies are discussed in the chapter on religious periodicals.

It may be surprising to think of these great, somewhat scholarly periodicals in connection with reviews of children's books. Indeed, reviews of children's books are not frequent in their pages. Enough are to be found, however, to make a brief discussion of them worthwhile.

THE NORTH AMERICAN REVIEW

By the beginning of our period, 1865, *The North American Review,* founded in 1815, was already an old periodical. At no time did it systematically review children's books, though, before the beginning of 1865, it did review an occasional one, such as Horace E. Scudder's anonymously published *Dream Children* in 1864.[2] During our period children's books were discussed in only two issues. In January, 1866, an article, "Children's Books of the Year," written by Thomas Wentworth

Higginson appeared, and in January, 1874, an anonymous article, "Works of Jules Verne."

Higginson's essay was by far the more extensive, including twenty-two titles by such authors as Jacob Abbott, William T. Adams, Horatio Alger, Jr., Rebecca Clarke, Charles Carleton Coffin, William Henry Giles Kingston, and John T. Trowbridge, to name only a few of the most popular. None of these books, which were published in 1865, except an edition of the *House That Jack Built,* and *Old Mother Hubbard,* are still read today.

In discussing the books before him, Higginson, for the most part, confined himself to general comments, only partly dealing with specific books, partly relating them to others of their type, and partly setting forth his ideas on proper standards for children's books. Often his comments applied to the general work of a particular author rather than to the book reviewed. For example, he said of John T. Trowbridge that he "never writes ill, and rarely very well," a remark that obviously applied to Trowbridge's general output, not merely to *The Drummer Boy,* which Higginson was reviewing.[3]

Higginson's general comments on children's literature are highly interesting, revealing the tolerant and broad-minded attitude he held toward reading for the young. "Grown people have their prejudices and limitations," he said, "but children have none." [4] Describing the kind of literary fare desirable for a child he made the following comment.

> *A child is as much injured by being debarred his proper rations of fancy as of fact,—of fact as of fancy. Always floating in delicious equipoise, he can neither be made exclusively real nor altogether ideal.*[5]

Before discussing a group of adventure stories he made another pungent comment.

> *What a relief, indeed, (if the truth must be told,) would be the occasional demise of some virtuous boy, in the midst of some of these amazing exploits,—something to remind us that these heroes too are mortal. If, after escaping by ten different stratagems, the first ten grizzly bears, he could be irremediably and hopelessly eaten up by the eleventh, it would really afford almost the only new sensation of which this department of literature is now capable.*[6]

But he did make some excellent comments, also, on individual works. Though he poked kindly fun at Jacob Abbott's *John Gay, or, Work for Boys,* he described its style as "clear and sensible." [7] Perhaps the most startling comment he made was that, with Rebecca Clarke, who wrote under the pseudonym Sophie May, a "touch of genius" entered the picture.[8] He particularly praised her ability to create character. Miss Clarke's works were exceedingly popular, and were still being reprinted in the early decades of the twentieth century.

Mr. Higginson made two remarks that are of special interest, one because it is the same complaint that Anne Carroll Moore would make in the 1920's, and the other because it indicated an awareness of one vital function which some scholars have attributed to American children's books. Like Miss Moore, Higginson complained that there was no high standard applied in the criticism of children's books so that authors were tempted to and did practice a slovenly level of work.[9] The other remark resembles a theory of Henry Steele Commager, promulgated in a lecture delivered in various parts of the country in 1959, that the United States, lacking a real past and feeling an urgent need to create one, made use of children's literature. It was particularly true, he felt, with hordes of immigrant children arriving on America's shores needing to be assimilated, that children's books could help to give them that sense of nationality which comes from an historic past. Higginson's remark, which Commager may know, was as follows.

Indeed, it is singular how much more of the aroma of American nationality one can get from our children's books than from any others, although one would at first suppose that these little people must lead much the same life, wherever on the globe they dwell.[10]

The second article dealing with children's books, "Works of Jules Verne," discussed four titles, the *Tour of the World in Eighty Days, Twenty Thousand Leagues Under the Sea, Five Weeks in a Balloon,* and *The Fur Country.* The reviewer said that these works had "taken a high place in that department of literature which aims especially at entertaining the young." [11] In fact, he acknowledged, all ages liked them. He provided a brief description of the action of each book, and praised Verne's character drawing and his ability to provide a vivid picture of his settings. Despite a tendency to "overstrain probability," these works were both entertaining and instructive.

It can be seen that the contribution of the *North American Review* to actual reviewing of children's books was relatively minor. But it is not to be ignored. Thomas Wentworth Higginson spoke with authority and was an influential literary critic, reviewing for many of the important periodicals of the day. It is impossible to prove, but still likely, that Higginson's article may have aroused the interest of other periodicals in reviewing more children's books.

THE NEW ENGLANDER

Like the *North American Review,* the *New Englander,* later known as the *Yale Review,* dated its founding from an earlier period. Mott reports that it was founded in January, 1843, and that its policies were Congregational, Whig, anti-slavery, pro-education, and orthodoxy in morals.[12] By the period of this study, the Whig party was dead, opposition to slavery was a dead issue, and none of the other policies are reflected in the tiny handful of reviews of children's books. It was another era.

Actually, only eight books and periodicals were reviewed in the entire seventeen years, 1865–1881, and those in exceedingly brief notices. Thomas Wentworth Higginson's *Young Folks' History of the United States* was praised as a model that might well be imitated by the writers of school histories.[13] Henry T. Coates's *The Children's Book of Poetry* had a good index, was well selected, and of interest to children.[14] Mrs. Edward Ashley Walker's *From the Crib to the Cross* and *The Pilgrim's Progress,* both in words of one syllable, were "very successful." [15] The only longer review dealt with William Elliot Griffis' *Japanese Fairy World,* but this review, even though of a children's book, was from a scholar's point of view, with objections to tampering with the original tales.[16]

The few reviews that did appear in the *New Englander* were printed in the midst of reviews of scholarly works, with no attempt to segregate them. Too few books were reviewed to provide a consistent pattern. It is not even possible to conjecture why, out of hundreds of works published, these eight should have been chosen for notice unless it is assumed that in some way, each was an unusual work. This cannot be assumed, however, except for a few books, such as Higginson's history and the strange productions of Mrs. Walker.

THE INTERNATIONAL REVIEW

Unlike the *North American Review* and the *New Englander, The International Review* was a product of the post-bellum world, founded in January, 1874, and unlike them, it was never a quarterly, but was a bimonthly magazine. It reviewed an even smaller number of children's books—three. The "Frontispiece" bound into Volume I of the periodical set forth its policies.

> *The chief object of the REVIEW is the sifting and telling treatment of great questions of our age and country above mere sect or party; literary, scientific, social, national, religious.*
> *It brings to its pages the best culture of Europe and America, and*

seeks to be a medium of communication for representative thinkers of the age.

It aims not to address merely scholars and divines, but to furnish guidance and information in pleasing popular forms to practical men in business and the professions.[17]

One thing it did not promise to do was to review children's books in a fair and impartial manner.

Of the three books it reviewed, one, *Spenser for Children,* by M. H. Towry, was recommended.[18] But Charles Carleton Coffin's *The Story of Liberty* and Frank R. Stockton's *A Jolly Fellowship* were roundly condemned. Coffin's book was biased, had illustrations that had done service elsewhere, and was, in any case, "a farrago of scraps of history . . . put together after a fashion hard to be understood by a child who is not old enough to seek his history in more authentic volumes." [19] The reviewer also objected to Coffin's use of the present tense, and to his dedication "to the boys and girls of America."

But the strangest review is that of *A Jolly Fellowship.* After a brief description of the action, the reviewer continued in this vein.

Boys are easily amused, and there may be stray boys who will derive amusement from this book in spite of the disagreeable self-sufficiency of the hero. It might strike maturer minds as harmless, were it not for the expression, "I would be drowned in less than a minute," which occurs early in the story. An accurate knowledge of English grammar is, perhaps, too much to require of writers for the young, but we had supposed everybody to be too familiar with the Frenchman's blunder, "I will drown, nobody shall save me," to run against so obvious a snag. But very likely we are too exacting.[20]

It is difficult not to agree. Perhaps he was.

Perhaps the attitude of the periodical is best revealed in an article by James Mascarene Hubbard, "Fiction and Public Libraries," which appeared in 1881. Hubbard not only objected to the quality of most fiction and to the use of taxpayers' money to provide it, but demanded that rigid censorship be applied to all books that might make their way to children.[21] Fortunately, for American children, this censorship never developed and was never put into the hands of the writers and editors of *The International Review.* Though a higher standard of criticism of children's books may have been needed, the few reviews in this periodical were not of a sort to provide it.

RELIGIOUS PERIODICALS

The number of religious periodicals published during the period of this study is so great that a complete examination of them would provide a study in itself. Only a selected few are examined here, not necessarily as representative of the whole, for the existence of a variety of such periodicals implies differing editorial and doctrinal points of view, but to illustrate the interest of the religious periodical press in children's literature.

That the religious periodicals should have reviewed children's books is not surprising, for the church publishing houses, under the names of societies, boards, or committees were among the more important and prolific producers of books for the young. Through the ubiquitous Sunday school libraries, churches were also major consumers of them. Several Protestant groups published approved lists of books for the Sunday school libraries of their sect, notably the Unitarians and the Episcopalians. Dodd, Mead's *Sunday-School Annual for 1871* carried a list of books published since 1868 for the Sabbath school libraries.[1] The same volume included an article by the Rev. Lyman Abbott, reviewer for *Harper's New Monthly Magazine,* on Sunday school libraries.

In choosing the periodicals to examine, an attempt has been made to include different points of view. Each of the periodicals discussed represents a different church group, Congregational, Unitarian, and Roman Catholic. At least two of the periodicals included with literary monthlies might easily have been included with this group instead. *Hours at Home,* while published by the trade house of Scribner, held an orthodox Presbyterian viewpoint and declared, in its subtitle, that it was "A Popular

Monthly Devoted to Religious and Useful Literature." Each issue in its first several volumes included a "Short Sermon to Sunday-School Teachers," and other articles concerning religious questions. Edward Everett Hale's *Old and New* also had close church affiliations. In fact, the Unitarian Association provided part of its financial support. And among the scholarly reviews, *The New Englander* was closely allied with Congregationalism.

THE INDEPENDENT

Founded in 1848 as a Congregationalist and anti-slavery weekly, *The Independent* was still vigorous after the Civil War had ended and one of its major causes had been removed. The periodical had been edited by Henry Ward Beecher during the early war years, but in 1863 Theodore Tilton became editor, and in 1870 Henry Chandler Bowen.[2] Though the periodical had been Congregationalist from its beginning, after the middle of 1867 Tilton attempted to make it a non-denominational Protestant periodical with a less religious tone. Mott says that it became more religious again after Tilton left the editorship.[3] Physically, *The Independent* was more a newspaper than a magazine, though its reduction in the 1870's to tabloid size gave it somewhat more the appearance of a magazine. Its size was that of a newspaper, and its format, with a multicolumn page, was certainly that of a newspaper.

The magazine carried a regular book review section in which, from time to time throughout the year, children's books were reviewed, sometimes grouped together under a special heading, but more often included with other books. In fact, this periodical reviewed more books, at times other than the pre-holiday seasons, than did any other examined. The reviews and notices of children's books ranged in length from single sentences of a dozen words to well over a hundred words. None were signed, except a single longer review, more than 700 words, of Miss Alcott's *Eight Cousins,* by Caroline H. Dall. Justin McCarthy was literary editor in 1868–1869, but it is not possible to determine whether he wrote any of the children's book reviews.

One striking characteristic of the reviews themselves is the greater concern expressed with books for the Sunday school libraries. Repeatedly the reviewer recommended a book for these libraries, declared such books were improving, or found books to be unsuitable for them. Besides a greater number of story books for Sunday schools, a greater number of nonfiction books of a religious nature were reviewed in *The Independent.* The books represented the output of many of the denominational publishers as well as the output of trade publishers who catered to

193

the religious trade. Only rarely were fewer than twenty-five books reviewed in a single year. Frequently more than 50 books were noticed. In 1879, 75 books were reviewed.

The reviews of Sunday school library books form such a large percentage of the reviews of children's books and, in some ways, differ so much from other reviews as to demand examination. At the end of 1865, in an editorial "Chat About Books," the magazine detected an improvement in Sunday school library books, and wondered if the improvement in tone in this type of literature might not be attributed to the influence of Henry Ward Beecher.[4] The newer books had a healthier tone and less of the "traditional dismality" which was so common earlier.

The reviewers for *The Independent* did not, however, assume that a book would be good merely because it was avowedly prepared for the Sunday school. *Ned Nevins, the Newsboy; or, Street Life in Boston,* by Henry Morgan, the third edition of which appeared in 1867, was sensational and unnatural. The reviewer said the "mere fact that it is intended for Sunday school libraries is no sufficient reason why it should be endorsed by the religious press."[5] In other reviews, the qualities expected of such books were clearly indicated. *My New Home* was a good religious juvenile with better writing and greater interest than the average book of its class. The reviewer declared it was not just a religious book with a thin coating of story, but rather an "interesting story, permeated with the holy influence of Christ."[6] Alexander MacLeod's *The Wonderful Lamp* was another Sunday school book of the better class. It was of interest to children, and not "stupidly good."[7]

On occasion, the reviewer dealt with the religious content of a book. Failure to give pre-eminence to Christianity in *The Childhood of Religions,* by Edward Clodd, led the reviewer to insist that the book not be given to children without "supplementary instruction" so that they would see the book in a proper frame of reference.[8] On the other hand, excessive partisanship was not acceptable. W. H. Daniels' *That Boy; Who Shall Save Him?* was a very poor book, with bad style and worse tone, for it was intended to make Methodist children hate Calvinism.[9]

In other books, not especially designed for Sunday school libraries, the reviewers were concerned with morality. Philip Gilbert Hamerton's *Harry Blount* was a "good, wholesome story, and wholesomeness is always profitable."[10] On the other hand Harry Castlemon's *Buried Treasure* was not a desirable book for children's reading because the "romantic adventures of a bad boy . . . are not the best reading for a good boy."[11] The same author's *Mail Carrier,* because it had low characters, was to be kept away from boy readers.[12]

The Independent reviewed more temperance books for children than did other periodicals, and was a little more kindly disposed toward them, recommending some of them for Sunday school libraries. *Bessie Lovell; or, The Power of a Loving Child* was recommended because it emphasized God's help in overcoming the curse of drink, rather than the more common pledge.[13] M. Alice Sweet's *Coals of Fire* was "a temperance story of the better sort" and could be recommended for Sunday schools.[14] But a far larger number of temperance stories were condemned as sensational. Sarah A. Mather's *Young Life* was fairly typical. The reviewer described it as "a stupid story of a decidedly priggish boy—the typical 'good boy' of old style Sunday-school literature." [15] The frontispiece, a picture showing a drunkard dead in a snow drift, made the book even worse.

The reviews in the periodical showed, actually, considerable concern with literary quality, and with the author's use of language. In several reviews the truth of character and incident was questioned. The chief fault of Susan Warner's *Melbourne House* was the "impossible perfection of the little heroines." [16] Martha F. Finley's *Elsie's Motherhood* was "goody-goody." [17] Susan C. Pindar's *The Wentworths; Their Home and Friends* was not consistently poor, but the chapters dealing with college life were completely fantastic.[18]

Often, the author's style was criticized. The style of the Rev. P. C. Headley's *Life and Naval Career of Vice-Admiral David Glasgow Farragut* showed marks of haste and carelessness.[19] The same author's *Life and Military Career of Major-General Philip Henry Sheridan* suffered from the same fault.[20] It might have been "valuable as well as popular" if written without such haste. C. A. Stephens' works suffered from the same fault, the reviewer said, in his notice of *On the Amazon*.[21]

The use of slang was not acceptable to *The Independent*. Even though Noah Brooks's *The Fairport Nine* was a highly readable book, on the whole a good one, it was not to be recommended because boys would be hurt by the slang it contained.[22] Nora Perry's *Bessie's Trials at Boarding School* on the other hand was,

> one of the best books for girls we have lately seen. Miss Perry writes well, and her pleasant stories are free from the modern and fashionable but objectionable slang talk.[23]

Several of the outstanding children's books of the period were reviewed, *Hans Brinker* no less than four times as different editions appeared. Two of Louisa May Alcott's books were reviewed, *Cupid and Chow-Chow* and *Eight Cousins*. Actually, *Cupid and Chow-Chow* received only a brief notice, in which the reviewer acceded to the judgment of children, who would be sure to like it.[24] Caroline H. Dall's review of *Eight Cousins* was the longest review of a children's book in *The*

195

Independent, and the only signed one. Mrs. Dall felt that *Eight Cousins* was Miss Alcott's best book since *Little Women,* with a better style and more individualized characters than the intervening ones.[25] Much of the review dealt with Miss Alcott's particular virtues and weaknesses as a writer, rather than with *Eight Cousins.* Mrs. Dall attributed Miss Alcott's success to the fact that her books had a sound and healthy moral tone, and to their cheerfulness.

Twelve of the tales of Jules Verne were reviewed, including all the more famous ones. The *Tour of the World in Eighty Days, Twenty Thousand Leagues Under the Sea,* and *In Search of the Castaways* were reviewed together. The reviewer predicted they would be widely read, and made the following analysis of Verne's success.

> *They are romantic narrative, intelligibly and imaginatively told, and are told in so circumstantial a way, too, that their young readers will be likely to accept them in good faith, like the veracious history of "Robinson Crusoe," though they are as full of inaccuracies and impossibilities as they can well be.*[26]

In a collective review of *From the Earth to the Moon, Five Weeks in a Balloon,* and *Fur Country,* Verne was reported to be the most popular of authors, judging by the rapidity with which his books were being translated into English.[27] The reviewer predicted, however, that Verne's fame was sure to fade. *The Mysterious Island* was declared to be Verne's best book.[28]

Some attention was given to the appearance of the books and to their illustrations, though no attempt was made to analyze the artistry. Sharp criticism was directed at the Lothrop house for printing in garish gold letters "$1000 Prize Series" on three books to which they had awarded prizes. Two even had the check printed on them. The reviewer said, tongue in cheek, that "such barbaric gold should never have found place upon books which bear the stamp of 'classic' Boston." [29] The reviewer sharply attacked Harper & Brothers for their use of "old torture" woodcuts to illustrate a portion of Coffin's *Story of Liberty.*[30] More often, the reviewer merely mentioned the illustrations or their source. He declared Mrs. Molesworth's *The Cuckoo Clock* to be "worth buying, if only for Walter Crane's illustrations." [31] In other reviews he pointed out the various sources of illustrations; that some of the pictures, for example, in Coffin's *The Boys of '76* were from Lossing's *Field-Book of the Revolution,*[32] and that many in William M. Davis' *Nimrod of the Sea* had done prior service in *Harper's New Monthly Magazine.*[33] One comment that throws some light on a particular kind of illustrating is to be found in the review of Paul Cobden's *Good Luck* published by Lee & Shepard. Since, in the illustration on page 176, Christy, represented as a boy, was actually a girl, it is doubtful whether the illustrator read the book he was illustrating.[34]

A number of works of history and biography were reviewed. The review of William M. Thayer's *A Youth's History of the Rebellion,* with its strongly pro-Northern bias, reveals the bias of *The Independent.* The reviewer described the book in this manner.

> *This history is written in a thoroughly loyal, freedom-loving spirit, and the author does not lack in plain speaking when alluding to treason and slavery. The young people who read this story of the great rebellion, as told by Mr. Thayer, will gain a true idea of the spirit and purpose of Northern and Southern traitors.*[35]

The other reviews were different. Higginson's *Young Folks' History of the United States* was praised for its clarity, accuracy, and stylistic excellence.[36] It was so good that it should be substituted for the history text books used in the schools. Charlotte Yonge's *Young Folks' History of England* was given similarly high praise. The reviewer declared it to be one of the best histories of England for children ever written.[37]

Titles from both Eggleston's and Towle's biography series were reviewed. While Towle's *Voyages and Discoveries of Vasco da Gama* was by no means perfect, with some details over-emphasized, and others slighted, but judging by what it was, rather than by what it was not, it could still be highly recommended.[38] His *Marco Polo,* however, contained "vain and useless fiction." [39] Eggleston's *Brant and Red Jacket* was called an excellent book.[40]

Among other works of nonfiction *What Mr. Darwin Saw in his Voyage Round the World in the Ship "Beagle"* was reviewed in a largely descriptive review and recommended for young readers.[41] Champlin's *Young Folks' Cyclopaedia of Common Things* received a brief notice. The reviewer described Champlin's method and declared the book to represent a good idea well carried out.[42]

Other categories of books reviewed included two of Lanier's books, several of Scudder's "Bodley" books, Butterworth's *Zigzag Journeys in Europe* and Knox's *Adventures of Two Youths in a Journey to Japan and China.* Only the Butterworth and Knox reviews are of special interest. Butterworth's book impressed the reviewer as one well-equipped to teach history to a boy.[43] He gave to it the top position among the year's holiday books so far that season. He found Knox's book, on the other hand, to be "designed to be instructive and less interesting in proportion." [44]

The reviewer frequently compared one author to another, usually in connection with some lesser aspect of the work, rather than in the actual evaluation. He declared that Elijah Kellogg, for example, was as prolific as though "his name were Abbott." [45] With two different books, Leland's *Johnnykin and the Goblins*[46] and Elizabeth Tabor Stephenson's work *Pansie's Flour-Bin*[47] he pointed out a resemblance to *Alice's Adventures in Wonderland*. William Henry Giles Kingston, an exceedingly prolific English writer of books for boys, was called an "English Oliver Optic." [48]

One other reference, though not a comparison of one author to another, is highly amusing. Reviewing E. H. Knatchbull-Hugessen's *Queer Folk,* the reviewer reported that "some dolt" in Parliament had reproached the Honorable Mr. Knatchbull-Hugessen, M.P., with "frittering away his time in the composition of story-books for children," an ability the reviewer would have welcomed in one of our own Congressmen such as "the chairman of the House Committee on Education." [49]

With the works of some authors the reviewer felt little need to discuss the book, because the author's reputation would itself guarantee the quality. Charlotte Tucker was one such author. In his notice of her *Exiles in Babylon,* the reviewer declared that A.L.O.E. was too well known to need commendation.[50] Rebecca Clarke was given the same honor in the notice of *Miss Thistledown,* but here the reviewer quoted authority, referring to Higginson's praise of Miss Clarke in the *North American Review.*[51]

One other special review feature in *The Independent* was a column, "Children's Books," that appeared in the November 21, 1867, issue.[52] This column was prepared in the form of a little story, included a letter from Santa Claus, and was slightly longer than usual reviews. The reviews themselves were written in a simple style, obviously intended to arouse the interest of children.

To evaluate the contribution of *The Independent* to the reviewing of children's books is made difficult by the fact that the productions of the Sunday school presses loomed so large among the books reviewed. Few of these books were reviewed in secular periodicals. Certain facts are obvious. *The Independent* reviewed a very large number of books for children each year, indicating its concern with children's literature. Many of the reviews, however, amounted to mere notices, bringing the books to the attention of its subscribers, but providing little knowledge of the contents or style of the books. Nevertheless, enough books were reviewed in some detail to make it possible to say that the readers of the magazine would have had a fair notion of the quantity and quality of the children's books of the period.

Though *The Unitarian Review* is little known today, Mott ascribes to it much that is of interest.[53] The periodical, a monthly, was founded in Boston in 1874 with Charles Lowe as editor. Lowe, however, died after four numbers were published, and subsequent years saw a variety of editors, Henry Wilder Foote, John Hopkins Morison, Henry H. Barber, and James De Normandie, before the end of 1881. Though theology was the primary interest of this magazine, literature was its secondary interest. Through its association with the Ladies' Commission on Sunday-School Books of the American Unitarian Association it made a notable contribution to general criticism of children's books, if not to reviewing itself.

The actual reviews printed in *The Unitarian Review* were few, thirty-eight of them between 1874 and the end of 1881. One review was signed with the initials, M. P. L., while two reviews were provided by the Ladies' Commission. The Ladies' Commission reviews were printed chiefly to show the methods used in evaluating books for their lists. The reviews ranged from one- or two-sentence notices to a review of over 1,000 words of S. F. Smith's *Myths and Heroes,* one of the "test" reviews of the Ladies' Commission.

An early issue of the periodical included an article by a member of the Commission setting forth the standards by which it judged children's books.[54] The same issue contained reviews of two books to illustrate the method of the Commission. The review of Smith's *Myths and Heroes* amounted to a vigorous attack. The reviewer demonstrated that the book was bigoted, contained poor scholarship and, worst of all, had plagiarized Edward Clodd's *Childhood of the World.*[55] Ninety pages were taken directly from Clodd without a word of acknowledgment. A description of the book and liberal quotations were used to illustrate its faults and errors.

The second book reviewed was Abby Morton Diaz's *Lucy Maria.* The reviewer described its good points and its bad ones, explaining that it was rejected because of confusion of characters, a poor style and lack of refinement.[56] Again, description and quotation were used to illustrate both the virtues and faults of the work.

Religion was rarely mentioned in the reviews of *The Unitarian Review,* and only on rare occasions a moral. One group of books, though, described as having literary defects, was listed because the reviewer felt that many people would feel that the "intense religiousness" would adequately compensate for lack of other merits.[57] Robert Lowell's *Antony Brade,* though it had no "moral" in the narrower sense, had "high principles and Christian spirit." [58] The morals in Miss C. D. Bell's *Which Is My Likeness?* were described as not too prominent.[59] George M. Baker's

Running to Waste was a book with a good purpose, but was too sensational and not refined enough in style.[60] Passages were described to show the bad moral pictures presented.

Usually the reviews dealt with more literary matters. Philip Gilbert Hamerton's *Harry Blount,* though not wholly successful, had still "fresh and vigorously written chapters" on various aspects of English boys' school and vacation life.[61] The style of the Rev. John Hall's *Familiar Talks to Boys* won the reviewer's respect. It was sensible, manly, and direct, and avoided all slang.[62] The dialogue in Mrs. L. B. Monroe's *The Story of Our Country,* however, was objectionable, even though other features of the book were admirable.[63] The author's use of the dialogue form was not successful. The children's remarks were flat and too mature.

At least one book was judged unsuited to children. Louisa T. Cragin's (Ellis Gray) *Long Ago* was about children rather than for them.[64] N. S. Dodge's *A Grandfather's Stories About American History* was admirably suited to its purpose for children, since it was intended to "keep alive the sentiment of patriotism in another generation." [65] The reviewer reported using one book, Louise Chandler Moulton's *New Bed-Time Stories,* with children.[66] The children liked it, but the reviewer felt that the book was not sufficiently uplifting.

Very little attention was given to illustrations. The shadow pictures by Helen Maria Hind for Edward E. Hale's *Silhouettes and Songs* won the reviewer's praise.[67] J. W. Champney's illustrations for his wife's *In the Sky Garden* were very ordinary, though the book itself was recommended.[68]

Two topical references are of some interest. The reviewer called the attention of the reader to the part played by the Ku Klux Klan disturbances in the plot of Martha F. Finley's *Elsie's Motherhood.*[69] And in the review of Joel Chandler Harris' *Uncle Remus; His Songs and Sayings,* the reviewer said, "Happy race! says the writer, we fancy. Shall the alphabet and the ballot spoil their joy?" [70]

The reviews were few in *The Unitarian Review,* too few to have greatly influenced the reading of children in the post-Civil War period, and, except for the reviews contributed by the Ladies' Commission, were very brief. Yet, through the Ladies' Commission on Sunday-School Books and its work, there can be no doubt that it did have an influence. Its greatest contribution was in the encouragement given the Commission and in the forum it provided for the pronouncements of that body.

Father Isaac T. Hecker, a priest of the Community of Paulist Fathers, founded *The Catholic World* in April, 1965. Though the periodical began as an eclectic journal, its content was soon almost entirely original.[71] In October, 1865, "Eclectic" was dropped from the title. Mott describes the periodical as one with a Catholic point of view, but not a theological journal.[72] It had, he says, a "high standard in literary tone and editorial enterprise." An examination of the early volumes gives the reader the feeling that the editor was frequently on the defensive and frequently engaged in controversy. This is apparent, to some extent, even in the reviews of children's books.

Between 1865 and 1881, *The Catholic World* printed reviews and notices of 134 children's titles, from one to twenty each year. Most of the books were Catholic Sunday school library books from the presses of Peter F. Cunningham of Philadelphia, D. & J. Sadlier & Company of New York, publishers of "The Young Catholic's Library," Kelly, Piet & Company of Baltimore, Patrick O'Shea of New York, and The Catholic Publication Society of New York. Perhaps two-thirds of the books reviewed were Catholic children's books. Since almost none of these books were reviewed elsewhere, it is obvious that the magazine was performing a valuable service for parents and children of that faith, as well as for the Sunday schools.

Most of the reviews in *Catholic World* were very short, and included a brief description, a remark that a book was or was not well written, and a recommendation, though in a few reviews the treatment was a little more extended. Many of the volumes in "The Young Catholic's Library," and in O'Shea's "Illustrated Catholic Sunday-School Library" were discussed in group reviews. *The Catholic World* did not, by any means, automatically recommend them. *Count Leslie,* for example, was badly translated.[73] The reviewer pointed out a line in which *him* is used instead of *he*. The periodical, *Spare Hours,* for Catholic children, was criticized for its failure to credit sources.[74]

In a review of several volumes of "The Young Catholic's Library," the magazine's general attitude was revealed. Writers for children, the reviewer felt, put too much of the romantic and unreal in their books, creating in children "a feverish desire for romance" that was all too apt to lead to the reading of novels in later years.[75] "There is," he said, "enough in the realities of life to startle and fix the attention of any child if properly presented."

The longest reviews that appeared in *The Catholic World* were those of books which the reviewer felt were, because of their bias, unsuitable for Catholic children. *Hans Brinker,* otherwise an excellent book for children, could not be recommended because of the stories of the Inquisition included in it.[76] *Shawl-Straps* was condemned because of anti-Catholicism. The reviewer quoted six passages to show Miss Alcott's prejudice.

> *We can scarcely believe that this book is from the same pen as* Little Women, *and we think it would be far better, when one is only willing to see things through their ignorances and prejudices, not to attempt to make others see with their eyes.*[77]

The most violent feelings were aroused by Coffin's *Story of Liberty* which was criticized by other periodicals for the same faults. The reviewer said that the first two hundred pages consisted of a fierce attack on "the pope, the priests, and every institution of the Catholic Church." [78] The illustrations were equally bad. Though the reviewer's attack on Coffin's book may have been excessive, in this case there seem to have been solid reasons behind his objections.

Equally interesting was the review of William T. Adams' *Shamrock and Thistle; or Young America in Ireland and Scotland.* The reviewer admitted that the "style is somewhat inflated, and it has a general tone of boyish exaggeration throughout." [79] But whatever its faults, the reviewer approved Adams' book because of the "fairness exhibited by him in speaking of Ireland."

The reviewer of *The Catholic World* had little taste for fairy stories, even when he was forced to acknowledge that one was a good example of its type. *Alice's Adventures in Wonderland* was excellent, but the reviewer regretted that children did not read instead "some probable or possible adventures." [80] Jean Ingelow, he felt, was a good guide to fairy land in her *Mopsa, the Fairy,* but she still could not make fairy land "half so fair or interesting as our own every-day world." [81] Yet, he was not happy either with Jean Macé's manner of presenting morals in *Home Fairy Tales.* Here, the coating of sugar over the pill of the moral was so thin as to be unpalatable.[82]

Perhaps the most enthusiastic review was that of *Little Women,* which the reviewer declared was "a charming story, full of life, full of fun, full of human nature, and therefore full of interest." [83] He praised the tone of the book and the earnestness of the four March sisters, urging his readers to make their acquaintance. *Eight Cousins,* though recommended for its "many useful lessons" and its "charming freshness," did not evoke the same enthusiasm.[84] He particularly objected to the "spirit of self-assertion in the heroine," which he felt to be an all too prevalent fault of American girls.

Some notices show little evidence that the reviewer had actually read the book. Frequently, he recommended a book on the basis of the author's past record or his popularity. In the review of William T. Adams' *Bear and Forbear* he recommended it with the statement, "Oliver Optic's books are always great favorites with the young people. This is quite as interesting as the rest of the series." [85] But on the whole, allowing for the magazine's aversion to the fairy tale and its defensive attitude regarding all that touched the Catholic Church, the reviewing in *The Catholic World* was not too different from that in other periodicals of its type, unless it be that this periodical put a little more emphasis on contents than did most others.

This has not been a complete examination of the reviewing of children's books in religious periodicals, but it is sufficient to make possible certain generalizations concerning their reviewing practices. Though their standards were not too different from those of many other periodicals, a difference is found in their reviews chiefly because of the larger number of Sunday school library books which they included. Many of them reviewed large numbers of books, indicating those which they considered suitable for Sunday schools, thus performing a needed service. While they did review many of the trade publications and often reviewed them well, their unique contribution was in their criticism of the Sunday school books.

16

PEDAGOGICAL PERIODICALS

It would be expected that periodicals serving the professional educator would be a rich source of reviews of children's books. Such was not the case. Lamenting in May, 1872, that juvenile books were so little reviewed, Edward Everett Hale urged the editors of journals of education to assist in a severe scrutiny of children's books.[1] Only one periodical responded by reviewing any considerable number of juvenile books, and it is questionable that Hale's plea had any connection with the reviewing in that periodical, *The New England Journal of Education.* Two other periodicals reviewed a limited number of children's books, *The Ohio Educational Monthly* and the *American Educational Monthly and New York Teacher.* The outstanding educational periodical of the period, Henry Barnard's *American Journal of Education* never reviewed a children's book. Indeed, this scholarly periodical was more concerned with comparative education and with the problems of higher education, than with elementary education at home, so that it is not surprising to discover that children's books had no place in its pages.

THE OHIO EDUCATIONAL MONTHLY

Published at Columbus, *The Ohio Educational Monthly* was not a new periodical at the beginning of our period. In fact, the 1865 volume was volume VI in a new series and volume XIV in the original series. Only an occasional review of a children's book appeared in the periodical, and then with no special logic in the choice of the book reviewed. Included were a children's periodical, *Our Young Folks,* history and biography, Champlin's *Young Folks' Cyclopaedia of Common Things* and a Jules Verne romance. It can only be assumed that an occasional book that came to the reviewer's hands was reviewed along with the more common pedagogical fare. The review of *Our Young Folks* is characteristic of the few reviews, and is therefore quoted in full.

> *"Our Young Folks," tried by the two-fold test of interest and influence, is unquestionably the best juvenile magazine published in this country. It is readable without being trashy, sparkling without being delusive, and instructive without being dull and prosaic. It hits, most happily, the golden mean between childish insipidity and staid erudition, combining, in due proportion, the sparkle and vivacity of youth with the wisdom of age.*
>
> *Believing that a wide circulation of this magazine will do much to correct the too-prevalent habit of reading trashy and pernicious works, we most cordially commend it to all parents and friends of youth.*[2]

No special mention is made of any use the periodical might have in school, nor was such a possible use suggested for other works reviewed. In the review of John D. Champlin, Jr.'s *Young Folks' Cyclopaedia of Common Things,* the reviewer stressed the importance of students' learning to use reference books, but so did periodicals which were not concerned with formal education.[3]

Too few children's books were reviewed in the *Ohio Educational Monthly* to make possible valid conclusions. The only possible conclusion to be drawn is that the editors were little concerned with the educational possibilities of books other than text books for children.

AMERICAN EDUCATIONAL MONTHLY

The *American Educational Monthly,* published in New York City, was founded in 1864, and, according to its subtitle was "Devoted to Popular Instruction and Literature." A few books for children were reviewed in its pages, the reviews appearing in the regular review section with other books, but never more than one or two in a season. None of the outstanding books were reviewed, and those reviewed were provided with only brief notices of thirty to fifty words.

Most of the books reviewed were recommended for their high moral purpose or for their ability to instruct. *Our Young Folks,* for example, was "full of sound American principles." [4] Edmund Morris' *Farming for Boys,* a book written with the avowed purpose of encouraging boys to

205

stay on the farm instead of migrating to the cities, was praised for its good purpose, despite its use of bad grammar and objectionable jargon.[5] One review of two little known books, a "well-written temperance story," *The Kemptons,* by Mrs. H. K. Potwin and a "well written moral tale," *Captain Christie's Granddaughter,* by Mrs. Ruth Buck Lamb, were recommended for teachers' lists.[6] None of the other reviews contained anything of special interest or significance.

Like the reviews in the *Ohio Educational Monthly,* the reviews of juvenile literature in the *American Educational Monthly* were remarkable only for their scarcity. Though one review spoke of teachers' lists, the periodical did little to provide teachers with material for such lists.

THE NEW ENGLAND JOURNAL OF EDUCATION

Among educational periodicals, only *The New England Journal of Education* reviewed a considerable number of children's books. It is difficult to determine how influential this Boston periodical may have been, but certainly it was read outside New England, for in mid-year, 1881, it changed its name to *The Journal of Education, New England and National.* The magazine was founded in 1874, and only slowly began to review children's books. The journal reviewed three books in 1875, ten in 1876, twenty-four in 1880, and thirty-nine in 1881.

Nearly every type of children's book published was reviewed, but the reviews emphasized, for the most part, the educational value of the books. Many books were particularly recommended either to teachers, to teachers and parents, and, in one case, to teachers to recommend to parents.[7] With this emphasis on the educational value of children's books came an increased emphasis on the value of the book's content, rather than its literary value, and greater attention to its moral. In fact, very few of the reviews exhibit concern for strictly literary qualities, except, in a few cases, to indicate realism in characterization. The reviewer said that the characters in Kate Tannatt Woods' *Six Little Rebels* were "finely drawn, fresh and natural," [8] but such comments were infrequent.

More typical was the comment on Julia A. Eastman's *Striking for the Right,* that anyone who reads the book must end by being "a great deal wiser and better than the average of mortals." [9] Similarly, Daniel Wise's *Winwood Cliff; or Oscar, the Sailor's Son,* was "healthy in tone, and useful in showing to the young the contrasts of good and evil actions in their effect upon their characters." [10]

Several of the travelogue story books were reviewed, but with little attention to their method, and much attention to their content. Butterworth's *Zigzag Journeys in Europe* would provide instruction to the young at the same time it delighted them.[11] The reviewer judged this volume to be the most elegant and interesting children's book, "for the price," that had been produced in America. The educational possibilities of Thomas W. Knox's works were discussed in the review of his *Adventures of Two Youths in a Journey to Siam and Java.*[12] Edward Greéy's *Young Americans in Japan* was declared to be "undoubtedly the best book on Japan for young folks yet published," but no mention was made of the author's literary skill which other periodicals had praised.[13]

Several books of history for children were reviewed in *The New England Journal of Education,* including Butterworth's, Drake's, and Scudder's books on Boston, Butterworth's *Young Folks' History of America,* Brook's *French History for English Children,* and Champlin's *Young Folks' History of the War for the Union.* Here, dealing with a nearly factual type of book, the reviews differ less from those in literary periodicals except that they are, perhaps, somewhat less critical. The reviewer recognized Butterworth's *Young Folks' History of America* as little more than a reprint of Robert Mackenzie's 1870 work, but still he praised it as "brilliant, original, fresh, taking, and handsomely presented." [14] This was said despite the fact that the work had no mention of the founding of Massachusetts Colony, nor even of the city of Boston. However, the reviewer stated that he hoped Mr. Butterworth might someday prepare an original history of his country.

The review of John D. Champlin, Jr.'s *Young Folks' History of the War for the Union* was a better review, examining the author's qualifications, describing his method, and praising his style.[15] Of particular note is the fact that this periodical, as did all except *The Critic,* praised Champlin's objectivity.

The two reference books by John D. Champlin, Jr., his *Young Folks' Cyclopaedia of Common Things* and his *Young Folks' Cyclopaedia of Persons and Places* were both reviewed. When the first one appeared, the reviewer recommended it for every school and home, emphasizing the desirability of children learning the reference habit.[16] The second volume made available to the child the whole world of people and places "which are outside of ordinary school text-books." [17] The two together, the reviewer felt, provided an excellent nucleus for a child's library.

Most reviews stressed, as the review of Champlin's reference books did, the educational value of the book reviewed. *The Young Folks' Book of Poetry,* edited by Loomis J. Campbell, was "well adapted for reading aloud and for paraphrasing; as an aid in practical composition." [18] Forbes E. Winslow's *Children's Fairy Geography,* "a charming specimen of the 'sugar-coated educational pills'," was "as fascinating as fairy stories and much more useful." [19]

A notable exception to this educational approach was in the reviews of two volumes by Laura E. Richards. Her *Five Mice in a Mouse-Trap by the Man in the Moon* showed a "wonderful facility and adaptation to the demands of young children," and would make an ideal gift for a young child.[20] Her *Sketches and Scraps* was declared to be a charming book.[21]

In some cases, the highest praise given to a book was that its English was pure, free from slang. Such was the praise given to Mrs. Ewing's *Jan of the Windmill*.[22] William T. Adams' *Vine and Olive,* on the other hand, despite its quantities of useful information, contained far too much slang to meet with full approval.[23]

The New England Journal of Education did attempt to inform its readers of children's books which might be useful to them, and succeeded in reviewing a considerable number. The reviews were unquestionably weighted in the direction of defining the usefulness of the books in the instruction of the young. But, since pedagogy was the purpose of the periodical, this is to be expected. The magazine did review children's books, calling to the attention of teachers those that seemed worthy, and, through the teachers, recommending them to parents. Whatever the merits of the individual reviews, they did show the concern of the editors that children's books be critically examined.

CHILDREN'S PERIODICALS

One of the interesting phenomena of the period following the Civil War was the publication of a considerable number of magazines for the young, among them the best this country has produced. *Our Young Folks, The Riverside Magazine for Young People,* and *St. Nicholas,* were only the brightest stars among a galaxy. But most of them, however, shone brightly for a little time and then blinked out. Only *St. Nicholas,* of the postwar crop of children's periodicals, lived on to vie with the still older *Youth's Companion,* and finally to outlive it.

It would not be surprising to find that the children's magazines were a rich source of reviews and comment on children's books; yet, with a few notable exceptions, this was not the case. *Harper's Young People,* founded in 1879, for example, had no reviews at all, though it did carry advertisements for its publisher's juvenile books. Even *St. Nicholas,* which reviewed more books than any other children's magazine, reviewed far fewer books than many periodicals aimed at an adult reading public. *The Riverside Magazine,* frequently referred to as a pioneer in criticism of children's literature, did not attempt to review the current output of books as they appeared, but rather, attempted to criticize a wide range of newer and older books which the editor felt worthy of children's reading, producing, therefore, true literary criticism, rather than reviews. But there were enough reviews to repay examination.

Founded April 16, 1827, *The Youth's Companion* was a seasoned veteran when the Civil War ended, and was to outlive many a younger periodical, finally merging with *The American Boy* in 1929.[1] A weekly publication, with appeal to the entire family, the magazine achieved a circulation unequalled by any periodical for young or old during the nineteenth century.[2] The magazine set out to be both instructive and entertaining, and provided a varied diet for its readers—stories, poems, puzzles, riddles, games, and a weekly summary of important events—but only a few, intermittent reviews of books. Often, the few reviews were of books that had appeared in whole or in part in the pages of *The Youth's Companion.*

The reviews, or more exactly, book notices, were usually very short and were frequently merely descriptive. At times the books were merely listed under the heading, "Books Received," or "New Books." Actual reviews appeared under such headings as "A Word to Parents and Youths," or "Books Which I Should Read." The average length of the reviews was about forty words though some were considerably shorter, and a few somewhat longer.

The most notable book reviewed in *The Youth's Companion* was *Hans Brinker,* but it was reviewed, not when it first appeared, but when a new edition was published in 1874. Then, as though to make up for the years of neglect, the book was reviewed in two successive issues. The first review, or notice, was the briefer of the two.

Hans Brinker is a story of domestic life in Holland, by Mary Mapes Dodge, a lady whose literary work does credit to her profession, and who in this delightful volume presents an engaging picture of one of the most peculiar countries in the world.[3]

The comment on the author is typical and even more space is given to her in the second review.

The story of Hans Brinker and the "darling little girl who won the silver skates" is one that we can heartily commend, and without any mental reservation. As a picture of Holland, the "queerest country in all the world," it is as natural and breezy as the sea-winds that turn the old wind-mills on the hills. The plot holds the reader, be he young or old, and Mrs. Dodge's literary work does credit to her profession, in which she is an artist, and which she evidently loves.[4]

210

The admiration of *The Youth's Companion* for Mrs. Dodge was further revealed when it reviewed her *Rhymes and Jingles,* which the reviewer declared exceeded in quality the English nursery rhymes.[5]

One book by another famous author was reviewed—Horatio Alger, Jr.'s *Strive and Succeed* was high-toned, vigorous, and filled with real human nature, *The Youth's Companion* said.[6] The reviewer said it was "a very admirable specimen of the right kind of story-telling for boys."

Except for these special cases, the typical children's books of the period received no mention in *The Youth's Companion.* Though there can be no doubt the magazine was influential in the world of children's literature, its influence was exerted through the stories and serials it printed, rather than through the books it reviewed.

OUR YOUNG FOLKS

Even before the Civil War ended, this first of the post-war children's magazines had appeared. The first issue was published in January, 1865, under the joint editorship of Lucy Larcom, John Townsend Trowbridge, and Gail Hamilton, pseudonym of Mary Abigail Dodge. Miss Dodge, after a bitter battle with the publishers, Ticknor & Fields, which she made public in her *Battle of the Books,* soon departed from the staff. This periodical set a new standard in children's magazines, though it would later be surpassed by the *Riverside Magazine* and by *St. Nicholas.* The editors attracted a notable group of contributors and had the distinction of publishing both Thomas Bailey Aldrich's *Story of a Bad Boy* and Lucretia P. Hale's *Peterkin Papers.*

Occasional book reviews and notices appeared in the magazine, often in the special column, "Our Letter Box," and were written, where the authorship is identified, by Lucy Larcom. No reviews were printed in the magazine until 1869, but from 1869 on a few appeared each year until the magazine was sold to *Scribner's Monthly* and merged in *St. Nicholas* early in 1874. Only a few of the reviews were more than 50 words long, and many were notices of a single sentence. On one occasion Miss Larcom, listing ten books without comment, said merely that she had had time only to glance at the books.[7] On other occasions, it is obvious that Miss Larcom was reporting books that she had not read, nor even, in some cases, seen.

For the most part, the reviews in *Our Young Folks* seemed to be aimed at the adult, rather than the child reader. The review of Carové's *Story Without an End* is a fair example of a review that would appeal more to adults.

It . . . has taken us entirely captive. It is more a dream than a story, and the pictures are the blossoms of the dream. A dream-child appears in them, wandering on from page to page among real morning-glories and violets and hepaticas, between the stars of earth and the stars of heaven, and is last seen as a small, shrouded chrysalis, so light as not to bend the grass-blades where it hangs, under the smile of the blue, eternal skies.

This lovely picture-book is one of the things that almost make us wish ourselves children again. Not because we should have been likely to own it, had it been written or translated then,—for Santa Claus was hardly acclimated in cold New England during our childhood, and, had he been, he would have brought no book so costly as this down our humble, old-fashioned chimney,—but because the story haunts us like a memory that slips away and returns again in glimpses and flashes. It is the poem that every imaginative child's heart sings to itself,—the vision that flits before every newly opening life, seen more or less dimly by each and by all. If not fully understood, (and what grown-up child understands his own life?) it cannot fail to bring beautiful dreams: and that is much, in a world where there are so many realities which are not beautiful.[8]

She writes of children rather than for them.

Her review of *The Story of a Bad Boy,* just before its publication in book form, however, is more clearly written for child readers.

We are almost sorry to speak of the publication of the "Story of a Bad Boy" in book form because it is, in fact, writing that bright little fellow's obituary, so far as our magazine is concerned. But Tom Bailey is only to take a new lease on life. He is to be dressed up new, in whatever style those who send for him may desire, and go a-visiting all the Young Folks who want to see him, to stay until his clothing, not his welcome, is worn out. This last could scarcely happen anywhere, for Tom Bailey is the best story-teller of all the boys we know,—excepting, perhaps, Tom Brown, of Rugby. He is both witty and well behaved,—two qualities not always found together; and we know that his story will read better as a whole than in fragments, as we have had to offer it to our readers.[9]

That this is not truly a review is obvious. The writer here assumes that her readers are already familiar with the book she is discussing, so that there is no need to describe or analyze. A fairer example of the best reviewing in *Our Young Folks* is the review of Jules Verne's *Twenty Thousand Leagues Under the Sea,* in which Miss Larcom described the action of the book, and then gave an evaluation, ranking it as "one of the most unique and entertaining romances of the sea since Robinson Crusoe." [10]

Nearly the same conclusion must be drawn concerning the reviewing in *Our Young Folks* as was drawn for the *Youth's Companion*. So few books were actually reviewed that the magazine, as far as reviewing is concerned, could have had little influence. Hardly more than a dozen books were given more than a mere listing.

OLIVER OPTIC'S MAGAZINE

In some ways the strangest children's magazine published in America was *Oliver Optic's Magazine*. It was published weekly in Boston by the house of Lee & Shepard, beginning January 5, 1867, under the editorship of William T. Adams. Though the magazine did carry serials by other Lee & Shepard authors, such as Elijah Kellogg, the bulk of the writing was done by Adams himself, under his pseudonym, Oliver Optic. Each semi-annual volume carried two of his stories for boys, some special columns, and plates from the newest Lee & Shepard books, chiefly by Optic. Beginning with the January, 1871, issue, the magazine became a monthly.

But what made the periodical unique among American children's magazines were its editorial columns. Mr. Adams was frequently engaged in controversy with his critics and the critics of his publishers. His editorial columns became his forum for scathing attacks on everyone who had the temerity to question the merit of his books for boys. Louisa May Alcott, Emily Huntington Miller, and Edward Eggleston were among those who felt his wrath.

About ten books were reviewed in *Oliver Optic's Magazine* between 1867 and its discontinuance following Lee & Shepard's bankruptcy in 1875. Most of the books reviewed were Lee & Shepard publications, though a few were from other Boston publishing houses, but no book published outside Boston was ever reviewed in it. Among the books reviewed was *Oliver Optic's Almanac for Our Boys and Girls* which was recommended as an "attractive, entertaining, and useful" book.[11]

A typical review from the magazine might be the one of Mary N. Prescott's *Matt's Follies,* which is here quoted in its entirety.

> *This is one of the pleasantest books for the younger readers that we have seen for a long time. The stories are lively and humorous, and full of interest. There is nothing tame or prosaic about them, and they will exactly suit the wide-awake boys or girls for whom they were written. Miss Prescott is too well known to our readers to need any*

endorsement from us; and we are sure our young friends will have a good time over the book.[12]

Adams was obviously reviewing a book by one of his own contributors and took much the same attitude Lucy Larcom had taken concerning Aldrich's *The Story of a Bad Boy,* that since the readers of the magazine knew the author or the book, little need be said.

The review of John T. Trowbridge's *Fast Friends* is especially interesting because of the presence of a note of bitterness. Adams was, by this time, under fairly steady attack because of the "sensational" elements in his books for boys. *Fast Friends,* Adams said, "is a very good story . . . and we find no 'wicked sensationalism' in it, to demoralize boys, unless we except the opportune recovery of the hero's money." [13] But even this is more a contribution to the understanding of Mr. Adams than to the record of the reviewing of children's books.

So few reviews actually appeared, and those few limited to the books of so few Boston publishers, that *Oliver Optic's Magazine* can hardly be considered a reviewing periodical. Though Mr. Adams' editorials and prolific writings indicate his concern with books for the young, this concern was not reflected in extensive reviewing in his periodical.

ST. NICHOLAS

In the July, 1873, issue of *Scribner's Monthly,* an unsigned article "Children's Magazines," was printed. In this article Mary Mapes Dodge, set forth the policy that was to govern the editing of *St. Nicholas,* the first issue of which would appear in November of the same year. Basically, her philosophy was that "a child's magazine is its pleasure ground." [14] This dictum, and the skill of Mrs. Dodge and her associate editor, Frank R. Stockton, made *St. Nicholas* the best of all children's magazines.

Mrs. Dodge set forth her policy concerning reviewing of books in the first issue of the periodical. In an article entitled "Books for Boys and Girls" she said "we shall try now and then to point out as they appear, the new books that are worthy of a boy's or girl's attention." [15] Donald G. Mitchell, she announced, would write articles on older books while "we" would review the newer ones.

Though there was no consistency from year to year in the number of books reviewed or noticed, 124 new books were discussed in the nine years from 1873 through 1881, most often under the heading, "Books Received." Though the reviews were not great in number, Mrs. Dodge disarmed criticism on this score by her remark that "it would be better to read no new books than to read too many of them." [16] The number of books reviewed in a single year ranged from twenty-seven in 1876 to none in 1881.

Works by such notable authors as Louisa May Alcott, Susan Coolidge, Jules Verne, Mrs. Ewing, and Mrs. Molesworth were reviewed, as well as books by the popular Horatio Alger, Jr., and William T. Adams. Several adult books were reviewed and recommended to older boys and girls, including anthologies by Clarence Stedman and John Greenleaf Whittier. A considerable number of the books reviewed had appeared originally in the pages of *St. Nicholas* itself. But, probably, in part because of Mrs. Dodge's selective policy, many of the most common types of children's books were not reviewed. Only one of the travelogue story books, unless one includes the early "Bodley" books of Horace E. Scudder in this classification, was reviewed, Hezekiah Butterworth's *Zigzag Journeys in Europe*.[17] Only M. H. Towry's *Spenser for Children,* of the many rewritten or edited classics was reviewed.[18] In fact, with only a few exceptions, all the books reviewed were either fiction or poetry.

The reviews were clearly aimed at the young readers of the magazine, written in language they could understand and intended to arouse their interest in reading the books. The review of Susan Coolidge's *Nine Little Goslings* provides an excellent picture of the style of these reviews.

> *A delightful book of stories and pictures. The first chapter tells how Johnny, who is not a boy, had a very narrow escape from something which was not an accident; the next and next, up to the ninth and last, give each an interesting history of events which seem as if they must have happened somewhere; while one and all are most originally and pleasantly told in the service of Mother Goose's melodies. We cordially advise all of our young friends of eight to eighty years to read this book.*[19]

The reviews of those books originally published in *St. Nicholas* received comments similar to the remarks of Lucy Larcom on *The Story of a Bad Boy* in *Our Young Folks*. Louisa May Alcott's *Eight Cousins* was published serially in *St. Nicholas* in 1875 before it was issued in book form for the Christmas trade the same year. Mrs. Dodge reviewed it and Trowbridge's *The Young Surveyor* in the following January issue.

> *EIGHT COUSINS, now published in book form by Roberts Bros., Boston, met with such a cordial reception in ST. NICHOLAS, that it must become one of Miss Alcott's most popular books. Everywhere, the children, the girls especially, take the greatest interest in Rose. Each of her seven cousins has his admirers, to be sure, and there are people who almost worship Uncle Alec; but Rose is the queen of the*

story. We think, too, that "Jo" of "Little Women" will have a power-
ful rival in this delightful young girl, who is as pretty as she is good,
and who is so very good. These stories of Mr. Trowbridge and Miss
Alcott have gone side by side through ST. NICHOLAS, and now that
they have separated and passed out into the wide world, we wish them
the best of good fortune.[20]

In the review of Bayard Taylor's *Boys of Other Countries,* Mrs. Dodge
regretted that only one of the tales in it had appeared in *St. Nicholas.*[21]

Most of the reviews consisted largely of descriptions of the books'
contents, with sometimes a sentence indicating approval, though every
book reviewed was one to be recommended. On one occasion Mrs. Dodge
compared one book with another, though not in detail. Jane G. Austin's
Moonfolk, she said, would have been "very interesting and original if
Alice in Wonderland had never been written." [22] As it was, Miss Austin's
book was largely a repetition of the same kind of things that were already familiar.

The factual books reviewed were largely books that would be useful
in hobbies, such as J. Walter Scott's *The International Postage-Stamp
Album* and Maurice Thompson's *The Witchery of Archery.* However,
John D. Champlin, Jr.'s *Young Folks' Cyclopaedia of Common Things*
was reviewed. This dealt more with a description of what an encyclopedia is and can be used for, than with the book itself.[23]

Though Mrs. Dodge remarked on occasion that engravings were attractive, she did not attempt to analyze illustrations in detail. She called
the illustrations in Horace E. Scudder's *Doings of the Bodley Family in
Town and Country* charming, and the cover quaint.[24] Of H. S. and W. O.
Perkins' *The Shining River,* she made the following remark.

We wonder anew, at sight of this, why, with all due regard to econ-
omy, the covers of the Sunday-school song-books cannot be made just
a little less ugly and uninviting.[25]

But this was not a book intended for the individual child's perusal.

The *St. Nicholas* reviews were so different from those appearing in
adult periodicals that it is difficult to compare them. While the adult
periodicals considered literary merit, interest to children, and, often, the
moral values of a book, this children's periodical wrote to inspire the
child to read. The judgment exercised lay in the selection of a book for
notice, rather than in any comment made in the review. Mrs. Dodge
would not, surely, have said that she was reviewing all the books that
were good for children. But what her choice did imply was that every
book she reviewed was good for children. Widely circulated as it was, *St.*

216

Nicholas must have greatly increased the interest of children in those books about which Mrs. Dodge wrote.

THE RIVERSIDE MAGAZINE FOR YOUNG PEOPLE

Horace E. Scudder, in 1867, launched *The Riverside Magazine for Young People,* one of the finest American children's periodicals. The quality of the magazine is revealed by an examination of even a partial list of the contributors, which included Jacob Abbott, Frank R. Stockton and Sarah Orne Jewett. Some of Andersen's tales made their first American appearance in the pages of the *The Riverside Magazine.*[26]

In the first issue Scudder began a column, "Books for Young People," in which he set forth, in part at least, the qualities he looked for in books for children. The column was not to be merely a department for bringing the new books to the attention of his young readers. On the contrary, he set out to write a column for the parents, who were beset with the gravest problems when they were forced to select, from the host of books available, those which they could be sure were suitable for their children. He would not, he said, consider only those books published in the last twenty years or so, nor just those written expressly for children, but all books, either old or new, that were "worth giving to a child." [27] Up to this time, he felt, very little attention had been given to children's books, and their serious consideration and criticism was overdue.

> *A literature is forming which is destined to act powerfully on general letters; hitherto it had been little disturbed by critics, but the time must soon come, if it has not already come, when students of literature must consider the character and tendency of* Children's Letters; *when all who have at heart the best interest of the Kingdom of Letters must look sharply to this Principality.*[28]

With this comment he set out to give books for children the kind of critical consideration he felt they deserved.

In subsequent columns Scudder discussed the value of Shakespeare's plays as literature for children's reading, biography, poetry, the novels of Sir Walter Scott, the Arabian Nights, and the works of Bjornson, none of them strictly children's books, but books from which children might profit. He did not discuss particular editions in any of these columns. The actual reviews divided neatly into groups; poetry and songs for young children, vacation reading for children, stories of family life, an 1868 survey of a few children's books, and an 1869 survey.

In the two columns dealing with poetry and songs for young children, Scudder discussed eight titles, comparing and contrasting them, and pointing out the special virtues and faults of each. He felt that Mrs. Silsbee's *Willie Winkie's Nursery Songs of Scotland,* published by Ticknor & Fields, was the best book of nursery-age songs available.[29] It achieved its effects through "a quick succession of little pictures that hold the mind a moment, and release it only to show another." M. O. Ward's *Songs for the Little Ones at Home,* published by the American Tract Society, was too didactic.[30] *Hymns for Mothers and Children* was written too much for mothers and not enough for children.[31] The work contained too many poems that were "merely pretty and on the general subject of children, and . . . plainly meant in many cases for mothers after the children had gone to bed or to school." [32] Other collections had other faults. None of them was entirely satisfactory.

Selecting books for summer vacation reading was a task Scudder found difficult. Besides a book of games for rainy days, the chief need was for nature books to answer the child's questions. The only book of this type he could recommend heartily was Dr. Worthington Hooker's *The Child's Book of Nature,* which began with simple facts and progressed to more complex ones.[33] He felt that the book was educational, but in no way pedantic, and with no danger of "weighing down of the child's mind with disconnected facts." The only other books he could even mildly recommend were *A First Lesson in Natural History,* by Actea, and two books by J. G. Wood, *Common Objects in the Woods* and *By the Seashore.* But the latter two were English books to be used with caution since they might be describing something quite different, but with the same name.[34]

The chief difficulty with family life stories, in which children were portrayed in their day-to-day existence, was that too often they were presented from an adult point of view. Since so many books of this type suffered from this fault, Scudder could find only two to recommend, Mary Howitt's *The Children's Year,* and Miss Catherine Sinclair's *Holiday House.*[35] The two books were very different, but both had the child's point of view.

In a group of reviews of recent publications in 1868, Scudder found five titles which he especially recommended, *Gertie and May,* Oscar Pletsch's picture books, Harriet Beecher Stowe's *Queer Little People,* Jean Macé's *Home Fairy Tales,* and Helen C. Weeks' *Grandpa's House.*[36] Pletsch was recommended for his frankness, his conscientiousness, and his humor, *Gertie and May* for the grace of its style and the refinement of its sentiments. *Grandpa's House* was merry and had abundant incident and "insight into the characteristic human nature of children." Though Scudder felt some distrust of all books of fairy stories, because the authors did not really believe in what they wrote, he found Macé's book to be made up of clever stories filled with "homely virtue."

The second group of recent publications contained four titles, two of which had appeared in part in *The Riverside Magazine,* Helen C. Weeks' *The Ainslee Stories,* and Elizabeth Prentiss' *Little Lou's Sayings and Doings.*[37] The Rev. Elijah Kellogg's *Lion Ben of Elm Island* was a mixture of good and bad. Individual sections were excellent, but the books suffered from poor connecting sections linking the parts together. Its greatest virtues lay in its "rugged honesty," "scorn at meanness," and "indignation at frivolity." The fourth title was William Barnes' *Rural Poems,* which was "honest and natural" in sentiment and at the same time picturesque.

After the April, 1867, issue, gaps, ever widening, began to appear between the "Books for Young People" as the pressure of many contributions to go into limited space began to crowd out and to postpone Scudder's column. By the time the magazine was sold to *Scribner's Monthly* in 1870, the column had all but ceased to exist. Scudder's plan for his column was ambitious, but the promise of it was only partly fulfilled. The reviews he published were good, but they were all too few. That fact, coupled with the briefness of the life of *The Riverside Magazine,* limited the influence Scudder had through this medium, though his influence was most certainly felt elsewhere in the world of children's books. The conclusion must be drawn, taken all in all, that the contribution of children's magazines to the reviewing of children's books was minor compared to that of several important adult periodicals.

18

BOOK TRADE PERIODICALS
AND A SCIENTIFIC
PERIODICAL

When the first issue of the periodical that was to be called, in its second year, *The Publishers' Weekly,* appeared it announced on its title page that it included the *American Literary Gazette and Publishers' Circular,* which had been established in 1852. *The Publishers' and Stationers' Weekly Trade Circular,* together with its predecessor, provided service to the book trade rather than to the general public. Both periodicals printed brief book reviews and notices, largely descriptive, but with some critical comments. They provided the richest source of information on the development of publishing and the book trade in the United States, for they were concerned not merely with keeping the members of the trade informed, but also with providing a kind of conscience to it. Children's books and trends in children's literature were covered along with all other aspects of the book world.

AMERICAN LITERARY GAZETTE
AND PUBLISHERS' CIRCULAR

The *American Literary Gazette* was published in Philadelphia by George W. Childs. Each semimonthly issue contained announcements of new books, articles, often very brief, concerning new developments in the book trade, statistics of the trade, and a small section of book notices and reviews. The "Book Notices" section was normally divided into groups, usually by subject, though frequently there was a section headed "Juveniles," in which one or several children's books were noticed.

220

Some of the books were given brief reviews, though a larger number were merely listed under the names of their publishers. A majority of the brief reviews were from twenty to forty words in length, though an occasional one was longer. One or two examples will provide an adequate picture of the style and method used in the average brief notice. The following is a notice of Daniel C. Eddy's *Walter's Tour in the East,* published by Sheldon & Company of New York.

> *This is a series deservedly popular for it mingles instruction with entertainment. It will close with the next volume, which will conduct the young reader to Athens.*[1]

Other reviews attempted to indicate the style of the writing or to give some notion of the content. The following review of Warren Ives Bradley's *Jack Arcombe; the Story of a Waif,* published by Andrew F. Graves of Boston, is an example.

> *The story has plenty of incident without much episodical "preaching" and the style of writing is graphic and spirited.*[2]

Only when the reviewer felt the book was of unusual significance, or when it touched on a subject he felt to be of great importance, was more space devoted to a work.

One such topic was the treatment of the Civil War in children's books. When Horatio Alger, Jr.'s *Frank's Campaign; or, What Boys Can Do on the Farm for the Camp* was reissued in early 1865, with the war still in progress, the notice was favorable.[3] The reviewer described the work in one sentence, and then commented that the author was careful to provide authentic pictures of camp life. J. R. Gilmore's (Edmund Kirke) *Patriot Boys and Prison Pictures,* near the end of 1865, brought a slightly weary response, the reviewer saying that "Mr. Kirke, in this volume endeavors to interest boys in war sketches, but we fear that sort of material is well nigh exhaustion." [4] The review of Charles Carleton Coffin's *Winning His Way,* in the latter half of which the hero is a soldier in the war, was merely descriptive.[5] But the reviewer's tone changed sharply in a review of the final volume of William M. Thayer's *A Youth's History of the Rebellion.*

> *The "Youth's History" consists of four volumes, of which this is the concluding one. We trust this sort of book will now come to an end. War is bad enough at best, but to have it served up to us in a perverted partisan story-telling and sensational style, and thrust into our faces in*

*the nursery and at the fireside, all for the good of small writers, specu-
lating publishers, and insidious propagandists, is adding to it an additional and more protracted terror.*[6]

In a review of *Frank's Search for Sea Shells,* by Helen F. Parker, the
reviewer found new cause for annoyance.

*We would call attention particularly to the "Search for Sea Shells,"
which will be found a pleasant introduction to the department of natural history to which it relates, though we do not see the good taste of
dragging slavery, the North and the South, and that sort of thing, into
an introduction to conchology.*[7]

With the anonymously published *Patriotism at Home* the reviewer's patience was exhausted.

*The seemingly interminable series of juveniles about the war and
politics, is protracted in this volume. This sort of literary capital is
nearly exhausted, and we hope soon to see it come to an end utterly.*[8]

Exhausted or not, the reviewer did not comment again on a book of this
type.

A few prominent authors received somewhat longer than usual reviews. *Hans Brinker* was not one of them, though it did receive a brief
favorable notice.[9] *Little Women* received even briefer treatment.[10] *An
Old-Fashioned Girl,* however, received a review nearly twice as long as
usual, though it was almost entirely descriptive.[11] The review of *Little
Men* was longer still, though the bulk of it was devoted to an explanation
of the workings of the British copyright law, of which Miss Alcott was
taking advantage.

*Miss Alcott has taken advantage of the law by which American
citizens may secure copyright for their books, both in America and
throughout the British dominions, by residing on British soil when the
book is simultaneously published in both countries. This also has the
further advantage of making the book copyright throughout Europe,
as nearly every country has an international copyright treaty with England. Curiously enough, this law only operates one way, and British
subjects cannot by any arrangement secure copyright in England and
America.*[12]

Aldrich's *The Story of a Bad Boy* was given a brief, but enthusiastic

222

notice.[13] The reviewer called it a capital book, which had humor and spirit, and would be sure to be popular with boys.

Even in such brief notices the reviewer revealed that he was fully aware of what was appealing to children. His notice of Nellie Eyster's *Sunny Hours* is almost a listing of such appealing elements.

> *It is written in a style perfectly intelligible to them; the narrative is occupied with incidents, and free from long passages of sermonizing. It is what it purports to be—a real picture of child life.*[14]

The review of Harriet B. McKeever's *Rupert Lawrence* lists another element, the presence of which was distasteful to boys—sentimentality.[15]

Two other reviews are worth mentioning for their topical interest. *Bread Winners,* by "A Lady of Boston," was an anti-women's-suffrage story, expressing an attitude with which the reviewer heartily agreed. "The wild ravings and absurd theories of the female advocates of the ballot-box are held up to ridicule," he reported with some degree of satisfaction.[16] The other review contained a verbal thrust at the supposed self-satisfaction of the people of Boston. Reviewing Madame J. Michelet's *The Story of My Childhood,* the reviewer poked fun at Mary Frazier Curtis' introduction to the work.

> *The translator thinks this is one of the sweetest and strangest pictures of child life "that has ever been offered to New England readers." The self-complacency of the allusion to New England readers exclusively, is like that of the Boston editor who spoke of a prayer made at a public celebration in that city as one of the most admirable that had ever been offered to a Boston audience.*[17]

It is hardly possible to compare the reviewing of this periodical with reviewing in periodicals intended for the general public. Though many books were discussed, and many more listed, the reviews were so brief that it is at least open to question whether they can properly be classified as reviews. Brief as they were, they indicate that this organ of the book trade was alive to the trends of its age in the reviewing of children's books. Like the literary and other magazines that reviewed children's books, the *American Literary Gazette* recognized that the books that would be most acceptable had some pretension to merit, and appeal to children.

223

When *Publishers' Weekly* began publication in January, 1872, as *The Publishers' and Stationers' Weekly Trade Circular,* it announced that in it was incorporated the older *American Literary Gazette and Publishers' Circular.* Issued from New York, it was edited and published by Frederick Leypoldt.

Nearly every issue included a "Books Received" or "Advance Book Notes" section, in which children's books were regularly included, sometimes merely listed, but at other times reviewed in brief notices ranging from a half-dozen to over a hundred words. Most of the notices consisted of fewer than 50 words, and with exceedingly few exceptions, were laudatory. Each year, in a special Christmas number, the "Juvenile Books of the Year" were listed, and an annual review of children's books arranged alphabetically by publisher provided. These were not in any sense book reviews, however, for often several titles were included in a single sentence. In 1879, the book notices were dropped, although the Christmas number included a number of pages, with one book per page, in which children's books were described and illustrations from the books reproduced. These notices are difficult to classify. The notes are almost exclusively descriptive and entirely laudatory. To the twentieth-century observer, they have more the appearance of advertisements than book reviews.

An examination of the notices that appeared in "Books Received" soon makes it obvious that the *Publishers' Weekly* considered its function to be that of informing the booksellers about the content and general tone of books, rather than criticism that would lead to any great degree of discrimination. Not that the editor did not recognize that many books of little merit were published, for in an editorial he pointed out the poor quality of many juvenile books.[18] It would seem, rather, that he selected for notices only from among those that could be recommended. The only unfavorable review, and that only mildly so, was the review of Roth's translation of Jules Verne's *Off On a Comet,* published by Claxton, Remsen, & Haffelfinger of Philadelphia. Roth, the reviewer said, had altered the book in translating it in order to make it the kind of book that would "instruct rather than amuse" the children, and in doing so changed a wild extravaganza into "an amusing textbook." [19]

More of the reviews were like that of Virginia W. Johnson's *The Catskill Fairies.* After a description of the action, the reviewer continued with this commendation:

The pretty conceits of the stories, the bright way in which they are told, and their odd humor and quaint mixing of fact and fancy, make the volume one of the loveliest specimens of a child's book one could imagine.[20]

Repeatedly, books were declared to be "one of the most charming books yet written for the young," [21] a book unequalled by "anything in the juvenile line published in a long time," [22] or "one of the best juveniles out." [23] The three books about which these remarks were made were all reviewed between October and December, 1874.

The reviews in *Publishers' Weekly* exhibited many of the same characteristics found in other periodicals. In many reviews those elements which appeal to children were indicated. John T. Trowbridge's *Doing His Best* was "full of incidents and clever conversations, and the interest . . . maintained to the end." [24] Though pointing out the healthful influence a book might have, the reviewer was careful to underscore the fact that the moral of the book would not impede the interest of children. The morals in Isabella F. Mayo's (Edward Garrett) *The Magic Flower-Pot, and Other Stories* were "so delightfully hidden in the charming style of the author" that the children would be almost unaware they were being instructed.[25] Truth to life was praised. *Nix's Offering*, by Mary H. Henry (Howe Benning), even though a religious book, had a believable heroine and a "natural plot." [26]

Several of the outstanding authors' books received notices. Two of the many editions of *Hans Brinker* were reviewed. *Eight Cousins, Under the Lilacs,* and one volume of *Aunt Jo's Scrap Bag* were given brief notices, recommending them. Jules Verne's works were consistently praised.

Illustrations were frequently mentioned, though not analyzed in detail. Typical of the comments on illustrations is this sentence from a review of *Hans Brinker*. "It contains at least sixty original illustrations, and is very beautifully printed on tinted paper, and is in a most gorgeous binding." [27] A very detailed description was given of the binding of Horace E. Scudder's *Bodleys Telling Stories*.

The greatest novelty is the binding, which is a new departure altogether, nothing like it having hitherto been attempted. It is fancy boards, Japanese in character, but so eccentric in design that it is almost impossible to describe it. On the outside of the two covers the design extends diagonally across the back from the upper right hand corner to the lower left, one half being a pale gray ground with light blue figures upon it, with the firm's monogram in gold, red, black, and blue on the front cover; the other half, a dead black, bears the title in front, in odd-looking red letters, while the back cover is adorned with gold stars, a young moon, and some striking red lines which might be forked lightning. The linings are even more elaborate than the exte-

225

rior. Light blue is the dominant color here, the illuminations being in scarlet, gold, and black, the design extending across the lining of the cover and its accompanying leaf. Nothing so novel, pretty, and attractive, and so elaborate and artistic, has been shown before in the binding line. All the mechanical parts of the book are of the finest workmanship.[28]

The reviews and notices in *Publishers' Weekly* do not make a contribution to the reviewing of children's books in the same sense that those of periodicals intended for the general public do. As far as their effect is concerned, though, the impact may well have been even greater, for *Publishers' Weekly* had its greatest influence with the booksellers, whose stock must have been affected to no small degree by the notices in this trade journal. Though the reviews were not critical for the most part, the trade would have turned more to the books noticed than to those merely listed. The listings were extensive. In fact, with the annual summaries of children's books, *Publishers' Weekly* provides the most nearly complete record of children's books published in the period.

THE POPULAR SCIENCE MONTHLY

The American public's interest in science immediately after the war helped in the creation of *The Popular Science Monthly* in 1872.[29] Edward Livingston Youmans was the editor from 1872 to 1877, and joint editor, with William J. Youmans, from 1877 to 1887. Mott gives to Youmans, himself, part of the credit for the great interest in science.[30] The New York firm of D. Appleton & Company was the publisher.

The periodical carried a book review section, chiefly, though not exclusively, devoted to the review of works in science. Occasional reviews of children's books were included. Most of the children's books were in science, also, but a few titles dealing with other subjects were included. No works of fiction were reviewed. Ten books for children were reviewed between 1872 and 1881, the reviews ranging in length from about 50 words to over 1,000, though most of them were one hundred or fewer. The longest, a review of Arabella B. Buckley's *Life and Her Children,* was actually quoted from the English periodical, *Nature.*[31]

The review of Edward Clodd's *Childhood of the World* provides an example of the method of reviewing.

It is written in attractive style and sure to gratify the young folk. The author contrives to convey a very large amount of information in very small space and in very simple language; he can simplify without debasing and can instruct the young without ever resorting to un-

worthy tricks or making drafts on their credulity, which maturer years would lead them to discount.[32]

The reviewer emphasized the style of the author, and his ability to convey complex meanings in a satisfactorily simple way.

Each review was a favorable one, but many science books for children were, of course, ignored. Presumably, the periodical only brought to the attention of the reader a few unusual books. Its contribution cannot be considered of importance in the reviewing of children's books. It is an interesting contribution, however, in that it reveals the attention given, even in a highly specialized field, to the reading of the young.

19

REVIEWING OF SELECTED BOOKS

Though the extensiveness of the reviewing of children's books from 1865 to 1881 has been illustrated in the preceding chapters, it is possible to provide further insight into this reviewing by examining the reviews of selected books of the period, drawing together all the reviews so that differences and similarities can be easily seen. For this purpose, a number of books widely known, and still widely read have been selected.

The books selected were, for the most part, given widespread acclaim at the time of first publication and have remained a part of the reading of children through subsequent generations. They are discussed here in the same chronological order in which the first reviews of them appeared. In a few cases this differs from the actual order of composition and publication. Included are Mary Mapes Dodge's *Hans Brinker; or, The Silver Skates*, Lewis Carroll's *Alice's Adventures in Wonderland* and *Through the Looking-Glass*, Louisa May Alcott's *Little Women*, Thomas Bailey Aldrich's *The Story of a Bad Boy*, and Samuel Langhorne Clemens' *The Adventures of Tom Sawyer* and *The Prince and the Pauper*. Several of them represented new types of children's books which might well have put the reviewers to the test, and might indicate better than some others, the actual quality of the reviewing.

THE GENESIS OF A CLASSIC: HANS BRINKER

Mary Mapes Dodge's classic, *Hans Brinker; or, The Silver Skates,* received more reviews than any other children's book published between 1865 and 1881. That it received twenty-two separate reviews was in part due to the fact that it was published repeatedly in new editions, but the republication was, in itself, testimony to the popularity of the book and to the high regard in which it was held. Even the first edition received six reviews, far more than most books received in 1866. This was the more surprising because the book was published by a relatively obscure publisher, James O'Kane, in an edition which was not nearly so attractive as the tale told by the author. Subsequent editions were published by Scribner, Armstrong & Company, and by Charles Scribner's Sons.

The six reviews of the first edition of *Hans Brinker* differed greatly in length, ranging from thirty-five words to over a thousand. The briefest notice appeared in *Harper's New Monthly Magazine*.

Hans Brinker; or, the Silver Skates, *by Mary E. Dodge, is a pleasant story, wrought out in all its details with the minuteness of a Dutch painting, of life in Holland in the olden time.*[1]

Though containing a word or two of praise, this review is largely a brief description of the subject of the book. Judgments were passed, however, in both the word "pleasant" and in the phrase "with the minuteness of a Dutch painting."

The notice in the *American Literary Gazette* was also brief and similar in nature to the review in *Harper's*.

Such juveniles as these are instructive as well as entertaining. In the form of a domestic tale, we are furnished here with a vivid picture of Holland, its resources, and the every-day life of its inhabitants.[2]

This review is more a descriptive note, and less a critical annotation.

With the *Nation* we find an actual review, though a brief one, of slightly more than 150 words.

Though a little late for the holidays, this boys' and girls' book is appropriate to the season, and yet quite independent of it. To be sure the plot is woven about a skating match, and there is a grand tour on skates undertaken by a band of clever Dutch youngsters. But this is really incidental to most agreeable descriptions of Amsterdam, Haarlem, and Leyden, and the Hague; to scraps of Dutch history; to pictures of the general scenery, position, popular life, and manners of Holland; and to the instructive development of character in the hero and heroine; just as good reading, every bit, for midsummer as for midwinter. The authoress has shown in her former works for the young a very rare ability to meet their wants, but she has produced nothing better than this charming tale, alive with incident and action, adorned rather than freighted with useful facts, and moral without moralization.[3]

One could ask little more of a longer review, except greater detail. The reader is provided with a description of the action, and with an evaluation of the merits of the book. It is related to the author's other writing of a similar type, and judged in relation to that writing.

The *Independent* reviewed the book at similar length, and in a similar manner.

> *To lay the scene of a story among the dykes and windmills of Holland is not a common procedure. Charles Reade, if not the only writer who has hitherto made the attempt, is certainly the only one who has achieved a notable success in so doing. As exquisite a story, however, as is The Cloister and the Hearth, the present volume does not suffer by a comparison with it. Though a story for and about boys, Hans Bunker [sic] presents as true a picture of Holland life as though its characters had been exclusively men and women; and, dealing, as it does, with the sentiments of duty and generosity common to men as well as children, it has an interest for us all. It is by no means an ordinary book. It contains passages of genuine humor and of the truest pathos, and evinces descriptive power of a high order. Were the author to write a strictly legitimate novel, it could scarcely fail of being a success; but should she continue to write books of the same class as Hans Brinker, no one will be dissatisfied. To write in such a way as to touch the feelings and awaken the best impulses of young and old is one of the rarest and most precious of gifts.*[4]

Again we find a comparison, but here with the work of another author who had used the same setting. This review, from a religious periodical, was somewhat more concerned with the tone of the book, but not to the exclusion of a consideration of literary merit, for the author's ability to create "genuine humor," "pathos" and excellent description was praised. The description of the content of the book was less adequate, though not absent, for the reviewer provided his readers with a picture of the setting.

The only review which was, in part at least, unfavorable, was *The Catholic World*'s review, and its criticism was doctrinal rather than literary. But for one objection, this review would have been not unlike those of the *Nation* and the *Independent*.

> *We could cordially recommend this well-written story were it not for one passage relating to* autos da fe *and the Inquisition. Those who*

have charge of Catholic youth are bound to be extremely careful what books they place in their hands, and this becomes often a cause of perplexity, as there are so few which are entirely unexceptionable. Those who write with the express purpose of inculcating the distinctive principles of Protestantism are not amenable to our criticism. But those who do not write with this intention, and who merely seek to afford entertainment to the youthful mind with a modicum of instructive information, may perhaps consider it worth while to respect the religion of a large and increasing class of the reading public. We are not very exacting. We desire only that books written for the instruction and amusement of the young public at large should contain a sound and wholesome morality and nothing offensive to Catholics. We could not desire a better specimen of this class of books than the work of our gifted authoress, which we have read with pleasure, with the exception of the single passage alluded to; and this might have been left out without any injury to the purpose of the story. Those who are disposed to profit by our hints will find us always ready to assist the circulation of their books by our recommendation, if their literary merit renders them worthy of it.[5]

The passage to which the reviewer refers is one of the several stories of Dutch history which the author permits her young characters to tell as they tour the major cities of the country. This one deals with the sieges of Leyden and Haarlem by the Spaniards, though it is difficult to see why it should have been offensive to an American Catholic 300 years later. Certainly there is nothing in Mrs. Dodge's tale which could be properly called anti-Catholic. The reviewer's concern with this one point left him with too little space to adequately describe the book, though he did praise the way in which it was written.

The longest review of *Hans Brinker* appeared in the *Atlantic Monthly*, a review of more than 1,000 words, discussing the book in great detail. It differed most from the other reviews in that it described the plot and quoted representative passages to illustrate the quality of the author's writing.

Hans Brinker is a charming domestic story of some three hundred and fifty pages, which is addressed, indeed, to young people, but which may be read with pleasure and profit by their elders. The scene is laid in Holland, a land deserving to be better known than it is; and the writer evinces a knowledge of the country, and an acquaintance with the spirit and habits of its stout, independent, estimable people, which must have been gathered not from books alone, but from living sources.

Graphically, too, is the quaint picture sketched, and with a pleasant touch of humor. We all know the main features of Dutch scenery; but they are seldom brought to our notice with livelier effect.[6]

The reviewer then quoted a long descriptive passage of about 200 words. He praised the tone of the book and its appeal to children, and quoted an entire incident on the canal to show this appeal. The review concluded with the following passage.

There is no formal moral, obtruding itself in set phrase. The lessons inculcated, elevated in tone, are in the action of the story and the feelings and aspirations of the actors. A young lady, for example, has been on a visit to aid and console a poor peasant-girl, whom, having been in deep affliction, she found unexpectedly relieved. Engrossed by her warm sympathy with her humble friend, she forgets the lapse of time.

"Hilda was reprimanded severely that day for returning late to school after recess, and for imperfect recitation.

"She had remained near the cottage until she heard Dame Brinker laugh, and heard Hans say, 'Here I am, father!' and then she had gone back to her lessons. What wonder that she missed them! How could she get a long string of Latin verbs by heart when her heart did not care a fig for them, but would keep saying to itself, 'O, I am so glad! I am so glad!' "

The book contains two things,—a series of lifelike pictures of an interesting country and of the odd ways and peculiarities and homely virtues of its inhabitants; and then, interwoven with these, a simple tale, now pathetic, now amusing, and carrying with it wholesome influences on the young heart and mind.[7]

This review, much longer than any of the others, provided a most adequate picture of the book to its potential readers. By the addition of quotations, not possible in a brief review, the reviewer was able to provide some of the flavor of the author's writing, along with his description of the contents and his evaluation of the merits of the book. In this review, and in others, there was clear-cut recognition of the very great merit of the work.

Many of the reviews of later editions of *Hans Brinker* appeared in the same periodicals that had reviewed the first edition, though there were many in other periodicals as well. The edition that appeared late in 1873 had new illustrations by Darley, Nast, and other artists and was, in appearance, better than the first edition. Both the *Independent* and the *Nation* devoted brief notices to this new edition, and *Appleton's Journal*,

The Galaxy, Publishers' Weekly, Scribner's Monthly, and the *Youth's Companion* reviewed it; *Appleton's Journal* twice.

The Independent declared that *Hans Brinker* needed no new commendation, limiting itself to only a few words.[8] *Appleton's Journal* noted the fact of a new edition and declared that *Hans Brinker* was "among the very first of the books that should be bought for children."[9] The *Nation,* on the other hand, devoted more space to this edition, discussing the fact that the book, eight years old, had continued to grow in popularity and prestige.[10] The reviewer declared it was an excellent children's book with excellent character development. He declared that, of all American juvenile books, this was the one most deserving to become a classic.

The review in *Publishers' Weekly* was as long as those the *Nation* and the *Independent* had devoted to the first edition.

> *This charming story holds a special place of its own among books designed for young readers. It is carefully and gracefully written, and combines instruction with amusement. The story is a simple domestic one, the scene of which is placed in Holland. One might think Mrs. Dodge had drawn from life, so vivid and so minute are her descriptions of the manners and customs of the Hollanders. She unites in her story all the charm of a book of travels with a plot well developed, and richly filled in with character sketches and interesting incidents. The volume is illustrated by Darley and Nast, and handsomely bound.*[11]

This review includes an evaluation, a description of the story and its setting, and a statement about the physical book.

The second review of this edition of *Hans Brinker* in *Appleton's Journal* was little longer than its first, simply reiterating what it had said before, that it was an excellent book for children.[12] The reviews in *The Galaxy, Scribner's Monthly* and the *Youth's Companion,* which, like the *Appleton's Journal* review, appeared early the next year, were longer. The review in the *Youth's Companion* was the shortest of the three.

> *The story of Hans Brinker and the "darling little girl who won the silver skates" is one that we can heartily commend, and without any mental reservation. As a picture of Holland, the "Queerest country in all the world," it is as natural and breezy as the sea-winds that turn the old wind-mills on the hills. The plot holds the reader, be he young or old, and Mrs. Dodge's literary work does credit to her profession, in which she is an artist, and which she evidently loves.*[13]

Though the reader might question the enthusiasm of the reviewer who puts the windmills on hills in Holland, the same basic ingredients of an adequate review are here, the description of the story and the evaluation, the awareness of the audience for whom the book was intended.

The review in *Scribner's Monthly* put even more emphasis on Mrs. Dodge's ability to interest children.

> *One of the charms of* Hans Brinker *is that it seems to be written by an author who has no Ideal Child in her mind, whom she seeks to interest and instruct; not even an ideal Real Child—that precious creature who is the bane of much of the finer sort of juvenile literature of our day. In style it is straightforward, earnest, simple without a shadow of any kind of affectation; it has all that glow and shimmer of wit, that vivacious, genial element which is the very essence of healthy, joyous childhood, and which, when caught into literature, wins to the book, all, no matter what their ages in years, who have, at heart, the freshness of youth.*[14]

Only *The Galaxy* had anything but praise for the book. This review was one of the longest, nearly 1,000 words of searching criticism. The reviewer praised the author's careful descriptive detail, and her skill in telling the story of the Brinkers. He felt, however, that the conversation of the aristocratic boys and girls was not always natural, and that the sections dealing with the "history, antiquities, and present customs of Holland" were "at times a little tedious." [15] All in all, however, he judged the book "a very creditable one." Nearly three-quarters of this review was devoted to a description of the plot.

Another edition of *Hans Brinker* appeared in time to be reviewed just before Christmas in 1875. This edition had another set of illustrations, pictures which had, the review in *Scribner's Monthly* informed the reader, first appeared with the French edition of the book.[16] This edition received four, possibly five, reviews. Susan Coolidge did not make clear which edition she was reviewing in the *Literary World* in January, 1878, but from what she says about it, it is possible that she had this same edition in hand. Each review dwelt on the superior appearance of this edition.

The review in the *Independent* was the briefest, the third review of this title to appear in that periodical.

> *That delightful juvenile,* Hans Brinker: or, The Silver Skates, *by Mrs. Dodge, the editor of* St. Nicholas, *has been brought out by Scribner, Armstrong & Co. in a style worthy of its merits. The book is of that square shape book-lovers like, the handsomely printed page is a pleasant and open one; there are plenty of good illustrations, and the binding is pretty indeed.*[17]

The review in *Publishers' Weekly,* though a little longer, dealt with the same aspects of the book as the *Independent,* and added a brief descriptive sentence about the story.

> *The boys and girls who are not fortunate enough to have read "Hans Brinker" are in luck this year, for nothing could be prettier than this new edition of one of the most charming and popular stories ever written. It contains at least sixty original illustrations, and is very beautifully printed on tinted paper, and is in a most gorgeous binding. Besides presenting a most fascinating story, the author gives a minute and perfect account of life in Holland, adding to her descriptions the embellishment of both pathos and humor. Nothing so intrinsically good and desirable in the way of a Christmas book is now in the market.[18]*

The reviewer in *Scribner's Monthly* devoted only part of his space to a discussion of the merits of the book. The bulk of his review was devoted to detailing the reception of the book at home and abroad, feeling no doubt, that *Hans Brinker* was by that time so well-known that little needed to be said about its contents.

> *"Hans Brinker; or the Silver Skates," has such a firmly established reputation, that the profusely illustrated edition of the book just published by Scribner, Armstrong & Co., will be received with applause and satisfaction. Mrs. Dodge has made the story one of her brightest and most limpid of realistic tales. Its current flows like a living stream; the characters have warmth and humanity. Moreover, the nameless something which we call "tone" is so healthful, that each reader is sure to rise from its perusal with quickened impulses for good.*
>
> *Very few American books, certainly none so unambitious and modest as this, have received in foreign lands the cordial welcome given to Mrs. Dodge's artistic story. "Hans Brinker" was written for American young people with the purpose of giving them correct information about life, manners and art in Holland. But the book has been reproduced in several European languages; and the youthful Hollanders delightedly read "Hans Brinker" in their own native language. This new American edition outshines all others issued in this country in the beauty of its typography and the profusion and spirit of its illustrations,—which are identical with those accompanying the latest French edition.[19]*

The third review of *Hans Brinker* to appear in *Appleton's Journal* was by far the longest, though it is clearly a review of a book that the reviewer assumes has established itself.

One of the most tasteful of the children's books which the season has produced is the new illustrated edition of "Hans Brinker; or, The Silver Skates," by Mrs. Mary Mapes Dodge (New York: Scribner, Armstrong & Co.). This story was first published several years ago; as the author says, "boys who were babies when it was first told can read every word of it now without skipping a single big word; better yet, they are old enough to find whatever is worth remembering in the book, and to take heart from its examples of Dutch heroism and love." Its fidelity and attractiveness are certified by the fact that it has become a general favorite in Holland, where the scene of the story is laid, as well as in our own country; and by the additional fact that, during years of competition with the copious juvenile literature of the period, it has gained rather than lost in popularity. The new edition is beautifully printed and bound, and possesses every attraction that illustration can bestow upon a text which affords exceptional opportunities to the artist.[20]

Though more poetic, the review by Susan Coolidge in *Literary World* chiefly welcomed the attractiveness of the new edition.

One occasionally sees a gingham-clad child, noble-looking enough to be a princess, and now and then we hear of a princess whose appearance befits gingham rather than royal ermine; the singular good-fortune is to find the royal mien and the royal robes combined. It is therefore with a pleasure enhanced by surprise, that we descry our old favorite Hans Brinker, *best and most charming of all juvenile stories which have appeared on this side of the sea, glittering in the brave garb with which the Messrs. Scribner have lately provided it, and in which it stands confessed, a real princess of holiday volumes, properly dressed at last, but no more bewitching (how could it be?) than when it shone in plain gingham, and only* deserved *the royal robes at last accorded it.*[21]

The *Independent* welcomed another new edition in the 1879 Christmas season, an edition with still another set of illustrations, "quaint Dutch" pictures this time.[22] The reviewer merely identified the book and remarked on the illustrations, the popularity of the story, and the effective way in which the information was presented, in a review of two sentences. *Harper's Magazine*'s review in January, 1880, also was confined largely to the edition rather than to the work itself.[23] The reviewer expressed his pleasure that an edition had appeared at so low a cost "as to make it accessible to thousands of young folk to whom it has been denied hitherto." The *Nation* provided the statement that summarized what had been happening to *Hans Brinker* in its review of this new, inexpensive edition. "There is no better sign in juvenile literature than the survival of what deserves to endure—the genesis of a new classic." [24]

This was the reviewing of *Hans Brinker* in the magazines studied. It is a record of respectable reviewing. The periodicals recognized the merit of the book at the outset, even though, in providing a picture of natural and normal children, it was different from most books that had preceded it. If Hans seems almost too good to be true to the modern reader, how real he must have seemed to a generation who had read the Rollo books. How well he paved the way for even more natural boys to come. But the chief point here is that the reviews of this book were concerned with literary merit and with the appeal of the book to children. The reviewers recognized a first-class book for children and, to some extent, helped to make it into a children's classic. *The Galaxy* provided the only unfavorable comments, although it praised the book as a whole. Even those comments are probably legitimate, for anyone who has watched children squirm while waiting to get through the travelogue and back to the story of the Brinkers would have to agree that the book, at those times, does drag a little. This was reviewing that would meet any standards.

A NEW KIND OF CLEVERNESS: ALICE'S ADVENTURES IN WONDERLAND

The year 1866 produced, in addition to *Hans Brinker,* another very different book, *Alice's Adventures in Wonderland,* an import from England. The story of how the Appleton firm secured the suppressed first edition and published it in America is too well-known to need repetition here. It is sufficient to say that the *Nation,* reviewing the Appleton edition, did not detect the bad printing of the illustrations which had so disturbed the author and the illustrator.

The *Nation* was the only periodical to review the first American edition of Carroll's classic nonsense story, though Lee & Shepard's 1869 edition was reviewed in a great many periodicals. Because of the excellence of the reviewing exhibited, the *Nation*'s review is quoted in its entirety, despite its great length.

"Alice's Adventures in Wonderland" is a last year's London book, imported by the Messrs. Appleton, and invested with their title-page. This, also, is very neatly printed and bound. The story is exactly such an one as a smart story-teller reels off to children, their questions suggesting new adventures, and the tale running on with no reason for stopping in one place rather than in another, except weariness or

237

"other engagements." But, off-hand as it is, it is wonderfully clever, and quite bristles with points and runs over with fun. The whole thing is a dream, as it finally turns out, and just the effect of a dream is given to it by the sudden and amusingly absurd changes, and the unastonished calmness with which Alice regards them all. Thus the baby she holds turns into a pig in her arms; Alice feels relieved to see it trot away quietly into the wood, and says to herself, "If it had grown up it would have been a dreadfully ugly child, but it makes rather a handsome pig, I think." The Cheshire cat, who always wears a grin, as in duty bound to fulfil the proverb, annoys Alice, who remonstrates: "I wish you wouldn't keep appearing and vanishing so suddenly; you make one quite giddy." "All right," said the cat, and this time it vanished quite slowly, beginning with the end of the tail and ending with the grin. All sorts of real and unreal creatures pass through her experience, and are unreasonable and rude, and wholly nonsensical. And nothing can be more like a fanciful child's dream than the croquet ground, where the balls were rolled-up hedgehogs, the mallets flamingoes, and both sorts of creatures manage to give considerable trouble by acting up to their natural gifts at the wrong time. Alice's particular flamingo twists up its long neck when she tries to make a stroke, "and looks in her face with such a puzzled expression that she could not help laughing;" which is continually the case with the reader of this most amusing of little books. Even the jokes help it, strange to say. We have had occasion to complain of Tom Hood's forced puns in "Fairy Realm" and "Jingles and Jokes," because not only poor and flat in themselves, but wholly unintelligible, or, at least, unattractive, to children. But this author can make puns that children laugh at and heartily enjoy. "The schoolmaster was an old turtle," says the Mock-Turtle to Alice; "we called him Tortoise." "Why did you call him Tortoise, if he wasn't one?" Alice asked. "We called him Tortoise because he taught us," said the Mock-Turtle, angrily; "really, you are very dull." "What are shoes made of under the sea?" "Soles and eels, of course," the Gryphon replied, rather impatiently; "any shrimp could have told you that." There are not a great many of these jokes, but what there are, are provocative of laughter—a good thing in jokes.

There is considerable merit in the delineation of character in these fanciful dramatis personae. *The melancholy Mock-Turtle and the nervous and ill-bred Gryphon toward the end are not better than the White Rabbit and the Dodo at the beginning. If the author does not write novels he ought to do so, for besides the merits of which we have already spoken, he is quite a master of dialogue; and that is to have one of the rarest of the minor gifts. Thus, when Alice is in the White*

238

Rabbit's house, and his servants are trying to get down the chimney to get at her, she hears their confused talk outside:

"Where's the other ladder? Why, I hadn't to bring but one; Bill's got the other. Bill, fetch it here, lad! Here, put 'em up at this corner. No, tie 'em together first; they don't reach half high enough yet. Oh! they'll do well enough; don't be particular. Here, Bill, catch hold of this rope. Will the roof bear? Mind that loose slate—oh, it's coming down! Heads below! (A loud crash.) Now, who did that? It was Bill, I fancy. Who's to go down the chimney?"

And so on. Some of the creatures are amusingly vulgar, and their talk has always a character suitable to the utterers.

The parodies of popular songs are excellent, parodies introduced by requests to Alice from the Caterpillar, the Gryphon, and the others to repeat poetry. Nearly all children have had their Saturdays made miserable by such stuff as,

"You are old, Father William, Theophilus cried,
    The few hairs that are left you are grey;
You are still, Father William, a cheerful old man—
    Now tell me the reason, I pray?"

And those who know it cannot but enjoy seeing it suffer punishment in the way it has to in Mr. Carroll's hands.

This is one of the best children's books we ever met with—a delightful addition to a delightful branch of literature. The illustrations also are excellent, for Mr. Tenniel always excels in such things. His pictures of the animated cards, and his portraits of the Mock-Turtle, the Hatter, the Duchess, and the Cheshire Cat are immensely funny. The drawings are full of spirit and expression, and very elegant in design.[25]

This review is as fully detailed, and as carefully analytical as any review of an adult book. The reviewer began by classifying the book as a fantasy with humor, describing certain incidents that illustrate the amusing qualities of the book, the sudden and unexpected changes, the ludicrousness of certain situations, the jokes. Then he dealt with the special virtues of characterization and of dialogue, quoting from the work to show the reader the qualities he was talking about. He compared Carroll's use of puns with Tom Hood's use of them. Finally, he discussed the illustrations and provided an evaluation of the book that it was one of the best children's books published.

The 1869 edition of *Alice's Adventures in Wonderland* was reviewed in five periodicals. These reviews dealt, of course, with a book already well-established. *Catholic World* provided the only review that was unenthusiastic.[26] The reviewer for that magazine regretted "that children should be entertained in this way instead or by some probable or possible adventures." He did, however, acknowledge that the book was well-written and well-illustrated. The review in *Harper's Magazine* opened with a descriptive sentence, but was mostly devoted to a discussion of the illustrator and to a comparison between the English edition by Macmillan and the American edition by Lee & Shepard.[27] The reviewer felt the American edition was quite as good as the English.

The *Overland Monthly* printed a review giving very high praise to the book.

To say that this little volume is the most originally entertaining and delightful child's story that ever a grown reader enjoyed, may appear extravagant and not very comprehensive criticism. But we know no other way to describe the pleasure that we get from Alice's adventures— a pleasure that is as difficult to analyze as the sensation we experience in that odd mixture of childish simplicity and archness which we call "cunning." It is not only the grown-up humor with which the story overflows—as in the idea of representing the Mock Turtle as a bona fide creature, or the delicious description of the trial of the Knave of Hearts before a jury of small and bewilderingly stupid animals—but the remarkable skill with which this grown-up humor is made to appear entirely consistent with the odd fancies of a clever girl of six years. Outside of the works of the world's few great humorists we know of nothing as truly and laughably grotesque as the "Mad Tea Party," which Alice attended in all the naïve and sweet seriousness of childhood. And in the capital conceit of making the animals argue with Alice about her lessons, snap her up on verbal mistakes, infelicities and improprieties of conduct, and in short, reflect in this wonderful dream of hers what must have been the frequent experiences of her waking moments, there is Art of no common quality.[28]

The reviewer continued in this vein, analyzing and praising Carroll's fantasy and recognizing in this work a truly original contribution to children's literature.

Strangely the reviewer for *Putnam's Magazine,* while declaring the work excellent and sure to be popular with ten year-old girls, declared that the nonsense was incomprehensible to adults. Only the pictures, he felt, were equally appealing to the child and his elders.[29] But he was the only reviewer who failed to see the unusual appeal of *Alice's Adventures in Wonderland* to most adults.

The *Literary World,* on the other hand, emphasized the delight of adults in it, though it did not ignore the appeal to children.[30] This review appeared belatedly, for the magazine did not begin publication until the year following Lee & Shepard's edition, and then because *Through the Looking-Glass* had been announced and the editor wished to call his readers' attention to the same author's earlier work. The review was long, over 2,000 words, and began with a section on fairy stories. It declared that "among recent publications we know of no book which combines so many of the requirements of a purely fanciful child's story," and that the book was "infinitely laughable." Much of the review was devoted to long quotations.

Again we find that the reviewers of the post-Civil War period were alert to merit in a new kind of children's book, and that they considered the book for itself, and in terms of its literary merit and appropriateness for children. Though some of the reviews were so brief as to amount to little more than notices, at least two of them were as long as the reviews given most adult books.

Through the Looking-Glass was only reviewed in the *Nation*. Since the rights to this book were retained by the English publishers, it may well be that most American periodicals failed to receive copies. The *Nation* reviewed it with enthusiasm, declaring it had "all the excellence of the former work as a true picture of a shifting dream." [31] The reviewer felt that the idea of an inverted looking-glass land was actually a cleverer idea than that of a rabbit hole. Again the dialogue and the parodies were praised.

Though only one review of this book appeared, that one illustrates again the superior quality of reviewing in the magazine in which it appeared. The *Nation* emphasized literary quality and intrinsic merit, relating the book to the author's previous book and judging it as a children's book intended to give a child pleasure.

THE NATURAL FAMILY STORY: LITTLE WOMEN

As *Hans Brinker* and *Alice's Adventures in Wonderland* were innovations in children's literature, so was Louisa May Alcott's *Little Women*. Most of the reviewers did not, self-consciously, proclaim that something new had appeared in children's books, although *The Galaxy* declared Miss Alcott had "struck a vein that will bear working." [32] Almost without exception, the reviewers did recognize that she had written a first-rate book for the young.

Both Parts I and II, published in 1868 and 1869 respectively, of *Little Women,* were reviewed in several periodicals. Part I received four reviews, Part II seven. The reviews of Part I tended to be shorter than the reviews of the second part, often merely notices, but all of them praised it.

The notice in *Hours at Home* cannot be labelled a review, for it consisted of only five words, "A capital story for girls," with no other comment.[33] The *American Literary Gazette* did not provide much more information, though it did declare that the story contained "plenty of incident and of sprightly conversation." [34] Both *Putnam's Magazine* and the *Nation* printed longer notices, Putnam's quoting a higher authority to defend its judgment; a twelve year-old girl.

One of the pleasantest books we have read for a long time is Little Women *(Roberts Bro's), the story of four young girls, Meg, Jo, Beth, and Amy. This is a thoroughly natural and charming book, fresh and full of life, and we heartily recommend it to all young people, big or little. We gave it to a little girl of twelve to read, for whose opinion we have great respect, and she pronounced it just the* nicest *book. "I could read it right through three times, and it would be nicer and funnier every time." And to our certain knowledge, she read it twice in one week, and would have read it again, had not the book been carried off.*[35]

The *Nation* pronounced *Little Women* an "agreeable little story," well suited to the reading of children." [36] The characters were admirable and well drawn. Only the illustrations, by Miss Alcott's sister, May, failed to win the approval of the reviewer.

When Part II appeared the praise devoted to the entire story was all but universal. The *Nation* called it "a hearty, unaffected, and 'genial' description of family life," and recommended it for all young people.[37] *Hours at Home* devoted more space than it had to the first part.

Miss Alcott is justly a great favorite with young readers, and her "Little Women" in both its parts, strikes us as one of the best of her many productions. It is really a charming story, thoroughly natural, fresh and full of interest. It will delight and improve the class to whom it is especially addressed.[38]

Putnam's Magazine provided one of the few notices which was at all critical. Though the reviewer for that magazine recommended the book, he questioned whether there was not "perhaps, a slight dullness, or lack of interesting action" in the second part.[39]

The longest review, and the most detailed, was printed in *The Galaxy*, though even here no space was devoted to a description of the action of the story.

Miss Alcott's dear "Little Women," Meg, Jo, Beth, and Amy, are already bosom friends to hundreds of other little women, who find in their experiences the very mirror of their own lives. In Part First we find them four natural, sweet girls, with well-defined characters, which in Part Second, are developed to womanhood through such truthful and lifelike scenes as prove Miss Alcott to be a faithful student of nature. It isn't à la mode *now to be moved over stories, but we pity the reader who can repress a few tears as well as many hearty laughs over the lives of these little women. We are glad to hear that Miss Alcott is to give us some "Little Men," too. She has struck a vein that will bear working.*[40]

Only *Catholic World* emphasized the moral quality of the book, praising its high tone more than its air of reality, but it did not ignore other qualities.

This is a charming story, full of life, full of fun, full of human nature, and therefore full of interest. The little women play at being pilgrims when they are children, and resolve to be true pilgrims as they grow older. Life to them was earnest; it had its duties, and they did not overlook them or despise them. Directed by the wise teachings and the good example of a good mother, they became in the end true and noble women. Make their acquaintance; for Amy will be found delightful, Beth very lovely, Meg beautiful, and Jo splendid; that there is a real Jo somewhere we have not the slightest doubt.[41]

The reviewer for *Harper's New Monthly Magazine* emphasized the autobiographical element in *Little Women.*[42] He praised the naturalness of the story, but questioned its suitability for very young readers. The children grew up too rapidly, so that the second part assumed the status of a full blown novel with adult love, marriage, and family life.

The seventh notice, in *Our Young Folks,* was exceedingly brief. The writer declared that it was too late to speak in detail about the book, since the second part had already appeared, but he did want his readers to know about it, since it was engrossing and "as natural as life." [43]

The reviews of *Little Women* were not as adequate as those of *Hans Brinker* or of *Alice's Adventures in Wonderland.* They failed to describe the action of the story, though, without exception they praised the naturalness of both character and action. Only one periodical emphasized the moral tone of the story, but even that periodical, the denominational *Catholic World,* considered other aspects of the book to be equally important. Certainly, *Little Women* was brought to the attention of a great many readers.

THE BAD BOY IN CHILDREN'S LITERATURE: TOM
BAILEY AND TOM SAWYER

Though Thomas Bailey Aldrich's *The Story of a Bad Boy* and Samuel
L. Clemens' *The Adventures of Tom Sawyer* were published seven years
apart, they were the two most important contributions to the "bad boy"
genre of American children's books. One of them was reviewed widely,
and was widely acclaimed. The other received only one review, a very
good one, but that fact can be explained by causes other than the myopia
of the reviewers.

The Story of a Bad Boy had six reviews, most of them long and analytical. Only the reviews in *Our Young Folks,* probably written by Lucy
Larcom, were short, and the relationship of that periodical to Aldrich's
book was different from any other, because it had first appeared serially
in that magazine. Miss Larcom's notice was more a "Godspeed" than an
actual review.

> *We are almost sorry to speak of the publication of the "Story of a
> Bad Boy" in book form, because it is, in fact, writing that bright little
> fellow's obituary, so far as our magazine is concerned. But Tom
> Bailey is only to take a new lease of life. He is to be dressed up new, in
> whatever style those who send for him may desire, and go a-visiting all
> the Young Folks who want to see him, to stay until his clothing, not
> his welcome, is worn out. This last could scarcely happen anywhere,
> for Tom Bailey is the best story-teller of all the boys we know,—ex-
> cepting, perhaps, Tom Brown, of Rugby. He is both witty and well
> behaved,—two qualities not always found together; and we know that
> his story will read better as a whole than in fragments, as we have had
> to offer it to our readers.[44]*

When the book actually had appeared, *Our Young Folks* devoted two
more sentences to it. "The 'Story of a Bad Boy' makes a very attractive
volume, without and within. 'Tom Bailey' will doubtless have a wide
popularity, during the holidays and long afterwards." [45]

The *American Literary Gazette's* review was also short, but was,
nonetheless, a true review rather than a mere notice, for it provided the
reader with some notion of the content of the book, with a statement
concerning the author's manner and an evaluation.

> *This is a capital book for boys, recounting all sorts of adventures
> and scrapes which befell the hero. It is written in the most amusing
> vein, with plenty of life and spirit, and will be a source of genuine*

*delight to all boys who read it. The work contains upward of forty
humorous illustrations.*[46]

The other three reviews, though praising the book no more highly,
provided the reader with more careful analyses, showing those elements
that made the book appealing and those which made it a new departure
in books for the young. The *Nation,* not declaring it a great book, judged
The Story of a Bad Boy one of the best that the 1869 season had produced.

> *Mr. T. B. Aldrich's "Story of a Bad Boy" they have rather stupidly
> rechristened in England, and there it is the story of "a not very bad
> boy." He was indeed about as bad—our young hero who went to
> school at Rivermouth—as the boys usually are who get the name he
> got, and his English godfathers were not far out of the way. He is
> certainly an amusing and interesting person, and the narrative of his
> various adventures is such as boys will recognize as possible and prob-
> able, while the older reader will find in it a humorous and clever rec-
> ord of the impressions made upon them by boyish performances—
> whether their own as they recollect them, or those of boys who are
> living under their observant eyes. This is perhaps hinting pretty
> strongly that Mr. Aldrich's book produces a slightly confused impres-
> sion, and that we have boy and man mingled in its pages in a way not
> possible out of literature, and in perfect literature not possible either.
> But perfect books are a little scarce, and so are pleasant books; and
> among the not many pleasant books for boys which this year has given
> us, the "Story of a Bad Boy" takes a high place. It is healthy reading,
> and may be safely commended to all buyers of holiday wares.*[47]

The reviewer in the *Overland Monthly* dealt specifically with Tom's
character as a bad boy, pointing out how natural he actually was, and
celebrating the fact that Aldrich had done justice to boys of this type.
After enumerating a number of the scrapes in which Tom Bailey found
himself, the reviewer declared his doubt that young readers would be any
more influenced to try such tricks themselves, as a result of reading this
book, than they had been restrained from them by reading the stories of
"those very nice boys who 'love their book,' and come to a righteous, but
premature end." [48] Much of Tom's apparent badness was only relative, in
any case, seeming larger because of the "puritanic austerity of the quaint
New England town where he lived." The reviewer praised the author's
skill in character delineation and in the omission of vulgar detail. He
described particular incidents that were amusing or well drawn, placing

the work high in children's literature. The review ran to more than 300 words.

Still longer and more detailed was the review written by William Dean Howells in the *Atlantic Monthly*.[49] Howells declared that Aldrich had produced a really new thing in American literature, "an absolute novelty," in producing a book about a boy which showed him as he was, not as he ought to be. In a review of nearly 2,000 words, Howells analyzed characterization, described incidents and discussed style. His praise was tempered by a shrewd recognition of certain faults. He described the same kind of mixing of point of view which the *Nation* had detected, and decribed one character as too much a stock theatrical type. The final evaluation, however, was full and laudatory.

> *Mr. Aldrich is a capital* conteur; *the narrative is invariably good, neither hurried nor spun out, but easily discursive, and tolerant of a great deal of anecdote that goes finally to complete the charm of a life-like and delightful little story, while the moralizing is always as brief as it is pointed and generous. When he comes to tell a tale for older heads,—as we hope he some day will,—we shall not ask him to do it better than this in essentials, and in less important particulars shall only pray him to be always himself down to the very last word and smallest turn of expression. We think him good enough.*[50]

Unlike *The Story of a Bad Boy,* with six reviews or notices, *The Adventures of Tom Sawyer* received only one. It would be too easy to condemn the lack of taste of the reviewers, if other evidence were not at hand to explain this dearth of attention. Clemens published his book with the American Publishing Company, of Hartford, Connecticut, a subscription publisher, rather than a trade publisher. As a result, *The Adventures of Tom Sawyer* was not distributed to reviewing periodicals as the normal trade book would have been. It is inconceivable that the *Nation* or the *Literary World* would not have reviewed this book, had review copies been available to them. Both periodicals listed books received in a regular department, but neither of them listed *The Adventures of Tom Sawyer*. Only a few of the books they received from publishers failed to get some notice. Without question, Clemens picked a lucrative method of publishing his book. By the time it was available to most periodicals, it was probably already in the great majority of homes reached by subscription books salesmen. But in choosing the method of publication that would net him the most money, the author prevented his book from receiving the immediate kind of critical attention it might otherwise have had. This lack of reviews may have aggravated the objections to the book about which later commentators have made such an issue.

The one review that did appear was full of praise for the book, and, indeed, was written by one of the most distinguished American literary critics of the time, William Dean Howells.[51] Howells probably had a copy of the book for reviewing largely because he was a close friend of the author, and because he had served as his literary advisor. The review ran to about 1,200 or 1,500 words, analyzing the book carefully from a literary point of view. Howells compared the book with Aldrich's, finding them similar in many ways; Clemens having dealt with the natural boy in a Western setting in a manner not unlike that with which Aldrich dealt with the same kind of boy in New England. He described the quality of characterization, particularly the skillful development of Tom's personality, showing that Tom was actually a realistic boy, mischievous but not bad, and related various incidents that added to the appeal of the book. He concluded that Tom Sawyer was at least the equal of Tom Brown and Tom Bailey, high praise indeed from the reviewer who had pronounced *The Story of a Bad Boy* a true innovation in American literature.

THE PRINCE AND THE PAUPER

The view that the reviewers had not deliberately ignored *The Adventures of Tom Sawyer* is fortified with additional evidence by the fact that *The Prince and the Pauper* was widely reviewed. It appeared at the very end of 1881, so that only two reviews are included in the issues of periodicals examined for this study, but many more reviews appeared in the early months of 1882. This second book, which Clemens wrote for children, was published by a trade publisher, James R. Osgood & Company, so that review copies were distributed as a matter of routine. Though this work cannot be classified as "bad boy" literature, it is mentioned here to show that when Clemens published his books through normal channels they were reviewed just as any other author's books were.

Both the *Critic* and *Atlantic Monthly* gave long reviews to this work. The *Critic* praised its "subdued and often delicate description," its "local tone and color," and its "harmony with historic period." [52] The reviewer called it "a sweet and wholesome tale," but less distinctly for children than *Tom Sawyer* had been. Discussing the plot, he said, "one shudders to think what it would have become in the hands of those who supply the literature of the Sunday-school libraries," but he felt that Clemens had handled it superbly.

The review in the *Atlantic Monthly* was the longest given any children's book in any of the periodicals examined, running to nearly three full two-column pages.[53] The review, in essence, said the same things that had been said in the *Critic,* that the book was more for older readers than *Tom Sawyer* had been, that its use of local color and historical materials was excellent, and that it was a delightful tale. The *Atlantic Monthly* reviewer dwelt at great length on the fact that Clemens, departing entirely from his accepted role as a writer, had achieved a great success. In fact, the reviewer placed *The Prince and the Pauper* above all the author's previous works.

But to return to the "bad boy" literature, the reviews of both *The Story of a Bad Boy* and *The Adventures of Tom Sawyer* again show the reviewing in the period from 1865 to 1881 to have been of high quality, and receptive to new developments in children's books, recognizing, as new departures occurred, their excellence as literature and as desirable books for children. Whether the books were stories of natural boys, like the tales of the two Toms, stories of domestic life for girls, nonsense fantasy, or a combination travelogue story of children in a far-off land, the reviewers were quick to recognize their merits and their appeal to children. None of these books, and they are only representative of the many books reviewed, were discussed for their morals, for their uses as collateral reading, nor for any purpose but the delight of children. The standards by which they were evaluated were literary standards, and the judgments passed were judgments of literature, even though it was for the juvenile group of readers.

20

CONCLUSION

Reviews by thousands and thousands of books! That is the story of reviewing of children's books in the seventeen years following the Civil War. It would be a specious claim to pretend that this is the extent of such reviewing. Thirty-six periodicals are only representative of American publishing during that time. The reviewing in religious periodicals would provide a large study in themselves. The reviewing in the daily and weekly newspapers would bulk many times larger than reviewing in magazines. An advertisement in the back of the 1876 edition of Helen Aldrich De Kroyft's *The Story of Little Jakey* contains quotations from thirty-one different reviews of that book, not one of them a review from a magazine examined for this study.[1] Many magazines issued briefly for regional consumption must have reviewed children's books as well. Even if the magazines examined here represent a major part of such reviewing, there can be no doubt that children's books were reviewed in enormous number.

Nearly every type of magazine reviewed some children's books. The largest numbers of reviews, and in large measure, the best reviews, were in periodicals that concentrated on reviewing books, such as *The Literary World, The Dial, The Critic,* and *The Nation,* though the reviewing of books was only one part of the latter magazine's broad interests. Literary monthlies, almost without exception, reviewed children's books; *The Atlantic Monthly* and *Scribner's Monthly* providing some of the finest of these reviews, and *Harper's New Monthly Magazine* reviewing a quantity equalled only by the *Nation* and the *Literary World.* Children's magazines, religious magazines, scholarly reviews and pedagogical peri-

249

odicals all reviewed children's books to a greater or lesser extent, indicating the importance attached by all to the reading of the young.

Nor was this reviewing merely protective, aimed at keeping from children those things which might harm them, but was chiefly of a positive nature, examining children's books to display their virtues and to discover their appeal to children. The period was one of new freedom for children, of new emphasis on the rights of children as human beings. This new attitude was reflected in their books and in the criticism of those books. Basically, this meant that the reviewers expected children's books to be a part of their play, to provide delight and not merely instruction. The older standards set by Mrs. Trimmer, Mrs. Barbauld, Samuel Goodrich, even Jacob Abbott, were not acceptable to the postwar critics. In their books children were to see themselves as they were, not as they ought to be.

The day of the priggish child was gone, or at least doomed. The children in children's books henceforth had to be recognizable children, neither all good nor all bad, but rather as they were to be found in real life. Reviewers could devote their energies to the literary quality of children's books, concerning themselves only with morals in a broader sense, in the sense of a healthful tone, rather than a maxim. Tom Bailey took the place of Peter Parley. Tom Sawyer involved himself in mischief and was still a hero.

It is true that not only had the books for children changed, but also the publishers had discovered a steady market of unprecedented proportions for their juvenile books. The production of children's books steadily increased, creating an ever greater need for critical examination. It was to this need that the periodicals responded.

Though Anne Carroll Moore has charged that these critics reviewed children's books to discover their moral influence, to display their ability to instruct and to determine their usefulness in various other ways, this charge is impossible to defend. A few periodicals undoubtedly did this. *Hours at Home* was concerned more with morals than with literary quality, but it represented an older attitude and a religious one. Some of the reviews were concerned with the value of books in instructing children. Some of the books were frankly intended to instruct, for nonfiction for children blossomed after the war. But Miss Moore's thesis can only be defended if the bulk of the evidence is ignored.

The correct statement about reviewing of children's books in the period from 1865 to 1881 might be that at no other time have such fine critics, such gifted authors, such discerning minds, devoted so much intelligent energy to a critical examination of children's books. What critic with the stature of William Dean Howells has reviewed children's books in the twentieth century? What children's authors so gifted as Mary

Mapes Dodge, Susan Coolidge, or even Horace E. Scudder have turned their creative minds to the analysis of books by other authors? Even the countless anonymous reviews of the time provide ample evidence that children's books were held to be important, important enough to merit careful reviewing and close examination.

It is not the purpose of this study to compare the reviewing of children's books a hundred years ago with reviewing today, but it is difficult to avoid doing so. In the post-Civil War period, every periodical of importance took some responsibility for children's literature. The *Harper's Magazine* of that day reviewed hundreds of children's books. The *Atlantic Monthly* provided reviews as long and as careful as any reviews of adult books. The *Nation* provided a consistently high quality of reviewing of children's books. These magazines, though under different ownership, still exist. But neither they, nor their modern companions review children's books as they once did. Today the reviewing of children's books is left to the periodicals published for libraries, to the Sunday supplements of a few metropolitan newspapers, and to the occasional pre-Christmas issues of a few other magazines. *The Horn Book* devotes itself to children's literature, it is true, but it reviews no more children's books in a year than did the *Literary World* which included children's literature as a part of all literature.

The end of the Civil War saw a great awakening to the importance of children's books. With that recognition of their importance came a great upsurge of criticism and of reviewing of children's books. It would be too much to call this period a "Golden Age" in the reviewing of children's books. That term has been used too often and with too little cause. Yet, it is true, those who selected children's books in the years following the Civil War had guidance from critics which must have enabled them to choose with admirable discrimination. The children of that day were fortunate indeed.

FOOTNOTES

CHAPTER 1

1. *The Independent,* XVII (April 6, 1865), 4.
2. *The Youth's Companion,* LII (August, 1879), 288.
3. *Ibid.,* LIV (February 3, 1881), 41.
4. *Ibid.,* LIII (July 29, 1880), 256.
5. Review of *Farming for Boys,* in *Hours at Home,* VII (May, 1868), 192.
6. William T. Adams, "Editorial Chit-Chat," *Oliver Optic's Magazine,* XIII (January, 1873), 78.
7. Adams, "The Great Jubilee," *Oliver Optic's Magazine,* XII (August, 1872), 557.
8. *The Youth's Companion,* XLIX (June 22, 1876), 201–02.
9. *Ibid.,* L (May 24, 1877), 166.
10. *Harper's New Monthly Magazine,* LIV (January, 1877), 307.
11. *The Youth's Companion,* L (August 23, 1877), 272.
12. *Ibid.,* LI (March 14, 1878), 84.
13. *Ibid.,* L (November 15, 1877), 392.
14. *Ibid.,* L (May 3, 1877), 142.
15. George M. Baker, "Original Dialogues: Shall Our Mothers Vote," *Oliver Optic's Magazine,* XVIII (July, 1875), 543–48.
16. *The Youth's Companion,* L (April 5, 1877), 108.
17. *Ibid.,* LI (March 21, 1878), 92.
18. *Ibid.,* LI (August 8, 1876), 256.
19. *Ibid.,* XLIX (August 3, 1876), 252.
20. *Ibid.,* LI (April 11, 1878), 118.
21. *Ibid.,* LI (August 15, 1878), 264.
22. *Ibid.,* LIII (January 1, 1880), 4.
23. Alice M. Jordan, *From Rollo to Tom Sawyer and Other Papers* (Boston: The Horn Book, Inc., c. 1948), p. 14.

24. Amy Cruse, *The Victorians and Their Reading* (Boston and New York: Houghton Mifflin Co., 1936), p. 309.
25. Cruse, *op. cit.*, p. 297.
26. Hellmut Lehmann-Haupt, *The Book in America; A History of the Making and Selling of Books in the United States* (2nd ed.; New York: R. R. Bowker Co., 1951), p. 196.
27. *The Independent*, XVII (November 18, 1875), 7.
28. *Weekly Trade Circular*, I (January 25, 1872), 41.
29. *Overland Monthly*, VI (February, 1871), 199.
30. *Ibid.*, I (November, 1868), 487–88.
31. *Putnam's Magazine*, N. S. II (December, 1868), 760.
32. *Old and New*, V (May, 1872), 608.
33. *Ibid.*, V (May, 1872), 611.
34. Jordan, *op. cit.*, p. 14.
35. Frank Luther Mott, *A History of American Magazines, 1865–1885* (Cambridge: Harvard University Press, 1938), p. 5.
36. Ann Carroll Moore, *The Three Owls, Third Book; Contemporary Criticism of Children's Books, 1927–1930* (New York: Coward-McCann, 1931), p. 2.
37. Cornelia Meigs *et al.*, *A Critical History of Children's Literature; A Survey of Children's Books in English from Earliest Times to the Present* (New York: The Macmillan Co., 1953), p. 421.
38. Louise Seaman Bechtel, "Books in Search of Children," *Bowker Lectures on Book Publishing* (New York: R. R. Bowker Co., 1957), p. 179.
39. Samuel C. Chew, *Fruit Among the Leaves: An Anniversary Anthology* (New York: Appleton-Century-Crofts, 1950) p. 33–34.
40. *The Nation*, III (December 13, 1866), 466–67.
41. *Ibid.*, II (January 25, 1866), 119–20.

CHAPTER 2

1. *Old and New*, III (January, 1871), 108.
2. *Ibid.*, XI (February, 1875), 210.
3. *Hours at Home*, IV (April, 1867), 572.
4. *Putnam's Magazine*, N. S. IV (July, 1869), 124.
5. *Independent*, XXIX (June 21, 1877), 9.
6. *Weekly Trade Circular*, II (October 3, 1872), 340.
7. *Old and New*, III (January, 1871), 108.
8. *Hours at Home*, II (November, 1865), 99.
9. *The Independent*, XVIII (October 25, 1866), 2–3.
10. *Old and New*, IV (October, 1871), 471.
11. *The Literary World*, I (March 1, 1871), 152.
12. *Publishers' Weekly*, IV (September 27, 1873), 319.
13. *Ibid.*, IV (November 8, 1873), 511.
14. *Ibid.*, IV (November 15, 1873), 530–31.
15. William T. Adams, "Valedictory," *Oliver Optic's Magazine*, XVIII (December, 1875), 958–59.
16. *Publishers' Weekly*, VIII (September 4, 1875), 405.
17. *Ibid.*, X (Christmas Number, 1876) 804.
18. *Scribner's Monthly*, XIII (January, 1877), 424.
19. *Publishers' Weekly*, XIV (August 25, 1877), 192.
20. *Ibid.*, XV (January 4, 1879), 6.
21. *Ibid.*, XVII(January 3, 1880), 6.
22. *The Literary World*, V (August, 1874), 41.
23. *Ibid.*, V (December, 1874), 104.
24. *Publishers' Weekly*, XII (September 8, 1877), 247.
25. *Old and New*, III (January, 1871), 108.
26. *Scribner's Monthly*, XIV (May, 1877), 108.
27. *Publishers' Weekly*, XVII (June 15, 1871), 98.

28. *Scribner's Monthly*, XIV (September, 1877), 720–21.
29. *Ibid.*, XIV (September, 1877), 721.
30. *St. Nicholas*, V (November, 1877), 69.
31. *Hours at Home*, X (January, 1870), 290.
32. *Literary World*, I (November 1, 1870), 88.
33. *Ibid.*, I (October 1, 1870), 72.
34. *Overland Monthly*, XII (February, 1874), 199.
35. *Scribner's Monthly*, XI (December, 1875), 296–97.
36. *The Dial*, II (December, 1881), 181.
37. *Publishers' Weekly*, XIV (August 10, 1878), 159.
38. *Ibid.*
39. *Literary World*, VII (June, 1877), 5–6.
40. *Lippincott's Magazine*, V (April, 1870), 463.
41. *Literary World*, II (September 1, 1871), 56.
42. *Old and New*, V (May, 1872), 607–11.
43. *The Dial*, II (December, 1881), 182.
44. *Hours at Home*, X (December, 1869), 196.
45. *Ibid.*, VII (July, 1868), 287.
46. *Literary World*, XII (September 24, 1881), 327.

CHAPTER 3

1. *Literary World*, XII (September 24, 1881), 327.
2. *Ibid.*, X (December 6, 1879), 401.
3. *Hours at Home*, X (January, 1870), 291.
4. *Lippincott's Magazine*, XXV (January, 1880), 136.
5. Horace E. Scudder, *Mr. Bodley Abroad* (Boston: Houghton, Mifflin & Co., 1881), p. 157.
6. Hezekiah Butterworth, *Zigzag Journeys in Classic Lands; or, Tommy Toby's Trip to Mt. Parnassus* (Boston: Estes & Lauriat, [c.1880]), frontispiece.
7. *Literary World*, XI (December, 4, 1880), 442.
8. *The Independent*, XXIX (August 16, 1877), 9.
9. Martha F. Finley, *Mildred Keith* (New York: Dodd, Mead & Co., 1878).
10. Helen Aldrich De Kroyft, *The Story of Little Jakey* (New York: Hurd & Houghton, 1871), p. 132.
11. De Kroyft, *op. cit.*, pp. 129–30.
12. William Dean Howells, review of *The Story of a Bad Boy*, by Thomas Bailey Aldrich in *Atlantic Monthly*, XXV (January, 1870), 124.
13. Howells, review of *The Adventures of Tom Sawyer*, by Samuel L. Clemens in *Atlantic Monthly*, XXXVII (May, 1876), 621.
14. *Atlantic Monthly*, XLII (December, 1878), 779.
15. *Old and New*, I (January, 1870), 84.
16. *Publishers' Weekly*, III (March 1, 1873), 220.
17. *The Nation*, V (December 24, 1867), 524.
18. *Penn Monthly*, VII (December, 1876), 987.
19. William T. Adams, "Books for Boys," *Oliver Optic's Magazine*, III (February 15, 1868), 112.
20. Adams, "Books for Boys and Girls," *op. cit.*, XI (March, 1872), 206.
21. Adams, "Independent Criticism," *op. cit.*, XV (May, 1874), 398.
22. Adams, "Juvenile Writing," *op. cit.*, XVII (June, 1875), 477–78.
23. The italics do not appear in the original publication in *St. Nicholas*, but do appear in the book form of the story.
24. Louisa May Alcott, "Eight Cousins," *St. Nicholas*, II (August, 1875), 616–17.
25. *Appleton's Journal*, XIV (November 6, 1875), 601.
26. *Scribner's Monthly*, XI (April, 1876), 897.
27. Adams, "Sensational Books," *op. cit.*, XVIII (September, 1875), 718.
28. *Ibid.*
29. Adams, "Sunday-School Books," *op. cit.*, XVI (December, 1874), 957–58.

30. *Scribner's Monthly,* III (December, 1871), 255.
31. *The Nation,* XXI (November 18, 1875), 329.
32. Leone F. Harvey, "Hunter's Fare; A Book Inquiry Department," *The Horn Book Magazine,* XXIV (May-June, 1948), 224.
33. *Appleton's Journal,* VI (December 9, 1871), 668.
34. *Ibid.,* XIV (December 25, 1875), 825.
35. *Penn Monthly,* VII (April, 1876), 332–33.
36. *The Nation,* III (December 27, 1866), 517.
37. *The Californian,* IV (December, 1881), 537.
38. *Harper's New Monthly Magazine,* LIV (January, 1877), 307.
39. *The Nation,* V (December 12, 1867), 474.
40. *Ibid.,* IX (October 14, 1869), 321.
41. Mary Godolphin, *Sandford and Merton, in Words of One Syllable.* (New York: McLoughlin Bros., n.d.), pp. 107–08.
42. *Literary World,* XII (June 4, 1881), 201.
43. Howells, review of *The Children's Crusade,* by George Zabriskie Gray in *Atlantic Monthly,* XXVII (February, 1871), 261–62.
44. Virginia Haviland, *The Travelogue Storybook of the Nineteenth Century. A Caroline Hewins Lecture.* (Boston: The Horn Book, Inc., 1950).
45. *The Nation,* XI (December 22, 1870), 424.

CHAPTER 4

1. Alice M. Jordan, *From Rollo to Tom Sawyer and Other Papers* (Boston: The Horn Book, Inc., c.1948), pp. 24–25.
2. "Osgood, Samuel," *Appleton's Cyclopaedia of American Biography* (New York: D. Appleton & Co., 1888) IV, pp. 600–01.
3. Samuel Osgood, "Books for Our Children," *Atlantic Monthly,* XVI (December, 1865), 724.
4. Osgood, *op. cit.,* 725.
5. Osgood, *op. cit.,* 725–26.
6. Osgood, *op. cit.,* 726.
7. Osgood, *op. cit.,* 727.
8. *Ibid.*
9. *Ibid.*
10. Osgood, *op. cit.,* 728.
11. *Ibid.*
12. Osgood, *op. cit.,* 729.
13. Osgood, *op. cit.,* 732.
14. Osgood, *op. cit.,* 733.
15. Osgood, *op. cit.,* 732.
16. George B. Bacon, "The Literature of Our Sunday-Schools. No. I," *Hours at Home,* X (February, 1870), 295.
17. Bacon, *op. cit.,* 296.
18. Bacon, *op. cit.,* 299.
19. *Ibid.*
20. Bacon, "The Literature of Our Sunday-Schools, No. II," *Hours at Home* X (March, 1870), 452.
21. Bacon, *op. cit.,* 455.
22. Bacon, *op. cit.,* 456.
23. Bacon, *op. cit.,* 458.
24. Bacon, "The Literature of Our Sunday Schools, No. III," *Hours at Home,* X (April, 1870), 559–60.
25. Bacon, *op. cit.,* 561.
26. *Ibid.*
27. Bacon, *op. cit.,* 566.
28. *Old and New,* IV (November, 1871), 626–29.
29. *Ibid.,* I (May, 1870), 709–12.

30. *Publishers' Weekly,* IV (November 22, 1873), 584.
31. *Ibid.*
32. *Unitarian Review,* I (June, 1874), 354–59.
33. *Literary World,* X (April 26, 1879), 136.
34. "Sunday School Books," *Literary World,* XI (July 31, 1880), 260.
35. Kate Gannett Wells, "The Responsibility of Parents in the Selection of Reading for the Young," *The Library Journal,* IV (September-October, 1879), 325–30.
36. Martha H. Brooks, "Sunday School Libraries," *The Library Journal,* IV (September-October, 1879), 338–41.
37. M. A. Bean, "The Evil of Unlimited Freedom in the Use of Juvenile Fiction," *The Library Journal,* IV (September-October, 1879), 341–43.
38. S. S. Green, "Sensational Fiction in Public Libraries," *The Library Journal,* IV (September-October, 1879), 345–55.
39. James Freeman Clarke, "Address," *The Library Journal,* IV (September-October, 1879), 355–57.
40. Thomas Wentworth Higginson, "Address," *The Library Journal,* IV (September-October, 1879), 357–59.
41. Higginson, *op. cit.,* 357.
42. Higginson, *op. cit.,* 358–59.
43. William P. Atkinson, "Address," *The Library Journal,* IV (September-October, 1879), 359–62.
44. Mellen Chamberlain, "Address," *The Library Journal,* IV (September-October, 1879), 362–66.
45. Mary Mapes Dodge, "Children's Magazines," *Scribner's Monthly,* VI (July, 1873), 352–54.
46. Dodge, *op. cit.,* 354.
47. Dodge, *op. cit.,* 355.
48. *Literary World,* IV (November, 1873), 88.

CHAPTER 5

1. Wayne Gard, *Book Reviewing* (New York: Alfred A. Knopf, 1928), p. 14.
2. Gard, *op. cit.,* p. 15.
3. Gard, *op. cit.,* p. 16.
4. Virginia S. Woolf, *Captain's Death Bed and Other Essays* (New York: Harcourt, Brace & Co., 1950), p. 130.
5. Leonard Woolf, "Note," *op. cit.,* p. 143.
6. Henry S. Canby, "On Reviewing," *Saturday Papers; Essays on Literature from The Literary Review; The First Volume of Selections from The Literay Review of The New York Evening Post,* by Henry Seidel Canby, William Rose Benet, Amy Loveman. (New York: Macmillan Co., 1921), p. 103.
7. W. Soskin, "Business of Book Reviewing," *Writing for Love or Money,* Norman Cousins, ed. (New York: Longmans, Green, & Co., 1949), p. 219.
8. *Ibid.,*
9. Herschel Brickell, "Book Review," *Writers on Writing* (Garden City, N.Y.: Doubleday & Co., 1949), p. 174.
10. Gard, *op. cit.,* pp. 13–14.
11. Soskin, *op. cit.,* p. 220.
12. Anne Carroll Moore, *The Three Owls, Third Book; Contemporary Criticism of Children's Books, 1927–1930* (New York: Coward-McCann, 1931), p. 1.
13. Moore, *op. cit.,* p. 2.
14. Anne Carroll Moore, "The Creation and Criticism of Children's Books," *ALA Bulletin,* XXVIII (August, 1934), 693–701.
15. Cornelia Meigs et al., *A Critical History of Children's Literature; A Survey of Children's Books in English from Earliest Times to the Present* (New York: The Macmillan Co., 1953), p. 421.

16. Louise Seaman Bechtel, "Books in Search of Children," *Bowker Lectures on Book Publishing* (New York: R. R. Bowker Co., 1957) p. 179.
17. Alice M. Jordan, *From Rollo to Tom Sawyer and Other Papers* (Boston: The Horn Book, Inc., c.1948), p. 14.

CHAPTER 6

1. *New Eclectic,* I (February, 1868), 238.
2. *Publishers' Weekly,* IV (November 22, 1873), 584.
3. *Literary World,* III (March 1, 1873), 152.
4. *Athenaeum,* No. 2225 (June 18, 1870), 803.
5. *Ibid.,* No. 2355 (December 14, 1872), 767.
6. *Ibid.,* No. 2473 (March 20, 1875), 392.
7. *Ibid.,* No. 1990 (December 16, 1865), 844.
8. *Ibid.,* No. 2303 (December 16, 1871), 787.
9. *Saturday Review,* XXXII (December 16, 1871), 789.

CHAPTER 7

1. Frank Luther Mott, *A History of American Magazines, 1865–1885* (Cambridge: Harvard University Press, 1938), p. 40.
2. Mott, *op. cit.,* p. 333.
3. Daniel C. Haskell, *The Nation, Volumes 1–105, New York, 1865–1917. Index of Titles and Contributors. Volume 1. Index of Titles.* (New York: New York Public Library, 1951), *passim.*
4. *The Nation,* VII (December 10, 1868), 483.
5. *Ibid.,* V (December 12, 1867), 474.
6. *Ibid.,* VI (February 20, 1868), 154.
7. *Ibid.,* VIII (May 13, 1869), 380–81.
8. *Ibid.,* XXVII (December 19, 1878), 389.
9. *Ibid.,* II (May 8, 1866), 582–83.
10. *Ibid.,* XVII (November 27, 1873), 358.
11. *Ibid.,* XVIII (November 2, 1865), 567.
12. *Ibid.,* I (December 14, 1865), 757.
13. *Ibid.,* III (December 27, 1866), 517.
14. *Ibid.,* VII (December 17, 1868), 508.
15. *Ibid.,* XXIX (December 18, 1879), 427.
16. *Ibid.,* I (August 17, 1865), 220.
17. *Ibid.,* XIII (December 21, 1871), 405.
18. *Ibid.,* XXI (December 16, 1875), 391.
19. *Ibid.,* XXVII (November 7, 1878), 288.
20. *Ibid.,* XVII (December 11, 1873), 389–90.
21. Titus M. Coan, review of *Children of the Olden Time,* by Mrs. Henry Mackarness in *The Nation,* XVII (November 27, 1873), 357.
22. *The Nation,* II (April 26, 1866), 536–37.
23. *Ibid.,* III (October 18, 1866), 307.
24. *Ibid.,* VII (December 10, 1868), 484.
25. *Ibid.,* XIII (December 21, 1871), 405.
26. William Francis Allen, review of *The Boys and Girls of the Revolution,* by Charles H. Woodman in *The Nation,* XXIII (December 7, 1876), 345.
27. *The Nation,* I (December 28, 1865), 816.
28. *Ibid.,* XXXI (December 16, 1880), 431–32.
29. *Ibid.,* XXV (December 20, 1877), 385.
30. *Ibid.,* XXI (November 18, 1875), 329.
31. *Ibid.,* III (December 13, 1866), 466.
32. *Ibid.*
33. *Ibid.,* VII (December 18, 1868), 507.
34. *Ibid.,* IX (December 16, 1869), 541–42.

35. *Ibid.*, XXV (November 15, 1877), 304.
36. *Ibid.*, XXV (December 6, 1877), 352.
37. *Ibid.*, VII (December 17, 1868), 508.
38. *Ibid.*, IX (December 16, 1869), 542.
39. *Ibid.*, XXIII (December 21, 1876), 373.
40. *Ibid.*, XXXIII (December 15, 1881), 477.
41. *Ibid.*
42. *Ibid.*, IX (December 23, 1869), 569.
43. *Ibid.*, XIX (November 19, 1874), 335.
44. *Ibid.*
45. *Ibid.*, XIX (December 3, 1874), 369.
46. *Ibid.*, XVII (December 4, 1873), 373.
47. *Ibid.*, XVII (December 11, 1873), 389.
48. *Ibid.*, XVII (December 4, 1873), 373–74.
49. *Ibid.*, IX (August 19, 1869), 155.
50. *Ibid.*, XIV (February 8, 1872), 95.
51. *Ibid.*, XIV (March 7, 1872), 159.
52. *Ibid.*
53. *Ibid.*, XIX (December 10, 1874), 384.
54. *Ibid.*, XXIII (December 14, 1876), 359.
55. *Ibid.*, XXXI (December 9, 1880), 416.
56. *Ibid.*, XXV (November 15, 1877), 305.
57. *Ibid.*, XXV (December 6, 1877), 353.
58. *Ibid.*, XXIII (December 14, 1876), 359.
59. *Ibid.*, IX (December 30, 1869), 587–88.
60. *Ibid.*, XI (December 22, 1870), 425.
61. *Ibid.*, V (October 24, 1867), 329.
62. *Ibid.*, VII (December 24, 1868), 531.
63. *Ibid.*, V (December 26, 1867), 523–24.
64. *Ibid.*, VIII (April 29, 1869), 339.
65. *Ibid.*, XXV (December 20, 1877), 385.
66. *Ibid.*, IX (December 16, 1869), 543–44.
67. *Ibid.*, IX (December 16, 1869), 540.
68. *Ibid.*, VIII (April 15, 1869), 295.
69. *Ibid.*
70. *Ibid.*, IV (January 10, 1867), 29.
71. *Ibid.*, IX (December 16, 1869), 542.
72. *Ibid.*, IX (December 16, 1869), 542–43.
73. *Ibid.*, XXV (December 6, 1877), 353.
74. *Ibid.*, III (December 20, 1866), 493.
75. *Ibid.*
76. *Ibid.*, VI (May 7, 1868), 376.
77. *Ibid.*, VII (November 12, 1868), 397–98.
78. *Ibid.*, XXVII (November 28, 1878), 339.
79. *Ibid.*, XXXIII (December 8, 1881), 457.
80. *Ibid.*, II (January 25, 1866), 119–20.
81. *Ibid.*, XVII (December 11, 1873), 389.
82. *Ibid.*, XXIX (December 11, 1879), 408.
83. *Ibid.*, II (December 13, 1866), 467–68.
84. Caroline M. Hewins, "Letter," in *The Nation*, VIII (April 15, 1869), 295.
85. *The Nation*, VII (October 22, 1868), 335.
86. *Ibid.*, VIII (May 20, 1869), 400.
87. *Ibid.*, XI (July 14, 1870), 30–31.
88. *Ibid.*, IX (December 30, 1869), 588.
89. *Ibid.*, I (December 14, 1865), 757.
90. *Ibid.*, IX (December 30, 1869), 587.
91. *Ibid.*, XIX (December 3, 1874), 368.

92. *Ibid.*, I (December 14, 1865), 757.
93. *Ibid.*, I (December 28, 1865), 818.
94. *Ibid.*, V (December 26, 1867), 523.
95. *Ibid.*, VII (August 20, 1868), 154–55.
96. *Ibid.*, XIX (December 17, 1874), 401.
97. *Ibid.*, XXV (December 6, 1877), 352–53.
98. *Ibid.*
99. *Ibid.*, XXI (November 18, 1880), 363.
100. *Ibid.*, I (September 21, 1865), 379.
101. *Ibid.*, I (December 14, 1865), 757.
102. *Ibid.*
103. *Ibid.*, II (March 1, 1866), 281.
104. *Ibid.*, IV (April 4, 1867), 273.
105. *Ibid.*, IV (January 31, 1867), 90.
106. Harold North Fowler, "Allen, William Francis," *Dictionary of American Biography* (New York: Charles Scribner's Sons, 1928) I, p. 211.
107. William Francis Allen, review of *The Boys and Girls of the Revolution,* by Charles H. Woodman in *The Nation,* XXIII (December 7, 1876), 345.
108. Allen, review of *The Story of Liberty,* by Charles Carleton Coffin in *The Nation,* XXVII (December 19, 1878), 389.
109. Allen, review of *Short History of France for Young People,* by Elizabeth Stansbury Kirkland in *The Nation,* XXVII (December 19, 1878), 389.
110. Allen, review of *Raleigh, His Exploits and Voyages,* by George M. Towle in *The Nation,* XXXIII (December 8, 1881), 456.
111. Allen, review of *Montezuma and the Conquest of Mexico,* by Edward Eggleston in *The Nation,* XI (November 18, 1880), 364.
112. Allen, review of *Marco Polo,* by George M. Towle in *The Nation,* XXI (November 18, 1880), 364.
113. Allen, review of *Magellan; or, The First Voyage Round the World,* by George M. Towle in *The Nation,* XXIX (December 4, 1879), 392.
114. Allen, review of *Young Folks' History of the War for the Union,* by John D. Champlin, Jr. in *The Nation,* XXXIII (November 24, 1881), 419–20.
115. Allen, review of *Young Folks' History of America,* by Hezekiah Butterworth in *The Nation,* XXXIII (August 25, 1881), 160.
116. Allen, review of *Zigzag Journeys in Europe,* by Hezekiah Butterworth in *The Nation,* XXIX (December 18, 1879), 427.
117. *The Nation,* XXIX (December 4, 1879), 392.
118. *Ibid.*, XXXIII (December 15, 1881), 478.
119. *Ibid.*, VII (September 17, 1868), 234–35.
120. *Ibid.*, XI (July 14, 1870), 31.
121. *Ibid.*, XV (August 8, 1872), 93–94.
122. *Ibid.*, XVII (November 27, 1873), 358.
123. *Ibid.*, XXI (December 16, 1875), 391.
124. *Ibid.*, XXIX (October 16, 1879), 263.
125. E. H. Hall, "Trowbridge, John," *Dictionary of American Biography* (New York: Charles Scribner's Sons, 1928) XVIII, pp. 654–55.
126. *The Nation,* XVIII (May 8, 1879), 324.
127. *Ibid.*, XXIII (December 14, 1876), 359.
128. *Ibid.*, XXXI (November 18, 1880), 363.
129. *Ibid.*, XXVII (December 19, 1878), 389.
130. *Ibid.*, XXIX (December 18, 1879), 428.
131. *Ibid.*, XXXI (December 9, 1880), 416.
132. *Ibid.*, XXXIII (November 24, 1881), 419.
133. William Crary Brownell, review of *The Two Gray Girls and Their Opposite Neighbors,* by Ellen Haile in *The Nation,* XXXI (December 9, 1880), 417.
134. *The Nation,* XXXIII (December 15, 1881), 478.
135. *The Critic,* I (December 3, 1881), 337–38.

136. *The Dial,* II (December, 1881), 181–82.
137. *Literary World,* XII (December 17, 1881), 478.
138. *The Nation,* V (December 26, 1867), 524.
139. *Ibid.,* XXIII (December 7, 1876), 345.
140. *Ibid.,* XXVII (November 7, 1878), 288.
141. *Ibid.,* XXIX (December 4, 1879), 392.
142. *Ibid.,* XV (December 12, 1872), 388–89.
143. *Ibid.,* XXI (December 16, 1875), 391–92.
144. *Ibid.,* V (December 12, 1867), 474.
145. *Ibid.,* VI (June 18, 1868), 496.
146. *Ibid.,* IX (October 14, 1869), 321.
147. Allen, review of *The Boy's Froissart,* by Sidney Lanier in *The Nation,* XXIX (December 4, 1879), 392.
148. Allen, review of *The Boy's King Arthur,* by Sidney Lanier in *The Nation,* XXXI (November 18, 1880), 364.
149. Allen, review of *The Boy's Mabinogion,* by Sidney Lanier in *The Nation,* XXXIII (November 24, 1881), 419.
150. *The Nation,* XXXI (November 18, 1880), 364.
151. *Ibid.,* XXXIII (December 15, 1881), 478.
152. *Ibid.*
153. *Ibid.,* IX (December 30, 1869), 388.
154. *Ibid.,* XIV (May 2, 1872), 294–95.
155. *Ibid.,* III (December 20, 1866), 493.
156. *Ibid.,* VII (December 10, 1868), 485.
157. *Ibid.,* XIX (November 19, 1874), 335–36.

CHAPTER 8

1. Frank Luther Mott, *A History of American Magazines, 1865–1885* (Cambridge: Harvard University Press, 1938), p. 25.
2. Mott lists *Nation, Critic, Dial,* and *Atlantic* as the magazines with the most consistently high quality reviewing. (*A History of American Magazines, 1865–1885,* p. 232).
3. J. Henry Harper, *The House of Harper; A Century of Publishing in Franklin Square* (New York: Harper & Bros., 1912), p. 129.
4. Howard Allen Bridgman, "Abbott, Lyman," *Dictionary of American Biography* (New York: Charles Scribner's Sons, 1928), I. p. 24.
5. Lyman Abbott, *Reminiscences* (Boston and New York: Houghton Mifflin Co., 1915), p. 284–85.
6. Abbott, *op. cit.,* p. 297.
7. *Harper's New Monthly Magazine,* XLVI (December, 1872), 140.
8. *Ibid.,* XLII (January, 1871), 305.
9. *Ibid.,* XLIV (December, 1871), 142.
10. *Ibid.,* XLVI (April, 1873), 774–75.
11. *Ibid.,* XL (January, 1870), 299.
12. *Ibid.,* XLII (January, 1871), 303.
13. *Ibid.,* XLII (January, 1871), 303–04.
14. *Ibid.,* LIV (March, 1877), 618.
15. *Ibid.,* XLVI (January, 1873), 303; XLVI (April, 1873), 774.
16. *Ibid.,* XLIV (January, 1872), 299.
17. *Ibid.,* XXXIV (January, 1867), 266.
18. *Ibid.,* XXVI (December, 1867), 128.
19. *Ibid.,* XLIV (January, 1872), 297.
20. *Ibid.,* L (January, 1875), 289.
21. *Ibid.,* XLII (February, 1871), 463.
22. *Ibid.,* XLII (March, 1871), 622.
23. *Ibid.,* LX (December, 1879), 155.
24. *Ibid.,* LIV (May, 1877), 924.

25. *Ibid.,* XXXIX (August, 1869), 455–56.
26. *Ibid.,* XLII (January, 1871), 304.
27. *Ibid.*
28. *Ibid.,* L (March, 1875), 601.
29. *Ibid.,* LX (December, 1879), 155.
30. *Ibid.,* XXXIX (November, 1869), 925.
31. *Ibid.,* XXXIX (August, 1869), 455.
32. *Ibid.,* XLIV (January, 1872), 300.
33. *Ibid.,* XLII (January, 1871), 304.
34. *Ibid.,* XLIII (August, 1871), 459.
35. Herbert R. Mayes, *Alger, A Biography Without a Hero* (New York: Macy-Masius, 1928), p. 104.
36. *Harper's New Monthly Magazine,* XLIII (August, 1871), 459.
37. *Ibid.,* XLVI (January, 1873), 303.
38. *Ibid.,* XLIV (December, 1871), 142.
39. *Ibid.,* XLVI (April, 1873), 774–75.
40. *Ibid.,* LXII (December, 1880), 155.
41. *Ibid.,* XLII (January, 1871), 304.
42. *Ibid.,* XLIII (July, 1871), 301.
43. *Ibid.,* XLVIII (January, 1874), 298.
44. *Ibid.,* XLVI (January, 1873), 303.
45. *Ibid.*
46. *Ibid.,* LVII (August, 1878), 465.
47. *Ibid.,* LVIII (April, 1879), 786.
48. *Ibid.,* XXXIX (November, 1869), 925.
49. *Ibid.,* XLII (January, 1871), 304.
50. *Ibid.,* XLII (April, 1871), 780.
51. *Ibid.,* XLIII (August, 1871), 457.
52. *Ibid.,* L (February, 1875), 449.
53. *Ibid.*
54. Abbott, *op. cit.,* p. 125 *et passim.*
55. *Harper's New Monthly Magazine,* XXXIX (August, 1869), 455–56.
56. *Ibid.,* XLI (June, 1870), 144.
57. *Ibid.,* XLIV (December, 1871), 142.
58. *Ibid.,* LVI (February, 1878), 470.
59. *Ibid.,* LIV (February, 1877), 471.
60. *Ibid.,* XLIII (October, 1871), 785.
61. Mott, *op. cit.,* p. 391.
62. *Harper's New Monthly Magazine,* XXXVIII (May, 1869), 855.
63. *Ibid.,* XLIV (January, 1872), 301.
64. *Ibid.,* L (January, 1875), 289.
65. *Ibid.,* XLVIII (December, 1873), 140.
66. *Ibid.,* XLII (January, 1871), 304–05.
67. *Ibid.,* XLII (January, 1871), 305.
68. *Ibid.,* LVI (January, 1878), 308.
69. *Ibid.,* LVI (April, 1878), 787–88.
70. *Ibid.,* LVIII (March, 1879), 631.
71. *Ibid.,* XXIX (November, 1869), 925.
72. *Ibid.,* XLIII (August, 1871), 459.
73. *Ibid.,* LVI (January, 1878), 311.
74. *Ibid.,* XL (May, 1870), 929.
75. *Ibid.,* L (January, 1875), 289.
76. *Ibid.,* XLVIII (January, 1874), 298.
77. *Ibid.,* XLI (June, 1870), 144.
78. *Ibid.,* XLII (January, 1871), 304.
79. *Ibid.,* XLVIII (January, 1874), 298.
80. *Ibid.,* XLIII (September, 1871), 624.

81. *Ibid.,* XLIV (January, 1872), 300.
82. *Ibid.,* XLVI (January, 1873), 303.
83. *Ibid.*
84. *Ibid.,* LXIII (August, 1881), 476.
85. *Ibid.,* XXXVIII (January, 1869), 276.
86. *Ibid.,* XLII (January, 1871), 249.
87. *Ibid.,* XLII (January, 1871), 303.
88. *Ibid.,* XLIV (January, 1872), 299.
89. *Ibid.,* LX (December, 1879), 154–55.
90. *Ibid.,* LX (January, 1880), 314–15.
91. *Ibid.,* LX (January, 1880), 315.
92. *Ibid.,* XXXVIII (May, 1869), 855.
93. *Ibid.,* XXXIX (August, 1869), 455.
94. *Ibid.,* XXXIX (November, 1869), 925.
95. *Ibid.,* XLII (January, 1871), 303.
96. *Ibid.,* XLVI (December, 1872), 140.
97. *Ibid.,* L (January, 1875), 289.
98. *Ibid.,* XLVI (January, 1873), 301–02.
99. *Ibid.,* XXXVII (August, 1868), 425.
100. *Ibid.,* LIX (July, 1879), 310–11.
101. *Ibid.,* LX (December, 1879), 155.
102. *Ibid.,* XLIV (January, 1872), 297.
103. *Ibid.,* XXXII (March, 1866), 525.
104. *Ibid.,* XLVI (March, 1873), 613.
105. *Ibid.,* L (May, 1875), 914.
106. *Ibid.*
107. *Ibid.,* LVII (August, 1878), 465.
108. *Ibid.,* LVIII (March, 1879), 631.
109. *Ibid.,* LX (February, 1880), 475.
110. *Ibid.,* XLIII (September, 1871), 624.
111. *Ibid.,* XLVI (April, 1873), 774.
112. *Ibid.,* LVI (January, 1878), 310.
113. *Ibid.,* LX (December, 1879), 155–56.
114. *Ibid.,* LXI (November, 1880), 955–56.
115. *Ibid.,* LX (January, 1880), 315.
116. *Ibid.,* LX (January, 1880), 314–15.
117. *Ibid.,* LVI (February, 1878), 470.
118. *Ibid.,* LVII (June, 1878), 149.
119. *Ibid.,* LIX (July, 1879), 310.
120. *Ibid.,* LVIII (February, 1879), 468.
121. *Ibid.,* LX (February, 1880), 474.
122. Mott, *op. cit.,* p. 361.
123. *Ibid.,* p. 375.
124. *Ibid.*
125. J. F. Meline, "Current Literature," *The Galaxy,* IX (January, 1870), 137.
126. *The Galaxy,* XI (January, 1871), 145–46.
127. *Ibid.,* XIII (February, 1872), 277.
128. *Ibid.*
129. *Ibid.,* XXIII (January, 1877), 139.
130. *Ibid.,* XVII (January, 1874), 143.
131. *Ibid.,* XXXIII (February, 1877), 285.
132. *Ibid.,* IX (May, 1870), 711–12.
133. *Ibid.,* IX (June, 1870), 853.
134. *Ibid.,* XIX (May, 1875), 718.
135. *Ibid.,* XXII (September, 1876), 427.
136. Mott, *op. cit.,* p. 381.
137. *Ibid.,* p. 417.

138. *Ibid.*, p. 421.
139. *Appleton's Journal,* XI (June 27, 1874), 827.
140. *Ibid.*, XIV (December 11, 1875), 761.
141. *Ibid.*, XV (January 29, 1876), 153.
142. *Ibid.*, XV (January 22, 1876), 123.
143. *Ibid.*, XII (November 21, 1874), 668.
144. *Ibid.*, XIV (November 6, 1875), 601.
145. *Ibid.*, X (December 20, 1873), 797.
146. *Ibid.*, XI (January 17, 1874), 91.
147. *Ibid.*, IX (January 1, 1873), 28.
148. *Ibid.*, IX (January 4, 1873), 61.
149. *Ibid.*, N. S. II (January, 1877), 96.
150. *Ibid.*, N. S. IX (November, 1880), 473.
151. *Ibid.*, N. S. X (January, 1881), 95.
152. *Ibid.*, XI (January 17, 1874), 91.
153. *Ibid.*, XII (November 21, 1874), 668.
154. *Ibid.*, XIV (December 11, 1875), 761.
155. *Ibid.*, XI (January 31, 1874), 155.
156. *Ibid.*
157. *Ibid.*, XII (October 24, 1874), 539.
158. *Ibid.*, VI (December 9, 1871), 668.
159. *Ibid.*, VII (February 17, 1872), 192.
160. *Ibid.*, IX (January 4, 1873), 61.
161. *Ibid.*, XIV (November 20, 1875), 665.
162. *Ibid.*, XIV (July 24, 1875), 118–19.
163. *Ibid.*, N. S. VII (December, 1879), 575–76.
164. *Ibid.*, N. S. II (January, 1877), 96.
165. *Ibid.*, N. S. V (November, 1878), 480.
166. *Ibid.*, N. S. VIII (February, 1880), 192.
167. *Ibid.*, N. S. XI (July, 1881), 96.
168. *Ibid.*
169. *Ibid.*, N. S. IV (January, 1878), 96.
170. *Ibid.*, N. S. V (August, 1878), 192.
171. *Ibid.*, N. S. VI (June, 1879), 576.
172. *Ibid.*, N. S. VIII (January, 1880), 96.
173. *Ibid.*, XII (December 19, 1874), 796.
174. *Ibid.*, XIV (December 11, 1875), 761.
175. *Ibid.*, X (December 13, 1873), 765.
176. *Ibid.*, XII (August 1, 1874), 155.
177. *Ibid.*, X (July 19, 1873), 93.
178. *Ibid.*, XIV (November 27, 1875), 695–96.
179. *Ibid.*, N. S. II (April, 1877), 384.
180. *Ibid.*, XIII (May 15, 1875), 631.
181. *Ibid.*, VII (January 6, 1872), 24.
182. *Ibid.*, XIV (November 27, 1875), 695–96.
183. Mott, *op. cit.,* pp. 32–33.
184. *Hours at Home,* IX (May, 1869), 100.
185. *Ibid.*, VIII (April, 1869), 579.
186. *Ibid.*, X (December, 1869), 195.
187. *Ibid.*
188. *Ibid.*, IV (February, 1867), 384.
189. *Ibid.*, VII (June, 1868), 191–92.
190. *Ibid.*, VII (June, 1868), 191.
191. *Ibid.*, VII (July, 1868), 287.
192. *Ibid.*, IX (August, 1869), 385.
193. *Ibid.*, XI (June, 1870), 196.
194. *Ibid.*, VI (January, 1868), 286.

195. *Ibid.*, XI (July, 1870), 292.
196. Mott, *op. cit.*, pp. 428–30.
197. *Putnam's Magazine*, N. S. II (December, 1868), 760.
198. *Ibid.*, N. S. II (July, 1868), 120.
199. *Ibid.*, N. S. I (March, 1868), 383–84.
200. *Ibid.*, N. S. II (December, 1868), 760.
201. *Ibid.*, N. S. V (January, 1870), 129.
202. *Ibid.*, N. S. II (November, 1868), 633.
203. *Ibid.*, N. S. IV (July, 1869), 124.
204. *Ibid.*, N. S. IV (September, 1869), 380–81.
205. *Ibid.*, N. S. V (January, 1870), 129.
206. Mott, *op. cit.*, pp. 457–58.
207. *Scribner's Monthly*, XI (April, 1876), 898.
208. *Ibid.*
209. *Ibid.*, III (December, 1871), 254.
210. *Ibid.*, V (January, 1873), 399.
211. *Ibid.*, IX (January, 1875), 388.
212. *Ibid.*, XXI (December, 1880), 322.
213. *Ibid.*, XIV (May, 1877), 120.
214. *Ibid.*, XV (December, 1877), 282–83.
215. *Ibid.*, XIII (January, 1877), 424.
216. *Ibid.*, XXI (December, 1880), 323.
217. *Ibid.*, III (March, 1872), 639.
218. *Ibid.*, XIV (May, 1877), 120.
219. *Ibid.*, XIV (September, 1877), 720–21.
220. *Ibid.*, I (February, 1871), 462.
221. *Ibid.*
222. *Ibid.*, XV (January, 1878), 440.
223. *Ibid.*, I (February, 1871), 462.
224. *Ibid.*, XXI (December, 1880), 321–22.
225. *Ibid.*, I (February, 1871), 462.
226. *Ibid.*, XI (December, 1875), 296–97.
227. *Ibid.*, III (January, 1872), 383.
228. *Ibid.*, II (October, 1871), 668–69.
229. *Ibid.*, IX (January, 1875), 388.
230. *Ibid.*, XI (December, 1875), 296–97.
231. *Ibid.*, XXII (October, 1881), 954.
232. *Ibid.*, III (January, 1872), 383.
233. *Ibid.*, XIX (December, 1879), 314.
234. *Ibid.*, XXI (January, 1881), 481.
235. *Ibid.*, II (August, 1871), 447.
236. *Ibid.*, IX (April, 1875), 768–69.
237. *Ibid.*, XIX (December, 1879), 316.
238. *Ibid.*, XIX (December, 1879), 313–14.
239. *Ibid.*, II (August, 1871), 446–47.
240. *Ibid.*, XIX (December, 1879), 315.
241. *Ibid.*, XXI (January, 1881), 481.
242. *Ibid.*, XI (April, 1876), 898.
243. *Ibid.*, VII (February, 1874), 507.
244. *Ibid.*, XV (December, 1877), 283.

CHAPTER 9

1. Frank Luther Mott, *A History of American Magazines, 1850–1865*, (Cambridge: Harvard University Press, 1938), pp. 32–33.
2. Van Wyck Brooks, *New England: Indian Summer* (New York: E. P. Dutton & Co., Inc., 1950), p. 1.
3. Mott, *op. cit.*, p. 507.

4. Horace E. Scudder, "Andersen's Short Stories," *Atlantic Monthly,* XXXVI (November, 1875), 598–602.
5. F. C. Hopkinson, review of *Florence and John,* by Jacob Abbott in *Atlantic Monthly,* V (February, 1860), 247–50.
6. Hopkinson, *op. cit.,* 247.
7. *Ibid.*
8. Mott, in *A History of American Magazines, 1850–1865,* pp. 501–07, describes, in detail, the changes and emendations forced upon contributors by the first three editors of the *Atlantic.*
9. *Atlantic Monthly,* XLI (January, 1878), 136–37.
10. *Ibid.,* XLIII (January, 1879), 123.
11. *Ibid.,* XXV (June, 1870), 753.
12. *Ibid.,* XXIX (January, 1872), 109.
13. *Ibid.,* XLI (January, 1878), 137.
14. *Ibid.,* XLVII (January, 1881), 123.
15. *Ibid.,* XLVIII (October, 1881), 574.
16. "Mark Twain's New Departure," *Atlantic Monthly,* XLVIII (December, 1881), 844.
17. *Atlantic Monthly,* XLV (January, 1880), 128.
18. *Ibid.,* XLII (December, 1878), 780.
19. *Ibid.,* XXV (June, 1870), 752.
20. *Ibid.,* XLVIII (December, 1881), 858.
21. *Ibid.,* XLVII (January, 1881), 124.
22. *Ibid.,* XL (December, 1877), 761.
23. *Ibid.,* XXIV (December, 1869), 767.
24. *Ibid.,* XL (December, 1877), 761.
25. *Ibid.,* XLII (December, 1878), 779.
26. *Ibid.,* XLI (January, 1878), 137–39.
27. *Ibid.,* XLIII (January, 1879), 125.
28. *Ibid.,* XLVII (January, 1881), 126.
29. *Ibid.,* XLII (December, 1878), 779.
30. William Dean Howells, review of *The Adventures of Tom Sawyer,* by Samuel L. Clemens in *Atlantic Monthly,* XXXVII (May, 1876), 621.
31. *Atlantic Monthly,* XLIII (January, 1879), 125.
32. "Mark Twain's New Departure," *Atlantic Monthly,* XLVIII (December, 1881), 845.
33. *Atlantic Monthly,* XXVII (February, 1871), 261–62.
34. *Ibid.,* XXIX (January, 1872), 109–10.
35. *Ibid.,* XLIII (January, 1879), 123.
36. *Ibid.*
37. *Ibid.,* XXVII (April, 1871), 525.
38. *Ibid.,* XLV (January, 1880), 127.
39. Howells, review of *The Story of a Bad Boy,* by Thomas Bailey Aldrich in *Atlantic Monthly,* XXV (January, 1870), 124.
40. Howells, review of *The Adventures of Tom Sawyer,* by Samuel L. Clemens in *Atlantic Monthly,* XXXVII (May, 1876), 622.
41. *Atlantic Monthly,* XL (December, 1877), 764.
42. *Ibid.,* XL (December, 1877), 763.
43. *Ibid.*
44. *Ibid.,* XLIII (January, 1879), 124.
45. *Ibid.,* XLVII (January, 1881), 123.
46. *Ibid.,* XLVII (February, 1881), 302.
47. Scudder, *op. cit.,* 601.
48. *Atlantic Monthly,* XXVII (April, 1871), 525.
49. *Ibid.,* XLVII (January, 1881), 124.
50. *Ibid.,* XLVII (February, 1881), 302.
51. *Ibid.,* XXIX (January, 1872), 109–10.

52. *Ibid.,* XVII (June, 1866), 780.
53. Howells, review of *Stories from My Attic,* by Horace E. Scudder in *Atlantic Monthly,* XXIV (December, 1869), 767.
54. *Atlantic Monthly,* XLII (December, 1878), 780.
55. *Ibid.,* XLV (January, 1880), 128.
56. *Supra.,* p. 133.
57. Howells, *op. cit.,* 767.
58. *Atlantic Monthly,* XLI (January, 1878), 139.
59. *Ibid.,* XLI (January, 1878), 138.
60. *Ibid.,* XLII (December, 1878), 779.
61. *Ibid.,* XXIX (January, 1872), 109–10.
62. *Ibid.,* XLV (January, 1880), 129.
63. *Ibid.,* XLVII (January, 1881), 122–23.
64. *Ibid.,* XLV (January, 1880), 131.
65. *Ibid.,* XLIII (January, 1879), 123.
66. *Ibid.,* XLVIII (December, 1881), 857.
67. *Ibid.*
68. *Ibid.,* XLVII (January, 1881), 126.
69. *Ibid.,* XLVII (February, 1881), 301.
70. *Ibid.,* XLVII (January, 1881), 125.
71. *Ibid.*
72. *Ibid.,* XLV (January, 1880), 131.
73. *Ibid.*
74. *Ibid.,* XLVII (January, 1881), 125.
75. *Ibid.,* XLVII (April, 1881), 592.
76. *Ibid.,* XXV (June, 1870), 753.
77. *Ibid.,* XLIII (January, 1879), 124.
78. *Ibid.,* XVIII (May, 1879), 685.
79. Frank Luther Mott, *A History of American Magazines, 1865–1885,* (Cambridge: Harvard University Press, 1938) p. 436.
80. Mott, *op. cit.,* p. 437.
81. Edward Everett Hale, "The Examiner," *Old and New,* I (January, 1870), 81–82.
82. Mott, *op. cit.,* p. 438.
83. *Old and New,* II (December, 1870), 739.
84. *Ibid.*
85. *Ibid.,* III (January, 1871), 107.
86. *Ibid.,* IX (May, 1874), 638.
87. *Ibid.,* III (February, 1871), 239.
88. *Ibid.*
89. *Ibid.,* III (June, 1871), 748.
90. *Ibid.,* I (May, 1870), 709–12.
91. *Ibid.,* IX (January, 1874), 139–40.
92. *Ibid.,* IV (December, 1871), 701.
93. *Ibid.,* III (February, 1871), 239.
94. *Ibid.,* V (May, 1872), 607.

CHAPTER 10

1. Frank Luther Mott, *A History of American Magazines, 1865–1885,* (Cambridge: Harvard University Press, 1938), p. 396.
2. Mott, *op. cit.,* p. 398.
3. *Lippincott's Magazine,* XX (December, 1877), 776.
4. *Ibid.,* II (October, 1868), 456.
5. *Ibid.*
6. *Ibid.,* VI (August, 1870), 231.
7. *Ibid.,* XX (December, 1877), 776.
8. *Ibid.,* V (April, 1870), 463.

9. *Ibid.,* XXI (January, 1878), 135–36.
10. *Ibid.,* XXVII (January, 1881), 112.
11. *Ibid.,* XX (December, 1877), 776.
12. *Ibid.,* XXI (January, 1878), 136.
13. *Ibid.,* XXVII (January, 1881), 112.
14. *Ibid.,* XX (December, 1877), 776.
15. *Ibid.,* XXI (January, 1878), 135–36.
16. *Ibid.,* XXV (January, 1880), 135.
17. *Ibid.,* VII (February, 1871), 232.
18. *The Nation,* XI (December 22, 1870), 424–25.
19. *Lippincott's Magazine,* XXI (January, 1878), 136.
20. *Ibid.,* XXV (January, 1880), 135.
21. *Ibid.,* XXV (January, 1880), 135–36.
22. *Ibid.,* XXVII (January, 1881), 112.
23. *Ibid.,* XXV (January, 1880), 135–36.
24. *Ibid.,* II (October, 1868), 456.
25. *Ibid.,* VI (August, 1870), 231.
26. *Ibid.,* XXVII (January, 1881), 112.
27. *Ibid.,* II (October, 1868), 456.
28. *Ibid.,* V (April, 1870), 463.
29. *Ibid.,* XXVII (January, 1881), 112.
30. *Ibid.,* XXI (January, 1878), 136.
31. *Ibid.,* XIX (February, 1877), 264.
32. Mott, *op. cit.,* p. 34–35.
33. *Penn Monthly Magazine,* IV (June, 1873), 433.
34. *Ibid.,* VII (December, 1876), 988.
35. *Ibid.,* IV (September, 1873), 666.
36. *Ibid.,* VII (December, 1876), 988–89.
37. *Ibid.,* VII (December, 1876), 989.
38. *Ibid.,* VII (December, 1876), 987.
39. *Ibid.,* VII (January, 1876), 80–81.
40. *Ibid.,* VII (December, 1876), 987–88.
41. *Ibid.,* VII (December, 1876), 989.
42. *Ibid.*
43. *Ibid.,* VII (January, 1876), 80–81.
44. *Ibid.,* XII (April, 1881), 320.
45. *Ibid.,* XII (January, 1881), 79–80.
46. *Ibid.,* VI (April, 1875), 306–07.
47. *Ibid.,* V (February, 1874), 165–66.
48. *Ibid.*
49. *Ibid.,* VII (February, 1876), 159.
50. *Ibid.,* XII (December, 1881), 956–57.
51. *Ibid.,* VII (December, 1876), 989.
52. *Ibid.,* VII (December, 1876), 988–89.
53. *Ibid.*
54. *Ibid.,* VII (December, 1876), 989.
55. *Ibid.,* VII (January, 1876), 80–81.
56. *Ibid.,* VII (December, 1876), 987.

CHAPTER 11

1. Frank Luther Mott, *A History of American Magazines, 1865–1885,* (Cambridge: Harvard University Press, 1938), p. 413–16.
2. *The Western Monthly,* II (August, 1869), 129–30.
3. *The Lakeside Monthly,* IX (January, 1873), 74.
4. *Ibid.,* IX (January, 1873), 73.
5. *Ibid.,* XI (January, 1874), 94.
6. *Ibid.*

7. *Ibid.,* IX (January, 1873), 73.
8. *The Western Monthly,* II (August, 1869), 129–30.
9. *Ibid.,* II (August, 1869), 129.
10. *The Lakeside Monthly,* X (July, 1873), 75–76.
11. *Ibid.,* X (July, 1873), 75.
12. *Ibid.,* IX (January, 1873), 73.
13. Mott, *op. cit.,* p. 51.
14. *Western,* VII (January, 1881), 110.
15. *Ibid.,* I (April, 1875), 262.
16. *Ibid.,* V (March, 1879), 212.
17. *Ibid.,* III (May, 1877), 310.
18. *Ibid.,* IV (January-February, 1878), 84.
19. *Ibid.,* VII (January, 1881), 110.

CHAPTER 12

1. Frank Luther Mott, *A History of American Magazines, 1865–1885,* (Cambridge: Harvard University Press, 1938), pp. 402–09.
2. *The Overland Monthly,* XV (November, 1875), 493.
3. *Ibid.,* I (August, 1868), 199–200.
4. *Ibid.,* IV (March, 1870), 294.
5. *Ibid.,* VII (September, 1871), 294.
6. *Ibid.,* XV (November, 1875), 493.
7. *Ibid.,* VII (September, 1871), 295.
8. *Ibid.,* II (May, 1869), 486.
9. *Ibid.*
10. *Ibid.,* I (August, 1868), 200.
11. *Ibid.,* I (November, 1868), 487.
12. *Ibid.,* VI (February, 1871), 199.
13. *Ibid.,* IV (April, 1870), 391.
14. *Ibid.,* XII (February, 1874), 199.
15. *Ibid.,* III (July, 1869), 102.
16. *Ibid.,* I (November, 1868), 488.
17. *Ibid.*
18. *Ibid.,* III (July, 1869), 102.
19. *Ibid.,* VI (June, 1871), 580.
20. *Ibid.,* XV (November, 1875), 494.
21. *Ibid.,* I (November, 1868), 487.
22. *Ibid.,* II (March, 1869), 293.
23. *Ibid.,* VII (September, 1871), 290.
24. *Ibid.,* XII (January, 1874), 103.
25. *Ibid.,* XV (November, 1875), 492.
26. *Ibid.,* VII (September, 1871), 290.
27. *Ibid.*
28. *Ibid.,* XII (April, 1874), 391.
29. *Ibid.,* XV (November, 1875), 492–93.
30. *Ibid.,* I (November, 1868), 487–88.
31. *Ibid.*
32. *Ibid.*
33. *Ibid.*
34. *Ibid.,* II (March, 1869), 293.
35. *Ibid.,* III (December, 1869), 579–80.
36. *Ibid.,* III (December, 1869), 579.
37. *Our Young Folks,* V (December, 1869), 854.
38. *Overland Monthly,* IV (April, 1870), 392.
39. *Ibid.,* VII (December, 1871), 584.
40. *Ibid.,* XII (February, 1874), 199.
41. *Ibid.,* VIII (January, 1872), 103.

42. Mott, *op. cit.*, p. 407.
43. *The Californian,* III (January, 1881), 92.
44. *Ibid.,* IV (November, 1881), 448.
45. *Ibid.,* IV (December, 1881), 537.
46. *Ibid.,* IV (July, 1881), 93.
47. *Ibid.,* IV (July, 1881), 92.
48. *Ibid.,* IV (December, 1881), 537.
49. *Ibid.,* II (July, 1880), 92.
50. *Ibid.,* III (January, 1881), 92.
51. *Ibid.*
52. *Ibid.,* III (January, 1881), 91–92.
53. *Ibid.,* IV (October, 1881), 361.
54. *Ibid.,* III (January, 1881), 92.
55. *Ibid.,* III (February, 1881), 192.

CHAPTER 13

1. Susan Coolidge, "Holiday Books for Children. I," *The Literary World,* VIII (December, 1877), 123–24.
2. Coolidge, "Holiday Books for Children. II," *The Literary World,* VIII (January, 1878), 142–43.
3. *The Literary World,* VIII (November, 1877), 94.
4. *Ibid.,* X (February 15, 1879), 55.
5. *Ibid.,* I (November 1, 1870), 88.
6. *Ibid.,* II (June 1, 1871), 8.
7. *Ibid.,* IV (January, 1874), 120.
8. *Ibid.,* VI (September, 1875), 48.
9. *Ibid.,* I (July 1, 1870), 23–24.
10. *Ibid.,* V (June, 1874), 13.
11. *Ibid.,* X (December 20, 1879), 439.
12. *Ibid.,* X (December 6, 1879), 403.
13. *Ibid.,* XI (December 4, 1880), 442.
14. *Ibid.,* I (August 1, 1870), 40.
15. *Ibid.,* I (November 1, 1870), 91.
16. *Ibid.,* I (December 1, 1870), 110.
17. *Ibid.,* III (February 1, 1873), 139.
18. *Ibid.,* VI (October, 1875), 68–69.
19. *Ibid.,* I (July 1, 1870), 23–24.
20. *Ibid.,* XI (October 23, 1880), 373.
21. *Ibid.,* XI (December 4, 1880), 441.
22. *Ibid.,* I (October 1, 1870), 73.
23. *Ibid.,* I (November 1, 1870), 91.
24. *Ibid.,* I (August 1, 1870), 40.
25. *Ibid.,* VIII (January, 1878), 143.
26. *Ibid.,* II (October 1, 1871), 68.
27. *Ibid.,* III (October 1, 1872), 76.
28. *Ibid.,* I (July 1, 1870), 25–26.
29. *Ibid.,* III (March 1, 1873), 155.
30. *Ibid.,* VIII (March, 1878), 181–82.
31. *Ibid.,* X (December 20, 1879), 439.
32. *Ibid.,* IX (June, 1878), 16.
33. *Ibid.,* I (December 1, 1870), 109.
34. *Ibid.,* II (July 1, 1871), 29.
35. *Ibid.,* III (March 1, 1873), 155.
36. *Ibid.,* X (December 6, 1879), 403.
37. *Ibid.,* XII (March 26, 1881), 119.
38. *Ibid.,* XI (October 23, 1880), 374.
39. *Ibid.,* I (September 1, 1870), 52.

40. *Ibid.,* VII (December, 1876), 104.
41. *Ibid.,* II (July 1, 1871), 24.
42. *Ibid.,* XI (December 18, 1880), 467.
43. *Ibid.*
44. *Ibid.,* IX (June, 1878), 7.
45. *Ibid.,* X (March 1, 1879), 76.
46. *Ibid.,* X (December 6, 1879), 402.
47. *Ibid.,* XI (November 6, 1880), 395–96.
48. *Ibid.,* XI (December 4, 1880), 441.
49. *Ibid.,* XII (December 3, 1881), 449.
50. *Ibid.,* VI (October, 1875), 68.
51. *Ibid.,* IX (November, 1878), 95.
52. *Ibid.,* X (December 6, 1879), 402.
53. *Ibid.,* XI (December 4, 1880), 442.
54. *Ibid.,* X (November 8, 1879), 360.
55. *Ibid.,* X (December 6, 1879), 402.
56. *Ibid.,* XI (December 4, 1880), 441.
57. *Ibid.,* XII (September 24, 1881), 327.
58. *Ibid.,* XII (November 5, 1881), 398.
59. *Ibid.,* XII (November 19, 1881), 419.
60. *Ibid.,* X (April 26, 1879), 135.
61. *Ibid.,* X (October 25, 1879), 342–43.
62. *Ibid.,* XI (December 18, 1880), 467.
63. *Ibid.,* I (November 1, 1870), 85–86.
64. *Ibid.,* III (December 1, 1872), 108.
65. *Ibid.,* V (February, 1875), 135.
66. *Ibid.,* XII (June 4, 1881), 201.
67. *Ibid.,* XII (December 3, 1881), 451.
68. *Ibid.,* XII (December 3, 1881), 449–50.
69. *Ibid.*
70. *Ibid.,* IX (June, 1878), 16.
71. *Ibid.,* XI (November 6, 1880), 395.
72. *Ibid.,* XI (October 23, 1880), 374.
73. *Ibid.,* X (October 11, 1879), 332.
74. *Ibid.,* XII (February 12, 1881), 51.
75. *Ibid.,* XI (December 4, 1880), 442.
76. *Ibid.,* XII (December 17, 1881), 478.
77. *Ibid.,* VIII (June, 1877), 5–6.
78. *Ibid.,* IX (December 10, 1878), 124.
79. *Ibid.,* XI (December 4, 1880), 442.
80. *Ibid.,* XI (October 23, 1880), 374.
81. *Ibid.,* XII (January 1, 1881), 11.
82. *Ibid.,* XII (December 3, 1881), 449.
83. Frank Luther Mott, *A History of American Magazines, 1865–1885,* (Cambridge: Harvard University Press, 1938), p. 539.
84. *The Dial,* I (December, 1880), 163–64.
85. *Ibid.,* II (December, 1881), 183.
86. *Ibid.,* I (December, 1880), 163–64.
87. *Ibid.,* II (December, 1881), 184.
88. *Ibid.,* II (December, 1881), 181–82.
89. *Ibid.,* I (December, 1880), 163–64.
90. *Ibid.,* II (October, 1881), 123.
91. *Ibid.,* I (December, 1880), 163–64.
92. *Ibid.,* II (December, 1881), 181–82.
93. *Ibid.*
94. *Ibid.,* I (December, 1880), 163–64.

95. *Ibid.,* II (December, 1881), 182–83.
96. *Ibid.,* I (December, 1880), 163–64.
97. *Ibid.,* II (December, 1881), 183.
98. *Ibid.,* II (December, 1881), 184.
99. *Ibid.,* II (December, 1881), 183–84.
100. *Ibid.,* II (December, 1881), 184.
101. *Ibid.,* II (December, 1881), 185.
102. *Ibid.,* II (December, 1881), 180.
103. Mott, *op. cit.,* p. 549.
104. *Ibid.,* p. 551.
105. *The Critic,* I (October 8, 1881), 275.
106. *Ibid.,* I (November 5, 1881), 307.
107. *Ibid.,* I (December 3, 1881), 337–38.
108. *Ibid.,* I (November 5, 1881), 307.
109. *Ibid.,* I (November 19, 1881), 322–23.
110. *Ibid.,* I (November 19, 1881), 323.
111. *Ibid.,* I (December 31, 1881), 369.
112. *Ibid.,* I (September 10, 1881), 247.
113. *Ibid.,* I (December 31, 1881), 368.
114. *Ibid.,* I (December 3, 1881), 337–38.
115. *Ibid.*
116. *Ibid.,* I (November 5, 1881), 307.
117. *Ibid.*
118. *Ibid.,* I (December 31, 1881), 369.
119. *Ibid.,* I (October 8, 1881), 275.
120. *Ibid.,* I (November 19, 1881), 320.
121. *Ibid.,* I (December 31, 1881), 369.

CHAPTER 14

1. Frank Luther Mott, *A History of American Magazines, 1850–1865,* (Cambridge: Harvard University Press, 1938), p. 312.
2. *North American Review,* XCVIII (January, 1864), 304.
3. Thomas Wentworth Higginson, "Children's Books of the Year," *North American Review,* CII (January, 1866), 242.
4. *Ibid.,* 237.
5. *Ibid.*
6. *Ibid.,* 240–41.
7. *Ibid.,* 245.
8. *Ibid.,* 243.
9. *Ibid.,* 242.
10. *Ibid.,* 248.
11. "Works of Jules Verne," *North American Review,* CXVIII (January, 1874), 192–93.
12. Mott, *op. cit.,* p. 312.
13. *The New Englander,* XXXIV (July, 1875), 599.
14. *Ibid.,* XXXIX (January, 1880), 152.
15. *Ibid.,* XXVIII (October, 1869), 810.
16. *Ibid.,* XL (January, 1881), 133–34.
17. "Frontispiece," *The International Review,* I.
18. *The International Review,* V (March, 1878), 275.
19. *Ibid.,* VI (January, 1879), 103.
20. *Ibid.,* IX (December, 1880), 723.
21. James Mascarene Hubbard, "Fiction and Public Libraries," *The International Review,* X (February, 1881), 177.

CHAPTER 15

1. Review of *Sunday-School Annual for 1871,* in *The Literary World,* II (August 1, 1871), 46.
2. Frank Luther Mott, *A History of American Magazines, 1741–1850,* (Cambridge: Harvard University Press, 1938), p. 374.
3. *Ibid.,* 375.
4. *The Independent,* XVII (December 28, 1865), 3.
5. *Ibid.,* XIX (May 9, 1867), 2.
6. *Ibid.,* XVII (October 12, 1865), 2.
7. *Ibid.,* XXV (May 8, 1873), 587.
8. *Ibid.,* XXVII (September 2, 1875), 10.
9. *Ibid.,* XXX (June 13, 1878), 10.
10. *Ibid.,* XXVII (April 29, 1875), 10.
11. *Ibid.,* XXXI (January 2, 1879), 12.
12. *Ibid.,* XXXII (March 4, 1880), 11.
13. *Ibid.,* XVII (December 7, 1865), 2.
14. *Ibid.,* XXX (October 24, 1878), 10.
15. *Ibid.,* XXV (September 11, 1873), 1130.
16. *Ibid.,* XVII (December 21, 1865), 2.
17. *Ibid.,* XXVIII (October 26, 1876), 9.
18. *Ibid.,* XXVIII (July 6, 1876), 9.
19. *Ibid.,* XVII (December 21, 1865), 2.
20. *Ibid.,* XVIII (January 4, 1866), 3.
21. *Ibid.,* XXVI (January 15, 1874), 10.
22. *Ibid.,* XXXII (November 4, 1880), 12.
23. *Ibid.,* XXVIII (January 13, 1876), 10.
24. *Ibid.,* XXVI (January 15, 1874), 10.
25. Caroline H. Dall, review of *Eight Cousins,* by Louisa May Alcott in *The Independent,* XXVII (October 7, 1875), 9.
26. *The Independent,* XXV (July 10, 1873), 872.
27. *Ibid.,* XXVI (January 8, 1874), 10.
28. *Ibid.,* XXVII (November 25, 1875), 8.
29. *Ibid.,* XXV (March 13, 1873), 331.
30. *Ibid.,* XXXI (March 27, 1879), 11.
31. *Ibid.,* XXIX (December 6, 1877), 10.
32. *Ibid.,* XVIII (December 7, 1876), 8.
33. *Ibid.,* XXVI (September 17, 1874), 11.
34. *Ibid.,* XXVI (January 15, 1874), 10.
35. *Ibid.,* XVIII (January 25, 1866), 3.
36. *Ibid.,* XXVII (March 4, 1875), 10.
37. *Ibid.,* XXXI (April 3, 1879), 11.
38. *Ibid.,* XXX (June 6, 1878), 10.
39. *Ibid.,* XXXII (November 4, 1880), 12.
40. *Ibid.,* XXXII (January 1, 1880), 10.
41. *Ibid.,* XXXI (October 9, 1879), 9.
42. *Ibid.,* XXXI (July 17, 1879), 12.
43. *Ibid.,* XXXI (November 27, 1879), 10.
44. *Ibid.,* XXXI (December 25, 1879), 9.
45. *Ibid.,* XXVII (June 10, 1875), 10.
46. *Ibid.,* XXVIII (December 14, 1876), 8.
47. *Ibid.,* XXXII (December 23, 1880), 11.
48. *Ibid.,* XXIX (October 11, 1877), 9.
49. *Ibid.,* XXVI (January 15, 1874), 10.
50. *Ibid.,* XVII (November 2, 1865), 2.
51. *Ibid.,* XXVI (January 15, 1874), 10.
52. *Ibid.,* XIX (November 21, 1867), 2.

53. Frank Luther Mott, *A History of American Magazines, 1865–1885,* (Cambridge: Harvard University Press, 1938), pp. 506–07.
54. "Literature for the Young," *The Unitarian Review,* I (June, 1874), 354–59.
55. Ladies' Commission on Sunday-School Books, review of *Myths and Heroes,* by S. F. Smith in *The Unitarian Review,* I (June, 1874), 491–95.
56. Ladies' Commission on Sunday-School Books, review of *Lucy Maria,* by Abby Morton Diaz in *The Unitarian Review,* I (June, 1874), 496–98.
57. *The Unitarian Review,* VII (January, 1877), 108.
58. *Ibid.,* III (March, 1875), 325–26.
59. *Ibid.,* IV (July, 1875), 110–11.
60. *Ibid.,* III (May, 1875), 536–37.
61. *Ibid.,* IV (November, 1875), 543.
62. *Ibid.,* VI (November, 1876), 566.
63. *Ibid.,* VII (February, 1877), 226.
64. *Ibid.,* VII (January, 1877), 108.
65. *Ibid.,* I (March, 1874), 94.
66. *Ibid.,* XV (February, 1881), 192.
67. *Ibid.,* V (January, 1876), 107.
68. *Ibid.,* VII (January, 1877), 108.
69. *Ibid.*
70. *Ibid.,* XVI (August, 1881), 196.
71. Mott, *op. cit.,* pp. 329–30.
72. *Ibid.,* p. 330.
73. *The Catholic World,* I (June, 1865), 432.
74. *Ibid.,* II (February, 1866), 718.
75. *Ibid.,* III (August, 1866), 720.
76. *Ibid.,* II (February, 1866), 719–20.
77. *Ibid.,* XVII (April, 1873), 142–43.
78. *Ibid.,* XXIX (April, 1879), 142.
79. *Ibid.,* VI (January, 1868), 574.
80. *Ibid.,* IX (June, 1869), 429.
81. *Ibid.,* X (October, 1869), 140.
82. *Ibid.,* VI (March, 1868), 860.
83. *Ibid.,* IX (July, 1869), 576.
84. *Ibid.,* XXII (December, 1875), 431–32.
85. *Ibid.,* XII (December, 1870), 431.

CHAPTER 16

1. *Old and New,* V (May, 1872), 611.
2. *Ohio Educational Monthly,* XIV (December, 1865), 416.
3. *Ibid.,* XXVIII (October, 1879), 338.
4. *American Education Monthly,* II (November, 1865), 349–51.
5. *Ibid.,* V (July, 1868), 296.
6. *Ibid.,* III (November, 1866), 446–47.
7. *The New England Journal of Education,* XIV (October 27, 1881), 274.
8. *Ibid.,* IX (May 22, 1879), 333.
9. *Ibid.,* II (November 13, 1875), 227.
10. *Ibid.,* IV (November 25, 1876), 240.
11. *Ibid.,* X (October 30, 1879), 249.
12. *Ibid.,* XII (November 18, 1880), 346.
13. *Ibid.,* XIV (November 24, 1881), 346.
14. *Ibid.,* XIII (June 16, 1881), 408.
15. *Ibid.,* XIV (November 10, 1881), 310.
16. *Ibid.,* X (November 27, 1879), 310.
17. *Ibid.,* XII (December 23, 1880), 436.
18. *Ibid.,* XI (May 27, 1880), 346.
19. *Ibid.,* XII (December 16, 1880), 416.

20. *Ibid.*
21. *Ibid.*, XIV (December 15, 1881), 402.
22. *Ibid.*, IV (December 16, 1876), 275.
23. *Ibid.*, IV (December 9, 1876), 263.

CHAPTER 17

1. Anne Thaxter Eaton, "Magazines for Children in the Nineteenth Century," *A Critical History of Children's Literature,* Cornelia Meigs, ed., (New York: Macmillan Co., 1953), p. 284.
2. Frank Luther Mott, *A History of American Magazines, 1865–1885,* (Cambridge: Harvard University Press, 1938), p. 6.
3. *The Youth's Companion,* XLVII (January 15, 1874), 23.
4. *Ibid.*, XLVII (January 22, 1874), 31.
5. *Ibid.*, XLVII (December 10, 1874), 312–13.
6. *Ibid.*, XLV (December 12, 1872), 405.
7. *Our Young Folks,* V (December, 1869), 854.
8. *Ibid.*, V (March, 1869), 201–02.
9. *Ibid.*, V (November, 1869), 784.
10. *Ibid.*, IX (February, 1873), 127.
11. *Oliver Optic's Magazine,* XI (January, 1872), 79.
12. *Ibid.*, XV (April, 1874), 319.
13. *Ibid.*, XVII (January, 1875), 79.
14. Mary Mapes Dodge, "Children's Magazines," *Scribner's Monthly,* VI (July, 1873), 353–54.
15. Mary Mapes Dodge, "Books for Boys and Girls," *St. Nicholas,* I (November, 1873), 44–45.
16. *Ibid.*, 44.
17. *St. Nicholas,* VII (December, 1879), 188.
18. *Ibid.*, V (January, 1878), 238.
19. *Ibid.*, III (January, 1876), 203.
20. *Ibid.*
21. *Ibid.*, V (November, 1877), 70.
22. *Ibid.*, II (January, 1875), 190.
23. *Ibid.*, VII (December, 1879), 188.
24. *Ibid.*, III (January, 1876), 103.
25. *Ibid.*, III (January, 1876), 104.
26. Virginia Haviland, *The Travelogue Story Book of the Nineteenth Century. A Caroline Hewins Lecture.* (Boston: The Horn Book, Inc., 1950), p. 14.
27. Horace E. Scudder, "Books for Young People," *The Riverside Magazine for Young People,* I (January, 1867), 44.
28. *Ibid.*
29. *The Riverside Magazine for Young People,* I (March, 1867), 141–42.
30. *Ibid.*, I (March, 1867), 142.
31. *Ibid.*, I (April, 1867), 189–90.
32. *Ibid.*
33. *Ibid.*, I (July, 1867), 333–34.
34. *Ibid.*
35. *Ibid.*, I (December, 1867), 572–3.
36. *Ibid.*, II (February, 1868), 93–94.
37. *Ibid.*, III (January, 1869), 46.

CHAPTER 18

1. *American Literary Gazette,* IV (January 2, 1865), 148.
2. *Ibid.*, XI (May 15, 1868), 44.
3. *Ibid.*, IV (January 2, 1865), 148.
4. *Ibid.*, VI (December 15, 1865), 132.
5. *Ibid.*, VI (January 1, 1866), 159.

6. *Ibid.*, VI (February 15, 1866), 228.
7. *Ibid.*, VIII (November 1, 1866), 11.
8. *Ibid.*, VIII (November 15, 1866), 53.
9. *Ibid.*
10. *Ibid.*, XII (November 2, 1868), 16.
11. *Ibid.*, XIV (April 15, 1870), 342.
12. *Ibid.*, XVII (June 15, 1871), 98.
13. *Ibid.*, XIV (December 1, 1869), 14.
14. *Ibid.*, VI (November 15, 1865), 49.
15. *Ibid.*, XIII (October 1, 1869), 340.
16. *Ibid.*, XVII (June 1, 1871), 66.
17. *Ibid.*, X (January 1, 1868), 160.
18. *Publishers' Weekly,* XIX (January 29, 1881), 88.
19. *Ibid.*, XIII (June 8, 1878), 557.
20. *Ibid.*, VIII (November 6, 1875), 712.
21. *Ibid.*, VI (Christmas Supplement, 1874), 14.
22. *Ibid.*, VI (October 17, 1874), 428–29.
23. *Ibid.*, VI (November 7, 1874), 518.
24. *Ibid.*, IV (November 22, 1873), 581.
25. *Ibid.*, XIV (September 21, 1878), 359.
26. *Ibid.*, IV (November 8, 1873), 514.
27. *Ibid.*, VIII (December 25, 1875), 957.
28. *Ibid.*, XII (September 22, 1877), 345–46.
29. Frank Luther Mott, *A History of American Magazines, 1865–1885,* (Cambridge: Harvard University Press, 1938), pp. 495–99.
30. *Ibid.*, p. 496.
31. *Popular Science Monthly,* XVIII (March, 1881), 701.
32. *Ibid.*, III (June, 1873), 249.

CHAPTER 19

1. *Harper's New Monthly Magazine,* XXXII (March, 1866), 526.
2. *American Literary Gazette,* VIII (November 15, 1866), 53.
3. *The Nation,* II (January 25, 1866), 119–20.
4. *The Independent,* XVIII (April 19, 1866), 3.
5. *The Catholic World,* II (February, 1866), 719–20.
6. *Atlantic Monthly,* XVII (July, 1866), 779–80.
7. *Ibid.*, XVII (July, 1866), 780.
8. *The Independent,* XXV (December 18, 1873), 1577.
9. *Appleton's Journal,* X (December 20, 1873), 797.
10. *The Nation,* XVII (December 11, 1873), 389.
11. *Publishers' Weekly,* IV (November 29, 1873), 625.
12. *Appleton's Journal,* XI (January 17, 1874), 91.
13. *The Youth's Companion,* XLVII (January 22, 1874), 31.
14. *Scribner's Monthly,* VII (February, 1874), 507.
15. *The Galaxy,* XVII (February, 1874), 284–85.
16. *Scribner's Monthly,* XI (December, 1875), 296.
17. *The Independent,* XXVII (December 30, 1875), 8.
18. *Publishers' Weekly,* VIII (December 25, 1875), 957.
19. *Scribner's Monthly,* XI (December, 1875), 296.
20. *Appleton's Journal,* XV (January 8, 1876), 58.
21. Susan Coolidge, review of *Hans Brinker,* by Mary Mapes Dodge in *The Literary World,* VIII (January, 1878), 143.
22. *The Independent,* XXXI (December 25, 1879), 9.
23. *Harper's New Monthly Magazine,* LX (January, 1880), 315.
24. *The Nation,* XXIX (December 11, 1879), 409.
25. *Ibid.*, III (December 13, 1866), 466–67.
26. *The Catholic World,* IX (June, 1869), 429.

27. *Harper's New Monthly Magazine*, XXXIX (August, 1869), 455.
28. *Overand Monthly*, III (July, 1869), 102.
29. *Putnam's Magazine*, IV (July, 1869), 124.
30. *The Literary World*, I (July 1, 1870), 23–24.
31. *The Nation*, XIV (February 8, 1872), 95.
32. *The Galaxy*, VIII (July, 1869), 141.
33. *Hours at Home*, VIII (November, 1868), 100.
34. *American Literary Gazette*, XII (November 2, 1868), 16.
35. *Putnam's Magazine*, N. S. II (December, 1868), 760.
36. *The Nation*, VII (October 22, 1868), 335.
37. *Ibid.*, VIII (May 20, 1869), 400.
38. *Hours at Home*, IX (June, 1869), 196.
39. *Putnam's Magazine*, N. S. IV (July, 1869), 124.
40. *The Galaxy*, VIII (July, 1869), 141.
41. *The Catholic World*, IX (July, 1869), 576.
42. *Harper's New Monthly Magazine*, XXXIX (August, 1869), 455–56.
43. *Our Young Folks*, V (September, 1869), 640.
44. *Ibid.*, V (November, 1869), 784.
45. *Ibid.*, VI (January, 1870), 71.
46. *American Literary Gazette*, XIV (December 1, 1869), 14.
47. *The Nation*, IX (December 30, 1869), 588.
48. *Overland Monthly*, IV (March, 1870), 294.
49. William Dean Howells, review of *The Story of a Bad Boy*, by Thomas Bailey Aldrich in *Atlantic Monthly*, XXV (January, 1870), 124–25.
50. *Ibid.*, 125.
51. Howells, review of *The Adventures of Tom Sawyer*, by Samuel L. Clemens in *Atlantic Monthly*, XXXVII (May, 1876), 621–22.
52. The Critic, I (December 31, 1881), 368.
53. "Mark Twain's New Departure," *Atlantic Monthly*, XLVIII (December, 1881), 843–45.

CHAPTER 20

1. Helen Aldrich De Kroyft, *The Story of Little Jakey* (New York: Hurd & Houghton, 1876), p. 132 ff.

APPENDIX

A BIBLIOGRAPHY OF REVIEWS

The bibliography which follows is included as an appendix to this study of the reviewing of children's books, in order to provide the interested scholar and student with a complete list of the reviews discussed in the text, and a partial list of the books available to American children between 1865 and 1881. It is not intended to be an exhaustive bibliography of such books. Rather, it is a beginning for such a bibliography, bringing together information otherwise available only in scattered sources.

The works listed are arranged by the year in which they were reviewed. Because of this chronological arrangement, dates of publication have been omitted, but, in the case of editions of works, sufficient information has been provided to distinguish between different editions of the same book.

Within the basic chronological arrangement, the books are arranged alphabetically by author. Anonymous works are interfiled alphabetically by title. Pseudonymous works are consistently listed under the real name of the author even though, in a few cases, this has meant that a less well-known name has been used. The author's pseudonym has been included in parentheses following his real name, so that this information would be readily available to students who might find this list useful. Each title has been checked in the *The American Catalogue* which has been used as the basic authority for names and titles in this list.

Abbott, Jacob. *American History. Vol. III, War of the Revolution.* (New York: Sheldon & Co.)
American Literary Gazette, IV (January 2, 1865), 148.

Mary Gay; or, Work for Girls. (New York: Hurd & Houghton)
American Literary Gazette, VI (November 15, 1865), 49.
Independent, XVII (December 7, 1865), 2.

Adams, William T. (Oliver Optic). *The Sailor Boy; or, Jack Somers in the Navy.* (Boston: Lee & Shepard)
American Literary Gazette, IV (January 16, 1865), 167–68.

Work and Win. (Boston: Lee & Shepard)
Nation, I (December 28, 1865), 818.

The Yankee Middy. (Boston: Lee & Shepard)
American Literary Gazette, VI (December 15, 1865), 132.
Nation, I (December 14, 1865), 757.

The Young Lieutenant; or, the Adventures of an Army Officer. (Boston: Lee & Shepard)
American Literary Gazette, V (July 1, 1865), 102.

Alden, Isabella M. (Pansy). *Helen Lester.* (Cincinnati: American Reform Tract and Book Society)
American Literary Gazette, IV (February 15, 1865), 212.

Alger, Horatio, Jr. *Frank's Campaign; or, What Boys Can Do on the Farm for the Camp.* (Boston: A. K. Loring)
American Literary Gazette, IV (January 2, 1865), 148.

Paul Prescott's Charge. (Boston: A. K. Loring)
American Literary Gazette, VI (November 15, 1865), 49.
Nation, I (December 14, 1865), 757.

Anderson, Mary E. *Scenes in the Hawaiian Islands and California.* (Boston: American Tract Society)
American Literary Gazette, V (May 15, 1865), 28.

Androclus the Slave. (Philadelphia: Thurston, Herline & Co.)
American Literary Gazette, VI (December 15, 1865), 132.

Aston, Miss D. *The Babe and the Princess and Other Poems for Children.* (New York: Carlton & Porter)
American Literary Gazette, V (February 15, 1865), 212.

Baché, Richard Meade. *The Young Wrecker of the Florida Reef; or, the Trials and Adventures of Fred Ransom.* (Philadelphia: James S. Claxton)
American Literary Gazette, VI (December 21, 1865), 132.
Independent, XVII (December 21, 1865), 2.

Baker, Harriet N. W. (Aunt Hattie; Mrs. Madeline Leslie). *The Hole in the Pocket.* (Boston: Graves & Young)
Independent, XVII (October 26, 1865), 2.

Ballantyne, Robert Michael. *Freaks on the Fells; or, Three Months' Rustication, and Why I Did Not Become a Sailor.* (Boston: Crosby & Ainsworth)
American Literary Gazette, IV (January 2, 1865), 148.

Barbauld, Anna Letitia. *Hymns in Prose for Children.* (New York: Hurd & Houghton)
American Literary Gazette, VI (December 15, 1865), 132.
Nation, I (December 14, 1865), 757.

Barlow, Mrs. C. J. *Helen MacGregor; or, The Conquest and Sacrifice* (Philadelphia: J. C. Garrigues & Co.)
American Literary Gazette, VI (November 15, 1865), 49.

Barrows, Fanny (Aunt Fanny). *Good Little Hearts; or, Stories About Children.* (New York: Hurd & Houghton)
American Literary Gazette, VI (December 1, 1865), 88.
Nation, I (December 14, 1865), 757.

Bessie Lovell; or, The Power of a Loving Child. (Boston: American Tract Society)
Independent, XVII (December 7, 1865), 2.

Blum, George and Louis Wahl. *Seaside and Fireside Fairies.* Translated from the German by A. L. Wister. (Philadelphia: Ashmead & Evans)
Atlantic Monthly, XV (May, 1865), 640.

Bradley, Mrs. M. E. *Grace's Visit; or, The Wrong Way to Cure a Fault.* (Boston: Crosby & Ainsworth)
American Literary Gazette, IV (January 2, 1865), 148.

Brehat, Alfred de. *Adventures of a Little French Boy.* (New York: Hurd & Houghton)
American Literary Gazette, VI (December 1, 1865), 88–89.
Nation, I (December 14, 1865), 757.

Bulwer-Lytton, Edward. *The Wooing of Master Fox.* Arranged for Children by O. D. Martin. (Philadelphia: Ashmead & Evans)
American Literary Gazette, VI (December 1, 1865), 89.

Calcott, Maria Hutchins. *The Two Firesides; or, The Mechanic and the Tradesman; A Tale of Ninety Years Ago.* (Philadelphia: Perkinpine & Higgins)
Independent, XVII (December 14, 1865), 2.

Charles, Elizabeth R. *The Song Without Words.* (New York: M. W. Dodd)
Nation, I (December 28, 1865), 818.

The Two Vocations; or, The Sisters of Mercy at Home. (New York: Robert Carter & Brothers)
American Literary Gazette, IV (March 1, 1865), 243.

The Children of the Valley; or, The Ghost of the Ruins. Translated from the French. (Philadelphia: Peter F. Cunningham; New York: D. & J. Sadlier & Co.)
Catholic World, I (June, 1865), 432.

Christie; or, Where the Tree Fell. (New York: Carlton & Porter)
American Literary Gazette, IV (February 15, 1865), 212.

Clacy, Ellen. *Wonderful Works; or, The Miracles of Christ.* (Boston: American Tract Society)
American Literary Gazette, V (May 15, 1865), 28.

Clarke, Rebecca (Sophie May). *Little Prudy.* (Boston: Lee & Shepard)
Nation, I (December 14, 1865), 757.

Coffin, Charles Carleton (Carleton). *Following the Flag, from August, 1861, to November, 1862, with the Army of the Potomac.* (Boston: Ticknor & Fields)
American Literary Gazette, IV (January 16, 1865), 167.

Count Leslie; or, The Triumphs of Filial Piety. A Catholic Tale. From the French. (Philadelphia: Peter F. Cunningham; New York: D. & J. Sadlier & Co.)
Catholic World, I (June, 1865), 432.

Cousin Carrie (pseud.). *Sun-Rays from Fair and Cloudy Skies.* (New York: D. Appleton & Co.)
Nation, I (December 28, 1865), 818.

Davis, Caroline E. K. (Caroline E. Kelley). *Arthur Merton; or, Sinning and Sorrowing.* (Philadelphia: J. C. Garrigues & Co.)
American Literary Gazette, V (September 15, 1865), 217.
Independent, XVII (November 23, 1865), 2.

Defoe, Daniel. *The Life and Adventures of Robinson Crusoe.* (New York: Hurd & Houghton)
Independent, XVII (December 14, 1865), 2.

Disosway, G. P. *The Children's Book of Sermons.* (New York: Carlton & Porter) American Literary Gazette, IV (February 15, 1865), 212.

Dodge, Mary Mapes. *Irvington Stories.* 4th ed. (New York: James O'Kane) American Literary Gazette, V (June 1, 1865), 52.

Dunning, Mrs. A. K. (Nellie Grahame). *Tim Harrison; or, The Boy Who Couldn't Say No.* (Philadelphia: Presbyterian Board of Publication) American Literary Gazette, V (May 15, 1865), 28.

Eddy, Daniel C. *Walter's Tour in the East.* (New York: Sheldon & Co.) American Literary Gazette, IV (January 2, 1865), 148.

Edgeworth, Maria. *Moral Tales.* (Philadelphia: Ashmead & Evans) American Literary Gazette, V (May 1, 1865), 7.

Popular Tales. (Philadelphia: Ashmead & Evans) American Literary Gazette, V (May 1, 1865), 7.
Independent, XVII (October 26, 1865), 2.

Ellen Vincent and the Blank Sheet. (Boston: Henry Hoyt) Nation, I (December 14, 1865), 757.

Ernest; or, No Humbug. (New York: Carlton & Porter) American Literary Gazette, IV (February 15, 1865), 212.

Eyster, Nellie. *Sunny Hours; or, Child-Life of Tom and Mary.* (Philadelphia: Ashmead & Evans) American Literary Gazette, VI (November 15, 1865), 49.

Faith the Cripple; or, Songs in the Night. (New York: Carlton & Porter) American Literary Gazette, IV (February 15, 1865), 212.

Finley, Martha F. (Martha Farquharson). *Mysie's Work and How She Did It.* (Philadelphia: Presbyterian Board of Publication) Independent, XVII (September 14, 1865), 2.

Fosdick, Charles Austin (Harry Castlemon). *Gunboat Series.* (Cincinnati: R. W. Carroll & Co.) American Literary Gazette, VI (November 1, 1865), 9.
Independent, XVII (December 7, 1865), 2.
Nation, I (December 14, 1865), 757.

Frost, Mrs. J. (C. Brandon). *David Woodburn, the Mountain Missionary.* (Boston: Henry Hoyt) Independent, XVII (November 2, 1865), 2–3.
Nation, I (December 14, 1865), 757.

Gilmore, J. R. (Edmund Kirke). *Patriot Boys and Prison Pictures.* (Boston: Ticknor & Fields) American Literary Gazette, VI (December 15, 1865), 132.
Nation, I (December 28, 1865), 818.

Gray, Alice. *Jolly and Katy in the Country.* (New York: Robert Carter & Brothers) American Literary Gazette, V (October 16, 1865), 271.
Nation, I (December 14, 1865), 757.

Greene, Mrs. R. J. *Cushions and Corners; or, Holidays at Old Orchard.* (Boston: E. P. Dutton & Co.) American Literary Gazette, VI (December 15, 1865), 132–33.
Nation, I (December 28, 1865), 817.

Guernsey, Clara F. *The Silver Cup.* (Philadelphia: American Sunday-School Union) American Literary Gazette, V (October 16, 1865), 271.
Independent, XVII (November 2, 1865), 2.

Harrison, Jennie. *On the Ferry-Boat.* (New York: Hurd & Houghton) American Literary Gazette, VI (December 15, 1865), 132.
Nation, I (December 14, 1865), 757.

Headley, P. C. *Life and Military Career of Major-General Philip Henry Sheridan.* (New York: Wm. H. Appleton)
Nation, I (December 28, 1865), 816.

Life and Military Career of Major-General William Tecumseh Sherman. (New York: Wm. H. Appleton)
American Literary Gazette, V (May 1, 1865), 6–7.

Life and Naval Career of Vice-Admiral David Glasgow Farragut. (New York: Wm. H. Appleton)
Independent, XVII (December 21, 1865), 2.
Nation, I (December 28, 1865), 816.

The Miner Boy and His Monitor; or, The Career and Achievements of John Ericsson, the Engineer. (New York: Wm. H. Appleton)
American Literary Gazette, IV (January 16, 1865), 167.

The Patriot Boy; or, The Life and Career of Major-General Ormsby M. Mitchell. (New York: Wm. H. Appleton)
American Educational Monthly, II (January, 1865), 32.

Hepworth, Mrs. G. H. (Una Savin). *The Little Gentleman in Green.* (Boston: A. K. Loring)
American Literary Gazette, VI (November 15, 1865), 49.
Nation, I (December 14, 1865), 757.

Heston, Newton. *The Anniversary Speaker; or, Young Folks on the Sunday-School Platform.* 2nd Ser. (Philadelphia: Perkinpine & Higgins)
American Literary Gazette, V (October 2, 1865), 242.

Hinsdale, Grace Webster. *Coming to the King; A Book of Daily Devotions for Children.* (New York: A. D. F. Randolph)
Independent, XVII (June 29, 1865), 2.

Hotchkin, B. B. *Manliness for Young Men and Their Well-Wishers.* (Philadelphia: Presbyterian Publication Committee)
American Literary Gazette, IV (January 16, 1865), 167.

Kingston, William Henry Giles. *The Cruise of the Frolic.* (Boston: J. E. Tilton & Co.)
Independent, XVII (December 14, 1865), 2.

Die Klugheit und Gelehrigheit der Thiere; Ein Bilderbuch für Kinder mit Funfzig Kleinen Erzahlungern. (St. Louis: Conrad Witter)
American Literary Gazette, VI (December 1, 1865), 89.

Lander, Sarah W. *Spectacles for Young Eyes: Berlin.* (Boston: Walker, Fuller & Co.)
American Literary Gazette, V (May 15, 1865), 28.

Spectacles for Young Eyes: Rome. (Boston: Walker, Fuller & Co.)
Nation, I (December 28, 1865), 818.

Lilian; A Tale of Three Hundred Years Ago. (New York: Carlton & Porter)
American Literary Gazette, V (August 15, 1865), 161–62.
Independent, XVII (December 14, 1865), 2.

Little Aggie's Library. (New York: Carlton & Porter)
Independent, XVII (December 7, 1865), 2.

The Little Corporal (periodical).
Nation, I (September 21, 1865), 379.
Nation, I (December 14, 1865), 757.

Little Kitty's Library. (New York: Robert Carter & Brothers)
American Literary Gazette, V (October 2, 1865), 242.
Independent, XVII (December 7, 1865), 2.

McKeever, Harriet B. *The Woodcliff Children.* (Philadelphia: Lindsay & Blakiston)
American Literary Gazette, VI (December 15, 1865), 132.

Marryatt, Frederick. *Privateersman*. (Boston: Roberts Brothers)
Nation, I (December 14, 1865), 757.

Mary Woodman and Her Grandmother; or, The Story of a Girl Who Wished for a Little More. (New York: Carlton & Porter)
American Literary Gazette, V (August 15, 1865), 161–62.

May Carleton's Story; or, The Catholic Maiden's Cross. The Miller's Daughter. Catholic Tales. (Philadelphia: Peter F. Cunningham; New York: D. & J. Sadlier & Co.)
Catholic World, I (June, 1865), 432.

Meaney, Mary L. *The Confessors of Connaught; or, The Tenants of a Lord Bishop*. (Philadelphia: Peter F. Cunningham; New York: D. & J. Sadlier & Co.)
Catholic World, I (July, 1865), 574–75.

Cottage Evening Tales for Young People. (Philadelphia: Peter F. Cunningham; New York: D. & J. Sadlier & Co.)
Catholic World, I (June, 1865), 432.

Grace Morton; or, The Inheritance. (Philadelphia: Peter F. Cunningham; New York: D. & J. Sadlier & Co.)
Catholic World, I (July, 1865), 574–75.

Philip Hartley; or, A Boy's Trials and Triumphs. (Philadelphia: Peter F. Cunningham; New York: D. & J. Sadlier & Co.)
Catholic World, I (June, 1865), 432.

The Mother's Picture Alphabet. (New York: Carlton & Porter)
American Literary Gazette, IV (February 15, 1865), 212.

Myrtle, Harriet. *The Water Lily*. (New York: Hurd & Houghton)
American Literary Gazette, VI (December 15, 1865), 132.
Independent, XVII (December 28, 1865), 3.
Nation, I (December 14, 1865), 757.

The Old Flag. (Philadelphia: American Sunday-School Union)
Independent, XVII (December 21, 1865), 2.

Our Young Folks (periodical).
American Educational Monthly, II (November, 1865), 349–51.
Independent, XVII (February 2, 1865), 2–3.
Nation, I (December 14, 1865), 757.
Ohio Educational Monthly, XIV (December, 1865), 416.

Pretty Annie. (Philadelphia: Thurston, Herline & Co.)
American Literary Gazette, VI (December 15, 1865), 132.

Rachel; or, The City Without Walls. (New York: Carlton & Porter)
American Literary Gazette, IV (February 15, 1865), 212.

Reid, Mayne. *The Boy Slaves*. (Boston: Ticknor & Fields)
American Literary Gazette, IV (February 1, 1865), 191.

Robbins, Mrs. S. S. *My New Home*. (New York: Robert Carter & Brothers)
Independent, XVII (October 12, 1865), 2.

Turning a New Leaf; or, The Story of Charles Terry. (New York: Robert Carter & Brothers)
Independent, XVII (November 23, 1865), 2.

Robert Merry's Third Book of Puzzles. (New York: F. A. Brown)
American Literary Gazette, VI (December 15, 1865), 132.

The Scottish Minister. New ed. (Boston: Henry Hoyt)
Nation, I (December 14, 1865), 757.

Scudder, Horace Elisha. *Dream Children*. (Cambridge, Mass.: Sever & Francis)
Nation, I (December 14, 1865), 757.

Seymour, Mary Alice. *Christmas Holidays at Cedar Grove*. 3rd ed. (Boston: E. P. Dutton & Co.)

American Literary Gazette, VI (December 15, 1865), 132–33.
Nation, I (December 28, 1865), 817.

Something New for My Little Friends; Stories in Verse. (Philadelphia: J. B. Lippincott & Co.)
American Literary Gazette, VI (December 1, 1865), 89.
Nation, I (December 28, 1865), 817.

The Star Dollars. (Philadelphia: Thurston, Herline & Co.)
American Literary Gazette, VI (December 15, 1865), 132.

Stephens, H. L. (illus.) *The House That Jack Built.* (New York: Hurd & Houghton)
American Literary Gazette, VI (November 15, 1865), 49.
Nation, I (December 14, 1865), 757.

Old Mother Hubbard and Her Dog. (New York: Hurd & Houghton)
American Literary Gazette, VI (November 15, 1865), 49.
Nation, I (December 14, 1865), 757.

Stoddard, Richard Henry. *The Children in the Wood.* (New York: Hurd & Houghton)
American Literary Gazette, VI (November 15, 1865), 49.
Nation, I (November 2, 1865), 567.

Thayer, William M. *A Youth's History of the Rebellion from the Capture of Roanoke Island to the Battle of Murfreesboro.* (Boston: Walker, Fuller & Co.)
American Literary Gazette, V (May 15, 1865), 28–29.

A Youth's History of the Rebellion from the Battle of Murfreesboro to the Massacre at Fort Pillow. (Boston: Walker, Fuller & Co.)
Nation, I (December 28, 1865), 818.

Tilton, Theodore. *The Fly.* (New York: Sheldon & Co.)
Nation, I (December 14, 1865), 757.

Golden-haired Gertrude. (New York: Tibbals & Whiting)
Nation, I (November 2, 1865), 568.

Two Hungry Kittens. (New York: Tibbals & Whiting)
Nation, I (December 28, 1865), 818.

Trowbridge, John Townsend (Paul Creyton). *The Three Scouts.* (Boston: J. E. Tilton & Co.)
American Literary Gazette, IV (February 15, 1865), 212.

Tucker, Charlotte (A.L.O.E.). *Exiles in Babylon; or, The Children of Light.* (New York: Carlton & Porter)
American Literary Gazette, V (May 1, 1865), 8.
American Literary Gazette, V (October 2, 1865), 242.
Independent, XVII (November 2, 1865), 2.

Giles Oldham; or, Miracles of Heavenly Love. (New York: Robert Carter & Brothers)
American Literary Gazette, V (May 1, 1865), 8.

Ned Franks; or, The Christian's Panoply. (New York: Robert Carter & Brothers)
American Literary Gazette, IV (March 1, 1865), 243.

The Silver Casket; or, The World and Its Wiles. (New York: Carlton & Porter)
American Literary Gazette, IV (January 2, 1865), 148.

Warner, Susan Bogert (Elizabeth Wetherell). *Melbourne House.* (New York: Robert Carter & Brothers)
Independent, XVII (December 21, 1865), 2.

The Ways of God. (Philadelphia: Thurston, Herline & Co.)
American Literary Gazette, VI (December 15, 1865), 132.

Whitney, Adeline Dutton Train. *Boys at Chequasset; or, "A Little Leaven."* (Boston: A. K. Loring)
American Literary Gazette, VI (November 15, 1865), 49.

Wildermuth, Ottalie. *Ottalie's Stories for the Little Folk.* (Boston: E. P. Dutton & Co.; New York: Hurd & Houghton)
American Literary Gazette, VI (December 15, 1865), 132–33.
Nation, I (December 28, 1865), 817.

Wise, Daniel (Francis Forrester: Lawrence Lancewood) *Sydney de Grey.* (Boston: Graves & Young)
American Literary Gazette, V (October 16, 1865), 271.
Independent, XVII (October 26, 1865), 2.
Nation, I (December 14, 1865), 757.

The Yankee Boy from Home. (New York: James Miller)
American Literary Gazette, IV (March 1, 1865), 243.

Yonge, Charlotte M. *A Book of Golden Deeds of All Times and All Countries.* (Cambridge, Mass.: Sever & Francis)
American Literary Gazette, IV (April 1, 1865), 287.
Nation, I (August 17, 1865), 220.

Countess Kate; A Story for Girls. (Boston: A. K. Loring)
American Literary Gazette, VI (November 15, 1865), 49.
Nation, I (December 14, 1865), 757.

BOOKS REVIEWED IN 1866

Abbott, Jacob. *John Gay; or, Work for Boys.* (New York: Hurd & Houghton)
North American Review, CII (January, 1866), 236–49.

Adams, William T. (Oliver Optic). *Army and Navy Stories.* (Boston: Lee & Shepard)
North American Review, CII (January, 1866), 236–49.

Boat Club Series. (Boston: Lee & Shepard)
North American Review, CII (January, 1866), 236–49.

Outward Bound; or, Young America Afloat. (Boston: Lee & Shepard)
Nation, III (December 20, 1866), 492–93.

Aesop. *The Fables of Aesop; With a Life of the Author.* (New York: Hurd & Houghton)
Hours at Home, II (January, 1866), 292.

Alger, Horatio, Jr. *Paul Prescott's Charge.* (Boston: A. K. Loring)
North American Review, CII (January, 1866), 236–49.

Andersen, Hans Christian. *What the Moon Saw, and Other Tales.* (New York: James Miller)
Nation, III (December 20, 1866), 493.

Andrews, Jane. *The Seven Little Sisters Who Live on the Round Ball That Floats in the Air.* (Boston: Ticknor & Fields)
North American Review, CII (January, 1866), 236–49.

The Arabian Nights' Entertainments. Edited by Rev. George Fyler Townsend. (New York: Hurd & Houghton)
American Literary Gazette, VIII (December 1, 1866), 97.
Nation, III (December 27, 1866), 517.

Ashton, Mrs. S. G. *The Mothers of the Bible.* (New York: Wm. H. Appleton)
Independent, XVIII (January 18, 1866), 3.

Baker, Harriet N. W. (Aunt Hattie; Mrs. Madeline Leslie). *Lost But Found; or, The Jewish Home.* (Boston: Graves & Young)
American Literary Gazette, VII (May 15, 1866), 35.

Balleydier, Alphonse(?). *The Blighted Flower, and Other Tales.* Translated from

the French of Balleydier by Mrs. J. Sadlier. (New York: D. & J. Sadlier & Co.)
Catholic World, III (August, 1866), 720.

Ten Stories. Translated from the French of Balleydier by Mrs. J. Sadlier. (New York: D. & J. Sadlier & Co.)
Catholic World, III (August, 1866), 720.

Valeria; or, The First Christians and Other Stories. Translated from the French of Balleydier and Madame Bowdon by Mrs. J. Sadlier. (New York: D. & J. Sadlier & Co.)
Catholic World, III (August, 1866), 720.

Berkley, Cora. *The Beauforts. A Story of the Alleghanies.* (Philadelphia: Peter F. Cunningham)
Catholic World, III (August, 1866), 720.

Bissell, Mary L. *Ned Grant's Quest.* (Boston: E. P. Dutton & Co.)
Nation, III (December 13, 1866), 466.

Blackburn, William M. *College Days of Calvin.* (Philadelphia: Presbyterian Board of Publication)
American Literary Gazette, VIII (November 1, 1866), 11.

Young Calvin in Paris, and the Little Flock That He Fed. (Philadelphia: Presbyterian Board of Publication)
American Literary Gazette, VIII (November 1, 1866), 11.

Bonner, John. *Child's History of the United States. Vol. III, P. 2, History of the Great Rebellion.* (New York: Harper & Brothers)
Harper's Magazine, XXXII (March, 1866), 525.
Nation, II (April 26, 1866), 536–37.

Brace, Charles Loring. *Short Sermons to Newsboys.* (New York: Charles Scribner & Co.)
American Literary Gazette, VII (May 15, 1866) 35.
Hours at Home, III (July, 1866), 289.
Independent, XVIII (May 31, 1866), 3.
Nation, II (May 8, 1866), 582–83.

Bradley, William Ives (Glance Gaylord). *Boys at Dr. Murray's.* (Boston: Graves & Young)
American Literary Gazette, VII (May 1, 1866), 10.
Nation, II (May 1, 1866), 551–52.

Browning, Elizabeth Barrett. *Poems of Childhood.* (New York: James Miller)
Nation, III (December 27, 1866), 517.

Bulfinch, Maria H. *Frank Stirling's Choice.* (Boston: E. P. Dutton & Co.)
Nation, III (December 13, 1866), 466.

Charles, Elizabeth R. *Song Without Words.* (New York: M. W. Dodd)
American Literary Gazette, VI (January 1, 1866), 159–60.
Independent, XVIII (March 22, 1866), 2.

Winifred Bertram and the World She Lived In. (New York: M. W. Dodd)
Independent, XVIII (January 11, 1866), 2.
Nation, II (February 1, 1866), 147–48.

Charles and Frederick; or, A Mother's Prayer, and Rose Blanche; or, Twelfth Night in Brittany. (Philadelphia: Peter F. Cunningham)
Catholic World, III (August, 1866), 720.

The Children of the Frontier. (New York: D. Appleton & Co.)
Nation, III (December 20, 1866), 493.

Christmas Greens. (Philadelphia: American Sunday-School Union)
Independent, XVIII (January 18, 1866), 3.

Clarke, Rebecca (Sophie May). *Little Prudy.* (Boston: Lee & Shepard)
North American Review, CII (January, 1866), 243.

Coffin, Charles Carleton (Carleton). *Following the Flag, from August, 1861, to November, 1862, with the Army of the Potomac.* (Boston: Ticknor & Fields) North American Review, CII (January, 1866), 241–42.

My Days and Nights on the Battlefield. (Boston: Ticknor and Fields) North American Review, CII (January, 1866), 241–42.

Winning His Way. (Boston: Ticknor & Fields) American Literary Gazette, VI (January 1, 1866), 159.

Constance and Edith; or, Incidents of Home Life. (New York: Robert Carter & Brothers) Independent, XVIII (April 19, 1866), 3.

Cooper, James Fenimore. *Stories of the Woods; or, Adventures of Leatherstocking.* (New York: J. G. Gregory) North American Review, CII (January, 1866), 236–49.

Dawes, Mrs. S. E. *Hours with Mamma.* (New York: American Tract Society) American Literary Gazette, VII (October 15, 1866), 291.

Dodge, Mary Abigail (Gail Hamilton). *Red-Letter Days in Applethorpe.* (Boston: Ticknor & Fields) American Literary Gazette, VIII (November 1, 1866), 11 Independent, XVIII (November 29, 1866), 3 Nation, III (December 20, 1866), 493.

Dodge, Mary Mapes. *Hans Brinker; or, The Silver Skates.* (New York: James O'Kane) American Literary Gazette, VIII (November 15, 1866), 53. Atlantic Monthly, XVII (June, 1866), 779–80. Catholic World, II (February, 1866), 719–20. Harper's Magazine, XXXII (March, 1866), 526. Independent, XVIII (April 19, 1866), 3. Nation, II (January 25, 1866), 119–20.

Dodgson, Charles L. (Lewis Carroll) *Alice's Adventures in Wonderland.* (New York: D. Appleton & Co.) Nation, III (December 13, 1866), 466–67.

Dora Darling, the Daughter of the Regiment. (Boston: J. E. Tilton & Co.) North American Review, CII (January, 1866), 242

Dyer, Sidney. *The Drunkard's Child; or, The Triumphs of Faith.* (New York: Sheldon & Co.) American Literary Gazette, VI (February 15, 1866), 228.

Elwes, Alfred. *Paul Blake; or, The Story of a Boy's Perils.* (New York: James Miller) Nation, III (December 20, 1866), 492.

Eyster, Nellie. *Chincapin Charlie.* (Philadelphia: Duffield Ashmead) American Literary Gazette, VIII (December 15, 1866), 136. Nation, III (December 20, 1866), 493.

Fosdick, Charles Austin (Harry Castlemon) *Gun Boat Series.* (Cincinnati: R. W. Carroll & Co.) American Literary Gazette, VIII (November 15, 1866), 53.

Gilbert, William. *The Magic Mirror; a Round of Tales for Young and Old.* (London and New York: A. Strahan) Nation, III (December 13, 1866), 466.

Gillett, E. H. *England Two Hundred Years Ago.* (Philadelphia: Presbyterian Publication Committee; New York: A. D. F. Randolph) American Literary Gazette, VIII (November 1, 1866), 11. Independent, XVIII (November 8, 1866), 3.

Gilmore, J. R. (Edmund Kirke). *Patriot Boys and Prison Pictures.* (Boston: Ticknor & Fields)

Independent, XVIII (February 1, 1866), 3.

Gordon, Clarence (Vieux Moustache). *Our Fresh and Salt Tutors.* (New York: Hurd & Houghton)
American Literary Gazette, VII (November 15, 1866), 526.

Greenwood, James. *The Adventures of Reuben Davidger; Seventeen Years and Four Months Captive Among the Dyaks of Borneo.* (New York: Harper & Brothers)
Nation, II (May 11, 1866), 598.

Guernsey, Lucy Ellen. *Milly; or, The Hidden Cross.* (Boston A. K. Loring)
Nation, III (December 20, 1866), 493.

Hale, Anne G. *Fannie and Robbie; A Year Book for Children of the Church.* (Boston: E. P. Dutton & Co.)
Nation, III (December 13, 1866), 466.

Headley, P. C. *The Girls of the Bible.* (New York: Wm. H. Appleton)
Independent, XVIII (January 18, 1866), 3.

Life and Military Career of Major-General Philip Henry Sheridan. (New York: Wm. H. Appleton)
Independent, XVIII (January 4, 1866), 3.

Helena Butler; A Story of the Rosary and the Shrine of the "Star of the Sea." (Philadelphia: Peter F. Cunningham)
Catholic World, III (August, 1866), 720.

Hepworth, Mrs. G. H. (Una Savin). *The Little Gentleman in Green.* (Boston: A. K. Loring).
North American Review, CII (January, 1866), 236–49.

Herbert, Sarah A. F. *Trust; or, A Peep at Eaton Parsonage.* (New York: A. D. F. Randolph)
American Literary Gazette, VII (May 15, 1866), 35.

Hillyard, W. H. *The Little Trapper.* (New York: James Miller)
Nation III (December 20, 1866), 492.

Hinsdale, Grace Webster. *Coming to the King and Thinking Aloud; A Book of Daily Meditations for Children.* (New York: A. D. F. Randolph)
American Literary Gazette, VI (February 1, 1866), 205.
Independent, XVIII (March 29, 1866), 3.

Hood, Thomas (the younger). *Fairy Realm; A Collection of the Favorite Old Tales.* (London: Ward, Lock & Tyler)
Nation, III (October 18, 1866), 307–08.

Jingles and Jokes for the Little Folks. (London: Cassell, Petter & Galpin)
Nation, II (January 11, 1866), 54.

Hymns for Mothers and Children. (Boston: Walker, Fuller & Co.)
Independent, XVIII (January 25, 1866), 3.

Ingelow, Jean. *Poor Matt; or, The Clouded Intellect.* (Boston: Roberts Brothers)
American Literary Gazette, VII (May 15, 1866), 35.

Stories Told to a Child. (Boston: Roberts Brothers)
American Literary Gazette, VI (March 15, 1866), 279.
Independent, XVII (June 14, 1866), 3.

Isa Graeme's World. (Philadelphia: American Sunday-School Union)
Independent, XVIII (January 25, 1866), 3.

Johnson, Virginia W. (Cousin Virginia). *The Kettle Club Series.* (Boston: Nichols & Noyes)
Nation, III (December 13, 1866), 466–67.

Kingston, William Henry Giles. *The Cruise of the Frolic.* (Boston: J. E. Tilton & Co.)
North American Review, CII (January, 1866), 240–41.

Laboulaye, Edouard. *Fairy Tales of All Nations.* Translated from the French by Mary L. Booth. (New York: Harper & Brothers)
American Literary Gazette, VIII (December 15, 1866), 136.
Nation, III (December 27, 1866), 514.

Lamb, Mrs. Joseph (Ruth Buck). *Captain Christie's Granddaughter.* (New York: M. W. Dodd)
American Educational Monthly, III (November, 1866), 447.
Hours at Home, III (October, 1866), 575.

Lander, Sarah W. *Spectacles for Young Eyes: Rome.* (Boston: Walker, Fuller & Co.)
American Literary Gazette, VI (January 1, 1866), 160.
Independent, XVIII (January 11, 1866), 2.

Lippincott, Sara Jane (Grace Greenwood). *Stories of Many Lands.* (Boston: Ticknor & Fields)
American Literary Gazette, VIII (December 1, 1866), 99.
Independent, XVIII (November 29, 1866), 3.
Nation, III (December 13, 1866), 467.

Llewellyn, E. L. *Dove's Nest and Benny Avert.* (Philadelphia: Ashmead & Evans)
American Literary Gazette, VI (February 15, 1866), 228.

Lucy's Half Crown, and Other Stories. (New York: James Miller)
Nation, III (December 20, 1866), 492.

McClellan, Kate. *Annie and Pierre; or, Our Father's Letter: A Book for the Holidays.* (New York: Protestant Episcopal Society for the Promotion of Evangelical Knowledge)
American Literary Gazette, VI (February 1, 1866), 204.

Mackay, Mrs. Colonel. *The Wycliffites; or, England in the Fifteenth Century.* (New York: Robert Carter & Brothers)
American Literary Gazette, VI (April 16, 1866), 338–39.

Mann, Mary. *The Flower People.* (Boston: Ticknor & Fields)
North American Review, CII (January, 1866), 245.

Manning, Anne. *Cherry and Violet; A Tale of the Great Plague.* (New York: M. W. Dodd)
Hours at Home, III (May, 1866), 100.
Independent, XVIII (June 7, 1866), 3.

Marshall, Emma. *The Lost Lilies; A Story for Children.* (Philadelphia: J. P. Skelly & Co.)
American Literary Gazette, VII (May 15, 1866), 35–36.

Mary Bruce; or, The Two Physicians. (London: Religious Tract Society; Boston: Henry Hoyt)
Independent, XVIII (March 15, 1866), 2.

Mathews, Julia A. (Alice Gray). *Golden Ladder Series.* (New York: Robert Carter & Brothers)
American Literary Gazette, VII (October 1, 1865), 252.

Meaney, Mary L. *A Father's Tales of the French Revolution.* 1st Ser. (Philadelphia: Peter F. Cunningham)
Catholic World, III (August, 1866), 720.

Ralph Berrien, and Other Stories of the French Revolution. 2nd Ser. (Philadelphia: Peter F. Cunningham)
Catholic World, III (August, 1866), 720.

Silver Grange; A Catholic Tale, and Phillipine; A Tale of the Middle Ages. (Philadelphia: Peter F. Cunningham)
Catholic World, III (August, 1866), 720.

Miss Matt; or, Our Youngest Passenger. (Boston: E. P. Dutton & Co.)
Nation, III (December 13, 1866), 467.

Newton, Dr. R. *The Great Pilot and His Lessons.* (New York: Robert Carter & Brothers)
American Literary Gazette, VIII (November 15, 1866), 53.

Oldfellow, Alfred. *Tom Randall; or, The Way to Success.* (New York: James Miller)
Nation, III (December 20, 1866), 492.

Our Young Folks (periodical).
Independent, XVIII (June 28, 1866), 3.
Independent, XVIII (July 26, 1866), 3.
New Englander, XXV (January, 1866), 178.

Parker, Helen F. *Frank's Hunt for Sea-Shells.* (Boston: American Tract Society)
American Literary Gazette, VII (November 1, 1866), 11.

Patriotism at Home. (Boston: William V. Spencer)
American Literary Gazette, VIII (November 15, 1866), 53.

Peabody, Andrew P. *Sermons for Children.* (Boston: American Unitarian Association)
American Literary Gazette, VI (February 15, 1866), 227–28.
Independent, XVIII (February 29, 1866), 3.

Perrault, Charles. *Les Contes de Perrault.* (Paris: Hetzel)
Nation, III (October 18, 1866), 307.

Phelps, Miss Elizabeth Stuart. *Gypsy Breynton.* (Boston: Graves & Young)
American Literary Gazette, VII (June 15, 1866), 86.

Planche, James Robinson. *An Old Fairy Tale Told Anew in Pictures and Verse.* (London: George Routledge & Sons)
Nation, III (October 18, 1866), 308.

The Play Room; or, In-door Games for Boys and Girls: A Complete Collection of Home Recreations. (New York: Dick & Fitzgerald)
American Literary Gazette, VIII (December 15, 1866), 136.

Potwin, Mrs. H. K. *The Kemptons.* (New York: M. W. Dodd)
American Educational Monthly, III (November, 1866), 446–47.
Hours at Home, III (October, 1866), 575.

Reid, Mayne. *Afloat in the Forest; or, A Voyage Among the Tree Tops.* (Boston: Ticknor & Fields)
American Literary Gazette, VIII (December 15, 1866), 136.

Riverside Magazine for Young People (periodical).
Independent, XVIII (December 27, 1866), 2.

Rosedale Library for Boys and Girls. (Philadelphia: Perkinpine & Higgins)
American Literary Gazette, VI (April 16, 1866), 339.

Sadlier, Mrs. J. *Aunt Honor's Keepsake.* (New York: D. & J. Sadlier & Co.)
Catholic World, III (August, 1866), 720.

The Exile of Tadmer, and Other Tales. Translated from the French by Mrs. J. Sadlier. (New York: D. & J. Sadlier & Co.)
Catholic World, III (August, 1866), 720.

Saint-Pierre, Jacques H. B. de. *Paul and Virginia. Rasselas. Elizabeth of Siberia. Undine. Sentram.* (New York: James Miller)
North American Review, CII (January, 1866), 236–49.

Savage, John. *Eva; A Goblin Romance, in Five Parts.* (New York: James B. Kirker) American Literary Gazette, VI (February 15, 1866), 228.

School and Home; or, Leaves from a Boy's Journal. (New York: Robert Carter & Brothers)
American Literary Gazette, VII (May 1, 1866), 9.

Sleeper, Martha G. *The Fonthill Recreations.* (Boston: Gould & Lincoln; New York: Sheldon & Co.)

American Literary Gazette, VI (January 1, 1866), 160.
Nation, III (December 13, 1866), 467.

The Mediterranean Islands. (Boston: Gould & Lincoln)
American Literary Gazette, VI (January 1, 1866), 160.

Smith, William W. *The Juvenile Definer.* (New York: A. S. Barnes & Co.)
Nation, III (October 25, 1866), 328–29.

Spare Hours: A Monthly Miscellany for the Young (periodical).
Catholic World, II (February, 1866), 718.

Stephens, H. L. (illus.) *The House That Jack Built.* (New York: Hurd & Houghton)
North American Review, CII (January, 1866), 244.

Old Mother Hubbard and Her Dog. (New York: Hurd & Houghton)
North American Review, CII (January, 1866), 244.

Stevenson, William Fleming. *Praying and Working, Being Some Account of What Men Can Do When in Earnest.* (New York: Robert Carter & Brothers)
American Literary Gazette, VI (April 16, 1866), 338–39.

Stewart, Agnes M. *Disappointed Ambition; or, Married and Single.* (New York: D. & J. Sadlier & Co.)
American Literary Gazette, VII (October 1, 1866), 252.

Stories on the Beatitudes. (New York: D & J. Sadlier & Co.)
Catholic World, III (August, 1866), 720.

Stoddard, Richard Henry. *The Story of Red Riding Hood, Told in Verse.* (New York: Hurd & Houghton)
North American Review, CII (January, 1866), 244.

Terhune, Mary Virginia Hawes (Marion Harland). *The Christmas Holly.* (New York: Sheldon & Co.)
Independent, XVIII (December 20, 1866), 2.

Thayer, William M. *A Youth's History of the Rebellion from the Battle of Murfreesboro to the Massacre at Fort Pillow.* (Boston: Walker, Fuller & Co.)
American Literary Gazette, VI (January 1, 1866), 160.
Independent, XVIII (January 25, 1866), 3.

A Youth's History of the Rebellion from the Massacre at Fort Pillow to the End. (Boston: Walker, Fuller & Co.)
American Literary Gazette, VI (February 15, 1866), 228.
Independent, XVIII (March 15, 1866), 2–3.

Thomes, W. H. *The Bushrangers; A Yankee's Adventures During His Second Visit to Australia.* (Boston: Lee & Shepard)
North American Review, CII (January, 1866), 236–49.

Tilton, Theodore. *The Fly.* (New York: Sheldon & Co.)
Methodist Quarterly Review, Fourth Series, XVIII (January, 1866), 163–64.

Golden-Haired Gertrude; A Story for Children. (New York: Tibbals & Whiting)
North American Review, CII (January, 1866), 244.

King's Ring. (New York: Hurd & Houghton)
American Literary Gazette, VIII (December 1, 1866), 97.

Two Hungry Kittens. (New York: Hurd & Houghton)
North American Review, CII (January, 1866), 244.

Trowbridge, John Townsend (Paul Creyton). *The Drummer Boy.* (Boston: J. E. Tilton & Co.)
North American Review, CII (January, 1866), 242.

Tucker, Charlotte (A.L.O.E.). *A Nutshell of Knowledge.* (New York: Robert Carter & Brothers)
American Literary Gazette, VII (May 1, 1866), 9.

Rescued from Egypt. (New York: Robert Carter & Brothers)
American Literary Gazette, VII (May 1, 1866), 9.
Independent, XVIII (June 14, 1866), 3.

A Visit to Aunt Agnes, for Very Little Children. (New York: Carlton & Porter)
American Literary Gazette, VI (February 15, 1866), 227.

Walsh, Viscount. *Tales and Stories.* Translated from the French by Mrs. J. Sadlier.
(New York: D. & J. Sadlier & Co.)
Catholic World, III (August, 1866), 720.

Watts, Isaac. *Divine and Moral Songs for Children.* (New York: Hurd & Houghton)
American Literary Gazette, VI (January 1, 1866), 159.

Watts, John G. *Little Lays for Little Folk.* (London and New York: George Routledge & Sons)
Nation, III (December 13, 1866), 467.

Whateley, Miss ——. *The Story of Martin Luther.* (New York: Robert Carter & Brothers)
American Literary Gazette, VIII (December 1, 1866), 97.

Whatley, Miss M. L. *Child-Life in Egypt.* (Philadelphia: American Sunday-School Union)
Independent, XVIII (December 20, 1866), 2.

Whitgift, Andrew. *Cripple Dan.* (New York: Robert Carter & Brothers)
American Literary Gazette, VIII (December 1, 1866), 97.

Whitney, Adeline Dutton Train. *A Summer in Leslie Goldthwaite's Life.* (Boston: Ticknor & Fields)
Nation, III (December 20, 1866), 493.

Wilberforce, W. *The Children and the Lion, and Other Sunday Stories.* (New York: Carlton & Porter)
American Literary Gazette, VI (February 15, 1866), 227.
Independent, XVIII (March 8, 1866), 3.

Willett, Edward. *Aspinax; or, The Enchanted Dwarf.* (New York: T. W. Strong)
American Literary Gazette, VIII (December 1, 1866), 97.

Myrtil; or, The Enchanted Island. (New York: T. W. Strong)
American Literary Gazette, VIII (December 1, 1866), 97.

Williams, Henry L., Jr. *The Boys of the Bible.* (New York: Wm. H. Appleton)
Independent, XVIII (January 18, 1866), 3.

The Wonderful Stories of Buz-Buz, the Fly, and Mother Grabem, the Spider.
(Philadelphia: J. B. Lippincott & Co.)
American Literary Gazette, VIII (December 15, 1866), 137.
Nation, III (December 20, 1866), 493.

Yonge, Charlotte M. *Countess Kate; A Story for Girls.* (Boston: A. K. Loring)
North American Review, CII (January, 1866), 245.

BOOKS REVIEWED IN 1867

Actea (pseud.). *A First Lesson in Natural History.* (Boston: Little, Brown & Co.)
Riverside Magazine, I (July, 1867), 333–34.

Adams, William T. (Oliver Optic). *Seek and Find; or, The Adventures of a Smart Boy.* (Boston: Lee & Shepard)
Nation V (December 26, 1867), 524.

The Arabian Nights' Entertainment. (New York: Hurd & Houghton)
Independent, XIX (January 24, 1867), 3.

Auerbach, Berthold. *The Little Barefoot.* Translated by Eliza Buckminster Lee.
(Boston: H. B. Fuller & Co.)

American Literary Gazette, IX (May 1, 1867), 14.
Independent, XIX (June 27, 1867), 2.

Aunt Effie's Rhymes for Children. (Boston: Ticknor & Fields)
Riverside Magazine, I (April, 1867), 189–90.

Aunt Zelpeth's Baby. (Boston: W. V. Spencer)
Nation, V (December 12, 1867), 474.

Barber, J. Warner. *Thrilling Incidents in American History.* (New York: George Routledge & Sons)
Nation, V (December 19, 1867), 498–99.

Barrow, Mrs. Fanny (Aunt Fanny). *Little Pet Books.* (New York: James O'Kane)
Catholic World, VI (November, 1867), 288.

Breed, William P. *Home-Songs for Home-Birds.* (Philadelphia: Presbyterian Board of Publication)
American Literary Gazette, VIII (February 1, 1867), 222.

Brock, Carey. *Copsley Annals Preserved in Proverbs.* (Boston: E. P. Dutton & Co.)
American Literary Gazette, X (December 16, 1867), 136.
Nation, V (December 12, 1867), 474.

Browning, Elizabeth Barrett. *Poems of Childhood.* (New York: James Miller)
Independent, XIX (March 7, 1867), 3.

Caroline; or, Self Conquest. (Philadelphia: Peter F. Cunningham)
Catholic World, V (August, 1867), 720.

Carové, Friedrich Wilhelm. *The Story Without an End.* (New York: Scribner, Welford & Co.)
Independent, XIX (December 5, 1867), 2–3.
Nation, V (December 19, 1867), 499.

Catlin, George. *Last Rambles Among the Indians of the Rocky Mountains and the Andes.* (New York: D. Appleton & Co.)
Nation, V (December 26, 1867), 523.

Life Among the Indians: A Book for Youth. (New York: D. Appleton & Co.)
Nation, V. (December 26, 1867), 523.

Charlesworth, Maria Louisa. *Blind Basket-Maker Library; A Sequel to Ministering Children.* (New York: Robert Carter & Brothers)
American Literary Gazette, VIII (April 1, 1867), 326.
Hours at Home, IV (April, 1867), 572.
Independent, XIX (March 14, 1876), 2.

Chellis, Mary Dwinell. *Old Sunapee* (Boston: Henry Hoyt)
Independent, XIX (July 17, 1867), 2.

Child, Lydia Maria. *Fact and Fiction: A Collection of Stories.* (New York: James Miller)
Nation, V (August 15, 1867), 127–28.

Rainbows for Children. (Boston: Ticknor & Fields)
American Literary Gazette, IX (October 15, 1867), 341.
Independent, XIX (November 21, 1867), 3.
Nation, V (October 24, 1867), 330.

The Children of the Frontier. (New York: D. Appleton & Co.)
Independent, XIX (March 14, 1867), 2–3.

Children's Own Book of Standard Fairy Tales. (Philadelphia: Duffield Ashmead)
American Literary Gazette, X (November 15, 1867), 49.

The Children's Poetry Book; A Selection of Narrative Poetry for the Young. (New York: George Routledge & Sons)
Nation, V (December 19, 1867), 500.

Clarke, Rebecca (Sophie May). *Dotty Dimple at Her Grandmother's.* (Boston: Lee & Shepard)
Nation, V (December 12, 1867), 474.

Denison, Mary Andrews. *Among the Squirrels.* (New York: George Routledge & Sons)
Nation, V (October 24, 1867), 330.

Douglas, Amanda M. *Stephen Dane.* (Boston: Lee & Shepard)
Oliver Optic's Magazine, I (May 11, 1867), 223.

Eiloart, Mrs. C. J. (Elizabeth Eiloart) *The Boys of Beechwood.* (New York: George Routledge & Sons)
Nation, V (December 19, 1867), 499.

Ellis, Mary. *Dick and His Cat; An Old Tale in a New Garb.* (Philadelphia: Mrs. J. Hamilton)
American Literary Gazette, VIII (February 15, 1867), 249–50.

Ervie. *Echo Bank: A Temperance Tale.* (New York: National Temperance Society)
Nation, V (December 12, 1867), 474.

Foe, Eugenie. *Boy Artists; or, Sketches of the Childhood of Michael Angelo, Mozart, Haydn, Watteau and Sebastian Gomez.* (Boston: E. P. Dutton & Co.)
American Literary Gazette, X (December 2, 1867), 88.
Nation, V (December 12, 1867), 474.

Frothingham, O. Brooks. *The Child's Book of Religion.* (Boston: Walker, Wise & Co.)
Independent, XIX (January 10, 1867), 3.
Nation, IV (January 10, 1867), 29.

Fuller, Jane G. *The Brownings: A Tale of the Great Rebellion.* (New York: M. W. Dodd)
Independent, XIX (March 7, 1867), 3.
Lucy Lee; or, All for Christ. (New York: M. W. Dodd)
Independent, XIX (March 7, 1867), 3.

Geiger, Herman. *Lydia; A Tale of the Second Century.* Translated from the German. (Philadelphia: Eugene Cummisky)
American Literary Gazette, VIII (January 15, 1867), 195.

Godolphin, Mary. *Robinson Crusoe, in Words of One Syllable.* (New York: George Routledge & Sons)
Nation, V (December 12, 1867), 475.

Goodwin, Lavinia L. *Little Helper; A Memoir of Florence Annie Caswell.* (Boston: Lee & Shepard)
Oliver Optic's Magazine, II (August 10, 1867), 408.

Gordon, Clarence (Vieux Moustache) *Our Fresh and Salt Tutors.* (New York: Hurd & Houghton)
New Englander, XXVI (January, 1867), 186.

Greene, Mrs. R. J. *A Winter and Summer at Burton Hall.* (Boston: E. P. Dutton & Co.)
Nation, V (December 12, 1867), 474.

Greenwood, James. *The Purgatory of Peter the Cruel.* (New York: George Routledge & Sons)
Nation, V (December 19, 1867), 499.

Grimm, Jacob L. and Wilhelm C. *Grimm's Goblins. Selected from the Household Stories of the Brothers Grimm.* (Boston: Ticknor & Fields)
American Literary Gazette, IX (October 15, 1867), 341
Independent, XIX (November 21, 1867), 3.
Nation, V (October 24, 1867), 329–30.

Headley, P.C. *Half Hours in Bible Lands.* (Philadelphia: John E. Potter & Co.)
American Literary Gazette, X (December 16, 1867), 136.

Home Twilight Stories. (Boston: Gould & Lincoln)
American Literary Gazette, X (December 16, 1867), 135.

Hooker, Worthington. *The Child's Book of Nature.* (New York: Harper & Brothers)
Riverside Magazine, I (July, 1867), 333–34.

How Paul's Penny Became a Pound. (New York: Robert Carter & Brothers)
Hours at Home, V (July, 1867), 288.

How Peter's Pound Became a Penny. (New York: Robert Carter & Brothers)
Hours at Home, V (July, 1867), 288.

Howitt, Mary. *The Children's Year.* (Boston: Crosby & Ainsworth)
Riverside Magazine, I (December, 1867), 572–73.

Our Four-Footed Friends. (New York: George Routledge & Sons)
Nation, V (December 26, 1867), 524.

Hymns for Mothers and Children. 2nd Ser. (Boston: Walker, Fuller & Co.)
Riverside Magazine, I (April, 1867), 189–90.

Laboulaye, Edouard. *Fairy Tales of All Nations.* Translated by Mary L. Booth. (New York: Harper & Brothers)
Harper's Magazine, XXXIV (January, 1867), 266.
Independent, XIX (February 21, 1867), 3.

Lippincott, Sara Jane (Grace Greenwood). *Stories and Sights of France and Italy.* (Boston: Ticknor & Fields)
American Literary Gazette, X (November 15, 1867), 48.

Stories of Many Lands. (Boston: Ticknor & Fields)
Hours at Home, IV (January, 1867), 288.

Little Songs for Little People. (New York: A. D. F. Randolph)
Riverside Magazine, I (March, 1867), 142.

MacDonald, George. *Dealings with the Fairies.* (London & New York: A. Strahan)
Nation, V. (October 24, 1867), 330.

Macé, Jean. *The History of a Mouthful of Bread, and Its Effects on the Organization of Men and Animals.* Translated from the French by Mrs. Alfred Gatty. (New York: American News Co.)
Hours at Home, IV (February, 1867), 383–84.
Independent, XIX (January 17, 1867), 2.

Macé's Fairy Book. Translated by Mary L. Booth. (New York: Harper & Brothers)
Harper's Magazine, XXXVI (December, 1867), 128.

McKeever, Harriet B. *Heavenward—Earthward.* (Philadelphia: J. B. Garrigues & Co.)
American Literary Gazette, X (December 2, 1867), 88.

Miller, Thomas. *The Boy's Own Country Book: Descriptive of the Seasons and Rural Amusements.* (New York: George Routledge & Sons)
Nation, V (December 19, 1867), 499.

The Child's Country Story Book. (London: George Routledge & Sons)
Nation, V (December 26, 1867), 523.

Moore, Mrs. J. F. *The Clifford Household.* (New York: M. W. Dodd)
Nation, V (December 26, 1867), 524.

Morgan, Henry. *Ned Nevins, the Newsboy; or, Street Life in Boston.* (Boston: Lee & Shepard)
Independent, XIX (May 9, 1867), 2.

Newman, May Wentworth (May Wentworth). *Fairy Tales from Gold Lands.* (San

Francisco: A. Roman & Co.)
American Literary Gazette, IX (October 15, 1867), 341.

Newton, Richard. *Bible Jewels.* (New York: Robert Carter & Brothers)
Hours at Home, VI (December, 1867), 190.

Nowell, Harriet P. H. (May Mannering). *Billy Grimes' Favorite; or, Johnny Greenleaf's Talent.* (Boston: Lee & Shepard)
Nation, V (December 12, 1867), 475.

Climbing the Rope; or, God Helps Those Who Help Themselves. (Boston: Lee & Shepard)
Nation, V (December 12, 1867), 475.

O'Connor, William D. *Nellie Renton; or, The Ghost.* (New York: G. P. Putnam & Son)
American Literary Gazette, X (December 16, 1867), 135.

Our Young Folks (periodical).
New Englander, XXVI (January, 1867), 186.
New Englander, XXVI (April, 1867), 397.

Parker, Rosa Abbot. *Alexis the Runaway; or, Afloat in the World.* (Boston: Lee & Shepard)
Nation, V (December 12, 1867), 475.

Tommy Hickup; or, A Pair of Black Eyes. (Boston: Lee & Shepard)
Nation, V (December 26, 1867), 524.

Phelps, Miss Elizabeth Stuart. *Gypsy's Sowing and Reaping.* (Boston: Graves & Young)
Independent, XIX (March 7, 1867), 3.

Pike, Mary H. *Striving and Gaining.* (Boston: Nichols & Noyes)
Nation, V (December 12, 1867), 474.

The Play Room; or, Indoor Games for Boys and Girls. A Complete Collection of Home Recreations. (New York: Dick & Fitzgerald)
Nation, IV (February 14, 1867), 129.

Pletsch, Oscar. *Little Folks.* (Boston: E. P. Dutton & Co.)
American Literary Gazette, X (December 2, 1867), 88
Nation, V (December 12, 1867), 475.

Schnick Schnack. Trifles for the Little Ones. (New York: George Routledge & Sons)
Nation, V (December 12, 1867), 475.

Schnik Schnak. Trifles for the Little Ones. (Boston: E. P. Dutton & Co.)
American Literary Gazette, X (December 2, 1867), 88.
Nation, V (December 12, 1867), 475.

Ploennies, Louisa von. *Princess Ilse: A Story of the Hartz Mountains.* (Boston: Gould & Lincoln)
American Literary Gazette, X (December 16, 1867), 135.
Nation, V (December 26, 1867), 524.

Reid, Mayne. *Afloat in the Forest; A Voyage Among the Tree Tops.* (Boston: Ticknor & Fields)
Independent, XIX (March 14, 1867), 2.

The Giraffe-Hunters. (Boston: Ticknor & Fields)
Hours at Home, IV (February, 1867), 384.
Independent, XIX (March 7, 1867), 3.

Riverside Magazine for Young People (periodical).
New Englander, XXVI (January, 1867), 186.
New Englander, XXVI (April, 1867), 397.

Robbins, Mrs. S. S. *Weighed in the Balance.* (New York: Robert Carter & Brothers)

Hours at Home, VI (December, 1867), 190.

Routledge, Edmund. *Every Boy's Book; A Complete Encyclopaedia of Sports and Amusements.* (New York: George Routledge & Sons)
Nation, V (December 26, 1867), 523–24.
Routledge's Every Boy's Annual; An Entertaining Miscellany of Original Literature. (New York: George Routledge & Sons)
Nation, V (December 19, 1867), 499.

Sage, Abby. *Pebbles and Pearls for the Young Folks.* (Hartford, Conn.: American Publishing Co.)
Independent, XIX (December 26, 1867), 6.

Samuels, Edward A. *Among the Birds; A Series of Sketches for Young Folks.* (Boston: Nichols & Noyes)
Nation, V (December 12, 1867), 474.

Scudder, Horace Elisha. *Dream Children.* (Cambridge, Mass.: Sever & Francis)
Nation, V (December 12, 1867), 474–75.

The Seven Corporal Works of Mercy and Mattie's Troubles. (Philadelphia: Peter F. Cunningham)
Catholic World, V (August, 1867), 720.

Sewell, Elizabeth M. *Home Life.* (New York: D. Appleton & Co.)
Nation, V (September 19, 1867), 231.

Shakings—Etchings from the Naval Academy. By a Member of the Class of 1867. (Boston: Lee & Shepard)
Oliver Optic's Magazine, I (May 18, 1867), 235.

Sheppard, Mrs. Edwin. *Judge Not; or, Hester Power's Girlhood.* (Boston: A. K. Loring)
Nation, V (December 19, 1867), 499.

Shields, Mrs. S. A. (Sarah Annie Frost). *Dialogues for Young Folks.* (New York: Dick & Fitzgerald)
American Literary Gazette, IX (October 15, 1867), 341.

Silsbee, Mrs. ——. *Willie Winkie's Nursery Songs of Scotland.* (Boston: Ticknor & Fields)
Riverside Magazine, I (March, 1867), 141–42.

Sinclair, Catherine. *Holiday House.* (New York: Robert Carter & Brothers)
Riverside Magazine, I (December, 1867), 572–73.

Sleeper, Martha G. *Sweden and Norway; Sketches and Stories of Their Scenery Customs, History, Legends, etc.* (Boston: Gould & Lincoln)
American Literary Gazette, X (December 16, 1867), 136.

Stale Bread; or, Letta, the Beggar Girl. (Philadelphia: American Baptist Publication Society)
American Literary Gazette, IX (October 15, 1867), 341.

Stories and Sketches by Our Best Authors. (Boston: Lee & Shepard)
Independent, XIX (September 5, 1867), 2.
Oliver Optic's Magazine, II (July 13, 1867), 344.

Stories on the Commandments. (Philadelphia: Peter F. Cunningham)
Catholic World, V (August, 1867), 720.

Stowe, Harriet Beecher. *Queer Little People.* (Boston: Ticknor & Fields)
Independent, XIX (November 21, 1867), 3.
Nation, V (December 19, 1867), 500.

Taylor, Ann and Jane. *Original Poems for Infant Minds.* (New York: Robert Carter & Brothers)
Riverside Magazine, I (March, 1867), 142.

Tenney, Sanborn and Abby A. *Natural History of Animals.* (New York: Charles Scribner & Co.)
Independent, XIX (March 7, 1867), 3.

Trimmer, Sarah Kirby. *The Little Fox; or, The Story of Sir F. L. McClintock's Arctic Expedition.* (New York: M. W. Dodd)
Nation, V (December 26, 1867), 524.

Tucker, Charlotte (A.L.O.E.). *David Aspinall, the Wanderer in Africa.* (New York: Robert Carter & Brothers)
Hours at Home, V (July, 1867), 288.

Lake of the Woods. (New York: Robert Carter & Brothers)
Hours at Home, V (July, 1867), 288.

Sunday Chaplet of Stories. (New York: Robert Carter & Brothers)
Hours at Home, V (July, 1867), 288. .

Ward, M. O. *Songs for the Little Ones at Home.* (New York: American Tract Society)
Riverside Magazine, I (March, 1867), 142.

Warner, Susan Bogert. (Elizabeth Wetherell) *The Word. A Star Out of Jacob.* (New York: Robert Carter & Brothers)
American Literary Gazette, VIII (March 15, 1867), 297.
Independent, XIX (May 23, 1867), 2.

Whateley, Miss ———. *The Story of Martin Luther.* (New York: Robert Carter & Brothers)
Independent, XIX (January 17, 1867), 3.

The Story of Martin Luther. (Philadelphia: Presbyterian Publication Committee; New York: A. D. F. Randolph)
American Literary Gazette, IX (May 15, 1867), 45.
Independent, XIX (June 6, 1867), 2.

Whitgift, Andrew. *Cripple Dan.* (New York: Robert Carter & Brothers)
Independent, XIX (January 17, 1867), 3.

Whitney, Adeline Dutton Train. *A Summer in Leslie Goldthwaite's Life.* (Boston: Ticknor & Fields)
Hours at Home, IV (February, 1867), 384.

Wood, J. G. *By the Seashore.* (New York: George Routledge & Sons)
Riverside Magazine, I (July, 1867), 333–34.

Common Objects in the Woods. (New York: George Routledge & Sons)
Riverside Magazine, I (July, 1867), 333–34.

BOOKS REVIEWED IN 1868

Adams, H. G. *The Weaver Boy Who Became a Missionary; Being the Story of the Life and Labors of David Livingstone.* (New York: Robert Carter & Brothers)
American Literary Gazette, X (March 16, 1868), 270.

Adams, William T. (Oliver Optic). *Breaking Away; or, The Fortunes of a Student.* (Boston: Lee & Shepard)
Catholic World, VI (January, 1868), 575.

Dikes and Ditches; or, Young America in Holland and Belgium. (Boston: Lee & Shepard)
Hours at Home, VII (September, 1868), 479.

Our Standard Bearer. (Boston: Lee & Shepard)
Putnam's Magazine, New Series II (November, 1868), 633.

Seek and Find; or, The Adventures of a Smart Boy. (Boston: Lee & Shepard)
Hours at Home, VI (February, 1868), 384.

Shamrock and Thistle; or, Young America in Ireland and Scotland. (Boston: Lee & Shepard)
Catholic World, VI (January, 1868), 574.

Young America Afloat. (Boston: Lee & Shepard)
Hours at Home, VI (April, 1868), 571.

Aesop. *The Fables of Aesop.* (New York: Charles Scribner & Co.)
Hours at Home, VI (January, 1868), 285.

Alcott, Louisa May. *Little Women; or, Meg, Jo, Beth, and Amy.* (Boston: Roberts Brothers)
American Literary Gazette, XII (November 2, 1868), 16.
Hours at Home, VIII (November, 1868), 100.
Nation, VII (October 22, 1868), 335.
Putnam's Magazine, New Series II (December, 1868), 760.

Alger, Horatio, Jr. *Ragged Dick; or, Street Life in New York with the Bootblacks.* (Boston: A. K. Loring)
American Literary Gazette, XI (May 15, 1868), 44.
Putnam's Magazine, New Series II (July, 1868), 120.

The Alphabet in Rhyme. (New York: American News Co.)
Nation, VII (December 17, 1868), 508.

Appleton's Juvenile Annual for 1869. (New York: D. Appleton & Co.)
Nation, VII (December 10, 1868), 485.

Ballantyne, Robert M. *The Coral Island; A Tale of the Pacific.* (New York: Thomas Nelson & Sons)
Catholic World, VI (February, 1868), 717–18.

Morgan Rattler; or, A Boy's Adventures in Brazil. (New York: Thomas Nelson & Sons)
Catholic World, VI (February, 1868), 717–18.

Ungava; A Tale of Esquimaux Land. (New York: Thomas Nelson & Sons)
Catholic World, VI (February, 1868), 717–18.

The Young Fur Trader; A Tale of the Far North. (New York: Thomas Nelson & Sons)
Catholic World, VI (February, 1868), 717–18.

The Bird and the Arrow. (Philadelphia: Presbyterian Publication Committee)
Hours at Home, VII (July, 1868), 287–88.

Bowen, Mrs. C. E. *Jack the Conqueror; or, Difficulties Overcome.* (New York: D. Appleton & Co.)
Nation, VII (December 17, 1868), 508.

Bowman, Anne. *The Boy Foresters; A Tale of the Days of Robin Hood.* (New York: George Routledge & Sons)
Nation, VII (December 24, 1868), 531.

The Doctor's Ward. (New York: George Routledge & Sons)
Nation, VII (December 24, 1868), 531.

Bradford, Mrs. Sarah H. *Tales for Little Convalescents.* (New York: Hurd & Houghton)
Nation, VII (December 17, 1868), 508.

Bradley, Warren Ives (Glance Gaylord). *Jack Arcombe; the Story of a Waif.* (Boston: Andrew F. Graves)
American Literary Gazette, XI (May 15, 1868), 44.

Miss Patience Hathaway; Her Friends and Her Enemies, and How She Returned Them Good for Evil. (Boston: Henry Hoyt)
Nation, VII (December 17, 1868), 507.

Bremer, Fredrika. *The Butterfly's Gospel, and Other Stories.* Translated by Margaret Howitt. (Philadelphia: Claxton, Remsen & Haffelfinger)
Nation, VII (December 10, 1868), 484.

Carové, Friedrich Wilhelm. *The Story Without an End.* Translated from the German by Sarah Austin. (New York: Scribner, Welford & Co.)
Hours at Home, VI (January, 1868), 286.

The Child's Auction, and Other Stories. (Boston: John L. Shorey)
Nation, VII (December 10, 1868), 484.

Clarke, Rebecca (Sophie May). *Dottie Dimple at Her Grandmother's.* (Boston: Lee & Shepard)
Catholic World, VI (January, 1868), 576.
Hours at Home, VI (January, 1868), 288.

The Cliff Hut; or, The Future of a Fisherman's Family. (Philadelphia: Presbyterian Publication Committee)
Hours at Home, VII (July, 1868), 287–88.

Comfort, Lucy Randall. *Folks and Fairies.* (New York: Harper & Brothers)
American Literary Gazette, X (January 15, 1868), 182.
Catholic World, VII (April, 1868), 144.

Conant, Helen S. *The Butterfly Hunters.* (Boston: Ticknor & Fields)
American Educational Monthly, V (July, 1868), 296.
American Literary Gazette, XI (May 15, 1868), 44.
Hours at Home, VII (June, 1868), 191–92.
Nation, VI (June 18, 1868), 496.
Putnam's Magazine, New Series II (December, 1868), 760.

Cooper, James Fenimore. *Stories of the Prairie, and Other Adventures of the Border.* (New York: Hurd & Houghton)
Nation, VII (December 24, 1868), 530.

Cousin Sue, (pseud.). *Wild Roses.* (Philadelphia: Presbyterian Publication Committee)
Hours at Home, VII (July, 1868), 287–88.

Daryl, Sidney. *Told in the Twilight; or, Short Stories for Long Evenings.* (Philadelphia: Claxton, Remsen & Haffelfinger)
Nation, VII (December 10, 1868), 484.

DeWitt, Madame (née Guizot). *A French Country Family.* Translated by Dinah Mulock Craik. (New York: Harper & Brothers)
American Literary Gazette, X (February 15, 1868), 221.

Diaz, Abby Morton. *The Entertaining Story of King Bronde, His Lily, and His Rosebud.* (Boston: Ticknor & Fields)
Nation, VII (December 10, 1868), 485.

Dickens, Charles. *Child-Pictures from Dickens.* (Boston: Ticknor & Fields)
Hours at Home, VI (February, 1868), 384.
Nation, VI (February 20, 1868), 154.

Dolly's Christmas Chickens. (New York: Robert Carter & Brothers)
Hours at Home, VII (July, 1868), 286.

Donald Fraser. (New York: Robert Carter & Brothers)
American Literary Gazette, IX (May 1, 1867), 14.

Donat Clare; or, The Manuscript Man. (Boston: Henry Hoyt)
Youth's Companion, XLI (October 15, 1868), 168.

Doublet, Victor. *Logic for Young Ladies.* Translated from the French. (New York: P. O'Shea)
Catholic World, VIII (October, 1868), 143.

Du Chaillu, Paul. *Stories of the Gorilla Country.* (New York: Harper & Brothers)
American Literary Gazette, X (February 1, 1868), 201.

Wild Life Under the Equator. (New York: Harper & Brothers)
Nation, VII (December 24, 1868), 530.

Emery, S. E. *Uncle Rod's Pet.* (Boston: E. P. Dutton & Co.)
Nation, VII (December 24, 1868), 530–31.

Farming for Boys. (Boston: Ticknor & Fields)
Hours at Home, VII (May, 1868), 192.

Father Cleveland; or, The Jesuit. (Boston: Patrick Donahoe)
American Literary Gazette, XI (August 1, 1868), 162.

Finley, Martha F. (Martha Farquharson). *Elsie Dinsmore.* (New York: M. W. Dodd)
Hours at Home, VI (February, 1868), 384.

Holidays at Roselands. (New York: M. W. Dodd)
American Literary Gazette, XI (June 15, 1868), 98.
Hours at Home, VII (July, 1868), 286–87.

The Shannons; or, From Darkness to Light. (Philadelphia: Presbyterian Publication Committee)
Hours at Home, VII (July, 1868), 287.

The Fisherman's Daughters, and Other Stories. (Boston: Henry Hoyt)
Youth's Companion, XLI (October 15, 1868), 168.

Foster, Sarah H. *Watchwords for Little Soldiers.* (Boston: Sunday-School Union; New York: James Miller)
Hours at Home, VII (July, 1868), 287.

The Foster Brothers; or, Pleasing Better Than Teasing. (Boston: W. V. Spencer)
Nation, VII (December 24, 1868), 530.

Frere, M. *Old Deccan Days; or, Hindoo Fairy Legends Current in Southern India.* (Philadelphia: J. B. Lippincott & Co.)
Lippincott's Magazine, II (December, 1868), 677–78.
Nation, VII (August 20, 1868), 154–55.

Frölich, Lorenz *Boasting Hector.* (Boston: Roberts Brothers)
Nation, VII (December 10, 1868), 484.

Foolish Zoe. (Boston: Roberts Brothers)
Nation, VII (December 10, 1868), 484.

Mischievous John. (Boston: Roberts Brothers)
Nation, VII (December 10, 1868), 484.

Gardette, Charles D. *Johnnie Dodge; or, The Freaks and Fortunes of an Idle Boy.* (Philadelphia: J. W. Daughaday & Co.)
American Literary Gazette, X (March 2, 1868), 246.

Gertie and May. (Boston: W. V. Spencer)
Riverside Magazine, II (February, 1868), 94.

Giles, Chauncey. *The Magic Spectacles.* (New York: Joseph R. Putnam)
Nation, VII (November 12, 1868), 397–98.

Godolphin, Mary. *Robinson Crusoe, in Words of One Syllable.* (New York: George Routledge & Sons)
Nation, VI (June 18, 1868), 496.

The Great Secret and Other Stories for the Youngest Readers. (Boston: John L. Shorey)
Nation, VII (December 10, 1868), 484.

Greenwood, James. *The Purgatory of Peter the Cruel.* (New York: George Routledge & Sons)
Putnam's Magazine, New Series I (January, 1868), 131.

Happy Hours of Childhood. (New York: P. O'Shea)
Catholic World, VI (January, 1868), 576.

Headley, P. C. *The Court and Camp of David.* (Boston: Henry Hoyt)
Youth's Companion, XLI (October 15, 1868), 168.

Hibbard, Shirley. *Clever Dogs, Horses, etc., with Anecdotes of Other Animals.* (New York: George Routledge & Sons)
Nation, VII (December 24, 1868), 531.

Hildeburn, Mrs. Mary J. *Carrie's Peaches; or, Forgive Your Enemies.* (Philadelphia: Presbyterian Publication Committee)

Hours at Home, VII (July, 1868), 288.

Dr. Leslie's Boys. (Philadelphia: Presbyterian Publication Committee)
Hours at Home, VII (July, 1868), 288.

Howitt, Mary. *Our Four-Footed Friends.* (New York: George Routledge & Sons)
Putnam's Magazine, New Series I (January, 1868), 131.

Pictures from Nature. (New York: George Routledge & Sons)
Nation, VII (December 24, 1868), 531.

The Illustrated Catholic Sunday-School Library. 1st Ser. (New York: The Catholic
Publication Society)
Catholic World, VII (June, 1868), 432.

The Illustrated Catholic Sunday-School Library. 2nd Ser. (New York: The Catholic Publication Society)
Catholic World, VIII (November, 1868), 286.

Ingelow, Jean. *A Sister's Bye-Hours.* (New York: George Routledge & Sons; Bos-
ton: Roberts Brothers)
American Literary Gazette, XI (May 1, 1868), 16.
Hours at Home, VII (June, 1868), 191.
Nation, VI (May 7, 1868), 376.

Stories Told to a Child. (Boston: Roberts Brothers)
New Eclectic, I (February, 1868), 238.

Johnson, Virginia W. (Cousin Virginia). *The Cricket's Friends. Tales Told by the
Cricket, Teapot, and Saucepan.* (Boston: Nichols & Noyes)
Nation, VII (December 10, 1868), 485.

Kingston, William Henry Giles. *Washed Ashore; or, The Tower of Stormount Bay.*
(Philadelphia: Claxton, Remsen & Haffelfinger)
Nation, VII (December 10, 1868), 485.

Koch, Rosalie. *Holly and Mistletoe.* Tales translated from the German of Rosalie
Koch. (New York: P. O'Shea)
Catholic World, VI (January, 1868), 576.

The Laughter Book for Little Folks. (New York: James Miller)
Nation, VII (December 24, 1868), 531.

Linton, W. J. *The Flower and the Star, and Other Stories for Children.* (Boston:
Ticknor & Fields)
Nation, VII (November 26, 1868), 442–43.

Little Rosy's Travels; or, Country Scenes in the South of France. (New York: A.
D. F. Randolph)
Nation, VII (December 10, 1868), 484.

Llewellyn, E. L. (Uncle John). *The Children's Album of Pretty Pictures, with
Short Stories.* (New York: D. Appleton & Co.)
Nation, VII (December 17, 1868), 508.

Luyster, Miss I. M. (trans.). *Narrative of a Voyage Round the World, Planned by
Four Adventurers; Miss Lily's Voyage Round the World Undertaken in Company with Masters Paul and Toto, Her Two Cousins, and Little Peter.* Translated from the French . . . (Boston: Roberts Brothers)
Nation, VII (December 17, 1868), 507–08.

Macé, Jean. *Grandpa's Arithmetic: A Story of Two Little Apple Merchants.* (New
York: P. S. Wynkoop & Son)
American Literary Gazette, XI (July 15, 1868), 146.
Nation, VII (September 17, 1868), 235.

*The History of a Mouthful of Bread and Its Effects on the Organization of
Men and Animals.* (New York: Harper & Brothers)
Harper's Magazine, XXXVII (August, 1868), 425.
Hours at Home, VII (September, 1868), 479.

Nation, VII (September 17, 1868), 234–35.
Putnam's Magazine, New Series I (March, 1868), 383–84.

Home Fairy Tales. (New York: Harper & Brothers)
Catholic World, VI (March, 1868), 860.
Nation, VII (September 17, 1868), 235.
Riverside Magazine, II (February, 1868), 94.

The Servants of the Stomach. (New York: Harper & Brothers)
Harper's Magazine, XXXVII (August, 1868), 425.
Hours at Home, VII (September, 1868), 479.
Nation, VII (September 17, 1868), 234–35.

McKeever, Harriet B. *Children with the Poets.* (Philadelphia: Claxton, Remsen & Haffelfinger)
American Literary Gazette, XI (October 1, 1868), 259.
Nation, VII (December 10, 1868), 484.

Maggie and the Sparrows. (New York: Robert Carter & Brothers)
Hours at Home, VII (July, 1868), 286.

Mathews, Joanna H. *Bessie and Her Friends.* (New York: Robert Carter & Brothers)
American Literary Gazette, XI (October 1, 1868), 259.

Bessie in the City. (New York: Robert Carter & Brothers)
Hours at Home, VII (June, 1868), 191.

May (pseud.). *I Will, and Other Stories.* (New York: P. S. Wynkoop & Son)
Nation, VII (December 10, 1868), 485.

May, Carrie L. *Ruth Lovell; or, Holidays at Home.* (Boston: Wm. H. Hill, Jr. & Co.)
Nation, VII (December 10, 1868), 484–85.

Michelet, Madame J. *The Story of My Childhood.* Translated from the French by Mary Frazier Curtis. (Boston: Little, Brown & Co.)
American Literary Gazette, X (January 1, 1868), 160.

Moore, Mrs. J. F. *The Clifford Household.* (New York: M. W. Dodd)
Hours at Home, VI (February, 1868), 384.

Morris, Edmund. *Farming for Boys.* (Boston: Ticknor & Fields)
American Educational Monthly, V (July, 1868), 296.
American Literary Gazette, XI (May 15, 1868), 44.
Hours at Home, VII (June, 1868), 192.
Nation, VI (June 18, 1868), 496.

Mountain Adventures in the Various Countries of the World; Selected from the Narratives of Celebrated Travellers. (Boston: Roberts Brothers)
Nation, VII (December 17, 1868), 508.

Nowell, Harriet P. H. (May Mannering). *Billy Grime's Favorite; or, Johnny Greenleaf's Talent.* (Boston: Lee & Shepard)
Catholic World, VI (January, 1868), 575.
Hours at Home, VI (January, 1868), 288.
Hours at Home, VI (February, 1868), 384.

Climbing the Rope; or, God Helps Those Who Help Themselves. (Boston: Lee & Shepard)
Catholic World, VI (January, 1868), 575.
Hours at Home, VI (January, 1868), 288.

O'Shea's Popular Juvenile Library. 1st Ser. (New York: P. O'Shea)
Catholic World, VII (August, 1868), 719.

Osten, Mary (Emile Eyler) *Grandmamma's Curiosity Cabinet.* From the German by Anna B. Cooke. (Boston: E. P. Dutton & Co.)
Nation, VII (December 17, 1868), 508.

Our Young Folks (periodical).
   Nation, VII (December 17, 1868), 508.

Palgrave, Francis Turner. *The Five Days' Entertainment at Wentworth Grange.* (Boston: Roberts Brothers)
   Nation, VII (December 17, 1868), 508.

Parker, Rosa Abbott (Rosa Abbott). *Alexis the Runaway; or, Afloat in the World.* (Boston: Lee & Shepard)
   Catholic World, VI (January, 1868) 575–76.
   Hours at Home, VI (January, 1868), 288.
      Tommy Hickup; or, A Pair of Black Eyes. (Boston: Lee & Shepard)
      Hours at Home, VI (February, 1868), 384.

Peebles, Mary L. (Lynde Palmer). *One Day's Weaving.* (Troy, N.Y.: Moore & Nims; New York: Wynkoop & Sherwood)
   Hours at Home, VII (July, 1868), 268.

The Pet Lamb, and Lambs of the Flock. (Philadelphia: Presbyterian Publication Committee)
   Hours at Home, VII (July, 1868), 287–88.

Poems Written for a Child by Two Friends. (New York: George Routledge & Sons)
   Nation, VII (August 6, 1868), 116.

Porter, J. L. *The Giant Cities of Bashan, and the Northern Border Land.* (Philadelphia: American Baptist Publication Society)
   American Literary Gazette, XI (August 1, 1868), 162.

Potwin, Mrs. H. K. *The Orphan's Triumphs; The Story of Lily and Harry Grant.* (New York: M. W. Dodd)
   Nation, VII (December 10, 1868), 484.

Prentiss, Elizabeth. *Little Lou's Sayings and Doings.* (New York: Hurd & Houghton)
   Nation, VII (December 17, 1868), 508.

Preston, Laura. *A Boy's Trip Across the Plains.* (San Francisco: A. Roman & Co.)
   Overland Monthly, I (November, 1868), 488.

Rands, William Brighty. *Lilliput Levee; Poems of Childhood.* (New York: Wynkoop & Sherwood)
   Nation, VII (August 6, 1868), 116.

The Riverside Magazine for Young People (periodical).
   Nation, VII (December 17, 1868), 508.

Robbins, Mrs. S. S. *Girding on the Armor.* (New York: Robert Carter & Brothers)
   Hours at Home, VII (July, 1868), 288.
      Robert Linton; or, What Life Taught Him. (New York: Robert Carter & Brothers)
      Hours at Home, VII (July, 1868), 286.

Rosa Lindesay, the Light of Kilmain. (Philadelphia: American Baptist Publication Society)
   American Literary Gazette, XI (August 1, 1868), 162.

Routledge, Edmund. *Every Boy's Book: A Complete Encyclopedia of Sports and Amusements.* (New York: George Routledge & Sons)
   Nation, VII (December 24, 1868), 531.

Sauvage, Elie. *The Little Gypsy.* Translated by I. M. Luyster. (Boston: Roberts Brothers)
   Nation, VII (December 10, 1868), 484.

The Sick Doll and Other Stories, for Youngest Readers. (Boston: John L. Shorey)
   Nation, VII (December 10, 1868), 484.

Sleeper, Martha G. *The Fonthill Recreations.* (Boston: Gould & Lincoln; New York: Sheldon & Co.)
Youth's Companion, XLI (January, 9, 1868), 11.

Squire Downing's Heirs. (New York: Robert Carter & Brothers)
Hours at Home, VII (June, 1868), 191.

The Story of a Round Loaf. (London: Seely, Jackson & Halliday)
Nation, VII (August 6, 1868), 117.

Stowe, Harriet Beecher. *Queer Little People.* (Boston: Ticknor & Fields)
Riverside Magazine, II (February, 1868), 94.

Talks with a Child on the Beatitudes. (Philadelphia: J. B. Lippincott & Co.)
American Literary Gazette, XI (October 1, 1868), 259.

Taylor, Ann (Ann Gilbert). *My Mother.* (New York: George Routledge & Sons)
Nation, VII (December 24, 1868), 531.
Putnam's Magazine, New Series I (January, 1868), 131.

Trimmer, Sarah Kirby. *The Little Fox; or, The Story of Captain Sir F. L. McClintock's Arctic Expedition.* (New York: M. W. Dodd)
Hours at Home, VII (February, 1868), 384.

Tucker, Charlotte (A.L.O.E.). *House Beautiful; or, The Bible Museum.* (New York: Robert Carter & Brothers)
Hours at Home, VII (June, 1868), 191.

Living Jewels. (New York: Robert Carter & Brothers)
Hours at Home, VII (July, 1868), 286.

On the Way; or, Places Passed by Pilgrims. (New York: Robert Carter & Brothers)
Hours at Home, VII (June, 1868), 191.

Warner, Susan Bogert (Elizabeth Wetherell). *Three Little Spades.* (New York: Harper & Brothers)
American Literary Gazette, X (March 16, 1868), 270.

Daisy, Continued from "Melbourne House." (Philadelphia: J. B. Lippincott & Co.)
Lippincott's Magazine, II (October, 1868), 456.
Overland Monthly, I (August, 1868), 199–200.

Weeks, Helen C. *Grandpa's House.* (New York: Hurd & Houghton)
Hours at Home, VI (April, 1868), 571.
Riverside Magazine, II (February, 1868), 93–94.

What Makes Me Grow? or, Walks and Talks with Amy Dudley. (New York: G. P. Putnam & Son)
Nation, VII (October 29, 1868), 355.
Putnam's Magazine, New Series II (December, 1868), 760–61.

White, Rhoda E. *Memoirs and Letters of Jenny C. White.* (Boston: Patrick Donahoe)
American Literary Gazette, XI (July 15, 1868), 146.

Wright, Julia McNair. *The Golden Fruit.* (Boston: Henry Hoyt)
Youth's Companion, XLI (October 15, 1868), 168.

Wright, Mrs. Washington (Carrie Carlton). *Inglenook: A Story for Children.* (San Francisco: A. Roman & Co.)
Overland Monthly, I (November, 1868), 488.

You-Sing; The Chinaman in California: a True Story of the Sacramento Flood. (Philadelphia: Presbyterian Publication Committee; New York: A. D. F. Randolph)
Nation, VII (December 10, 1868), 483–85.

BOOKS REVIEWED IN 1869

Alcott, Louisa May. *Little Women; or, Meg, Jo, Beth, and Amy.* Part Second.
(Boston: Roberts Brothers)
Catholic World, IX (July, 1869), 576
Galaxy, VIII (July, 1869), 141.
Harper's Magazine, XXXIX (August, 1869), 455–56.
Hours at Home, IX (June, 1869), 196.
Nation, VIII (May 20, 1869), 400.
Our Young Folks, V (September, 1869), 640.
Putnam's Magazine, New Series IV (July, 1869), 124.
Aldrich, Thomas Bailey. *The Story of a Bad Boy.* (Boston: Fields, Osgood & Co.)
American Literary Gazette, XIV (December 1, 1869), 14.
Nation, IX (December 30, 1869), 588.
Our Young Folks, V (November, 1869), 784.
Alger, Horatio, Jr. *Rough and Ready.* (Boston: A. K. Loring)
Nation, IX (December 30, 1869), 587.
Appleton, Anna E. *Stories for Eva.* (Boston: American Unitarian Association)
Nation, VIII (April 15, 1869), 295.
Appleton's Juvenile Annual for 1869. (New York: D. Appleton & Co.)
Harper's Magazine, XXXVIII (January, 1869), 276.
Putnam's Magazine, New Series III (January, 1869), 120.
Aunt Florida (pseud.). *Phebe Travers; or, One Year at a Boarding-School.* (San Francisco: A. Roman & Co.)
American Literary Gazette, XIV (November 1, 1869), 14.
Overland Monthly, III (December, 1869), 579–80.
Bache, Anna. *Legends of Fairy Land.* (Philadelphia: Claxton, Remson & Haffelfinger)
American Literary Gazette, XIII (August 2, 1869), 179–80.
Baker, Harriet N. W. (Aunt Hattie; Mrs. Madeline Leslie). *Paul Barton; or, The Drunkard's Son.* (Boston: Andrew F. Graves; Philadelphia: American Baptist Publication Society)
American Literary Gazette, XIII (August 16, 1869), 227.
Walter and Frank; or, The Apthorp Farm. (Boston: Andrew F. Graves)
Nation, IX (December 16, 1869), 541–42.
Baker, Sir Samuel W. *Cast Up by the Sea.* (New York: Harper & Brothers; Philadelphia: J. B. Lippincott & Co.)
American Educational Monthly, VI (April, 1869), 167.
Nation, VIII (March 25, 1869), 240.
Overland Monthly, II (May, 1869), 486.
Ballantyne, Robert Michael. *Deep Down; A Tale of the Cornish Mines.* (Philadelphia: J. B. Lippincott & Co.)
Nation, VIII (April 29, 1869), 339.
Erling the Bold: A Tale of the Norse Sea-Kings. (Philadelphia: J. B. Lippincott & Co.)
Nation, IX (December 30, 1869), 587.
Shifting Winds; A Tough Yarn. (Philadelphia: Porter & Coates)
American Literary Gazette, XIII (October 1, 1869), 340.
Barnes, William. *Rural Poems.* (Boston: Roberts Brothers)
Riverside Magazine, III (January, 1869), 46.
Barrows, William. *The General: or, Twelve Nights in the Hunter's Camp.* (Boston: Lee & Shepard)
Harper's Magazine, XXXIX (August, 1869), 455–56.

Hours at Home, IX (July, 1869), 292.
Putnam's Magazine, New Series IV (July, 1869), 124.

Before the Throne; or, Daily Devotions for a Child. (New York: M. W. Dodd)
Hours at Home, VIII (April, 1869), 580.

Bourne, H. R. F. *Famous London Merchants; A Book for Boys.* (New York: Harper & Brothers)
American Literary Gazette, XIII (August 2, 1869), 180.

Bowen, Mrs. C. E. *Jack the Conqueror; or, Difficulties Overcome.* (New York: Robert Carter & Brothers)
Hours at Home, IX (May, 1869), 100.

Boyd, Mrs. E. E. *Farmer Burt's Seed.* (Philadelphia: J. P. Skelly & Co.)
American Literary Gazette, XIV (November 15, 1869), 64.

Carové, Friedrich Wilhelm. *The Story Without an End.* Translated from the German by Sarah Austin. (New York: Scribner, Welford & Co.)
Our Young Folks, V (March, 1869), 201–02.

Chellis, Mary Dwinell. *Aunt Dinah's Pledge.* (New York: National Temperance Society)
Nation, IX (December 16, 1869), 542–43.

Effie Wingate's Work. (Boston: H. A. Young & Co.)
American Literary Gazette, XIII (October 15, 1869), 385.

Child-World. (New York: George Routledge & Sons)
Nation, VIII (May 13, 1869), 380–81.

Clarke, Rebecca (Sophie May). *Dotty Dimple at Play.* (Boston: Lee & Shepard)
Our Young Folks, V (September, 1869), 639.

Dotty Dimple at School. (Boston: Lee & Shepard)
Catholic World, IX (June, 1869), 428–29.
Harper's Magazine, XXXIX (August, 1869), 455–56.
Our Young Folks, V (September, 1869), 639.
Putnam's Magazine, New Series IV (July, 1869), 124.

Dotty Dimple's Flyaway. (Boston: Lee & Shepard)
Our Young Folks, V (December, 1869), 855.

Coxe, Arthur Cleveland. *Stories for Sundays Illustrating the Catechism.* By Mrs. Sherwood. Revised by A. C. Coxe. (Philadelphia: J. B. Lippincott & Co.)
American Literary Gazette, XIV (December 1, 1869), unnumbered.

Dall, Caroline H. *Patty Gray's Journey to the Cotton Islands.* (Boston: Lee & Shepard)
Harper's Magazine, XXXIX (November, 1869), 925.

Davis, Caroline E. K. *John Brett's Household.* (Philadelphia: J. K. Garrigues & Co.)
Hours at Home, X (December, 1869), 195.

Denison, Mary Andrews. *Anne and Tilly.* (Philadelphia: Alfred Martien)
American Literary Gazette, XIV (November 15, 1869), 64.

Dodge, Mary Mapes. *A Few Friends; or, How They Amused Themselves: A Tale in Nine Chapters; Containing Descriptions of Twenty Pastimes and Games and a Fancy-Dress Party.* (Philadelphia: J. B. Lippincott & Co.)
Catholic World, VIII (March, 1869), 856–57.
Hours at Home, VIII (March, 1869), 483.

Dodgson, Charles L. (Lewis Carroll). *Alice's Adventures in Wonderland.* (Boston: Lee & Shepard)
Catholic World, IX (June, 1869), 429.
Harper's Magazine, XXXIX (August, 1869), 455.
Overland Monthly, III (July, 1869), 102.
Putnam's Magazine, New Series IV (July, 1869), 124.

Dolliver, Clara G. *The Candy Elephant and Other Stories.* (San Francisco: A. Roman & Co.)
Overland Monthly, III (December, 1869), 579–80.

No Babies in the House and Other Stories for Children. (San Francisco: A. Roman & Co.)
Overland Monthly, II (March, 1869), 293.

Don't Wait; or, The Story of Maggie. (New York: A. D. F. Randolph)
Hours at Home, V (May, 1867), 94.

Dorr, Julia C. R. *Sybil Huntington.* (New York: G. W. Carleton)
Our Young Folks, V (October, 1869), 710.

Du Chaillu, Paul. *Lost in the Jungle.* (New York: Harper & Brothers)
Nation, IX (December 16, 1869), 542.

Wild Life Under the Equator. (New York: Harper & Brothers)
Harper's Magazine, XXXVIII (January, 1869), 276.
Hours at Home, VIII (March, 1869), 483.

Edgeworth, Maria. *The Parent's Assistant; or, Stories for Children.* (Baltimore: Kelly, Piet & Co.)
Catholic World, X (December, 1869), 430–31.

Erickson, D. S. *The Station-Master's Daughter and Her Friends.* (Boston: Congregational Sabbath-School and Publishing Society)
Hours at Home, VIII (April, 1869), 578.

Eyster, Nellie. *Tom Harding and His Friends.* (Philadelphia: Duffield Ashmead)
Nation, IX (December 16, 1869), 542.

Freeman, Edward A. *Old English History for Children.* (New York: Macmillan & Co.)
Nation, IX (December 16, 1869), 543.

Frölich, Lorenz. *Boasting Hector.* (Boston: Roberts Brothers)
Our Young Folks, V (March, 1869), 202.

Foolish Zoe. (Boston: Roberts Brothers)
Our Young Folks, V (March, 1869), 202.

Mischievous John. (Boston: Roberts Brothers)
Our Young Folks, V (March, 1869), 202.

Fuller, Jane G. *Uncle John's Flower-Gatherer: A Companion for the Woods and the Fields.* (New York: M. W. Dodd)
Hours at Home, IX (August, 1869), 386.

Glimpses of Pleasant Homes. (New York: Catholic Publication Society)
American Literary Gazette, XIII (June 1, 1869), 587–88.
Catholic World, IX (June, 1869), 423–24.
Nation, IX (December 30, 1869), 588.

Godolphin, Mary, *The Swiss Family Robinson in Words of One Syllable.* (New York: George Routledge & Sons)
Nation, IX (October 14, 1869), 321.

Gordon, Clarence (Vieux Moustache). *Two Lives in One.* (New York: Hurd & Houghton)
Nation, IX (December 23, 1869), 568.

Gourand, Julie. *A Little Boy's Story.* Translated from the French by Howard Glyndon. (New York: Hurd & Houghton)
Catholic World, X (December, 1869), 426.
Putnam's Magazine, New Series IV (December, 1869), 765–66.

Greene, Mrs. R. J. *Filling Up the Chinks.* (New York: E. P. Dutton & Co.)
Nation, IX (December 23, 1869), 568.

Greenwood, James. *Wild Sports of the World; A Book of Natural History and Adventure.* (New York: Harper & Brothers)

American Literary Gazette, XIV (December 1, 1869), unnumbered.

Hayes, Isaac I. *Cast Away in the Cold.* (Boston: Fields, Osgood & Co.)
Harper's Magazine, XXXVIII (January, 1869), 276.

Hosmer, Margaret. *Juliet the Heiress.* (Philadelphia: J. P. Skelly & Co.)
American Literary Gazette, XIII (October 1, 1869), 340.

Hotchkin, B. B. *Upward from Sin Through Grace to Glory.* (Philadelphia: Presbyterian Publication Committee)
Hours at Home, IX (May, 1869), 100.

The Illustrated Catholic Sunday-School Library. 3rd Ser. (New York: The Catholic Publication Society)
Catholic World, IX (May, 1869), 286–87.

Ingelow, Jean. *Mopsa, the Fairy.* (Boston: Roberts Brothers)
American Literary Gazette, XIII (July 1, 1869), 119.
Catholic World, X (October, 1869), 140.
Harper's Magazine, XXXIX (November, 1869), 925.
Hours at Home, IX (August, 1869), 385.
Nation, IX (August 19, 1869), 155.
Our Young Folks, V (September, 1869), 639–40.
Putnam's Magazine, New Series IV (September, 1869), 380–81.
Western Monthly, II (August, 1869), 129–30.

Kellogg, Elijah. *The Ark of Elm Island.* (Boston: Lee & Shepard)
Catholic World, IX (June, 1869), 428.
Harper's Magazine, XXXIX (August, 1869), 455–56.

Lion Ben of Elm Island. (Boston: Lee & Shepard)
Riverside Magazine, III (January, 1869), 46.

Kingston, William Henry Giles. *Count Ulrich; A Tale of the Reformation in Germany.* (Philadelphia: American Baptist Publication Society)
American Literary Gazette, XII (February 15, 1869), 203.

Kirby, Mary and Elizabeth. *The World at Home; or, Pictures and Scenes from Far Off Lands.* (New York: Thomas Nelson & Sons)
American Literary Gazette, XIV (December 1, 1869), unnumbered.

Kirkland, Caroline Matilda. *Garland of Poetry for the Young.* (New York: Charles Scribner & Co.)
Hours at Home, VIII (March, 1869), 482.

Kuntze, E. J. *The Mystic Bells.* (New York: G. P. Putnam & Sons)
American Literary Gazette, XIV (December 1, 1869), unnumbered.
Nation, IX (December 30, 1869), 588.
Putnam's Magazine, New Series IV (December, 1869), 765.

Lathrop, Mrs. H. *Allerton Homes.* (Philadelphia: J. P. Skelly & Co.)
American Literary Gazette, XIII (September 15, 1869), 301.

Linton, W. J. *The Flower and the Star, and Other Stories for Children.* (Boston: Fields, Osgood & Co.)
Harper's Magazine, XXXVIII (January, 1869), 276.
Our Young Folks, V (March, 1869), 202.

Little Drops of Rain. (New York: Robert Carter & Brothers)
American Literary Gazette, XIII (October 1, 1869), 340.

Little Effie's Home. (New York: Robert Carter & Brothers)
American Literary Gazette, XIII (September 15, 1869), 301.

Little Freddie Feeding His Soul. (New York: Robert Carter & Brothers)
Hours at Home, IX (May, 1869), 100.

Little Rosy's Travels; or, Country Scenes in the South of France. (New York: A. D. F. Randolph)
Hours at Home, VIII (January, 1869), 292.

The Lost Father, a Story of a Philadelphia Boy. (Philadelphia: Presbyterian Publication Committee)
Hours at Home, IX (May, 1869), 100.

Luyster, Miss I. M. (trans.). *Miss Lily's Voyage Round the World.* (Boston: Roberts Brothers)
Our Young Folks, V (March, 1869), 202.

M., M. E. *Philip Brantley's Life Work, and How He Found It.* (New York: M. W. Dodd)
Hours at Home, IX (August, 1869), 386.

McKeever, Harriet B. *Jack and Florie; or, The Pigeon's Wedding.* (Philadelphia: Claxton, Remsen & Haffelfinger)
Nation, IX (December 16, 1869), 544.

 Rupert Lawrence; or, A Boy in Earnest. (Philadelphia: J. P. Skelly & Co.)
American Literary Gazette, XIII (October 1, 1869), 340.

Manning, Anne. *The Spanish Barber.* (New York: M. W. Dodd)
Nation, IX (December 30, 1869), 588.

Mathews, Joanna H. *Bessie Among the Mountains.* (New York: Robert Carter & Brothers)
Hours at Home, IX (May, 1869), 100.

 Bessie At School. (New York: Robert Carter & Brothers)
American Literary Gazette, XIII (October 15, 1869), 385.
Harper's Magazine, XL (December, 1869), 139.

Meunier, Victor. *Adventures on the Great Hunting Grounds of the World.* (New York: Charles Scribner & Co.)
American Literary Gazette, XIV (November 1, 1869), 14.

Miller, Emily Huntington. *The Royal Road to Fortune.* (Chicago: Alfred L. Sewell & Co.)
American Literary Gazette, XIV (December 1, 1869), unnumbered.

Miller, Lydia Falconer. *Cats and Dogs; or, Notes and Anecdotes of Two Great Families of the Animal Kingdom.* (Boston: D. Lothrop & Co.)
Nation, IX (December 23, 1869), 568.

Mudge, Z. A. *Views From Plymouth Rock; A Sketch of the Early History of the Plymouth Colony.* (New York: Carlton & Lanahan)
Hours at Home, VIII (April, 1869), 579.

Nanny's Christmas; A Story for Children. (Philadelphia: Claxton, Remsen & Haffelfinger)
Nation, IX (December 23, 1869), 568.

Napier, Charles Ottley Groom. *Tommy Try, and What He Did in Science.* (New York: D. Appleton & Co.)
American Literary Gazette, XIII (June 1, 1869), 61.
Hours at Home, IX (June, 1869), 195–96.
Nation, IX (July 8, 1869), 35–36.
Putnam's Magazine, New Series IV (July, 1869), 124–25.

Neal, John. *Great Mysteries and Little Plagues.* (Boston: Roberts Brothers)
American Literary Gazette, XIV (December 1, 1869), unnumbered.
Nation, IX (December 16, 1869), 543.

Newman, May Wentworth (May Wentworth). *Fairy Tales from Gold Lands.* (San Francisco: A. Roman & Co.)
American Literary Gazette, XIV (December 1, 1869), unnumbered.
Harper's Magazine, XXXVIII (May, 1869), 855.

 The Golden Dawn, and Other Stories. (New York and San Francisco: A. Roman & Co.)
American Literary Gazette, XIV (December 1, 1869), unnumbered.
Overland Monthly, III (December, 1869), 579–80.

Golden Gate Series. (San Francisco: A. Roman & Co.)
Our Young Folks, V (December, 1869), 854.

Nowell, Harriet P. H. (May Mannering). *Salt-Water Dick.* (Boston: Lee & Shepard)
Catholic World, IX (June, 1869), 428.
Harper's Magazine, XXXIX (August, 1869), 455–56.
Putnam's Magazine, New Series IV (July, 1869), 124.

Nursery Carols. (Philadelphia: J. B. Lippincott & Co.)
Harper's Magazine, XL (December, 1869), 139.

O'Shea's Popular Juvenile Library. Second Series. (New York: P. O'Shea)
Catholic World, VIII (January, 1869), 573.

Our Young Folks (periodical).
Harper's Magazine, XXXVIII (January, 1869), 276.

Peckham, Mary C. *Father Gabrielle's Fairy.* (Boston: American Unitarian Association)
Nation, VIII (April 15, 1869), 295.

Phelps, Miss Elizabeth Stuart. *The Trotty Book.* (Boston: Fields, Osgood & Co.)
Nation, IX (December 16, 1869), 540–41.

Prentiss, Elizabeth. *Little Lou's Sayings and Doings.* (New York: Hurd & Houghton)
Riverside Magazine, III (January, 1869), 46.

Nidworth, and His Three Magic Wands. (Boston: Roberts Brothers)
American Literary Gazette, XIV (November 1, 1869), 14.
Nation, IX (December 23, 1869), 569.
Putnam's Magazine, New Series IV (December 1869), 765.

Pressense, Madame E. de. *Rosa.* (Philadelphia: Presbyterian Board of Publication)
American Literary Gazette, XII (February 15, 1869), 203.

Ralston, W. R. S. (trans.). *Krilof and His Fables.* (New York: George Routledge & Sons)
Nation, IX (December 30, 1869), 588.

Robbins, Mrs. S. S. *Butterfly Flights.* (New York: Robert Carter & Brothers)
American Literary Gazette, XIV (December 1, 1869), unnumbered.

Rodney, Marion L. L. (Fadette). *Sea Drift.* (Philadelphia: Claxton, Remsen & Haffelfinger)
American Literary Gazette, XIII (August 2, 1869), 179.

Saintine, Xavier Boniface. *Dame Nature and Her Three Children; A Grandpap's Talks and Stories about Natural History and Things of Daily Use.* Translated from the French. (New York: Hurd & Houghton)
American Literary Gazette, XIII (October 15, 1869), 385.
Nation, IX (December 23, 1869), 568.

Sanborn, Kate A. *Home Pictures from English Poets, for Fireside or School.* (New York: D. Appleton & Co.)
Our Young Folks, V (April, 1869), 270.

Sauvage, Elie. *The Little Gypsy.* Translated from the French by I. M. Luyster. (Boston: Roberts Brothers)
American Literary Gazette, XII (February 15, 1869), 203.
Catholic World, VIII (January, 1869), 574.
Galaxy, VII (January, 1869), 137–38.

Scudder, Horace Elisha. *Stories from My Attic.* (New York: Hurd & Houghton)
Atlantic Monthly, XXIV (December, 1869), 766–67.
Hours at Home, X (December, 1869), 195.
Nation, IX (December 30, 1869), 587–88.

Scudder, Mrs. Joseph. *Captain Waltham; A Tale of Southern India.* (Philadelphia: Presbyterian Publication Committee)
American Literary Gazette, XII (February 15, 1869), 203.

Sherwood, Mary Martha. *The Lily Series.* (New York: Robert Carter & Brothers)
Hours at Home, IX (May, 1869), 100.

Stockton, Frank R. *Ting-a-ling.* (New York: Hurd & Houghton)
Nation, IX (December 23, 1869), 569.

Tales from Alsace; or, Scenes and Pictures from the Days of the Reformation. (New York: Robert Carter & Brothers)
American Literary Gazette, XII (March 1, 1869), 226.
Harper's Magazine, XXXVIII (May, 1869), 855.

Taney, Mrs. Sanborn. *Pictures and Stories of Animals for the Little Ones at Home.* (New York: Sheldon & Co.)
Harper's Magazine, XXXVIII (January, 1869), 276.

Thurston, Louise M. *How Charley Roberts Became a Man.* (Boston: Lee & Shepard)
Our Young Folks, V (December, 1869), 854–55.

How Eva Roberts Gained Her Education. (Boston: Lee & Shepard)
Our Young Folks, V (December, 1869), 855.

Todd, Dr. J. *Sunset Land; or, The Great Pacific Slope.* (Boston: Lee & Shepard)
Our Young Folks, V (December, 1869), 855.

Tucker, Charlotte (A.L.O.E.). *John Carey; or, What is a Christian?* (New York: Robert Carter & Brothers)
American Literary Gazette, XII (March 1, 1869), 226.

Uncle Sam Series for American Children. (Boston: Fields, Osgood & Co.)
American Literary Gazette, XIV (December 1, 1869), unnumbered.
Our Young Folks, V (December, 1869), 855.

Veitch, Agnes. *Frank Fielding; or, Debts and Difficulties.* (Philadelphia: Alfred Martien)
American Literary Gazette, XIV (November 15, 1869), 64.

Verne, Jules. *Five Weeks in a Balloon; or, Journeys and Discoveries in Africa by Three Englishmen.* (New York: D. Appleton & Co.)
Harper's Magazine, XXXVIII (May, 1869), 854.
Hours at Home, VIII (April, 1869), 579.

Walker, Mrs. Edward Ashley. *From the Crib to the Cross; A Life of Christ in Words of One Syllable.* (New York: George A. Leavitt)
New Englander, XXVIII (October, 1869), 810.
Our Young Folks, V (December, 1869), 855.

The Pilgrim's Progress from This World to That Which Is to Come. By John Bunyan. In Words of One Syllable. (New York: George A. Leavitt)
New Englander, XXVIII (October, 1869), 810.
Our Young Folks, V (December, 1869), 855.

Walker, Mary Spring. *The Rev. Dr. Willoughby and His Wine.* (New York: National Temperance Society)
American Literary Gazette, XIV (December 1, 1869), unnumbered.
Nation, IX (December 16, 1869), 543.

Warner, Susan Bogert (Elizabeth Wetherell). *Daisy.* 2nd Ser. (Philadelphia: J. B. Lippincott & Co.)
Nation, IX (December 23, 1869), 568.

Weeks, Helen C. *The Ainslee Stories.* (New York: Hurd & Houghton)
Riverside Magazine, III (January, 1869), 46.

An American Family in Paris. (New York: Hurd & Houghton)
Nation, IX (December 16, 1869), 543–44.

White and Red: Life Among the Northwest Indians. (New York: Hurd & Houghton)
Nation, IX (December 30, 1869), 588.

Weston, H. H., C. Clark, and L. Gibbons. *The Fairy Egg and What It Contained.* (Boston: Fields, Osgood & Co.)
Nation, IX (December 16, 1869), 543.
Our Young Folks, V (December, 1869), 855.

Wise, Daniel (Francis Forrester; Lawrence Lancewood). *Peter Clinton; the Story of a Boy.* (Boston: H. A. Young & Co.)
American Literary Gazette, XIII (October 15, 1869), 385.

Wright, Julia McNair. *John and Demijohn.* (Boston: Henry Hoyt)
Nation, IX (December 16, 1869), 543.

Wright, Mrs. Washington (Carrie Carlton). *Inglenook Series.* (San Francisco: A. Roman & Co.)
American Literary Gazette, XIV (December 1, 1869), 103.
Our Young Folks, V (December, 1869), 854.

Y., T. R. *Emily Douglas; or, A Year with the Camerons.* (New York: A. D. F. Randolph)
Hours at Home, IX (August, 1869), 386.

Yonge, Charlotte M. *A Book of Golden Deeds.* (Boston and Cambridge: Sever & Francis)
American Literary Gazette, XII (March 1, 1869), 226.
Nation, VIII (March 11, 1869), 195.

Young Christian's Library. (Philadelphia: Henry McGrath)
Catholic World, IX (August, 1869), 719.

BOOKS REVIEWED IN 1870

Abbott, Jacob. *Hubert.* (New York: Dodd & Mead)
American Literary Gazette, XVI (November 1, 1870), 8.
Literary World, I (December 1, 1870), 109.

Juno and Georgie. (New York: Dodd & Mead)
American Literary Gazette, XV (June 15, 1870), 108.
Hours at Home, XI (July, 1870), 292.

Juno on a Journey. (New York: Dodd & Mead)
American Literary Gazette, XVI (November 1, 1870), 8.
Literary World, I (December 1, 1870), 109.

Mary Osborne. (New York: Dodd & Mead)
Hours at Home, XI (July, 1870), 292.

The Rollo and Lucy Books of Poetry. (New York: Dodd & Mead)
American Literary Gazette, XVI (December 1, 1870), 19.
Nation, XI (December 1, 1870), 373.

Adams, William T. (Oliver Optic). *Bear and Forbear; or, The Young Skipper of Lake Ucayga.* (Boston: Lee & Shepard)
Catholic World, XII (December, 1870), 431.
Old and New, II (December, 1870), 739.

Down the Rhine; or, Young America in Germany. (Boston: Lee & Shepard)
Hours at Home, X (February, 1870), 388.

Alcott, Louisa May. *An Old-Fashioned Girl.* (Boston: Roberts Brothers)
American Literary Gazette, XIV (April 15, 1870), 342.
Atlantic Monthly, XXV (June, 1870), 752–53.
Galaxy, IX (May, 1870), 710.
Harper's Magazine, XLI (June, 1870), 144.
Hours at Home, XI (June, 1870), 196.

Lippincott's Magazine, VI (August, 1870), 230–32.
Nation, XI (July 14, 1870), 30–31.

Aldrich, Thomas Bailey. *The Story of a Bad Boy.* (Boston: Fields, Osgood & Co.)
Atlantic Monthly, XXV (January, 1870), 124–25.
Our Young Folks, VI (January, 1870), 71.
Overland Monthly, IV (March, 1870), 294.

Allingham, William. *In Fairy Land.* (New York: D. Appleton & Co.)
Our Young Folks, V (January, 1870), 72.

Andersen, Hans Christian. *Wonder Tales Told for Children.* (New York: Hurd & Houghton)
American Literary Gazette, XIV (March 1, 1870), 249.

Aunt Mattie's Library. (Boston: Gould & Lincoln)
Literary World, I (November 1, 1870), 84–85.

B., C. E. *Work for All, and Other Tales.* (New York: E. P. Dutton & Co.)
Nation, XI (December 22, 1870), 425.

Ballantyne, Robert Michael. *Erling the Bold; a Tale of the Norse Sea-Kings.* (Philadelphia: J. B. Lippincott & Co.)
American Literary Gazette, XIV (January 1, 1870), 106.

Barnard, Charles Francis, Jr. (Jane Kingsford). *The Tone Masters.* (Boston: Lee & Shepard)
Hours at Home, XI (May, 1870), 97.
Literary World, I (July 1, 1870), 28–29.

The Tone Masters. Vol. II. (Boston: Lee & Shepard)
Literary World, I (December 1, 1870), 109.

Bowen, Mrs. C. E. *The Young Potato Roaster and The Boy Guardian.* (New York: Robert Carter & Brothers)
American Literary Gazette, XVI (November 1, 1870), 9.

Bradley, M. E. and K. J. Neely, *Proverb Stories.* 2nd Ser. (Boston: Lee & Shepard)
Old and New, II (December, 1870), 740.

Bund, Ludwig. *Puck's Nightly Pranks.* Translated from the German by Charles T. Brooks. (Boston: Roberts Brothers)
Nation, XI (December 15, 1870), 409.

Busch, William. *Max and Maurice; A Juvenile History in Seven Tricks.* From the German by Charles T. Brooks. (Boston: Roberts Brothers)
Nation, XI (December 22, 1870), 424.

Carter, Mrs. ——. *Rainy Day in the Nursery.* (Boston: Lee & Shepard)
Harper's Magazine, XL (January, 1870), 299.

Chaplin, Ada C. *Christ's Cadets.* (Philadelphia: American Baptist Publication Society)
American Literary Gazette, XV (June 15, 1870), 108.

Chatterbox, 1870. (New York: Pott & Amery)
American Literary Gazette, XVI (December 1, 1870), 18.

Clare Maitland. (New York: D. & J. Sadlier & Co.)
Catholic World, XII (October, 1870), 141–42.

Clarke, Rebecca (Sophie May). *Little Folks Astray.* (Boston: Lee & Shepard)
Literary World, I (October 1, 1870), 73–74.
Old and New, II (December, 1870), 739.

Clever Jack; or, The Adventures of a Donkey. Written by Himself. (Philadelphia: J. B. Lippincott & Co.)
Nation, XI (December 15, 1870), 409–10.

Conant, Helen S. *The Butterfly Hunters.* (Boston: Fields, Osgood & Co.)
Galaxy, IX (June, 1870), 853.

Corbet, Robert St. John. *The Holiday Camp; or, Three Days Picnic.* (New York: George Routledge & Sons)
Nation, XI (December 1, 1870), 373.

Cox, Mrs. W. N. (Percy Curtiss). *Amy Garnett, the Alms House Girl.* (Boston: A. F. Graves)
Literary World, I (September 1, 1870), 52.

Curious Facts for Little People: About Animals. (New York: E. P. Dutton & Co.)
Nation, XI (December 18, 1870), 392.

Daisy's Companions; or, Scenes from Child Life. (Boston: Roberts Brothers)
Nation, XI (November 24, 1870), 356.

Dall, Caroline H. *Patty Gray's Journey: From Boston to Baltimore; From Baltimore to Washington; On the Way—At Mount Vernon.* (Boston: Lee & Shepard)
Literary World, I (August 1, 1870), 40–41.

Darling, Mary G. *Battles at Home.* (Boston: H. B. Fuller)
Literary World, I (November 1, 1870), 91.

Davidson, Ellis A. *Happy Nursery.* (New York: Cassell, Petter & Galpin)
Nation, XI (December 22, 1870), 424.

De Liefde, J. *The Golden Cap; or, The Beautiful Legend Fostedina and Adgillus, and Other Stories.* (New York: Robert Carter & Brothers)
Hours at Home, XI (May, 1870), 97.

De Mille, James. *B. O. W. C.* (Boston: Lee & Shepard)
Literary World, I (October 1, 1870), 69–70.

The Boys of Grand Prè School. (Boston: Lee & Shepard)
Literary World, I (October 1, 1870), 69–70.
Old and New, II (December, 1870), 738.

de Stolz, Madame. *House on Wheels; or, The Stolen Child.* Translated from the French by Miss E. F. Adams. (Boston: Lee & Shepard)
Old and New, II (December, 1870), 739.

Dodgson, Charles L. (Lewis Carroll). *Alice's Adventures in Wonderland.* (Boston: Lee & Shepard)
Literary World, I (July 1, 1870), 23–24.

Doré, Gustave (illus.). *Popular Fairy Tales.* (New York: James Miller)
Nation, XI (December 15, 1870), 409.

Du Chaillu, Paul. *Lost in the Jungle.* (New York: Harper & Brothers)
American Literary Gazette, XIV (January 1, 1870), 101.
Harper's Magazine, XL (February, 1870), 461–62.
Hours at Home, X (January, 1870), 291.

My Apingi Kingdom; with Life in the Great Sahara. (New York: Harper & Brothers)
American Literary Gazette, XVI (December, 1870), 18.
Nation, XI (December 22, 1870), 425.

Elliot, J. W. *National Nursery Rhymes and Songs.* (New York: George Routledge & Sons)
Nation, XI (December 1, 1870), 373.

Everett, William. *Double Play; or, How Joe Handy Chose His Friends.* (Boston: Lee & Shepard)
Literary World, I (December 1, 1870), 102.

Ewing, Juliana Horatia (Aunt Judy). *Brownies and Other Tales.* (Boston: Roberts Brothers)
Nation, XI (November 24, 1870), 356.

Fette, W. Eliot (ed.). *Dialogues from Dickens for School and Home Amusement.* (Boston: Lee & Shepard)
Hours at Home, XI (May, 1870), 97.

Forbes, J. H. (Arthur Locker). *Stephen Scudamore the Younger; or, The Fifteen-Year-Olds.* (New York: George Routledge & Sons)
Nation, XI (December 8, 1870), 392.

Freeman, Edward A. *Old English History for Children.* (London: Macmillan & Co.)
Old and New, I (February, 1870), 258–59.

Good Stories for Young People. (Philadelphia: J. B. Lippincott & Co.)
American Literary Gazette, XVI (December 1, 1870), 17.

Good Words for the Young: An Illustrated Monthly Magazine (periodical).
Lippincott's Magazine, V (March, 1870), 350.

Gordon, Clarence (Vieux Moustache). *Two Lives in One.* (New York: Hurd & Houghton)
American Literary Gazette, XIV (January 15, 1870), 143.

Gourand, Julie. *A Little Boy's Story.* Translated from the French by Howard Glyndon. (New York: Hurd & Houghton)
Harper's Magazine, XL (January, 1870), 299.

Gray, George Zabriskie. *The Children's Crusade: An Episode of the 13th Century.* (New York: Hurd & Houghton)
Literary World, I (November 1, 1870), 85–86.
Nation, XI (December 22, 1870), 424.

Greenwood, James. *Wild Sports of the World.* (New York: Harper & Brothers)
Hours at Home, X (January, 1870), 291.

Guernsey, Clara F. *The Merman and the Figure-Head.* (Philadelphia: J. B. Lippincott & Co.)
Nation, XI (December 22, 1870), 424.

Hackländer, F. W. *Enchanting and Enchanted.* Translated from the German by Mrs. A. L. Wister. (Philadelphia: J. B. Lippincott & Co.)
Nation, XI (December 22, 1870), 425.

Heaton, Mrs. Charles. *Routledge's Album for Children.* (New York: George Routledge & Sons)
Nation, XI (December 22, 1870), 424.

The History of Brittany. (New York: Carlton & Lanahan)
Hours at Home, XI (May, 1870), 97.

History of the Crusades. (New York: Carlton & Lanahan)
Hours at Home, XI (May, 1870), 97.

Holiday Pleasures. (New York: Pott & Amery)
American Literary Gazette, XVI (December 1, 1870), 18.
Nation, XI (November 24, 1870), 355–56.

Home Chats with Our Young Folks on People and Things They See and Hear About. (New York: D. Appleton & Co.)
Appleton's Journal, IV (December 17, 1870), 744.

Hosmer, Margaret, and Julia Dunlap, *Under the Holly; or, A Week at Hopeton House.* (Philadelphia: Porter & Coates)
American Literary Gazette, XIV (January 1, 1870), 105.
Nation, XI (December 22, 1870), 425.

Howitt, William. *Jack of the Mill.* (New York: George Routledge & Sons)
Nation, XI (December 8, 1870), 392.

Hughes, Thomas. *Tom Brown's School-Days.* (New York: Harper & Brothers)
Harper's Magazine, XL (May, 1870), 929.
Hours at Home, XI (May, 1870), 97.

Jackson, Thomas. *Our Feathered Companions, or, Conversations of a Father with His Children About Sea-Birds, Song-Birds, and Other Feathered Tribes That Live in or Visit the British Isles* . . . (New York: George Routledge & Sons)
Nation, XI (December 1, 1870), 373.

John Whopper, the Newsboy. (Boston: Roberts Brothers)
Literary World, I (December 1, 1870), 103.
Nation, XI (December 8, 1870), 392.

Jones, Meredith. *The Story of Captain Cook's Three Voyages Round the World.* (Boston: Lee & Shepard)
Literary World, I (December 1, 1870), 110.

Kellogg, Elijah. *The Ark of Elm Island.* (Boston: Lee & Shepard)
Literary World, I (July 1, 1870), 25–26.

The Boy Farmer of Elm Island. (Boston: Lee & Shepard)
Catholic World, X (March, 1870), 860.
Hours at Home, X (February, 1870), 388.
Literary World, I (July 1, 1870), 25–26.

Charlie Bell, The Waif of Elm Island. (Boston: Lee & Shepard)
Literary World, I (July 1, 1870), 25–26.

The Hard Scrabble of Elm Island. (Boston: Lee & Shepard)
Catholic World, XII (November, 1870), 288.
Literary World, I (July 1, 1870), 25–26.
Old and New, II (December, 1870), 739.

Lion Ben of Elm Island. (Boston: Lee & Shepard)
Literary World, I (July 1, 1870), 25–26.

The Young Shipbuilders of Elm Island. (Boston: Lee & Shepard)
Catholic World, XII (November, 1870), 288.
Literary World, I (July 1, 1870), 25–26.

King, R. *Keightly Hall, and Other Tales.* (New York: D. & J. Sadlier & Co.)
Catholic World, XII (October, 1870), 141–42.

Kingston, William Henry Giles. *Count Ulrich of Lindburg.* (New York: Carlton & Lanahan)
Hours at Home, XI (May, 1870), 97.

Knatchbull-Hugessen, E. H. *Puss-Cat Mew, and Other Stories.* (New York: Harper & Brothers)
Nation, XI (December 22, 1870), 424–25.

Knevels, Mrs. D. C. (Francis Eastwood). *Geoffry the Lollard.* (New York: Dodd & Mead)
American Literary Gazette, XVI (December, 1870), 19.

Konewka, Paul, (illus.). *Black Peter.* Scissor Pictures by Paul Konewka. With rhymes from the German. (New York: Hurd & Houghton)
Nation, XI (December 15, 1870), 409.

Kuntze, E. J. *The Mystic Bells.* (New York: G. P. Putnam & Son)
Harper's Magazine, XL (January, 1870), 299.

Lear, Edward. *A Book of Nonsense.* (New York: James Miller)
Nation, XI (December 15, 1870), 409.

Letters Everywhere. (Boston: Lee & Shepard)
Old and New, II (December, 1870), 739.

The Library of Good Example. (New York: P. O'Shea)
Catholic World, X (February, 1870), 719.

The Little Red Riding-Hood Picture Book. (New York: George Routledge & Sons)
Nation, XI (December 1, 1870), 372.

Lorimer, Mary. *Among the Trees.* (New York: Hurd & Houghton)
Putnam's Magazine, V (January, 1870), 129.

Lowell, Anna C. *Posies for Children.* (Boston: Roberts Brothers)
Nation, XI (December 22, 1870), 424.

McCabe, James D., Jr. *Planting the Wilderness; or, The Pioneer Boys.* (Boston: Lee & Shepard)
Catholic World, X (March, 1870), 860.
Hours at Home, X (February, 1870), 388.

MacDonald, George. *Ranald Bannerman's Boyhood.* (Philadelphia: J. B. Lippincott & Co.)
American Literary Gazette, XVI (December, 1870), 18.
Nation, XI (December 1, 1870), 373.

McKeever, Harriet B. *Little Mary and the Fairy.* (Philadelphia: Claxton, Remsen & Haffelfinger)
American Literary Gazette, XVI (December, 1870), 18.

Manning, Annie. *One Trip More, and Other Stories.* (New York: Cassell, Petter & Galpin)
Nation, XI (December 15, 1870), 410.
The Spanish Barber. (New York: M. W. Dodd)
Hours at Home, X (February, 1870), 388.

Marcet, Jane. *Mary's Grammar.* (New York: D. Appleton & Co.)
American Literary Gazette, XIV (April 1, 1870), 313.

Mathews, Joanna H. *Bessie on Her Travels.* (New York: Robert Carter & Brothers)
Hours at Home, XI (May, 1870), 97.

Mayo, Isabella F. (Edward Garrett and Ruth Garrett). *White As Snow.* (New York: A. D. F. Randolph)
Hours at Home, XI (October, 1870), 576.

Moncrieff, Robert Hope (Ascott R. Hope). *My Schoolboy Friends; A Story of Whiteminster Grammar School.* (New York: Virtue & Yorsten)
American Literary Gazette, XVI (December, 1870), 18.
Nation, XI (December 22, 1870), 425.

Morrow, J. *A Voice from the Newsboys.* (New York: A. S. Barnes & Co.)
American Literary Gazette, XIV (February 15, 1870), 218.

Mother Goose. *Mother Goose's Melodies.* (Philadelphia: Porter & Coates)
Nation, XI (November 24, 1870), 355.

Nellie's Dark Days. (New York: Dodd & Mead)
American Literary Gazette, XVI (November 1, 1870), 9.

Newhall, C. S. (Carl). *Joe and the Howards.* (Boston: A. F. Graves)
Literary World, I (September 1, 1870), 53–54.

Nowell, Harriet P. H. (May Mannering). *Little Maid of Oxboy.* (Boston: Lee & Shepard)
Old and New, II (December, 1870), 739.

The Nursery (periodical). (Boston: John L. Shorey)
Literary World, I (September 1, 1870), 61.

On the Seas; A Book for Boys. (New York: George Routledge & Sons)
Nation, XI (December 8, 1870), 392.

Pardon, G. F. (Captain Crawley). *The Book of Manly Games for Boys.* (London: William Tegg)
American Literary Gazette, XIV (January 1, 1870), 105.

Parker, Rosa Abbott (Rosa Abbott). *Pinks and Blues; or, The Orphan Asylum.* (Boston: Lee & Shepard)
Old and New, II (December, 1870), 739–40.

Parkes-Belloc, Bessie. *Peoples of the World.* (New York: Cassell, Petter & Galpin)
Nation, XI (December 15, 1870), 410.

Pearson, C. H. *The Cabin on the Prairie.* (Boston: Lee & Shepard)
Catholic World, X (March, 1870), 860.
Hours at Home, X (February, 1870), 388.

Peebles, Mary L. (Lynde Palmer). *The Magnet Stories. John-Jack.* (Troy, New York: H. B. Nims & Co.)
Nation, XI (December 22, 1870), 425.

Phelps, Miss Elizabeth Stuart. *Gates Ajar.* (New York: Charles Scribner & Sons)
Our Young Folks, VI (January, 1870), 71.

The Gypsy Series. (Boston: H. A. Young & Co.)
Literary World, I (August, 1870), 40.

Trotty Book. (Boston: Fields, Osgood & Co.)
Our Young Folks, VI (January, 1870), 71.

Phelps, W. D. *Fore and Aft; or, Leaves from the Life of an Old Sailor.* (Boston: Nichols & Hall)
Literary World, I (December 1, 1870), 103.

The Picture Story-Book, Containing Fred Lee's Voyage and Other Illustrated Stories. (New York: American Tract Society)
Literary World, I (October 1, 1870), 76.

Porter, Rose. *Summer Drift-Wood for the Winter Fire.* (New York: A. D. F. Randolph)
Hours at Home, XI (October, 1870), 575–76.

Prentiss, Elizabeth. *Nidworth and His Three Magic Wands.* (Boston: Roberts Brothers)
Catholic World, X (February, 1870), 716.
Harper's Magazine, XL (January, 1870), 299–300.

Stepping Heavenward. (New York: A. D. F. Randolph)
Harper's Magazine, XL (January, 1870), 299–300.

Putnam, May. *Freddie Fighting His Way.* (New York: Robert Carter & Brothers)
American Literary Gazette, XVI (November 1, 1870), 9.

Recollections of Eton. (New York: Harper & Brothers)
Hours at Home, XI (October, 1870), 575.

Reid, Mayne. *The Castaways: A Story of Adventure in the Wilds of Borneo.* (New York: Sheldon & Co.)
American Literary Gazette, XVI (December, 1870), 18.
Literary World, I (December 1, 1870), 110.

Routledge's Annual for 1871. (New York: George Routledge & Sons)
Old and New, II (December, 1870), 740.

S., F. M. *A Lost Piece of Silver.* (New York: Pott & Amery)
American Literary Gazette, XVI (December, 1870), 18.

Sadlier, Mrs. J. (trans.). *The Mysterious Hermit; or, The Grotto of Beatus and Other Tales.* (New York: D. & J. Sadlier & Co.)
Catholic World, XII (October, 1870), 141–42.

Saintine, Xavier Boniface. *Dame Nature and Her Three Daughters.* (New York: Hurd & Houghton)
American Education Monthly, VII (March, 1870), 128.
Putnam's Magazine, New Series V (January, 1870), 129.

Samuels, Mrs. S. B. C. *The Springdale Stories.* (Boston: Lee & Shepard)
Nation, XI (December 8, 1870), 392.

Sargent, G. E. *Chronicles of the Old Manor-House.* (Philadelphia: Presbyterian Board of Publication)
American Literary Gazette, XV (June 15, 1870), 108.

Scudder, Horace Elisha. *Stories from My Attic.* (New York: Hurd & Houghton)
American Literary Gazette, XIV (January 1, 1870), 106.

Harper's Magazine, XL (January, 1870), 299.
Putnam's Magazine, New Series V (January, 1870), 129.

Ségur, Comtesse Eugienie de. *Fairy Tales for Little Folks.* Translated from the French by Mrs. Chapman Coleman and her daughter. (Philadelphia: Porter & Coates)
American Literary Gazette, XIV (January 1, 1870), 105.

The Snow-White and Rose-Red Picture Book. (New York: George Routledge & Sons)
Nation, XI (December 1, 1870), 372.

Stockton, Frank R. *Ting-a-ling.* (New York: Hurd & Houghton)
American Literary Gazette, XIV (January 1, 1870), 105.
Lippincott's Magazine, V (April, 1870), 463.

Stories of Old England. (New York: Carlton & Lanahan)
Hours at Home, XI (May, 1870), 97.

Taylor, Miss T. *Marguerite; or, The Huguenot Child.* (Cincinnati: Hitchcock & Walden; New York: Carlton & Lanahan)
American Literary Gazette, XVI (November 1, 1870), 9.

Thurston, Louise M. *Charley and Eva's Home in the West.* (Boston: Lee & Shepard) Literary World, I (December 1, 1870), 98–99.
Old and New, II (December, 1870), 739.

How Charley Roberts Became a Man. (Boston: Lee & Shepard)
Literary World, I (December, 1870), 98–99.

How Eva Roberts Gained Her Education. (Boston: Lee & Shepard)
Literary World, I (December 1, 1870), 98–99.

Tucker, Charlotte M. (A.L.O.E.). *A Braid of Cords.* (New York: Robert Carter & Brothers)
Hours at Home, XI (May, 1870), 97.

The Two Voyages; or, Midnight and Daylight. (Philadelphia: Presbyterian Board of Publication)
American Literary Gazette, XV (June 15, 1870), 108.

Weeks, Helen C. *An American Family in Paris.* (New York: Hurd & Houghton)
Putnam's Magazine, New Series V (January, 1870), 129.

White and Red: Life Among the Northwest Indians. (New York: Hurd & Houghton)
American Literary Gazette, XIV (January 1, 1870), 106.
Putnam's Magazine, New Series V (January, 1870), 129.

Weston, H. H., C. Clark and L. Gibbons. *The Fairy Egg, and What It Contained.* (Boston: Fields, Osgood & Co.)
American Literary Gazette, XIV (January 1, 1870), 106.
Our Young Folks, VI (January, 1870), 71.
Overland Monthly, IV (April, 1870), 391–92.

The Fairy Folk Series. (Boston: A. K. Loring)
Literary World, I (December 1, 1870), 109.
Nation, XI (December 8, 1870), 392.

Winnifred Jones; or, The Very Ignorant Girl. (New York: D. & J. Sadlier & Co.)
Catholic World, XII (October, 1870), 141–42.

Wood, Ellen P. *The Orville College Boys.* (New York: George Routledge & Sons)
Nation, XI (December 8, 1870), 392.

Wood, J. G. *Our Domestic Pets.* (New York: George Routledge & Sons)
Nation, XI (December 15, 1870), 410.

Wright, Julia McNair. *Jug-or-Not.* (New York: National Temperance Society)
American Literary Gazette, XV (June 15, 1870), 107–08.

Youmans, Eliza D. *The First Book of Botany*. (New York: D. Appleton & Co.)
Appleton's Journal, III (May 14, 1870), 555.
Catholic World, XI (June, 1870), 431.
Galaxy, IX (May, 1870), 711–12.
Hours at Home, XI (October, 1870), 576.
Nation, XI (July 14, 1870), 31.

Zschokke, Heinrich. *Labor Stands on Golden Feet: A Holiday Story*. Translated by
John Yates, LL.D. (New York: Dodd & Mead)
American Literary Gazette, XVI (December, 1870), 19.
Literary World, I (December 1, 1870), 109.
Nation, XI (November 24, 1870), 356.

BOOKS REVIEWED IN 1871

Abbott, Jacob. *The August Stories*. (New York: Dodd & Mead)
Appleton's Journal, VI (December 23, 1871), 724.

Heat. (New York: Harper & Brothers)
American Literary Gazette, XVII (May 1, 1871), 10.
Harper's Magazine, XLII (March, 1871), 623.
Literary World, I (May 1, 1871), 188.

Hubert. (New York: Dodd & Mead)
Harper's Magazine, XLII (January, 1871), 304.
Scribner's Monthly, I (February, 1871), 462.

Juno on a Journey. (New York: Dodd & Mead)
Harper's Magazine, XLII (January, 1871), 304.
Scribner's Monthly, I (February, 1871), 462.

Light. (New York: Harper & Brothers)
Harper's Magazine, XLIII (August, 1871), 457.
Literary World, II (July 1, 1871), 29.

The Rollo and Lucy Books of Poetry. (New York: Dodd & Mead)
Harper's Magazine, XLII (January, 1871), 304.

Adams, William T. (Oliver Optic). *Bear and Forbear; or, The Young Skipper of
Lake Ucayga*. (Boston: Lee & Shepard)
Harper's Magazine, XLII (January, 1871), 304.

Cringle and Cross-Tree; or, The Sea-Swashes of a Sailor. (Boston: Lee &
Shepard)
American Literary Gazette, XVII (October 16, 1871), 363.

Desk and Debit; or, The Catastrophe of a Clerk. (Boston: Lee & Shepard)
American Literary Gazette, XVII (May 15, 1871), 39.

Field and Forest; or, The Fortunes of a Farmer. (Boston: Lee & Shepard)
Catholic World, XII (March, 1871), 859–60.
Old and New, III (January, 1871), 109.
Our Young Folks, VII (January, 1871), 63.

Plane and Plank; or, The Mishaps of a Mechanic. (Boston: Lee & Shepard)
Catholic World, XII (March, 1871), 859–60.

Up the Baltic; or, Young America in Norway, Sweden and Denmark. (Boston:
Lee & Shepard)
American Literary Gazette, XVII (July, 1871), 122.
Literary World, II (July 1, 1871), 29.

The Upward and Onward Series. (Boston: Lee & Shepard)
Overland Monthly, VI (February, 1871), 199–200.

Young America Abroad. (Boston: Lee & Shepard)
Harper's Magazine, XLIII (September, 1871), 624.

Aikin, J. *The Children's Album of Pretty Pictures with Stories.* (Boston: Lee & Shepard)
American Literary Gazette, XVII (October 16, 1871), 363.
Literary World, II (November 1, 1871), 91.

Alcott, Louisa May. *Aunt Jo's Scrap-Bag.* (Boston: Roberts Brothers)
Literary World, II (December 1, 1871), 106.

Little Men; Life at Plumfield with Joe's Boys. (Boston: Roberts Brothers)
American Literary Gazette, XVII (June 15, 1871), 98.
Harper's Magazine, XLIII (August, 1871), 458.
Literary World, II (June 1, 1871), 6–7.
Old and New, IV (July, 1871), 102.
Overland Monthly, VII (September, 1871), 293–94.
Scribner's Monthly, II (August, 1871), 446–47.

Alger, Horatio, Jr. *Tattered Tom.* (Boston: A. K. Loring)
Harper's Magazine, XLIII (August, 1871), 459.

Andersen, Hans Christian. *Fairy Tales and Sketches.* (London: Bell & Daldy)
Overland Monthly, VI (June, 1871), 580.

Stories and Tales. (New York: Hurd & Houghton)
Literary World, I (March 1, 1871), 156.

Baché, Richard Meade. *American Wonderland.* (Philadelphia: Claxton, Remsen & Haffelfinger)
American Literary Gazette, XVII (September 15, 1871), 288.
Nation, XIII (December 21, 1871), 405.

Baker, G. M. *Social Stage.* (Boston: Lee & Shepard)
Harper's Magazine, XLII (January, 1871), 304.
Our Young Folks, VI (January, 1871), 63.

Ballantyne, Robert Michael. *The Floating Light of Goodwin Sands.* (Philadelphia: Claxton, Remsen & Haffelfinger)
Literary World, I (January 1, 1871), 123.

Ballard, Julia P. *Building Stones.* (Boston: D. Lothrop & Co.)
American Literary Gazette, XVI (February 15, 1871), 158.

Barnard, Charles Francis, Jr. (Jane Kingsford). *The Tone Masters, Vol. III.* (Boston: Lee & Shepard)
Literary World, I (January 1, 1871), 123.
Our Young Folks, VII (January, 1871), 63.

Bates, Lizzie. *How It Was Paid.* (Philadelphia: Alfred Martien)
American Literary Gazette, XVII (October 2, 1871), 324.

Begon, Comtesse de F. (Mme. de Stolz). *House on Wheels (La Maison Roulante); or, The Stolen Child.* Translated by Miss E. F. Adams. (Boston: Lee & Shepard)
Harper's Magazine, XLII (January, 1871), 304.
Our Young Folks, VII (January, 1871), 63.

Bennett, Mary E. *Six Boys; A Mother's Story as Told in Extracts from Her Journal.* (Boston: American Tract Society)
American Literary Gazette, XVII (June 15, 1871), 98.
Harper's Magazine, XLIII (September, 1871), 624.

Biart, Lucien. *Adventures of a Young Naturalist in Mexico.* Edited and Adapted by Parker Gilmore. (New York: Harper & Brothers)
American Literary Gazette, XVI (January 2, 1871), 66–67.
Harper's Magazine, XLII (January, 1871), 301.
Lippincott's Magazine, VII (February, 1871), 232.
Old and New, III (February, 1871), 238.
Overland Monthly, VI (February, 1871), 199–200.

Bradley, Mrs. M. E. and K. J. Neely. *Proverb Stories; A Wrong Confessed Is Half Redressed.* (Boston: Lee & Shepard)
  Catholic World, XII (January, 1871), 574–75.
  Harper's Magazine, XLII (January, 1871), 304.
  Scribner's Monthly, I (February, 1871), 462.

Brave Ballads for American Children. (Boston: Fields, Osgood & Co.)
  Our Young Folks, VII (January, 1871), 63–64.

Bread Winners. (Boston: Nichols & Hall)
  American Literary Gazette, XVII (June 1, 1871), 66.

Broome, Mary A. (Lady Barker). *A Christmas Cake in Four Quarters.* (London and New York: Macmillan & Co.)
  Nation, XIII (December 21, 1871), 405–06.

Bund, Ludwig. *Puck's Nightly Pranks.* Translated from the German by Charles T. Brooks. (Boston: Roberts Brothers)
  Old and New, III (January, 1871), 107.

Bunyan, John. *Pilgrim's Progress.* (New York: E. P. Dutton & Co.)
  Harper's Magazine, XLII (January, 1871), 305.

Busch, William. *Max and Maurice; A Juvenile History in Seven Tricks.* Translated from the German by Charles T. Brooks. (Boston: Roberts Brothers)
  Old and New, III (February, 1871), 239.

Charles, Elizabeth R. *The Victory of the Vanquished.* (New York: Dodd & Mead)
  American Literary Gazette, XVI (January 1, 1871), 66.

Chatterbox, 1871. (New York: Pott, Young & Co.)
  Literary World, II (June 1, 1871), 13.
  Nation, XIII (December 14, 1871), 389.

Chellis, Mary Dwinell. *The Hermit of Holcombe.* (Boston: H. A. Young & Co.)
  Literary World, I (May 1, 1871), 188.

Cheney, Mrs. E. D. *Faithful to the Light.* (Boston: American Unitarian Association)
  Literary World, I (January 1, 1871), 123.

Child, Louise Maria. *The Children of Mount Ida, and Other Stories.* (New York: D. G. Francis)
  American Literary Gazette, XVII (June 15, 1871), 98.

Children's Magazine. (New York: Church Book Society)
  Nation, XIII (December 14, 1871), 389.

The Children's Treasure. (Boston: Lee & Shepard)
  Literary World, II (December 1, 1871), 109.

Cinderella. (Boston: Fields, Osgood & Co.)
  Our Young Folks, VII (January, 1871), 64.

Clarke, Rebecca (Sophie May). *Dotty Dimple.* (Boston: Lee & Shepard)
  Overland Monthly, VI (February, 1871), 199–200.

  Dotty Dimple's Fly Away. (Boston: Lee & Shepard)
  Overland Monthly, VI (February, 1871), 199–200.

  Little Folks Astray. (Boston: Lee & Shepard)
  Catholic World, XII (January, 1871), 575.
  Harper's Magazine, XLII (January, 1871), 304.
  Old and New, III (February, 1871), 240.
  Our Young Folks, VII (January, 1871), 63.
  Scribner's Monthly, I (February, 1871), 462.

  Prudy Keeping House. (Boston: Lee & Shepard)
  Old and New, III (February, 1871), 240.

Cobden, Paul. *The Beckoning Series.* (Boston: Lee & Shepard)
  Overland Monthly, VI (February, 1871), 199–200.

Going on a Mission. (Boston: Lee & Shepard)
Catholic World, XII (March, 1871), 859–60.
Harper's Magazine, XLII (March, 1871), 623.
Old and New, III (January, 1871), 107.
Our Young Folks, VII (January, 1871), 63.

Who Will Win? (Boston: Lee & Shepard)
Catholic World, XII (March, 1871), 859–60.
Harper's Magazine, XLII (March, 1871), 623.
Old and New, III (January, 1871), 107.
Our Young Folks, VII (January, 1871), 63.

Conant Farm. (New York: Robert Carter & Brothers)
Harper's Magazine, XLII (January, 1871), 305.
Scribner's Monthly, I (February, 1871), 462.

Conwell, R. H. *Why and How: Why the Chinese Emigrate.* (Boston: Lee & Shepard)
Our Young Folks, VII (January, 1871), 63.

The Countess of Glosswood; a Tale. Translated from the French. (Baltimore: Kelly, Piet & Co.)
American Literary Gazette, XVI (April 1, 1871), 234.

Craik, Dinah Mulock. *Adventures of a Brownie, As Told to My Child.* (New York: Harper & Brothers)
Harper's Magazine, XLVI (December, 1871), 140.

The Fairy Book. (New York: Macmillan & Co.)
Nation, XIII (December 14, 1871), 389.

Is It True? (New York: Harper & Brothers)
Harper's Magazine, XLVI (December, 1871), 140.

Little Sunshine's Holiday; A Picture from Life. (New York: Harper & Brothers)
American Literary Gazette, XVII (July 1, 1871), 122.
Literary World, II (July 1, 1871), 29.
Nation, XIII (September 14, 1871), 182.

Craik, Georgiana M. *The Cousin from India.* (New York: Harper & Brothers)
American Literary Gazette, XVII (September 1, 1871), 262.
Literary World, II (September 1, 1871), 61.
Nation, XIII (December 21, 1871), 406.

Curious Facts About Animals. (New York: E. P. Dutton & Co.)
Harper's Magazine, XLII (January, 1871), 305.

Darling, Mary G. *Battles at Home.* (Boston: H. B. Fuller)
Harper's Magazine, XLIII (August, 1871), 459.
Old and New, III (February, 1871), 239.

In the World. (Boston: H. B. Fuller)
Harper's Magazine, XLIII (August, 1871), 459.
Literary World, I (May 1, 1871), 183.
Old and New, IV (July, 1871), 102.

Davy's Motto; or, Deeds Speak Louder Than Words. (Boston: A. F. Graves)
Literary World, I (May 1, 1871), 188.

De Kroyft, Helen Aldrich. *The Story of Little Jakey.* (New York: Hurd & Houghton)
Literary World, II (November 1, 1871), 92.

De Mille, James D. *The Boys of Grand Prè School.* (Boston: Lee & Shepard)
Harper's Magazine, XLII (January, 1871), 304.
Our Young Folks, VII (January, 1871), 63.

Fire in the Woods. (Boston: Lee & Shepard)
Literary World, II (October 1, 1871), 68–69.

Nation, XIII (December 14, 1871), 390.

Lost in the Fog. (Boston: Lee & Shepard)
Catholic World, XII (March, 1871), 859–60.
Literary World, I (January 1, 1871), 123.
Old and New, III (February, 1871), 239.

Denison, Mrs. M. A. (Clara Vance). *The Talbury Girls.* (Boston: D. Lothrop & Co.)
Literary World, II (November 1, 1871), 92–93.
Our Young Folks, VII (December, 1871), 767.

Devereux, George H. *Sam Shirk: A Tale of the Woods of Maine.* (New York: Hurd & Houghton)
Literary World, I (January 1, 1871), 123.
Old and New, III (February, 1871), 239.

Diaz, Abby Morton. *The William Henry Letters.* (Boston: Fields, Osgood & Co.)
Atlantic Monthly, XXVII (April, 1871), 524–25.
Literary World, I (January 1, 1871), 123.
Our Young Folks, VII (January, 1871), 63.

Dickens, Charles. *A Child's Dream of a Star.* (Boston: Fields, Osgood & Co.)
Atlantic Monthly, XXVII (February, 1871), 269–70.
Harper's Magazine, XLII (January, 1871), 303.
Literary World, I (January, 1871), 118.
Overland Monthly, VI (February, 1871), 199–200.

Doré, Gustave (illus.). *Popular Fairy Tales.* (New York: James Miller)
Harper's Magazine, XLII (January, 1871), 303.

Down the Steps. (New York: Robert Carter & Brothers)
Harper's Magazine, XLII (January, 1871), 305.
Scribner's Monthly, I (February, 1871), 462.

Du Chaillu, Paul. *The Country of the Dwarfs.* (New York: Harper & Brothers)
Nation, XIII (December 21, 1871), 405.

My Apingi Kingdom. (New York: Harper & Brothers)
Harper's Magazine, XLII (January, 1871), 303–04.
Lippincott's Magazine, VII (February, 1871), 232.
Literary World, I (January 1, 1871), 123.
Old and New, III (February, 1871), 238–39.
Overland Monthly, VI (February, 1871), 199–200.
Scribner's Monthly, I (February, 1871), 463.

Dunning, Mrs. A. K. *Mistaken; A Story of Four Lives.* (Boston: D. Lothrop & Co.)
Literary World, II (October 1, 1871), 75.

Duval, J. C. *Adventures of Big-Foot Wallace.* (Philadelphia: Claxton, Remsen & Haffelfinger)
Harper's Magazine, XLII (January, 1871), 305.

Eastman, Julia A. *The Romneys of Ridgemont.* (Boston: D. Lothrop & Co.)
Our Young Folks, VII (December, 1871), 767.

Eggleston, Edward. *Book of Queer Stories and Stories Told on a Cellar Door.* (Chicago: Adams, Blackmer & Lyon Publishing Co.)
Scribner's Monthly, II (June, 1871), 221.

Mr. Blake's Walking Stick. (Chicago: Adams, Blackmer & Lyon Publishing Co.)
Scribner's Monthly, II (June, 1871), 221.

Emma Parker; or, Scenes in the Homes of the City Poor. (New York: A. D. F. Randolph)
American Literary Gazette, XVI (March 15, 1871), 208.
Harper's Magazine, XLII (May, 1871), 931.

Scribner's Monthly, II (June, 1871), 221.

Everett, William. *Double-Play; or, How Joe Hardy Chose His Friends*. (Boston: Lee & Shepard)
Catholic World, XII (March, 1871), 859–60.
Harper's Magazine, XLII (March, 1871), 623.
Our Young Folks, VII (January, 1871), 63.

Familiar Discourses to the Young. (New York: Catholic Publication Society)
Catholic World, XIII (May, 1871), 288

Field, Mrs. Frederick. *By-and-By*. (New York: Leavitt & Allen Brothers)
Scribner's Monthly, I (February, 1871), 462.

I Didn't Hear. (New York: Leavitt & Allen Brothers)
Scribner's Monthly, I (February, 1871), 462.

I Forgot. (New York: Leavitt & Allen Brothers)
Scribner's Monthly, I (February, 1871), 462.

Finley, Martha F. (Martha Farquharson). *The Old-Fashioned Boy*. (Philadelphia: W. B. Evans & Co.)
Literary World, II (September 1, 1871), 60.

Goldschmidt, M. *The Flying Mail*. (Boston: Sever & Francis)
Harper's Magazine, XLII (January, 1871), 305.

Goldsmith, Christabel. *Brazen Gates*. (New York: G. W. Carleton & Co.)
Literary World, II (December 1, 1871), 108.

Good Stories. (Philadelphia: J. B. Lippincott & Co.)
Harper's Magazine, XLII (January, 1871), 305.

Good Words for the Young (periodical).
Harper's Magazine, XLII (January, 1871), 305.

Goulding, F. R. *Nacouchee; or, Boy Life on the Mountains*. (Philadelphia: Claxton, Remsen & Haffelfinger)
Scribner's Monthly, II (June, 1871), 221.

Saloquah; or, Boy Life Among the Indians. (Philadelphia: Claxton, Remsen & Haffelfinger)
Scribner's Monthly, II (June, 1871), 221.

Sapelo; or, Child Life on the Tidewater. (Philadelphia: Claxton, Remsen & Haffelfinger)
Scribner's Monthly, II (June, 1871), 221.

Gray, George Zabriskie. *The Children's Crusade; An Episode of the 13th Century*. (New York: Hurd & Houghton)
Atlantic Monthly, XXVII (February, 1871), 261–62.
Harper's Magazine, XLII (March, 1871), 622.
Old and New, III (January, 1871), 107.
Scribner's Monthly, II (June, 1871), 216–17.

Grimm, Jacob and Wilhelm. *The Household Stories*. (New York: James Miller)
Harper's Magazine, XLII (January, 1871), 303.

Guernsey, Clara F. *The Merman and the Figure-Head*. (Philadelphia: J. B. Lippincott & Co.)
American Literary Gazette, XVI (January 1, 1871), 66.

Hackländer, F. W. *Enchanting and Enchanted*. Translated from the German by Mrs. A. L. Wister. (Philadelphia: J. B. Lippincott & Co.)
Harper's Magazine, XLII (January, 1871), 303.

Hale, Edward Everett. *How to Do It*. (Boston: James R. Osgood & Co.)
Literary World, II (October 1, 1871), 75.

Harnard, Lois. *Coco, the Monkey*. Translated from Madame Dumont. (Philadelphia: Claxton, Remsen, & Haffelfinger)
Old and New, III (January, 1871), 108.

Harrison, Jennie. *The Old Back Room.* (New York: Dodd & Mead)
Appleton's Journal, VI (December 23, 1871), 724.

Holt, Emily Sarah. *Ashcliffe Hall.* (New York: Robert Carter & Brothers)
American Literary Gazette, XVII (May 15, 1871), 40.
Harper's Magazine, XLIII (July, 1871), 301.

How Nelly Found the Fairies. (Philadelphia: J. B. Lippincott & Co.)
American Literary Gazette, XVI (January 2, 1871), 66.

Hughes, Thomas. *Tom Brown's School Days, and Tom Brown at Oxford.* (New York: Harper & Brothers)
Old and New, III (January, 1871), 108.

The Illustrated Catholic Sunday-School Library. 4th Ser. (New York: The Catholic Publication Society)
Catholic World, XIII (July, 1871), 573–74.

The Infant's Delight. (Boston: Lee & Shepard)
Literary World, II (December 1, 1871), 109.

Ivan and Vasilesa; or, Modern Life in Russia. (Philadelphia: Presbyterian Board of Publication)
Scribner's Monthly, I (February, 1871), 462.

John Whopper, the News Boy. (Boston: Roberts Brothers)
Harper's Magazine, XLII (February, 1871), 463.

Johnson, E. *The Judge's Pets.* (New York: Hurd & Houghton)
Harper's Magazine, XLIV (December, 1871), 142.
Literary World, II (November 1, 1871), 92.
Nation, XIII (December 21, 1871), 405.
Our Young Folks, VII (December, 1871), 767.
Scribner's Monthly, III (December, 1871), 254.

Keeler, Ralph. *Vagabond Adventures.* (Boston: Fields, Osgood & Co.)
Our Young Folks, VII (January, 1871), 64.

Kellogg, Elijah. *Arthur Brown, the Young Captain.* (Boston: Lee & Shepard)
Catholic World, XIII (April, 1871), 143–44.
Harper's Magazine, XLII (March, 1871), 623.

The Hard Scrabble of Elm Island. (Boston: Lee & Shepard)
Harper's Magazine, XLII (January, 1871), 304.

The Spark of Genius. (Boston: Lee & Shepard)
Literary World, II (November 1, 1871), 92.

The Young Deliverers of Pleasant Cove. (Boston: Lee & Shepard)
American Literary Gazette, XVII (July 1, 1871), 122.
Literary World, II (July 1, 1871), 29.

The King's God-Child. (Philadelphia: Claxton, Remsen & Haffelfinger)
Literary World, II (October 1, 1871), 75.

Kingsbury, O. A. *Hints for Living; A Book for Young People.* (Boston: D. Lothrop & Co.)
American Literary Gazette, XVII (August 15, 1871), 233.

Kingsley, Henry. *The Lost Child.* (New York: Macmillan & Co.)
Literary World, II (December 1, 1871), 108.

Kirby, Alfred F. P. *Green Island; A Tale for Youth.* (Baltimore: Kelly, Piet & Co.)
Catholic World, XII (January, 1871), 575.

The Maltese Cross and Other Tales. (Baltimore: Kelly, Piet & Co.)
Catholic World, XII (January, 1871), 575.

Knatchbull-Hugessen, E. H. *Moonshine.* (London and New York: Macmillan & Co.)
Literary World, II (December 1, 1871), 108.

Nation, XIII (December 21, 1871), 406–07.

Puss-Cat Mew, and Other Stories. (New York: Harper & Brothers)
American Literary Gazette, XVI (January 1, 1871), 66.
Harper's Magazine, XLII (January, 1871), 303.
Literary World, I (January 1, 1871), 123.

Knevels, Mrs. D. C. (F. Eastwood). *Geoffrey the Lollard.* (New York: Dodd & Mead)
Harper's Magazine, XLII (January, 1871), 304.

Konewka, Paul (illus.). *Black Peter.* Scissor Pictures by Paul Konewka. With Rhymes from the German. (New York: Hurd & Houghton)
Atlantic Monthly, XXVII (February, 1871), 269–70.
Harper's Magazine, XLII (January, 1871), 305.

Krauth, Dr. C. P. *Iron Age of Germany.* From the German. (Philadelphia: Lutheran Publishing House)
Harper's Magazine, XLII (January, 1871), 304.

Lear, Edward. *Nonsense Songs, Stories, Botany and Alphabets.* (Boston: J. R. Osgood & Co.)
Literary World, II (July 1, 1871), 28.
Our Young Folks, VII (October, 1871), 639.
Scribner's Monthly, II (October, 1871), 668–69.

Letters Everywhere. (Boston: Lee & Shepard)
Harper's Magazine, XLII (January, 1871), 304.
Our Young Folks, VII (January, 1871), 63.

Lever, Charles. *A Rent in the Cloud.* (Philadelphia: T. B. Peterson & Brothers)
Old and New, III (January, 1871), 108.

Lewis, A. H. (Henry Louis). *The Boston Boy.* (Boston: Graves & Ellis)
Literary World, II (November 1, 1871), 92.

Linda Newton. (Boston: A. F. Graves)
Literary World, I (May 1, 1871), 188.

Little Folks: A Magazine for the Young. (New York: American News Co.)
Nation, XIII (December 14, 1871), 389.

Little Red Riding Hood. (Boston: Fields, Osgood & Co.)
Our Young Folks, VII (January, 1871), 64.

Little Redcap; A Tale for Boys. (Boston: D. Lothrop & Co.)
American Literary Gazette, XVI (April 1, 1871), 234.

Lonely Ways; or, The Diary of a Poor Young Lady. From the German, by F. E. B. (Philadelphia: Claxton, Remsen & Haffelfinger)
American Literary Gazette, XVII (October 2, 1871), 324.

Lowell, Anna C. *Posies for Children.* (Boston: Roberts Brothers)
Harper's Magazine, XLII (March, 1871), 624.
Old and New, III (February, 1871), 239–40.

Ludlow, Park. *The Red Shanty Boys; or, Pictures of New England School Life Thirty Years Ago.* (Boston: Henry A. Young & Co.)
Literary World, II (November 1, 1871), 93.

Lukin, J. *The Young Mechanic.* (New York: G. P. Putnam & Son)
Harper's Magazine, XLIII (October, 1871), 785.
Overland Monthly, VII (September, 1871), 290–91.
Scribner's Monthly, II (August, 1871), 447.

MacDonald, George. *At the Back of the North Wind.* (London: A. Strahan & Co.)
Overland Monthly, VII (September, 1871), 294–95.
Ranald Bannerman's Boyhood. (Philadelphia: J. B. Lippincott & Co.)
Harper's Magazine, XLII (January, 1871), 305.

Mackarness, M. A. *The Children's Sunday Album.* (Boston: Lee & Shepard)

327

American Literary Gazette, XVII (October 16, 1871), 363.
Literary World, II (November 1, 1871), 91.

Marsh, Caroline. *The Rift in the Clouds.* (New York: Robert Carter & Brothers)
American Literary Gazette, XVII (October 2, 1871), 324.
Harper's Magazine, XLIV (December, 1871), 142.

Marshall, Emma. *Little Primrose; or, The Bells of Old Effingham.* (New York:
Robert Carter & Brothers)
Harper's Magazine, XLII (January, 1871), 305.

Mathews, Joanna H. *Dora's Motto.* (New York: Robert Carter & Brothers)
Harper's Magazine, XLIII (July, 1871), 301.

Flowerets. (New York: Robert Carter & Brothers)
Harper's Magazine, XLII (January, 1871), 305.
Scribner's Monthly, I (February, 1871), 462.

Jessie's Parrot. (New York: Robert Carter & Brothers)
Harper's Magazine, XLIV (December, 1871), 142.

Lilly Norris's Enemy. (New York: Robert Carter & Brothers)
Harper's Magazine, XLIV (December, 1871), 142.

Mathews, Julia A. *Allan Haywood.* (New York: Robert Carter & Brothers)
Harper's Magazine, XLII (January, 1871), 305.
Scribner's Monthly, I, (February, 1871), 462.

Christy's Grandson. (New York: Robert Carter & Brothers)
Scribner's Monthly, I (February, 1871), 462.

Grandfather's Faith. (New York: Robert Carter & Brothers)
Harper's Magazine, XLIV (December, 1871), 142.

Lawrence Bronson's Victory. (New York: Robert Carter & Brothers)
Scribner's Monthly, I (February, 1871), 462.

Montgomery, Florence. *Misunderstood.* (New York: A. D. F. Randolph)
Harper's Magazine, XLII (January, 1871), 304.

A Very Simple Story. (New York: A. D. F. Randolph)
Harper's Magazine, XLIII (July, 1871), 301.

Mother Anthony's Family. (Boston: Congregational Publishing Society)
Literary World, I (February 1, 1871), 140.

Mudge, Z. A. *Shell Cove; A Story of the Seashore and of the Sea.* (Boston: D.
Lothrop & Co.)
American Literary Gazette, XVII (October 2, 1871), 324.
Literary World, II (October 1, 1871), 75.
Our Young Folks, VII (December, 1871), 767.

Mumford, Mary E. *Hila Dart, a Born Romp.* (Philadelphia: W. B. Evans & Co.)
Literary World, II (December 1, 1871), 109.

Munroe, Anna. *The Model Sunday-School Speaker.* (Boston: Lee & Shepard)
Literary World, II (December 1, 1871), 109.

My Young Days. (New York: E. P. Dutton & Co.)
Literary World, II (December 1, 1871), 109.

Newton, Richard. *Nature's Wonders.* (New York: Robert Carter & Brothers)
American Literary Gazette, XVII (September 15, 1871), 288.

Norris, Emilia M. *Adrift on the Sea; or, The Children's Escape.* (New York: E. P.
Dutton & Co.)
Nation, XII (December 14, 1871), 389.

Nowell, Harriet P. H. (May Mannering). *The Little Maid of Oxboy.* (Boston: Lee
& Shepard)
Catholic World, XII (January, 1871), 575.
Harper's Magazine, XLII (January, 1871), 304.

The Old World Seen with Young Eyes. (New York: T. Whittaker)
American Literary Gazette, XVII (June 15, 1871), 98.

Our Country Home. (New York: Pott, Young & Co.)
Literary World, II (December 1, 1871), 108.

Parker, Rosa Abbott (Rosa Abbott). *Pinks and Blues; or, The Orphan Asylum.*
(Boston: Lee & Shepard)
Catholic World, XII (January, 1871), 574.
Harper's Magazine, XLII (January, 1871), 304.
Scribner's Monthly, I (February, 1871), 462.

The Patranas Library; Spanish Stories, Legendary and Traditional. (Baltimore:
Kelly, Piet & Co.)
American Literary Gazette, XVI (January, 2, 1871), 67.

Pearson, C. H. *The Young Pioneers of the Northwest.* (Boston: Lee & Shepard)
Literary World, I (February 1, 1871), 140.

Pilpay. *The Fables of Pilpay.* (New York: Hurd & Houghton)
Literary World, II (October 1, 1871), 75.
Nation, XIII (December 21, 1871), 407.

Prentiss, Elizabeth. *Little Threads.* (New York: A. D. F. Randolph)
Harper's Magazine, XLII (January, 1871), 304.

The Percys. (New York: A. D. F. Randolph)
Harper's Magazine, XLII (March, 1871), 623.

The Story Lizzie Told. (New York: A. D. F. Randolph)
Harper's Magazine, XLII (April, 1871), 780.

Priest, Miss S. M. *Little Pieces for Little Speakers.* (Boston: Lee & Shepard)
Literary World, II (December 1, 1871), 109.

Pritchard, Sarah J. *Rose Marbury.* (New York: Robert Carter & Brothers)
Harper's Magazine, XLII (January, 1871), 305.

Pro and Con. (Boston: D. Lothrop & Co.)
Our Young Folks, VII (December, 1871), 767.

Prosser, Mrs. ——. *The Clacketts of Inglesbrook Hall.* (New York: A. D. F.
Randolph)
American Literary Gazette, XVII (August 1, 1871), 184.

Putnam, May. *Freddie Fighting His Way.* (New York: Robert Carter & Brothers)
Harper's Magazine, XLII (January, 1871), 305.

Raymond, Rossiter W. *The Children's Week.* (New York: J. B. Ford & Co.)
American Literary Gazette, XVI (January 2, 1871), 67.
Harper's Magazine, XLII (April, 1871), 623.
Literary World, I (January 1, 1871), 123–24.
Overland Monthly, VI (February, 1871), 199–200.

Reed, E. *Idle Word Series.* (Philadelphia: Claxton, Remsen, & Haffelfinger)
Old and New, III (January, 1871), 107.

She Hath Done What She Could. (Philadelphia: Claxton, Remsen & Haffelfinger)
Old and New, III (January, 1871), 107.

Reid, Mayne. *The Castaways: A Story of Adventure in the Wilds of Borneo.* (New
York: Sheldon & Co.)
Galaxy, XI (January, 1871), 145–46.
Harper's Magazine, XLII (January, 1871), 305.
Old and New, III (January, 1871), 109.

Richardson, Abby Sage. *Stories from Old English Poetry.* (New York: Hurd &
Houghton)
Literary World, II (October 1, 1871), 75.
Nation, XIII (December 21, 1871), 407.

329

Our Young Folks, VII (December, 1871), 767.
Overland Monthly, VII (November, 1871), 483–84.

Robert Merry's Midsummer Volume (Merry's Museum, January to June, 1871). (Boston: H. B. Fuller)
Literary World, II (August 1, 1871), 46.

Robinson, Annie Douglas (Marion Douglas). *Picture Poems for Young Folks.* (Boston: J. R. Osgood & Co.)
Nation, XIII (December 21, 1871), 405.

Samuels, Mrs. S. B. C. *The Springdale Stories.* (Boston: Lee & Shepard)
Harper's Magazine, XLII (January, 1871), 304.
Our Young Folks, VII (January, 1871), 63.
Scribner's Monthly, I (February, 1871), 462.

Sanford, Mrs. D. P. *Five Happy Children.* (New York: E. P. Dutton & Co.)
Nation, XIII (December 21, 1871), 406.

Two Happy Children. (New York: E. P. Dutton & Co.)
Literary World, II (December 1, 1871), 109.

Smith, Caroline L. *The American Home Book of In-Door Games, Recreations and Occupations.* (Boston: Lee & Shepard)
Literary World, II (December 1, 1871), 109.

Smith, Hannah (Hesba Stretton). *David Lloyd's Last Will.* (New York: A. D. F. Randolph)
American Literary Gazette, XVII (August 15, 1871), 233.
Harper's Magazine, XLIV (December, 1871), 142.

Max Kromer; A Story of the Siege of Strasburg. (New York: Dodd & Mead)
American Literary Gazette, XVI (April 15, 1871), 257.
Literary World, I (April 1, 1871), 173.
Scribner's Monthly, II (June, 1871), 220.

Nelly's Dark Days. (New York: Dodd & Mead)
Harper's Magazine, XLII (January, 1871), 304.
Scribner's Monthly, I (February, 1871), 462.

Stephenson, Eliza Tabor. *Nine Years Old.* (New York: Macmillan & Co.)
Nation, XIII (December 14, 1871), 390.

When I Was a Little Girl. (New York: Macmillan & Co.)
Nation, XIII (December 14, 1871), 390.

Stevenson, W. F. *Lives and Deeds Worth Knowing About.* (New York: Robert Carter & Brothers)
Harper's Magazine, XLII (January, 1871), 305.

Stowe, Harriet Beecher. *Little Pussy Willow.* (Boston: Fields, Osgood & Co.)
Catholic World, XIII (April, 1871), 144.

A Tale of a Nest. (New York: E. P. Dutton & Co.)
Literary World, II (December 1, 1871), 109.
Nation, XIII (December 21, 1871), 407.

Tefft, Lyman B. *Curiosities of Heat.* (Philadelphia: Bible & Publication Society)
American Literary Gazette, XVII (August 1, 1871), 184.

Testas, Marie Felicie. *The Virtues and Faults of Childhood.* Translated from the French by Mrs. Susan Harris. (Baltimore: Kelly, Piet & Co.)
American Literary Gazette, XVI (January 16, 1871), 97.

Thurston, Louise M. *Charley and Eva Roberts' Home in the West.* (Boston: Lee & Shepard)
Catholic World, XII (January, 1871), 575.
Harper's Magazine, XLII (January, 1871), 304.

Trowbridge, John Townsend (Paul Creyton). *Jack Hazard and His Fortunes.* (Boston: J. R. Osgood & Co.)

Nation, XIII (December 14, 1871), 390.

Lawrence's Adventures Among the Ice-Cutters, etc. (Boston: Fields, Osgood & Co.)
Literary World, I (January 1, 1871), 123.
Our Young Folks, VII (January, 1871), 63.

Tucker, Charlotte (A.L.O.E.). *A.L.O.E.'s Picture Story Book.* (New York: Robert Carter & Brothers)
American Literary Gazette, XVII (September 15, 1871), 288.

Warner, Anna B. *Stories of Vinegar Hill.* (New York: Robert Carter & Brothers)
Harper's Magazine, XLIV (December, 1871), 142.

Warner, Susan Bogert (Elizabeth Wetherell). *The House in Town.* (New York: Robert Carter & Brothers)
American Literary Gazette, XVII (September 15, 1871), 288.
Harper's Magazine, XLIV (December, 1871), 142.

Opportunities. (New York: Robert Carter & Brothers)
American Literary Gazette, XVI (March 1, 1871), 180.
Harper's Magazine, XLII (May, 1871), 93.
Scribner's Monthly, II (June, 1871), 220.

What She Could. (New York: Robert Carter & Brothers)
Harper's Magazine, XLII (January, 1871), 305.
Scribner's Monthly, I (February, 1871), 462.

Weeks, Helen C. *Four and What They Did.* (New York: Hurd & Houghton)
Literary World, II (October 1, 1871), 76.
Our Young Folks, VII (December, 1871), 767.
Overland Monthly, VII (December, 1871), 584.
Scribner's Monthly, VII (December, 1871), 254.

Wells, Kate G. *In the Clearings.* (Boston: American Unitarian Association)
Literary World, I (January 1, 1871), 123.

Weston, H. H. *Daffy-Down Dilly and Her Friends.* (Boston: A. K. Loring)
Our Young Folks, VII (January, 1871), 64.

What Shauny Did to the Light-House. (New York: Robert Carter & Brothers)
Harper's Magazine, XLIII (July, 1871), 301.

White, Alexina B. *Little Folk Songs.* (New York: Hurd & Houghton)
Harper's Magazine, XLIV (December, 1871), 142.
Literary World, II (October 1, 1871), 76.
Nation, XIII (December 14, 1871), 390.
Our Young Folks, VII (December, 1871), 767.
Scribner's Monthly, III (December, 1871), 254.

Whitney, Adeline Dutton Train. *Real Folks.* (Boston: James R. Osgood & Co.)
Literary World, II (October 1, 1871), 73–74.
Our Young Folks, VII (December, 1871), 767.

We Girls. (Boston: Fields, Osgood & Co.)
Literary World, I (January 1, 1871), 118–19.

Whittier, John Greenleaf. *Child-Life; A Collection of Poems.* (Boston: James R. Osgood & Co.)
Appleton's Journal, VI (December 9, 1871), 668.
Literary World, II (December 1, 1871), 108.

Woolsey, Sarah Chauncey (Susan Coolidge). *A New Year's Bargain.* (Boston: Roberts Brothers)
Literary World, II (December 1, 1871), 106.
Scribner's Monthly, III (December, 1871), 254–55.

Wright, Julia McNair. *The Best Fellow in the World.* (New York: American Temperance Society)
Harper's Magazine, XLIII (September, 1871), 624.

Y., T. R. *Belle Lovel.* (New York: A. D. F. Randolph)
Harper's Magazine, XLIII (August, 1871), 459.

Yonge, Charlotte. *Little Lucy's Wonderful Globe.* (New York: Macmillan & Co.)
Literary World, II (December 1, 1871), 108.

The Young Catholic's Guide. A Monthly Magazine. (Chicago: John Graham)
Catholic World, XII (February, 1871), 720.

Zschokke, Heinrich. *Labor Stands on Golden Feet.* (New York: Dodd & Mead)
Harper's Magazine, XLII (January, 1871), 304.
Scribner's Monthly, I (February, 1871), 462.

BOOKS REVIEWED IN 1872

Abbott, Jacob. *August and Elvie.* (New York: Dodd & Mead)
Harper's Magazine, XLIV (January, 1872), 300.

Force. (New York: Harper & Brothers)
Weekly Trade Circular, II (November 21, 1872), 537–38.

Granville Valley. (New York: Dodd & Mead)
Weekly Trade Circular, II (November 7, 1872), 488.

Water and Land. (New York: Harper & Brothers)
Harper's Magazine, XLIV (January, 1872), 297.
Literary World, II (February 1, 1872), 140.

Adams, William T. (Oliver Optic). *Bivouac and Battle.* (Boston: Lee & Shepard)
Literary World, II (January 1, 1872), 124.
Youth's Companion, XLV (January 25, 1872), 31.

Northern Lands. (Boston: Lee & Shepard)
Literary World, II (April 1, 1872), 171.

Sea and Shore; or, The Tramps of a Traveller. (Boston: Lee & Shepard)
Literary World, III (July 1, 1872), 27.

Aikin, J. *Children's Album of Pretty Pictures with Stories.* (Boston: Lee & Shepard)
Harper's Magazine, XLIV (January, 1872), 299.

Alcott, Louisa May. *Aunt Jo's Scrap-Bag.* (Boston: Roberts Brothers)
Appleton's Journal, VII (January 6, 1872), 24.
Harper's Magazine, XLIV (March, 1872), 463.

Shawl-Straps. (Boston: Roberts Brothers)
Literary World, III (December 1, 1872), 99.

Alger, Horatio, Jr. *Phil the Fiddler; or, The Young Street Musician.* (Boston: A. K. Loring)
Literary World, III (June 1, 1872), 11.

Strive and Succeed; or, The Progress of Walter Conrad. (Boston: A. K. Loring)
Literary World, III (November 1, 1872), 93.
Youth's Companion, XLV (December 12, 1872), 405.

Alice Leigh's Mission. (New York: Nelson & Phillips)
Nation, XV (December 19, 1872), 410.

Aunt Fanny's Present. (Philadelphia: Peter F. Cunningham)
Catholic World, XV (June, 1872), 432.

Baker, George M. *A Baker's Dozen.* (Boston: Lee & Shepard)
Catholic World, XV (September, 1872), 859.

Bates, Lizzie. *The Seymours.* (New York: National Temperance Society)
Harper's Magazine, XLIV (January, 1872), 301.

Black, Harriet M. (Hannah Maria). *Dolly's Resolutions; or, Letters from Abroad.*
(Philadelphia: Claxton, Remsen & Haffelfinger)

Weekly Trade Circular, II (September 12, 1872), 256.

Blue Mantle Series. (New York: Carlton & Lanahan; San Francisco: E. Thomas; Cincinnati: Hitchcock & Walden)
Nation, XV (December 19, 1872), 409.

Broome, Mrs. Frederick N. (Lady Barker). *Christmas Cake in Four Quarters.* (London and New York: Macmillan & Co.)
Scribner's Monthly, III (March, 1872), 639.

Ribbon Stories. (New York: Macmillan & Co.)
Nation, XV (December 19, 1872), 410.

By the Seaside. (New York: P. O'Shea)
Catholic World, XV (September, 1872), 859.

Chester, John. *Derwent; or, Recollections of Young Life in the Country.* (New York: A. D. F. Randolph)
Nation, XV (December 19, 1872), 408.

The Christian Hero; or, Robert Annan. (Boston: Henry Hoyt)
Youth's Companion, XLV (June 13, 1872), 169.

Christine. (pseud.). *Ambition's Contest; or, Faith and Intellect.* (Boston: P. Donahoe)
Catholic World, XVI (October, 1872), 144.

Clarke, Rebecca (Sophie May). *Aunt Madge's Story.* (Boston: Lee & Shepard)
Catholic World, XV (April, 1872), 144.

The Doctor's Daughter. (Boston: Lee & Shepard)
Our Young Folks, VIII (March, 1872), 189.
Youth's Companion, XLV (January 25, 1872), 31.

Little Grandmother. (Boston: Lee & Shepard)
Literary World, III (July 1, 1872), 27.

Cobden, Paul. *The Turning Wheel.* (Boston: Lee & Shepard)
Our Young Folks, VIII (March, 1872), 189.

Craig (Knox), Isa. *The Young Folks' History of England.* (Boston: Lee & Shepard)
Literary World, III (December 1, 1872), 108.

Craik, Dinah Mulock. *The Adventures of a Brownie, As Told to My Child.* (New York: Harper & Brothers)
Literary World, III (October 1, 1872), 76.
Our Young Folks, VIII (December, 1872), 762–63.

Is It True? (New York: Harper & Brothers)
Literary World, III (July 1, 1872), 28.
Weekly Trade Circular, I (June 6, 1872), 527.

Twenty Years Ago; From the Journal of a Girl in Her Teens. (New York: Harper & Brothers)
Literary World, II (April 1, 1872), 173.
Weekly Trade Circular, I (February 8, 1872), 99.

Cupples, Ann Jane. *Singular Creatures; or, Tappy's Chicks.* (Boston: Lee & Shepard)
Our Young Folks, VIII (March, 1872), 189.

Davis, Caroline E. K. *Aunt Lois; or, Happiness to Others.* (Boston: Henry Hoyt)
Youth's Companion, XLV (December 5, 1872), 397.

De Kroyft, Helen Aldrich. *The Story of Little Jakey.* (New York: Hurd & Houghton)
Harper's Magazine, XLIV (January, 1872), 300.
Overland Monthly, VIII (January, 1872), 104.

De Mille, James. *Among the Brigands.* (Boston: Lee & Shepard)
Our Young Folks, VIII (March, 1872), 189.

Fire in the Woods. (Boston: Lee & Shepard)
Overland Monthly, VIII (January, 1872), 104.

Picked Up Adrift. (Boston: Lee & Shepard)
Literary World, III (October 1, 1872), 76.

The Young Dodge Club. (Boston: Lee & Shepard)
Literary World, III (December 1, 1872), 108.
Nation, XV (December 19, 1872), 409.

Diaz, Abby Morton. *William Henry and His Friends.* (Boston: James R. Osgood & Co.)
Atlantic Monthly, XXIX (January, 1872), 109–10.

Distant Cousins. (Boston: Roberts Brothers)
Harper's Magazine, XLIV (January, 1872), 299.

Dodge, Mary Abigail (Gail Hamilton). *Little Folk Life.* (New York: Harper & Brothers)
Harper's Magazine, XLV (November, 1872), 784.
Literary World, III (October 1, 1872), 76.
Our Young Folks, VIII (December, 1872), 762.
Weekly Trade Circular, II (August 22, 1872), 174.

Dodgson, Charles L. (Lewis Carroll). *Through the Looking-Glass, and What Alice Found There.* (New York and London: Macmillan & Co.)
Nation, XIV (February 8, 1872), 95.

Douglas, Amanda M. *Kathie's Stories for Young People.* (Boston: Lee & Shepard)
Harper's Magazine, XLIV (March, 1872), 463.
Overland Monthly, VIII (January, 1872), 103–04.

Du Chaillu, Paul. *The Country of the Dwarfs.* (New York: Harper & Brothers)
Harper's Magazine, XLV (January, 1872), 299.
Literary World, II (January 1, 1872), 123.

Elliot, J. W. *Mother Goose Set to Music.* (New York: G. W. Carleton & Co.)
Overland Monthly, VIII (January, 1872), 103–04.

Father Muller; or, The Good Heart. Translated from the German. (Boston: Henry Hoyt)
Youth's Companion, XLV (December 12, 1872), 405.

Fawcett, Edgar. *Short Poems for Short People.* (New York: F. B. Felt & Co.)
Appleton's Journal, VII (February 17, 1872), 192.

Fidelity Rewarded; or, Little George. (Boston: Henry Hoyt)
Youth's Companion, XLV (July 11, 1872), 225.

Finding Shelter; or, Little Nan. (Boston: Henry Hoyt)
Youth's Companion, XLV (June 13, 1872), 193.

Fuller, Jane G. *Bending Willow.* (New York: Robert Carter & Brothers)
Harper's Magazine, XLIV (January, 1872), 301.

G., J. E. *Houses Not Made with Hands.* (New York: G. W. Carleton & Co.)
Overland Monthly, VIII (January, 1872), 103–04.

Giberne, Agnes. *Not Forsaken or; The Old Home in the City.* (New York: E. P. Dutton & Co.)
Literary World, III (December 1, 1872), 107.

Goodrich, Frank B. *Remarkable Voyages.* (Philadelphia: J. B. Lippincott & Co.)
Nation, XV (December 19, 1872), 410.

Gordon, Clarence (Vieux Moustache). *Boarding School Days.* (New York: Hurd & Houghton)
Literary World, III (November 1, 1872), 92.
Our Young Folks, VIII (December, 1872), 762.
Weekly Trade Circular, II (September 19, 1872), 287.

Gould, Jeanie T. *Marjorie's Quest*. (Boston: James R. Osgood & Co.)
Our Young Folks, VIII (December, 1872), 762.

Grace Martin; or, Poor, Not Friendless. (Boston: Henry Hoyt)
Youth's Companion, XLV (May 23, 1872), 169.

Gray, Asa. *Botany for Young People*. (New York: Ivison, Blakeman & Taylor)
Nation, XV (August 8, 1872), 93–94.

Hale, Edward Everett. *How to Do It*. (Boston: James R. Osgood & Co.)
Scribner's Monthly, III (April, 1872), 511.

Harrison, Jennie. *Old Back Room*. (New York: Dodd & Mead)
Harper's Magazine, XLIV (January, 1872), 300.

Heavenward Paths for Little Feet. (New York: E. P. Dutton & Co.)
Literary World, III (December 1, 1872), 108.

Hood, Thomas, the younger. *Puss and Robin*. (New York: Macmillan & Co.)
Harper's Magazine, XLIV (January, 1872), 299.
Scribner's Monthly, III (January, 1872), 383.

Hopkins, Miss I. T. *Summer in the Forest*. (New York: American Tract Society)
Harper's Magazine, XLIV (January, 1872), 300.

Hymn Stories. (New York: E. P. Dutton & Co.)
Literary World, III (December 1, 1872), 107–08.

Hymns for Mothers and Children. 4th ed. (Boston: Nichols & Hall)
Literary World, II (March 1, 1872), 155–56.

The Illuminated Scripture Text-Book. (New York: E. P. Dutton & Co.)
Literary World, III (December 1, 1872), 108.

Keene, Mrs. S. F. *Guy's Life Lesson*. (Boston: Henry Hoyt)
Youth's Companion, XLV (April 4, 1872), 113.

Kellogg, Elijah. *The Child of the Island Glen*. (Boston: Lee & Shepard)
Literary World, III (October 1, 1872), 77.

Sophomores of Radcliffe. (Boston: Lee & Shepard)
Literary World, II (January 1, 1872), 124.
Our Young Folks, VIII (March, 1872), 189.
Youth's Companion, XLV (January 25, 1872), 31.

Whispering Pine. (Boston: Lee & Shepard)
Literary World, III (July 1, 1872), 27.

Kingsley, Henry. *The Lost Child*. (New York: Macmillan & Co.)
Harper's Magazine, XLIV (January, 1872), 299.
Scribner's Monthly, III (January, 1872), 383.

Knatchbull-Hugessen, E. H. *Moonshine*. (London and New York: Macmillan & Co.)
Harper's Magazine, XLIV (January, 1872), 299.

Tales at Tea-Time. (London and New York: Macmillan & Co.)
Literary World, III (December 1, 1872), 107.
Nation, XV (December 12, 1872), 388–89.

Knatchbull-Huggessen, Lois. *The History of Prince Perrypets*. (New York: Macmillan & Co.)
Literary World, III (December 1, 1872), 108.

Konewka, Paul (illus.). *Catastrophe of the Hall*. (Philadelphia: Porter & Coates)
Harper's Magazine, XLIV (January, 1872), 298.

Laing, Mrs. C. H. B. *The Seven Kings of the Seven Hills*. (Philadelphia: Porter & Coates)
Nation, XV (December 19, 1872), 409.

Lamb, Charles and Mary. *Poetry for Children*. (London: Basil Montagu Pickering)
Old and New, VI (August, 1872), 196–97.

The Life and Times of Conrad the Squirrel. (London and New York: Macmillan & Co.)
  Literary World, III (December 1, 1872), 108.
  Nation, XV (December 5, 1872), 369.

Lifted Up; or, Walter Douglas. (Boston: Henry Hoyt)
  Youth's Companion, XLV (June 13, 1872), 169.

Little Pierre, the Pedlar of Alsace. (New York: Catholic Publication Society)
  Catholic World, XV (May, 1872), 284–85.

Lockyer, Lisa. *A Child's Influence; or, Katheleen and Her Great Uncle.* (New York: E. P. Dutton & Co.)
  Literary World, III (December 1, 1872), 107.

MacDonald, George. *The Princess and the Goblin.* (Philadelphia: J. B. Lippincott & Co.)
  Nation, XIV (March 7, 1872), 159.
  Scribner's Monthly, IV (September, 1872), 646.

Mackarness, M. A. *Children's Sunday Album.* (Boston: Lee & Shepard)
  Harper's Magazine, XLIV (January, 1872), 299.

Mazini, Linda. *In the Golden Shell; A Story of Palermo.* (London and New York: Macmillan & Co.)
  Nation, XV (December 19, 1872), 411.

Mead, M. Gertrude. *Nannie and Our Boys.* (Boston: Congregational Publishing Society)
  Scribner's Monthly, IV (May, 1872), 127.

Moore, Mrs. J. F. *A Home in a Rough Suburb.* (Boston: Henry Hoyt)
  Youth's Companion, XLV (May 23, 1872), 169.

Morris, Francis Orpen. *Dogs and Their Doings.* (New York: Harper & Brothers)
  Harper's Magazine, XLIV (January, 1872), 299.

Newton, A. E. *Lessons for Children About Themselves.* (Boston: Newton & Co.)
  Our Young Folks, VIII (December, 1872), 763.

Oliphant, Margaret O. W. *Agnes Hopetoun's Schools and Holidays.* (London and New York: Macmillan & Co.)
  Literary World, III (December 1, 1872), 107.
  Nation, XV (December 5, 1872), 368–69.

Oliver Optic's Almanac for Our Boys and Girls. (Boston: Lee & Shepard)
  Oliver Optic's Magazine, XI (January, 1872), 79.

O'Reilly, Mrs. Robert. *Daisy's Companions.* (Boston: Roberts Brothers)
  Literary World, III (December 1, 1872), 107.
  Our Young Folks, VIII (December, 1872), 762.

  Deborah's Drawer. (Boston: Roberts Brothers)
  Literary World, III (December 1, 1872), 107.

  The Doll World; or, Play and Earnest. (Boston: Roberts Brothers)
  Literary World, III (December 1, 1872), 107.

  Little Grig and the Tinker's Letter. (New York: Nelson & Phillips; Cincinnati: Hitchcock & Walden)
  Nation, XV (December 19, 1872), 410.

Phillips, Philip. *Song Life for Sunday-Schools.* (New York: Harper & Brothers)
  Harper's Magazine, XLV (September, 1872), 625.
  Literary World, III (November 1, 1872), 91.

Powers, Stephen. *Muskingum Legends.* (Philadelphia: J. B. Lippincott & Co.)
  Harper's Magazine, XLIV (January, 1872), 300.

Prentiss, Elizabeth. *Aunt Jane's Hero.* (New York: A. D. F. Randolph)
  Harper's Magazine, XLIV (January, 1872), 301.

Real Robinson Crusoes; or, Life on Desolate Islands. (New York: Nelson & Phillips; Cincinnati: Hitchcock & Walden)
Nation, XV (December 19, 1872), 410.

Richardson, Abby Sage. *Stories from Old English Poetry.* (New York: Hurd & Houghton)
Atlantic Monthly, XXIX (January, 1872), 109–10.
Harper's Magazine, XLIV (January, 1872), 301.

Robbins, Alice. *Chauntry's Boy.* (Boston: Henry Hoyt)
Youth's Companion, XLV (April 4, 1872), 113.

Robinson, Annie Douglas (Marion Douglas). *Picture-Poems for Young Folks.* (Boston: James R. Osgood & Co.)
Literary World, II (January 1, 1872), 123.

Rossetti, Christina G. *Sing-Song.* (Boston: Roberts Brothers)
Appleton's Journal, VII (January 6, 1872), 24.
Harper's Magazine, XLIV (January, 1872), 299.
Nation, XIV (May 2, 1872), 294–95.

The Runaway; A Story for the Young. (New York: Macmillan & Co.)
Nation, XV (December 19, 1872), 410.

Sadlier, Mrs. J., (trans.). *Legends of St. Joseph.* (New York: D. & J. Sadlier & Co.)
Catholic World, XV (August, 1872), 719.

Samuels, Adelaide F. *Dick and Daisy Series.* (Boston: Lee & Shepard)
Harper's Magazine, XLIV (March, 1872), 463.

Sanford, Mrs. D. P. *The Rose Dale Books.* (New York: E. P. Dutton & Co.)
Harper's Magazine, XLIV (January, 1872), 299.

Saxe, John Godfrey. *Fables and Legends of Many Countries.* (Boston: James R. Osgood & Co.)
Harper's Magazine, XLV (July, 1872), 297–98.
Literary World, III (June 1, 1872), 11.
Nation, XV (October 13, 1872), 253.
Weekly Trade Circular, I (May 30, 1872), 491–92.

Shipton, Anna. *The Cottage on the Rock.* (Boston: Henry Hoyt)
Youth's Companion, XLV (May 23, 1872), 169.

Following Fully; or, Giving Up All for Christ. (Boston: Henry Hoyt)
Youth's Companion, XLV (May 23, 1872), 169.

Smith, Caroline L. *The American Home Book of In-Door Games, Recreations and Occupations.* (Boston: Lee & Shepard)
Catholic World, XIV (February, 1872), 720.
Overland Monthly, VIII (January, 1872), 103–04.

Stephens, Charles Asbury. *Camping Out.* (Boston: James R. Osgood & Co.)
Literary World, III (November 1, 1872), 93.
Nation, XV (December 5, 1872), 367–68.

Stephenson, Eliza Tabor. *Nine Years Old.* (New York: Macmillan & Co.)
Harper's Magazine, XLIV (March, 1872), 463.
Scribner's Monthly, III (March, 1872), 639.

Stockton, Frank R. *Roundabout Rambles in Lands of Fact and Fancy.* (New York: Scribner, Armstrong & Co.)
Catholic World, XVI (December, 1872), 432.
Literary World, III (November 1, 1872), 92.
Nation, XV (December 12, 1872), 388–89.
Our Young Folks, VIII (December, 1872), 762.

Terhune, Marion Virginia Hawes (Marion Harland). *Marion Harland's Recipe Book.* (New York: Charles Scribner & Sons)
Overland Monthly, VIII (January, 1872), 103–04.

337

Tiny Library. (London: S. W. Partridge & Co.)
Our Young Folks, VIII (March, 1872), 189.

Trowbridge, John Townsend (Paul Creyton). *A Chance for Himself.* (Boston:
James R. Osgood & Co.)
Appleton's Journal, VIII (November 23, 1872), 585.
Nation, XV (December 12, 1872), 388.
Our Young Folks, VIII (December, 1872), 763.

Tuttle, Edmund B. *The Boy's Book About Indians.* (Philadelphia: J. B. Lippincott
& Co.)
Nation, XV (December 5, 1872), 368.

Underwood, Francis H. *Cloud Pictures.* (Boston: Lee & Shepard)
Our Young Folks, VIII (March, 1872), 189.

Weeks, Helen C. *Four, and What They Did.* (New York: Hurd & Houghton)
Harper's Magazine, XLIV (January, 1872), 300.

What the World Made Them. (New York: G. P. Putnam & Son)
Harper's Magazine, XLIV (January, 1872), 301.

White, Alexina B. *Little-Folk Songs.* (New York: Hurd & Houghton)
Galaxy, XIII (February, 1872), 277.

Whitney, Adeline Dutton Train. *Real Folks.* (Boston: James R. Osgood & Co.)
Atlantic Monthly, XXIX (January, 1872), 109–10.
Harper's Magazine, XLIV (March, 1872), 463.
Scribner's Monthly, III (February, 1872), 502–05.

Whittier, John Greenleaf. *Child-Life; A Collection of Poems.* (Boston: James R.
Osgood & Co.)
Atlantic Monthly, XXIX (January, 1872), 109.

Williams, Katherine. *Tiptoe.* (New York: American Tract Society)
Harper's Magazine, XLIV (January, 1872), 300–01.

The Wood Carvers; or, A Visit to the Seashore. (New York: Nelson & Phillips)
Nation, XV (December 19, 1872), 410.

Woodland Cottage, and Other Tales. (Philadelphia: Peter F. Cunningham)
Catholic World, XV (June, 1872), 432.

Woolsey, Sarah Chauncey (Susan Coolidge). *The New Year's Bargain.* (Boston:
Roberts Brothers)
Nation, XIV (January 25, 1872), 62–63.

What Katy Did. (Boston: Roberts Brothers)
Literary World, III (December 1, 1872), 105–06.

Wright, B. E. *A Home Tour with Aunt Bessie.* (New York: Nelson & Phillips;
Cincinnati: Hitchcock & Walden)
Nation, XV (December 19, 1872), 410.

Yonge, Charlotte M. *A Book of Golden Deeds of All Times and All Countries.*
(New York: Macmillan & Co.)
Harper's Magazine, XLIV (March, 1872), 463.
Scribner's Monthly, III (March, 1872), 639.

Little Lucy's Wonderful Globe. (New York: Macmillan & Co.)
Harper's Magazine, XLIV (January, 1872), 299.
Scribner's Monthly, III (January, 1872), 383.

P's and Q's; or, The Question of Putting Upon. (New York: Macmillan & Co.)
Nation, XV (December 19, 1872), 411.

A Storehouse of Stories. (London and New York: Macmillan & Co.)
Nation, XV (December 19, 1872), 408–09.

Youmans, Eliza D. *The First Book of Botany.* New edition. (New York: D. Appleton & Co.)
Popular Science Monthly, I (May, 1872), 120–22.

Abbott, Edna A. *Parables for Children.* (London: Macmillan & Co.)
Independent, XXV (September 11, 1873), 1130.

Abbott, Jacob. *Force.* (New York: Harper & Brothers)
Harper's Magazine, XLVI (January, 1873), 301–02.
Literary World, III (January 1, 1873), 123.
Methodist Quarterly Review, XXV (January, 1873), 179.

Light. (New York: Harper & Brothers)
Methodist Quarterly Review, XXV (January, 1873), 179.

Water and Land. (New York: Harper & Brothers)
Methodist Quarterly Review, XXV (January, 1873), 179.

Adams, William T. (Oliver Optic). *Cross and Crescent; or, Young America in Turkey and Greece.* (Boston: Lee & Shepard)
Catholic World, XVI (March, 1873), 859.
Independent, XXV (March 20, 1873), 363.
Literary World, III (March 1, 1873), 155.

Little Bobtail. (Boston: Lee & Shepard)
Literary World, III (March 1, 1873), 155.

Money-Maker; or, The Victory of the Basilisk. (Boston: Lee & Shepard)
Publishers' Weekly, IV (December 13, 1873), 668–69.

Sunny Shores; or, Young America in Italy and Austria. (Boston: Lee & Shepard)
Publishers' Weekly, IV (Christmas Supplement, 1873), 14.

The Yacht Club; or, The Young Boat Builders. (Boston: Lee & Shepard)
Publishers' Weekly, IV (October 4, 1873), 350.

Adventures by Sea and Land. (Philadelphia: Porter & Coates)
Literary World, IV (November, 1873), 91.
Publishers' Weekly, IV (November 22, 1873), 580.
St. Nicholas, I (November, 1873), 45.

The Adventures of Robinson Playfellow. (New York: George Routledge & Sons)
Harper's Magazine, XLVI (January, 1873), 303.

Alcott, Louisa May. *Shawl-Straps.* (Boston: Roberts Brothers)
Catholic World, XVII (April, 1873), 142–43.
St. Nicholas, I (November, 1873), 45.

Alger, Horatio, Jr. *Try and Trust; or, The Story of a Bound Boy.* (Boston: A. K. Loring)
St. Nicholas, I (December, 1873), 102.

Alice Porter. (New York: Reformed Church Board of Publications.)
Independent, XXV (December 4, 1873), 1514.

Anderson, Mary E. *New Songs for Little People.* (Boston: Lee & Shepard)
Publishers' Weekly, IV (December 27, 1873), 707.

Arnot, W. *Anchor of the Soul.* (New York: American Tract Society)
Independent, XXV (December 4, 1873), 1514.

Auerbach, Berthold. *Little Barefoot; or, Strive and Trust.* (New York: George Routledge & Sons)
Harper's Magazine, XLVI (January, 1872), 303.

B., M. A. *Constance and Marion; or, The Cousins.* (Baltimore: Kelly, Piet & Co.)
Catholic World, XVII (June, 1873), 432.

Benjamin, Mrs. E. Bedell. *Brightside.* (New York: Robert Carter & Brothers)
Independent, XXV (June 26, 1873), 843.
St. Nicholas, I (December, 1873), 103.

339

Borg, Selma and Marie A. Brown (trans.). *Northern Lights; Tales from the Swedish and Finnish.* (Philadelphia: Porter & Coates)
Appleton's Journal, X (December 20, 1873), 797.
Galaxy, XVI (December, 1873), 863–64.
Nation, XVII (November 27, 1873), 357–58.
St. Nicholas, I (December, 1873), 102.

Broome, Mrs. Frederic Napier (Lady Barker). *Ribbon Stories.* (New York: Macmillan & Co.)
Literary World, III (January 1, 1873), 124.

Busch, William. *Buzz-a-Buzz; or, The Bees.* Translated from the German by Hezekiah Watkins. (New York: Henry Holt & Co.)
Independent, XXV (December 25, 1873), 1610.
Nation, XVII (December 11, 1873), 389.
Publishers' Weekly, IV (November 29, 1873), 625.

Cary, Alice and Phoebe. *Ballads for Little Folk.* (New York: Hurd & Houghton)
Appleton's Journal, V (December 20, 1873), 797.
Independent, XXV (December 18, 1873), 1577.

Chatterbox for 1873. (New York: American News Co.)
Independent, XXV (December 18, 1873), 1577.

Chellis, Mary Dwinell. *Two Boys Saved; or, A Plain Woman.* (Boston: Congregational Publishing Society)
Independent, XXV (September 11, 1873), 1130.

Cheney, Ednah D. *Sally Williams, the Mountain Girl.* (Boston: Lee & Shepard)
Harper's Magazine, XLVI (April, 1873), 774.

Clarke, Mrs. Henry Steele. *The Marble Preacher.* (Boston: D. Lothrop & Co.)
Literary World, IV (June 1, 1873), 12.

Clarke, J. Erskine. *Sunday Reading for the Young.* (New York: American News Co.)
Independent, XXV (December 18, 1873), 1577.

Clarke, Rebecca (Sophie May). *Little Grandfather.* (Boston: Lee & Shepard)
Independent, XXV (December 14, 1873), 1514.

Miss Thistledown. (Boston: Lee & Shepard)
Publishers' Weekly, IV (December 13, 1873), 669.

Clodd, Edward. *The Childhood of the World.* (Boston: Shepard & Gill)
Lakeside Monthly, X (July, 1873), 75–76.
Literary World, IV (November, 1873), 91.
Nation, XVII (November 27, 1873), 358.
Popular Science Monthly, III (June, 1873), 249.

Conscience, Hendrik. *The Fisherman's Daughter and the Amulet.* (Baltimore: John Murphy & Co.)
Catholic World, XVII (July, 1873), 575.

Craig (Knox), Isa. *The Young Folks' History of England.* (Boston: Lee & Shepard)
Harper's Magazine, XLVI (March, 1873), 613.

Craik, Dinah Mulock. *Adventures of a Brownie, As Told to My Child.* (New York: Harper & Brothers)
Penn Monthly, IV (June, 1873), 433.

The Cumberstone Contest. (New York: Dodd & Mead)
Publishers' Weekly, IV (December 13, 1873), 668.

Cunningham, E. *Seven Autumn Leaves from Fairy Lands.* (Boston: A. Williams & Co.)
Literary World, III (February 1, 1873), 139.

Cupples, George. *The Deserted Ship.* (Boston: Shepard & Gill)
Literary World, III (January 1, 1873), 123.

De Mille, James. *The Treasure of the Seas.* (Boston: Lee & Shepard)
Catholic World, XVI (March, 1873), 859.
Independent, XXV (March 20, 1873), 363.
Literary World, III (March 1, 1873), 155.

DeWitt, P. *An Only Sister.* (New York: Harper & Brothers)
Appleton's Journal, IX (January 25, 1873), 156–57.
Harper's Magazine, XLVI (April, 1873), 774.
Literary World, III (February 1, 1873), 139.

Diaz, Abby Morton. *Lucy Maria.* (Boston: James R. Osgood & Co.)
Independent, XXV (December 18, 1873), 1577.
Literary World, IV (December, 1873), 107.
Publishers' Weekly, IV (November 22, 1873), 582.

Dodge, Mary Abigail (Gail Hamilton). *Child World.* (Boston: Shepard & Gill)
Independent, XXV (December 18, 1873), 1577.
Literary World, III (February 1, 1873), 139.
Nation, XVII (December 4, 1873), 374.

Little Folk Life. (New York: Harper & Brothers)
Lakeside Monthly, IX (January, 1873), 73.

Dodge, Mary Mapes. *Hans Brinker; or, The Silver Skates.* Illustrated by Darley, Nast and others. (New York: Scribner, Armstrong & Co.)
Appleton's Journal, X (December 20, 1873), 797.
Independent, XXV (December 18, 1873), 1577.
Nation, XVII (December 11, 1873), 389.
Publishers' Weekly, IV (November 29, 1873), 625.

Eastman, Julia. *Striking for the Right.* (Boston: D. Lothrop & Co.)
Independent, XXV (March 13, 1873), 331.
Literary World, III (March 1, 1873), 155.

Edson, N. I. *Silent Tom.* (Boston: D. Lothrop & Co.)
Independent, XXV (March 13, 1873), 331.
Literary World, III (March 1, 1873), 155.

Eiloart, Mrs. C. J. *Boy with an Idea.* (New York: G. P. Putnam's Sons)
Independent, XXV (December 4, 1873), 1514.
Publishers' Weekly, IV (October 4, 1873), 350.

Faithful But Not Famous. (Philadelphia: American Sunday-School Union)
Independent, XXV (September 11, 1873), 1130.

Finished or Not. (Boston: D. Lothrop & Co.)
Literary World, IV (June 1, 1873), 11.

Finely, Martha F. (Martha Farquharson). *Elsie's Girlhood.* (New York: Dodd & Mead)
Literary World, III (February 1, 1873), 139.

Floyd, Cornelia. *Honest and Earnest.* (New York: A. D. F. Randolph)
Harper's Magazine, XLVI (April, 1873), 774–75.

Gilman, Arthur. *First Steps in English Literature.* (New York: Hurd & Houghton)
St. Nicholas, I (November, 1873), 45.

Gow, Alexander M. *Good Morals and Gentle Manners.* (Cincinnati: Wilson, Hinkle & Co.)
Independent, XXV (July 24, 1873), 929.

Hale, Edward Everett. *Ups and Downs.* (Boston: Roberts Brothers)
Appleton's Journal, IX (June 7, 1873), 766.
Lakeside Monthly, IX (June, 1873), 510.

Hallowell, Mrs. Joshua L. *Bec's Bedtime.* (Philadelphia: Porter & Coates)
Publishers' Weekly, IV (December 20, 1873), 687.

Harcourt, Helen. *Bertram Raymond; or, The Cruise of the Dolphin.* (Philadelphia: Claxton, Remsen & Haffelfinger)

Independent, XXV (March 20, 1873), 363.

Hedges, Mary J. *Working and Winning.* (New York: American Tract Society)
Harper's Magazine, XLVI (January, 1873), 303.

Henry, Mary H. (Howe Benning). *Nix's Offering.* (New York: Warren & Wyman)
Publishers' Weekly, IV (November 8, 1873), 514.

Hetzel, Pierre-Jules (P. J. Stahl). *Davie and Dot; Their Pranks and Pastimes.*
Adapted from the French. (New York: Pott, Young & Co.)
Nation, XVII (December 11, 1873), 389.

Good Little Children. Adapted from the French. (New York: Pott, Young
& Co.)
Nation, XVII (December 11, 1873), 389.

Hodder, Edna. *Old Merry's Travels on the Continent.* (Philadelphia: J. B. Lippincott & Co.)
Independent, XXV (December 4, 1873), 1514.

Holt, Mrs. M. A. *John Bentley's Mistake.* (New York: National Temperance Society)
Independent, XXV (September 11, 1873), 1130.

Hosmer, Margaret. *Courts and Corners.* (Boston: Congregational Publishing Society)
Independent, XXV (December 4, 1873), 1514.

Lilly's Hard Words. (Philadelphia: Claxton, Remsen & Haffelfinger)
Independent, XXV (June 12, 1873), 747.

Howard, Marion. *Fred's Hard Fight.* (New York: National Temperance Society)
Independent, XXV (September 11, 1873), 1130.

Howitt, Mary. *Sketches of Natural History; or, Songs of Animal Life.* (New York:
Thomas Nelson & Sons)
Nation, XVII (December 11, 1873), 390.

Hugo, Victor. *Gavroche, the Gamin of Paris.* Translated and adapted by M. C.
Pyle. (Philadelphia: Porter & Coates)
Literary World, III (January 1, 1873), 123.
Nation, XVII (November 28, 1873), 357.

Hyde, Anna M. *Work, Play and Profit; or, Gardening for Young Folks Expl. in a
Story.* (Philadelphia: J. B. Lippincott & Co.)
Independent, XXV (July 10, 1873), 872.

The Illustrated Catholic Sunday-School Library. (New York: The Catholic Publication Society)
Catholic World, XVII (June, 1873), 430.

Kellogg, Elijah. *John Godsoe's Legacy.* (Boston: Lee & Shepard)
Publishers' Weekly, IV (October 11, 1873), 378.

A Stout Heart; or, The Student from Over the Sea. (Boston: Lee & Shepard)
Publishers' Weekly, IV (December 27, 1873), 707.

Winning His Spurs. (Boston: Lee & Shepard)
Literary World, III (March 1, 1873), 156.

The King and the Cloister; or, Legends of the Dissolution. (London: Stewart)
Catholic World, XVII (June, 1873), 430.

Knatchbull-Hugessen, E. H. *Queer Folk.* (London and New York: Macmillan &
Co.)
Literary World, IV (December, 1873), 108.
Nation, XVII (December 4, 1873), 373.

Laing, Mrs. C. H. B. *The Seven Kings of the Seven Hills.* (Philadelphia: Porter &
Coates)
Literary World, III (January 1, 1873), 123.

Larned, Augusta. *Country Stories.* (New York: Nelson & Phillips)

Independent, XXV (December 18, 1873), 1577.

Holiday Stories. (New York: Nelson & Phillips)
Independent, XXV (December 18, 1873), 1577.

Stories for Leisure Hours. (New York: Nelson & Phillips)
Independent, XXV (December 18, 1873), 1577.

Ledyard, Laura W. *Very Young Americans.* (Boston: Roberts Brothers)
St. Nicholas, I (November, 1873), 45.

Lee, Minnie Mary. *Myrrha Lake; or, Into the Light of Catholicity.* (New York: Catholic Publication Society)
Independent, XXV (June 26, 1873), 843.

The Life and Times of Conrad the Squirrel. (London and New York: Macmillan & Co.)
Harper's Magazine, XLVI (January, 1873), 303.

The Life of a Bear. (New York: Pott, Young & Co.)
Nation, XVII (December 11, 1873), 390.

Ling Bank Cottage. (New York: American Tract Society)
Independent, XXV (September 11, 1873), 1130.

Little Laddie. (New York: Thomas Nelson & Sons)
Nation, XVII (December 11, 1873), 390.

McConaughy, Mrs. J. E. *The Fire Fighters.* (New York: American Temperance Society)
Harper's Magazine, XLVI (January, 1873), 303.

Mackarness, M. A. *Children of the Olden Time.* (London: Griffith & Farran; New York: Scribner, Welford & Armstrong)
Independent, XXV (December 4, 1873), 1514.
Nation, XVII (November 27, 1873), 357.

MacLeod, Alexander. *The Wonderful Lamp.* (New York: Robert Carter & Brothers)
Independent, XXV (May 8, 1873), 587.

Maggie's Mistake; A School Girl's Story. (New York: Pott, Young & Co.)
Nation, XVII (December 11, 1873), 389–90.

Maguire, John Francis. *Young Prince Marigold, and Other Fairy Stories.* (London and New York: Macmillan & Co.)
Independent, XXV (December 18, 1873), 1577.
Nation, XVII (December 4, 1873), 373–74.

Malot, Hector. *Romain Kalbris; His Adventures by Sea and Land.* Translated from the French by Mrs. Julia McNair Wright. (Philadelphia: Porter & Coates)
Appleton's Journal, X (November 1, 1873), 573.
Independent, XXV (November 30, 1873), 1450.
Publishers' Weekly, IV (November 22, 1873), 582.
St. Nicholas, I (December, 1873), 102.

March, Ann. *The Old Stone House.* (Boston: D. Lothrop & Co.)
Independent, XXV (March 13, 1873), 331.
Literary World, IV (June 1, 1873), 12.

Marshall, Emma. *Matthew Frost; or, Little Snowdrop's Mission.* (New York: Robert Carter & Brothers)
Harper's Magazine, XLVI (April, 1873), 774.

Martineau des Chesnez, Baroness E. *Lady Green-Satin and Her Maid Rosette; or, The History of Jean Paul and His Little White Mice.* Translated from the French. (Philadelphia: Porter & Coates)
Appleton's Journal, X (December 20, 1873), 797.
Harper's Magazine, XLVIII (December, 1873), 140.
Literary World, IV (October, 1873), 75.

Nation, XVII (November 27, 1873), 357.
Publishers' Weekly, IV (November 22, 1873), 581.
St. Nicholas, I (December, 1873), 102.

Mason, James. *The Old Fairy Tales.* (New York: Cassell, Petter & Galpin)
Independent, XXV (December 18, 1873), 1577.

Mather, Sarah A. *Young Life; or, The Boys and Girls of Pleasant Valley.* (Cincinnati: Hitchcock & Walden)
Independent, XXV (September 11, 1873), 1130.

Mathews, Joanna H. *Fanny's Birthday Gift.* (New York: Robert Carter & Brothers)
Independent, XXV (November 20, 1873), 1450.
Publishers' Weekly, IV (October 11, 1873), 379.

Fun and Work. (New York: Robert Carter & Brothers)
Independent, XXV (December 4, 1873), 1514.

Kitty and Lulu Books. (New York: Robert Carter & Brothers)
Harper's Magazine, XLVI (January, 1873), 303.

Kitty's Scrap-Book. (New York: Robert Carter & Brothers)
Independent, XXV (June 26, 1873), 843.

The White Rabbit. (New York: Robert Carter & Brothers)
Harper's Magazine, XLVI (April, 1873), 774.

Miller, Mary E. *Little Margery.* (New York: American Tract Society)
Publishers' Weekly, IV (December 13, 1873), 669.

Mother Anne and Her Little Maggie. (New York: A. D. F. Randolph)
Publishers' Weekly, IV (November 22, 1873), 580.

Moulton, Louise Chandler. *Bed-Time Stories.* (Boston: Roberts Brothers)
Literary World, IV (November, 1873), 91.
Publishers' Weekly, IV (November 1, 1873), 486.
St. Nicholas, I (November, 1873), 102.
Scribner's Monthly, VII (November, 1873), 125.

Munson, Mrs. C. A. *Oline; or, One Year at the Nest.* (New York: N. Tibbals & Son)
Independent, XXV (September 11, 1873), 1130.

My Pet's Album. (New York: George Routledge & Sons)
Harper's Magazine, XLVI (April, 1873), 775.

Newton, Richard. *Leaves from the Tree of Life.* (New York: Robert Carter & Brothers)
Independent, XXV (December 4, 1873), 1514.

Oliphant, Mrs. Margaret O. W. *Agnes Hopetoun's Schools and Ho idays.* (New York: Macmillan & Co.)
Harper's Magazine, XLVI (April, 1873), 774–75.

O'Reilly, Mrs. Robert. *Doll World; or, Play and Earnest.* (Boston: Roberts Brothers)
Harpers' Magazine, XLVI (January, 1873), 303.

Gile's Minority; or, Scenes at the Red House. (Boston: Roberts Brothers)
Independent, XXV (December 18, 1873), 1577.
Literary World, IV (December, 1873), 103.

Our Western Home. (Philadelphia: American Sunday-School Union)
Independent, XXV (December 4, 1873), 1514.

Peebles, Mary L. (Lynde Palmer). *Helps Over Hard Places; for Boys.* (Troy, New York: H. B. Nims & Co.)
Harper's Magazine, XLVI (April, 1873), 775.

Perilous Incidents in the Lives of Sailors and Travellers. Translated from the German. (Philadelphia: Porter & Coates)

Independent, XXV (December 18, 1873), 1577.
Literary World, IV (November, 1873), 91.
Publishers' Weekly, IV (November 22, 1873), 580.

Peter's Journey and Other Tales. (New York: Catholic Publication Society)
Catholic World, XVII (May, 1873), 285–86.

Phelps, Miss Elizabeth Stuart. *Trotty's Wedding-Tour.* (Boston: James R. Osgood & Co.)
Independent, XXV (December 25, 1873), 1610.

Power, Philip Bennett. *Truffle Nephews.* (New York: Robert Carter & Brothers)
Independent, XXV (November 20, 1873), 1450.

Pratt, Mary E. *Rhoda Thornton's Girlhood.* (Boston: Lee & Shepard)
Nation, XVII (December 11, 1873), 390.
Publishers' Weekly, IV (December 6, 1873), 646.

Prescott, Mary N. *Matt's Follies.* (Boston: James R. Osgood & Co.)
Independent, XXV (November 20, 1873), 1450.

Pritchard, Sarah J. *Aunt Sadie's Cow.* (New York: Robert Carter & Brothers)
Independent, XXV (June 26, 1873), 843.
St. Nicholas, I (December, 1873), 103.

Raffensperger, Mrs. A. F. *My Pet's Picture Book.* (New York: American Tract Society)
Independent, XXV (December 4, 1873), 1614.

Robbins, Mrs. S. S. *Who Won?* (New York: Robert Carter & Brothers)
Harper's Magazine, XLVI (January, 1873), 303.

The Runaway; A Story for the Young. (New York: Macmillan & Co.)
Literary World, III (January 1, 1873), 123.

St. Nicholas (periodical).
Independent, XXV (November 13, 1873), 1418.
Scribner's Monthly, VII (November, 1873), 115.

Shields, Mrs. S. A. (Sarah Annie Frost). *Sunshine for Rainy Days.* (New York: American Tract Society)
Publishers' Weekly, IV (November 22, 1873), 581–82.

Shipley, Mary E. *Jessie's Work; or, Faithfulness in Little Things.* (Boston: American Tract Society)
Independent, XXV (June 12, 1873), 747.

Standard Fairy Tales. (Philadelphia: Porter & Coates)
Publishers' Weekly, IV (December 13, 1873), 668.

Stephens, Charles Asbury. *Camping Out.* (Philadelphia: Porter & Coates.)
Harper's Magazine, XLVI (January, 1873), 303.

Fox Hunting. (Philadelphia: Porter & Coates)
Independent, XXV (November 20, 1873), 1450.

Left on Labrador. (Philadelphia: Porter & Coates.)
Harper's Magazine, XLVI (April, 1873), 774.
Literary World, III (January 1, 1873), 123.
Our Young Folks, IX (February, 1873), 127.

Off to the Geysers. (Philadelphia: Porter & Coates.)
Appleton's Journal, IX (January 4, 1873), 61.
Harper's Magazine, XLVI (April, 1873), 774.
Independent, XXV (March 20, 1873), 363.
Literary World, III (January 1, 1873), 124.
Our Young Folks, IX (February, 1873), 127.

On the Amazon, (Philadelphia: Porter & Coates.)
Literary World, IV (December, 1873), 107.

Stockton, Frank R. *Roundabout Rambles in Lands of Fact and Fancy*. (New York: Scribner, Armstrong & Co.)
Harper's Magazine, XLVI (April, 1873), 775.

Stories for the Fireside. (New York: American Tract Society)
Harper's Magazine, XLVI (January, 1873), 303.

The Story of the Carrier Dove. (New York: Robert Carter & Brothers)
Independent, XXV (June 26, 1873), 843.

Tardieu, J. de (J. T. de Saint-Germain). *Only a Pin*. Translated from the French. (New York: Catholic Publication Society)
Independent, XXV (June 26, 1873), 843.

Taylor, J. E. *Geological Stories*. (New York: G. P. Putnam's Sons)
Publishers' Weekly, IV (October 4, 1873), 350.

Temple, Crona. *Little Wavie, the Foundling of Glenderg*. (Boston: Congregational Publishing Society)
Independent, XXV (September 11, 1873), 1130.

Tilton, S. Willis. *Songs for Our Darlings*. (Boston: J. E. Tilton & Co.)
Nation, XVI (March 20, 1873), 200.

Todd, John. *Lectures to Children*. (Northampton: Bridgman & Childs)
Independent, XXV (December 18, 1873), 1577.

Townsend, Virginia F. *Only Girls*. (Boston: Lee & Shepard)
Harper's Magazine, XLVI (April, 1873), 774.

Trowbridge, John Townsend (Paul Creyton). *A Chance for Himself*. (Boston: James R. Osgood & Co.)
Atlantic Monthly, XXXI (January, 1873), 109.
Harper's Magazine, XLVI (January, 1873), 303.

Doing His Best. (Boston: James R. Osgood & Co.)
Independent, XXV (December 25, 1873), 1610
Literary World, IV (December, 1873), 107.
Publishers' Weekly, IV (November 22, 1873), 581.

Tucker, Charlotte (A.L.O.E.). *The Silver Keys*. (New York: Robert Carter & Brothers)
Independent, XXV (December 4, 1873), 1514.

Uncle Hardy (pseud.). *Notable Shipwrecks*. (New York: Cassell, Petter & Galpin)
Independent, XXV (December 18, 1873), 1577.

Verne, Jules. *Five Weeks in a Balloon*. (Boston: James R. Osgood & Co.)
Literary World, IV (December, 1873), 100–01.
Publishers' Weekly, IV (December 20, 1873), 687.

From the Earth to the Moon. (New York: Scribner, Armstrong & Co.)
Appleton's Journal, X (December 20, 1873), 797.
Appleton's Journal, X (December 27, 1873), 830.
Publishers' Weekly, IV (December 20, 1873), 687.

The Fur Country; or, 70 Degrees North Latitude. (Boston: James R. Osgood & Co.)
Appleton's Journal, X (December 13, 1873), 765.

In Search of the Castaways. (Philadelphia: J. B. Lippincott & Co.)
Independent, XXV (July 10, 1873), 872.

Journey to the Center of the Earth. (New York: Scribner Armstrong & Co.)
Appleton's Journal, X (December 20, 1873), 797.
Literary World, IV (October 1873), 71.
St. Nicholas, I (November, 1873), 45.

The Tour of the World in Eighty Days. (Boston: James R. Osgood and Co.)
Appleton's Journal, X (July 19, 1873), 93.
Independent, XXV (July 10, 1873), 872.

Literary World, IV (July, 1873), 23.

Penn Monthly, IV (September, 1873), 666.

Twenty Thousand Leagues Under the Sea. (Boston: James R. Osgood & Co.)
Harper's Magazine, XLVI (April, 1873), 774.
Independent, XXV (July 10, 1873), 872.
Our Young Folks, IX (February, 1873), 127.

Warner, Susan Bogert (Elizabeth Wetherell). *The Little Camp on Eagle Hill.*
(New York: Robert Carter & Brothers)
Harper's Magazine, XLVIII (December, 1873), 140.
Independent, XXV (November 20, 1873), 1450.
Publishers' Weekly, IV (October 4, 1873), 350–51.
St. Nicholas, I (November, 1873), 45.

Warren, Israel P. *The Three Judges; Story of the Men Who Beheaded Their King.*
(New York: Warren & Wyman)
Nation, XVII (December 4, 1873), 374.

Washington, Nina. *Ethel's Pearls.* (New York: American Tract Society)
Harper's Magazine, XLVI (January, 1873), 303.

Whittier, John Greenleaf. *Child-Life in Prose.* (Boston: James R. Osgood & Co.)
Appleton's Journal, X (November 15, 1873), 637.
Independent, XXV (November 20, 1873), 1450.

Wilberforce, Samuel. *Little Wanderers and Other Sunday Stories.* (New York: G.
W. Carleton & Co.)
Independent, XXV (December 18, 1873), 1577.

Woolsey, Sarah Chauncey (Susan Coolidge). *The New Year's Bargain.* (Boston:
Roberts Brothers)
St. Nicholas, I (November, 1873), 45.

What Katy Did. (Boston: Roberts Brothers)
Appleton's Journal, IX (January 1, 1873), 28.
Harper's Magazine, XLVI (April, 1873), 774.
Lakeside Monthly, IX (January, 1873), 74.
Scribner's Monthly, V (January, 1873), 399.

What Katy Did at School. (Boston: Roberts Brothers)
Independent, XXV (December 18, 1873), 1577.
Literary World, IV (December, 1873), 102–03.

Wright, Caleb E. *Marcus Blair.* (Philadelphia: J. B. Lippincott & Co.)
Independent, XXV (December 4, 1873), 1514.

Wright, Julia McNair. *Nothing to Drink.* (New York: American Temperance Society)
Independent, XXV (September 11, 1873), 1130.

Yonge, Charlotte M. *A Storehouse of Stories.* (New York: Macmillan & Co.)
Literary World, III (January, 1873), 124.

BOOKS REVIEWED IN 1874

Abbott, Edna A. *The Child's Christmas Sheaf from the Bible Fields.* (New York:
American Tract Society)
Literary World, IV (April, 1874), 173.

Adams, William T. (Oliver Optic). *The Dorcas Club; or, Our Girls Afloat.* (Boston: Lee & Shepard)
Publishers' Weekly, VI (December 19, 1874), 677.

Sunny Shores. (Boston: Lee & Shepard)
Literary World, V (November, 1874), 92.

Adventures by Sea and Land. (Philadelphia: Porter & Coates)
Harper's Magazine, XLVIII (January, 1874), 298.

Alcott, Louisa May. *Cupid and Chow-Chow*. (Boston: Roberts Brothers)
Independent, XXVI (January 15, 1874), 10.
Literary World, IV (January, 1874), 125.

Alden, Isabella (Pansy). *The King's Daughter*. (Boston: D. Lothrop & Co.)
Independent, XXVI (March 26, 1874), 9.

Wise or Otherwise. (Boston: D. Lothrop & Co.)
Independent, XXVI (March 26, 1874), 9.

Alger, Horatio, Jr. *Brave and Bold*. (Boston: A. K. Loring)
Literary World, V (December, 1874), 108.

Risen from the Ranks; or, Harry Walton's Success. (Boston: A. K. Loring)
Nation, XIX (December 3, 1874), 368.

The Ancient Nation: A Sign and a Wonder. (New York: Pott, Young & Co.)
Literary World, V (September, 1874), 60.

Anderson, Mary E. *New Songs for Little People*. (Boston: Lee & Shepard)
Literary World, IV (January, 1874), 124.

Asbjornsen, P. C. *Tales from the Fjeld*. Translated by George W. Dasent.
Independent, XXVI (April 16, 1874), 9.

Austin, Mrs. George L. *Little People of God*. (Boston: Shepard & Gill)
Literary World, IV (January, 1874), 124.

Austin, Jane G. *Moonfolk: A True Account of the Home of the Fairy Tales*. (New York: G. P. Putnam's Sons)
Appleton's Journal, XII (October 24, 1874), 539.
Independent, XXVI (November 19, 1874), 11.
Literary World, V (November, 1874), 91.
Nation, XIX (December 10, 1874), 384–85.
Publishers' Weekly, VI (October 17, 1874), 428–29.

Baker, George M. *Running to Waste*. (Boston: Lee & Shepard)
Publishers' Weekly, VI (October 3, 1874), 363.
Youth's Companion, XLVII (December 17, 1874), 421.

Ballard, Julia P. *Seven Years from Tonight*. (Boston: Congregational Publishing Society)
Independent, XXVI (March 12, 1874), 10.

Bickersteth, E. H. *The Reef and Other Parables*. (New York: Robert Carter & Brothers)
Independent, XXVI (April 16, 1874), 10.

Boyesen, Hjalmar H. *Gunnar; A Norse Romance*. (Boston: James R. Osgood & Co.)
Youth's Companion, XLVII (November 19, 1874), 388–89.

A Boy's Kingdom; or, Four Years in a Cave. (New York: Thomas Nelson & Sons)
Publishers' Weekly, VI (Christmas Supplement, 1874), 13.

The Boys of England and America; a Young Gentleman's Journal of Sport, Sensation, Fun and Instruction. (London: Edwin J. Brett)
Scribner's Monthly, VII (January, 1874), 370–71.

Busch, William. *Buzz-a-Buzz; or, The Bees*. Translated from the German by Hezekiah Watkins. (New York: Henry Holt & Co.)
Galaxy, XVII (February, 1874), 287.

Canby, Margaret T. *Birdie and His Fairy Friends*. (Philadelphia: Claxton, Remsen & Haffelfinger)
Harper's Magazine, XLVIII (January, 1874), 299.

Caroll, M. *How Marjorie Helped*. (Boston: Lee & Shepard)
Unitarian Review, II (October, 1874), 308.

Chaney, George L. *F. Grant & Co.; or, Partnerships*. (Boston: Roberts Brothers)

Independent, XXVI (December 17, 1874), 9.
Publishers' Weekly, VI (December 19, 1874), 678.

The Charity Stories. (New York: American Tract Society)
Harper's Magazine, XLVIII (January, 1874), 298.

Cheney, Ednah D. *The Child of the Tide.* (Boston: Lee & Shepard)
Literary World, V (December, 1874), 108.
Publishers' Weekly, VI (Christmas Supplement, 1874), 13.

Children of Mary. (Baltimore: Kelly, Piet & Co.)
Catholic World, XIX (July, 1874), 576.

The Children's Hymn and Chant Book. (London: John Marshall & Co.)
Unitarian Review, II (October, 1874), 308.

Clarke, Rebecca (Sophie May). *The Doctor's Daughter.* (Boston: Lee & Shepard)
Harper's Magazine, XLVIII (January, 1874), 299.

Miss Thistledown. (Boston: Lee & Shepard)
Independent, XXVI (January 15, 1874), 10.
Literary World, IV (January, 1874), 123.

Our Helen. (Boston: Lee & Shepard)
Literary World, V (December, 1874), 108.
Publishers' Weekly, VI (Christmas Supplement, 1874), 13.

Clodd, Edward. *The Childhood of the World.* (Boston: Shepard & Gill)
Independent, XXVI (January 8, 1874), 10.
Old and New, IX (January, 1874), 139–40.
Penn Monthly, V (February, 1874), 165–66.

Cobden, Paul. *Good Luck.* (Boston: Lee & Shepard)
Independent, XXVI (January 15, 1874), 10.
Publishers' Weekly, V (January 17, 1874), 50.

Take a Peek. (Boston: Lee & Shepard)
Independent, XXVI (October 22, 1874), 11.

Cozzens, Samuel Woodworth. *The Marvellous Country; or, Three Years in Arizona and New Mexico, the Apache's Home.* (Boston: Shepard & Gill)
Youth's Companion, XLVII (February 26, 1874), 71.

Craik, Dinah Mulock. *The Little Lame Prince.* (New York: Harper & Brothers)
Independent, XXVI (December 3, 1874), 9.
Publishers' Weekly, VI (December 12, 1874), 653.

Craik, Georgiana M. *Miss Moore.* (New York: Harper & Brothers)
Appleton's Journal, XII (July 18, 1874), 93.
Literary World, V (July, 1874), 27.
Publishers' Weekly, VI (July 4, 1874), 12.

Davidson, Ellis A. *The Boy-Joiner and Model-Maker.* (New York: Cassell, Petter & Galpin)
Nation, XIX (December 3, 1874), 369.

Davis, William M. *Nimrod of the Sea; or, The American Whaleman.* (New York: Harper & Brothers)
Independent, XXVI (September 17, 1874), 11.
Publishers' Weekly, VI (September 19, 1874), 310.
Youth's Companion, XLVII (November 19, 1874), 388.

De Liefde, Jacob. *The Great Dutch Admirals.* (New York: George Routledge & Sons)
Nation, XIX (December 17, 1874), 402.

Densel, Mary. *Lloyd Dalan.* (New York: E. P. Dutton & Co.)
Publishers' Weekly, VI (November 21, 1874), 579.

Diaz, Abby Morton. *Lucy Maria.* (Boston: James R. Osgood & Co.)
Harper's Magazine, XLVIII (April, 1874), 748.

Unitarian Review, I (June, 1874), 496–98.

Dodge, Mary Abigail (Gail Hamilton). *Little Folk Life*. (Boston: Wm. F. Gill & Co.)
Independent, XXVI (December 17, 1874), 9.
Nation, XIX (December 19, 1874), 402.

Dodge, Mary Mapes. *Hans Brinker; or, The Silver Skates*. Illustrated by Darley, Nast, and others. (New York: Scribner, Armstrong & Co.)
Appleton's Journal, XI (January 17, 1874), 91.
Galaxy, XVII (February, 1874), 284–85.
Scribner's Monthly, VII (February, 1874), 507.
Youth's Companion, XLVII (January 15, 1874), 23.
Youth's Companion, XLVII (January 22, 1874), 31.

Rhymes and Jingles. (New York: Scribner, Armstrong & Co.)
Appleton's Journal, XII (December 19, 1874), 796.
Independent, XXVI (December 3, 1874), 9.
Nation, XIX (December 3, 1874), 369.
Youth's Companion, XLVII (December 10, 1874), 412–13.

Dodge, N. S. *A Grandfather's Stories About American History*. (Boston: Lee & Shepard)
Independent, XXVI (January 15, 1874), 10.
Literary World, IV (February, 1874), 140.
Publishers' Weekly, V (January 3, 1874), 18.
Unitarian Review, I (March, 1874), 94.

Dog Life: Narratives Exhibiting Instinct, Intelligence, Fidelity, Sympathy, Attachment, and Sorrow. (New York: Thomas Nelson & Sons)
Nation, XIX (November 19, 1874), 335.
Publishers' Weekly, VI (Christmas Supplement, 1874), 12.

Douglas, Amanda M. *The Old Woman That Lived in a Shoe*. (Boston: Wm. F. Gill & Co.)
Nation, XIX (December 17, 1874), 401.
Publishers' Weekly, VI (November 7, 1874), 518.

Dulcken, H. W. *Happy Day Stories for the Young*. (London and New York: George Routledge & Sons)
Nation, XIX (December 3, 1874), 367–68.

Eastman, Julia A. *Kitty Kent's Troubles*. (Boston: D. Lothrop & Co.)
Independent, XXVI (March 26, 1874), 9.
Publishers' Weekly, V (January 31, 1874), 110.

The Easy Book for Little Children. (Boston: John L. Shorey)
Literary World, IV (February, 1874), 140.

Estes, Dana. *Chimes for Childhood; A Collection of Songs for Little Ones*. (Boston: Estes & Lauriat)
Nation, XIX (December 17, 1874), 402.

Firth, Frank R. *The Young Engineer: Memoir of F. R. Firth*. (Boston: Lee & Shepard)
Youth's Companion, XLVII (November 19, 1874), 389.

Follen, Eliza Lee. *Little Songs*. (Boston: Lee & Shepard)
Independent, XXVI (December 17, 1874), 9.

Foote, E. B. *Science in Story; or, Sammy Tubbs, the Boy Doctor, and Sponsie, the Troublesome Monkey*. (The Murray Hill Publishing Co.)
Independent, XXVI (November 26, 1874), 9.

Fosdick, Charles A. (Harry Castlemon). *The Sportsman's Club Afloat*. (Philadelphia: Porter & Coates)
Literary World, V (June, 1874), 13.
Publishers' Weekly, V (May 30, 1874), 513.

Gilman, Arthur. *Seven Historic Ages.* (New York: Hurd & Houghton)
Independent, XXVI (April 16, 1874), 9.
Literary World, IV (March, 1874), 157.

The Golden Fence, and Other Tales. (Philadelphia: J. B. Lippincott & Co.)
Nation, XIX (December 17, 1874), 402.

Greenwood, James. *Legends of Savage Life.* (New York: G. P. Putnam's Sons)
Harper's Magazine, XLVIII (January, 1874), 298.

Hallowell, Mrs. Joshua L. *Bec's Bedtime.* (Philadelphia: Porter & Coates)
Appleton's Journal, XI (January 17, 1874), 91.
Nation, XIX(November 19, 1874), 335.

Hamerton, Eugenie. *The Mirror of Truth, and Other Marvelous Histories.* (Boston: Roberts Brothers)
Independent, XXVI (December 31, 1874), 9.

Hamerton, Phillip Gilbert. *Chapters on Animals.* (Boston: Roberts Brothers)
Independent, XXVI (May 28, 1874), 9.
Youth's Companion, XLVII (November 19, 1874), 388.

The Happy Hour. (New York: D. Appleton & Co.)
Appleton's Journal, XII (December 19, 1874), 797.
Independent, XXVI (December 3, 1874), 9.

Haweis, Hugh Reginald. *Pet; or, Pastimes and Penalties.* (New York: Harper & Brothers)
Independent, XXVI (March 12, 1874), 10.
Publishers' Weekly, V (March 7, 1874), 255.

Heaton, Mrs. Charles. *Happy Spring Time.* (New York: Macmillan & Co.)
Independent, XXVI (January 15, 1874), 10.

A Hieroglyphic Geography of the United States, Pt. I; Containing the New England States and New York. (New York: E. P. Dutton & Co.)
Independent, XXVI (December 10, 1874), 9.
Nation, XIX (December 10, 1874), 385.

Hosmer, Margaret. *Little Rosie's First Play Days.* (Philadelphia: Porter & Coates)
Literary World, IV (January, 1874), 124.

Johnson, Helen Kendrick. *Roddy's Romance.* (New York: G. P. Putnam's Sons)
Independent, XXVI (December 31, 1874), 9.
Literary World, V (November, 1874), 92.

Kellogg, Elijah. *The Fisher Boys of Pleasant Cove.* (Boston: Lee & Shepard)
Literary World, IV (April, 1874), 187.
Publishers' Weekly, V (May 16, 1874), 477.

Sowed by the Wind; or, The Poor Boy's Fortune. (Boston: Lee & Shepard)
Independent, XXVI (December 31, 1874), 9.

A Stout Heart. (Boston: Lee & Shepard)
Independent, XXVI (January 15, 1874), 10.
Literary World, IV (February, 1874), 140.

Knatchbull-Hugessen, E. H. *Queer Folk.* (New York: Macmillan & Co.)
Independent, XXVI (January 15, 1874), 10.

Whispers from Fairy-Land. (New York: D. Appleton & Co.)
Appleton's Journal, XII (December 19, 1874), 797.
Independent, XXVI (December 3, 1874), 9.

Knox, Kathleen. *Fairy Gifts; or, A Wallet of Wonders.* (New York: Pott, Young & Co.)
Nation, XIX (December 17, 1874), 402.

Laing, Mrs. C. H. B. *The Heroes of the Seven Hills.* (Philadelphia: Porter & Coates)
Independent, XXVI (April 16, 1874), 9–10.

Literary World, V (June, 1874), 12.

Larcom, Lucy. *Childhood Songs.* (Boston: James R. Osgood & Co.)
Independent, XXVI (December 3, 1874), 9.
Literary World, V (December, 1874), 108.

Larned, Augusta. *Talks With Girls.* (New York: Nelson & Phillips; Cincinnati: Hitchcock & Walden)
Independent, XXVI (October 29, 1874), 11.
Nation, XIX (December 3, 1874), 368.

Leander, Richard. *Fantastic Stories.* (New York: George Routledge & Sons)
Nation, XIX (December 10, 1874), 385.

The Life of an Elephant. (New York: Pott, Young & Co.)
Nation, XIX (December 10, 1874), 385.

Little Blue Eyes, and Other Field and Flower Stories. (New York: Thomas Nelson & Sons)
Publishers' Weekly, VI (Christmas Supplement, 1874), 14.

Lorimer, George C. *Under the Evergreens; or, A Night with St. Nicholas.* (Boston: Shepard & Gill)
Independent, XXVI (January 15, 1874), 10.
Literary World, IV (January, 1874), 124.
Youth's Companion, XLVII (January 15, 1874), 23.

Lottie Eames; or, Do Your Best and Leave the Rest. (Boston: Lee & Shepard)
Harper's Magazine, XLVIII (January, 1874), 298.

Lowell, Robert Traill Spence. *Antony Brade.* (Boston: Roberts Brothers)
Independent, XXVI (October 15, 1874), 10.
Publishers' Weekly, VI (October 31, 1874), 485.

Mackarness, M. A. *Children of the Olden Time.* (New York: Scribner, Armstrong & Co.)
St. Nicholas, I (January, 1874), 174.

McKeever, Harriet B. *The Nursery Treasury.* (Philadelphia: Claxton, Remsen & Haffelfinger)
Harper's Magazine, XLVIII (January, 1874), 299.

Mann, Mary Peabody. *The Flower People.* (Boston: James R. Osgood & Co.)
Independent, XXVI (December 10, 1874), 9.

Mathews, Joanna H. *Fanny's Birthday Gift.* (New York: Robert Carter & Brothers)
St. Nicholas, I (January, 1874), 174.

The New Scholars. (New York: Robert Carter & Brothers)
Independent, XXVI (April 16, 1874), 10.

Rosalie's Pet. (New York: Robert Carter & Brothers)
Publishers' Weekly, VI (October 31, 1874), 485.

Mathews, Julia A. *Giuseppe's Home.* (New York: Robert Carter & Brothers)
Independent, XXVI (March 12, 1874), 10.
Publishers' Weekly, V (February 28, 1874), 232.

Miller, Mary E. *The Holly Books.* (New York: American Tract Society)
Harper's Magazine, XLVIII (January, 1874), 298.

Mrs. Mouser; or, Tales of a Grandmother. (New York: Pott, Young & Co.)
Nation, XIX (December 17, 1874), 401–02.

Mother Anne and Her Little Maggie. (New York: A. D. F. Randolph)
Harper's Magazine, XLVIII (January, 1874), 298.

Moulton, Louise Chandler. *Bed-Time Stories.* (Boston: Roberts Brothers)
Galaxy, XVII (January, 1874), 143.
Lakeside Monthly, XI (January, 1874), 94–95.

More Bed-Time Stories. (Boston: Roberts Brothers)

Independent, XXVI (November 19, 1874), 9.
Literary World, V (December, 1874), 108–09.
Publishers' Weekly, VI (Christmas Supplement, 1874), 14.
Youth's Companion, XLVII (December 17, 1874), 420–21.

The Mountain Girl. (Boston: Lee & Shepard)
Harper's Magazine, XLVIII (January, 1874), 299.

Naaké, John T. *Slavonic Fairy Tales, Collected and Translated from the Russian, Polish, Servian, and Bohemian.* (New York: George Routledge & Sons)
Nation, XIX (December 17, 1874), 401.

Neally, A. R. *The Children's Bible Story-Book.* (New York: E. P. Dutton & Co.)
Publishers' Weekly, VI (Christmas Supplement, 1874), 14.

Norris, Emilia Marryat. *The Sea-Side Home and Smuggler's Cave.* (New York: Pott, Young & Co.)
Publishers' Weekly, VI (November 28, 1874), 601.

O'Reilly, Mrs. Robert. *Gile's Minority; or, Scenes at the Red House.* (Boston: Roberts Brothers)
Old and New, IX (May, 1874), 638.
Youth's Companion, XLVII (February 26, 1874), 71.

The Stories They Tell Me; or, Sue and I. (New York: E. P. Dutton & Co.)
Publishers' Weekly, VI (September 19, 1874), 310–11.

Owen, F. M. *The Soldier and Patriot; Story of George Washington.* (New York: Cassell, Petter & Galpin)
Independent, XXVI (January 15, 1874), 10.

Parker, Caroline E. R. *Wilson's Kindling Depot.* (New York: American Tract Society)
Harper's Magazine, XLVIII (January, 1874), 298.

Parsons, Mrs. ——. *Twelve Tales for the Young.* (London: Burns & Oates)
Catholic World, XIX (July, 1874), 576.

Paws and Claws; Being True Stories of Clever Creatures, Tame and Wild. (London, Paris and New York: Cassell, Petter & Galpin)
Nation, XIX (December 3, 1874), 368.
Publishers' Weekly, VI (Christmas Supplement, 1874), 12.

Phelps, Mrs. E. B. *Memoirs of Washington.* (Cincinnati: Robert Clarke & Co.)
Nation, XIX (November 19, 1874), 335–36.

Phelps, Miss Elizabeth Stuart. *Trotty's Wedding-Tour.* (Boston: James R. Osgood & Co.)
Harper's Magazine, XLVIII (January, 1874), 299.
St. Nicholas, I (January, 1874), 174.

Pollard, Josephine. *Gipsy in New York.* (New York: Nelson & Phillips)
Independent, XXVI (January 15, 1874), 10.

Gipsy's Travels. (New York: Nelson & Phillips)
Independent, XXVI (October 29, 1874), 11.

Pratt, Mary E. *Rhoda Thornton's Girlhood.* (Boston: Lee & Shepard)
Catholic World, XVIII (January, 1874), 575.

Prescott, Mary N. *Matt's Follies.* (Boston: James R. Osgood & Co.)
Harper's Magazine, XLVIII (January, 1874), 298.
Oliver Optic's Magazine, XV (April, 1874), 319.
St. Nicholas, I (January, 1874), 174.

Purbrick, Edward Ignatius. *May Papers.* (London: Burns & Oates)
Catholic World, XIX (June, 1874), 432.

Raffensperger, Mrs. A. F. *My Pet's Picture Book.* (New York: American Tract Society)
Harper's Magazine, XLVIII (January, 1874), 298.

Raymond, Rossiter W. (Robertson Gray). *The Man in the Moon and Other People*. (New York: J. B. Ford & Co.)
Independent, XXVI (December 17, 1874), 9.
Publishers' Weekly, VI (December 19, 1874), 678.

Raynal, F. E. *Wrecked on a Reef; or, Twenty Months Among the Auckland Isles*. (New York: Thomas Nelson & Sons)
Publishers' Weekly, VI (Christmas Supplement, 1874), 13.

Robbins, Mrs. S. S. *Doors Outward*. (New York: Robert Carter & Brothers)
Publishers' Weekly, VI (October 31, 1874), 485.

Rossetti, Christina G. *Speaking Likenesses*. (Boston: Roberts Brothers)
Independent, XXVI (December 10, 1874), 9.

Rover, Winnie. *The Neptune Outward Bound*. (New York: P. O'Shea)
Appleton's Journal, XI (June 27, 1874), 827.

S., M. F. *Catherine Hamilton*. (New York: Catholic Publication Society)
Catholic World, XIX (June, 1874), 432.

St. Nicholas for 1875. (New York: Scribner & Co.)
Appleton's Journal, XII (December 19, 1874), 797.
Independent, XXVI (October 1, 1874), 11.
Publishers' Weekly, VI (Christmas Supplement, 1874), 12–13.
Scribner's Monthly, IX (December, 1874), 260.
Youth's Companion, XLVII (January 15, 1874), 23.

Sanford, Mrs. D. P. *Pussy Tip-Toe's Family*. (New York: E. P. Dutton & Co.)
Nation, XIX (December 10, 1874), 385.
Publishers' Weekly, VI (September 19, 1874), 310.

Ségur, Comtesse Eugenie de. *French Fairy Tales*. (Philadelphia: Porter & Coates)
Appleton's Journal, XII (December 19, 1874), 797.

Shields, Mrs. S. A. (Sarah Annie Frost). *Sunshine for Rainy Days*. (New York: American Tract Society)
Harper's Magazine, XLVIII (January, 1874), 298.

Very Little Tales. (New York: American Tract Society)
Harper's Magazine, XLVIII (January, 1874), 298.

Smith, S. Francis. *Knights and Sea-Kings; or, The Middle Ages*. (Boston: D. Lothrop & Co.)
Publishers' Weekly, VI (November 21, 1874), 579.

Myths and Heroes; or, The Childhood of the World. (Boston: D. Lothrop & Co.)
Independent, XXVI (March 26, 1874), 9.
Unitarian Review, I (June, 1874), 491–95.

Standard Fairy Tales. (Philadelphia: Porter & Coates)
Appleton's Journal, XII (December 19, 1874), 797.
Harper's Magazine, XLVIII (January, 1874), 298.

Stanley, Henry M. *My Kalulu, Prince, King and Slave: Story of Central Africa*. (New York: Scribner, Armstrong & Co.)
Appleton's Journal, XI (January 13, 1874), 155.
Literary World, IV (February, 1874), 140.
Overland Monthly, XII (April, 1874), 390–91.
Publishers' Weekly, V (January 10, 1874), 33.

Stedman, Edmund Clarence. *Poems*. (Boston: James R. Osgood & Co.)
St. Nicholas, I (January, 1874), 174.

Stephens, Charles Asbury. *On the Amazon*. (Boston: James R. Osgood & Co.)
Harper's Magazine, XLVIII (January, 1874), 299.
Independent, XXVI (January 15, 1874), 10.

Stockton, Frank R. *What Might Have Been Expected*. (New York: Dodd, Mead)
Appleton's Journal, XII (November 21, 1874), 668.

Independent, XXVI (November 19, 1874), 9.
Nation, XIX (November 19, 1874), 335.
Publishers' Weekly, VI (November 7, 1874), 518–19.

Stoddard, R. H. *Lolly Dink's Doings.* (Boston: Wm. F. Gill & Co.)
Independent, XXVI (December 17, 1874), 9.
Independent, XXVI (December 31, 1874), 9.
Nation, XIX (December 17, 1874), 402.

Stories for Children by Eleven Sophomores. (Boston: Roberts Brothers)
Independent, XXVI (December 10, 1874), 9.

The Story of a Summer Day. (New York: Thomas Nelson & Sons)
Nation, XIX (November 19, 1874), 335.
Publishers' Weekly, VI (Christmas Supplement, 1874), 13.

Sylvia, and Other Dramas. (New York: P. M. Haverty)
Catholic World, XIX (July, 1874), 576.

Symington, Maggie. *Working to Win.* (New York: E. P. Dutton & Co.)
Publishers' Weekly, VI (September 5, 1874), 245.

Taylor, J. E. *Geological Stories.* (New York: G. P. Putnam's Sons)
Overland Monthly, XII (January, 1874), 103.

Thorne, Olive. *Little Folks in Feathers and Fur, and Others in Neither.* (Hartford: Dustin, Gilman & Co.)
Independent, XXVI (November 19, 1874), 9.

Tomlinson, Mrs. Charles. *First Steps in General Knowledge.* (New York: Pott, Young & Co.)
Independent, XXVI (August 27, 1874), 11.

Townsend, Virginia F. *That Queer Girl.* (Boston: Lee & Shepard)
Independent, XXVI (December 31, 1874), 9.

Trafton, Adeline. *An American Girl Abroad.* (Boston: Lee & Shepard)
Harper's Magazine, XLVIII (January, 1874), 299.

Trowbridge, John Townsend (Paul Creyton). *Doing His Best.* (Boston: James R. Osgood & Co.)
Harper's Magazine, XLVIII (January, 1874), 298.
Oliver Optic's Magazine, XV (January, 1874), 78.

Fast Friends. (Boston: James R. Osgood & Co.)
Independent, XXVI (October 29, 1874), 11.
Publishers' Weekly, VI (Christmas Supplement, 1874), 12.
Youth's Companion, XLVII (December 10, 1874), 413.

Ugly Girl. (Boston: Lee & Shepard)
Harper's Magazine, XLVIII (January, 1874), 299.

Varney, George J. *The Young People's History of Maine to 1842.* (Portland, Me.: Dresser, McClellan & Co.)
Publishers' Weekly, V (January 10, 1874), 32.

Verne, Jules. *Doctor Ox and Other Stories.* (Boston: James R. Osgood & Co.)
Appleton's Journal, XII (August 1, 1874), 155.
Literary World, V (August, 1874), 43.

Five Weeks in a Balloon. (Boston: James R. Osgood & Co.)
Independent, XXVI (January 8, 1874), 10.
North American Review, CXVIII (January, 1874), 192–93.
Oliver Optic's Magazine, XV (January, 1874), 78.
Overland Monthly, XII (February, 1874), 198–99.

From the Earth to the Moon. (New York: Scribner, Armstrong & Co.)
Independent, XXVI (January 8, 1874), 10.
Literary World, IV (January, 1874), 124.
Overland Monthly, XII (April, 1874), 391.

The Fur Country; or 70 Degrees North Latitude. (Boston: James R. Osgood & Co.)
Independent, XXVI (January 8, 1874), 10.
North American Review, CXVIII (January, 1874), 192–93.

The Mysterious Island, Pt. I. (Boston: H. L. Shepard & Co.)
Literary World, V (November, 1874), 91.

The Tour of the World in Eighty Days. (Boston: James R. Osgood & Co.)
North American Review, CXVIII (January, 1874), 192–93.

Twenty Thousand Leagues Under the Sea. (Boston: James R. Osgood & Co.)
North American Review, CXVIII (January, 1874), 192–93.

Viollet-le-Duc, Eugene E. *The Story of a House.* Translated from the French by George M. Towle. (Boston: James R. Osgood & Co.)
Youth's Companion, XLVII (December 10, 1874), 412.

Ward, Hetta L. H. *Davy's Jacket.* (Boston: D. Lothrop & Co.)
Independent, XXVI (March 26, 1874), 9.

Warner, Mrs. S. E. *Our Baby.* (New York: American Tract Society)
Appleton's Journal, XI (January 17, 1874), 91.

Warner, Susan Bogert (Elizabeth Wetherell). *Willow Brook.* (New York: Robert Carter & Brothers)
Independent, XXVI (March 12, 1874), 12.
Publishers' Weekly, V (February 28, 1874), 232.

Washburn, Mary L. *Christmas Week at Grandmother Cheeryheart's.* (Boston: Congregational Publishing Society)
Independent, XXVI (March 12, 1874), 10.

Weir, Marion Eliza. *Rockbourne, a Tale.* (New York: Robert Carter & Brothers)
Independent, XXVI (March 26, 1874), 9.

Whittier, John Greenleaf. *Child-Life in Prose.* (Boston: James R. Osgood & Co.)
Harper's Magazine, XLVIII (January, 1874), 298.
Overland Monthly, XII (January, 1874), 104.
St. Nicholas, I (January, 1874), 174.

Wise, Daniel (Francis Forrester; Lawrence Lancewood). *Story of a Wonderful Life.* (Cincinnati: Hitchcock & Walden)
Independent, XXVI (January 15, 1874), 10.

Wood, J. G. *Trespassers: Showing How the Inhabitants of Earth, Air, and Water Are Enabled to Trespass on Domains Not Their Own.* (New York: Thomas Nelson & Sons)
Nation, XIX (December 3, 1874), 369.

Woolsey, Sarah Chauncey (Susan Coolidge). *Mischief's Thanksgiving, and Other Stories.* (Boston: Roberts Brothers)
Independent, XXVI (November 19, 1874), 9.
Literary World, V (December, 1874), 108.
Publishers' Weekly, VI (Christmas Supplement, 1874), 14.

What Katy Did at School. (Boston: Roberts Brothers)
Youth's Companion, XLVII (February 26, 1874), 71.

Yonge, Charlotte M. *Ashley Priors.* (New York: Macmillan & Co.)
Literary World, V (September, 1874), 59.

BOOKS REVIEWED IN 1875

Achard, Émile. *The History of My Friends; or, Home Life with Animals.* (New York: G. P. Putnam's Sons)
Independent, XXVII (November 18, 1875), 8.
Nation, XXI (December 16, 1875), 391.
Publishers' Weekly, VIII (November 13, 1875), 742.

Adams, H. C. *Sunday Evenings at Home.* (New York: George Routledge & Sons)
Harper's Magazine, L (January, 1875), 289.

Adams, William T. (Oliver Optic). *The Dorcas Club; or, Our Girls Afloat.* (Boston: Lee & Shepard)
Literary World, V (January, 1875), 124.

Going West. (Boston: Lee & Shepard)
Publishers' Weekly, VIII (December 18, 1875), 936.

Ocean Born; or, The Cruise of the Clubs. (Boston: Lee & Shepard)
Publishers' Weekly, VII (June 5, 1875), 597.

Albertsen, Frank. *The Four-Footed Lovers.* (Boston: Lee & Shepard)
Independent, XXVII (December 9, 1875), 8.

Alcott, Louisa May. *Eight Cousins; or, The Aunt-Hill.* (Boston: Roberts Brothers)
Appleton's Journal, XIV (November 6, 1875), 601.
Catholic World, XXII (December, 1875), 431–32.
Independent, XXVII (October 7, 1875), 9.
Literary World, VI (October, 1875), 68–69.
Overland Monthly, XV (November, 1875), 493–94.
Publishers' Weekly, VIII (October 9, 1875), 567.

Alden, Isabella (Pansy). *Four Girls at Chautauqua.* (Boston: D. Lothrop & Co.)
Indepedent, XXVIII (August 10, 1876), 11.

Alger, Horatio, Jr. *Brave and Bold; or, The Story of a Factory-Boy.* (Boston: A. K. Loring)
St. Nicholas, II (January, 1875), 190.

Jack's Ward; or, The Boy Guardian. (Boston: A. K. Loring)
Independent, XXVII (December 2, 1875), 8.

Risen from the Ranks; or, Harry Walton's Success. (Boston: A. K. Loring)
St. Nicholas, II (January, 1875), 190.

Andersen, Hans Christian. *Andersen's Fairy Tales.* (New York: Scribner, Armstrong & Co.)
St. Nicholas, II (January, 1875), 190.

Animals and Their Young. (New York: George Routledge & Sons)
Harper's Magazine, L (January, 1875), 289.

Austin, Jane G. *Moonfolk: A True Account of the Home of the Fairy Tales.* (New York: G. P. Putnam's Sons)
Harper's Magazine, L (January, 1875), 290.
St. Nicholas, II (January, 1875), 190.
Scribner's Monthly, IX (January, 1875), 387–88.

Baker, George M. *Running to Waste.* (Boston: Lee & Shepard)
Unitarian Review, III (May, 1875), 536–37.

Ballantyne, Robert M. *Rivers of Ice.* (New York: Pott, Young & Co.)
Independent, XXVII (November 18, 1875), 8.

Barker, Mrs. Sale. *Little Wide-Awake.* (New York: George Routledge & Sons)
Harper's Magazine, L (January, 1875), 289.

Bartlett, G. B. *Parlor Amusements for the Young Folks.* (Boston: James R. Osgood & Co.)
Independent, XXVII (February 11, 1875), 11.
Publishers' Weekly, VII (January 30, 1875), 112.

Bell Miss C. D. *Which Is My Likeness?; or, Seeing Others As We See Ourselves.* (New York: Thomas Nelson & Sons)
Unitarian Review, IV (July, 1875), 110–11.

Bowen, Mrs. C. E. *Alice Neville and Riversdale.* (New York: Robert Carter & Brothers)
Publishers' Weekly, VII (April 3, 1875), 358.

Brenda (pseud.). *Froggy's Little Brother.* (New York: Robert Carter & Brothers) Publishers' Weekly, VII (February 27, 1875), 238.

Buckland, Frank T. *Log-Book of a Fisherman and Zoologist.* (Philadelphia: J. B. Lippincott & Co.)
Nation, XXI (December 16, 1875), 391.

Campbell, Emma F. R. *Toward the Mark; or, Grace Allen's Aim.* (Philadelphia: Garrigues Brothers)
Independent, XXVII (November 18, 1875), 8.

Chaney, George L. *F. Grant & Co.; or Partnerships.* (Boston: Roberts Brothers) Literary World, V (January, 1875), 125.

Charles, Elizabeth R. *The Bertram Family.* (New York: Dodd & Mead) Publishers' Weekly, VIII (November 20, 1875), 772.

Chatterbox (periodical).
Independent, XXVII (December 2, 1875), 8.

Chellis, Mary Dwinell. *All for Money.* (New York: National Temperance Society) Independent, XXVII (November 4, 1875), 9.

Clarke, Mary Cowden. *The Girlhood of Shakespeare's Heroines.* (New York: G. P. Putnam's Sons)
St. Nicholas, II (January, 1875), 190.

Clarke, Rebecca (Sophie May). *The Asbury Twins.* (Boston: Lee & Shepard) Independent, XXVII (December 30, 1875), 9.
Publishers' Weekly, VIII (December 25, 1875), 957.

Clodd, Edward. *The Childhood of Religions.* (New York: D. Appleton & Co.) Appleton's Journal, XIV (July 24, 1875), 118–19.
Independent, XXVII (September 2, 1875), 10.

Coffin, Charles Carleton (Carleton). *Caleb Krinkle.* (Boston: Lee & Shepard) Catholic World, XXI (April, 1875), 144.
Publishers' Weekly, VII (January 16, 1875), 57.
Youth's Companion, XLVIII (January 14, 1875), 12.

Craik, Dinah Mulock. *The Little Lame Prince.* (New York: Harper & Brothers) Appleton's Journal, XIII (January 2, 1875), 21.
Harper's Magazine, L (January, 1875), 289.

Songs of Our Youth. (New York: Harper & Brothers)
Harper's Magazine, L (May, 1875), 914–15.
Independent, XXVII (April 29, 1875), 10.
Literary World, V (May, 1875), 187.
Publishers' Weekly, VII (April 3, 1875), 359.

Diaz, Abby Morton. *A Story-Book for the Young Folks.* (Boston: James R. Osgood & Co.)
Independent, XXVII (November 4, 1875), 9.
Literary World, VI (November, 1875), 83–84.
Publishers' Weekly, VIII (November 6, 1875), 712.

Dodge, Mary Mapes. *Hans Brinker; or, The Silver Skates.* (New York: Scribner, Armstrong & Co.)
Independent, XXVII (December 30, 1875), 9.
Publishers' Weekly, VIII (December 25, 1875), 957.
Scribner's Monthly, XI (December, 1875), 296.

Rhymes and Jingles. New Edition. (New York: Scribner, Armstrong & Co.) Catholic World, XX (January, 1875), 576.
Harper's Magazine, L (March, 1875), 601.
Independent, XXVII (October 7, 1875), 10.
Publishers' Weekly, VIII (October 9, 1875), 568.
Scribner's Monthly, XI (December, 1875), 296.

Dog Life: Narratives Exhibiting Instinct, Intelligence, Fidelity, Sympathy, Attach-
ment, and Sorrow. (New York: Thomas Nelson & Sons)
Harper's Magazine, L (January, 1875), 289.

Drinkwater, Jennie M. *Fred and Jeanie; How They Learned About God.* (New
York: Robert Carter & Brothers)
Independent, XXVII (November 18, 1875), 8.
Publishers' Weekly, VIII (November 6, 1875), 713.

Eastman, Julia A. *Striking for the Right.* (Boston: D. Lothrop & Co.)
New England Journal of Education, II (November 13, 1875), 227.
Young Rick. (Boston: D. Lothrop & Co.)
Independent, XXVII (December 30, 1875), 9.

Eggleston, George Cary. *The Big Brother: Story of Indian War.* (New York: G. P.
Putnam's Sons)
Publishers' Weekly, VIII (November 6, 1875), 712.

Emerson, Nannette S. *Little Folks' Letters.* (New York: G. W. Carleton & Co.)
Independent, XXVII (December 2, 1875), 8.
Publishers' Weekly, VIII (November 20, 1875), 773.

Engleback, A. H. *Two Campaigns; A Tale of Old Alsace.* (London: Society for
Promoting Christian Knowledge; New York: Pott, Young & Co.)
Independent, XXVII (November 4, 1875), 9.
Nation, XXI (November 18, 1875), 328.

Ewing, Juliana Horatia (Aunt Judy). *Six to Sixteen.* (Boston: Roberts Brothers)
Independent, XXVII (November 18, 1875), 8.
Publishers' Weekly, VIII (November 13, 1875), 742.

Farman, Ella. *The Cooking Club of Tu-Whit Hollow.* (Boston: D. Lothrop &
Co.)
Independent, XXVII (August 10, 1875), 11.

Finley, Martha F. (Martha Farquharson). *Elsie's Womanhood.* (New York: Dodd
& Mead)
Independent, XXVII (November 4, 1875), 9.
Literary World, VI (December, 1875), 100–101.
Publishers' Weekly, VIII (October 9, 1875), 567.

Floyd, Cornelia (Neil Forrest). *Mice at Play.* (Boston: Roberts Brothers)
Independent, XXVII (November 18, 1875), 8.
Publishers' Weekly, VIII (November 13, 1875), 742.

Follen, Eliza Lee. *Little Songs.* (Boston: Lee & Shepard)
Harper's Magazine, L (March, 1875), 601.

Foster, Emilie. *The Haven Children; or, Frolics at the Funny Old House on Funny
Street.* (New York: E. P. Dutton & Co.)
Literary World, VI (October, 1875), 69.
Publishers' Weekly, VIII (September 11, 1875), 437.

Foster, Mrs. I. H. (Faye Huntington). *Mr. MacKenzie's Answer.* (New York:
National Temperance Society)
Independent, XXVII (November 4, 1875), 9.

Gardner, Mrs. H. C. *Mehetabel, a Story of the Revolution.* (New York: Nelson &
Phillips)
Independent, XXVII (December 9, 1875), 8.

Giberne, Agnes. *Floss Silverthorn.* (New York: Robert Carter & Brothers)
Publishers' Weekly, VII (February 13, 1875), 182.

Gilmar, Arthur. *Apples of Gold.* (Boston: American Tract Society)
Independent, XXVII (December 9, 1875), 8.

Girardin, J. *Adventures of Johnny Ironsides.* From the French. (New York:
George Routledge & Sons)
Nation, XXI (December 16, 1875), 392.

Goatland; A Story of Country Life. (New York: Thomas Nelson & Sons)
Nation, XXI (December 16, 1875), 391.

The Goody Two Shoes Picture Book. (New York: George Routledge & Sons)
Harper's Magazine, L (January, 1875), 289.

Guernsey, Clara F. *The Mallory Girls; or, The Wrong and the Right Way.* (Philadelphia: American Sunday-School Union)
Independent, XXVII (November 4, 1875), 9.

Guernsey, Lucy Ellen. *Grandmother Brown's School Days; or, Education As It Was Seventy Years Since.* (Philadelphia: American Sunday-School Union)
Independent, XXVII (November 4, 1875), 9.

Guild, Mrs. C. S. *Hymns and Rhymes; For Home and School.* (Boston: Nichols & Hall)
Publishers' Weekly, VII (January 30, 1875), 111.

   Hymns for Mothers and Children. (Boston: Nichols & Hall)
   Literary World, V (January, 1875), 125.

Hale, Edward Everett (ed.). *Silhouettes and Songs Illustrative of the Months.* Illus. by H. M. Hind. (Boston: Lockwood, Brooks & Co.)
Nation, XXI (December 23, 1875), 403.

Half-Hours with the Animals. (New York: Thomas Nelson & Sons)
Nation, XXI (December 16, 1875), 391.

Hamerton, Philip Gilbert. *Harry Blount; Passages in a Boy's Life on Land and Sea.* (Boston: Roberts Brothers)
Independent, XXVII (April 29, 1875), 10.
Literary World, V (May, 1875), 188.
Publishers' Weekly, VII (April 24, 1875), 439.
Scribner's Monthly, X (June, 1875), 256.
Unitarian Review, IV (November, 1875), 543.

Higginson, Thomas Wentworth. *Young Folks' History of the United States.* (Boston: Lee & Shepard)
Galaxy, XIX (May, 1875), 718.
Harper's Magazine, L (May, 1875), 914.
Independent, XXVII (March 4, 1875), 10.
Literary World, V (February, 1875), 135.
New Englander, XXXIV (July, 1875), 599.
Penn Monthly, VI (April, 1875), 306–07.
Scribner's Monthly, IX (April, 1875), 768–69.
Western, I (April, 1875), 262.

Hoffmann, Ernest Theodore. *Nutcracker and Mouseking.* (Boston: Lockwood, Brooks & Co.)
Independent, XXVII (December 16, 1875), 8.

Holt, Emily Sarah. *Imogene; A Story of the Mission of Augustine.* (New York: Robert Carter and Brothers)
Independent, XXVII (November 4, 1875), 9.

The House That Jack Built.
Nation, XXI (December 16, 1875), 392.

Huntington, Emily. *Little Lessons for Little Housekeepers.* (New York: A. D. F. Randolph)
Publishers' Weekly, VIII (November 20, 1875), 773.

Jerrold, Alice. *Cruise of the Acorn.*
Nation, XXI (December 16, 1875), 392.

Johnson, Helen Kendrick. *Roddy's Reality.* (New York: G. P. Putnam's Sons)
Independent, XXVII (December 23, 1875), 8.
Nation, XXI (December 16, 1875), 392.

Roddy's Romance. (New York: G. P. Putnam's Sons)
Appleton's Journal, XIII (January 2, 1875), 21.

Johnson, Virginia W. (Cousin Virginia). *The Catskill Fairies.* (New York: Harper
& Brothers)
Appleton's Journal, XIV (November 20, 1875), 664–65.
Harper's Magazine, LII (December, 1875), 147.
Independent, XXVII (November 18, 1875), 7.
Literary World, VI (November, 1875), 83.
Nation, XXI (November 18, 1875), 329.
Publishers' Weekly, VIII (November 6, 1875), 712.

Kellogg, Elijah. *Brought to the Front.* (Boston: Lee & Shepard)
Independent, XXVII (December 23, 1875), 8.
Publishers' Weekly, VIII (December 18, 1875), 936.

Sowed by the Wind. (Boston: Lee & Shepard)
Literary World, V (January, 1875), 124.
Publishers' Weekly, VII (January 16, 1875), 58.

Wolf Run; or, The Boys of the Wilderness. (Boston: Lee & Shepard)
Independent, XXVII (June 10, 1875), 10.
Publishers' Weekly, VII (June 5, 1875), 597.

Knatchbull-Hugessen, E. H. *Higgledy-Piggledy.* (New York: D. Appleton & Co.)
Appleton's Journal, XIV (December 11, 1875), 761.
Nation, XXI (December 16, 1875), 392.

Knox, Kathleen. *Fairy Gifts; or, A Wallet of Wonders.* (New York: Pott, Young &
Co.)
Harper's Magazine, L (January, 1875), 290.

Land of the Lion; or, Adventures Among the Wild Animals of Africa. (New York:
Thomas Nelson & Sons)
Nation, XXI (December 16, 1875), 391.

Larcom, Lucy. *Childhood Songs.* (Boston: James R. Osgood & Co.)
Harper's Magazine, L (March, 1875), 601.
St. Nicholas, II (January, 1875), 190.
Unitarian Review, IV (August, 1875), 216.

The Life of an Elephant. (New York: Pott, Young & Co.)
Harper's Magazine, L (January, 1875), 289.

Lippincott, Sara J. (Grace Greenwood). *Heads and Tails: Studies and Stories of
Pets.* (New York: J. B. Ford & Co.)
Literary World, V (January, 1875), 125.
Publishers' Weekly, VII (January 9, 1875), 31.

Little Folks (periodical).
Independent, XXVII (December 2, 1875), 8.

Little Rosebud's Album. (New York: George Routledge & Sons)
Harper's Magazine, L (January, 1875), 289.

Logie, Sarah E. C. (Sarah E. Chester). *Proud Little Dody.* (New York: American
Tract Society)
Publishers' Weekly, VIII (November 6, 1875), 713.

Longfellow, Henry Wadsworth. *The Hanging of the Crane.* (Boston: James R.
Osgood & Co.)
St. Nicholas, II (January, 1875), 190.

Lowell, Robert (Traill Spence). *Antony Brade.* (Boston: Roberts Brothers)
St. Nicholas, II (January, 1875), 189.
Unitarian Review, III (March, 1875), 325–26.

MacDonald, George. *A Double Story.* (New York: Dodd & Mead)
Appleton's Journal, XIII (June 26, 1875), 824.

McKean, May F. *Agnes and Mattie.* (Philadelphia: American Baptist Publication Society)
   Literary World, V (January, 1875), 124.
Marguerite's Journal; A Story for Girls. (New York: G. W. Carleton & Co.)
   Independent, XXVII (November 18, 1875), 8.
Marshall, Emma. *Little Brothers and Sisters.* (New York: Robert Carter & Brothers)
   Publishers' Weekly, VII (June 19, 1875), 646.
   Now-a-days; or, King's Daughters. (New York: E. P. Dutton & Co.)
   Literary World, V (March, 1875), 157.
Mathews, Joanna H. *Eleanor's Visit.* (New York: Robert Carter & Brothers)
   Publishers' Weekly, VII (April 3, 1875), 358.
   Elsie's Santa Claus. (New York: Robert Carter & Brothers)
   Independent, XXVII (November 4, 1875), 9.
   Publishers' Weekly, VIII (October 3, 1875), 664.
May's Own Boy. (New York: Pott, Young & Co.)
   Harper's Magazine, L (January, 1875), 289.
Mrs. Mouser. (New York: Pott, Young & Co.)
   Harper's Magazine, L (January, 1875), 289.
Moulton, Louise Chandler. *More Bed-Time Stories.* (Boston: Roberts Brothers)
   Harper's Magazine, L (February, 1875), 449.
   Oliver Optic's Magazine, XVIII (November, 1875), 767.
   St. Nicholas, II (January, 1875), 190.
Mulholland, Rosa. *Puck and Blossom.* (New York: Pott, Young & Co.)
   Nation, XXI (December 16, 1875), 392.
Murray, C. O. *The Merry Elves; or, Little Adventures in Fairy Land.* (New York: Thomas Nelson & Sons)
   Harper's Magazine, L (January, 1875), 290.
Newton, Dr. R. *The Wonder Case.* (New York: Robert Carter & Brothers)
   Harper's Magazine, L (January, 1875), 289.
The Nursery (periodical).
   Independent, XXVII (January 28, 1875), 12.
Palgrave, Francis Turner. *Children's Treasury of English Song.* (New York: Macmillan & Co.)
   Appleton's Journal, XIV (December 25, 1875), 825.
   Nation, XXI (December 16, 1875), 392.
   New England Journal of Education, II (December 18, 1875), 287.
   Publishers' Weekly, VIII (December 4, 1875), 890.
Payne, Annie Mitchell. *The Odd One.* (New York: Robert Carter & Brothers)
   Independent, XXVII (November 4, 1875), 9.
The Peep Show (periodical).
   Independent, XXVII (December 23, 1875), 8.
Phil Derry; The Western Boy Who Became a Sunday-School Missionary. (Philadelphia: American Sunday-School Union)
   Independent, XXVII (December 9, 1875), 8.
Raymond, Rossiter W. (Robertson Gray). *The Man in the Moon and Other People.* (New York: J. B. Ford & Co.)
   Harper's Magazine, L (February, 1875), 449.
   Literary World, V (January, 1875), 125.
Richardson, Abby Sage. *The History of Our Country.* (New York: Hurd & Houghton)
   Atlantic Monthly, XXXVI (August, 1875), 244–45.
   Overland Monthly, XV (November, 1875), 492–93.

Robbins, Mrs. S. S. *Brentford Parsonage*. (New York: Robert Carter & Brothers)
Independent, XXVII (November 4, 1875), 9.

St. Nicholas (periodical).
Independent, XXVII (October 28, 1875), 9.

Sanford, Mrs. D. P. *Frisk and His Flock*. (New York: E. P. Dutton & Co.)
Independent, XXVII (December 2, 1875), 8.
Literary World, VI (October, 1875), 68.
Nation, XXI (November 18, 1875), 328–29.
Publishers' Weekly, VIII (September 11, 1875), 437.
Scribner's Monthly, XI (December, 1875), 297.

Pussy Tip-Toe's Family. (New York: E. P. Dutton & Co.)
Harper's Magazine, L (January, 1875), 289.

Sawyer, George A. *Fret-Sawing and Wood-Carving for Amateurs*. (Boston: Lee & Shepard)
Youth's Companion, XLVIII (March 25, 1875), 92.

Scudder, Horace Elisha. *Doings of the Bodley Family in Town and Country*. (New York: Hurd & Houghton)
Appleton's Journal, XIV (December 11, 1875), 761.
Independent, XXVII (October 28, 1875), 8.
Literary World, VI (October, 1875), 68.
Nation, XXI (November 18, 1875), 329.
Publishers' Weekly, VIII (October 2, 1875), 534–35.
Scribner's Monthly, XI (December, 1875), 296.

Seaton, Thomas. *A Manual of Fret-Cutting and Wood-Carving*. (London and New York: George Routledge & Sons)
Nation, XXI (November 18, 1875), 329.

Shields, Mrs. S. A. (Sarah Annie Frost). *Sunshine for Rainy Days*. (New York: American Tract Society)
Publishers' Weekly, VIII (November 6, 1875), 713.

Smith, Mary P. Wells (P. Thorne). *Jolly Good Times; or, Child Life on a Farm*. (Boston: Roberts Brothers)
Independent, XXVII (November 4, 1875), 9.
Literary World, VI (November, 1875), 79.
Nation, XXI (November 18, 1875), 329.
Publishers' Weekly, VIII (November 13, 1875), 742.

Stevenson, Sarah Hackett. *Boys and Girls in Biology: Simple Studies of Lower Forms of Life; Based Upon Lectures of T. H. Huxley*. (New York: D. Appleton & Co.)
Publishers' Weekly, VII (May 8, 1875), 494.

Stockton, Frank R. *Tales Out of School*. (New York: Scribner, Armstrong & Co.)
Appleton's Journal, XIV (December 11, 1875), 761.
Independent, XXVII (December 9, 1875), 8.
Nation, XXI (December 16, 1875), 391–92.
Scribner's Monthly, XI (December, 1875), 296–97.

What Might Have Been Expected. (New York: Dodd & Mead)
Scribner's Monthly, IX (January, 1875), 388.

Stoddard, R. H. *Lolly Dink's Doings*. (Boston: William F. Gill & Co.)
Literary World, V (January, 1875), 124.
St. Nicholas, II (January, 1875), 190.

Story of a Summer Day. (New York: Thomas Nelson & Sons)
Harper's Magazine, L (1875), 289.

Stowe, Harriet Beecher. *Betty's Bright Idea*. (New York: J. B. Ford & Co.)
Publishers' Weekly, VIII (December 18, 1875), 937.

Sunday Reading for the Young (periodical).
Independent, XXVII (December 2, 1875), 8.

Thorne, Olive. *Little Folks in Feathers and Fur, and Others in Neither.* (Hartford, Conn.: Dustin, Gilman & Co.)
St. Nicholas, II (January, 1875), 190.

Townsend, Virginia F. *That Queer Girl.* (Boston: Lee & Shepard)
Literary World, V (January, 1875), 124.
Publishers' Weekly, VII (January 16, 1875), 57.
Youth's Companion, XLVIII (January 14, 1875), 12–13.

Trimmer, Sarah Kirby. *History of the Robins; for Instruction of Children on Treatment of Animals.* (New York: Thomas Nelson & Sons)
Appleton's Journal, XIV (December 11, 1875), 761.
Independent, XXVII (November 18, 1875), 8.
Nation, XXI (December 16, 1875), 391.

Trowbridge, John Townsend (Paul Creyton). *Fast Friends.* (Boston: James R. Osgood & Co.)
Oliver Optic's Magazine, XVII (January, 1875), 79.
St. Nicholas, II (January, 1875), 189.

The Young Surveyor. (Boston: James R. Osgood & Co.)
Appleton's Journal, XIV (November 20, 1875), 665.
Independent, XXVII (November 4, 1875), 9.
Publishers' Weekly, VIII (November 6, 1875), 713.

Tucker, Charlotte (A.L.O.E.). *Fairy Frisket; or, Peeps at Insect Life.* (New York: Robert Carter & Brothers)
Publishers' Weekly, VII (February 13, 1875), 182.

The Little Maid [also] *Living Jewels.* (New York: Robert Carter & Brothers)
Publishers' Weekly, VII (April 3, 1875), 358.

Verne, Jules. *Adventures of Captain Hatteras.* (Boston: James R. Osgood & Co.)
Independent, XXVII (October 28, 1875), 8.
Publishers' Weekly, VIII (October 16, 1875), 639.

The Mysterious Island. Complete in 3 vols. (New York: Scribner, Armstrong & Co.)
Independent, XXVII (December 30, 1875), 9.

The Mysterious Island. Abandoned. (New York: Scribner, Armstrong & Co.)
Publishers' Weekly, VIII (December 4, 1875), 889.

The Mysterious Island. Dropped from the Clouds. (New York: Scribner, Armstrong & Co.)
Appleton's Journal, XIV (November 27, 1875), 695–96.
Independent, XXVII (November 25, 1875), 8.
Literary World, VI (December, 1875), 100.
Publishers' Weekly, VIII (November 13, 1875), 742.

The Mysterious Island. The Secret of the Island. (New York: Scribner, Armstrong & Co.)
Publishers' Weekly, VIII (December 25, 1875), 957.

The Wreck of the "Chancellor". (Boston: James R. Osgood & Co.)
Appleton's Journal, XIII (May 15, 1875), 631.

Warner, Susan Bogert (Elizabeth Wetherell). *Bread and Oranges.* (New York: Robert Carter & Brothers)
Independent, XXVII (November 4, 1875), 9.
Publishers' Weekly, VIII (October 30, 1875), 687.

The Rapids of Niagara. (New York: Robert Carter & Brothers)
Independent, XXVII (November 18, 1875), 7–8.

Whittier, John Greenleaf. *Hazel Blossoms.* (Boston: James R. Osgood & Co.)
St. Nicholas, II (January, 1875), 189.

Whymper, Frederick. *The Heroes of the Arctic.* (New York: Pott, Young & Co.)
Independent, XXVII (November 18, 1875), 8.
Publishers' Weekly, VIII (November 13, 1875), 742.

Wide Awake; An Illustrated Magazine for Girls and Boys for 1875.
Publishers' Weekly, VIII (December 18, 1875), 936.
Unitarian Review, IV (October, 1875), 440.

Winthrop, Sophy. *Faith and Patience; or, The Harrington Girls.* (New York: A. D. F. Randolph)
Independent, XXVII (October 7, 1875), 10.
Publishers' Weekly, VIII (October 23, 1875), 663.

Wood, J. G. *Popular Illustrated Natural History.* (New York: George Routledge & Sons)
Nation, XXI (December 16, 1875), 391.

Trespassers; Showing How Inhabitants of Earth, Air, and Water Are Enabled to Trespass on Domains Not Their Own. (New York: Thomas Nelson & Sons)
Harper's Magazine, L (January, 1875), 290.

Woods, Edgar. *Golden Apples.* (New York: Robert Carter & Brothers)
Harper's Magazine, L (January, 1875), 289.

Woolsey, Sarah Chauncey (Susan Coolidge). *Mischief's Thanksgiving, and Other Stories.* (Boston: Roberts Brothers)
Harper's Magazine, L (February, 1875), 449.
St. Nicholas, II (January, 1875), 190.

Nine Little Goslings. (Boston: Roberts Brothers)
Independent, XVII (November 4, 1875), 9.
Literary World, VI (November, 1875), 79.
Nation, XXI (November 18, 1875), 329.
New England Journal of Education, II (October 30, 1875), 204.
Publishers' Weekly, VIII (November 13, 1875), 742–43.

BOOKS REVIEWED IN 1876

Abbott, Edward. *Long Look House.* (Boston: Noyes, Snow & Co.)
Independent, XXVIII (December 19, 1876), 8.
Literary World, VII (December, 1876), 103.
Nation, XXIII (December 14, 1876), 359.
New England Journal of Education, IV (December 9, 1876), 263.
Publishers' Weekly, X (December 2, 1876), 946.

Abbott, John S. C. *George Washington.* (New York: Dodd & Mead)
Appleton's Journal, XV (January 29, 1876), 153.

Achard, Émile. *History of My Friends; or, Home Life with Animals.* (New York: G. P. Putnam's Sons)
Penn Monthly, VII (February, 1876), 159.
St. Nicholas, III (January, 1876), 204.

Adams, William T. (Oliver Optic). *Going West; or, The Perils of a Poor Boy.* (Boston: Lee & Shepard)
Literary World, VI (January, 1876), 116.

In Doors and Out; or, Views from the Chimney Corner. (Boston: Lee & Shepard)
Catholic World, XXII (April, 1876), 720.
New England Journal of Education, III (January 1, 1876), 12.

Vine and Olive; or, Young America in Spain and Portugal. (Boston: Lee & Shepard)
New England Journal of Education, IV (December 9, 1876), 263.
Publishers' Weekly, X (December 2, 1876), 947.

Albertsen, Frank. *The Four-Footed Lovers.* (Boston: Lee & Shepard)
Youth's Companion, XLIX (January 6, 1876), 5.

Alcott, Louisa May. *Eight Cousins; or, The Aunt-Hill.* (Boston: Roberts Brothers)
St. Nicholas, III (January, 1876), 203.
Scribner's Monthly, XI (April, 1876), 897–98.

Rose in Bloom. (Boston: Roberts Brothers)
Literary World, VII (December, 1876), 104.
Nation, XXIII (December 21, 1876), 373.

Silver Pitchers. (Boston: Roberts Brothers)
Publishers' Weekly, IX (June 17, 1876), 793.

Alden, Isabella (Pansy). *Pansy's Picture Book.* (Boston: D. Lothrop & Co.)
Publishers' Weekly, X (November 25, 1876), 919.

The Randolphs. (Boston: D. Lothrop & Co.)
Publishers' Weekly, X (December 2, 1876), 947.

Alger, Horatio, Jr. *Sam's Chance and How He Improved It.* (Boston: A. K. Loring)
Independent, XXVIII (May 18, 1876), 10.

Apples of Gold (periodical).
Independent, XXVIII (December 21, 1876), 8.
New England Journal of Education, IV (December 16, 1876), 275.
Publishers' Weekly, X (December 16, 1876), 1007.

Austin, Mrs. G. Lowell. *The Little People of God, and What the Poets Have Said of Them.* (Boston: Lee & Shepard)
Nation, XXIII (December 14, 1876), 359.

Barnum, P. T. *Lion Jack; or, How Menageries Are Made.* (New York: G. W. Carleton & Co.)
Independent, XXVIII (December 7, 1876), 8.
Publishers' Weekly, X (November 25, 1876), 919–20.

Brackett, Anna C. and I. M. Eliot. *Poetry for Home and School.* (New York: G. P. Putnam's Sons)
Independent, XXVIII (May 4, 1876), 10.
Nation, XXIII (July 6, 1876), 15.
Unitarian Review, V (May, 1876), 568.

Brooks, Noah. *The Boy Emigrants.* (New York: Scribner, Armstrong & Co.)
Independent, XXVIII (December 7, 1876), 8.
Literary World, VII (December, 1876), 104.
Nation, XXIII (December 7, 1876), 345.
Publishers' Weekly, X (November 25, 1876), 919.
St. Nicholas, V (December, 1876), 150.

Brown, Theron. *Walter Neal's Example.* (Boston: D. Lothrop & Co.)
Independent, XXVIII (July 6, 1876), 9.
Publishers' Weekly, X (July 8, 1876), 137.

Brown, Thomas (Park Ludlow). *The Taxidermist's Manual.* (New York: G. P. Putnam's Sons)
St. Nicholas, III (January, 1876), 204.

Butts, Mrs. M. F. *Three Girls.* (Boston: Congregational Publishing Society)
Independent, XXVIII (May 25, 1876), 9.
Publishers' Weekly, IX (March 25, 1876), 407–08.

Cahun, Leon. *The Adventures of Captain Mago; or, A Phoenician Expedition, 1000 B.C.* (New York: Scribner, Armstrong & Co.)
Independent, XXVIII (November 2, 1876), 9.
Literary World, VII (November, 1876), 80.
Publishers' Weekly, X (October 28, 1876), 702.

Carleton, Will. *Young Folks' Centennial Rhymes.* (New York: Harper & Brothers)
Harper's Magazine, LIII (September, 1876), 628–29.
Penn Monthly, VII (December, 1876), 989.
Publishers' Weekly, X (August 12, 1876), 328.

Champney, Lizzie W. *In the Sky Garden.* (Boston: Lockwood, Brooks & Co.)
Independent, XXVIII (December 21, 1876), 8.
Nation, XXIII (December 14, 1876), 359.
New England Journal of Education, IV (December 16, 1876), 275.
Publishers' Weekly, X (December 16, 1876), 1007.

Chellis, Mary Dwinell. *Ten Cents.* (New York: National Temperance Society)
Publishers' Weekly, X (October 28, 1876), 704.

Clarke, Rebecca (Sophie May). *Flaxie Frizzle.* (Boston: Lee & Shepard)
Independent, XXVIII (December 7, 1876), 8.
Literary World, VII (December, 1876), 104–05.
Publishers' Weekly, X (November 25, 1876), 919.

The Horn of Plenty. (Boston: W. F. Gill & Co.)
Appleton's Journal, XV (January 15, 1876), 89.
Independent, XXVIII (January 6, 1876), 11.

Clemens, Samuel Langhorne (Mark Twain). *The Adventures of Tom Sawyer.* (Hartford: American Publishing Co.)
Atlantic Monthly, XXXVII (May, 1876), 621–22.

Clodd, Edward. *The Childhood of Religions.* (New York: D. Appleton & Co.)
Popular Science Monthly, IX (July, 1876), 372.

Cobb, James F. and H. A. Page. *Stories of Success.* (Boston: D. Lothrop & Co.)
Independent, XXVIII (July 6, 1876), 9.

Coffin, Charles Carleton (Carleton). *The Boys of '76.* (New York: Harper & Brothers)
Independent, XXVIII (December 7, 1876), 8.
Penn Monthly, VII (December, 1876), 988–89.
Publishers' Weekly, X (December 2, 1876), 948.

Cozzens, S. Woodworth. *The Young Trail-Hunters.* (Boston: Lee & Shepard)
Nation, XXIII (December 7, 1876), 345.
Publishers' Weekly, X (December 2, 1876), 947–48.

Cragin, Louisa T. (Ellis Gray). *Long Ago; A Year of Child Life.* (Boston: Lockwood, Brooks & Co.)
Independent, XXVIII (December 21, 1876), 8.
Nation, XXIII (December 21, 1876), 373.
Publishers' Weekly, X (December 16, 1876), 1010.

Craigie, Mary E. *Once Upon a Time: Stories of the Ancient Gods and Heroes.* (New York: G. P. Putnam's Sons)
Independent, XXVIII (November 2, 1876), 9.

Craik, Dinah Mulock. *Songs of Our Youth.* (New York: Harper & Brothers)
Atlantic Monthly, XXXVII (February, 1876), 251–52.

Crane, Walter. *The Baby's Opera.* (New York: George Routledge & Sons)
Nation, XXIII (December 14, 1876), 359.

Davis, Elizabeth A. *Snip and Whip, and Some Other Boys.* (Boston: Lee & Shepard)
New England Journal of Education, IV (December 9, 1876), 263.
Publishers' Weekly, X (December 2, 1876), 948.

De Mille, James. *The Winged Lion; or, Stories of Venice.* (Boston: Lee & Shepard)
Independent, XXVIII (December 7, 1876), 8.
Literary World, VII (December, 1876), 104.
Publishers' Weekly, X (November 25, 1876), 919.

De Morgan, Mary. *On a Pincushion and Other Fairy Tales.* (New York: E. P. Dutton & Co.)
Publishers' Weekly, X (December 2, 1876), 946.

Dodge, Mary Mapes. *Hans Brinker; or, The Silver Skates.* (New York: Scribner, Armstrong & Co.)
Appleton's Journal, XV (January 8, 1876), 58.

Douglas, Amanda M. *There's No Place Like Home.* (Boston: W. F. Gill & Co.)
Literary World, VI (January, 1876), 117.

Eggleston, George Cary. *The Big Brother: Story of Indian War.* (New York: G. P. Putnam's Sons)
Penn Monthly, VII (January, 1876), 80–81.
St. Nicholas, III (January, 1876), 204.

Captain Sam; or, The Boy Scout of 1814. (New York: G. P. Putnam's Sons)
Independent, XXVIII (November 2, 1876), 9.
Literary World, VII (November, 1876), 89.
Penn Monthly, VII (December, 1876), 987–88.
Publishers' Weekly, X (October 28, 1876), 703.

Ewing, Juliana Horatia (Aunt Judy). *Jan of the Windmill; Story of the Plains.* (Boston: Roberts Brothers)
New England Journal of Education, IV (December 16, 1876), 275.
Publishers' Weekly, X (December 9, 1876), 976.

Six to Sixteen. (Boston: Roberts Brothers)
St. Nicholas, III (January, 1876), 204.

Finley, Martha F. (Martha Farquharson). *Elsie's Motherhood.* (New York: Dodd, Mead)
Independent, XXVIII (October 26, 1876), 9.
Publishers' Weekly, X (October 14, 1876), 632.

Floyd, Cornelia (Neil Forrest). *Mice at Play.* (Boston: Roberts Brothers)
St. Nicholas, III (January, 1876), 204.

Fosdick, Charles A. (Harry Castlemon). *Frank Nelson in the Forecastle.* (Philadelphia: Porter & Coates)
Literary World, VII (January, 1876), 116.
Publishers' Weekly, X (November 25, 1876), 921.

Snowed Up; or, The Sportsman's Club in the Mountains. (Philadelphia: Porter & Coates)
Independent, XXVIII (September 21, 1876), 12.
Literary World, VII (October, 1876), 71.
Penn Monthly, VII (December, 1876), 989.
Publishers' Weekly, X (September 16, 1876), 475.

Frothingham, Octavius Brooks. *Child's Book of Religion for Sunday-Schools and Homes.* (New York: G. P. Putnam's Sons)
Independent, XXVIII (December 7, 1876), 8.

Graham, Mary. *Grandfather's Last Work.* (Philadelphia: American Sunday-School Union)
Independent, XXVIII (December 21, 1876), 8.

Griffith, M. E. *Boys at Eastwick.* (Philadelphia: Presbyterian Board of Publication)
Publishers' Weekly, X (December 16, 1876), 1008.

Guernsey, Lucy E. and Clara F. *Washington and Seventy-Six.* (Philadelphia: American Sunday-School Union)
Independent, XXVIII (October 5, 1876), 9.
Publishers' Weekly, X (September 16, 1876), 474.

Hale, Edward Everett (ed.). *Silhouettes and Songs Illustrative of the Months.* Illus. by H. M. Hind. (Boston: Lockwood, Brooks & Co.)
Unitarian Review, V (January, 1876), 107.

Hall, John. *Familiar Talks to Boys.* (New York: Dodd, Mead & Co.)
Galaxy, XXII (September, 1876), 427.
Harper's Magazine, LIV (December, 1876), 150.
Independent, XXVIII (June 15, 1876), 10.
Publishers' Weekly, IX (June 3, 1876), 738.
Unitarian Review, VI (November, 1876), 569.

Hoffman, Professor ———. *Modern Magic.* (New York: George Routledge & Sons)
Nation, XXIII (December 21, 1876), 373.

Hopkins, I. T. *Floy Lindsley.* (New York: American Tract Society)
St. Nicholas, III (January, 1876), 204.

Hymns and Poems for Little Folks. (New York: Cassell, Petter & Galpin)
Publishers' Weekly, X (December 2, 1876), 948.

In Search of Truth; Conversations on the Bible and Popular Theology. (Publisher unknown)
Unitarian Review, VI (November, 1876), 566.

Jackson, Helen Hunt (H. H.) *Bits of Talk in Verse and Prose for Young Folks.* (Boston: Roberts Brothers)
Independent, XXVIII (November 23, 1876), 9.
Nation, XXIII (December 14, 1876), 359.
Publishers' Weekly, X (November 25, 1876), 920.

Johnson, Helen Kendrick. *Roddy's Ideal.* (New York: G. P. Putnam's Sons)
Independent, XXVIII (December 7, 1876), 8.
Nation, XXIII (December 7, 1876), 345.
Penn Monthly, VII (December, 1876), 989.
Publishers' Weekly, X (November 25, 1876), 920.

Johnson, Virginia W. (Cousin Virginia). *The Catskill Fairies.* (New York: Harper & Brothers)
Methodist Quarterly Review, XXVIII (January, 1876), 191.

Kavanagh, Bridget and Julia. *The Pearl Fountain and Other Fairy Tales.* (New York: Henry Holt & Co.)
Nation, XXIII (December 7, 1876), 345.
Publishers' Weekly, X (November 25, 1876), 918.

Kellogg, Elijah. *Brought to the Front.* (Boston: Lee & Shepard)
Literary World, VI (January, 1876), 116.

Kingston, William Henry Giles. *Snow-Shoes and Canoes; or, The Early Days of a Fur Trader in the Hudson Bay Territory.* (Philadelphia: J. B. Lippincott & Co.)
Nation, XXIII (December 21, 1876), 373.
Virginia; A Centennial Story. (Boston: D. Lothrop & Co.)
Independent, XXVIII (July 6, 1876), 9.
Publishers' Weekly, X (December 2, 1876), 948.

Kriege, Alma L. *Rhymes and Tales for the Kindergarten and Nursery.* (New York: E. Steiger)
Publishers' Weekly, X (November 25, 1876), 921.

Lathbury, Mary A. (Aunt May). *Fleda and the Voice.* (New York: Nelson & Phillips)
Publishers' Weekly, X (December 9, 1876), 977–78.

Lear, Edward. *Nonsense Songs.* (Boston: Roberts Brothers)
Publishers' Weekly, IX (June 17, 1876), 792–93.

Leland, Charles Godfrey. *Johnnykin and the Goblins.* (New York: Macmillan & Co.)

Independent, XXVIII (December 14, 1876), 8.
Nation, XXIII (December 14, 1876), 359.
Publishers' Weekly, X (November 25, 1876), 921.

Lippincott, Sara J. (Grace Greenwood). *Heads and Tails: Studies and Stories of Pets*. (New York: J. B. Ford & Co.)
St. Nicholas, III (January, 1876), 103.

Livingstone, Mrs. C. M. *Katy Hunter's Home*. (Boston: D. Lothrop & Co.)
Independent, XXVIII (July 6, 1876), 9.

Lloyd, Elizabeth. *Literature for Little Folks*. (New York: Sower, Potts & Co.)
Literary World, VI (April, 1876), 164.

Logie, Sarah E. C. (Sarah E. Chester). *Her Little World*. (New York: American Tract Society)
Publishers' Weekly, X (October 28, 1876), 703.
Proud Little Dody. (New York: American Tract Society)
St. Nicholas, III (January, 1876), 204.

Lukin, J. *Amongst Machines*. (New York: G. P. Putnam & Sons)
Independent, XXVIII (November 2, 1876), 9.
Literary World, VII (November, 1876), 88.

MacDonald, George. *A Double Story*. (Boston: D. Lothrop & Co.)
Scribner's Monthly, XI (February, 1876), 289.

Matéaux, Clara L. *Little Folks' Picture Album*. (New York: Cassell, Petter & Galpin)
Publishers' Weekly, X (November 25, 1876), 920.
Through Picture Land. (New York: Cassell, Petter & Galpin)
Publishers' Weekly, X (November 25, 1876), 920.

Mathews, Joanna H. and Julia A. *The Broken Mallet and the Pigeon's Eggs*. (New York: Robert Carter & Brothers)
Publishers' Weekly, X (November 4, 1876), 741.
Little Friends at Glenwood. (New York: Robert Carter & Brothers)
Publishers' Weekly, IX (April 8, 1876), 472.

Mathews, Julia A. *Uncle Joe's Thanksgiving*. (New York: Robert Carter & Brothers)
Publishers' Weekly, X (October 28, 1876), 703–04.

Millard, Harrison. *Silver Threads of Song*. (New York: S. T. Gordon & Son)
St. Nicholas, III (January, 1876), 204.

Miller, Emily Huntington. *What Tommy Did*. (Chicago: S. C. Griggs & Co.)
Independent, XXVIII (October 26, 1876), 9.
Publishers' Weekly, X (September 30, 1876), 572.

Miller, T. *Little Rosy's Pets*. (Boston: Congregational Publishing Society)
Independent, XXVIII (April 27, 1876), 10.
Publishers' Weekly, IX (April 8, 1876), 472.

Monroe, Mrs. L. B. *The Story of Our Country*. (Boston: Lockwood, Brooks & Co.)
Independent, XXVIII (October 26, 1876), 9.
Literary World, VII (November, 1876), 87.
New England Journal of Education, IV (November 11, 1876), 216.
Publishers' Weekly, X (October 14, 1876), 633–34.

Mulholland, Rosa. *Prince and Savior*. (Boston: Thomas B. Noonan & Co.)
Independent, XXVII (February 17, 1876), 12.

Newton, William W. *The Gate of the Temple*. (New York: T. Whittaker)
Independent, XXVIII (May 18, 1876), 9.
Publishers' Weekly, IX (May 6, 1876), 585.

Norton, John N. *The King's Ferryboat and Other Stories.* (New York: T. Whittaker)
Independent, XXVIII (November 23, 1876), 8.
Publishers' Weekly, X (November 25, 1876), 920.

Only a Dog. (New York: E. P. Dutton & Co.)
Publishers' Weekly, X (December 2, 1876), 947.

Palgrave, Francis Turner. *The Children's Treasury of English Song.* (New York: Macmillan & Co.)
Literary World, VI (January, 1876), 118.
Penn Monthly, VII (April, 1876), 332–33.
St. Nicholas, III (February, 1876), 270.

Perkins, H. S. and W. O. *The Shining River; A Collection of Music for Sunday-Schools.* (Boston: Oliver Ditson Co.)
St. Nicholas, III (January, 1876), 204.

Perry, Nora. *Bessie's Trials at Boarding School.* (Boston: D. Lothrop & Co.)
Appleton's Journal, XV (January 22, 1876), 123.
Independent, XXVIII (January 13, 1876), 10.

Phin, John. *Practical Hints on the Selection and Use of the Microscope.* (New York: Industrial Publication Society)
St. Nicholas, III (January, 1876), 204.

Pictures for Our Darlings. (Boston: D. Lothrop & Co.)
Publishers' Weekly, X (November 25, 1876), 919.

Pindar, Susan C. *The Wentworths; Their Home and Friends.* (Boston: D. Lothrop & Co.)
Independent, XXVIII (July 6, 1876), 9.

Pruyn, Mary. *Grandmama's Letters from Japan.* (Boston: James H. Earle)
Independent, XXVIII (December 21, 1876), 8.

Raffensperger, Mrs. A. F. *Little Stories for Good Little People.* (New York: American Tract Society)
Publishers' Weekly, X (November 4, 1876), 741.

Robinson, Leora Bettison. *The House with Spectacles.* (New York: G. P. Putnam & Sons)
Nation, XXIII (December 7, 1876), 345.
Publishers' Weekly, X (November 25, 1876), 920.

The Rose Library. (*Popular Literature of All Countries*). (New York: Scribner, Welford & Armstrong)
St. Nicholas, III (January, 1876), 204.

Samuels, Adelaide F. *Daisy Travers; or, The Girls of Hive Hall.* (Boston: Lee & Shepard)
Independent, XXVIII (December 7, 1876), 8.
Publishers' Weekly, X (November 25, 1876), 919.

Sanford, Mrs. D. P. *Frisk and His Flock.* (New York: E. P. Dutton & Co.)
St. Nicholas, III (January, 1876), 204.

Houseful of Children. (New York: E. P. Dutton & Co.)
Nation, XXIII (December 7, 1876), 345.
Publishers' Weekly, X (December 2, 1876), 946.

Sangster, Margaret E. *May Stanhope and Her Friends.* (New York: American Tract Society)
Publishers' Weekly, X (October 7, 1876), 602.

Splendid Times. (New York: American Tract Society)
St. Nicholas, III (January, 1876), 204.

Science in Sport Made Philosophy in Earnest. (New York: George Routledge & Sons)
Nation, XXIII (December 14, 1876), 359.

Scott, J. Walter. *The International Postage-Stamp Album.* (New York: J. W. Scott & Co.)
St. Nicholas, III (February, 1876), 270.

Scudder, Horace Elisha. *Doings of the Bodley Family in Town and Country.* (New York: Hurd & Houghton)
St. Nicholas, III (January, 1876), 103.

Shields, Mrs. S. A. (Sarah Annie Frost). *A Happy Summer; or, The Children's Journey.* (New York: American Tract Society)
Publishers' Weekly, X (October 7, 1876), 602.

Smith, Julia R. *How They Made a Man of Him.* (Springfield, Mass.: James D. Gill)
Publishers' Weekly, IX (April 29, 1876), 560.

Smith, Mary P. Wells (P. Thorne). *Jolly Good Times; or, Child Life on a Farm.* (Boston: Roberts Brothers)
St. Nicholas, III (January, 1876), 204.

Stedman, Edmund Clarence. *Victorian Poets.* (Boston: James R. Osgood & Co.)
St. Nicholas, III (January, 1876), 203.

Stockton, Frank R. *Tales Out of School.* (New York: Scribner, Armstrong & Co.)
St. Nicholas, III (January, 1876), 203.

Taylor, Bayard. *Boys of Other Countries.* (New York: G. P. Putnam's Sons)
Independent, XXVIII (November 2, 1876), 9.
Literary World, VII (November, 1876), 88.
Penn Monthly, VII (December, 1876), 988.
Publishers' Weekly, X (October 28, 1876), 702–03.

Terhune, Mary Virginia Hawes (Marion Harland). *My Little Love.* (New York: G. W. Carleton & Co.)
Publishers' Weekly, X (October 14, 1876), 634.

Tracy, C. C. *Myra; or, A Child's Story of Missionary Life.* (Boston: Congregational Publishing Society)
Independent, XXVIII (December 21, 1876), 8.
Publishers' Weekly, X (December 9, 1876), 977.

Trimmer, Sarah Kirby. *History of the Robins: for Instruction of Children on Treatment of Animals.* (London and New York: Thomas Nelson & Sons)
Harper's Magazine, LII (January, 1876), 297.

Trowbridge, John Townsend (Paul Creyton). *The Young Surveyor.* (Boston: James R. Osgood & Co.)
St. Nicholas, III (January, 1876), 203.

Tucker, Charlotte (A.L.O.E.). *The Golden Fleece.* (New York: Thomas Nelson & Sons)
Publishers' Weekly, IX (March 25, 1876), 407.

Uncle Herbert (pseud.). *The Prattler.* (Philadelphia: J. B. Lippincott & Co.)
Nation, XXIII (December 21, 1876), 373.

Verne, Jules. *Adventures of Captain Hatteras.* (Boston: James R. Osgood & Co.)
St. Nicholas, III (January, 1876), 204.

The Mysterious Island. (New York: Scribner, Armstrong & Co.)
Appleton's Journal, XV (January 8, 1876), 58.
Publishers' Weekly, IX (March 25, 1876), 407.

The Village School and Other Poems. (Philadelphia: J. B. Lippincott & Co.)
Independent, XXVIII (December 7, 1876), 8.

Water Lilies. (New York: National Temperance Society)
Independent, XXVIII (November 9, 1876), 9.
Publishers' Weekly, X (October 28, 1876), 703.

We Boys. Written by One of Us for the Amusement of Pa's and Ma's in General, Aunt Louisa in Particular. (Boston: Robert Brothers)

Independent, XXVIII (December 21, 1876), 8.
Nation, XXIII (December 21, 1876), 373.
New England Journal of Education, IV (December 16, 1876), 275.
Publishers' Weekly, X (December 9, 1876), 977.

Wendetè, Charles W. and H. S. Perkins. *The Sunny Side; A Book of Religious Songs for the Sunday-School and Home.* (New York: William A. Pond & Co.)
Unitarian Review, V (April, 1876), 452.

Whittier, John Greenleaf. *The Songs of Three Centuries.* (Boston: James R. Osgood & Co.)
St. Nicholas, III (March, 1876), 340.

Wide Awake Pleasure Book. (Boston: D. Lothrop & Co.)
Independent, XXVIII (December 21, 1876), 8.
Publishers' Weekly, X (November 25, 1876), 920.

Wise, Daniel (Francis Forrester; Lawrence Lancewood). *Winwood Cliff; or, Oscar, the Sailor's Son.* (Boston: Lee & Shepard)
Literary World, VII (December, 1876), 104.
New England Journal of Education, IV (November 25, 1876), 240.
Publishers' Weekly, X (December 2, 1876), 948.

Woodman, Charles H. *The Boys and Girls of the Revolution.* (Philadelphia: J. B. Lippincott & Co.)
Independent, XXVIII (December 7, 1876), 8.
Literary World, VII (December, 1876), 103.
Nation, XXIII (December 7, 1876), 345.
Publishers' Weekly, X (November 25, 1876), 920.

Woolsey, Sarah Chauncey (Susan Coolidge). *Nine Little Goslings.* (Boston: Roberts Brothers)
St. Nicholas, III (January, 1876), 203.
Scribner's Monthly, XI (April, 1876), 898.

Zerega, Katherine B. *The Children's Paradise.* (New York: G. P. Putnam & Sons)
Independent, XXVIII (December 21, 1876), 8.
Publishers' Weekly, X (December 9, 1876), 978.

BOOKS REVIEWED IN 1877

Abbott, Edward. *Long Look House.* (Boston: Noyes, Snow & Co.)
Appleton's Journal, N. S. II (January, 1877), 96.
Harper's Magazine, LIV (May, 1877), 924.

Out-Doors at Long Look. (Boston: Noyes, Snow & Co.)
Independent, XXIX (December 27, 1877), 11.
Nation, XXV (December 20, 1877), 385.

Adams, William T. (Oliver Optic). *Isles of the Sea; or, Young America Homeward Bound.* (Boston: Lee & Shepard)
Publishers' Weekly, XII (December 15, 1877), 824.

Out West; or, Roughing It on the Great Lakes. (Boston: Lee & Shepard)
Independent, XXIX (May 17, 1877), 10.

Alcott, Louisa May. *My Girls.* (Boston: Roberts Brothers)
Independent, XXIX (November 29, 1877), 10.

Rose in Bloom. (Boston: Roberts Brothers)
Unitarian Review, VII (January, 1877), 108.

Alden, Isabella (Pansy). *Chautauqua Girls at Home.* (Boston: D. Lothrop & Co.)
Independent, XXIX (August 23, 1877), 10.

Alger, Horatio, Jr. *Shifting for Himself; or, Gilbert Greyson's Fortunes.* (Boston: A. K. Loring)

Literary World, VII (January, 1877), 117.

Andrews, Jane. *Each and All; or, How the Seven Little Sisters Prove Their Sisterhood.* (Boston: Lee & Shepard)
Nation, XXV (December 6, 1877), 353.

Barker, Mrs. Sale. *Little Blue Bell's Picture Book.* (New York: George Routledge & Sons)
Literary World, VIII (December, 1877), 124.

Little Curly Pate's Story Book. (New York: George Routledge & Sons)
Literary World, VIII (December, 1877), 124.

Little Rosy Cheek's Picture Book. (New York: George Routledge & Sons)
Literary World, VIII (December, 1877), 124.

Barr, Lillie E. *Coral and Christian; or, The Children's Pilgrim's Progress.* (New York: W. B. Mucklow)
Publishers' Weekly, XII (November 10, 1877), 556.

Bartlett, Mary C. *Real Boys and Girls.* (Boston: Lockwood, Brooks & Co.)
Independent, XXIX (December 6, 1877), 10.

Bates, Clara Doty. *Classics of Babyland.* (Boston: D. Lothrop & Co.)
Independent, XXIX (January 4, 1877), 8.
Literary World, VII (January, 1877), 124.

Bayard, Emile. *The Story of a Wooden Horse.* Translated from the French by Mrs. Sale Barker. (New York: George Routledge & Sons)
Literary World, VIII (December, 1877), 124.

Ben Blinker. (Boston: Lee & Shepard)
Literary World, VIII (November, 1877), 94.

Brave Little Heart. (New York: George Routledge & Sons)
Literary World, VIII (December, 1877), 124.

Brooks, Noah. *The Boy Emigrants.* (New York: Scribner, Armstrong & Co.)
Appleton's Journal, N.S. II (January, 1877), 96.
Harper's Magazine, LIV (January, 1877), 308.
Scribner's Monthly, XIII (January, 1877), 424.

Cahun, Leon. *The Adventures of Captain Mago; or, A Phoenician Expedition, 1000 B.C.* (New York: Scribner, Armstrong & Co.)
Appleton's Journal, N.S. II (January, 1877), 96.
Harper's Magazine, LIV (January, 1877), 307.
Scribner's Monthly, XIII (January, 1877), 423.

Capron, Mary J. (Archie Fell). *Gold and Gilt; or, Maybee's Puzzle.* (Boston: Henry Hoyt & Co.)
Nation, XXV (December 6, 1877), 353.

Champney, Lizzie W. *All Around a Palette.* (Boston: Lockwood, Brooks & Co.)
Independent, XXIX (December 13, 1877), 10.
Literary World, VIII (December, 1877), 124.

In the Sky Garden. (Boston: Lockwood, Brooks & Co.)
Literary World, VII (January, 1877), 118.
Unitarian Review, VII (January, 1877), 108.

Chaney, George Leonard. *Tom: A Home Story.* (Boston: Roberts Brothers)
Independent, XXIX (November 29, 1877), 10.
Literary World, VIII (December, 1877), 123–24.

Charles, Elizabeth R. *Note Book of the Bertram Family.* (New York: Dodd, Mead & Co.)
Unitarian Review, VII (January, 1877), 108.

Chatterbox for 1876–1877. (New York: American News Co.)
Literary World, VII (January, 1877), 116.

Chatterbox for 1877–1878. (New York: American News Co.)
Publishers' Weekly, XII (November 3, 1877), 521.

Chatterbox Junior. (New York: World Publishing Co.)
Publishers' Weekly, XII (September 1, 1877), 213.

The Christmas Story-Teller: By Old Hands and New Ones. (New York: Scribner, Welford & Armstrong)
St. Nicholas, V (December, 1877), 166.

Clarke, Rebecca (Sophie May). *Doctor Papa.* (Boston: Lee & Shepard)
Independent, XXIX (June 21, 1877), 9.
Publishers' Weekly, XI (June 16, 1877), 659.
Unitarian Review, VIII (September, 1877), 348.

Quinnebasset Girls. (Boston: Lee & Shepard)
Publishers' Weekly, XII (December 15, 1877), 823–24.

Coffin, Charles Carleton (Carleton). *The Boys of '76.* (New York: Harper & Brothers)
Appleton's Journal, N.S. II (January, 1877), 96.
Harper's Magazine, LIV (January, 1877), 306.

Cox, G. W. *Tales of Ancient Greece.* 3rd ed. (Chicago: Jansen, McClurg & Co.)
Nation, XXV (December 6, 1877), 353.
Publishers' Weekly, XII (December 1, 1877), 782.

Cozzens, Samuel Woodworth. *Crossing the Quicksands.* (Boston: Lee & Shepard)
Independent, XXIX (June 21, 1877), 9.
Publishers' Weekly, XI (June 16, 1877), 658.

Cragin, Louisa T. (Ellis Gray). *The Cedars; More of Child Life.* (Boston: Lockwood, Brooks & Co.)
Literary World, VIII (December, 1877), 124.
Nation, XXV (December 20, 1877), 385.

Long Ago; A Year of Child Life. (Boston: Lockwood, Brooks & Co.)
Harper's Magazine, LIV (February, 1877), 471.
Unitarian Review, VII (January, 1877), 108.

Cragin, Mary A. (Joy Allison). *David Kent's Ambition.* (Boston: Congregational Publishing Society)
Publishers' Weekly, XII (December 15, 1877), 825.

Craigie, Mary E. *Once Upon a Time: Stories of the Ancient Gods and Heroes.* (New York: G. P. Putnam's Sons)
Harper's Magazine, LIV (January, 1877), 308.

Crane, Walter. *The Baby's Opera.* (New York: McLoughlin Brothers)
Literary World, VIII (June, 1877), 5–6.

The Baby's Opera. (New York: George Routledge & Sons)
Literary World, VIII (June, 1877), 5–6.

De Morgan, Mary. *On a Pincushion, and Other Fairy Tales.* (New York: E. P. Dutton & Co.)
Literary World, VIII (December, 1877), 124.
Nation, XXV (November 15, 1877), 305.

Deering, Mary S. *Phil, Rob, and Louis; or, Haps and Mishaps of Three Average Boys.* (Portland, Me.: Dresser, McClellan & Co.)
Publishers' Weekly, XII (November 17, 1877), 584.

Diaz, Abby Morton. *The Jimmyjohns and Other Stories.* (Boston: James R. Osgood & Co.)
Publishers' Weekly, XII (November 17, 1877), 583.

Dodge, Mary Mapes. *Baby Days.* (New York: Scribner & Co.)
Literary World, VIII (December, 1877), 123.

St. Nicholas, V (December, 1877), 166.
Scribner's Monthly, XV (December, 1877), 283.

Eckerson, Margaret H. *Flossy and Bossy Stories.* (Boston: D. Lothrop & Co.)
Nation, XXV (December 20, 1877), 385.

Eggleston, George Cary. *Captain Sam; or, The Boy Scout of 1814.* (New York: G. P. Putnam's Sons)
Appleton's Journal, N.S. II (January, 1877), 96.
Harper's Magazine, LIV (January, 1877), 308.

The Signal Boys; or, Captain Sam's Company. (New York: G. P. Putnam's Sons)
Nation, XXV (December 6, 1877), 352.
Publishers' Weekly, XII (November 17, 1877), 583.

Ewing, Juliana Horatia (Aunt Judy). *A Great Emergency, and Other Tales.* (Boston: Roberts Brothers)
Independent, XXIX (November 29, 1877), 10.
Literary World, VIII (December, 1877), 124.

Jan of the Windmill; Story of the Plains. (Boston: Roberts Brothers)
Harper's Magazine, LIV (March, 1877), 618.
Lippincott's Magazine, XIX (February, 1877), 264.
Scribner's Monthly, XIV (September, 1877), 720–21.
Unitarian Review, VII (January, 1877), 108.

Farman, Ella. *Mrs. Hurd's Niece.* (Boston: D. Lothrop & Co.)
Independent, XXIX (January 4, 1877), 8.

Field, Marie E. *The Wings of Courage.* (New York: G. P. Putnam's Sons)
Lippincott's Magazine, XX (December, 1877), 776.
Nation, XXV (November 15, 1877), 305.
Publishers' Weekly, XII (October 20, 1877), 305.
St. Nicholas, V (December, 1877), 166.

Finley, Martha F. (Martha Farquharson). *Elsie's Children.* (New York: Dodd, Mead & Co.)
Nation, XXV (November 15, 1877), 304.
Publishers' Weekly, XII (November 3, 1877), 521–22.

Elsie's Motherhood. (New York: Dodd, Mead & Co.)
Galaxy, XXXIII (February, 1877), 285.
Harper's Magazine, LIV (January, 1877), 307.
Unitarian Review, VII (January, 1877), 108.

Floyd, Cornelia (Neil Forrest). *Some Other Babies, Very Much Like Helen's Only More So.* (Boston: Roberts Brothers)
Literary World, VII (February, 1877), 143.

Follen, Eliza Lee. *A Well-Spent Hour.* (New York: T. Y. Crowell)
Independent, XXIX (August 16, 1877), 10.
Literary World, VIII (November, 1877), 94.

Gassett, Mrs. ———. *Sunbeam's Picture Books.* (New York: George Routledge & Sons)
Literary World, VIII (December, 1877), 124.

Hall, C. W. *Adrift in the Ice-Fields.* (Boston: Lee & Shepard)
Nation, XXV (November 15, 1877), 304.
Publishers' Weekly, XII (November 3, 1877), 519–20.

Hallowell, Sarah C. *Nan; the New-Fashioned Girl.* (Boston: D. Lothrop & Co.)
Nation, XXV (November 15, 1877), 304.

Hamilton, Kate W. (Fleeta). *We Three.* (Philadelphia: Presbyterian Board of Publication)
Publishers' Weekly, XII (September 29, 1877), 371.

Happy Days for Boys and Girls. (Philadelphia: Porter & Coates)

Independent, XXIX (November 1, 1877), 9.
Publishers' Weekly, XII (September 1, 1877), 213.

Higginson, Thomas Wentworth. *Young Folks' Book of American Explorers*. (Boston: Lee & Shepard)
Literary World, VII (April, 1877), 173–74.
Nation, XXIV (April 26, 1877), 254.
Publishers' Weekly, XI (April 14, 1877), 429.
Western, III (May, 1877), 310.

Hoffman, Professor ——. *Modern Magic*. (New York: George Routledge & Sons)
Literary World, VIII (December, 1877), 124.

Holt, Emily Sarah. *Lettice Eden*. (New York: Robert Carter & Brothers)
Publishers' Weekly, XII (December 15, 1877), 826.

Hope, Arthur. *A Manual of Sorrento and Inlaid Work for Amateurs, with Original Designs*. (Chicago: John Wilkinson; New York: G. P. Putnam's Sons)
Nation, XXV (December 6, 1877), 353.

Houdin, Robert. *Secrets of Conjuring and Magic*. (New York: George Routledge & Sons)
Literary World, VIII (December, 1877), 124.
Nation, XXV (December 6, 1877), 353.

Hoyt, Mrs. K. C. *Janet et Ses Amis*. (New York: D. Appleton & Co.)
Appleton's Journal, N.S. II (January, 1877), 96.
Atlantic Monthly, XXXIX (January, 1877), 116.

Hughes, Kate E. (trans.). *The Little Pearls; or, Gems of Virtue*. (New York: P. O'Shea)
Catholic World, XXV (August, 1877), 718.

Jackson, Helen Hunt (H. H.). *Bits of Talk in Verse and Prose for Young Folks*. (Boston: Roberts Brothers)
St. Nicholas, IV (January, 1877), 230.
Unitarian Review, VII (January, 1877), 108.

Johnson, Helen Kendrick. *Roddy's Ideal*. (New York: G. P. Putnam's Sons)
Appleton's Journal, N.S. II (January, 1877), 96.

Kavanagh, Bridget and Julia. *The Pearl Fountain, and Other Fairy Tales*. (New York: Henry Holt & Co.)
Appleton's Journal, N.S. II (January, 1877), 96.
Literary World, VII (January, 1877), 119.

Keary, Eliza. *The Magic Valley; or, Patient Antoine*. (London and New York: Macmillan & Co.)
Independent, XXIX (December 6, 1877), 10.
Nation, XXV (December 20, 1877), 385.

Kellogg, Elijah. *The Mission of the Black Rifle; or, On the Trail*. (Boston: Lee & Shepard)
Independent, XXIX (January 4, 1877), 8.
Literary World, VII (January, 1877), 117.

Kingston, William Henry Giles. *Voyage of the Steadfast*. (Boston: D. Lothrop & Co.)
Independent, XXIX (October 11, 1877), 9.
Literary World, VIII (November, 1877), 94.
Nation, XXV (December 6, 1877), 352.
Publishers' Weekly, XII (September 29, 1877), 371.

Kirkland, Elizabeth S. *Dora's Housekeeping*. (Chicago: Jansen, McClurg & Co.)
Nation, XXV (December 20, 1877), 385.

Six Little Cooks; or, Aunt Jane's Cooking Class. (Chicago: Jansen, McClurg & Co.)
Independent, XXIX (May 3, 1877), 10.

377

Literary World, VIII (June, 1877), 10.
Publishers' Weekly, XI (April 21, 1877), 14.
St. Nicholas, V (December, 1877), 166.

Lamb, Charles and Mary. *Poetry for Children and Prince Dorus.* (New York: Scribner, Armstrong & Co.)
Nation, XXV (December 20, 1877), 385–86.

Larned, August A. *Old Tales Retold from Grecian Mythology in Talks Around the Fire.* (New York: Nelson & Phillips; Cincinnati: Hitchcock & Walden)
Independent, XXIX (February 15, 1877), 10.
Methodist Quarterly Review, XXIX (April, 1877), 376.

Lathbury, Mary A. (Aunt May). *Fleda and the Voice.* (New York: Nelson & Phillips)
Independent, XXIX (January 4, 1877), 8.

Lawrence, Margaret W. *The Home Garden.* (New York: American Tract Society)
Harper's Magazine, LIV (January, 1877), 308.

Leland, Charles Godfrey. *Johnnykin and the Goblins* (New York: Macmillan & Co.)
Literary World, VII (January, 1877), 117.

Little Folks. (New York: American News Co.)
Literary World, VII (January, 1877), 116.

Logie, Sarah E. C. (Sarah E. Chester). *Betty and Her Cousin Harry.* (New York: American Tract Society)
St. Nicholas, V (December, 1877), 166.

Her Little World. (New York: American Tract Society)
Harper's Magazine, LIV (January, 1877), 307.

Lukin, J. *Amongst Machines.* (New York: G. P. Putnam's Sons)
Appleton's Journal, N. S. II (January, 1877), 96.
Harper's Magazine, LIV (January, 1877), 307.

Macy, W. H. *There She Blows! or; The Log of the Arethusa.* (Boston: Lee & Shepard)
Publishers' Weekly, XII (December 15, 1877), 824.

Matéaux, Clara L. *Through Picture Land.* (New York: Cassell, Petter & Galpin)
Harper's Magazine, LIV (January, 1877), 308.
Literary World, VII (January, 1877), 116.

Mathews, Cornelius. *The Enchanted Moccasins, and Other Legends of the American Indians.* 3rd ed. (New York: G. P. Putnam's Sons)
Nation, XXV (December 6, 1877), 352.

Mathews, Joanna H. and Julia A. *Blackberry Jam.* (New York: Robert Carter & Brothers)
Publishers' Weekly, XII (September 22, 1877), 347.

The Broken Mallet and the Pigeon's Eggs. (New York: Robert Carter & Brothers)
Harper's Magazine, LIV (January, 1877), 307.

Mathews, Julia A. *Jack Granger's Cousin.* (Boston: Roberts Brothers)
Literary World, VIII (November, 1877), 94.
Publishers' Weekly, XII (October 27, 1877), 492.

Uncle Joe's Thanksgiving. (New York: Robert Carter & Brothers)
Harper's Magazine, LIV (January, 1877), 307.

Miller, Emily Huntington. *Captain Fritz; His Friends and Adventures.* (New York: E. P. Dutton & Co.)
Literary World, VIII (December, 1877), 123.

What Tommy Did. (Chicago: S. C. Griggs & Co.)
Independent, XXIX (May 24, 1877), 10.

St. Nicholas, IV (January, 1877), 230.

Miller, Mrs. J. A. (Faith Latimer). *Dear Old Stories Told Once More.* (New York: American Tract Society)
Publishers' Weekly, XII (December 1, 1877), 782–83.

Mitchell, Donald G. (Ik. Marvel). *About Old Story-Tellers; Of How and When They Lived, and What Stories They Told.* (New York: Scribner, & Armstrong Co.)
Independent, XXIX (December 6, 1877), 10.
Nation, XXV (December 6, 1877), 353.
St. Nicholas, V (December, 1877), 166.

Molesworth, Mrs. Mary Louisa (Ennis Graham). *The Cuckoo Clock.* (London: Macmillan & Co.)
Independent, XXIX (December 6, 1877), 10.
Nation, XXV (December 6, 1877), 353.

Monroe, Mrs. L. B. *The Story of Our Country.* (Boston: Lockwood, Brooks & Co.)
Unitarian Review, VII (February, 1877), 226.

Mortimer, Mrs. M. *Peep of Day.* (New York: Robert Carter & Brothers)
Harper's Magazine, LIV (January, 1877), 308.

Mother Goose's Nursery Rhymes. (New York: McLoughlin Brothers)
Publishers' Weekly, XI (January 6, 1877), 18.

Newton, W. Wilberforce. *Little and Wise.* (New York: Robert Carter & Brothers)
Independent, XXIX (May 24, 1877), 9.
Publishers' Weekly, XI (March 24, 1877), 331.

Our Children's Songs. (New York: Harper & Brothers)
Harper's Magazine, LVI (December, 1877), 147.
Independent, XXIX (November 15, 1877), 10.
Literary World, VIII (December, 1877), 124.
Publishers' Weekly, XII (November 17, 1877), 582.

Pabke, Marie, and Marie J. Pitman. *Wonder-World Stories from the Chinese, French, German, Hebrew, Hindoostanee, Hungarian, Irish, Italian, Japanese, Russian, Swedish, and Turkish.* (New York: G. P. Putnam's Sons)
Nation, XXV (December 6, 1877), 352–53.
Publishers' Weekly, XII (December 1, 1877), 781.

Paull, Mrs. H. B. *Only a Cat; Autobiography of Tom Blackman.* (New York: T. Whittaker)
Independent, XXIX (December 13, 1877), 10.
Publishers' Weekly, XII (December 15, 1877), 826.

The Picture Album. (New York: Cassell, Petter, Galpin & Co.)
Harper's Magazine, LIV (January, 1877), 308.

Pollard, Josephine. *The Other Gypsy.* (New York: Nelson & Phillips)
Independent, XXIX (January 4, 1877), 8.

Robinson, Leora Bettison. *Patsy; A Story for Girls.* (New York: G. P. Putnam's Sons)
Lippincott's Magazine, XX (December, 1877), 776.
Publishers' Weekly, XII (October 27, 1877), 492.

Roe, E. Payson. *Near to Nature's Heart.* (New York: Dodd, Mead & Co.)
Unitarian Review, VII (January, 1877), 108.

Round, William M. F. (Rev. P. Pennot). *Child Marian Abroad.* (Boston: Lee & Shepard)
Independent, XXIX (December 13, 1877), 10.

St. Nicholas. (New York: Scribner & Co.)
Independent, XXIX (November 22, 1877), 10.
Literary World, VIII (December, 1877), 123.

Sanford, Mrs. D. P. *A Houseful of Children.* (New York: E. P. Dutton & Co.)
Literary World, VII (January, 1877), 124.

The Little Brown House and the Children Who Lived in It. (New York: E. P. Dutton & Co.)
Literary World, VIII (December, 1877), 124.
Publishers' Weekly, XII (December 1, 1877), 782.

Sangster, Margaret E. *May Stanhope and Her Friends.* (New York: American Tract Society)
Harper's Magazine, LIV (January, 1877), 307.

Scudder, Horace Elisha. *The Bodleys Telling Stories.* (New York: Hurd & Houghton)
Appleton's Journal, N. S. III (December, 1877), 576.
Atlantic Monthly, XL (December, 1877), 761–63.
Literary World, VIII (November, 1877), 94.
Nation, XXV (November 15, 1877), 304–05.
Publishers' Weekly, XII (September 22, 1877), 345–46.
St. Nicholas, V (December, 1877), 166.
Scribner's Monthly, XV (December, 1877), 282–83.

Doings of the Bodley Family in Town and Country. (New York: Hurd & Houghton)
Atlantic Monthly, XL (December, 1877), 761–63.

Sherwood, Mary Martha. *The Flowers of the Forest.* (New York: Robert Carter & Brothers)
Harper's Magazine; LIV (January, 1877), 307.

The Little Woodman. (New York: Robert Carter & Brothers)
Harper's Magazine, LIV (January, 1877), 307.

Shields, Mrs. S. A. (Sarah Annie Frost). *A Happy Summer; or, The Children's Journey.* (New York: American Tract Society)
Harper's Magazine, LIV (January, 1877), 308.

Smith, J. Moyr (illus.). *The Prince of Argolis.* (New York: Henry Holt & Co.)
Independent, XXIX (December 6, 1877), 10.
Nation, XXV (December 20, 1877), 385.

Smith, Mary P. Wells (P. Thorne). *Jolly Good Times at School; also Some Times Not Quite So Jolly.* (Boston: Roberts Brothers)
Independent, XXIX (November 29, 1877), 10.
Literary World, VIII (December, 1877), 124.

Talbot, C. R. (John Brownjohn; Magnus Merriwether). *Adventures of Miltiades Peterkin Paul.* (Boston: D. Lothrop & Co.)
Literary World, VIII (December, 1877), 124.
Publishers' Weekly, XII (November 17, 1877), 583.

Talbot, Eleanor W. *Jack O'Lantern.* (New York: Robert Carter & Brothers)
Publishers' Weekly, XII (September 29, 1877), 372.

Taylor, Bayard. *Boys of Other Countries.* (New York: G. P. Putnam's Sons)
Appleton's Journal, N. S. II (January, 1877), 96.
Galaxy, XXIII (January, 1877), 139.
Harper's Magazine, LIV (January, 1877), 307–08.
St. Nicholas, V (November, 1877), 70.
Scribner's Monthly, XIV (May, 1877), 120.

Uncle Herbert (pseud.). *The Prattler.* (Philadelphia: J. B. Lippincott & Co.)
Harper's Magazine, LIV (January, 1877), 308.
Literary World, VII (January, 1877), 118.

Uno (pseud.). *Baby Ballads.* (Boston: Lee & Shepard)
Literary World, VIII (December, 1877), 124.
Publishers' Weekly, XII (October 27, 1877), 492.

Verne, Jules. *Michael Strogoff, the Courier of the Czar.* Translated by W. H. G. Kingston. (New York: Scribner, Armstrong & Co.)
Appleton's Journal, N. S. II (April, 1877), 384.
Harper's Magazine, LIV (April, 1877), 772.
Independent, XXIX (February 8, 1877), 10.
Literary World, VII (March, 1877), 159
Publishers' Weekly, XI (January 27, 1877), 89.

Walton, Mrs. O. F. *A Peep Behind the Scenes.* (New York: Robert Carter & Brothers)
Independent, XXIX (July 19, 1877), 9.
Publishers' Weekly, XII (July 28, 1877), 121.

Warner, Anna B. (Amy Lothrop). *Vinegar Hill Stories.* (New York: Robert Carter & Brothers)
Harper's Magazine, LIV (January, 1877), 307.

Warner, Anna B. (Amy Lothrop) and Susan Bogert Warner (Elizabeth Wetherell). *The Gold of Chickaree.* (New York: G. P. Putnam's Sons)
Unitarian Review, VII (January, 1877), 108.

Warner, Charles Dudley. *Being a Boy.* (Boston: James R. Osgood & Co.)
Atlantic Monthly, XL (December, 1877), 763–64.
Literary World, VIII (December, 1877), 124.

Warner, Susan Bogert (Elizabeth Wetherell). *Pine Needles.* (New York: Robert Carter & Brothers)
Publishers' Weekly, XI (March 24, 1877), 330.

We Boys. Written by One of Us for the Amusement of Pa's and Ma's in General, Aunt Louisa in Particular. (Boston: Roberts Brothers)
Literary World, VII (January, 1877), 116.
Unitarian Review, VII (January, 1877), 108.

Wheaton, Campbell. *Six Sinners.* (New York: G. P. Putnam's Sons)
Lippincott's Magazine, XX (December, 1877), 776.
Nation, XXV (November 15, 1877), 304.
Publishers' Weekly, XII (October 20, 1877), 468–69.

Woodman, Charles H. *The Boys and Girls of the Revolution.* (Philadelphia: J. B. Lippincott & Co.)
Harper's Magazine, LIV (January, 1877), 308.

Wright, Julia McNair. *A Strange Sea Story.* (New York: National Temperance Society)
Independent, XXIX (January 4, 1877), 8.

BOOKS REVIEWED IN 1878

Adams, William T. (Oliver Optic). *Lake Breezes; or, The Cruise of the Sylvania.* (Boston: Lee & Shepard)
Literary World World, IX (December, 1878), 107.
Publishers' Weekly, XIV (November 2, 1878), 539.

Alcott, Louisa May. *My Girls.* (Boston: Roberts Brothers)
Harper's Magazine, LVI (February, 1878), 470.
Literary World, VIII (January, 1878), 142.
St. Nicholas, V (January, 1878), 238.

Under the Lilacs. (Boston: Roberts Brothers)
Literary World, IX (November, 1878), 95.
Publishers' Weekly, XIV (October 26, 1878), 506.

Alcott, Louisa May and Others. *Merry Times for Boys and Girls.* (Philadelphia: Porter & Coates)
Literary World, IX (December, 1878), 106.
Publishers' Weekly, XIV (November 2, 1878), 539.

Alden, Isabella (Pansy). *Links in Rebecca's Life.* (Boston: D. Lothrop & Co.)
Independent, XXX (June 13, 1878), 9.

Andrews, Jane. *Each and All; or, How the Seven Little Sisters Prove Their Sisterhood.* (Boston: Lee & Shepard)
Literary World, VIII (January, 1878), 143.

Aunt Effie's Rhymes for Little Children. (New York: George Routledge & Sons)
Literary World, IX (December, 1878), 106.

Aunt Kate's Gems. (New York: McLoughlin Brothers)
Literary World, IX (December, 1878), 106.

Barbaud, Anna Letitia. *Hymns in Prose.* (New York: Thomas Nelson & Sons)
Literary World, IX (December, 1878), 106.

Barker, Mrs. Sale. *Little Wide-Awake.* (New York: George Routledge & Sons)
Literary World, IX (December, 1878), 105.

Little Wide-Awake Picture Book. (New York: George Routledge & Sons)
Literary World, IX (December, 1878), 105–06.

Picture Story Album for Girls. (New York: George Routledge & Sons)
Literary World, VIII (January, 1878), 143.

Barkley, H. C. *My Boyhood.* (New York: E. P. Dutton & Co.)
Harper's Magazine, LVIII (December, 1878), 151.
Literary World, IX (December, 1878), 106.
Nation, XXVII (November 28, 1878), 340.
Publishers' Weekly, XIV (October 5, 1878), 420.

Bartlett, Mary C. *Real Boys and Girls.* (Boston: Lockwood, Brooks & Co.)
Literary World, VIII (January, 1878), 143.

Bates, Clara Doty. *More Classics of Babyland.* (Boston: D. Lothrop & Co.)
Literary World, IX (December 10, 1878), 125.

Bates, Miss L. *The Image Unveiled.* (New York: National Temperance Society)
Independent, XXX (June 13, 1878), 9.

Beesly, Mrs. ———. *Stories from the History of Rome.* (New York: Macmillan & Co.)
Nation, XXVII (November 7, 1878), 288.

Bell, Lucia C. *True Blue.* (Boston: D. Lothrop & Co.)
Literary World, IX (December 10, 1878), 124.

Bennett, William D. *A History of Methodism for Our Young People.* (Cincinnati: Hitchcock & Walden)
Methodist Quarterly Review, XXX (April, 1878), 387.

Bewick, Thomas. *Select Fables.* (London: Longmans, Green & Co.)
Nation, XXVII (November 28, 1878), 339.

Brenda (pseud.). *Lotty's Visit to Grandmamma.* (New York: E. P. Dutton & Co.)
Literary World, VIII (January, 1878), 143.

Brine, Mary D. *Bessie, the Cash Girl.* (New York: Nelson & Phillips; Cincinnati: Hitchcock and Walden)
Independent, XXX (June 13, 1878), 10.
Methodist Quarterly Review, XXX (April, 1878), 387.

Bunce, John Thackeray. *Fairy Tales; Their Origin and Meaning.* (New York: D. Appleton & Co.)
Nation, XXVII (December 19, 1878), 389.

Butts, Mrs. M. F. *Frolic and Her Friends.* (New York: American Tract Society)
Harper's Magazine, LVI (January, 1878), 311.

Caldecott, Randolph. *The House That Jack Built.* (New York: George Routledge & Sons)
Literary World, IX (December, 1878), 106.
Nation, XXVII (December 19, 1878), 389.

John Gilpin. (New York: George Routledge & Sons)
Literary World, IX (December, 1878), 106.
Nation, XXVII (December 19, 1878), 389.

Calkins, N. A., and Abby Morton Diaz. *Prang's Natural History Series for Children.* (Boston: L. Prang & Co.)
Nation, XXVII (December 12, 1878), 373.

Capron, Mary J. (Archie Fell). *Gold and Gilt; or, Maybee's Puzzle.* (Boston: Henry Hoyt)
Harper's LVI (February, 1878), 470.

Carey, Annie. *The History of a Book.* (London: Cassell, Petter, Galpin & Co.)
Western, IV (January-February, 1878), 84.

Champney, Lizzie W. *All Around a Palette.* (Boston: Lockwood, Brooks & Co.)
Harper's Magazine, LVI (February, 1878), 470.
St. Nicholas, V (February, 1878), 302.

Chaney, George Leonard. *Tom, a Home Story.* (Boston: Roberts Brothers)
Harper's Magazine, LVI (February, 1878), 470.

Charlesworth, Maria Louisa. *The Old Looking-Glass; or, Mrs. Dorothy Cope's Recollections.* (New York: Robert Carter & Brothers)
Publishers' Weekly, XIII (February 2, 1878), 142.

Childhood's Wonders. (New York: McLoughlin Brothers)
Literary World, IX (December, 1878), 106.

Church, Alfred J. *Stories from Homer.* (New York: Harper & Brothers)
Appleton's Journal, N.S. V. (August, 1878), 192.
Harper's Magazine, LVII (June, 1878), 149.
Literary World, IX (June, 1878), 7.
Publishers' Weekly, XIII (April 27, 1878), 425.

Clark, E. Warren. *Life and Adventures in Japan.* (New York: American Tract Society)
St. Nicholas, VI (December, 1878), 142.

Clarke, Rebecca (Sophie May). *Little Pitchers.* (Boston: Lee & Shepard)
Literary World, IX (December 10, 1878), 124.

Quinnebasset Girls. (Boston: Lee & Shepard)
Harper's Magazine, LVI (February, 1878), 470.
Literary World, VIII (January, 1878), 143.

Cobb, James F. *Heroes of Charity.* (New York: American Tract Society)
St. Nicholas, VI (December, 1878), 142.

Cobden, Paul. *Little Lights Along the Shore.* (New York: Robert Carter & Brothers)
Literary World, IX (December, 1878), 106.
Publishers' Weekly, XIV (October 19, 1878), 479.

Coffin, Charles Carleton (Carleton). *Story of Liberty.* (New York: Harper & Brothers)
Nation, XXVII (December, 1878), 389.

Colomb, Mary. *Uncle Chesterton's Heir.* (New York: George Routledge & Sons)
Literary World, IX (December 10, 1878), 124.

Cooke, F. E. *Guiding Lights.* (New York: American Tract Society)
St. Nicholas, VI (December, 1878), 142.

Cooke, Rose Terry. *Happy Dodd.* (Boston: Henry Hoyt)
Literary World, IX (December 10, 1878), 124.

Cox, G. W. *Tales of Ancient Greece.* (Chicago: Jansen, McClurg & Co.)
Literary World, VIII (February, 1878), 161.

Cragin, Louisa T. (Ellis Gray). *The Cedars; More of Child Life.* (Boston: Lockwood, Brooks & Co.)

Harper's Magazine, LVI (January, 1878), 311.

Crane, Walter. *Baby's Bouquet.* (New York: George Routledge & Sons)
Literary World, IX (December 10, 1878), 124.

The Baby's Opera. (New York: McLoughlin Brothers)
Literary World, IX (December, 1878), 106.

Cupples, George. *The Green Hand.* (New York: George Routledge & Sons)
Literary World, IX (December 10, 1878), 124.

Daniels, W. H. *That Boy; Who Shall Save Him?* (Cincinnati: Hitchcock & Walden)
Independent, XXX (June 13, 1878), 10.

De Morgan, Mary. *On a Pincushion, and Other Fairy Tales.* (New York: E. P. Dutton & Co.)
Atlantic Monthly, XLI (January, 1878), 137–38.

Defoe, Daniel. *The Life and Adventures of Robinson Crusoe.* (New York: James Miller)
Literary World, IX (December, 1878), 106.

Diaz, Abby Morton. *The Jimmyjohns and Other Stories.* (Boston: James R. Osgood & Co.)
Atlantic Monthly, XLI (January, 1878), 137–39.
Literary World, VIII (January, 1878), 143.

Dodge, Mary Mapes. *Hans Brinker; or, The Silver Skates.* (New York: Scribner, Armstrong & Co.)
Literary World, VIII (January, 1878), 143.

Eggleston, Edward and Mrs. L. E. Seelye. *Tecumseh and the Shawnee Prophet.* (New York: Dodd, Mead & Co.)
Literary World, IX (November, 1878), 95.

Eggleston, George Cary. *The Signal Boys; or, Captain Sam's Company.* (New York: G. P. Putnam's Sons)
Atlantic Monthly, XLI (January, 1878), 137–39.

Ellis, Mrs. Charles. *Summer in Normandy.* (New York: George Routledge & Sons)
Nation, XXVII (November 28, 1878), 339.

Every-day Experiences at Eton. (New York: George R. Lockwood)
St. Nicholas, V (January, 1878), 238.

Field, Marie E. *The Wings of Courage.* (New York: G. P. Putnam's Sons)
Atlantic Monthly, XLI (January, 1878), 137–39.
Harper's Magazine, LVI (January, 1878), 310.

Finley, Martha F. (Martha Farquharson). *Mildred Keith.* (New York: Dodd, Mead & Co.)
Literary World, IX (November, 1878), 95.

Fosdick, Charles A. (Harry Castlemon). *The Boy Traders; or, The Sportsman's Club Among the Boers.* (Philadelphia: Porter & Coates)
Literary World, VIII (March, 1878), 182.
St. Nicholas, V (February, 1878), 302.

The Boy Trapper. (Philadelphia: Porter & Coates)
Publishers' Weekly, XIV (October 19, 1878), 479.
St. Nicholas, VI (December, 1878), 141.

The Buried Treasure; or, Old Jordan's Haunt. (Philadelphia: Porter & Coates)
Literary World, IX (June, 1878), 16.
Publishers' Weekly, XIII (March 30, 1878), 353.

Foster, Mrs. I. H. (Faye Huntington). *Echoing and Re-Echoing.* (Boston: D. Lothrop & Co.)
Independent, XXX (June 13, 1878), 9.

Frith, Henry. *Picture-Story Album for Boys.* (New York: George Routledge & Sons)
Literary World, VIII (January, 1878), 143.

Gerstäcker, F. *The Strange Village, and Other Stories.* (Baltimore: Kelly, Piet & Co.)
Catholic World, XXVIII (October, 1878), 144.

Godolphin, Mary. *Robinson Crusoe, in Words of One Syllable.* (New York: McLoughlin Brothers)
Literary World, IX (December, 1878), 106.

Sandford and Merton in Words of One Syllable. (New York: McLoughlin Brothers)
Literary World, IX (December, 1878), 106.

Swiss Family Robinson in Words of One Syllable. (New York: McLoughlin Brothers)
Literary World, IX (December, 1878), 106.

Goodrich, Elizabeth, P. *The Young Folks' Opera; or, Child Life in Song.* (Boston: Lee & Shepard)
Literary World, IX (December 10, 1878), 125.

Goodridge, J. F. *Mother Goose in White.* (Boston: Lee & Shepard)
Nation, XXVII (November 28, 1878), 339.
Publishers' Weekly, XIV (November 2, 1878), 539.

Gordon, Janet. *Champions of the Reformation.* (New York: American Tract Society)
St. Nicholas, VI (December, 1878), 142.

Hall, C. W. *Adrift in the Ice-Fields.* (Boston: Lee & Shepard)
Literary World, VIII (March, 1878), 181.

Happy Days for Boys and Girls. (Philadelphia: Porter & Coates)
Harper's Magazine, LVI (January, 1878), 310.
St. Nicholas, V (January, 1878), 238.

Happy Moods of Happy Children. (Boston: D. Lothrop & Co.)
Literary World, IX (December 10, 1878), 124.

Harris, Mrs. F. McCready (Hope Ledyard). *Nan's Thanksgiving.* (New York: American Tract Society)
St. Nicholas, V (July, 1878), 637.

Heild, Mrs. ——. *Bright Sundays.* (New York: Cassell, Petter & Galpin)
Literary World, IX (December, 1878), 106.

Pet's Posy of Pictures and Stories. (New York: Cassell, Petter & Galpin)
Literary World, IX (December, 1878), 106.

Hering, Jeannie. *The Child's Delight.* (New York: George Routledge & Sons)
Literary World, IX (December, 1878), 106.

Higginson, Thomas Wentworth. *Young Folks' Book of American Explorers.* (Boston: Lee & Shepard)
Harper's Magazine, LVII (August, 1878), 466.
Unitarian Review, IX (March, 1878), 359–60.

The House in the Glen and the Boys Who Built It. (New York: Robert Carter & Brothers)
Independent, XXX (March 28, 1878), 10.

Hunt, Sara Keables. *Yusuf in Egypt and His Friends.* (New York: American Tract Society)
Harper's Magazine, LVII (August, 1878), 466.
St. Nicholas, V (July, 1878), 637.

Illustrated Book of Songs for Children. (New York: James Miller)
Literary World, IX (December, 1878), 106.

Jackson, Helen Hunt (H. H.). *Nelly's Silver Mine.* (Boston: Roberts Brothers)
 Atlantic Monthly, XLII (December, 1878), 779–80.
 Harper's Magazine, LVIII (December, 1878), 151.
 Independent, XXX (November 21, 1878), 9.
 Literary World, IX (November, 1878), 95.
 Publishers' Weekly, XIV (November 2, 1878), 538.

Jewett, Sarah Orne. *Play Days.* (Boston: Houghton, Osgood & Co.)
 Atlantic Monthly, XLII (December, 1878), 779.
 Literary World, IX (December, 1878), 106.
 Nation, XXVII (November 28, 1878), 339–40.
 Publishers' Weekly, XIV (November 2, 1878), 538.

Keary, Annie. *A York and a Lancaster Rose.* (New York: Macmillan & Co.)
 Literary World, VIII (January, 1878), 142.
 St. Nicholas, V (February, 1878), 302.

Kellogg, Elijah. *Burying the Hatchet; or, The Young Brave of the Delawares.* (Boston: Lee & Shepard)
 Literary World, IX (December 10, 1878), 124.

 Good Old Times. (Boston: Lee & Shepard)
 Literary World, VIII (March, 1878), 182.

Kendall, Mrs. E. D. *Mother Goose Masquerades.* (Boston: Lee & Shepard)
 Publishers' Weekly, XIII (April 6, 1878), 377.

Kingston, William Henry Giles. *Kidnapping in the Pacific.* (New York: George Routledge & Sons)
 Literary World, IX (December 10, 1878), 124.
 Nation, XXVII (December 12, 1878), 373.

Kirkland, Elizabeth Stansbury. *Dora's Housekeeping.* (Chicago: Jansen, McClurg & Co.)
 Harper's Magazine, LVI (February, 1878), 470–71.
 Literary World, VIII (March, 1878), 182.

 Short History of France for Young People. (Chicago: Jansen, McClurg & Co.)
 Nation, XXVII (December 19, 1878), 389.

 Six Little Cooks; or, Aunt Jane's Cooking Class. (Chicago: Jansen, McClurg & Co.)
 Literary World, VIII (January, 1878), 143.

Knatchbull-Hugessen, E. H. *Uncle Joe's Stories.* (New York: George Routledge & Sons)
 Literary World, IX (December 10, 1878), 124.

La Bédollièrre, Émile de. *The Story of a Cat.* Translated by Thomas Bailey Aldrich. (Boston: Houghton, Osgood & Co.)
 Independent, XXX (December 19, 1878), 11.
 Literary World, IX (December 10, 1878), 124.

Lamb, Charles and Mary. *Poetry for Children and Prince Dorus.* (New York: Scribner, Armstrong & Co.)
 Atlantic Monthly, XLII (October, 1878), 516–17.
 Harper's Magazine, LVI (February, 1878), 470.
 Scribner's Monthly, XV (February, 1878), 600–01.

Letters from Muskoka. By an Emigrant Lady. (London: Richard Bentley & Son)
 Atlantic Monthly, XLII (December, 1878), 778.

Lewis, Mrs. L. P. *Henri; or, The Little Savoyard in Paris.* Translated from the French. (New York: W. B. Mucklow)
 Literary World, IX (June, 1878), 16.

Little Chatterbox. (New York: R. Worthington)
 Literary World, IX (December 10, 1878), 125.

Little Folks. (New York: Cassell, Petter & Galpin)
Literary World, IX (December, 1878), 106.

Little Snowdrop's Picture-Book. (New York: George Routledge & Sons)
Literary World, IX (December, 1878), 106.

Little Speckly; or, The Adventures of a Chicken, Told by Herself. (New York: George Routledge & Sons)
Nation, XXVII (November 28, 1878), 339.

Little Violet's Picture Book. (New York: George Routledge & Sons)
Literary World, IX (December, 1878), 106.

Logie, Sarah, E. C. (Sarah E. Chester). *Betty and Her Cousin Harry.* (New York: American Tract Society)
Harper's Magazine, LVI (January, 1878), 311.
Literary World, VIII (January, 1878), 143.

Handsome Harry. (New York: American Tract Society)
Publishers' Weekly, XIV (October 19, 1878), 477.
St. Nicholas, VI (December, 1878), 142.

Lukin, J. *The Boy Engineers: What They Did and How They Did It.* (New York: G. P. Putnam's Sons)
Harper's Magazine, LVI (May, 1878), 940.
Literary World, IX (June, 1878), 16.
Nation, XXVII (November 7, 1878), 288.
Popular Science Monthly, XIII (July, 1878), 376.
St. Nicholas, V (October, 1878), 830.

Macduff, J. Ross. *Brighter Than the Sun; or, Christ the Light of the World.* (New York: Robert Carter & Brothers)
Harper's Magazine, LVI (January, 1878), 308.

Martineau, Harriet. *The Crofton Boys.* (New York: George Routledge & Sons)
Literary World, IX (December 10, 1878), 124–25.

Feats on the Fiord. (New York: George Routledge & Sons)
Literary World, IX (December 10, 1878), 124–25.

The Settlers at Home. (New York: George Routledge & Sons)
Literary World, IX (December 10, 1878), 124–25.

Matéaux, Clara L. *Old Folks at Home.* (New York: Cassell, Petter & Galpin)
Literary World, IX (December, 1878), 106.

Wee Willie Winkie: Story of a Boy Who Was Found. (New York: Cassell, Petter & Galpin)
Literary World, IX (December, 1878), 106.

Mathews, Cornelius. *The Enchanted Moccasins, and Other Legends of the American Indians.* 3rd Ed. (New York: G. P. Putnam's Sons)
Lippincott's Magazine, XXI (January, 1878), 136.

Mathews, Joanna H. *Daisybank.* (New York: American Tract Society)
St. Nicholas, VI (December, 1878), 142.

Mathews, Joanna H. and Julia A. *Blackberry Jam.* (New York: Robert Carter & Brothers)
Harper's Magazine, LVI (January, 1878), 311.

Milly's Whims. (New York: Robert Carter & Brothers)
Independent, XXX (June 13, 1878), 9.
Publishers' Weekly, XIII (March 2, 1878), 253.

Mathews, Julia A. *Bessie Harrington's Venture.* (Boston: Roberts Brothers)
Independent, XXX (June 13, 1878), 9.
Literary World, VIII (March, 1878), 182.
Publishers' Weekly, XIII (January 19, 1878), 62–63.

387

Jack Granger's Cousin. (New York: Robert Carter & Brothers)
Harper's Magazine, LVI (January, 1878), 311.
Literary World, VIII (January, 1878), 143.

Mayo, Isabella F. (Edward Garrett). *Magic Flower-Pot, and Other Stories.* (New York: Cassell, Petter & Galpin)
Independent, XXX (October 10, 1878), 9.
Literary World, IX (November, 1878), 95.
Nation, XXVII (December 12, 1878), 373.
Publishers' Weekly, XIV (September 21, 1878), 359.

Miller, Emily Huntington. *Captain Fritz, His Friends and Adventures.* (New York: E. P. Dutton & Co.)
Atlantic Monthly, XLI (January, 1878), 139.
Harper's Magazine, LVI (January, 1878), 310.

Little Neighbors. (New York: E. P. Dutton & Co.)
Harper's Magazine, LVIII (December, 1878), 151.
Literary World, IX (December, 1878), 106.
Publishers' Weekly, XIV (November 2, 1878), 539.

Miller, Mrs. J. A. (Faith Latimer). *Dear Old Stories Told Once More.* (New York: American Tract Society)
Harper's Magazine, LVI (January, 1878), 310.

Miller, Mary Esther. *Brother Ben* [also] *The Bird Summer.* (Boston: Congregational Publishing Society)
Nation, XXVII (December 12, 1878), 373.

Mitchell, Donald G. (Ik. Marvel). *About Old Story-Tellers; How and When They Lived, and What Stories They Told.* (New York: Scribner, Armstrong & Co.)
Harper's Magazine, LVI (February, 1878), 470.
Lippincott's Magazine, XXI (January, 1878), 136.
Literary World, VIII (January, 1878), 142.
Scribner's Monthly, XV (January, 1878), 439.

Molesworth, Mrs. Mary Louisa (Ennis Graham). *The Cuckoo Clock.* (New York: Macmillan & Co.)
Literary World, VIII (January, 1878), 142.

Grandmother Dear. (New York: Macmillan & Co.)
Nation, XXVII (December 19, 1878), 389.

Moore, Annie and Laura D. Nichols. *Overhead.* (Boston: D. Lothrop & Co.)
Literary World, IX (December 10, 1878), 124.

Moore, Clement C. *A Visit from St. Nicholas.* (Boston: Estes & Lauriat)
Literary World, IX (December 10, 1878), 125.

A Visit from St. Nicholas. (New York: McLoughlin Brothers)
Literary World, IX (December, 1878), 106.

Morley, Henry. *The Chicken Market and Other Fairy Tales.* (New York: Cassell, Petter & Galpin)
Independent, XXX (October 10, 1878), 9.
Literary World, IX (November, 1878), 95.
Nation, XXVII (November 28, 1878), 339.
Publishers' Weekly, XIV (September 21, 1878), 359.

Mother Goose's Melodies. (Boston: Houghton, Osgood & Co.)
Independent, XXX (December 19, 1878), 11.
Literary World, IX (December 10, 1878), 123–24.
Nation, XXVII (November 28, 1879), 339.

Narrative Poetry for the Young. (New York: George Routledge & Sons)
Literary World, VIII (January, 1878), 143.

Nesbitt, M. L. *Grammar Land; or, Grammar in Fun.* (New York: Henry Holt & Co.)

Literary World, IX (November, 1878), 95.
Nation, XXVII (November 7, 1878), 288.
Publishers' Weekly, XIV (November 2, 1878), 536.

Newton, Richard. *The King in His Beauty.* (New York: Robert Carter & Brothers)
Independent, XXX (June 13, 1878), 9.
Publishers' Weekly, XIII (April 6, 1878), 377.

Life of Christ for the Young. (Philadelphia: Gebbie & Barrie)
Harper's Magazine, LVI (April, 1878), 787–88.

Noble, Annette Lucille. *The Queer House in Rugby Court.* (New York: National Temperance Society)
Independent, XXX (Jun 13, 1878), 9–10.

Nursery Rhymes and Melodies of Mother Goose. (Boston: Lee & Shepard)
Independent, XXX (December 19, 1878), 11.
Literary World, IX (December 10, 1878), 124.

The Orphan of Alsace; A Tale of the Crusades. Translated from the French. (Baltimore: Kelly, Piet & Co.)
Catholic World, XXVIII (October, 1878), 144.

Our Sunday Fireside; or, Meditations for Children. (London: Burns & Oates)
Catholic World, XXVIII (August, 1878), 715–16.

Pabke, Marie and Marie J. Pitman. *Wonder-World Stories from the Chinese, French, German, Hebrew, Hindoostanee, Hungarian, Irish, Italian, Japanese, Russian, Swedish, Turkish.* (New York: G. P. Putnam's Sons)
Literary World, VIII (February, 1878), 161.
Scribner's Monthly, XV (January, 1878), 440.

Parkman, Alice. *Slices of Mother Goose.* (Boston: Lockwood, Brooks & Co.)
St. Nicholas, V (February, 1878), 302.

Parrots and Monkeys. (New York: R. Worthington)
Nation, XXVII (November 7, 1878), 288.

Pilgrim, T. (Arthur Morecamp). *Live Boys; Charley and Nasho in Texas.* (Boston: Lee & Shepard)
Literary World, IX (December, 1878), 107.

Pollard, M. M. *His Grandchild.* (New York: Robert Carter & Brothers)
Harper's Magazine, LVI (January, 1878), 311.

Powers, Mrs. S. D. *Behaving; or, Papers on Children's Etiquette.* (Boston: D. Lothrop & Co.)
Literary World, VIII (March, 1878), 182.

Pratt, Ella Farman. *The Children's Almanac.* (Boston: D. Lothrop & Co.)
Literary World, IX (December 10, 1878), 125.

Rand, E. A. *Christmas Jack.* (New York: American Tract Society)
Literary World, IX (December, 1878), 107.
Publishers' Weekly, XIV (October 19, 1878), 477.
St. Nicholas, VI (December, 1878), 142.

Rands, William Brighty. *Lilliput Land; or, The Children's Peep-Show.* (New York: Baker, Pratt, & Co.)
Lippincott's Magazine, XXI (January, 1878), 136.
St. Nicholas, V (January, 1878), 238.

Reid, Mayne. *Stories About Animals.* (New York: James Miller)
Literary World, IX (December, 1878), 106.

Robbins, Mrs. S. S. *Moore's Forge.* (New York: Robert Carter & Brothers)
Literary World, VIII (January, 1878), 143.

One Happy Winter; or, A Visit to Florida. (Boston: Lockwood, Brooks & Co.)
Literary World, VIII (January, 1878), 142–43.

Robinson, Leora Bettison. *Patsy; A Story for Girls*. (New York: G. P. Putnam's Sons)
Atlantic Monthly, XLI (January, 1878), 137.
Harper's Magazine, LVI (January, 1878), 310–11.

Round, William M. F. (Rev. P. Pennot). *Child Marian Abroad*. (Boston: Lee & Shepard)
Literary World, VIII (January, 1878), 143.

Routledge, Edmund. *Every Boy's Annual 1878*. (New York: George Routledge & Sons)
Literary World, IX (December, 1878), 105.

S., M. F. *Lily's Vocation, and Other Stories*. (Baltimore: Kelly, Piet & Co.)
Catholic World, XXVIII (October, 1878), 144.

Sanford, Mrs. D. P. *Aunt Elsie's Boys and Girls*. (New York: E. P. Dutton & Co.)
Literary World, IX (December, 1878), 106.

Aunt Sophy's Boys and Girls. (New York: E. P. Dutton & Co.)
Harper's Magazine, LVIII (December, 1878), 151.
Literary World, IX (December 10, 1878), 124.

Carl's First Days. (New York: E. P. Dutton & Co.)
Literary World, IX (December, 1878), 106.
Publishers' Weekly, XIV (November 2, 1878), 539.

Frisk and His Flock. (New York: E. P. Dutton & Co.)
Atlantic Monthly, XLI (January, 1878), 139.

The Little Brown House and the Children Who Lived In It. (New York: E. P. Dutton & Co.)
Atlantic Monthly, XLI (January, 1878), 139.
Harper's Magazine, LVI (January, 1878), 310.

Pussy Tip-Toe's Family. (New York: E. P. Dutton & Co.)
Atlantic Monthly, XLI (January, 1878), 138.

The Sunday Evening Hour. (New York: E. P. Dutton & Co.)
Harper's Magazine, LVI (January, 1878), 310.

Scudder, Horace Elisha. *The Bodleys on Wheels*. (Boston: Houghton, Osgood & Co.)
Independent, XXX (October 10, 1878), 10.
Literary World, IX (November, 1878), 95.
Nation, XXVII (November 7, 1878), 288.
Publishers' Weekly, XIV (October 5, 1878), 419.
St. Nicholas, VI (December, 1878), 141–42.

The Bodleys Telling Stories. (New York: Hurd & Houghton)
Harper's Magazine, LVI (January, 1878), 310.

Sewall, Frank. *Angelo, the Circus Boy*. (Philadelphia: J. B. Lippincott & Co.)
Literary World, IX (December 10, 1878), 124.
Nation, XXVII (December 12, 1878), 373.

Sherwood, Mary Martha. *Robert and Frederick*. (New York: George Routledge & Sons)
Literary World, VIII (January, 1878), 143.

Shillaber, B. P. (Mrs. Partington). *Ike Partington and His Friends*. (Boston: Lee & Shepard)
Literary World, IX (December 10, 1878), 124.

Shippen, E. *Thirty Years at Sea*. (Philadelphia: J. B. Lippincott & Co.)
Literary World, IX (December 10, 1878), 124.

Sleight, Mary B. *Prairie Days; or, The Boys and Girls of Osego*. (New York: E. P. Dutton & Co.)
Harper's Magazine, LVIII (December, 1878), 151.
Literary World, IX (November, 1878), 95.

Nation, XXVII (November 28, 1878), 340.
Publishers' Weekly, XIV (October 19, 1878), 478.

Smith, J. Moyr (illus.). *The Prince of Argolis.* (New York: Henry Holt & Co.)
Appleton's Journal, N. S. IV (January, 1878), 96.
Harper's Magazine, LVI (February, 1878), 470.
Lippincott's Magazine, XXI (January, 1878), 135–36.
Literary World, VIII (January, 1878), 146.

Smith, Lucy T. (L. T. Meade). *Water Gypsies.* (New York: Robert Carter & Brothers)
Literary World, IX (December, 1878), 106.

Stahl, P. J. (pseud.). *Little Miss Mischief, and Her Happy Thoughts.* Translated from the French by Mrs. Ella Farman Pratt. (Boston: D. Lothrop & Co.)
Literary World, IX (December 10, 1878), 124.

Stoddard, Richard Henry. *Adventures in Fairy Land.* (New York: James Miller)
Literary World, IX (December, 1878), 106.

The Story of Cecil and His Dog; or, The Reward of Virtue. (New York: James Miller)
Literary World, IX (December, 1878), 106.

Surr, Elizabeth. *Good Out of Evil.* (New York: Thomas Nelson & Sons)
Literary World, IX (December, 1878), 106–07.

Sweet, M. Alice. *Coals of Fire.* (New York: National Temperance Society)
Independent, XXX (October 24, 1878), 10.

Talbot, Eleanor W. *Jack O'Lantern.* (New York: Robert Carter & Brothers)
Literary World, VIII (January, 1878), 143.

Thayer, W. Makepeace (Uncle Juvinell). *Nelson; or, How a Country Boy Made His Way in the City.* (New York: T. Y. Crowell)
Literary World, IX (November, 1878), 95.

Thompson, Maurice. *The Witchery of Archery.* (New York: Charles Scribner's Sons)
St. Nicholas, V (September, 1878), 766.

The Three Wishes; A Tale for Girls. (Baltimore: Kelly, Piet & Co.)
Catholic World, XXVIII (October, 1878), 144.

Tilden, Louise W. *Karl and Gretchen's Christmas.* (Cincinnati: Robert Clarke & Co.)
Literary World, IX (December 10, 1878), 125.
Publishers' Weekly, XIV (November 2, 1878), 539.

Towle, George Makepeace. *Voyages and Adventures of Vasco da Gama.* (Boston: Lee & Shepard)
Appleton's Journal, N.S. V (November, 1878), 480.
Harper's Magazine, LVII (August, 1878), 465.
Independent, XXX (June 6, 1878), 10.
Literary World, IX (June, 1878), 16.
Nation, XXVII (November 7, 1878), 288.
St. Nicholas, V (August, 1878), 702.

Towry, M. H. *Spenser for Children.* (London: Chatto & Windus; New York: Scribner, Armstrong & Co.)
International Review, V (March, 1878), 275.
St. Nicholas, V (January, 1878), 238.

Trowbridge, John Townsend (Paul Creyton). *Bound in Honor; or, a Harvest of Wild Oats.* (Boston: Lee & Shepard)
Literary World, VIII (March, 1878), 181–82.

His Own Master. (Boston: Lee & Shepard)
Literary World, VIII (March, 1878), 181–82.

Tucker, Charlotte (A.L.O.E.). *The Giant Killers*. (New York: Robert Carter & Brothers)
Harper's Magazine, LVI (January, 1878), 311.

Uncle Herbert (pseud.). *My Picture Story Book*. (Philadelphia: J. B. Lippincott & Co.)
Literary World, IX (December 10, 1878), 124.

The Playmate. (Philadelphia: J. B. Lippincott & Co.)
Literary World, IX (December 10, 1878), 124.

Verne, Jules. *Hector Servadac; or, Career of a Comet*. (New York: Scribner, Armstrong & Co.)
Appleton's Journal, N. S. IV (February, 1878), 200.
Harper's Magazine, LVI (February, 1878), 470.
Independent, XXX (January 10, 1878), 12.

Off On a Comet; A Journey Through Space. (Philadelphia: Claxton, Remsen & Haffelfinger)
Independent, XXX (July 18, 1878), 12.
Ohio Educational Monthly, XXVII (August, 1878), 271.
Publishers' Weekly, XIII (June 8, 1878), 557.

To the Sun; Journey Through Planetary Space. (Philadelphia: Claxton, Remsen & Haffelfinger)
Catholic World, XXVII (May, 1878), 287–88.

Walton, Mrs. O. F. *A Peep Behind the Scenes*. (New York: Robert Carter & Brothers)
Harper's Magazine, LVI (January, 1878), 311.

Warner, Charles Dudley. *Being a Boy*. (Boston: James R. Osgood & Co.)
St. Nicholas, V (June, 1878), 572.

Warner, Susan Bogert (Elizabeth Wetherell). *The Broken Walls of Jerusalem, and the Rebuilding of Them*. (New York: Robert Carter & Brothers)
Literary World, IX (December, 1878), 106.
Publishers' Weekly, XIV (October 26, 1878), 507.

The Kingdom of Judah. (New York: Robert Carter & Brothers)
Independent, XXX (April 4, 1878), 11.

Wheaton, Campbell. *Six Sinners; or, School-Days in Buntam Valley*. (New York: G. P. Putnam's Sons)
Atlantic Monthly, XLI (January, 1878), 137.
St. Nicholas, V (February, 1878), 302.

The Wonderful Leaps of Sam Patch. (New York: McLoughlin Brothers)
Literary World, IX (December, 1878), 106.

Woodward, A. A. (Auber Forestier). *Echoes from Mist-land; or, The Nibelungen Lay Revealed*. (Chicago: S. C. Griggs & Co.)
Literary World, VIII (February, 1878), 161.

Worth a Threepenny Bit. (New York: E. P. Dutton & Co.)
Literary World, VIII (January, 1878), 143.

The Young Catholic. (New York: Catholic Publication Society)
Catholic World, XXVIII (September, 1878), 860.

Youth's Health-Book. (New York: Harper & Brothers)
Harper's Magazine, LVII (August, 1878), 468.

BOOKS REVIEWED IN 1879

Adams, Emily. *Six Months at Mrs. Prior's*. (Boston: D. Lothrop & Co.)
Independent, XXX (July 3, 1879), 10.

Adams, Sarah B. *Amy and Marion's Voyage Around the World*. (Boston: D. Lothrop & Co., 1879)

Independent, XXXI (March 20, 1879), 11.

Alcott, Louisa May. *Aunt Jo's Scrap-Bag.* (Boston: Roberts Brothers)
Independent, XXXI (October 23, 1879), 9.
Nation, XXIX (December 18, 1879), 427.
Scribner's Monthly, XIX (December, 1879), 315.

Alcott, Louisa May, and Others. *Sparkles for Bright Eyes.* (New York: T. Y. Crowell)
Independent, XXXI (October 23, 1879), 9.
Literary World, X (December 6, 1879), 401.

Alexander, Mrs. C. F. *Moral Songs.* (London: Masters & Co.)
Nation, XXIX (December 4, 1879), 392–93.

The Apple Blossom Books. (New York: Phillips & Hunt)
Independent, XXXI (December 25, 1879), 9.

Art in the Nursery. (Boston: D. Lothrop & Co.)
Independent, XXXI (December 25, 1879), 9.

Baker, Harriet N. W. (Aunt Hattie; Mrs. Madeline Leslie). *Out of the Depths; or, The Rector's Trial.* (Boston: Ira Bradley & Co.)
Literary World, X (December 6, 1879), 403.

The Sisters at Service; or, I Am for Jesus. (Boston: Ira Bradley & Co.)
Literary World, X (December 6, 1879), 403.

True and False Pride. (Boston: Ira Bradley & Co.)
Literary World, X (December 6, 1879), 403.

Balfour, Clara L. *Women Worth Emulating.* (New York: American Tract Society)
St. Nicholas, VII (December, 1879), 188.

Ballard, Julia P. *Caught and Fettered.* (New York: National Temperance Society)
Independent, XXXI (March 20, 1879), 11.

Insect Lives; or, Born in Prison. (Cincinnati: Robert Clarke & Co.)
Independent, XXXI (December 25, 1879), 9.
Literary World, X (December 20, 1879), 439.
Nation, XXIX (December 11, 1879), 408.
New England Journal of Education, X (December 11, 1879), 342.
St. Nicholas, VII (December, 1879), 188.

Bartlett, Mary C. *Little Figures and Other Stories.* (Boston: Lockwood, Brooks & Co.)
Independent, XXXI (March 20, 1879), 11.

Bates, Clara Doty. *Child Lore.* (Boston: D. Lothrop & Co.)
Independent, XXXI (December 25, 1879), 9.
Nation, XXIX (December 18, 1879), 428.

Bell, Lucia Chase. *True Blue.* (Boston: D. Lothrop & Co.)
New England Journal of Education, IX (January 16, 1879), 45.

Bismarck, Otto von. *Prince Bismarck's Letters.* (New York: Charles Scribner's Sons)
St. Nicholas, VI (January, 1879), 230.

Books for Our Birdies. (New York: American Tract Society)
St. Nicholas, VII (December, 1879), 188.

Books of Natural History. (Philadelphia: Claxton, Remsen & Haffelfinger)
Literary World, X (December 6, 1879), 403.

Brown, Emma. *Once Upon a Time.* (Boston: D. Lothrop & Co.)
Literary World, X (December 6, 1879), 401.

Buckley, Arabella B. *The Fairy-Land of Science.* (New York: D. Appleton & Co.)
Harper's Magazine, LIX (July, 1879), 310–11.
Independent, XXXI (May 1, 1879), 10.

Literary World, X (April 26, 1879), 135.
Nation, XXVIII (May 8, 1879), 324.

Bunce, John Thackeray. *Fairy Tales; Their Origin and Meaning.* (New York: D. Appleton & Co.)
Harper's Magazine, LIX (June, 1879), 148.

Butterworth, Hezekiah. *Zigzag Journeys in Europe; or, Vacation Rambles in Historic Lands.* (Boston: Estes & Lauriat)
Independent, XXXI (November 27, 1879), 10.
Independent, XXXI (December 25, 1879), 9.
Literary World, X (November 8, 1879), 360.
Nation, XXIX (December 18, 1879), 427–28.
New England Journal of Education, X (October 30, 1879), 249.
St. Nicholas, VII (December, 1879), 188.

Caldecott, Randolph. *The Babes in the Wood.* (New York: George Routledge & Sons)
Nation, XXIX (December 18, 1879), 428.
Elegy on the Death of a Mad Dog. (New York: George Routledge & Sons)
Nation, XXIX (December 18, 1879), 428.

Calkins Norman A., and Abby Morton Diaz. *Prang's Natural History Series for Children.* (Boston: L. Prang & Co.)
St. Nicholas, VI (February, 1879), 303.

Champlin, John D., Jr. *Young Folks' Cyclopaedia of Common Things.* (New York: Henry Holt & Co.)
Independent, XXXI (October 2, 1879), 9.
Literary World, X (October 11, 1879), 332.
Nation, XXIX (October 16, 1879), 262.
New England Journal of Education, X (November 27, 1879), 310.
Ohio Educational Monthly, XXVIII (October, 1879), 338.
St. Nicholas, VII (December, 1879), 188.
Scribner's Monthly, XIX (December, 1879), 316.

Charles, Elizabeth A. *Joan, the Maid, Deliverer of France and England.* (New York: Dodd, Mead & Co.)
Independent, XXXI (April 17, 1879), 10.

Chatterbox for 1879. (Boston: Estes & Lauriat)
Independent, XXXI (December 25, 1879), 9.
St. Nicholas, VII (December, 1879), 188.

Chatterbox Junior. (New York: R. Worthington)
Independent, XXXI (December 25, 1879), 9.

Chellis, Mary Dwinell. *The Brewery at Taylorville.* (New York: National Temperance Society)
Independent, XXXI (January 2, 1879), 12.

Church, Alfred J. *Stories from Virgil.* (New York: Scribner & Welford)
Western, V (March, 1879), 212.
Stories from Virgil. (New York: Harper & Brothers)
Harper's Magazine, LVIII (February, 1879), 468.

Clark, Mrs. S. R. Graham. *Yensie Walton.* (Boston: D. Lothrop & Co.)
Independent, XXXI (July 3, 1879), 10.

Clarke, Rebecca (Sophie May). *Little Pitchers.* (Boston: Lee & Shepard)
Atlantic Monthly, XLIII (January, 1879), 124.
Independent, XXXI (April 10, 1879), 10.
New England Journal of Education, IX (May 22, 1879), 333.

Coates, Henry T. *Children's Book of Poetry.* (Philadelphia: Porter & Coates)
Independent, XXXI (October 23, 1879), 9.
Literary World, X (November 22, 1879), 285–86.

Nation, XXIX (October 16, 1879), 263.

Coffin, Charles Carleton (Carleton). *Story of Liberty.* (New York: Harper & Brothers)
Atlantic Monthly, XLIII (January, 1879), 125.
Catholic World, XXIX (April, 1879), 141–42.
Harper's Magazine, LVIII (January, 1879), 312.
Independent, XXXI (March 27, 1879), 11.
International Review, VI (January, 1879), 103.

Cooke, John Esten. *Stories of the Old Dominion.* (New York: Harper & Brothers)
Harper's Magazine, LIX (July, 1879), 310.
Independent, XXXI (June 5, 1879), 10.
Literary World, X (August 16, 1879), 270.
Methodist Quarterly Review, XXXI (July, 1879), 603.
Unitarian Review, XII (November, 1879), 579.

Cooper, Vincent King. *Tales from Euripides.* (New York: Harper & Brothers)
Harper's Magazine, LIX (September, 1879), 633.

Corbin, Caroline Fairfield. *Belle and the Boys.* (Chicago: Jansen, McClurg & Co.)
Independent, XXXI (December 4, 1879), 9.
Literary World, X (December 6, 1879), 403.
Nation, XXIX (December 4, 1879), 391.
New England Journal of Education, X (December 25, 1879), 374.

Cousin Daisy (pseud.). *The Picture Alphabet.* Philadelphia: J. B. Lippincott & Co.)
St. Nicholas, VII (December, 1879), 188.

Damon, William E. *Ocean Wonders.* (New York: D. Appleton & Co.)
Literary World, X (April 26, 1879), 135.

Darwin, Charles Robert. *What Mr. Darwin Saw in His Voyage Round the World in the Ship "Beagle."* (New York: Harper & Brothers)
Appleton's Journal, N. S. VII (December, 1879), 575–76.
Harper's Magazine, LX (December, 1879), 155.
Independent, XXXI (October 9, 1879), 9.
Literary World, X (October 25, 1879), 342–43.
Nation, XXIX (October 16, 1879), 263.

Dayre, Sydney. *The Queer Little Wooden Captain.* (New York: Authors' Publishing Co.)
Independent, XXXI (October 23, 1879), 9.

Dodds, Mrs. M. L. *Rose Dunbar's Mistake; or, Who Have I in Heaven.* (New York: Robert Carter & Brothers)
Independent, XXXI (April 24, 1879), 10.

Dodge, Mary Mapes. *Baby Days.* (New York: Scribner & Co.)
Scribner's Monthly, XIX (December, 1880), 314.

Hans Brinker; or, The Silver Skates. (New York: Charles Scribner's Sons)
Independent, XXXI (December 25, 1879), 9.
Nation, XXIX (December 11, 1879), 409.

Drayton, Henry S. *Light in Dark Places; or, How the Camps Lived in Their Poverty.* (Philadelphia: Claxton, Remsen & Haffelfinger)
Independent, XXXI (December 4, 1879), 9.

Eggleston, Edward and Mrs. L. E. Seelye. *Brant and Red Jacket.* (New York: Dodd, Mead & Co.)
Nation, XXIX (December 18, 1879), 427.

Pocahontas. (New York: Dodd, Mead & Co.)
Literary World, X (December 6, 1879), 402.
Nation, XXIX (December 4, 1879), 391–92.

Eggleston, George Cary. *Red Eagle, and the Wars with the Creek Indians of Alabama.* (New York: Dodd, Mead & Co.)
Harper's Magazine, LVIII (March, 1879), 627.

Finley, Martha F. (Martha Farquharson). *Mildred at Roselands.* (New York: Dodd, Mead & Co.)
Independent, XXXI (December 4, 1879), 9.
Literary World, X (December 6, 1879), 403.
Nation, XXIX (December 4, 1879), 391.

Fosdick, Charles A. (Harry Castlemon). *The Buried Treasure; or, Old Jordan's Haunt.* (Philadelphia: Porter & Coates)
Independent, XXXI (January 2, 1879), 12.

Gladstone, Mrs. George. *Stick to the Raft.* (Boston: Congregational Publishing House)
Independent, XXXI (April 10, 1879), 10.

Gobright, L. A. *Echoes of Childhood.* (Philadelphia: Claxton, Remsen & Haffelfinger)
Independent, XXXI (December 4, 1879), 9.

Goodrich, Elizabeth P. *The Young Folks' Opera; or, Child Life in Song.* (Boston: Lee & Shepard)
Atlantic Monthly, XLIII (January, 1879), 125.

Greenaway, Kate. *Under the Window.* (London: George Routledge & Sons)
St. Nicholas, VII (December, 1879), 188.
Scribner's Monthly, XIX (December, 1879), 314.

Greenwood, James. *The Adventures of Reuben Davidger, Seventeen Years and Four Months a Captive Among the Dyaks of Borneo.* (New York: Harper & Brothers)
Harper's Magazine, LX (December, 1879), 155.

Guernsey, Clara F. *Sybil and the Sapphires.* (Philadelphia: American Sunday-School Union)
Independent, XXXI (December 4, 1879), 9.

Hale, Edward Everett. *Mrs. Merriam's Scholars.* (Boston: Roberts Brothers)
Harper's Magazine, LVIII (April, 1879), 786.
Unitarian Review, XI (January, 1879), 115.

Stories of War, Told by Soldiers. (Boston: Roberts Brothers)
Nation, XXIX (December 4, 1879), 392.

Hall, Theresa Oakey. *Nuts for Christmas Cracking.* (New York: T. Whittaker)
Independent, XXXI (December 25, 1879), 9.

Happy Home Stories. (New York: American Tract Society)
St. Nicholas, VII (December 1879), 188.

Hays, Mrs. W. J. *The Princess Idleways; A Fairy Story.* (New York: Harper & Brothers)
Literary World, X (December 6, 1879), 403.
Nation, XXIX (December 7, 1879), 391.

Higginson, Mary Thacher. *Room for One More.* (Boston: Lee & Shepard)
Literary World, X (December 6, 1879), 403.
Nation, XXIX (December 11, 1879), 408.
New England Journal of Education, X (November 27, 1879), 310.
Scribner's Monthly, XIX (December, 1880), 315.

Holiday Times for Boys and Girls. (Philadelphia: Porter & Coates)
Independent, XXXI (December 25, 1879), 9.
New England Journal of Education, X (December 25, 1879), 374.

Holt, Emily Sarah. *Lady Sybil's Choice.* (New York: Robert Carter & Brothers)
Independent, XXXI (December 25, 1879), 9.

Margery's Sons; A 15th Century Tale of the Court of Scotland. (New York: Robert Carter & Brothers)
Independent, XXXI (April 24, 1879), 10.

Hopkins, I. T. *The Signal Flag.* (New York: American Tract Society)
St. Nicholas, VII (December, 1879), 188.

Houghton, Louise Seymour. *Fifine.* (New York: American Tract Society)
St. Nicholas, VII (December, 1879), 188.

Howard, O. O. *Donald's School Days.* (Boston: Lee & Shepard)
Atlantic Monthly, XLIII (May, 1879), 685.
Independent, XXXI (April 10, 1879), 10.
Literary World, X (February 15, 1879), 55.

Hunt, Madeline Bonavia. *Little Hinges.* (New York: Cassell, Petter & Galpin)
Independent, XXXI (December 4, 1879), 9.
Literary World, X (December 6, 1879), 403.
New England Journal of Education, X (November 20, 1879), 294.

Jackson, Helen Hunt (H. H.) *Letters from a Cat.* (Boston: Roberts Brothers)
Independent, XXXI (December 4, 1879), 9.
Nation, XXIX (December 4, 1879), 392.

Johnson, Edwin A. *The Live Boy; or, Charley's Letters.* (New York: Nelson & Phillips)
Independent, XXXI (December 4, 1879), 9.

Kellogg, Elijah. *Burying the Hatchet; or, The Young Brave of the Delawares.* (Boston: Lee & Shepard)
Atlantic Monthly, XLIII (January, 1879), 125.
Independent, XXXI (March 20, 1879), 11.

Kingston, William Henry Giles. *Hendricks the Hunter; Tale of Zululand.* (New York: A. C. Armstrong & Co.)
Independent, XXXI (December 25, 1879), 9.

Notable Voyages from Columbus to Parry. (New York: George Routledge & Sons)
Nation, XXIX (December 18, 1879), 427.

Kirkland, Elizabeth S. *A Short History of France for Young People.* (Chicago: Jansen, McClurg & Co.)
Ohio Educational Monthly, XXVIII (June, 1879), 196.

Knox, Thomas W. *Boy Travellers in the Far East; Adventures of Two Youths on a Journey to Japan and China.* (New York: Harper & Brothers)
Independent, XXXI (December 25, 1879), 9.
Literary World, X (December 6, 1879), 402.
Nation, XXIX (December 4, 1879), 392.
New England Journal of Education, X (December 4, 1879), 326.

La Bédollière, Émile de. *The Story of a Cat.* Translated from the French by Thomas Bailey Aldrich. (Boston: Houghton, Osgood & Co.)
Atlantic Monthly, XLIII (January, 1879), 123.

Lamb, Charles. *The Adventures of Ulysses.* (New York: Harper & Brothers)
Harper's Magazine, LVIII (April, 1879), 786.

Lane-Clark, Theodora M. L. *Roman Violets and Where They Blossom.* (London: Burns & Oates)
Catholic World, XXIX (July, 1879), 575–76.

Lanier, Sidney. *The Boy's Froissart.* (New York: Charles Scribner's Sons)
Independent, XXXI (December 25, 1879), 9.
Literary World, X (December 6, 1879), 402.
Nation, XXIX (December 4, 1879), 392.
New England Journal of Education, X (December 4, 1879), 326.
Scribner's Monthly, XIX (December, 1879), 315.

Lynnde, Elmer. *Daphne Stories.* (New York: American Tract Society)
St. Nicholas, VII (December, 1879), 188.

Markham, Richard. *Around the Yule Log.* (New York: Dodd, Mead & Co.)
Independent, XXXI (December 25, 1879), 9.
Literary World, X (December 6, 1879), 401–02.
Nation, XXIX (December 4, 1879), 392.

Miller, Mrs. J. A. *Pictures and Stories of Long Ago.* (New York: American Tract Society)
St. Nicholas, VII (December, 1879), 188.

Miller, Mary Esther. *Books for Bright Eyes.* (New York: American Tract Society)
St. Nicholas, VI (January, 1879), 230.

Brother Ben [also] *The Bird Summer.* (Boston: Congregational Publishing Society)
Atlantic Monthly, XLIII (May, 1879), 685.
Independent, XXX (March 20, 1879), 11.

Miller, Olive Thorne. *Little Folks in Feathers and Fur, and Others in Neither.* (New York: E. P. Dutton & Co.)
Harper's Magazine, LX (December, 1879), 155.
Independent, XXXI (October 23, 1879), 9.
Literary World, X (December 6, 1879), 402.
Nation, XXIX (December 4, 1879), 392.
St. Nicholas, VII (December, 1879), 188.

Nimpo's Troubles. (New York: E. P. Dutton & Co.)
Harper's Magazine, LX (December, 1879), 155.
St. Nicholas, VII (December, 1879), 188.
Scribner's Monthly, VII (December, 1879), 188.

Molesworth, Mrs. Mary Louisa (Ennis Graham). *The Cuckoo Clock.* (London: Macmillan & Co.)
St. Nicholas, V (February, 1878), 302.

Grandmother Dear. (London: Macmillan & Co.)
Independent, XXXI (March 20, 1879), 11.
Literary World, X (February 15, 1879), 55.

Moncrieff, Robert Hope (Ascott R. Hope). *Spindle Stories.* (New York: George Routledge & Sons)
Nation, XXIX (December 11, 1879), 408.

Moore, Annie, and Laura D. Nichols. *Overhead.* (Boston: D. Lothrop & Co.)
Independent, XXXI (March 27, 1879), 11.

Mother Goose's Melodies; or, Songs for the Nursery. (Boston: Houghton, Osgood & Co.)
Atlantic Monthly, XLIII (January, 1879), 123.
St. Nicholas, VI (February, 1879), 303.

Nesbitt, M. L. *Grammar-Land; or, Grammar in Fun.* (New York: Henry Holt & Co.)
Harper's Magazine, LVIII (January, 1879), 312.

Newton, William W. *The Wicket-Gate.* (New York: Robert Carter & Brothers)
Independent, XXXI (April 24, 1879), 10.

Niebuhr, Barthold G. *Greek Hero-Stories.* Translated by B. Hoppin. (New York: Dodd, Mead & Co.)
Appleton's Journal, N. S. VI (June, 1879), 576.
Harper's Magazine, LIX (July, 1879), 310.
Literary World, X (April 12, 1879), 123.

Parrots and Monkeys. (New York: R. Worthington)
St. Nicholas, VI (January, 1879), 230.

Pilgrim, T. (Arthur Morecamp). *Live Boys; or, Charlie and Nasho in Texas.* (Boston: Lee & Shepard)
Independent, XXXI (March 20, 1879), 11.

Poetry for Children. (New York: E. P. Dutton & Co.)
Harper's Magazine, LX (December, 1879), 155.
Independent, XXXI (October 23, 1879), 9.
Literary World, X (December 6, 1879), 402.

Porter, Mary W. *Poor Papa.* (Boston: D. Lothrop & Co.)
Independent, XXXI (July 17, 1879), 12.

Proctor, Richard A. *Flowers of the Sky.* (New York: A. C. Armstrong & Son)
Literary World, X (December 6, 1879), 403.

Raffensperger, Mrs. A. F. *Sunny Hours.* (New York: American Tract Society)
St. Nicholas, VII (December, 1879), 188.

Rand, Edward A. *Nellie's New Year.* (New York: American Tract Society)
Literary World, X (December 6, 1879), 403.
St. Nicholas, VII (December, 1879), 188.

The Schooner on the Beach. (Philadelphia: American Sunday-School Union)
Independent, XXXI (August 28, 1879), 11.

Richardson, J. (Adam Stwin). *Eyes Right.* (Boston: D. Lothrop & Co.)
Independent, XXXI (March 27, 1879), 11.

Robertson, Margaret M. *David Fleming's Forgiveness.* (New York: A. D. F. Randolph)
Independent, XXXI (August 28, 1879), 11.

Rosebud's Menagerie. (New York: R. Worthington)
Independent, XXXI (December 25, 1879), 9.

Sanford, Mrs. D. P. *The Captain's Children.* (New York: E. P. Dutton & Co.)
Harper's Magazine, LX (December, 1879), 154–55.
Independent, XXXI (December 25, 1879), 9.
Literary World, X (December 6, 1879), 402.

Scudder, Horace Elisha. *The Bodleys Afoot.* (Boston: Houghton, Osgood & Co.)
Harper's Magazine, LX (December, 1879), 155–56.
Independent, XXXI (October 16, 1879), 10.
Literary World, X (October 25, 1879), 348.
Nation, XXIX (October 16, 1879), 263.
Scribner's Monthly, XIX (December, 1879), 315.

The Bodleys on Wheels. (Boston: Houghton, Osgood & Co.)
Atlantic Monthly, XLIII (January, 1879), 123.

Shaw, Flora L. *Castle Blair.* (Boston: Roberts Brothers)
Harper's Magazine, LVIII (March, 1879), 631–32.
Literary World, X (February 15, 1879), 55.

Sherwood, Mary Martha. *Stories on the Church Catechism.* (New York: T. Whittaker)
Literary World, X (December 6, 1879), 403.

Shillaber, B. P. (Mrs. Partington). *Ike Partington; or, The Adventures of a Human Boy and His Friends.* (Boston: Lee & Shepard)
Atlantic Monthly, XLIII (January, 1879), 124.
Independent, XXXI (March 6, 1879), 12.

Shinn, G. W. *Stories for the Happy Days of Christmas Time.* (New York: T. Whittaker)
Literary World, X (December 6, 1879), 403.

Smith, Hannah (Hesba Stretton). *In Prison and Out.* (New York: Dodd, Mead & Co.)
Independent, XXXI (December 4, 1879), 9.

Smith, J. Moyr. (illus.). *Tales of Old Thûle*. (Philadelphia: J. B. Lippincott & Co.)
Nation, XXIX (December 11, 1879), 408.

Smith, Lucy T. (L. T. Meade). *Dot and Her Treasures*. (New York: Robert Carter & Brothers)
Independent, XXXI (December 4, 1879), 9.

Storr, Francis and Hawes Turner. *Canterbury Chimes; or, Chaucer Tales Retold for Children*. (Boston: Roberts Brothes)
Literary World, X (March 1, 1879), 76.

Stuart, Esme. *The Little Brown Girl*. (New York: Dodd, Mead & Co.)
Independent, XXXI (August 28, 1879), 11.

Talbot, C. R. (John Brownjohn; Magnus Merriweather). *Royal Lowrie*. (Boston: D. Lothrop & Co.)
Independent, XXXI (March 20, 1879), 11.

Tiny's Natural History. (New York: George Routledge & Sons)
Nation, XXIX (December 11, 1879), 409.

Towle, George M. *Magellan; or, The First Voyage Round the World*. (Boston: Lee & Shepard)
Independent, XXXI (December 25, 1879), 9.
Literary World, X (December 6, 1879), 402.
Nation, XXIX (December 4, 1879), 392.

Pizarro. (Boston: Lee & Shepard)
Harper's Magazine, LVIII (March, 1879), 631.
Literary World, X (February 15, 1879), 55.

Trowbridge, Catherine M. *A Crown of Glory*. (New York: American Tract Society)
St. Nicholas, VII (December, 1879), 188.

Trowbridge, John Townsend (Paul Creyton). *Young Joe and Other Boys*. (Boston: Lee & Shepard)
Literary World, X (December 20, 1879), 439.
New England Journal of Education, X (December 11, 1879), 342.

Uncle Herbert (pseud.). *The Boys' and Girls' Treasury*. (Philadelphia: J. B. Lippincott & Co.)
St. Nicholas, VII (December, 1879), 188.

Van Marter, M. *Light for the Little Ones*. (New York: Phillips & Hunt)
Independent, XXXI (December 25, 1879), 9.

Verne, Jules. *Dick Sands, the Boy-Captain*. (New York: Charles Scribner's Sons)
Harper's Magazine, LVIII (April, 1879), 789.
Literary World, X (February 15, 1879), 55.

The Exploration of the World. (New York: Charles Scribner's Sons)
Appleton's Journal, N. S. VII (December, 1879), 576.
Literary World, X (December 6, 1879), 413.
New England Journal of Education, X (December 4, 1879), 326.
Scribner's Monthly, XIX (December, 1879), 313–14.

The Tribulations of a Chinaman in China. (Boston: Lee & Shepard)
New England Journal of Education, X (November 20, 1879), 294.

Warner, Susan Bogert (Elizabeth Wetherell). *The Broken Walls of Jerusalem and the Rebuilding of Them*. (New York: Robert Carter & Brothers)
Harper's Magazine, LVIII (March, 1879), 631.

The House of Israel. (New York: Robert Carter & Brothers)
Harper's Magazine, LVIII (March, 1879), 631.

The Kingdom of Judah. (New York: Robert Carter & Brothers)
Harper's Magazine, LVIII (March, 1879), 631.

The Star Out of Jacob. (New York: Robert Carter & Brothers)
Harper's Magazine, LVIII (March, 1879), 631.

Walks from Eden. (New York: Robert Carter & Brothers)
Harper's Magazine, LVIII (March, 1879), 631.

Wells, James. *Bible Children.* (New York: Robert Carter & Brothers)
Independent, XXXI (December 4, 1879), 9.

White, Alexina B. *Little Folk Songs.* (Boston: Estes & Lauriat)
St. Nicholas, VII (December, 1879), 188.
Scribner's Monthly, (December, 1879), 314.

Wise, Daniel (Francis Forrester; Lawrence Lancewood). *Roderick Ashcourt.* (Boston: Lee & Shepard)
Literary World, X (December 20, 1879), 439.

Woods, Kate Tannatt. *Six Little Rebels.* (Boston: D. Lothrop & Co.)
Independent, XXXI (July 3, 1879), 10.
New England Journal of Education, IX (May 22, 1879), 333.

Woolsey, Sarah Chauncey (Susan Coolidge). *Eyebright.* (Boston: Roberts Brothers)
Independent, XXXI (October 23, 1879), 9.
Nation, XXIX (December 18, 1879), 427.
Scribner's Monthly, XIX (December, 1879), 315.

Wray, J. Jackson. *A Man Every Inch of Him; or, The Story of Frank Fullerton's School-Days.* (New York: Cassell, Petter & Galpin)
Independent, XXXI (December 4, 1879), 9.
Literary World, X (December 6, 1879), 403.
New England Journal of Education, X (November 20, 1879), 294.

Yonge, Charlotte M. *The Story of the Christians and Moors of Spain.* (London: Macmillan & Co.)
Independent, XXXI (April 24, 1879), 10.

Young Folks' History of England. (Boston: Estes & Lauriat)
Harper's LIX (July, 1879), 311.
Independent, XXXI (April 3, 1879), 11.
Literary World, X (April 26, 1879), 139.
Nation, XXIX (November 20, 1879), 354.

Young Folks' History of Germany. (Boston: D. Lothrop & Co.)
Nation, XXVIII (May 29, 1879), 375.

Young Folks' History of Greece. (Cincinnati: Hitchcock & Walden)
Independent, XXXI (February 27, 1879), 12.

Young Folks' History of Rome. (Cincinnati: Hitchcock & Walden)
Literary World, X (December 6, 1879), 402–03.

BOOKS REVIEWED IN 1880

Alcott, Louisa May. *Aunt Jo's Scrap-Bag.* (Boston: Roberts Brothers)
Harper's Magazine, LX (January, 1880), 315.

Jack and Jill. (Boston: Roberts Brothers)
Literary World, XI (October 23, 1880), 373.

Little Women. Illus. Ed. (Boston: Roberts Brothers)
Dial, I (December, 1880), 163–64.

Alden, W. L. *The Moral Pirates.* (New York: Harper & Brothers)
Literary World, XI (December 4, 1880), 442.

Ames, Fanny B. *Christmas Day and All the Year.* (Boston: George H. Ellis)
Literary World, XI (December 18, 1880), 467.
New England Journal of Education, XI (December 23, 1880), 436.

Anderson, Mary E. *New Songs for Little People.* (Boston: Lee & Shepard)
Independent, XXXII (December 16, 1880), 9.
Literary World, XI (December 4, 1880), 441.

Arthur, Timothy Shay. *The Boys' and Girls' Treasury.* (Philadelphia: J. B. Lippincott & Co.)
New England Journal of Education, XI (February 12, 1880), 106.

Baby Land. (Boston: D. Lothrop & Co.)
Independent, XXXII (October 28, 1880), 10.

Baker, Sir Samuel W. *Cast Up by the Sea.* (New York: Harper & Brothers)
Harper's Magazine, LXI (November, 1880), 955–56.

Ballantyne, Robert Michael. *Philosopher Jack.* (London: James Nisbet)
Nation, XXXI (November 18, 1880), 364.

Ballard, Julia P. *Insect Lives; or, Born in Prison.* (Cincinnati; Robert Clarke & Co.)
Atlantic Monthly, XLV (January, 1880), 128.
Lippincott's Magazine, XXV (January, 1880), 135.

Barker, Mrs. Sale. *Little Wide-Awake's Painting-Book.* (New York: George Routledge & Sons)
Literary World, XI (December 4, 1880), 441.

Beach, Rebecca Gibbons. *Allie's Mistake.* (New York: G. P. Putnam's Sons)
Literary World, XI (December 4, 1880), 442.
Nation, XXXI (December 16, 1880), 432.

Beecher, Julia M. *Aim, Fire, Bang; Stories for Young Folks.* (Boston: Lee & Shepard)
Literary World, XI (December 18, 1880), 467.

Bell, N. R. E. (N. D'Anvers). *Story of a Dog; or, Pixie's Adventures.* (Philadelphia: J. B. Lippincott & Co.)
Literary World, XI (December 18, 1880), 467.
Nation, XXXI (December 9 ,1880), 416.

Biart, Lucien. *An Involuntary Voyage.* (New York: Harper & Brothers)
Harper's Magazine, LX (February, 1880), 475.

Brooks, Noah. *The Fairport Nine.* (New York: Charles Scribner's Sons)
Independent, XXXII (November 4, 1880), 12.
Literary World, XI (December 4, 1880), 441.
Nation, XXXI (November 18, 1880), 364.
Scribner's Monthly, XXI (December, 1880), 323.

Brown, Howard N. *Sunday Stories.* (Boston: Lockwood, Brooks & Co.)
Unitarian Review, XIII (January, 1880), 92–93.

Butterworth, Hezekiah. *Zigzag Journeys in Classic Lands; or, Tommy Toby's Trip to Mt. Parnassus.* (Boston: Estes & Lauriat)
New England Journal of Education, XII (December 23, 1880), 436.

Zigzag Journeys in Europe; or, Vacation Rambles in Historic Lands. (Boston: Estes & Lauriat)
Harper's Magazine, LX (January, 1880), 315.

Caldecott, Randolph. *The Three Jovial Huntsmen.* (New York: George Routledge & Sons)
Nation, XXXI (December 9, 1880), 416.

Campbell, Loomis J. (ed.). *The Young Folks' Book of Poetry.* (Boston: Lee & Shepard)
New England Journal of Education, XI (May 27, 1880), 346.

Chamberlain, Parthene B. *A Rare Piece of Work; or, Gilkie's Court.* (New York: T. Y. Crowell)
Literary World, XI (October 23, 1880), 374.

Champlin, John D., Jr. *The Child's Catechism of Common Things.* (New York: Henry Holt & Co.)
Scribner's Monthly, XIX (April, 1880), 949.
The Young Folks' Cyclopaedia of Common Things. (New York: Henry Holt & Co.)
Popular Science Monthly, XVI (January, 1880), 424.
The Young Folks' Cyclopaedia of Persons and Places. (New York: Henry Holt & Co.)
New England Journal of Education, XII (December 23, 1880), 436.

Chatterbox for 1880. (Boston: Estes & Lauriat)
Dial, I (December, 1880), 163–64.

Chatterbox Junior. (New York: R. Worthington)
Independent, XXXII (December 2, 1880), 10.

Clarke, Rebecca (Sophie May). *Twin Cousins.* (Boston: Lee & Shepard)
Literary World, XI (December 18, 1880), 467.

Coates, Henry T. *The Children's Book of Poetry.* (Philadelphia: Porter & Coates)
Appleton's Journal, N. S. VIII (January, 1880), 96.
New Englander, XXXIX (January, 1880), 152.

Coffin, Charles Carleton (Carleton). *Old Times in the Colonies.* (New York: Harper & Brothers)
Dial, I (December, 1880), 163–64.
Independent, XXXII (December 2, 1880), 10.
Literary World, XI (December 4, 1880), 441.
New England Journal of Education, XII (December 23, 1880), 436.

Corbin, Caroline Fairfield. *Belle and the Boys.* (Chicago: Jansen, McClurg & Co.)
Atlantic Monthly, XLV (January, 1880), 129.
Harper's Magazine, LX (January, 1880), 315.
Crossing the Atlantic. (New York: E. P. Dutton & Co.)
Literary World, XI (October 23, 1880), 374.

Cousin Daisy (pseud.). *The Youngster.* Illustrated by Kate Greenaway. (Philadelphia: J. B. Lippincott & Co.)
Independent, XXXII (December 16, 1880), 9.

Darwin, Charles Robert. *What Mr. Darwin Saw in His Voyage Round the World in the Ship "Beagle."* (New York: Harper & Brothers)
Atlantic Monthly, XLV (January, 1880), 131.

Davis, J. A. *The Chinese Slave-Girl.* (Philadelphia: Presbyterian Board of Publication)
Literary World, XI (December 18, 1880), 467.

Day, Thomas. *The History of Sandford and Merton.* (Boston: Roberts Brothers)
Literary World, XI (November 6, 1880), 395.

De Morgan, Mary. *Necklace of Princess Fiorimonde.* (New York: Macmillan & Co.)
Dial, I (December, 1880), 163–64.
Independent, XXXII (December 16, 1880), 9.
Literary World, XI (December 4, 1880), 442.
Nation, XXXI (November 18, 1880), 363.

Dodge, Mary Mapes. *Hans Brinker; or, The Silver Skates.* (New York: Charles Scribner's Sons)
Harper's Magazine, LX (January, 1880), 315.

Eggleston, Edward and Mrs. L. E. Seelye. *Brant and Red Jacket.* (New York: Dodd, Mead & Co.)
Appleton's Journal, N. S. VIII (February, 1880), 192.
Harper's Magazine, LX (February, 1880), 475.
Independent, XXXII (January 1, 1880), 10.

Unitarian Review, XIII (May, 1880), 480.

Montezuma and the Conquest of Mexico. (New York: Dodd, Mead & Co.)
Independent, XXXII (November 4, 1880), 12.
Literary World, XI (October 23, 1880), 374.
Nation, XXXI (November 18, 1880), 364.
New England Journal of Education, XII (November 25, 1880), 362.

Pocahontas. (New York: Dodd, Mead & Co.)
Appleton's Journal, N.S. VIII (February, 1880), 192.
Harper's Magazine, LX (February, 1880), 475.

Eliot, Samuel. *Poetry for Children.* (Boston: Lee & Shepard)
Literary World, XI (January 17, 1880), 27.
New England Journal of Education, XI (February 12, 1880), 106.

Six Stories from the Arabian Nights. (Boston: Lee & Shepard)
Literary World, XI (January 17, 1880), 27.
New England Journal of Education, XI (February 12, 1880), 106.

Emmet, Rosina (illus.). *Pretty Peggy and Other Ballads.* (New York: Dodd, Mead
& Co.)
Dial, I (December, 1880), 163–64.
Independent, XXXII (December 2, 1880), 10.
Literary World, XI (December 4, 1880), 440–41.
New England Journal of Education, XII (November 18, 1880), 346.

The Pretty Peggy Painting Book. (New York: Dodd, Mead & Co.)
Independent, XXXII (December, 23, 1880), 11.

Ewing, Juliana Horatia. *We and the World.* (Boston: Roberts Brothers)
Literary World, XI (December 4, 1880), 440.
Nation, XXXI (December 9, 1880), 417.

The Fifth of November, and Other Tales. (London: Burnes & Oates)
Catholic World, XXXII (October, 1880), 144.

Finley, Martha F. (Martha Farquharson). *Elsie's Widowhood.* (New York: Dodd,
Mead & Co.)
Harper's Magazine, LXI (August, 1880), 483–84.
Literary World, XI (November 6, 1880), 396.
Nation, XXXI (September 16, 1880), 209.

First Lessons in Natural History and Language. (New York: Harper & Brothers)
Harper's Magazine, LX (February, 1880), 475.

Follen, Eliza Lee. *Little Songs.* New Edition. (Boston: Lee & Shepard)
Independent, XXXII (December 16, 1880), 9.
Literary World, XI (December 4, 1880), 441.

Fosdick, Charles A. (Harry Castlemon). *The Mail Carrier.* (Philadelphia: Porter
& Coates)
Independent, XXXII (March 4, 1880), 11.

Gaskoin, Mrs. Herman. *Children's Treasury of Bible Stories. Pt. III. The Apostles,
St. James, St. Paul, St. John.* (New York: Macmillan & Co.)
Independent, XXXII (June 3, 1880), 10.
Literary World, XI (October 9, 1880), 354.

Gatty, Margaret Scott. *Parables from Nature.* (New York: G. P. Putnam's Sons)
Literary World, XI (December 4, 1880), 441.
Nation, XXXI (December 9, 1880), 416.
New England Journal of Education, XII (November 11, 1880), 330.

Giberne, Agnes. *Sun, Moon and Stars.* (New York: Robert Carter & Brothers)
Harper's Magazine, LXII (December, 1880), 155.

Golden Hours (periodical).
Independent, XXXII (October 28, 1880), 10.

Goodale, Elaine and Dora Read. *In Berkshire with the Wild Flowers.* (New York: G. P. Putnam's Sons)
Atlantic Monthly, XLV (January, 1880), 127.

Greenaway, Kate. *Kate Greenaway's Birthday-Book for Children.* Verses by Mrs. Sale Barker. (New York: George Routledge & Sons)
Dial, I (December, 1880), 163–64.
Literary World, XI (November 6, 1880), 395.

Trot's Journey; Pictures, Rhymes and Stories. (New York: R. Worthington)
Independent, XXXII (December 2, 1880), 10.

Griffis, William Elliot. *Japanese Fairy World.* (Schenectady, N.Y.: James H. Barhyte)
Nation, XXXI (November 18, 1880), 363.

Guernsey, Lucy Ellen. *The Mission Box; or, Doing Good and Getting Good.* (New York: American Sunday-School Union)
New England Journal of Education, XI (April 22, 1880), 267.

Habberton, John. *The Worst Boy in Town.* (New York: G. P. Putnam's Sons)
Appleton's Journal, N. S. IX (November, 1880), 473.
Harper's Magazine, LXII (December, 1880), 155.
Literary World, XI (October 9, 1880), 354.
Scribner's Monthly, XXI (December, 1880), 321–22.

Haile, Ellen. *The Two Gray Girls and Their Opposite Neighbors.* (New York: Cassell, Petter & Galpin)
Independent, XXXII (December 2, 1880), 10.
Literary World, XI (December 4, 1880), 441.
Nation, XXXI (December 9, 1880), 417.

Hale, Edward Everett. *Stories of the Sea, Told by Sailors.* (Boston: Roberts Brothers)
Literary World, XI (December 18, 1880), 467.
Nation, XXI (December 16, 1880), 432.

Stories of War, Told by Soldiers. (Boston: Roberts Brothers)
Unitarian Review, XIII (January, 1880), 95.

Hale, Lucretia P. *The Peterkin Papers.* (Boston: Houghton, Mifflin & Co.)
Literary World, XI (December 4, 1880), 441.
Nation, XXXI (December 9, 1880), 417.

Hall, C. W. *Drifting Round the World: A Boy's Adventures by Sea and Land.* (Boston: Lee & Shepard)
Independent, XXXII (December 16, 1880), 10.
Nation, XXXI (December 16, 1880), 431–32.

Hall, John. *Foundation Stones for Young Builders.* (Philadelphia: American Sunday-School Union)
Independent, XXXII (January 15, 1880), 13.

Hamilton, Kate W. (Fleeta). *The House That Jack Built.* (Philadelphia: Presbyterian Board of Publication)
Literary World, XI (December 18, 1880), 467.

Vagabond and Victor. (Philadelphia: Presbyterian Board of Publication)
Literary World, XI (October 9, 1880), 354.

Harper's Young People (periodical).
Dial, I (December, 1880), 163–64.
Independent, XXXII (October 28, 1880), 10.
New England Journal of Education, XII (December 2, 1880), 380.

Harris, Amanda B. *How We Went Birds'-Nesting.* (Boston: D. Lothrop & Co.)
Literary World, XI (December 4, 1880), 440.

Hathaway, Mary E. N. *In the Fields.* (Boston: D. Lothrop & Co.)
Independent, XXXII (December 30, 1880), 11.

Hays, Mrs. W. J. *The Princess Idleways; A Fairy Story.* (New York: Harper & Brothers)
Atlantic Monthly, XLV (January, 1880), 129.
Harper's Magazine, LX (January, 1880), 315.
Independent, XXXII (March 4, 1880), 11.

Higginson, Mary Thacher. *Room for One More.* (Boston: Lee & Shepard)
Atlantic Monthly, XLV (January, 1880), 129.
Harper's Magazine, LX (January, 1880), 315.
Independent, XXXII (March 4, 1880), 11.

Hill, Kate Neely. *The Flower Mission, and What Grew Out of It.* (New York: American Sunday-School Union)
Independent, XXXII (March 4, 1880), 11.
New England Journal of Education, XI (April 22, 1880), 266.

Ingersoll, Ernest. *Friends Worth Knowing.* (New York: Harper & Brothers)
Literary World, XI (December 18, 1880), 467.

Jackson, Helen Hunt (H. H.). *Letters from a Cat.* (Boston: Roberts Brothers)
Harper's Magazine, LX (January, 1880), 315.

Kellogg, Elijah. *A Strong Arm and a Mother's Blessing.* (Boston: Lee & Shepard)
Literary World, XI (December 18, 1880), 467.

Kingston, William Henry Giles. *Dick Cheveley.* (Philadelphia: J. B. Lippincott & Co.)
Literary World, XI (November 6, 1880), 395.
Nation, XXXI (December 16, 1880), 431.

In the Wilds of Florida. (New York: Thomas Nelson & Sons)
Literary World, XI (November 6, 1880), 396.
Nation, XXXI (December 9, 1880), 416.

Tale of the Shore and Ocean; or, The Heir of Kilfinnan. (New York: A. C. Armstrong & Son)
Nation, XXXI (December 9, 1880), 416.

Knox, Thomas W. *The Boy Travellers in the Far East; Adventures of Two Youths in a Journey to Japan and China.* (New York: Harper & Brothers)
Californian, II (July, 1880), 92.
Harper's Magazine, LX (January, 1880), 314–15.
Lippincott's Magazine, XXV (January, 1880), 135–36.

The Boy Travellers in the Far East; Adventures of Two Youths in a Journey to Siam and Java. (New York: Harper & Brothers)
Dial, I (December, 1880), 163–64.
Harper's Magazine, LXII (December, 1880), 154–55.
Literary World, XI (December 4, 1880), 441.
Nation, XXXI (November 18, 1880), 363–64.
New England Journal of Education, XII (November 18, 1880), 346.

Lanier, Sidney. *The Boy's Froissart.* (New York: Charles Scribner's Sons)
Appleton's Journal, N. S. VII (January, 1880), 96.
Atlantic Monthly, XLV (January, 1880), 130.
Harper's Magazine, LX (February, 1880), 474.
Lippincott's Magazine, XXV (January, 1880), 135.

The Boy's King Arthur. (New York: Charles Scribner's Sons)
Dial, I (December, 1880), 163–64.
Independent, XXXII (December 9, 1880), 10.
Literary World, XI (December 4, 1880), 441.
Nation, XXXI (November 18, 1880), 364.
New England Journal of Education, XII (December 9, 1880), 398.

Little Buttercup's Picture Book. (New York: George Routledge & Sons)
Literary World, XI (December 4, 1880), 441.

Little Folks' Bible Gallery. (New York: Cassell, Petter, Galpin & Co.)
Literary World, XI (December 4, 1880), 441.

Little Songs for Little People. (New York: A. D. F. Randolph)
Independent, XXXII (December 30, 1880), 11.

Little Tiny's Book of Objects. (New York: George Routledge & Sons)
Literary World, XI (December 4, 1880), 441.

Locker, Mrs. Frederick. *What the Blackbird Said.* (New York: George Routledge & Sons)
Literary World, XI (December 4, 1880), 442.
Nation, XXXI (December 9, 1880), 416.

Lodge, Henry Cabot. *Six Popular Tales.* (Boston: George A. Smith)
Literary World, XI (January 17, 1880), 27.
New England Journal of Education, XI (February 12, 1880), 106.

Lossing, Benson J. *Story of the United States Navy, for Boys.* (New York: Harper & Brothers)
Independent, XXXII (December 23, 1880), 11.
Nation, XXXI (December 16, 1880), 432.

Mark Dennison's Charge. (New York: George Routledge & Sons)
Literary World, XI (December 4, 1880), 442.

Markham, Richard. *Aboard the Mavis.* (New York: Dodd, Mead & Co.)
Literary World, XI (December 4, 1880), 441.
Nation, XXXI (December 9, 1880), 416–17.
New England Journal of Education, XII (December 16, 1880), 416.

Around the Yule Log. (New York: Dodd, Mead & Co.)
Harper's Magazine, LX (February, 1880), 475.

Materfamilias (pseud.). *Tales from the Odyssey for Boys and Girls.* (New York: Harper & Brothers)
Harper's Magazine, LX (April, 1880), 795.

Mathews, Joanna H. *Belle's Pink Boots.* (New York: E. P. Dutton & Co.)
Dial, I (December, 1880), 163–64.
Independent, XXXII (December 2, 1880), 10.
Literary World, XI (December 4, 1880), 441.

Merry Ballads of the Olden Time. (London: Scribner & Welford)
Dial, I (December, 1880), 163–64.

Middleton, Meade. *Now and Then, at Daisy Dingle Farm.* (Philadelphia: Presbyterian Board of Publication)
Literary World, XI (October 9, 1880), 354.

Miller, Olive Thorne. *Little Folks in Feathers and Fur, and Others in Neither.* (New York: E. P. Dutton & Co.)
New England Journal of Education, XI (April 22, 1880), 266.

Nimpo's Troubles. (New York: E. P. Dutton & Co.)
Independent, XXXII (March 4, 1880), 11.

Queer Pets at Marcy's. (New York: E. P. Dutton & Co.)
Dial, I (December, 1880), 163–64.
Harper's Magazine, LXII (December, 1880), 155.
Independent, XXXII (October 7, 1880), 12.
Literary World, XI (October 23, 1880), 373.
Nation, XXXI (November 18, 1880), 363.

Molesworth, Mrs. Mary Louisa (Ennis Graham). *A Christmas Child.* (New York: Macmillan & Co.)
Independent, XXXII (December 9, 1880), 10.
Literary World, XI (December 4, 1880), 441.
Nation, XXXI (December 9, 1880), 416.

Hermy. (New York: George Routledge & Sons)
Literary World, XI (December 4, 1880), 441.

The Tapestry Room. (New York: Macmillan & Co.)
Independent, XXXII (March 11, 1880), 11.

Moseley, Julia Daniels. *Little Zee; A Fairy Story*. (Chicago: H. A. Sumner & Co.)
Dial, I (December, 1880), 163–64.
New England Journal of Education, XII (December 23, 1880), 436.

Moulton, Louise Chandler. *Bed-Time Stories*. Vol. III. (Boston: Roberts Brothers)
Literary World, XI (October 23, 1880), 373–74.

The Nursery (periodical).
Independent, XXXII (October 28, 1880), 10.

Old Fashioned Fairy Tales. (Boston: Roberts Brothers)
Literary World, XI (November 6, 1880), 395.

Petrie, Helen. *The Little Pilgrim*. (New York: E. P. Dutton & Co.)
Literary World, XI (October 23, 1880), 374.

Phillips, E. C. *Meyrick's Promise; or, Little Fugitives from the Jamaica Rebellion in 1865*. (New York: George Routledge & Sons)
Literary World, XI (December 18, 1880), 467.

Pilgrim, T. (Arthur Morecamp). *Live Boys in the Black Hills; or, The Young Texan Gold-Hunters*. (Boston: Lee & Shepard)
Literary World, XI (December 18, 1880), 467.

Prince Darling's Story Book. (New York: George Routledge & Sons)
Literary World, XI (December 18, 1880), 467.
Nation, XXXI (December 16, 1880), 432.

Rand, E. A. *The Bark Cabin on the Kearsarge*. (Boston: D. Lothrop & Co.)
Independent, XXXII (July 1, 1880), 10.
Pushing Ahead; or, Big Brother Dave. (Boston: D. Lothrop & Co.)
Independent, XXXII (July 1, 1880), 10.
Literary World, XI (October 9, 1880), 354.

Raymond, Rossiter W. *The Merry Go Round*. (New York: Fords, Howard, & Hulbert)
New Englander, XXXIX (March, 1880), 304.

Richards, Laura E. *Five Mice in a Mouse-Trap by the Man in the Moon. Done in Vernacular from the Lunacular by Laura E. Richards*. (Boston: Estes & Lauriat)
New England Journal of Education, XII (December 16, 1880), 416.

Rousselet, Louis. *The Serpent-Charmer*. (New York: Charles Scribner's Sons)
Harper's Magazine, LX (February, 1880), 475.

Routledge, W. *Singing Quadrille and Children's Singing Lancers*. (New York: George Routledge & Sons)
Literary World, XI (December 4, 1880), 441.
Nation, XXXI (December 16, 1880), 432.

Roy's Dory. (Boston: D. Lothrop & Co.)
Literary World, XI (December 18, 1880), 467.

St. Nicholas (periodical).
Dial, I (December, 1880), 163–64.
Independent, XXXII (October 28, 1880), 10.

Scott, J. Walter. *A Revised List of Postage Stamps and Stamped Envelopes of All Nations*. (New York: Scott & Co.)
Harper's Magazine, LX (January, 1880), 315.

Scudder, Horace Elisha. *The Bodleys Afoot*. (Boston: Houghton, Mifflin & Co.)
Atlantic Monthly, XLV (January, 1880), 127.

Mr. Bodley Abroad. (Boston: Houghton, Mifflin & Co.)
Dial I (December, 1880), 163–64.
Harper's Magazine, LXI (November, 1880), 955–56.
Independent, XXXII (September 16, 1880), 12.
New England Journal of Education, XII (October 7, 1880), 250.
Scribner's Monthly, XXI (December, 1880), 321.

Seamer, Mary. *Shakespeare's Stories Simply Told.* (New York: Thomas Nelson & Sons)
Literary World, XI (November 6, 1880), 395–96.
Nation, XXXI (November 18, 1880), 364.

Sequel to Mamma's Bible Stories. (New York: Robert Carter & Brothers)
Independent, XXXII (February 5, 1880), 12.

Shillaber, B. P. *Cruises with Captain Bob on Sea and Land.* (Boston: Lee & Shepard)
Independent, XXXII (March 4, 1880), 11.

A Silver Key to a Golden Palace. (New York: George Routledge & Sons)
Literary World, XI (December 4, 1880), 441.

Smith, Mrs. F. Burge. *Cousin Minnie.* (New York: T. Whittaker)
Literary World, XI (October 9, 1880), 354.

Smith, J. Moyr (illus.). *Tales of Old Thûle.* (Philadelphia: J. P. Lippincott & Co.)
Harper's Magazine, LX (February, 1880), 475.
Independent, XXXII (March 11, 1880), 11.

The Wooing of the Water Witch. (New York: Henry Holt & Co.)
Independent, XXXII (December 16, 1880), 10.
Literary World, XI (December 18, 1880), 467.

Sowerby, J. G. and H. H. Emerson. *Afternoon Tea.* (New York: Scribner & Welford)
Dial, I (December, 1880), 163–64.

Stephenson, Elizabeth Tabor. *Pansie's Flour-Bin.* (New York: Macmillan & Co.)
Independent, XXXII (December 23, 1880), 11.
Literary World, XI (December 4, 1880), 441.
Nation, XXXI (December 9, 1880), 416.

Stockton, Frank R. *A Jolly Fellowship.* (New York: Charles Scribner's Sons)
Harper's Magazine, LXII (December, 1880), 155.
Independent, XXXII (October 7, 1880), 12.
International Review, IX (December, 1880), 723.
Literary World, XI (October 23, 1880), 373.
Nation, XXXI (November 18, 1880), 364.
Scribner's Monthly, XXI (December, 1880), 321.

Sunday. (periodical). (New York: E. P. Dutton & Co.)
Independent, XXXII (October 7, 1880), 12.
Literary World, XI (September 11, 1880), 312.
Literary World, XI (October 23, 1880), 373.

Sunday Chatterbox. (New York: R. Worthington)
Independent, XXXII (December 2, 1880), 10.

Talbot, Eleanor W. *Wonder Eyes, and What For?* (New York: Cassell, Petter, Galpin & Co.)
Independent, XXXII (December 2, 1880), 10.
Literary World, XI (December 4, 1880), 441.

Tales from Ariosto, Retold for Children. (Boston: Roberts Brothers)
Unitarian Review, XIII (January, 1880), 95.

Taneyhill, M. Ellen. *The Young Folks of Renfrew.* (New York: Phillips & Hunt)
Independent, XXXII (March 4, 1880), 11.

Tilsley, M. J. *Ups and Downs; All Smiles, No Frowns.* (New York: E. P. Dutton & Co.)

Dial, I (December, 1880), 163–64.
Independent, XXXII (December 2, 1880), 10.
Literary World, XI (October 23, 1880), 374.

Towle, George M. *Magellan; or, The First Voyage Round the World.* (Boston: Lee & Shepard)
Appleton's Journal, N. S. VIII (February, 1880), 192.
Atlantic Monthly, XLV (January, 1880), 131.
Harper's Magazine, LX (February, 1880), 474–75.

Marco Polo. (Boston: Lee & Shepard)
Independent, XXXII (November 4, 1880), 12.
Literary World, XI (November 6, 1880), 395.
Nation, XXXI (November 18, 1880), 364.

Trowbridge, John Townsend (Paul Creyton). *The Silver Medal.* (Boston: Lee & Shepard)
Literary World, XI (December 18, 1880), 467.

Young Joe, and Other Stories. (Boston: Lee & Shepard)
Independent, XXXII (March 4, 1880), 11.

Uncle Herbert (pseud.). *Feet and Wings.* (Philadelphia: J. B. Lippincott & Co.)
Literary World, XI (December 18, 1880), 467.
Nation, XXXI (December 16, 1880), 432.

Uno (pseud.). *Baby Ballads.* (Boston: Lee & Shepard)
Independent, XXXII (December 16, 1880), 9.
Literary World, XI (December 4, 1880), 441.

Vandegrift, Margaret. *Clover Beach.* (Philadelphia: Porter & Coates)
Literary World, XI (December 18, 1880), 467.

Verne, Jules. *The Exploration of the World.* (New York: Charles Scribner's Sons)
Harper's Magazine, LXII (December, 1880), 155.
Independent, XXXII (October 28, 1880), 10.
Lippincott's Magazine, XXV (January, 1880), 135.
New England Journal of Education, XII (October 21, 1880), 282.
Scribner's Monthly, XXI (December, 1880), 322.

The Tribulations of a Chinaman in China. (New York: E. P. Dutton & Co.)
Independent, XXXII (January 1, 1880), 11.
Literary World, XI (October 23, 1880), 374.

Viollet-le-Duc, Eugene E. *Learning to Draw; or, The Story of a Young Designer.* (New York: G. P. Putnam's Sons)
Nation, XXXI (December 16, 1880), 431.

Walton, Mrs. O. F. *Christie's Old Organ. Saved at Sea. Little Faith.* (New York: Robert Carter & Brothers)
Harper's Magazine, LXII (December, 1880), 155.

Weatherly, George. *Little Folk's Black and White Painting-Book.* (New York: Cassell, Petter, Galpin & Co.)
Independent, XXXII (December 2, 1880), 10.
Literary World, XI (November 6, 1880), 395.

Pictures to Paint. (New York: Cassell, Petter, Galpin & Co.)
Independent, XXXII (December 2, 1880), 10.
Literary World, XI (November 6, 1880), 395.

What Is a Gentleman? (Boston: A. K. Loring)
Independent, XXXII (February 26, 1880), 12.

What Rosa Did. (New York: R. Worthington)
Independent, XXXII (December 2, 1880), 10.

Wide-Awake (periodical).
Independent, XXXII (October 28, 1880), 10.

Winslow, Forbes E. *Child's Fairy Geography; A Merry Trip Round Europe.* (New York: Pott, Young & Co.)
Nation, XXXI (November 18, 1880), 364.
New England Journal of Education, XII (December 16, 1880), 416.

Winthrop, A. T. *Wilfred.* (New York: A. D. F. Randolph)
Literary World, XI (December 18, 1880), 467.

Wise, Daniel (Francis Forrester; Lawrence Lancewood). *Roderick Ashcourt.* (Boston: Lee & Shepard)
Independent, XXXII (March 4, 1880), 11.

Woods, Kate Tannatt. *Six Little Rebels.* (Boston: D. Lothrop & Co.)
Atlantic Monthly, XLV (January, 1880), 128–29.

Woolsey, Sarah Chauncey (Susan Coolidge). *Eyebright.* (Boston: Roberts Brothers)
Harper's Magazine, LX (January, 1880), 315.

A Guernsey Lily; or, How the Feud Was Healed. (Boston: Roberts Brothers)
Dial, I (December, 1880), 163–64.
Literary World, XI (December 4, 1880), 442.

Yonge, Charlotte M. *Bye-Words. A Collection of Tales New and Old.* (London and New York: Macmillan & Co.).
Independent, XXXII (May 16, 1880), 10.
Nation, XXX (March 11, 1880), 201.

Youth's Companion (periodical).
Independent, XXXII (October 28, 1880), 10.

BOOKS REVIEWED IN 1881

Abbott, Edward. *The Long Look Books.* Vols. I, II, & III. (Boston: Henry D. Noyes & Co.)
Journal of Education, XIV (November 24, 1881), 346.

Adams, H. C. *Who Did It? or, Holmwood Priory.* (New York: E. P. Dutton & Co.)
Critic, I (November 19, 1881), 321.

Adams, W. H. Davenport. *Some Heroes of Travel.* (New York: Pott, Young & Co.)
Atlantic Monthly, XLVII (January, 1881), 125.

Adams, William T. (Oliver Optic). *Down South; or, Yacht Adventures in Florida.* (Boston: Lee & Shepard)
Independent, XXXIII (January 13, 1881), 12.
New England Journal of Education, XII (January 6, 1881), 10.

Albertsen, Frank. *The Four-Footed Lovers.* (Boston: Lee & Shepard)
Californian, IV (December, 1881), 537.
Journal of Education, XIV (December 29, 1881), 442.

Alcott, Louisa May. *Jack and Jill.* (Boston: Roberts Brothers)
Atlantic Monthly, XLVII (January, 1881), 123.
Harper's Magazine, LXII (January, 1881), 314.
Scribner's Monthly, XXI (January, 1881), 481.

Alden, Isabella M. (Pansy). *The Pocket Measure.* (Boston: D. Lothrop & Co.)
Literary World, XII (October 22, 1881), 374.

Alden, W. L. *Cruise of the "Ghost"* (New York: Harper & Brothers)
Journal of Education, XIV (December 1, 1881), 364.
Nation, XXXIII (December 8, 1881), 456.

The Moral Pirates. (New York: Harper & Brothers)
Atlantic Monthly, XLVII (February, 1881), 301.
Harper's Magazine, LXII (January, 1881), 314–15.

Lippincott's Magazine, XXVII (January, 1881), 111–12.

Alger, Horatio, Jr. *From Canal Boy to President; or, The Boyhood and Manhood of James A. Garfield.* (New York: John R. Anderson & Co.)
Journal of Education, XIV (November 17, 1881), 328.
Ohio Educational Monthly, XXIX (December, 1881), 438.

Ames, Fanny B. *Christmas Day and All the Year.* (Boston: George H. Ellis)
Critic, I (October 8, 1881), 276.

Arrom, C. B. de F. (Fernan Caballero). *Spanish Fairy Tales.* (Philadelphia: J. B. Lippincott & Co.)
Critic, I (November 19, 1881), 321.
Dial, II (December, 1881), 183.
Nation, XXXIII (December 15, 1881), 477.
Literary World, XII (December 3, 1881), 450.

Baby Dear. (New York: R. Worthington)
Literary World, XII (September 24, 1881), 328.

Ballantyne, Robert Michael. *Giant of the North; or, Pokings Round the Pole.* (New York: Thomas Nelson & Sons)
Nation, XXXIII (November 17, 1881), 400.

Beach, Rebecca Gibbons. *Allie's Mistake; A Christmas Story.* (New York: G. P. Putnam's Sons)
Harper's Magazine, LXII (February, 1881), 476.

Beecher, Julia M. *Air! Fire! Bang! Stories for Young Folks.* (Boston: Lee & Shepard)
Independent, XXXIII (January 13, 1881), 12.
Lippincott's Magazine, XXVII (January, 1881), 112.

Boys' and Girls' First Story Book. (Philadelphia: J. B. Lippincott & Co.)
Literary World, XII (January 1, 1881), 11.

Brook, Sarah. *A French History for English Children.* (London and New York: Macmillan & Co.)
Journal of Education, XIV (December 29, 1881), 442.
Literary World, XII (December 3, 1881), 451.
Nation, XXXIII (December 8, 1881), 456.

Brooks, Noah. *The Fairport Nine.* (New York: Charles Scribner's Sons)
Atlantic Monthly, XLVII (January, 1881), 123.
Harper's Magazine, LXII (January, 1881), 314.

Buckley, Arabella B. *Life and Her Children.* (New York: D. Appleton & Co.)
Atlantic Monthly, XLVII (April, 1881), 592.
Literary World, XII (April 9, 1881), 135.
Popular Science Monthly, XVIII (March, 1881), 701.

Butterworth, Hezekiah. *Young Folks' History of America.* (Boston: Estes & Lauriat).
Californian, IV (October, 1881), 361.
Literary World, XII (June 4, 1881), 201.
Nation, XXXIII (August 25, 1881), 160.
New England Journal of Education, XIII (June 16, 1881), 408.

Young Folks' History of Boston. (Boston: Estes & Lauriat)
Journal of Education, XIV (November 24, 1881), 346.
Literary World, XII (December 3, 1881), 449–50.
Nation, XXXIII (November 17, 1881), 400.
Nation, XXXIII (December 15, 1881), 478.

Zigzag Journeys in Classic Lands; or, Tommy Toby's Trip to Mt. Parnassus. (Boston: Estes & Lauriat)
Atlantic Monthly, XLVII (February, 1881), 302.
Literary World, XII (January 1, 1881), 11.

Zigzag Journeys in the Orient; The Adriatic to the Baltic. (Boston: Estes & Lauriat)
Dial, II (December, 1881), 184.
Journal of Education, XIV (December 1, 1881), 364.
Literary World, XII (September 24, 1881), 327.
Nation, XXXIII (December 15, 1881), 478.

Carey, Annie. *School-Girls; or, Life at Montagu Hall.* (New York: Cassell, Petter, Galpin & Co.)
Critic, I (September 10, 1881), 247.
Literary World, XII (October 22, 1881), 373.

Cassell's Book of Indoor Amusements, Card Games and Fireside Fun. (New York: Cassell, Petter, Galpin & Co.)
Critic, I (December 3, 1881), 337–38.
Dial, II (December, 1881), 185.
Journal of Education, XIV (November 24, 1881), 346.
Literary World, XII (November 19, 1881), 418–19.
Nation, XXXIII (December 15, 1881), 478.

Cassell's Book of Sports and Pastimes. (New York: Cassell, Petter, Galpin & Co.)
Critic, I (December 3, 1881), 337–38.
Nation, XXXIII (December 15, 1881), 478.

Champlin, John D., Jr. *The Young Folks' Astronomy.* (New York: Henry Holt & Co.)
Atlantic Monthly, XLVIII (September, 1881), 432.
Critic, I (August 27, 1881), 233.
Nation, XXXIII (August 11, 1881), 122.
New England Journal of Education, XIV (August 11, 1881), 94.

The Young Folks' Cyclopaedia of Persons and Places. (New York: Henry Holt & Co.)
Atlantic Monthly, XLVII (February, 1881), 302.
Literary World, XII (February 12, 1881), 51.
Popular Science Monthly, XVIII (April, 1881), 848.

Young Folks' History of the War for the Union. (New York: Henry Holt & Co.)
Appleton's Journal, N. S. XI (July, 1881), 96.
Critic, I (November 19, 1881), 320.
Dial, II (December, 1881), 185.
Journal of Education, XIV (November 10, 1881), 310.
Nation, XXXIII (November 24, 1881), 419–20.

Chatterbox for 1881. (Boston: Estes & Lauriat)
Critic, I (December 3, 1881), 337–38.
Dial, II (December, 1881), 186.
Journal of Education, XIV (November 24, 1881), 346.
Literary World, XII (December 3, 1881), 450.

Chatterbox Junior. (New York: R. Worthington)
Literary World, XII (November 5, 1881), 398.

Chatterbox Packet. (Boston: Estes & Lauriat)
Dial, II (December, 1881), 186.

Chellis, Mary Dwinell. *Harold Dorsey's Fortune.* (Boston: Congregational Publishing Society)
Atlantic Monthly, XLVIII (October, 1881), 574.

Clemens, Samuel Langhorne (Mark Twain). *The Prince and the Pauper.* (Boston: James R. Osgood & Co.)
Atlantic Monthly, XLVIII (December, 1881), 843–45.
Critic, I (December 31, 1881), 368.

Coffin, Charles Carleton (Carleton). *Old Times in the Colonies*. (New York: Harper & Brothers)
    Appleton's Journal, N. S. X (January, 1881), 95.
    Atlantic Monthly, XLVII (January, 1881), 125–26.
    Harper's Magazine, LXII (January, 1881), 313–14.
    Lippincott's Magazine, XXVII (January, 1881), 111.

Cooke, Laura S. H. *Dimple Dopp*. (Boston: James R. Osgood & Co.)
    Nation, XXXIII (November 17, 1881), 399.

Corbett, Mrs. E. T. *Three Wise Old Couples*. (New York: Cassell, Petter, Galpin & Co.)
    Critic, I (December 3, 1881), 337–38.
    Journal of Education, XIV (November 24, 1881), 346.
    Literary World, XII (September 24, 1881), 327.
    Literary World, XII (November 19, 1881), 418.
    Nation, XXXIII (November 24, 1881), 419.

Cousin Daisy (pseud.). *The Youngster*. (Philadelphia: J. B. Lippincott & Co.)
    Literary World, XII (January 1, 1881), 11.

Cupples, Ann Jane. *Driver to Sea*. (Boston: A. Williams & Co.)
    Literary World, XII (December 3, 1881), 450.
    Nation, XXXIII (December 15, 1881), 478.

Cupples, George. *Deserted Ship*. (Boston: A. Williams & Co.)
    Literary World, XII (December 3, 1881), 450.
    Nation, XXXIII (December 15, 1881), 478.

Day, Thomas. *The History of Sandford and Merton*. (New York: George Routledge & Sons)
    Dial, II (December, 1881), 181–82.
    Literary World, XII (December 3, 1881), 450.

Defoe, Daniel. *Life and Adventures of Robinson Crusoe*. (London: Bickers & Son; New York: Scribner & Welford)
    Nation, XXXIII (December 8, 1881), 457.
    Life and Adventures of Robinson Crusoe. (New York: Harper & Brothers)
    Atlantic Monthly, XLVIII (July, 1881), 144.
    Harper's Magazine, LXIII (August, 1881), 476.

Diaz, Abby Morton. *King Grimalkum and Pussyanita; or, The Cat's Arabian Nights*. (Boston: D. Lothrop & Co.)
    Nation, XXXIII (November 17, 1881), 399.

Dodge, Mary Mapes. *Rhymes and Jingles*. (New York: Charles Scribner's Sons)
    Literary World, XII (January 1, 1881), 11.

Drake, Samuel Adams. *Around the Hub*. (Boston: Roberts Brothers)
    Critic, I (December 31, 1881), 369.
    Dial, II (December, 1881), 184.
    Journal of Education, XIV (November 17, 1881), 328.
    Literary World, XII (December 3, 1881), 449–50.
    Nation, XXXIII (November 17, 1881), 400.

Eddy, D. C. (Rupert Van Wert). *Rip Van Winkle's Travels in Foreign Lands*. (New York: Thomas Y. Crowell & Co.)
    Nation, XXXIII (December 15, 1881), 478.

Elliott, J. W., and J. M. Bentley. *The Little Folks' Album of Music*. (New York: Cassell, Petter, Galpin & Co.)
    Dial, II (December, 1881), 185.
    Journal of Education, XIV (November 24, 1881), 346.
    Literary World, XII (September 24, 1881), 327.
    Literary World, XII (November 19, 1881), 419.
    Nation, XXXIII (December 8, 1881), 456–57.

Emmet, Rosina (illus.). *Pretty Peggy and Other Ballads.* (New York: Dodd, Mead & Co.)
Scribner's Monthly, XXI (January, 1881), 481.

Pretty Peggy Painting Book. (New York: Dodd, Mead & Co.)
Literary World, XII (January 1, 1881), 11.

Engle, Alice B. *A Story of Four Acorns.* (Boston: D. Lothrop & Co.)
Journal of Education, XIV (November 24, 1881), 346.
Literary World, XII (December 3, 1881), 450.
Nation, XXXIII (December 8, 1881), 457.

Ewing, Juliana Horatia (Aunt Judy). *Mrs. Overtheway's Remembrances.* (Boston: Roberts Brothers)
Atlantic Monthly, XLVIII (December, 1881), 858.
Critic, I (November 19, 1881), 322–23.
Literary World, XII (October 22, 1881), 372.
Nation, XXXIII (November 17, 1881), 399.

We and the World. (Boston: Roberts Brothers)
Harper's Magazine, LXII (January, 1881), 314.

Finley, Martha F. (Martha Farquharson). *Mildred and Elsie.* (New York: Dodd, Mead & Co.)
Journal of Education, XIV (December 29, 1881), 442.

Fosdick, Charles A. (Harry Castlemon). *George at the Wheel; or, Life in a Pilot-House.* (Philadelphia: Porter & Coates)
Nation, XXXIII (December 15, 1881), 478.

Gatty, Margaret Scott. *Parables from Nature.* (New York: G. P. Putnam's Sons)
Atlantic Monthly, XLVII (February, 1881), 301.
Harper's Magazine, LXII (January, 1881), 314.
Lippincott's Magazine, XXVII (January, 1881), 112.
Scribner's Monthly, XXI (January, 1881), 482.

Gerson, Virginia. *Little Dignity.* (New York: George Routledge & Sons)
Critic, I (November 5, 1881), 307.
Dial, II (December, 1881), 181–82.
Literary World, XII (December 3, 1881), 449.
Nation, XXXIII (November 24, 1881), 419.

Gray, W. T. *A Bad Boy's Diary.* (New York: J. S. Ogilvie)
Atlantic Monthly, XLVII (February, 1881), 302.

Greenaway, Kate. *Kate Greenaway's Birthday-Book for Children.* Verses by Mrs. Sale Barker. (New York: George Routledge & Sons)
Literary World, XII (January 1, 1881), 11.

Mother Goose. (New York: George Routledge & Sons)
Critic, I (November 5, 1881), 307.
Dial, II (December, 1881), 181–82.
Literary World, XII (December 3, 1881), 449.
Nation, XXXIII (November 24, 1881), 419.

Greéy, Edward. *Young Americans in Japan; Adventures of the Jewett Family and Their Friend Oto Nambo.* (Boston: Lee & Shepard)
Californian, IV (December, 1881), 537.
Dial, II (December, 1881), 183–84.
Journal of Education, XIV (November 24, 1881), 346.
Literary World, XII (November 19, 1881), 419.
Nation, XXXIII (December 8, 1881), 456.
Penn Monthly, XII (December, 1881), 956–57.

Griffis, William Elliot. *Japanese Fairy World.* (Schenectady, N.Y.: James H. Barhyte)
Atlantic Monthly, XLVII (January, 1881), 125.
Californian, III (January, 1881), 92.

Lippincott's Magazine, XXVII (January, 1881), 112.
New Englander, XL (January, 1881), 133–34.
Scribner's Monthly, XXII (October, 1881), 954.

Guernsey, Lucy Ellen. *The Old Stanfield House; or, The Sin of Covetousness.* (Philadelphia: American Sunday-School Union)
Independent, XXXIII (January 13, 1881), 12.

Habberton, John. *Who Was Paul Grayson?* (New York: Harper & Brothers)
Atlantic Monthly, XLVIII (July, 1881), 144.
Californian, IV (July, 1881), 93.
Dial, II (June, 1881), 44.
New England Journal of Education, XIII (June 2, 1881), 374.

The Worst Boy in Town. (New York: G. P. Putnam's Sons)
Atlantic Monthly, XLVII (January, 1881), 123.
Lippincott's Magazine, XXVII (January, 1881), 112.

Haile, Ellen. *Hazel-Nut and Her Brothers.* (New York: Cassell, Petter, Galpin & Co.)
Critic, I (December 31, 1881), 369.
Journal of Education, XIV (November 24, 1881), 346.
Literary World, XII (September 24, 1881), 327.
Nation, XXXIII (December 8, 1881), 457.

Hale, Edward Everett. *Stories of Adventure, Told by Adventurers.* (Boston: Roberts Brothers)
Atlantic Monthly, XLVIII (December, 1881), 858.
Critic, I (November 15, 1881), 307.
Literary World, XII (October 22, 1881), 374.
Nation, XXXIII (December 15, 1881), 478.

Stories of War, Told by Soldiers. (Boston: Roberts Brothers)
Scribner's Monthly, XXI (January, 1881), 482.

Hale, Lucretia P. *Peterkin Papers.* (Boston: James R. Osgood & Co.)
Independent, XXXIII (January 6, 1881), 11–12.
Scribner's Monthly, XXII (October, 1881), 954.

Harper's Young People (periodical).
Dial, II (December, 1881), 186.
Journal of Education, XIV (November 24, 1881), 346.

Harris, G. Amanda. *The Little Folks' Everyday Book.* (Boston: D. Lothrop & Co.)
Dial, II (December, 1881), 181–82.

Harris, Joel Chandler. *Uncle Remus; His Songs and Sayings.* (New York: D. Appleton & Co.)
Appleton's Journal, N. S. X (January, 1881), 95.
Literary World, XII (March 26, 1881), 118.
Scribner's Monthly, XXI (April, 1881), 961–62.
Unitarian Review, XVI (August, 1881), 196.

Hauff, William. *The Arabian Days' Entertainment.* Translated by H. P. Curtis. (Boston: Houghton, Mifflin & Co.)
Nation, XXXIII (December 15, 1881), 477.

Little Mook and Other Fairy Tales. Translated by Percy Pinkerton. (New York: G. P. Putnam's Sons)
Critic, I (December 31, 1881), 369.
Literary World, XII (December 3, 1881), 450.
Nation, XXXIII (December 15, 1881), 477.

Tales of the Caravan, Inn, and Palace. Translated by Edward L. Stowell. (Chicago: Jansen, McClurg & Co.)
Dial, II (December, 1881), 183.
Nation, XXXIII (December 15, 1881), 477.

Hoffman, Professor ——. *Modern Magic*. (New York: Cassell, Petter, Galpin & Co.)
Dial, II (December, 1881), 185–86.

Parlor Amusements and Evening Party Entertainments. (New York: George Routledge & Sons)
Critic, I (December 3, 1881), 337–38.
Dial, II (December, 1881), 184.

Hoppin, A. (C. Auton). *Recollections of Auton House*. (Boston: Houghton, Mifflin & Co.)
Critic, I (December 3, 1881), 337–38.
Dial, II (December, 1881), 185.
Literary World, XII (December 3, 1881), 450.

Hulme, F. Edward. *Flower-Painting in Water-Colors*. (New York: Cassell, Petter, Galpin & Co.)
Literary World, XII (November 19, 1881), 418.

Hunt, Mrs. Holman. *Children at Jerusalem*. (London: Ward, Lock & Co.)
Literary World, XII (October 22, 1881), 373.

Ingersoll, Ernest. *Friends Worth Knowing*. (New York: Harper & Brothers)
Atlantic Monthly, XLVII (February, 1881), 302.
Lippincott's Magazine, XXVII (January, 1881), 112.
New England Journal of Education, XII (January 27, 1881), 64.

Jackson, Helen Hunt (H. H.). *Mammy Tittleback and Her Family*. (Boston: Roberts Brothers)
Critic, I (November 5, 1881), 307.
Literary World, XII (October 22, 1881), 373.
Nation, XXXIII (November 17, 1881), 399.

Jeffries, Richard. *Wood Magic*. (New York: Cassell, Petter, Galpin & Co.)
Atlantic Monthly, XLVIII (October, 1881), 574.

Johnson, E. K. (illus.). *Puss-in-Boots*. (New York: Thomas Nelson & Sons)
Nation, XXXIII (November 24, 1881), 419.

Johnson, Rossiter. *Phaeton Rogers*. (New York: Charles Scribner's Sons)
Atlantic Monthly, XLVIII (December, 1881), 858.
Critic, I (November 19, 1881), 321.
Journal of Education, XIV (November 17, 1881), 328.
Literary World, XII (November 5, 1881), 398.
Nation, XXXIII (November 17, 1881), 399.

Kaler, James Otis (James Otis). *Toby Tyler; or, Ten Weeks with a Circus*. (New York: Harper & Brothers)
Californian, IV (November, 1881), 448.
Critic, I (September 10, 1881), 247.
Dial, II (October, 1881), 123.
Harper's Magazine, LXIII (November, 1881), 953.
Nation, XXXIII (November 24, 1881), 420.

Keith, Leslie. *Nobody's Lad*. (New York: Robert Carter & Brothers)
Harper's Magazine, LXII (February, 1881), 476.

Kellogg, Elijah. *A Strong Arm and a Mother's Blessing*. (Boston: Lee & Shepard)
Atlantic Monthly, XLVII (February, 1881), 301.

The Unseen Hand; or, James Renfrew and His Boy Helpers. (Boston: Lee & Shepard)
Journal of Education, XIV (December 29, 1881), 442.

King Christmas. (New York: Dodd, Mead & Co.)
Dial, II (December, 1881), 181–82.

Kingston, William Henry Giles. *Dick Cheveley*. (Philadelphia: J. B. Lippincott & Co.)

Atlantic Monthly, XLVII (February, 1881), 301.
Independent, XXXIII (January 13, 1881), 12.
Lippincott's Magazine, XXVII (January, 1881), 112.

Peter Trawl; or, The Adventures of a Whaler. (New York: A. C. Armstrong & Son)
Literary World, XII (December 3, 1881), 450.
Nation, XXXIII (December 15, 1881), 478.

A Tale of the Shore and Ocean; or, The Heir of Kilfinnan. (New York: A. C. Armstrong & Son)
Independent, XXXIII (January 13, 1881), 12.

Knox, Thomas W. *The Boy Travellers in the Far East; Adventures of Two Youths in a Journey to Ceylon and India.* (New York: Harper & Brothers)
Dial, II (December, 1881), 183.
Journal of Education, XIV (December 1, 1881), 364.
Literary World, XII (December 3, 1881), 450.
Nation, XXXIII (December 15, 1881), 478.

The Boy Travellers in the Far East; Adventures of Two Youths in a Journey to Siam and Java. (New York: Harper & Brothers)
Appleton's Journal, N. S. X (January, 1881), 95.
Atlantic Monthly, XLVII (January, 1881), 125.
Californian, III (January, 1881), 92.
Lippincott's Magazine, XXVII (January, 1881), 111.
Scribner's Monthly, XXI (January, 1881), 482.

The Young Nimrods in North America; Hunting Adventures on Land and Sea. (New York: Harper & Brothers)
Appleton's Journal, N. S. XI (July, 1881), 96.
Atlantic Monthly, XLVIII (July, 1881), 144.
Californian, IV (July, 1881), 92.
Dial, II (June, 1881), 44.
Harper's Magazine, LXIII (August, 1881), 476.
Journal of Education, XIV (November 3, 1881), 292.

Lanier, Sidney. *The Boy's King Arthur.* (New York: Charles Scribner's Sons)
Atlantic Monthly, XLVII (January, 1881), 122–23.

The Boy's Mabinogion. (New York: Charles Scribner's Sons)
Dial, II (December, 1881), 182–83.
Journal of Education, XIV (November 24, 1881), 346.
Literary World, XII (December 3, 1881), 449.
Nation, XXXIII (November 24, 1881), 419.

Ledyard, Laura, and W. T. Peters. *Tutti-Fruitti.* (New York: George W. Harlan)
Catholic World, XXXIV (December, 1881), 432.
Critic, I (November 19, 1881), 321.
Dial, II (December, 1881), 186.
Literary World, XII (November 19, 1881), 418.

The Little Bugler; A Story for Boys. (St. Louis: G. I. Jones & Co.)
Western, VII (January, 1881), 110.

Little Folks. (New York: Cassell, Petter, Galpin & Co.)
Critic, I (December 3, 1881), 337–38.
Journal of Education, XIV (November 24, 1881), 346.
Literary World, XII (September 24, 1881), 327–28.
Literary World, XII (December 3, 1881), 451.

Little Folks' Illuminating Book. (New York: Cassell, Petter, Galpin & Co.)
Literary World, XII (September 24, 1881), 327.

Little Red-Riding Hood. (New York: Thomas Nelson & Sons)
Nation, XXXIII (November 24, 1881), 419.

Lossing, Benson J. *The Story of the United States Navy for Boys.* (New York: Harper & Brothers)
Atlantic Monthly, XLVII (February, 1881), 302.
Harper's Magazine, LXII (February, 1881), 476.
New England Journal of Education, XIII (January 6, 1881), 10.

Lothrop, Harriet Mulford (Margaret Sidney). *The Five Little Peppers and How They Grew.* (Boston: D. Lothrop & Co.)
Nation, XXXIII (December 8, 1881), 457.

Lukin, J. *Amongst Machines.* (New York: G. P. Putnam's Sons)
Popular Science Monthly, XVIII (March, 1881), 705.

The Boy Engineers. (New York: G. P. Putnam's Sons)
Popular Science Monthly, XIX (May, 1881), 125.

MacArthur, Blanche, and Jennie Moore. *Lessons in Figure Painting.* (New York: Cassell, Petter, Galpin & Co.)
Literary World, XII (November 19, 1881), 418.

McCabe, James D. *Our Young Folks Abroad.* (Philadelphia: J. B. Lippincott & Co.)
Atlantic Monthly, XLVIII (December, 1881), 857.
Critic, I (December 31, 1881), 369.
Literary World, XII (November 5, 1881), 398.
Nation, XXXIII (December 15, 1881), 478.

MacLeod, Alexander. *The Gentle Heart.* (New York: Robert Carter & Brothers)
Harper's Magazine, LXII (January, 1881), 314.

Matéaux, Clara L. *Around and About Old England.* (New York: Cassell, Petter, Galpin & Co.)
Literary World, XII (September 24, 1881), 327.

Old Proverbs with New Pictures. Illus. by Lizzie Lawson. (New York: Cassell, Petter, Galpin & Co.)
Critic, I (November 5, 1881), 307.
Dial, II (December, 1881), 181–82.
Journal of Education, XIV (November 24, 1881), 346.
Literary World, XII (September 24, 1881), 327.
Literary World, XII (November 19, 1881), 418.
Nation, XXXIII (November 24, 1881), 419.

Mathews, Joanna H. *Bessie Bradford's Secret.* (New York: Cassell, Petter, Galpin & Co.)
Journal of Education, XIV (November 24, 1881), 346.
Literary World, XII (September 24, 1881), 327.
Nation, XXXIII (December 8, 1881), 457.

Mathews, Margaret Harriet. *Dr. Gilbert's Daughters.* (Philadelphia: Porter & Coates)
Atlantic Monthly, XLVIII (December, 1881), 858.
Journal of Education, XIV (December 15, 1881), 402.
Literary World, XII (November 5, 1881), 397.

Memoirs of a New York Doll. (New York: Benziger Bros.)
Catholic World, XXXII (March, 1881), 860.

Merry Nursery. (Philadelphia: J. B. Lippincott & Co.)
Literary World, XII (January 1, 1881), 11.

Miller, Olive Thorne. *Queer Pets at Marcy's.* (New York: E. P. Dutton & Co.)
Scribner's Monthly, XXI (January, 1881), 481–82.

Moseley, Julia Daniels. *Little Zee.* (Chicago: H. A. Sumner & Co.)
Literary World, XII (January 1, 1881), 11.

Moulton, Louise Chandler. *New Bed-Time Stories.* (Boston: Roberts Brothers)
Harper's Magazine, LXII (January, 1881), 314.

Scribner's Monthly, XXI (January, 1881), 481.
Unitarian Review, XV (February, 1881), 192.

Old Crummels. (New York: Dodd, Mead & Co.)
Critic, I (December 3, 1881), 337–38.

Our Little Ones at Home and in School. (Boston: Lee & Shepard)
Californian, IV (December, 1881), 537.
Dial, II (December, 1881), 185.
Literary World, XII (December 3, 1881), 450.
Penn Monthly, XII (November, 1881), 879.

Patch, Olive. *Happy Little People.* (New York: Cassell, Petter, Galpin & Co.)
Literary World, XII (September 24, 1881), 327.

Pilgrim, T. (Arthur Morecamp). *Live Boys in the Black Hills.* (Boston: Lee & Shepard)
Independent, XXXIII (January 13, 1881), 12.

Plympton, Miss A. G. *The Glad Year Round for Boys and Girls.* (Boston: James R. Osgood & Co.)
Atlantic Monthly, XLVIII (December, 1881), 857.
Critic, I (December 3, 1881), 337–38.
Dial, II (December, 1881), 181–82.
Journal of Education, XIV (November 24, 1881), 346.
Literary World, XII (December 3, 1881), 449.
Nation, XXXIII (November 24, 1881), 419.
St. Nicholas, IX (December, 1881), 181.

Pollard, Josephine. *The Decorative Sisters.* (New York: A. D. F. Randolph)
Critic, I (December 3, 1881), 337–38.
Nation, XXXIII (November 24, 1881), 419.

Porter, Mary W. *Five Little Southerners.* (Boston: D. Lothrop & Co.)
New England Journal of Education, XIII (February 17, 1881), 120.

Proctor, Richard Anthony. *Flowers of the Sky.* (New York: A. C. Armstrong & Co.)
New England Journal of Education, XIII (May 19, 1881), 342.

Pyle, Howard. *Yankee Doodle.* (New York: Dodd, Mead & Co.)
Critic, I (December 3, 1881), 337–38.
Dial, II (December, 1881), 181–82.
Literary World, XII (December 17, 1881), 478.
Nation, XXXIII (December 15, 1881), 478.

Raymond, Robert R. *Shakespeare for the Young Folks.* (New York: Fords, Howard & Hulbert)
Critic, I (December 17, 1881), 356.
Dial, II (December, 1881), 185.
Nation, XXXIII (December 15, 1881), 478.

Richards, Laura E. *Five Mice in a Mouse-Trap by the Man in the Moon. Done in Vernacular from the Lunacular by Laura E. Richards.* (Boston: Estes & Lauriat)
Atlantic Monthly, XLVII (February, 1881), 302.
Californian, III (February, 1881), 192.
Literary World, XII (January 1, 1881), 11.

Sketches and Scraps. (Boston: Estes & Lauriat)
Critic, I (December 3, 1881), 337–38.
Journal of Education, XIV (December 15, 1881), 402.
Literary World, XII (December 17, 1881), 478.

Ross, Ellen. *Dora's Boy.* (New York: Thomas Y. Crowell & Co.)
New England Journal of Education, XIII (April 28, 1881), 290.

Rousselet, Louis. *Two Cabin Boys.* (Boston: Roberts Brothers)

Atlantic Monthly, XLVIII (December, 1881), 858.
Literary World, XII (November 5, 1881), 397–98.

Royal Chatterbox. (New York: R. Worthington)
Literary World, XII (September 24, 1881), 328.

St. Nicholas (periodical).
Critic, I (December 3, 1881), 337–38.
Dial, II (December, 1881), 186.

Scudder, Horace Elisha. *Boston Town*. (Boston: Houghton, Mifflin & Co.)
Critic, I (October 8, 1881), 275.
Harper's Magazine, XLIV (December, 1881), 155.
Journal of Education, XIV (October 20, 1881), 256.
Literary World, XII (December 3, 1881), 449–50.
Nation, XXXIII November 17, 1881), 400.

The Children's Book. (Boston: Houghton, Mifflin & Co.)
Atlantic Monthly, XLVIII (December, 1881), 857.
Critic, I (December 3, 1881), 337–38.
Dial, II (December, 1881), 184.
Journal of Education, XIV (November 3, 1881), 292.
Literary World, XII (November 5, 1881), 397.
Nation, XXXIII (November 24, 1881), 419.

Mr. Bodley Abroad. (Boston: Houghton, Mifflin & Co.)
Atlantic Monthly, XLVII (January, 1881), 125–26.
Californian, III (January, 1881), 92.

Segur, Comtesse Eugénie de. *Adventures of a Donkey*. (Baltimore: Kelly, Piet & Co.)
Atlantic Monthly, XLVII (March, 1881), 448.
Catholic World, XXXII (February, 1881), 576.

Shaw, Catherine. *In the Sunlight and Out of It: A Year of My Life Story*. (New York: Robert Carter & Brothers)
Harper's Magazine, LXII (February, 1881), 476.

Shaw, Flora L. *Hector*. (Boston: Roberts Brothers)
Critic, I (November 19, 1881), 323.
Literary World, XII (November 5, 1881), 397.
Nation, XXXIII (November 17, 1881), 400.

Smith, Lucy T. (Lucy T. Meade). *How Nora Crena Saved Her Own*. (New York: Robert Carter & Brothers)
Harper's Magazine, LXII (February, 1881), 476.

Stephens, Charles Asbury. *The Knockabout Club in the Woods*. (Boston: Estes & Lauriat)
Critic, I (December 31, 1881), 369.
Journal of Education, XIV (November 24, 1881), 346.
Literary World, XII (September 24, 1881), 327.

Stockton, Frank R. *The Floating Prince, and Other Fairy Tales*. (New York: Charles Scribner's Sons)
Critic, I (December 3, 1881), 337–38.
Dial, II (December, 1881), 185.
Literary World, XII (December 3, 1881), 450.
Nation, XXXIII (December 15, 1881), 477–78.

A Jolly Fellowship. (New York: Charles Scribner's Sons)
Atlantic Monthly, XLVII (January, 1881), 124.

Round-About Rambles in Lands of Fact and Fancy. New Edition. (New York: Charles Scribner's Sons)
Atlantic Monthly, XLVIII (December, 1881), 857.
Journal of Education, XIV (October 27, 1881), 274.

Literary World, XII (November 5, 1881), 398.

Tales Out of School. New Edition. (New York: Charles Scribner's Sons)
Atlantic Monthly, XLVIII (December, 1881), 857.
Journal of Education, XIV (October 27, 1881), 274.

Stoddard, William Osborn. *The Quartet*. (New York: Charles Scribner's Sons)
Critic, I (October 8, 1881), 276.
Literary World, XII (November 5, 1881), 398.
Nation, XXXIII (November 17, 1881), 399.

Stowe, Harriet Beecher. *A Dog's Mission; or, Story of the Old Avery House*. (New York: Fords, Howard & Hulburt)
Literary World, XII (December 3, 1881), 451.

Little Pussy Willow [also] *The Minister's Watermelons*. (New York: Fords, Howard & Hulburt)
Literary World, XII (December 3, 1881), 451.

Queer Little People. (New York: Fords, Howard & Hulburt)
Literary World, XII (December 3, 1881), 451.

Sugar and Spice and All That's Nice. (New York: R. Worthington)
Critic, I (December 3, 1881), 357–58.
Literary World, XII (September 24, 1881), 328.

Sunday. (New York: E. P. Dutton & Co.)
Atlantic Monthly, XLVIII (December, 1881), 857.

Swinton, William, and George R. Cathcart. *Golden Book of Tales*. (New York: Ivison, Blakeman, Taylor & Co.)
Dial, II (December, 1881), 186.
Literary World, XII (December 3, 1881), 450.
Nation, XXXIII (November 24, 1881), 419.

Tamenaga, Shunsui. *The Loyal Ronins*. Translated from the Japanese by Shiuichiro Saito and Edward Greéy. (New York: G. P. Putnam's Sons)
Californian, III (January, 1881), 92.

Thébaud, A. J. *The Twit-Twats; A Christmas Allegorical Story of Birds*. (New York: Catholic Publication Society)
Catholic World, XXXIV (November, 1881), 287.

Towle, George M. *Marco Polo, His Travels and Adventures*. (Boston: Lee & Shepard)
New England Journal of Education, XIII (January 6, 1881), 10.
Penn Monthly, XII (April, 1881), 320.

Raleigh, His Exploits and Voyages. (Boston: Lee & Shepard)
Nation, XXXIII (December 8, 1881), 456.

Townsend, Virginia F. *Lenox Dare*. (Boston: Lee & Shepard)
New England Journal of Education, XII (March 3, 1881), 154.

Trowbridge, John Townsend (Paul Creyton). *Pocket-Rifle*. (Boston: Lee & Shepard)
Nation, XXXIII (November 17, 1881), 399–400.

Valentine, Mrs. Laura. *Shakespearian Tales in Verse*. (New York: A. C. Armstrong & Son)
Critic, I (December 31, 1881), 369.
Nation, XXXIII (December 15, 1881), 478.

Vandegrift, Margaret. *Clover Beach*. (Philadelphia: Porter & Coates)
Atlantic Monthly, XLVII (February, 1881), 301.
New England Journal of Education, XIII (January 6, 1881), 10.

Under the Dog-Star. (Philadelphia: Porter & Coates)
Journal of Education, XIV (November 24, 1881), 346.
Literary World, XII (December 3, 1881), 450.

Nation, XXXIII (December, 1881), 457.

Verne, Jules. *Exploration of the World*. Pt. II. (New York: Charles Scribner's Sons)
Literary World, XII (January, 1881), 11.

The Tribulations of a Chinaman in China. (Boston: Lee & Shepard)
Journal of Education, XIV (December 29, 1881), 442.

Viollet-le-Duc, Eugene E. *Learning to Draw; or, The Story of a Young Designer*. (New York: G. P. Putnam's Sons)
Californian, III (January, 1881), 91–92.
Penn Monthly, XII (January, 1881), 79–80.

Warner, Susan Bogert (Elizabeth Wetherell). *Carl Krinken; His Christmas Stocking*. (New York: Robert Carter & Brothers)
Harper's Magazine, LXII (February, 1881), 476.

Waugh, Ida. *Holly Berries*. (New York: E. P. Dutton & Co.)
Critic, I (November 5, 1881), 307.
Dial, II (December, 1881), 181–82.
Nation, XXXIII (November 24, 1881), 419.

Wheeler, Candace. *The Prize Painting-Book: Good Times*. (New York: White & Stokes)
Dial, II (December, 1881), 181–82.
Literary World, XII (November 19, 1881), 418.
Nation, XXXIII (December 15, 1881), 478.

When I Was a Bachelor. (New York: Dodd, Mead & Co.)
Critic, I (December 3, 1881), 337–38.

Willett, Edward. *Cat's Cradle*. (New York: R. Worthington)
Journal of Education, XIV (November 24, 1881), 346.
Literary World, XII (September 24, 1881), 328.
Literary World, XII (December 3, 1881), 449.
Nation, XXXIII (November 24, 1881), 419.

Wingrave, Marion M. *The May Blossom; or, The Princess and Her People*. (New York: A. C. Armstrong & Son)
Critic, I (December 3, 1881), 337–38.
Dial, II (December, 1881), 181–82.
Literary World, XII (November 19, 1881), 418.
Nation, XXXIII (November 24, 1881), 419.
St. Nicholas, IX (December, 1881), 181.

Wise, Daniel (Francis Forrester; Lawrence Lancewood). *Thorncliffe Hall*. (Boston: Lee & Shepard)
Atlantic Monthly, XLVIII (December, 1881), 858.
Literary World, XII (December 3, 1881), 450.

Woods, Kate Tannatt. *Doctor Dick*. (Boston: D. Lothrop & Co.)
Journal of Education, XIV (December 1, 1881), 364.

Woolsey, Sarah Chauncey (Susan Coolidge). *Cross Patch*. (Boston: Roberts Brothers)
Atlantic Monthly, XLVIII (December, 1881), 857.
Critic, I (December 3, 1881), 337–38.
Literary World, XII (October 22, 1881), 373.
Nation, XXXIII (November 17, 1881), 399.

A Guernsey Lily; or, How the Feud Was Healed. (Boston: Roberts Brothers)
Harper's Magazine, LXII (February, 1881), 475–76.
Scribner's Monthly, XXI (January, 1881), 482.

Write Your Own Stories. (Boston: D. Lothrop & Co.)
Literary World, XII (November 19, 1881), 418.

Yonge, Charlotte M. *Young Folks' Bible History*. (Boston: D. Lothrop & Co.)
Literary World, XII (March 26, 1881), 119.

Young America's Picture-Book. (New York: R. Worthington)
Literary World, XII (September 24, 1881), 328.

The Young Folks' Robinson Crusoe. Paraphrased by Mrs. E. W. Farrar. Condensed
by William T. Adams. (Boston: Lee & Shepard)
Californian, IV (December, 1881), 537.
Literary World, XII (December 3, 1881), 450–51.
Nation, XXXII (November 24, 1881), 419.

Zimmerman, Jane Eggleston. *Gray Heads on Green Shoulders*. (Chicago: Women's
Temperance Publication Association)
Independent, XXXIII (January 13, 1881), 12.
New England Journal of Education, XIII (March 3, 1881), 154.

BIBLIOGRAPHY

BOOKS

Abbott, Lyman, *Reminiscences*. (Boston and New York: Houghton Mifflin Co., 1915), 509 pp.

Bechtel, Louise Seaman. "Books in Search of Children," *Bowker Lectures on Book Publishing*. (New York: R. R. Bowker Co., 1957) pp. 177–201.

Brickell, Herschel. "Book Review," *Writers on Writing*. (Garden City, N.Y.: Doubleday & Co., 1949), 309 pp.

Bridgman, Howard Allen. "Abbott, Lyman," *Dictionary of American Biography*. (New York: Charles Scribner's Sons, 1928), v. I, pp. 24–25.

Brooks, Van Wyck. *New England: Indian Summer*. (New York: E. P. Dutton & Co., Inc., 1950), 569 pp.

Burlingame, Roger. *Of Making Many Books: A Hundred Years of Reading, Writing and Publishing*. (New York: Charles Scribner's Sons, 1946), 347 pp.

Canby, Henry S. "On Reviewing," *Saturday Papers; Essays on Literature from The Literary Review; The First Volume of Selections from The Literary Review of the New York Evening Post,* by Henry Seidel Canby, William Rose Benet, Amy Loveman. (New York: The Macmillan Co., 1921), 133 pp.

Chew, Samuel C. *Fruit Among the Leaves; An Anniversary Anthology*. (New York: Appleton-Century-Crofts, 1950), 535 pp.

Cruse, Amy. *The Victorians and Their Reading*. (Boston and New York: Houghton Mifflin Co., 1936), 444 pp.

Fowler, Harold North. "Allen, William Francis," *Dictionary of American Biography*. (New York: Charles Scribner's Sons, 1928), v. I, p. 211.

Gard, Wayne. *Book Reviewing*. (New York: Alfred A. Knopf, 1927), 159 pp.

Hall, E. H. "Trowbridge, John," *Dictionary of American Biography*. (New York: Charles Scribner's Sons, 1928), v. XVIII, pp. 654–55.

Harper, J. Henry. *The House of Harper; A Century of Publishing in Franklin Square*. (New York: Harper & Bros., 1912), 689 pp.

Haskell, Daniel C. *The Nation, Volumes 1–105, New York, 1865–1917. Index of Titles and Contributors*. Volume I. *Index of Titles*. (New York: The New York Public Library, 1951), 577 pp.

Haviland, Virginia. *The Travelogue Storybook of the Nineteenth Century*. A Caroline Hewins Lecture. (Boston: The Horn Book, Inc., 1950), 70 pp.

Hewins, Caroline M. *A Midcentury Child and Her Books* [and] *Caroline M. Hewins and Books for Children* by Jennie D. Lindquist. (Boston: The Horn Book, Inc., 1954), 107 pp.

Jordan, Alice M. *From Rollo to Tom Sawyer and Other Papers*. (Boston: The Horn Book, Inc., [c.1948]), 160 pp.

Lehmann-Haupt, Hellmut. *The Book in America; A History of the Making and Selling of Books in the United States*. Second Edition. (New York: R. R. Bowker Co., 1951), 493 pp.

Mayes, Herbert R. *Alger, A Biography Without a Hero*. (New York: Macy-Masius, 1928), 241 pp.

Meigs, Cornelia, *et al. A Critical History of Children's Literature: A Survey of Children's Books in English from Earliest Times to the Present*. (New York: The Macmillan Co., 1953), 624 pp.

Moore, Anne Carroll. *The Three Owls, Third Book; Contemporary Criticism of Children's Books, 1927–1930*. (New York: Coward-McCann, 1931), 462 pp.

Morris, Richard B. *Encyclopedia of American History*. (New York: Harper & Bros., 1953), 776 pp.

Mott, Frank Luther. *Golden Multitudes; The Story of Best Sellers in the United States*. (New York: The Macmillan Co., 1947), 357 pp.
  A History of American Magazines, 1741–1850. (Cambridge: Harvard University Press, 1939), 848 pp.
  A History of American Magazines, 1850–1865. (Cambridge: Harvard University Press, 1938), 608 pp.
  A History of American Magazines, 1865–1885. (Cambridge: Harvard University Press, 1935), 649 pp.

"Osgood, Samuel," *Appleton's Cyclopaedia of American Biography*. (New York: D. Appleton & Co., 1888), v. IV, pp. 600–601.

Paine, Albert Bigelow. *Mark Twain's Autobiography*. (New York and London: Harper & Bros., 1924), 2 vs.

Soskin, W. "Business of Book Reviewing," *Writing for Love or Money*. Norman Cousins, ed. (New York: Longmans, Green, & Co., 1949), 278 pp.

Sheehan, Donald. *This Was Publishing: A Chronicle of the Book Trade in the Gilded Age*. (Bloomington: Indiana University Press, 1952), 288 pp.

Targ, William. *Bibliophile in the Nursery; A Bookman's Treasury of Collectors' Lore on Old and Rare Children's Books*. (Cleveland and New York: The World Publishing Co., [c.1957]), 503 pp.

Woolf, Virginia S. *Captain's Death Bed and Other Essays*. (New York: Harcourt, Brace & Co., 1950), 248 pp.

426

ARTICLES

Atkinson, William P. "Address," *The Library Journal,* IV (September-October, 1879), 359–62.

Bacon, George B. "The Literature of Our Sunday-Schools, I, II, III," *Hours at Home,* X (February, March, April, 1870), 393–400, 450–59, 558–67.

Bean, Miss M. A. "The Evil of Unlimited Freedom in the Use of Juvenile Fiction," *The Library Journal,* IV (September-October, 1879), 341–43.

Brooks, Martha H. "Sunday School Libraries," *The Library Journal,* IV (September-October, 1879), 338–41.

Chamberlain, Mellen. "Address," *The Library Journal,* IV (September-October, 1879), 362–66.

"Children's Magazines," *The Literary World,* IV (November, 1873), 88.

Clarke, James Freeman. "Address," *The Library Journal,* IV (September-October, 1879), 355–57.

[Dodge, Mary Mapes]. "Children's Magazines," *Scribner's Monthly,* VI (July, 1873), 352–54.

Green, S. S. "Sensational Fiction in Public Libraries," *The Library Journal,* IV (September-October, 1879), 345–55.

Harvey, Leone F. "Hunter's Fare; A Book Inquiry Department," *The Horn Book Magazine,* XXIV (May-June, 1948), 224.

Higginson, Thomas Wentworth. "Address," *The Library Journal,* IV (September-October, 1879), 357–59.

Hubbard, James Mascarene. "Fiction and Public Libraries," *The International Review,* X (February, 1881), 168–78.

"The Ladies' Commission," *Old and New,* IV (November, 1871), 626–29.

"The Ladies' Commission on Sunday-School Books," *Old and New,* I (May, 1870), 709–12.

"Literature for the Young," *The Unitarian Review and Religious Magazine,* I (June, 1874), 354–59.

Moore, Anne Carroll. "The Creation and Criticism of Children's Books," *ALA Bulletin,* XXVIII (August, 1934), 693–701.

Osgood, Samuel. "Books for Our Children," *Atlantic Monthly,* XVI (December, 1865), 724–35.

Scudder, Horace E. "Andersen's Short Stories," *Atlantic Monthly,* XXXVI (November, 1875), 598–602.

"Sunday-School Books—The Ladies' Commission," *Publishers' Weekly,* IV (November 22, 1873), 584.

Wells, Kate Gannett. "The Responsibility of Parents in the Selection of Reading for the Young," *The Library Journal,* IV (September-October, 1879), 325–30.

PERIODICALS - AMERICAN

American Educational Monthly. Vols. II–VII. (New York: Schermerhorn, Bancroft & Co., 1865–69)

American Literary Gazette and Publishers' Circular. Vols. IV–XVII. (Philadelphia: George W. Childs, 1865–71)

Appleton's Journal of Literature, Science and Art. Vols. I–XV. (New York: D. Appleton & Co., 1869–76)

Appleton's Journal: A Monthly Miscellany of Popular Literature. (Subtitle, 1879–81: *A Magazine of General Literature*) Vols. New Series I–XI (New York: D. Appleton & Co., 1876–81)

The Atlantic Monthly: A Magazine of Literature, Science, Art and Politics. Vols. XV–XLVIII. (Boston: Ticknor & Fields, 1865–68; Fields, Osgood & Co., 1868–70; John H. Osgood & Co., 1871–73; H. O. Houghton & Co., 1874–77; Houghton, Osgood & Co., 1878–79; Houghton, Mifflin & Co., 1880–81)

The Californian, A Western Monthly. Vols. I–IV (San Francisco: A. Roman Publishing Co., 1880–81)

The Catholic World: A Monthly Eclectic Magazine of General Literature and Science. Vols. I–XXXIV (New York: Catholic Publishing Society, 1865–81)

The Critic. Vols. I & II (New York: J. L. & J. B. Gilder, 1881; The Critic Printing & Publishing Co., 1881)

The Dial: A Monthly Review and Index of Current Literature. Vols. I–IV (Chicago: Jansen, McClurg & Co., 1881)

The Galaxy: An Illustrated Magazine of Entertaining Reading. Vols. I–XXV (New York: W. C. & F. P. Church, 1866–68; Sheldon & Co., 1868–78)

Harper's New Monthly Magazine. Vols. XXX–XLIV (New York: Harper & Bros., 1865–81)

Hours at Home. Vols. I–XI (New York: Charles Scribner & Co., 1865–70)

The Independent. Vols. XVII–XXXIII (New York: Henry Chandler Bowen, *et. al.*, 1865–81)

International Review. Vols. I–VIII (New York: A. S. Barnes & Co., 1874–81)

The Lakeside Monthly. Vols. V–XI (Chicago: Lakeside Publishing Co., 1871; Reed, Browne & Co., 1871; F. F. Browne & Co., 1873–74)

Lippincott's Magazine of Literature, Science and Education. (Title, 1871–81: *Lippincott's Magazine of Popular Literature and Science*) Vols. I–XXVIII (Philadelphia: J. B. Lippincott & Co., 1868–81)

The Literary World: A Review of Current Literature. (Subtitle, 1879–81: *A Fortnightly Review of Current Literature*) Vols. I–XII (Boston: S. R. Crocker, 1870–77; Edward H. Hames, 1877–81)

The Nation: A Weekly Journal Devoted to Politics, Literature, Science and Art. Vols. I–XXXIII (New York: Joseph H. Richards [for Nation Association] 1865–66; E. L. Godkin & Co., 1866–81)

The New Englander. Vols. XXIV–XL (New Haven: W. L. Kingsley, 1865–81)

The North American Review. Vols. CI–CXXXIII (Boston: Ticknor & Fields, 1865–67; Fields, Osgood & Co., 1868–69; James R. Osgood & Co. [A. T. Rice, owner, 1877] 1870–77. New York: D. Appleton & Co. [A. T. Rice, owner] 1878–80; A. T. Rice, 1881)

Ohio Educational Monthly. Vols. XIV–XXIX (Columbus: Ohio State Teachers Association, 1865–81)

Old and New. Vols. I–XI (Boston: H. O. Houghton & Co., 1870; Roberts Bros., 1870–74; Lee & Shepard, 1875. E. E. Hale and others, owners)

Oliver Optic's Magazine: Our Boys and Girls. (Subtitle dropped in 1874). Vols. I–XVIII (Boston: Lee & Shepard, 1867–75)

Our Young Folks. Vols. I–IX (Boston: Ticknor & Fields, 1865–73)

The Overland Monthly. Vols. I–XV (San Francisco: A. Roman & Co., 1868–69; John H. Carmany, 1869–75)

Penn Monthly Magazine. Vols. I–XIII (Philadelphia: University Press Co., 1870–81)

The Popular Science Monthly. Vols. I–XIX (New York: D. Appleton & Co., 1872–81)

The Publishers' Weekly (*The Publishers' and Stationers' Weekly Trade Circular,* 1872) Vols. I–XIX (New York: F. Leypoldt, 1872–79, 1880–81; R. R. Bowker, 1879–80)

Putnam's Magazine: Original Papers on Literature, Science, Art, and National Interests. Vols. New Series I–VI (New York: G. P. Putnam & Sons, 1868–70)

The Riverside Magazine for Young People. Vols. I–IV. (New York: Hurd & Houghton, 1868–70)

St. Nicholas: Scribner's Illustrated Magazine for Girls and Boys. Vols. I–IX. (New York: Scribner & Co., 1873–80; Century Co., 1881)

Scribner's Monthly, an Illustrated Magazine for the People. Vols. I–XXII (New York: Scribner & Co., 1873–81)

The Unitarian Review and Religious Magazine. Vols. I–XVI (Boston: Leonard C. Bowles, 1874–76; Unitarian Review, 1876–81)

The Western. Vols. I–VIII (St. Louis: Western Publishing Co., 1875–81)

The Western Monthly. Vols. I–IV (Chicago: H. V. Reed and E. C. Tuttle, 1869; Reed, Browne & Co., 1869; Western Monthly Co., 1870)

The Youth's Companion. Vols. XXXIX–XLII, XLV, XLVII–LIV (Boston: Olmstead & Co., 1865–67; Perry Mason & Co., 1867–81)

PERIODICALS - ENGLISH

The Athenaeum. Numbers 1990–2826. (London: John Francis, 1865–1881).

The Saturday Review of Politics, Literature, Science and Art. Vols. XIX–XXXIV. (London: The Chawton Publishing Co., Ltd., 1865–1872).

UNPUBLISHED MATERIAL

Erazmus, Dorothy, "Reviewing of Children's Books, 1882–1890." Unpublished Seminar Paper, Department of Library Science, University of Michigan, 1956. 174 pp.

INDEX

434

440

442

O

Ocean Wonders. W. E. Damon, 177

Off on a Comet. J. Verne, 224

Off to the Geysers. C. A. Stephens, 105, 111, 113

Ohio Educational Monthly (per.), 204–05

O'Kane, James, & Co., 229

Old and New (per.), 9, 13, 16, 17, 24, 33, 52, 89, 120, 126, 138–41

Old Deccan Days. M. Frere, 80

Old English History for Children. E. A. Freeman, 139

Old-Fashioned Girl. L. M. Alcott, 67, 79–80, 98, 102, 108, 117, 129, 130, 137, 143, 145, 146, 222

Old Mother Hubbard and Her Dog. H. L. Stephens (illus.), 188

Old Proverbs with New Pictures. L. Matéaux, 185

Old Times in the Colonies. C. C. Coffin, 131, 137, 145, 182

Oliver Optic's Almanac for Our Boys and Girls. W. T. Adams, 213

Oliver Optic's Magazine (per.), 3, 5, 18–19, 33–34, 37, 45, 81, 213–14

On a Pincushion. M. De Morgan, 76, 134

On the Amazon. C. A. Stephens, 195

Optic, Oliver (pseud.) see Adams, W. T.

O'Reilly, Mrs. R.
"Doll World" series, 27
Gile's Minority, 140

Osgood, James R., & Co., 14, 15, 27, 247

Osgood, S., 128
"Books for Our Children" (article), 46–50, 58, 59

O'Shea, Patrick, & Co., 201

Otis, James (pseud.) see Kaler, J. O.

Ouida (pseud.) see Ramée, L. de la

Our Baby. S. E. Warner, 111

Our Four-Footed Friends, M. Howitt, 85

Our Standard Bearer. W. T. Adams, 119

Our Young Folks (per.), 11, 31, 41, 81, 163, 204, 205, 209, 211–13, 243, 244

Our Young Folks Abroad. J. D. McCabe, 83, 177, 185

"Our Young Folks Abroad" series. W. T. Adams, 43

"Our Young Yachters" series. C. A. Stephens, 27, 43

Out-Doors at Long Look House. E. Abbott, 77

Outlook (per.), 90

Overland Monthly (per.), 8, 17, 32, 158–65, 240, 245

P

Pabke, M. and M. Dean
Wonder-World Stories, 81, 122

Palfrey, F. W., 71

Palfrey, J. G., 139

Palgrave, F. T.
Children's Treasury of English Song, 40

Pansie's Flour-Bin. E. T. Stephenson, 39, 76, 198

Pansy (pseud.) see Alden, I.

"Papers on Fiction and the Reading of School Children," 46, 55–58 see also Wells, K. G.; Brooks, M. H.; Bean, M. A.; Green, S. S.; Clarke, J. F.; Higginson, T. W.; Atkinson, W. P.; Chamberlain, M.

Parables from Nature. M. S. Gatty, 145

Parker, H. F.
Frank's Search for Sea Shells, 222

Parker, R. A.
Pinks and Blues, 122
"Rosa Abbott Stories" series, 27

Parley, Peter (pseud.) see Goodrich, S. G.

Patriot Boys and Prison Pictures. J. R. Gilmore, 221

Patriotism at Home, 222

Patsy. L. B. Robinson, 129, 143

Patty Gray's Journey to the Cotton Islands. C. Dall, 94, 101

Paul Prescott's Charge. H. Alger, Jr., 80

Paulist Fathers, Community of, 201

Pearl Fountain. B. and J. Kavanagh, 111

Peckham, M. C.
Father Gabrielle's Fairy, 77

Penn Monthly (per.), 33, 40, 147–152, 154

Perkins, W. O. and H. S. Perkins
Shining River, 216

Perkins, H. S. and W. O. Perkins
Shining River, 216

Perry, N.
Bessie's Trials at Boarding School, 11, 195

Peterkin Papers. L. P. Hale, 45, 123, 171–72, 211

Phebe Travers. Aunt Florida, 163

Phelps, E. B.
Memoirs of Washington, 87

Phelps, E. S.
Gypsy Series, 170, 172

Picked Up Adrift. J. De Mille, 173

Picture Poems for Young Folks. A. D.
  Robinson, 72
Pilgrim's Progress. J. Bunyan, 41
Pilgrim's Progress in Words of One
  Syllable. Mrs. E. A. Walker, 190
Pindar, S. C.
  Wentworths, 195
Pinks and Blues. R. A. Parker, 122
Pizarro. G. M. Towle, 105
Play Days. S. O. Jewett, 130, 134
Pletsch, O., 218
Plympton, A. G.
  Glad Year Round, 136
Pocahontas. E. Eggleston, 105, 113
Poems of Childhood. E. B. Browning,
  41, 71
Poetry for Children. C. and M.
  Lamb, 139
Police Gazette (per.), 56
Popular Fairy Tales. G. Doré, 102
Popular Science Monthly (per.), 44,
  226–27
Porter & Coates, 16, 40, 96
Potwin, H. K.
  Kemptons, 206
Prentiss, E.
  Little Lou's Sayings and Doings, 219
  Story Lizzie Told, 97
Prescott, M. N., Matt's Follies, 102, 213
Preston, L.
  Boy's Trip Across the Plains,
  160, 163
Pretty Peggy and Other Ballads. R. Em-
  met, 123
Prince and the Pauper. S. L. Clemens,
  129, 131–32, 137–38, 184, 185,
  247–48
Princess and the Goblin. G. MacDon-
  ald, 75, 124
Princess Idleways. W. J. Hays, 103
Pritchard, S. J.
  Rose Marbury, 100
"Proverb Stories" series. M. E. Bradley
  and K. J. Neely, 27, 122
Prince of Argolis. J. M. Smith, 106,
  113, 143, 145
Publishers' and Stationers' Weekly Trade
  Circular (per.), 220, 224
Publishers' Weekly (per.), 8, 13, 18, 19,
  23, 33, 53, 54, 220, 224–26, 233,
  235
Puss and Robin. T. Hood, 123
Pussy-Cat Mew. E. H. Knatchbull-
  Hugessen, 92
Putnam's, G. P., Sons, 14
Putnam's Magazine (per.), 9, 15, 89,
  118–19, 120, 240, 242

Pyle, H., 84, 182
  Yankee Doodle, 85, 170, 180,
  182, 185

Q

Queer Folk. E. H. Knatchbull-Huges-
  sen, 75, 198
Queer House in Rugby. A. L. Noble, 28
Queer Little People. H. B. Stowe, 218

R

Ragged Dick. H. Alger, Jr., 3, 119
Raleigh, His Exploits and Voyages.
  G. M. Towle, 82
Ramée, L. de la
  Dog of Flanders, 55
  Nurnberg Stove, 55
  Under Two Flags, 55
Ranald Bannerman's Boyhood. G. Mac-
  Donald, 147
Randolph, Anson D. F., & Co., 14, 15
Rands, W. B.
  Lilliput Land, 143
Rare Piece of Work. P. B. Chamber-
  lain, 174
Raymond, R. R.
  Shakespeare for the Young
  Folks, 87
Raymond, R. W.
  Man in the Moon, 98
Real Folks, A. D. T. Whitney, 134
Reid, M. 39, 112
  Castaways, 108, 171
Rhymes and Jingles. M. M. Dodge, 24,
  40, 74, 94, 114, 211
Richards, L. E., 175
  Five Mice in a Mouse-Trap by the
  Man in the Moon, 134, 167, 207
  Sketches and Scraps, 185, 208
Richardson, A. S.
  History of Our Country, 161–62
  Stories from Old English Poetry,
  132, 134
Richardson, C. F., 23
Ripley, G., 90
Risen from the Ranks. H. Alger, Jr., 80
Riverside Magazine for Young People
  (per.), 22, 44, 45, 81, 86, 209,
  211, 217–19
Robbins, S. S.
  My New Home, 194
Robert and Frederick. M. M. Sher-
  wood, 172
Roberts Bros., 15, 16, 27
Robinson, A. D.
  Picture Poems for Young Folks, 72

446

Robinson, L. B.
  Patsy, 129, 143
Robinson Crusoe. D. Defoe, 41, 93, 108
Robinson Crusoe in Words of One Syllable. M. Godolphin, 41, 86
Roddy's Ideal. H. K. Johnson, 149
Roderick Ashcourt. D. Wise, 173
Rollo and Lucy Books of Poetry. J. Abbott, 97
Rollo in Europe. J. Abbott, 185
Rollo's Tour in Europe, J. Abbott, 176
Roman, A., & Co., 17, 103, 158, 162
"Rosa Abbott Stories" series. R. A. Parker, 27
Rose in Bloom. L. M. Alcott, 174
Rose Marbury. S. J. Pritchard, 100
Rossetti, C., 41
  Sing-Song, 87, 115
Rough and Ready. H. Alger, Jr., 80
Roundabout Rambles in Lands of Fact and Fancy. F. R. Stockton, 86, 114
Rousselet, L.
  Two Cabin Boys, 130
Routledge, E.
  Every Boy's Book, 76
Routledge, George, & Sons, 15, 20–21, 180
Rover, W.
  Neptune Outward Bound, 110
Running to Waste. G. M. Baker, 199
Rupert Lawrence. H. B. McKeever, 223
Rural Poems. W. Barnes, 219

S

Sadlier, D. & J., & Co., 201
St. Nicholas (per.), 14, 21, 44, 45, 58, 75, 81, 120, 125, 209, 211, 214–17
Saito, S.
  Loyal Ronins (trans.), 166
Sand, G., 143
Sanford, D. P.
  Captain's Children, 103
  Houseful of Children, 85
Salt-Water Dick. H. P. H. Nowell, 94
Sangster, M. E. 29, 91
Saturday Review of Politics, Literature, Science, and Art, 68–69
"Science for the Young" series. J. Abbott, 44, 98, 104
Scott, J. W.
  International Postage Stamp Album, 216
Scott, Sir W., 217
Scribner, C. 120
Scribner & Co., 120

Scribner, Armstrong & Co., 24
Scribner, Charles, & Sons, 14, 20, 115
Scribner, Welford & Co., 40
Scribner's Monthly (per.), 19, 20–21, 22, 37, 39, 58, 89, 118, 120–25, 211, 219, 233–34, 235, 249
Scudder, H. E., 14, 39, 127, 133, 177, 217–19, 251
  "Bodley Family" series, 24, 43, 86, 130, 136, 197, 215
  Bodleys Afoot, 106, 132
  Bodleys on Wheels, 85, 176
  Bodleys Telling Stories, 105, 121, 130, 225–26
  Boston Town, 42, 179, 185, 207
  Children's Book, 40
  Doings of the Bodley Family in Town and Country, 130, 176, 216
  Dream Children, 187
  Mr. Bodley Abroad, 27, 106, 136–137, 167
  Stories from My Attic, 76, 92, 116, 119, 130, 134
Seamer, M.
  Shakespeare Stories Simply Told, 87, 175
Seek and Find. W. T. Adams, 80
Segur, Comtesse E. de
  Fairy Tales for Little Folk, 40
Servants of the Stomach. J. Macé, 84, 104
Seymours. L. Bates, 102
Shakespeare for the Young Folk. R. R. Raymond, 87
Shakespeare Stories Simply Told. M. Seamer, 87, 175
Shakespearian Tales in Verse. L. Valentine, 87, 185
Shamrock and Thistle. W. T. Adams, 202
Shaw, F. L.
  Hector, 185
Shawl-Straps. L. M. Alcott, 201
Sherwood, M. M.
  Robert and Frederick, 172
  Stories on the Church Catechism, 174
Shillaber, B. P.
  Ike Partington, 133
Shining River. H. S. and W. O. Perkins, 216
Short History of France for Young People. E. S. Kirkland, 82
Short Poems for Short People. E. Fawcett, 112
Short Sermons to Newsboys. C. L. Brace, 71

449

Z

INDEX TO ILLUSTRATIONS

452